Gospel Worship

Gospel Worship

BEING

An Attempt to Exhibit a Scriptural View

OF THE

Nature, Obligations, Manner, and Ordinances of the Worship of God

IN THE

New Testament

by Archibald Hall

John 5:39, *Search the scriptures.*
Matthew 28:20, *Observe all things whatsoever I have commanded you.*
1 Corinthians 11:2, *Now I praise you, brethren, that you…keep the ordinances, as I delivered them to you.*
Jeremiah 6:16, *Thus saith the* LORD, *Stand ye in the ways, and see, and ask for the old paths, where is the good way, and walk therein.*

Reformation Heritage Books
Grand Rapids, Michigan

Gospel Worship
© 2024 by Reformation Heritage Books

All rights reserved. No part of this book may be used or reproduced in any manner whatsoever without written permission except in the case of brief quotations embodied in critical articles and reviews. Direct your requests to the publisher at the following addresses:

Reformation Heritage Books
3070 29th St. SE Grand Rapids, MI 49512
616-977-0889
orders@heritagebooks.org
www.heritagebooks.org

Scripture taken from the King James Version. In the public domain.

ISBN 979-8-88686-156-3
Printed in the United States of America
24 25 26 27 29/10 9 8 7 6 5 4 3 2 1

Typeset with EB Garamond using LaTeX.
Logan West
www.texset.com

Contents

Editorial Note	xi
Foreword	xiii
Preface	xxxiii

Introductory Discourse — 1
   The Nature of Religious Worship — 4
   The Obligation on Mankind to Worship God — 18
   The Manner of Worshipping Him Acceptably — 23
   Some Remarks concerning Liturgies — 28
        The Opinion of Protestant Dissenters — 29
        Whether Liturgies are Authorized — 30
        That They Are Unreasonable Impositions — 35

Gospel Worship — 41

1 Reading the Holy Scriptures — 47
   1 What God Hath Appointed about Reading — 48
   2 It Is a Divine and Most Excellent Institution — 53
   3 Vindication from Some Objections — 58
   4 Some Directions for Advantage and Comfort — 61

2 Preaching the Gospel — 69
   1 The Nature — 69
   2 To Continue till the End of the World — 73
   3 Who May Warrantably Preach — 76
   4 Vindication From Some Objections — 79
   5 Describing the Manner — 83

3 Hearing the Word Preached — 95
   1 What God Hath Appointed — 95
   2 The Obligations to Honor This Ordinance — 97
   3 Pretenses for Neglecting to Hear Preaching — 102
   4 Directions for Hearing Preaching — 107

4 Singing the Praises of God — 115
1. The Nature of the Service — 115
2. The Obligations to Observe It — 116
3. Vindication Against Some Objections — 120
4. Answering a Few Questions Relative to It — 122
5. Directions concerning Right Performance — 132

5 Prayer — 135
1. The Nature of This Duty — 135
2. The Obligations to Pray — 139
3. Objections Obviated — 143
4. Questions Concerning It — 148
5. Rules for the Discharge of It — 159

6 The Public Blessing of the Congregation — 165
1. The Importance and Weight of This Service — 166
2. Necessary Directions about It — 173

7 The Sacraments in General — 177
1. Their Name — 177
2. Their Nature — 178
3. Their Ends — 181
4. Their Efficacy — 184
5. Their Use — 188
6. Their Number — 190
7. The Wisdom and Advantages — 197
8. The Persons That May Administer Them — 199

8 Baptism — 201
1. Its Name — 201
2. Its Nature — 212
3. Its Authority and Institution — 217
4. Its Excellency and Usefulness — 219
5. The Objections Made against It — 226
6. To Whom It Is to Be Administered — 228
7. The Manner of Performing This Duty — 248
8. The Directions Relative to It — 253

9   The Lord's Supper   263
    1   The Names of This Ordinance 263
    2   The Author of It 266
    3   Its Nature 267
    4   The Obligations to Observe It 275
    5   The Excellent Uses and Purposes of It 280
    6   Objections against It Removed 287
    7   Some Questions Relative to It Answered 290
    8   Practical Directions concerning It 299

10   The Observation of the Lord's Day   311
    1   The Names Given to This Day 312
    2   Its Original Institution 313
    3   Its Nature 318
    4   The Obligations to Observe It 321
    5   The Proper Employments of It 327
    6   Directions for the Sanctification of It 333
    7   Motives to Engage Our Regard to It 337

11   The Observation of Times of Thanksgiving   341
    1   The Nature of the Duty 341
    2   Showing the Reasonableness Thereof 345
    3   Representing the Ends of It 346
    4   Answering Some Questions Relative to It 348
    5   Directions concerning Its Performance 351

12   The Observation of Religious Fasts   357
    1   The Nature of a Religious Fast Considered 357
    2   That It Is a Divine Institution Proved 360
    3   The Ends to Which This Exercise Should Be Directed . . . 362
    4   Some Questions Relative to It Answered 364
    5   Directions concerning Its Observation 370
    6   Encouragements to This Service Proposed 378

13   Ministerial Visitations of the Flock   381
    1   General Principles 382
    2   General Duties 387
    3   Particular Duties of Christians Recommended 393

	To the Tempers of People	393
	To Their Stations	402
	To Their Manifold Relations	403
	To Magistrates and Subjects	404
	To Husbands and Wives	406
	To Parents and Children	408
	To Masters and Servants	411
	To Neighbors	414
	To Friends	416
	To Their Age as Children, Grown Men, or Old People	419
	To Their Employments in Life	426
	To Their Several Conditions in Respect of Prosperity or Adversity	429
4	Conclusion with Solemn Prayer	434

14 Ministerial Visitation of the Sick   437

1. Obligations upon Christians and Elders 437
2. An Account of the Manner of Elders Performing It 440
3. Directions to Christians Concerning the Use of It 447

15 Catechizing   451

1. The Nature of the Duty Represented 451
2. The Manner of Performing the Duty Considered 452
3. The Matter of It 453
4. The Obligation on Christians to Observe It 457
5. A Few Questions Relative to It Answered 462
6. Directions concerning It 466
   - To Teachers 466
   - To Those That Are Taught 468

16 Social Religious Meetings   473

1. The Nature of These Meetings Considered 474
2. Their Warrant from Scripture 474
3. The End and Design of Them Shown 480
4. The Manner of Conducting Them 485
5. Christians Excited to This Duty 491

TABLE OF CONTENTS

17 Family Religion — **495**
  1 The Various Parts of It Considered 495
  2 Arguments Proving It to Be a Duty 499
  3 The Seasons of Family Duties 503
  4 The Obligations on Heads of Families 504
  5 Causes of Its Neglect 505
  6 Arguments Pressing the Observation of It 508
  7 Objections against It Answered 512
  8 Directions Relative to It 515
      To Masters and Heads of Families 515
      To Members of Them 517

18 Personal Religion — **519**
  1 The Nature and Particular Branches of It 520
  2 Obligations on Christians to Practice It 523
  3 The Seasons of Personal Religion 525
  4 The Duty Pressed by Several Arguments 529
  5 Objections against It Answered 536
  6 Practical Directions respecting It 539

19 Liberality to the Poor Saints — **543**
  1 An Account of the Nature of the Duty 544
  2 The Obligations on Christians to It 546
  3 The Causes Why They Neglect It 550
  4 The Objects, Measure, Manner, and Season of It 555
  5 A Regard to the Duty Pressed 563

20 Swearing by the Name of God — **569**
  1 The Nature of an Oath 569
  2 The Warrant for Swearing by the Name of God 572
  3 The Manner in Which an Oath Should Be Taken 575
  4 The Ends for Which It Should Be Used 583
  5 Questions respecting It Answered 584
  6 Inferences from the Subject 587

21 Vowing to the Lord — **593**
  1 The Nature of a Vow 593
  2 The Warrant for It 595

	3	The Matters Which Vows Refer to	599
	4	For What Purposes They Should Be Made	601
	5	The Obligation of Them	603
	6	In What Capacity Christians May Vow	606
	7	Some Directions Relative to Their Vows	617

22 Casting of Lots — 623

1	The Principles on Which This Ordinance Proceeds	623
2	The Nature of Lotting	624
3	The Purposes for Which It Should Be Used	626
4	The Abuses of It	628
5	Directions concerning the Lawful Use of Lots	633

Appendix — 635

Love-Feasts 635
The Holy Kiss 640
Washing the Disciples' Feet 643
Abstaining from Blood, etc. 648

Archaic Words — 657

Bibliography — 659

Scripture Index — 665

Editorial Note

There are always difficult decisions which must be made when republishing an older book. The intent is to reproduce the author's work as accurately as possible with no abridgment or alteration of the content, while acknowledging advances in technology and typographical standards to which readers are more accustomed. The end result should be such that there is no detraction from, but only improvement, upon the original.

Spelling and punctuation have been almost entirely modernized but the original words and sentence structure left alone—with the exception of a few quotations where it was most proper to rearrange the author's self-bracketed comments to be outside the quote. Block quotations were not a typographical standard at the time of its original printing, yet they aid in clarifying presentation to the modern reader.

Hall was very free with his quotations from Scripture so I have modified these to conform to actual Scripture quotations where it does not harm the sense of his message. There was also an inconsistent manner of inserting Scripture references. These have been standardized as much as possible to be within parentheses at the end of the quotation.

Another addition are headings which have been added to the sections as an aid for navigation, and which were worded as closely as possible to the author's own descriptions of topics in each chapter. In a few instances typos or missing words (or an entire chapter missing from a list of contents), have simply been corrected.

I was greatly helped by the proofreaders provided by Reformation Heritage Books. We trust that the result is faithful to the author and will be agreeable to the reader as the best edition of this magnificent and edifying book.

Logan West
June, 2024

Foreword

Ah, bonnie Scotland! The very name conjures up images of pastoral scenes, of sheep gamboling on heather-covered hills, of clear streams, and of rugged coast lines pounded by sea-surf; of castles and cotters' cottages, of mist and fog, of the warmth of a hearth accompanied by the inner warmth of a wee dram of Drambuie or a 25-year single malt. One can almost hear the drone of the bagpipe, and the laughter of Tartan-clad lads and lasses.

But for those who are spiritually attuned, the real beauty of Scotland is not to be found in its natural wonders nor its mystical past, but rather in the fact that it was in this land that the Protestant Reformation found perhaps its highest and most mature theological expression. And particularly with regard to the doctrine and practice of worship, Scotland was second to none in doctrinal thought and formulation.

To understand and appreciate Scotland—to know what made it truly fascinating and truly great—you must look first and foremost to its religious, and particularly its Presbyterian, heritage. And it is because of that spiritual background that a work such as this present one, *Gospel Worship*, could appear.

The fierce, even barbaric, Scottish clansmen, having been conquered by the gospel of Christ in the early middle ages, experienced further refining in the 1520s as a result of the Lutheran reform. But the Scots went beyond Luther and embraced the more thoroughgoing reform promulgated by John Calvin (1509–1564) in Geneva.

One of the chief Scottish Calvinists was John Knox (c. 1513–1572); the efforts by him and others resulted in the Church of Scotland becoming Reformed in its theology, polity, and worship. In the seventeenth century, Scotland experienced its Second Reformation, highlighted by the Scottish National Covenant of 1638 and the Solemn League and Covenant of 1643. That latter pact joined together the Scottish Presbyterians and the English Puritans, and led directly to the convening of the Westminster Assembly, which produced the Confession of Faith and Catechisms of the same name.

Not that the forces of Roman Catholicism didn't fight back—they did. The consequent struggle stretched over many decades, flaming forth most prominently during the Killing Time when, over the course of a generation, from 1660 to 1688, at least 18,000 Scotsmen and Scotswomen and children were either murdered or imprisoned or sent into exile.

The Glorious Revolution of 1688 which brought William and Mary to the throne led to a time of external calm. But then, the Church of Scotland suffered internal controversies and dissensions and schisms. One of the most notable of the divisions was that of the Seceders. Originally comprising four ministers who were disciplined by the Established Church in 1733, the Seceders formed the Associate Presbytery.

The causes of this division largely revolved around the issue of legalism. The Seceders championed God's free grace, while the Established Church reflected a more legalistic approach to the gospel.[1]

The Seceder movement, with its evangelistic zeal and warm-hearted approach, grew rapidly. But more than that, the movement represented a rich theological heritage, profound thoughtfulness, and principled commitment. And it was in that environment that Archibald Hall was raised and it was in that context that he would minister.

A dozen miles south of the Scottish capital of Edinburgh, in the county of Mid-Lothian, is Penicuik. The name of the parish originally was Pen Y Cog, meaning "Hill of the Cuckoo" in the ancient language of Old Brythonic. Even before the Industrial Revolution got into high gear in the mid-1700s, Penicuik had transitioned to manufacturing: by the early eighteenth century, paper-making was the prime industry. Travel another five miles southwest, upstream along the meandering River North Esk, and you will come to Marfield, an agricultural community. It was there that Archibald Hall was born in 1736.

His parents, who were strongly religious, had a profound spiritual influence upon him. Even his suffering the loss of his mother before he was ten years old had good effect, as "the remembrance of the affection-

---

[1] For an exhaustive discussion, see David C. Lachman, *The Marrow Controversy: An Historical and Theological Analysis* (Edinburgh: Rutherford House, 1988).

ate and serious advices, which she gave on her death-bed, continued with him through life."[2]

Also affecting the young Archibald was his first teacher, John Brown, known to history as John Brown of Haddington. A self-taught scholar whose life breathed an intimate knowledge of Christ, John Brown would later become the Associate Synod's Professor of Divinity. From Brown, Hall learned Latin, Greek, and Hebrew. But he also developed a love of learning—and not just an intellectual knowledge, but an experiential learning, a love of learning Christ. Archibald studied mathematics, logic, and philosophy at the University of Edinburgh, and then was instructed in theology by the Rev. James Fisher of the Secession Church.[3]

We say "the Secession Church"; however, please note that there were at this time *two* Secession branches, a split having occurred in 1747 between the Burghers and the Anti-Burghers. The matter revolved around whether certain citizens of three significant cities, Edinburgh, Glasgow, and Perth, known as burgesses, could take their oath of office. "The issue was important to the Associate Synod because, within a burgh, none but burgesses were permitted to engage in commerce, belong to a trade guild, or enjoy the privilege of voting."[4] The controversy had to do with whether, after the Secession, the oath was pledging the burgesses to agree with the established Church of Scotland in its action of driving out the Seceders, or whether the oath should be understood merely in the historic sense of being against Roman Catholicism.

In 1758, the pro-burgher Associate Church licensed Archibald Hall, then around 22 years old, to preach the gospel. His first charge was at Torpichen, a small village in West Lothian. Seven years later, in 1765, he became the pastor to a Seceder congregation gathered in Well-street in an area of London called Hackney, about six miles northeast of Westminster Abbey.[5]

The record is clear—the young preacher was well liked and respected. An historical account two generations later averred that he showed "evi-

---

[2] John M'Kerrow, *History of the Secession Church* (Glasgow: A. Fullarton and Co., 1841), 872.
[3] Ibid.
[4] Sherman Isbell, "Burgess, Oath," in Nigel M. de S. Cameron, David F. Wright, David C. Lachman, and Donald E. Meek, eds., *Dictionary of Scottish Church History & Theology* (Downers Grove, Ill.: InterVarsity, 1993), 109.
[5] James Grant, *Sketches of London* (Philadelphia: Carey and Hart, 1839), Vol. II, 124.

dence of a masculine understanding richly stored with theology...while in common with the venerable *Dr. Jerment*, he contributed by the excellence of his regular ministrations to draw honour around the cause of the Secession in London."[6]

In Hackney, owing to the soil, farming was not feasible; accordingly, the agricultural pursuit was largely that of grazing. In addition to a place for cattle, it was also an area of manor houses. Under Henry VIII, the many religious orders in and around the village were broken up and their land given to the crown. That land was sold to nobility, who desired the healthy environment as well as the close proximity to London (less than three miles away); these country estates would provide the ability to retreat from the city for respite. In the eighteenth century, there were workhouses, too, in the general area—places where the poor could live and work. But what is perhaps most interesting is that the area was known for its religious nonconformity, which could include a variety of groups, including Quakers, Unitarians, Jews, and Baptists.[7]

It is not surprising, therefore, to find a Seceder congregation gathered here. The church met on Well-street, a half-mile long street which began at Mare Street and ran east before curving northeast. To the west of Well-street was a common called Well Street Fields. Nearby was a small hamlet on Well-street, which had two dozen people in the early seventeenth century.[8]

Though Hall's new charge was in what was largely a rural setting, nevertheless, it was just outside the national capital. Furthermore, in contrast to the homogeneity of West Lothian, there was much diversity, in terms of socio-economics, occupation, and religion. The wholly new experience must have been exhilarating for the youthful minister. This would have been true particularly because it was a place where there was much interaction of ideas. The Scottish Enlightenment was in full swing, and was influential not only in Scotland, but south of the border, in England, as well. And English philosophers were making their own mark, too.

---

[6] *Historical Sketch of the Origin of the Secession Church. By the Rev. Andrew Thomson, B.A.* and *The History of the Rise of the Relief Church. By the Rev. Gavin Struthers, D.D.* (Edinburgh and London: A. Fullarton and Co., 1848), 171.

[7] Hackney (London Borough), *London Borough of Hackney: Archaeological Priority Areas Appraisal* (N.p. [Oxford, England?]: Oxford Archaeology South, 2017), 6, 20, 24.

[8] Ibid., 55.

Appropriately, Archibald Hall would demonstrate his own contribution to the life of the mind. He proved to be an adept writer, penning a variety of works.

Produced just prior to his death and published posthumously some years later was *A Treatise on the Faith and Influence of the Gospel*; this lengthy book (more than 450 pages) is a sincere call to avoid hypocrisy. Another of his writings, consisting of two communion sermons, shows his pastoral heart as well as his interest in the doctrine and practice of worship.[9] Several of his writings reflect his role as a churchman. In 1771, he wrote *An Impartial Survey of the Religious Clause in Some Burgess-Oaths*, defending the position of the Associate Synod. He dealt with church polity in *An Humble Attempt to Exhibit a Scriptural View of the Constitution, Order, Discipline, and Fellowship of the Gospel Church*.[10] And in 1770, he published his magnum opus, this present volume, on the doctrine and practice of worship.

Hall's writings are both theoretical and practical; intellectual but also applicatory. Those characteristics are on full display in *Gospel Worship*. And it bears noting that he was continuing a long line of Reformed thinking on worship.

The general outline of what sparked the Protestant Reformation is well known. Martin Luther, upset with the sale of indulgences, preached against them, and also nailed his Ninety-five Theses to the door (serving sort of like a bulletin board or an ancient version of Facebook) of the castle church at Wittenberg. The papacy reacted to Luther's attack on the Church's corruption and also condemned his and the other Reformers' insistence that justification is by faith alone based upon the imputation of Christ's righteousness alone.

---

[9] The full title is *GRACE AND HOLINESS: OR, Complete Redemption effected by the SON of GOD, without the LAW; AND Believers Death to the Law, a Doctrine according to GODLINESS. Being the Substance of TWO DISCOURSES, DELIVERED AT Well's-Street, near Oxford-Street, August 4th and 5th, 1776; And now published, (by particular desire) with considerable Enlargements* (LONDON: Printed for G. Keith, in Gracechurch-Street; J. Mathews, N° 18, in the Strand; W. Watts, Upper-Moorfields; and D. Murray, Poultney-Court, Golden-Square, 1777).

[10] Other writings of his that have appeared in print are a tract on church fellowship, and a small collection of his letters.

However, that account is only part of the story. The battle over salvation was matched by an early modern era version of worship wars.

Perhaps the best recounting of this part of the religious conflict is Carlos N. M. Eire's *War Against the Idols*. The basic thrust of this *tour de force* is that "John Calvin, in defending the heritage of the Reformed attitude toward idolatry, forged a new, scripturally based, theological metaphysics in which the boundaries between the spiritual and the material were more clearly drawn than ever; and that his reaffirmation of the centrality of 'spiritual' worship, with its consequent denial of compromise, provided a solid ideological foundation for much of the social and political unrest that accompanied the spread of Calvinism."[11]

Calvinism unabashedly promoted a "pure" and "spiritual" worship which would brook no compromise—a rejection of idolatry that led to iconoclasm, which had both social and political ramifications. Our intention, however, is not to focus on the cultural, social, and political dimensions of the Reformation's worship wars. Beyond smashing idols, Calvinists also sought, positively, to establish "primitive" worship—that is to say, not primitive in the sense of crude or backwards or anti-intellectual, but primitive in the sense of reflecting the practice of apostolic Christianity.

Calvin, Knox, and numerous other Reformers promoted a thoroughgoing reformation of worship. In contrast to Luther's accommodationist position, Calvin and his followers sought to employ in worship only those practices which were divinely commanded.

This approach, which would later have the name "regulative principle of worship" attached to it,[12] characterized the Western branch of the Reformation. The Swiss Reformed, the French Reformed, the German Reformed, the Dutch Reformed, the English Puritans, and the Scots and Irish Presbyterians, all emulated this strict principle—at least in theory. The various Calvinistic churches put into practice simple, Bible-based services of worship. Musical instruments were largely swept away. All 150 psalms were put into meter so that the congregation could more readily

---

[11] Carlos N. M. Eire, *War Against the Idols: The Reformation of Worship from Erasmus to Calvin* (Cambridge: Cambridge University Press, 1990), 3.

[12] See Frank J. Smith (with Chris Coldwell), "The Regulative Principle of Worship: Sixty Years in Reformed Literature. Part One (1946–1999)," *The Confessional Presbyterian*, 2 (2006): 89–164, and "The Regulative Principle of Worship: Sixty Years in Reformed Literature. Part Two (2000-2006)," *The Confessional Presbyterian*, 3 (2007): 155–215.

participate in the singing. All manmade ceremonies and accouterments were abolished. The Word of God, both read and preached, became essential to the worship experience. The sacraments were reduced from seven to two (baptism and the Lord's Supper), and they were returned to their New Testament simplicity.

At least some of the confessions and creeds coming out of the Reformation and Post-Reformation eras directly reflect this commitment. In Scotland, the First Book of Discipline (1560) condemns idolatry, by which it understands "the Mass, invocation of saints, adoration of images, and the keeping and retaining of the same; and, finally, all honouring of God not contained in his holy word." The Heidelberg Catechism was written in Germany in 1562; the catechism's Q. 96, which asks "What doth God require in the second commandment?", answers: "That we in no wise represent God by images, nor worship him in any other way than he has commanded in his word." In Switzerland, Bullinger's Second Helvetic Confession (1564) declares that "we teach that God is to be adored and worshipped as he himself has taught us to worship, namely, 'in spirit and in truth' (John 4:23 f.), not with any superstition, but with sincerity, according to his Word; lest at anytime he should say to us: 'Who has required these things from your hands?' (Isa. 1:12; Jer. 6:20). For Paul also says: 'God is not served by human hands, as though he needed anything,' etc. (Acts 17:25)."

But the most explicit expression of a strict view of worship would be found in the productions of the Westminster Assembly (1643–1649), which reflected the convictions of the Puritans in England and the Presbyterians of Scotland. Chapter XXI of the Westminster Confession of Faith declares that "the acceptable way of worshipping the true God is instituted by himself, and so limited by his own revealed will, that he may not be worshipped according to the imaginations and devices of men, or the suggestions of Satan, under any visible representation, or any other way not prescribed in the Holy Scripture." The Westminster Larger Catechism, Q/A 108, says: "The duties required in the second commandment are, the receiving, observing, and keeping pure and entire, all such religious worship and ordinances as God hath instituted in his Word." Similarly, "The sins forbidden in the second commandment are, all devising, counseling, commanding, using, and anywise approving, any religious worship not instituted by God himself" (Q/A 109).

Though the Westminster Standards were designed as a way of providing uniformity of doctrine, polity, and worship for the entire English-speaking world, the English, prodded by a monarchy committed against Puritanism, soon turned away from the Westminster perspective. It was left to the Scots to perpetuate the Westminster approach. Ever since the adoption of the Westminster Standards by the Church of Scotland General Assembly in 1647, Presbyterianism and Westminster have been intertwined and inseparable items. But the embrace of the theology of the Westminster Assembly by the Scots was not the discovery of new thinking; rather, it gave the Scots the opportunity to say "Amen!" to what they already believed.

Moreover, one should note that across the theological spectrum and the denominational landscape, not only intellectual stimulation but also a deep-seated spirituality epitomized Scottish church life. Or, we could say that the commitment to intellectual engagement was not merely hypothetical. The fact of widespread martyrdom reminded the Scots of the seriousness of their faith, and confirmed them in their desire to serve Christ. Even the doctrinal controversies, which often produced schism, served to stimulate their thinking and to enable an iron-sharpening-iron reality.

Scotland, then, in the 1700s was uniquely positioned for intense and mature reflection on the doctrine of worship—one which not only celebrated proper worship but which also inculcated the manner by which such regulated worship should come to expression and have a personal, heart-felt impact on the worshiper. Only in a land such as this could there have arisen the type of work found in Hall's *Gospel Worship*. It is not a 25-year Scotch, but a libation that was more than two centuries in the making.[13]

After a brief Preface, the author pens almost forty pages of Introductory Discourse. It is here that he distinguishes between civil honor or worship, and religious worship. When the term ("worship") "is applied to the

---

[13] Perhaps the best book on Presbyterian worship in Scotland is Charles Greig M'Crie, *The Public Worship of Presbyterian Scotland Historically Treated* (Edinburgh and London: William Blackwood and Sons, 1892). For a good treatment of the Westminster Directory, see Richard A. Muller and Rowland S. Ward, *Scripture and Worship: Biblical Interpretation and the Directory for Public Worship* (Phillipsburg, N.J.: P & R Publishing, 2007).

infinitely great and perfect God, denoting the adoration of our hearts, and suitable expressions of it in our words and actions, it is properly *Religious* or *Divine Worship*, and admits of no limitation, being founded on absolute supremacy, and all other infinite perfections of the divine nature. It lies in acknowledging the boundless perfections of the supreme Being, and owning our dependence on him, for what we are, and for what we have; for what we need, and for what we wish" (4).

This religious worship must be concerned not just with inward attitude but with the external expression: "the exercise of the heart is the principal thing in worshipping God; but they go to a very criminal extreme, that altogether exclude bodily service" (15). In other words, worshipping properly entails not merely the thinking of good things, but engaging in particular parts (or elements or practices) of worship that are prescribed.

Most importantly, then, "God is to be worshipped only *in the way of his own appointment*. The appointments of the Deity concerning his worship, are not to be gathered from the uncertain tradition of the elders, the authority of men, or the dictates of our own reason: no; they stand engrossed in the volume of *his book*, which is the *only* rule to direct us how we may glorify and enjoy him" (23). Furthermore,

> God is to be worshipped *by the assistance of his Spirit*...Those that would worship the living God with acceptance, ought to entertain such humble and grateful sentiments. All their just apprehensions, pure, spiritual, and holy affections, earnest desires, humble confidence, enlargedness of heart, peace and joy, freedom, fervor and propriety, and whatever else can be named, that enters into or constitutes evangelical and animated devotion; all come from the Spirit, and are all his own fruits. He must enlighten and impress the mind with suitable views of the object and nature of our adorations; incline and fix the heart in this heavenly exercise; administer boldness in entering into the holiest of all by the blood of Jesus; uphold, encourage, and assist with realizing manifestations of the truth in the conscience; and enable us to cry, *Abba, Father*; bearing witness with our spirits, that we are the children of God (25).

That Spirit-led worship should influence the one who is offering the worship:

God is to be worshipped *in the exercise of all suitable graces*, under the influence of his Spirit...We should seriously think of his greatness and our own nothingness, of his holiness and our vileness, of his righteousness and our guilt, of his transcendent excellence and our unworthiness, of his all-sufficiency and our necessity, of his incomprehensibleness and our darkness: we should take a survey of these to aggrandize him in our eyes, and to lay us low before him. And with what delight and gratitude should we reflect on the riches of his grace in Christ, and the various strong encouragements he has given us in him, and in the promises of his covenant, to relieve us under a sense of our multiplied discouragements in ourselves!...When we approach to him in any act of worship, we should look by faith to an atoning Savior, and yield up ourselves to stand in his righteousness before the throne of God, and so go to him in Christ as our God, as the Father of mercies, and our almighty Friend. We should relent with brokenness of heart, with ingenuous shame, and evangelical repentance, for our multiplied and aggravated offenses; and should surrender ourselves, and all our concerns, for time and eternity, into our Father's hands, and be ready to do and suffer his will in all things. Our hearts should rise above this world, and enter by faith, hope, desire, love and joy, into that within the veil, whither Jesus our Forerunner is entered for us; and we should be making the best of our way to that blessed world, with humble, firm dependences on God's covenant-faithfulness and love, that all things shall work together for our good; and that he will guide us by his counsel, and afterwards receive us to his glory. And all this should be done with earnestness and fervor, with integrity and uprightness of heart, that we may be sincere, and without offense, till the day of Christ (26).

Hall deals with one of the controverted matters between the Anglicans on the one hand, and the English Puritans and Scottish Presbyterians on the other, viz., the use of liturgies. In denying the legitimacy of the Anglican Book of Common Prayer, Hall contests the idea of there being an authorization of a binding form of words in any period of redemptive history, starting with the antediluvian era into the Christian age. For example, that "there is no vestige of any form of prayer given by God, far less drawn up and imposed by men, for ordinary public worship, *from Moses to David*." Similarly, "It cannot be proved, that there was any form of prayer used or imposed, *from the reign of David, till the captivity of the Jews*." And, "there is no satisfying evidence, that ever the Jewish church used a form of prayer, *from the captivity to Christ*" (32). In arguing that liturgies are "unreasonable impositions," Hall writes: "No creature has any right to impose anything on mankind in what concerns the worship and service of God" (37).

Hall offers a few more pages of prefatory material, in which he lists the chapters to follow; as he writes, his purpose "is to treat of the several ordinances of God, that belong to his worship." He also states: "My design is to hold forth such things as are of divine institution in each ordinance, that we may be furnished with knowledge to discern between the appointments of heaven, and the inventions of men" (45). A comparison of this list to the list of chapters in the Westminster Directory for Publick Worship reveals commonality.[14] At the same time, there are some differences.

For example, since Hall's focus is more than just public worship, he discourses on some matters that the Directory for Publick Worship does not.[15] That variation is simply a manifestation of a different scope. But more significantly, some of the items in Hall's list would not be regarded as an *ordinance* of God per se, but rather an *occasion* when religious exercises, including prayer, would be appropriate. Examples of this latter phenomenon include Hall's handling of "Ministerial visitations of the flock" and "Ministerial visitations of the sick."

---

[14] The chapters in the Westminster Directory are as follows: "Of the Assembling of the Congregation, and their Behaviour in the Publick Worship of God"; "Of Publick Reading of the Holy Scriptures"; "Of Publick Prayer before the Sermon"; "Of the Preaching of the Word"; "Of Prayer after Sermon"; "Of the Administration of the Sacraments, and First of Baptism"; "Of the Celebration of the Communion, or the Sacrament of the Lord's Supper"; "Of the Sanctification of the Lord's Day"; "The Solemnization of Marriage"; "Concerning Visitation of the Sick"; "Concerning Burial of the Dead"; "Concerning Publick Solemn Fasting"; "Concerning the Observation of Days of Publick Thanksgiving"; "Of Singing of Psalms"; and an appendix, "Touching Days and Places for Publick Worship." The astute observer will note that two of the elements of worship in the (exhaustive) list in Westminster Confession of Faith, Chapter XXI, viz., the taking of religious oaths and vows, are not handled by the Westminster Directory.

[15] Even the Directory includes some matters that are not public worship, including visitation of the sick. Hall includes even more topics that likewise are not public worship.

In a similar vein, Hall argues that showing mercy to the poor, because of the description of it being "pure religion, and undefiled before God and the Father" (James 1:27), is "a branch of holy worship, and to be performed out of respect to God. When it is practiced upon these principles, it becomes a sacrifice with which 'God is well pleased,' Heb 13:16." In his estimation, "Doing good, and communicating, are sacrifices in which God is said to be well pleased. Charitable donations are an odor of sweet smell, a sacrifice acceptable and well-pleasing unto God…Our glorified Redeemer in heaven, and his poor members on earth, are joined together in so close, intimate, and indissoluble an union, that what is done to his poor, is actually and truly done to him." When performed properly, "the *mercy* shown to the saints, becomes an act of truly sincere and uncorrupted *worship*" (545f).

But Hall's conclusion does not take into account that the Bible was using metaphorical language in order to impress upon believers the importance of such service, not to intimate that all such service is to be regarded as acts of worship per se. As a matter of fact, the same approach could appeal to Romans 12:1, 2 in order to try to demonstrate that all of life is worship—a proposition that would, of course, defeat the very point of talking about worship as something distinct. It would also conflict with the dialogical nature of worship, in which God speaks and men respond.[16]

What we are suggesting is that while all elements of worship are ordinances, not all ordinances are elements or parts of worship. Not everything that is of a religious nature, and that has been established by God, is necessarily an act of worship.

There is another issue in which Hall deviates from historic Presbyterianism, viz., in terms of church-state relations. Specifically, with regard to whether the church should be, in the words of Westminster Larger Catechism Q/A 191, "countenanced and maintained by the civil magistrate," Hall goes in a counter direction. He argues that churches in the New Testament age should have "no connection with civil powers, no dependence upon them, and no assistance from them, considered merely as churches"

---

[16] See Frank J. Smith, "The Nature of Worship," in Frank J. Smith and David C. Lachman, *Worship in the Presence of God: A collection of essays on the nature, elements, and historic views and practice of worship* (Greenville, S.C.: Greenville Seminary Press, 1992; rpt. Fellsmere, Fla.: Reformation Media and Press, 2006).

(609; cf. 613f). His view, which may very well have been influenced by Enlightenment ideas, was also manifest in American Presbyterianism, as his spiritual cousins across the pond, in adopting the Westminster Confession of Faith in 1788, modified Chapters XXIII and XXXI in a similar fashion.

But here's the problem: if the subject of divine worship is something which should not be within the purview of the civil magistrate, then the second commandment is no longer universally applicable—that is to say, binding upon all persons at all times. The end result is a secularization of the state, rather than its being, in principle, subject to the rule of God.[17] But that position runs counter to the Westminster Larger Catechism, Q/A 99, which maintains that the moral law is universally binding. Furthermore, in a subtle way, this position eats away at the notion of the content of worship as being totally objective. Yes, it is true that one could, for the moment, maintain a strict view of worship which is binding upon the church. Nevertheless, it is arguable that this modification of the conception of church-state relations is one of the reasons why American Presbyterian worship, in short order, started to turn away from the regulative principle, to a more pragmatic basis of determining worship practices.[18]

However, please note that while we take exception to Hall's conception of a few of these matters, that quibble should not detract from his overall wise counsel and direction regarding the practice of worship.

There is far too much material in this present volume to attempt to give even a brief synopsis of all of the chapters. But we do think it worthwhile and important to highlight several matters that may be of particular interest to today's reader.

---

[17] This conclusion is definitely not what Hall intended. He recognizes that the authority of civil magistrates "is originally in, and derived from the King of kings, and Lord of lords." Furthermore, these rulers "ought to fear God above all, to be prudent in their designs, courageous in their performances, faithful in their promises, wise in their counsels, careful observers of their own laws, zealous for their subjects' welfare, merciful to the oppressed, favorable to the good, terrible to the evil, and just to all." Indeed, they "must give an account unto the great God of all that trust he hath reposed in them" (405f). However, notice that there is no specific reference to the law of God as informing the civil magistrates as to how they should govern. In any case, denying the obligation of the civil magistrate to follow the second commandment, drives a wedge between the first table of the law and the second table of the law, which ultimately leads to governmental autonomy.

[18] For demonstration of how pragmatism influenced even Old School Presbyterianism, see Julius Melton, *Presbyterian Worship in America: Changing Patterns Since 1787* (rpt. Eugene, Ore.: Wipf and Stock Publishers, 2001).

In Chapter 1, "Of Reading the Holy Scriptures," Hall clearly agrees with the Westminster Directory in affirming that the reading of Scripture in public worship is to be done by someone who is called to such (48, 82f), and in distinguishing between reading and preaching (49).

In Chapter 4, "Of Singing the Praises of God," we find the observation that the singing of praise is perpetual because it "is a part of *moral worship*; whereas sacrifices are of *ceremonial institution:* the first may therefore be performed in a spiritual manner; but the last cannot, being a carnal commandment in the very nature of it, though subservient to a spiritual purpose." Accordingly, "This duty of singing remained in full force, after the ceremonial law, with all its instituted rites, was abolished." Indeed, we are *"under an obligation* to sing psalms, and hymns, and spiritual songs" (117). This obligation "to sing publicly the praises of God, is the *same* upon *women* and *men*. They are jointly members of his church, and heirs of his kingdom; and therefore, are equally bound to celebrate his praise. To be sure, women should keep silence in the churches: for it is not permitted for them to speak there (1 Cor. 14:34). It is neither decent, nor allowable for them to preach, or act the proper part of the man, in any public way of speaking… [B]ut this is no reason, why they may not bear a part in psalmody, and joining with the church to sing divine praise, since this is *no act of authority*; but a moral service, which concerns *equally* all the human species: let their glory, therefore, sing his praise" (124). With regard to the content of worship song, the author advocates the standard Presbyterian position of exclusive psalmody, and disproves the views of Isaac Watts (125ff). Hall justifies metrical singing as entirely proper, as well as the practice of lining out, and addresses the choice of tunes (129, 131f, 132).[19]

Chapters 11 and 12 deal with times of thanksgiving and religious fasts. Hall properly notes that both of these matters are occasional in nature. His counsel regarding how to engage in fasting is particularly helpful.

Chapter 16 discusses social religious meetings, which are defined as *"regular societies of Christians, who have voluntarily agreed to assemble together, at stated times and places of meeting, for obtaining, and communicating, the useful purposes of holy friendship one with another"* (474). Curiously, Hall argues that several passages that customarily have been regarded as references to the congregation in its public worship, such as Colossians

---

[19] See also pp. 522f for his discussion of singing in private worship.

3:16 and Hebrews 10:24–25, are actually proof texts for these voluntary meetings (477f).

The final chapter broaches a topic that is seemingly unique for a work on worship—the casting of lots. Hall writes that "*a lot* is an ordinance of the like *sacred* and *religious nature* with *an oath:* and, as in *taking an oath* upon any just occasion, God is to be regarded as the heart-searching and omniscient, as the righteous and tremendous Judge of all; so in *the use of a lot*, God is to be regarded as the immense Governor of the world, who knows all things, and who is able and has a right to control, direct, and dispose of all as he sees fit.... The lot is a special, particular, and solemn appeal to God, and supposes that he is present to determine the event which is put upon the issue of it, as an oath supposes that he is a present Witness of what is sworn" (625).

Lastly, the Appendix addresses several practices which "are supposed by some to be standing religious services, appointed by the Lord Jesus Christ, to continue till his second coming." They are love-feasts, the holy kiss, washing the disciples' feet, and abstaining from the eating of blood and of things strangled (635).

What we have in this massive tome is a significantly applicatory yet also highly intellectual consideration of the doctrine and practice of worship. The work is a manifestation not only of the seriousness, but also the genius of the Scots.

In 2001, a book appeared with the outrageous title *How the Scots Invented the Modern World*.[20] The title's claim is provocative, perhaps even extravagant, but the scholar does have a point. In numerous fields, including science (Charles Lyell's *Principles of Geology*), technology (James Watt's steam engine), industry (steel magnate Andrew Carnegie), communication (Alexander Graham Bell), transportation (macadamised roads named after John McAdam; John MacDonald's construction of the Canadian Pacific Railway), medicine (Alexander Munro, Sr.'s pioneering work in anatomy; John Lind's treatment of scurvy), literature (Robert Burns; Sir Walter Scott), economics (Adam Smith and his *Wealth of Nations*), education (the Scottish approach creating the American liberal arts college and

---

[20] Arthur Herman, *How the Scots Invented the Modern World: The True Story of How Western Europe's Poorest Nation Created Our World & Everything in It* (New York: Three Rivers Press, 2001).

the American university), politics (numerous politicians are from Scottish descent, including Andrew Jackson, John C. Calhoun, James Knox Polk, and Sam Houston), and philosophy (David Hume's empiricism; Thomas Reid's Scottish common sense realism), Scotsmen and their descendants have had an influence far vaster than the size of Scotland. Plus, the Scots and Scots-Irish brought their inventiveness and indomitable spirit and invincibility that conquered frontiers, to all the other continents. Indeed, Scots were in the forefront of American independence (Scottish Presbyterian minister John Witherspoon, president of what today is Princeton University, was the only clergyman to sign the Declaration of Independence; the Mecklenburg Declaration in North Carolina predated the July 4th, 1776 declaration in Philadelphia by more than a year).

The author even acknowledges (though a bit reluctantly) that those pesky old Presbyterians (such as John Knox) were at least partially responsible for establishing the foundation in which all this progress could be made. However, he posits that the real progress was possible only after ecclesiastical "moderates" came to the fore, and the Scottish Enlightenment replaced the radical commitment to the divine revelation of the Bible.

To secularists, the Scottish contribution to the world is found not in the spiritual realm, but in a rejection of it. But as modernist (or postmodernist) assumptions continue to take root, post-Christian Scotland will quickly discover that the inherent contradictions in its "brave new world" will result in the society falling apart. Even if Scotland might continue to lay claim to great discoveries and innovations (as a manifestation of residual blessing arising from the permeation of Christianity), Scotland's great days, for the moment, at least, most likely are long since gone. And one of the prime reasons for the downgrade is that Scotland has forgotten that the most important and influential and foundational factor in the prospering of a society is genuine religion—that is, biblical Christianity.

In its place have come secular humanism, atheism, Roman Catholicism, and Islam. There has also been a reawakened paganism, from which Scotland had been rescued and redeemed hundreds of years ago.

And what does this so-called progressive society look like? Really, a rather barbarian place. For the year ending March 31, 2019, violent crimes (murders, attempted murders, and serious assaults) were up more than ten percent in comparison to the previous year, and sexual crimes were up 7.3 per cent.[21] Drug abuse is rampant—so much so that Scotland's drug death rate is Europe's highest.[22] "Out-of-wedlock" is the new normal for pregnancies and births.[23] Gangs and street violence mirror Scotland's violent past when the Picts and other pagans ruled.[24] A new totalitarianism threatens the ability of Christians to maintain practices and opinions in accord with Scripture on various ethical matters, including abortion and sexuality.[25] Scotland has become the first nation to embrace the pro-perversity position with regard to sexuality, with school children being propagandized to parrot the absurd (and totally unscientific) view that there are multitudinous genders.[26] And much of the blame must be laid at the church's door: not only have church membership and attendance plummeted, but, more devastatingly, many of the churches which formerly were solid in their profession of Christianity have rejected that faith once delivered to the saints.

Sadly, in the twenty-first century, it is a not-so-bonnie Scotland that one finds. But the contrast between 1770 and 2020 makes Archibald Hall's work all the more poignant and significant. For only through a rediscovery of the spiritual truths with respect to worship found in this book will Scotland's true gift to the world be a blessing to that fabled land and more broadly as well.

In 1778, Archibald Hall was dying. His bodily frailty, manifest by a cough and labored breathing, had afflicted him for a number of years. Ascending into the pulpit took its toll physically—ministering the word was often painful. But a letter he wrote during his time of illness speaks of his joy of belonging to Christ:

---

[21] Chris Marshall, "Police Scotland record 'shocking' rise in number of violent crimes," *The Scotsman* (May 18, 2019)

[22] "Scotland drug death rate highest in Europe and still on rise," BBC Online (May 31, 2019).

[23] "Majority of Scottish babies born out of wedlock," *The Scotsman* (March 12, 2009).

[24] Ron McCay, "Murder, maiming and mayhem…Glasgow's gang wars are well and truly back," [Glasgow] *Evening Times* (May 13, 2018).

[25] One Scotland (https://onescotland.org/campaigns/hate-crime-campaign/).

[26] Matthew Robinson, "Scotland becomes first country to back teaching LGBTI issues in schools," CNN online (updated November 9, 2018); Jolene Campbell, "Primary one children will be told 'your gender is what you decide,'" *The Scotsman* (August 5, 2018, updated August 7, 2018); Diane Gaskins, "Gender War Update: Scottish Student Expelled For Believing in Two Genders," Pulpit and Pen website (July 6, 2019).

> I see no refuge for me in the prospect of change and war,[27] death and eternity, but only in the sovereignty of divine grace, and in the everlasting righteousness of Jesus, and surety of the better covenant. I see no other warrant, nor indeed any need of a further warrant, to believe my salvation by grace, to expect victory over death, and to appropriate eternal life, besides the free and faithful exhibition which God makes to me, as a sinner, of Jesus Christ, and all things with him. O that the view of things which stands clear to my understanding may be the daily ministration of the Spirit, and of all his saving and precious fruits to my soul! In the view of these truths, I hope to say, Farewell time and all its vanities, welcome eternity and all its realities.

Another letter also bears witness to his hope:

> The springs of life are wasting, though under many merciful circumstances, which render the decay comparatively very easy to nature. I have long believed the truth of the union between Christ and his people; I saw it was manifestly a Scripture doctrine; I believed it to be a very important one; but I think the consolation of it opens of late on my mind with a kind of evidence and satisfaction which I never before perceived. By this union, Christ's righteousness is my righteousness, his death my death, his life my life, his glory my glory! Here I often solace myself. In this medium, death and the grave are divested of all their gloom; judgment appears to be a joyful solemnity; eternity, a delightful, boundless object of expectation and desire.

After quoting these epistles, one author observed:

> Such were the sentiments that animated this good man in the prospect of bidding adieu to this world. He looked forward to the approaching change with a dignified composure. When any of his people visited him, during his illness, he was peculiarly urgent in

---

[27] The reference is to the War for American Independence, which had commenced in 1775, and was formalized with the Declaration of Independence in 1776.

admonishing them to attend to the concerns of their soul; and assured them that all the hopes of a happy eternity, which he cherished, rested solely on the merits of that Saviour, whom he had, during the course of ministrations, so frequently recommended to their regard. Some of his friends having paid him a visit, when he was near the close of his days, and weeping by his bedside at the prospect of the loss which they and the church of Christ would speedily sustain in his removal from them, he addressed them in the language of the Saviour: "If ye love me, ye would not weep, but rejoice, because I say I go to the Father." Soon after this he fell asleep in Jesus. He expired on the 6th of May, 1778, in the forty-second year of his age, and nineteenth of his ministry. His dust was deposited among the ashes of the non-conformists in Bunhill-fields.[28]

As demonstrated by the way that he faced death, he had appropriated the lessons he had laid out in this work on worship. This book is not only his magnum opus, but also his testimony. And it is also his legacy which he has left to us.

So, enjoy this volume. Sip it. Savor it. And relish the thought that this work not only will bring blessing to whatever land in which it is implemented, but that it will aid in leading you beside the still waters and into pastures green, in eternity.

Frank J. Smith, Ph.D., D.D.[29]
June, 2024

---

[28] M'Kerrow, *History of the Secession Church*, 873–74. Bunhill Fields is a cemetery in the London Borough of Islington, just north of the City of London. Among those who were buried there were numerous non-conformist ministers, including the famed theologian John Owen and John Bunyan, author of *The Pilgrim's Progress*.

[29] The author of the Foreword, Dr. Frank J. Smith, is President of Tyndale International University, Los Angeles; Lecturer of History at Georgia Gwinnett College; and Pastor of Atlanta Reformed Presbyterian Church.

Preface

The ordinances of gospel-worship are an important branch of the system of revealed truth, which is delivered to mankind in the Scriptures. The grace of God that bringeth salvation is the matter of our faith, and the guide to our practice; it is a firm ground of confidence and a spring of willing, spiritual obedience. That obedience, which arises from a belief of the truth, is most extensive—as the law, which is the rule of it, is exceeding broad. It includes all the dependence, service, and resignation due to God; and all the benevolence, honor, and good offices we owe to men.

Religious worship, in the full extent of it, is implied in *the obedience of faith*: and therefore, though some of *its outward circumstances* may be determined by *prudence*, everything that pertains to *the substance of its services* must be adjusted by *divine institution*. The *moral law* binds us to "receive and observe, to keep pure and entire, all such religious worship and ordinances as God hath appointed in his word." When worship is not conducted upon this principle it becomes odious in the sight of God, and so far unprofitable to them who are exercised in it with the greatest diligence and zeal. The verdict of heaven is clear and positive: "in vain do they worship me, teaching for doctrines the commandments of men" (Matt. 15:9).

These volumes are intended to exhibit that system of instituted worship which is delivered in the oracles of God. The subject is copious, important, and interesting; and the reader is entitled to judge of the execution of it. I must, however, be allowed to anticipate some of the objections that will probably be made against the work, by making a few observations relative to it, as,

1. I do not pretend to amuse the world with *original essays* upon the several branches of the subject. I gratefully acknowledge my obligations to the pious labors of such writers as I have had the happiness to consult, though I have not confined myself to the plan followed by any one of them. In a performance of this nature, it may be questioned whether *originality* (which has in many cases a claim to the highest esteem) would be a real merit. Perhaps a concise judicious *arrangement* of what is most

pertinent and weighty in the writings of these who have carefully examined the subject in its several parts, would answer a better purpose.

2. My design is not to write for *a party*, but with impartial candor to state and plead what I apprehend to *be the cause of God and truth*. I am not ashamed to declare myself a warm conscientious friend to the Reformation-system of doctrine, worship, discipline, and government, which is publicly professed in the *Church of Scotland*, and delineated in the *Confession of Faith* and *Catechisms*, in the *Directory for the Worship of God*, and in the *Form of Presbyterial Church-government*—all composed by *the Assembly* convened at *Westminster, annis* 1643–1647. But my attachment to this system arises neither from the authority of that assembly, nor from a devoted regard to my connections, whom I honor and esteem in the Lord, but from a conviction, upon inquiry, that this system for which our ancestors so nobly contended, is founded upon and agreeable to the oracles of God.

3. I intend no offense to any *man* or *party of men* by some strictures upon opinions or practices, wherein we differ upon principle. I only design to make an apology for my own sentiments and conduct, without violating that charity, which thinketh no evil, and rejoiceth in a manifestation of the truth (1 Cor. 13:5–6).

4. The same sentiments are sometimes repeated, but generally in a different light. Repetitions of this sort have their use and in writing on such a subject are not easy to be avoided. A critic may censure what a common reader (and for such this work is especially adapted) will perhaps reckon an advantage.

5. My highest ambition is to borrow all my arguments, authorities, and lights, from *The Word of God*. Human writings are often referred to in the following sheets to vouch facts and explain doctrines or duties, and sometimes to show the harmony of sentiments, but never to confirm an opinion. The *weight of names*, if admitted as a good argument in disputation, might embarrass the best cause in the world, and would soon reduce mankind to downright skepticism; or, which is not a great deal better, to build their faith on the most deceiving and precarious authority. But "we have a more sure word of prophecy, whereunto we do well to take heed" (2 Peter 1:19).

6. Though my conscience acquits me of a *design* to publish or vindicate any error, I readily acknowledge my liableness through prejudice, igno-

rance, or inadvertency, to mistakes upon some or all of the various weighty points under consideration. Therefore, notwithstanding the determining evidence that possesses my mind, I am still open to that conviction which arises from a faithful manifestation of Scripture truth, and will thankfully receive it from whatsoever quarter.

Upon the whole, I submit the performance to the judgment of the public, and recommend it, in a particular manner, to the careful perusal of *my own congregation*, to whom the substance of a considerable part of it was first delivered upwards of two years ago in several discourses, and for whose edification through the divine blessing, it is now, with various alterations and improvements, published in its present form—humbly beseeching the *Father of Mercies* to forgive all that is amiss; and to give a powerful testimony to whatever is *agreeable to his holy word*, in the conscience of every reader.

Archibald Hall
Castle-street, Oxford-road, London,
April 18, 1770

Introductory Discourse

I know not whither the dignity of sublime sentiment, or the propriety of judicious address, claims our first notice in Paul's speech to the men of Athens that is recorded in Acts 17:22–29. With the most prudent and engaging air, he acts the faithful *minister* and the tender *friend*; he joins the harmlessness of the innocent dove with the wisdom of the cunning serpent and insinuates the most profitable knowledge by an occasional hint taken from their avowed ignorance and superstition. Said he,

> Ye men of Athens, I perceive that in all things ye are too superstitious. For as I passed by, and beheld your devotions, I found an altar with this inscription, *To The Unknown God*. Whom therefore ye ignorantly worship, him declare I unto you. God that made the world, and all things therein, seeing that he is Lord of heaven and earth, dwelleth not in temples made with hands: neither is worshipped with men's hands, as though he needed any thing, seeing he giveth to all life, and breath, and all things; and hath made of one blood, all nations of men, for to dwell on all the face of the earth, and hath determined the times before appointed, and the bounds of their habitation: that they should seek the Lord, if haply they might feel after him, and find him, though he be not far from every one of us: for in him we live, and move, and have our being; as certain also of your own poets have said, For we are also his offspring. Forasmuch then as we are the offspring of God, we ought not to think that the Godhead is like unto gold, or silver, or stone graven by art and man's device.

Nor is the spirited and warm exclamation of Barnabas and Paul to the mob, that would have paid them divine honors, at Lystra, inferior to this in majesty, and force. The language is so simple, the sentiment so noble, and the evidence so strikingly clear, that it convinces the mind, awes the conscience, and offers a sacred violence to every movement of the heart. The text will be the best proof of this,

> Sirs, why do ye these things? We also are men of like passions with you, and preach unto you, that ye should turn from these vanities unto the living God, which made heaven, and earth, and the sea, and all things that are therein: who in times past suffered all nations to walk in their own ways. Nevertheless, he left not himself without witness, in that he did good, and gave us rain from heaven, and fruitful seasons, filling our hearts with food and gladness (Acts 14:15–17).

After such a speech, uttered with all the warmth of honest zeal, we are not much surprised to hear that the enthusiastic giddy populace were restrained from sacrificing unto them, though it was with difficulty.

It may be observed that in all ages and regions, the several nations of the world, however various and opposite in their characters, inclinations, and manners, have always united in one essential point: the inherent opinion of an adoration due to a supreme Being, and of external methods necessary to evidence such a belief. Into whatever country we cast our eyes we find priests, altars, sacrifices, festivals, religious ceremonies, temples or places consecrated to religious worship. In every people we discover a reverence and awe of the Deity, an homage and honor paid to him, and an open profession of an entire dependence upon him in all their undertakings and necessities, in all their adversities and dangers. Incapable of themselves to penetrate futurity and to ascertain events in their own favor, we find them intent upon consulting the Deity by oracles and by other methods of a like nature, and to merit his protection by prayers, vows, and offerings. It is by the same supreme authority they believe the most solemn treaties are rendered inviolable. That authority gives sanction to their oaths, and to that by imprecations is referred the punishment of such crimes and enormities as escape the knowledge and power of men. On their private occasions, voyages, journeys, marriages, diseases, the Divinity is still invoked. With him their every repast begins and ends. No war is declared, no battle fought, no enterprise formed, without his being first implored. To him the glory of their success is constantly ascribed by public acts of thanksgiving. Thus every nation will walk in the name of their god.

So general, so uniform, so perpetual a consent of all the nations of the universe—which neither the prejudice of the passions, the false reasoning of some philosophers, nor the authority and example of certain princes, have ever been able to weaken or vary—can proceed only from a first principle seated in the nature of man, from an inherent sense implanted in his heart by the Author of his being, and from an original tradition as ancient as the world itself. God hath not left himself without a witness in the things he hath made and in every man's conscience, and wherever this accumulated evidence has a due weight, it must convince us that he is and that he has a just claim to the homage of his creatures.

There are essential and eternal differences in the nature, stations, and conduct of beings, viewed in a comparison or relation to one another. One being excels another in glory and has a real, not an imaginary title to a preferable regard. These differences are the ground of all relative connections and account for the manifold subordination, dependence, and union of creatures, with regard to God and to one another.

Acknowledgments of superior worth and excellence, in an amiable, benevolent, and useful character, are a tribute due to justice and gratitude. Respect, esteem, honor, and reverence in external methods suitable to express such acknowledgments, are called *worship*, even where a fellow-mortal is the object of them (Luke 14:10). But we must not presume to degrade infinite perfection by any comparison, that would only show our extreme blindness and consummate folly. "To whom will ye liken God? or what likeness will ye compare unto him?" (Isa. 40:18). The eternal glories of his infinite perfection manifested to creatures in the manner and measure in which he is pleased to make them known, infallibly determine the kind and manner of that worship he requires. Would it be the height of blasphemy to acknowledge any creature to be equal to God? Would this be a bold invasion of the divine prerogative and a daring robbery? Surely the crime is no less if men will confer the worship of the Deity upon any creature.

Reason has universally perceived the necessary connection of this obvious inference with its principle, "God is, therefore he must be worshipped." Nor is this other inference less evident, "such as God is, such must the nature of his worship be." These conclusions may be illustrated, but they need no proof. Therefore, to give divine worship to a creature is a contradiction; it supposes the creature possessed of the transcendent glories of Godhead and yet to be but a creature still. A notorious absurdity!

In this introductory discourse, I beg leave to indulge some freedom of candid inquiry on the following heads, which will greatly contribute to answer the main design of this treatise. I shall attempt,
1. To explain the nature of religious worship;
2. To represent the obligation that lies on mankind to worship God;
3. To describe the manner of worshipping God with acceptance; and,
4. To make some remarks on liturgies, or forms of divine worship.

The Nature of Religious Worship
The first head leads me to explain the *nature of religious worship*. Worship in general is the respect or honor we pay to another on the account of his excellence or superiority. When *this* honor is applied to a creature, denoting the inward esteem or veneration we have of him, and *that* respect is the outward expression of regard we pay him, it is *civil honor* or *worship*, and is always subject to proper limitations, answerable to the limited excellence or superiority of its object. But when it is applied to the infinitely great and perfect God, denoting the adoration of our hearts and suitable expressions of it in our words and actions, it is properly *religious* or *divine worship*, and admits of no limitation, being founded on the absolute supremacy and all other infinite perfections of the divine nature. It lies in acknowledging the boundless perfections of the supreme Being and owning our dependence on him for what we are and for what we have, for what we need and for what we wish. Where there is not this *proper cause* of divine worship, to give it is *idolatry*; where there is this proper cause of divine worship, to withhold it is *atheism*. "Thou shalt worship the Lord thy God, and him only shalt thou serve" (Matt. 4:10).

Perhaps it may assist our apprehensions on this subject to review the emphatic terms used by the Holy Ghost, both in the Old and New Testament, to describe this worship. The Hebrews commonly express it by a word that comes from the root שחה, which properly denotes *bowing down*, either in order to do honor or on any other account. Most frequently indeed, though not always, it is applied to that honor and respect which inferiors pay to their superiors, by *bowing* the head, the body, the knees, or which was most respectful of all, by falling prostrate with their whole body on the earth with their arms stretched out. Accordingly, we often find these phrases of "bowing to the earth" (Gen. 33:3); "bowing to the ground" (Gen. 18:2). In eastern countries, the most profound obedience is paid by falling down with the face on the ground, to which we find several expressive allusions in the inspired writings (Ps. 72:9; Isa. 49:23; 65:25, besides many others). The application of this phrase to the worship of the most high God is so easy and natural that it is perceived as soon as it is proposed. I may only observe that this word is most commonly used in the conjugation *hithpahel*, and signifies in that form, "he bowed down himself," to express the voluntary, full, hearty, affectionate, and humble adorations of the true worshipers of the only living and true God.

In close connection with this the Hebrews use another word עבד, which carries the idea of *servitude*, and is more or less emphatic and significant, according to its object. Applied to God, it takes in the whole of practical religion in temper and behavior (Deut. 6:13; 28:47; Isa. 19:23). It is so called because it is a service prescribed by God and enjoined on man, and when performed is an instance of obedience that cannot claim a reward because it is only a performance of duty.

The New Testament is more copious and uses a greater variety of words in describing the worship of God. Among others I find it is expressed by words that are connected with the following roots, Σεβω, Θρησκος, Ευλαβης, Λατρευω, Δολευω, and προσκυνεω.

The verb Σεβω, or Σεβομαι, carries in it the signification of *warmth and fervor* in worship, and is a contrast both to cool indifferency, and lukewarmness in formal professions that are unattended with sincere affection; when it is compounded with the adverb ευ, as in ευσεβης it denotes "one that worships the true God *aright*, with a fervent spirit, in every proper expression of a temper impressed with the fear and love of God."

Θρεσκος, rendered *religious* (James 1:26), is supposed to be the same as "*Thracian*, or one belonging to the country of Thrace," in the original use of the word. Orpheus is said to have brought the rites of religious worship, that were afterwards used through all Greece, into that country; and then in honor of his country and the better to bind his countrymen to a persevering attachment to that system, he gave it the common name of his country. In after times it became a common character of a devout man. To be worshipers of the true God is the common characteristic of true Christians.

Ευλαβης, rendered *devout* (Luke 2:25), properly signifies "*one that takes well*, that is, with caution, prudence, and attention." Nothing can better express the cautious fear, the godly jealousy, and the circumspect attention of the people of God that should prevail especially in every part of his worship.

Λατρηια is another word frequently used to denote the worship due to God only; it is commonly and properly translated *service* (Rom. 12:1 and other places). It seems to answer exactly to the Hebrew word עבד taken notice of already.

The verb Δουλευειν, signifies "to devote one's self wholly to serve another." According to this sense of the word it is plain that no man can serve two masters (Luke 16:13). Everyone that has but a superficial acquaintance with the Popish controversy must know that the Romish church makes a mighty difference between the worship of Δουληια, and of Λατρηια; they appropriate this last to God and they pretend the other signifies a religious worship common to creatures. The harmonious judgment of *lexicographers* and *critics* of the *Protestant denomination* is, that these words are used promiscuously, and in strict propriety mean the same thing. If we suspect them of partiality in using this shift to support a party-quarrel against the creature-worshipers of the church of Rome, we may soon be satisfied for ourselves of the solid grounds of their judgment by considering (1.) the promiscuous use of these words in the best Greek writers.[1] And (2.) in the sacred writings: "they themselves shew of us…how ye turned [δουλευειν]…to serve the living and true God" (1 Thess. 1:9). "How much more shall the blood of Christ…purge your conscience from dead works [εις το λατρευειν] to serve the living God?" (Heb. 9:14).

> And I cannot but observe that several learned men of the Romish church have given up this long exploded distinction. Ludovicus Vives shows out of Suidas and Xenophon that these two words are usually taken for one another. Their learned Durantus allows the same as to Paul's use of the word. Cardinal Bellarmine and Vasquez are forced to own the distinction to be unscriptural. But the learned Nicolas Serrareus speaks out most freely on this head, and tells us that it is the opinion of the most and the wisest among them, that it is one and the same virtue of religion, which containeth both Λατρηια, and Δουληια.[2]

---

[1] See Edward Leigh. *Critica Sacra: Philological and Theological Observations upon the Greek Words of the New Testament, in Order Alphabetical*, on the word Δουληια.

[2] Obadiah Hughes. *Sermons Against Popery, Preached at Salters-Hall*, p. 16.

The last word I am to take any notice of is προσκυνειν, commonly translated *to worship*, as "thou shalt worship the Lord thy God" (Matt. 4:10). It answers to the Hebrew word שחה, which has been explained already. I shall only subjoin the substance of a remark made by the very learned Grotius on this word. It is to this purpose:

> Words frequently lose their original meaning and are confined to an adopted sense of them; this has actually happened to this Greek word προσκυνειν. It was first used of some gesture that testified some reverence, compare Matthew 8:2 with Luke 5:12. And then, as the outward sign is nearly related to what it signifies, it came to be used sometimes to signify the act of the mind itself. In general, and as it is used in the second commandment (Ex. 20:5), it denotes every act by which men use to show esteem, reverence, affection, and dependence.

That burning and shining light and ornament of the reformation, Mr. James Durham of Glasgow, in his excellent commentary on Revelation 19:10 has the following remark: "Worship implieth three things (1.) An act of the understanding, taking up an excellency in the object worshipped; (2.) An act of the will, yielding it conformly to that apprehended excellency; and (3.) An external act of the body."[3]

In explaining these weighty particulars every essential requisite of divine worship will naturally occur. I shall endeavor to be as concise and full as the importance of the subject, and my capacity, will admit on each of them.

1. An act of the understanding, whereby we discern an infinite excellency in the Lord our God, is implied in divine worship. He that cometh to God in the duties of religious worship, must believe that he is, and have some just apprehensions of his character. The most loyal subject would pay no more regard to his sovereign in disguise and incog, than his unknown assumed character in a stranger might reasonably expect. When men become vain in their imagination concerning the divine Majesty, they become absurd in their worship. We must know what we worship, or else our worship will be a vain oblation. The most high God, the Possessor of

---

[3] James Durham. *A Commentary upon the Book of the Revelation.*

heaven and earth, who is over all, God blessed forever, is the only worthy object of everlasting ascriptions of glory, honor, and blessing. He

> is a Spirit, in and of himself infinite in being, glory, blessedness, and perfection; all-sufficient, eternal, unchangeable, incomprehensible, every where present, almighty, knowing all things, most wise, most holy, most just, most merciful and gracious, long-suffering, and abundant in goodness and truth...[He] is but one only, the living and true God...There be three persons in the Godhead, the Father, the Son, and the Holy Ghost; and these three are one true, eternal God, the same in substance, equal in power and glory.[4]

This is the God we worship. How glorious and fearful is his name! How awful his majesty! And how amiable and excellent his whole character! Is he not rightly called the God of glory, and again, the God of all grace? Yes, thou, and only thou art worthy, O Lord, to receive all glory, and blessing, and honor, and power; for thou hast created all things, thou art the God of the whole earth, and what is superlatively good to sinful men, thou art in Christ the God and Father of the church. Thine awful and amiable glories shine on men with unutterable comfort, while thou sittest on thy throne, to look upon like a jasper, and a sardine stone, and a rainbow round about thy throne, in sight like unto an emerald (Rev. 4:2–3). May we come with humble boldness to the throne of thy grace, to receive mercy, and find grace to help us in the time of need! Let us daily ask the wisdom that is profitable to direct us, from the Father of lights, that we may with judgment and affection know himself, according to the plain revelation he has made of his perfections, counsels, and will, and of the way of salvation through the Messiah. Ignorant worship and blind devotion is the sacrifice of fools, it is abomination in the sight of God. Impressed views of the divine character are the only effectual means of producing such tempers as enter deep into the very nature of gospel-worship, such as humility, reverence, fear, trust, hope, esteem, and the like. These fruits of the Spirit live or die, abound or fail, according to our apprehensions of God. We must *truly know* or else we cannot *rightly serve the Lord.* Then shall we know that it is honorable, pleasing, profitable, and good to worship God, if we follow on to know

---

[4] *Westminster Larger Catechism*, questions 7–9.

the Lord. When the knowledge of the glory of the Lord fills the earth, a *pure offering* shall be offered in righteousness upon his altar; and when God shall be all in all in the heavenly state, his servants shall *serve* him.

2. That divine worship, which is our reasonable service, includes a hearty unreserved subjection of our wills to God, whom we apprehend to be so supremely glorious, so transcendently excellent. As we read we have reason to tremble at the alarming truth suggested in that awful text,

> The wrath of God is revealed from heaven against all ungodliness, and unrighteousness of men, who hold the truth in unrighteousness; because that which may be known of God, is manifest in them; for God hath shewed it unto them. For the invisible things of him from the creation of the world are clearly seen, being understood by the things that are made, even his eternal power and Godhead; so that they are without excuse: because that, when they knew God, they glorified him not as God, neither were thankful; but became vain in their imaginations, and their foolish heart was darkened. Professing themselves to be wise, they became fools: and changed the glory of the uncorruptible God into an image made like to corruptible man, and to birds, and fourfooted beasts, and creeping things. Wherefore God also gave them up to uncleanness through the lusts of their own hearts, to dishonour their own bodies between themselves: who changed the truth of God into a lie, and worshipped and served the creature more than the Creator, who is blessed for ever. Amen (Rom. 1:18–25).

Say not, O my soul, am I dog that I should do so? Rather implore the *free gift* of the *Spirit of love, and of a sound mind*, that thou mayest, under his benign influence, receive the truth in the love of it, and speak the truth in love in every approach to the throne of grace. The truths of God must not only be *put into our minds* but also *written in our hearts*, they must be apprehended in our understandings, and moreover, cordially embraced in our souls. This is of so great importance that we find the whole law is summed up and fulfilled in *love*. The want of this makes every religious service an abomination in the sight of God. Suppose the sentiments to be correct and the words good, yet if the heart is not sincere, God is dishonored, not glorified by such worship, if it may be called by that name.

Mere professions cannot deceive omniscience. He seeketh such as worship in spirit and in truth, to worship him. Devils believe that there is a God, and that he is a God of infinite excellency, and still they hate and tremble. We should believe that he is, and highly esteem, love, and honor him as a Being endued with attributes and perfections superlatively excellent, and making himself over in a covenant-grant to be our own God according to the tenor of his whole revealed character. This is called *a yielding ourselves to the Lord, following hard after him, being fervent in spirit, serving the Lord*, and *worshipping him in spirit and in truth.* In worshipping God the soul adores and reverenceth his majesty; is delighted with his amiableness; embraceth his goodness; dependeth wholly upon his veracity, power, and favor; enters into an intimate communion with this most lovely Object; admireth his works; believeth his word; approveth his actions; acquiesceth in his proceedings; patiently submits to his corrections; and centers his whole affections upon God alone. The true worshiper humbles himself before divine glory; is ashamed before divine purity; trusts in divine faithfulness; hopes in divine mercy; and comforts his soul in divine grace. In one word, he yields all the powers of his soul to be delightfully lost in conformity, dependence, and devotedness, to the Lord his God.

3. The third circumstance connected with the worship of God is an external act of the body. This is a fit adjunct of religious worship. Some are pleased to speak in very high terms about the nature and importance of bodily worship. Bishop King, in his book called *The Inventions of Man in the Worship of God*, is not content to say, "That bodily adoration is a part of God's worship"; though that is far enough from being proper or even true; he is pleased to add, "If we look into the Scriptures, we shall not find praying, praising, reading the Scriptures, or administering the sacraments, termed *worship*. Bending or bowing the body is *that* which is *properly* in Scripture called *worship, etc.*"[5] I shall contrast with this the remark of Mr. Boyse, who wrote an answer to this book, at the desire of the Presbyterian dissenters in Ireland, and printed it with their approbation:

> God requires external marks of our inward reverence when we offer up our prayers and thanksgivings, and accordingly it was the practice of holy men both in the Old and New Testament to offer these

---

[5] William King. *A Discourse concerning the Inventions of Men in the Worship of God*. 5th, p. 95.

parts of worship to God in such devout postures; and the Scriptures frequently call these external postures of devotion by the name of worship; not because these postures are immediate, direct worship, properly so called, but because these bodily actions are the external expressions of religious reverence and homage common to all the several parts of direct and immediate worship.[6]

Three things we earnestly plead: that the external acts of the body in religious worship are no distinct and separate part of that worship; that *of themselves* they are vain; and that they do not commend us to God. These things we ever assert and firmly believe. We also maintain and constantly affirm that "God is a Spirit: and they that worship him must worship him in spirit and in truth...for the Father seeketh such to worship him" (John 4:23-24). We daily urge the necessity of offering up *spiritual* sacrifices, and that the service of believers must be *reasonable*. We perseveringly recommend praying with the spirit, and with the understanding also; and to sing the praises of God with the spirit, and with the understanding also, with grace in the heart, making melody to the Lord.

But we must not imagine that outward worship is *needless* because inward worship is *so necessary and important*. Body and spirit must go on jointly in this *service*. Hence the apostle exhorts (1 Cor. 6:20), to glorify God in our bodies, and in our spirits which are God's. We must worship God with our bodies, not only using them in his service but *composing them to an allowable outward gesture*, as Mr. Boston has expressed himself on this point.[7] Ardent desire, unfeigned faith, lively hope, supreme love, holy fear, and judicious zeal, these most important and necessary ingredients in divine worship, far from excluding, do rather encourage, the uncovered head, the bended knee, the vocal song and supplication; or the table-posture in showing the Lord's death. We know that even the bodies of the saints are the temples of the Holy Ghost. The human frame is so constructed that we are apt, and cannot help it, to represent our inward affections by outward expressions; while the soul and body are vitally united they will naturally receive mutual impressions from each other. If there be

---

[6] Joseph Boyse. *Remarks on a Late Discourse*, p. 107.
[7] Thomas Boston. "The Distinguishing Character of Real Christians". In *Works, Volume 4*, p. 474.

any inward devotion and reverence in the mind, we cannot, without offering violence to our natures, forbear to express it by outward reverential signs, and gestures of adoration in the solemn worship of God. This is a ground in nature and reason, of all external acts of the body in divine worship. The words of that heathen poet, who says, *Format enim natura prius, etc.* that is, "nature forms us first to every shape of fortune," are drawn from that deep acquaintance with men and things, for which the writer is so justly admired.[8]

Whoever will be at pains to consult Fenelon of Cambray's dialogues concerning eloquence, with impartiality and attention, must be convinced that every inward prevailing temper of mind shows itself, in an external conduct or manner, that is perfectly natural; and where nature is most exactly followed men act most in character.

When we give honor to men, we do and we must use some bodily action to certify the person we honor, as well as others, that we would be thought to esteem and honor him in our minds, which cannot be known to fellow-creatures, but by such external signs. But when we worship God, it is wholly unworthy of his omniscience to suppose he needs to learn, to know what is in man, from such outward demonstrations. Nevertheless there are few points in the system of revelation, that are established with clearer and fuller evidence than this, "That the worship of God implies external actions of the body, corresponding to an hearty subjection of the will unto the sublime excellency of the Lord our God, truly apprehended in the understanding." For,

(1.) If we look into the Old Testament the evidence rises strong and flashes conviction. Examples are numberless: "Abraham's servant...worshipped the LORD, bowing himself to the earth" (Gen. 24:52); in the original it runs, "He bowed himself down to the earth, unto JEHOVAH"; "I bowed down my head, and worshipped [*Heb.* bowed myself unto] the LORD" (Gen. 24:48); "O come, let us worship and bow down: let us kneel before the LORD our maker" (Ps. 95:6); "Wherewith shall I come before the LORD, and bow myself before [worship] the high God?" (Mic. 6:6). But quotations might be multiplied to prove what is undeniable.

(2.) Let us in the next place inquire, what the New Testament has revealed on this point. And here we shall find an *exact harmony*, or more

---

[8] See Horace. *Ars Poetica: The Art of Poetry.*

properly, a *very sameness* in the account of divine worship, with what we have seen enjoined and observed under the Old Testament. The following examples may suffice for a specimen: "There came a leper, and worshipped him" (Matt. 8:2), "kneeling down to him" (Mark 1:40), "she came and worshipped" (Matt. 15:25), she "came and fell at his feet" (Mark 7:25), he "fell down before him" (Luke 8:28), "he worshipped him" (Mark 5:6), "he fell down at Jesus' feet" (Luke 8:41), "worshipped him" (Matt. 9:18), "Falling down on his face, he will worship God" (1 Cor. 14:25), "I fell down to worship at the feet of the angel...do it not...worship God" (Rev. 22:8–9). It will be rather too weak and absurd to insinuate, "that all these expressions are to be taken in a metaphorical and emblematical sense." I am apt to think a plea of that kind must be supported by principles that will enervate all the dictates of common sense, and render the Bible a useless system, because at best absurdly vague and of doubtful meaning. But if we should allow these to be figurative and that they only describe the exercises of the mind (which no prudent man will ask, as to the greater part of them), I would beg leave to suggest "that even this supposes a gesture of the body to which the disposition of the mind corresponds." So that such a plea and such a concession, admit the whole I am endeavoring to establish.

(3.) Let us now attend to some weighty examples of eminent characters; and they either expressly bear, or at least necessarily suppose "that bodily service is comprehended in divine worship." Holy angels, who are spirits and have not flesh and bones, are said in worshipping God to stand and cover their faces and feet (Isa. 6:2), or to fall down (Rev. 7:11). Devils are represented as doing homage to the Son of God, falling down (Mark 3:11). Stephen in his dying moments kneeled down, and prayed (Acts 7:60). Paul describes divine worship as a bowing the knee unto the God and Father of our Lord Jesus Christ (Eph. 3:14), and his exemplary conduct casts a beautiful luster on his description (Acts 20:36). The wise men that found the child Jesus by the direction of the star, worshipped him, falling down (Matt. 2:11). Mary Magdalene and the other Mary held Jesus by the feet and worshipped him (Matt. 28:9). Jesus has left us an example of this in worshipping his Father (Matt. 26:39; Luke 22:41) and has given directions concerning religious worship that includes bodily service (Mark 11:25). I might add that all religion is included in that expression, in "the name of Jesus every knee shall bow" (Phil. 2:10). And the same thing is meant in these pregnant texts: Romans 12:1 compared with 1 Peter 2:5 and 1 Corinthians 6:19–20.

(4.) I apprehend the apostle's reasoning in 1 Corinthians 11:4–15 furnishes another proof. Unless we suppose, that there is a visible decency and propriety in worshipping God with our bodies, we shall be still more at a loss than we are to find a tolerable sense of that difficult place.

(5.) An argument may be drawn from the second commandment. We are forbidden *to bow down ourselves unto graven images to serve them, because the Lord our God is a jealous God* (Ex. 20:5). To worship, and to bow down to an object, are allowed to have the same meaning (Isa. 2:8–9). This commandment, having a peculiar reference to the manner of religious worship, forbids the *false* and enjoins *the proper use* of the *modes of it*; we must not bow down to graven images because *such a manner of paying religious adoration is proper to God only*.

The general rule for using our bodies in a proper manner, while we are immediately engaged in the duties of divine worship, is laid down and supported by the polite and ingenious Witsius, in the following words,

> *Preces ordinariæ, statæ, etc.* Ordinary, stated prayers, in the closet, in the family, or in the sanctuary, require such gestures as are proper both to excite and demonstrate the humility, reverence, hope, zeal, and like affections of the mind: For (1.) In prayer, even our body should show that it is God's. (2.) We have the example of the saints, both under the Old and New Testament, and of Christ the King of saints to this purpose. (3.) We have the command of God to bind us. It is true, the repeated commands to bow down, to bend the knee, to stretch out our hands, *etc.* especially regard the soul; but it is plain, they suppose, *N.B.*, that gesture of the body, to which God would have the disposition of the soul to correspond. (4.) It is many ways expedient; for hereby we testify obedience and reverence to God; hereby fellow-worshipers, or present spectators, are stirred up to join with us; and hereby we are kept in mind that we speak to God; our very gestures being significant and instructive monitors.[9]

---

[9] Hermann Witsius. *Exercitationes Sacræ in Symbolum quod Apostolorum Dicitur et in Orationem Dominicam*, exercit. 4to. ss. 44ma.

The author is speaking indeed of prayer only, but what he says on that head may be also applied to other institutions that have the same object and the same tendency.

We are ever prone to sinful and dangerous extremes. While some zealously affect gaudiness, pomp, and show in the worship of God, and under pretense of decency model its divine institutions to please a vain and carnal mind, others show the utmost indifference about the external manner of their devotion; their plea is that if the heart be right with God, all is very well. To the former God says, "in vain do they worship me, teaching for doctrines the commandments of men" (Matt. 15:9), and to the latter he says glorify God with *your bodies* and your spirits (1 Cor. 6:20). Everyone must allow that the exercise of the heart is the principal thing in worshipping God; but they go to a very criminal extreme that altogether exclude bodily service. That text in John 4:23–24 is greatly perverted from its original meaning when it is adduced to prove that New Testament worship has no reference to the body, its gestures, and actions. This will best appear from a short view of the context.

In our Savior's time all the duties of religion were extremely sunk among the Jews; they were turned into merely bodily exercise, for the most part. The woman of Samaria, perceiving from a striking circumstance relating to her own private life that the Jew with whom she conversed was some extraordinary prophet, thought this was a favorable opportunity to obtain satisfaction upon a grand question of debate between the Samaritans and Jews touching the true place of divine worship: whether it was mount Gerizim, as the Samaritans held, or the temple at Jerusalem, according to the religion of the Jews? Our Savior, without hesitation declared in favor of the latter: "Ye worship ye know not what: we know what we worship: for salvation is of the Jews" (John 4:22), hereby not only condemning the defection of the Samaritans from the Jewish church, and that impure mixture of idolatry and heathenish superstition with which their commerce and affinity with the Assyrians had infected them, but also pronouncing the Jewish to be the true visible church of God: "salvation is of the Jews." In their custody is the law and the writings of the prophets; among them is the priesthood established by God, and that form of worship which he has appointed; and of them is the Messiah, the Christ. But our Savior, not content with setting her right in this particular (for new converts were to be made, not to Judaism, but to Christianity), acquaints her that all disputes about locality of worship were frivolous and unimportant, seeing that distinction of place, which had till then obtained in the offering up of sacrifices, and the more solemn celebration of divine worship, was upon the point of ceasing, and the time at hand, when God would be served in a more free and unconfined manner: "the hour cometh, and now is, when the true worshipers shall worship the Father in spirit and in truth: for the Father seeketh such to worship him. God is a Spirit: and they that worship him must worship him in spirit and in truth" (John 4:23–24).

Nothing is more plain than the strong and lively contrast between worshipping the Father in mount Gerizim, or at Jerusalem, and worshipping him in spirit and in truth; and that the last comes in the room of the former. To have just apprehensions of the former will very much assist us to obtain the true meaning of the latter. I suppose by the worshipping of the Father at Jerusalem, all will own we are to understand worshipping him by ceremonial rites, and carnal ordinances, and particularly as it was *then performed for the most part*, with merely external expressions and modes of religious adoration. This being granted—and I do not see how it can be denied—it is a necessary consequence that to worship God in spirit and in truth, is to testify our reverence of his name, and to perform every act of religious worship according to the spiritual and substantial dignity of gospel-institutions, settled by the authority of Jesus Christ who is risen from the dead and who has adapted the plan of his church equally to serve the purposes of Jew and Gentile, that they may be no longer distinct but one new man in himself.

That the phrase of "worshipping God in the spirit," may include a great deal more is readily granted; but that this is the proper sense of it in this place and in Philippians 3:3, is undeniably evident from the context. In both these passages the old and new dispensations of divine grace are supposed to be one in substance, scope, and design, though differing in their form: the first exhibiting in a figure what is substantial in the latter. This consideration alone excepted, the saints that lived before the gospel-church was set up, worshipped God in a spiritual manner, as well as those that have lived since that memorable era. This will be evident by observing,

(1.) That all of them, under each dispensation, worshipped God with their spirit, soul, and body; they were all internal worshipers; they joined inward to outward worship; they aimed at, and in some measure attained the spirituality of worship, which includes a regard to the command of God, love to his service, delight in the work, and single views to his honor.[10]

(2.) They all worshipped by the assistance and influence of his Holy Spirit. And,

(3.) They were all sincere and upright in their hearts, in the service of God.

In a word, whatever constitutes real, vital, powerful, and practical godliness, is characteristic of believers and their worship under each dispensation, and therefore as "the worshipping of God in the spirit," must denote something not confined to the Jewish saints *as such*, it must have a reference to the system of gospel-institutions appointed by Christ after his resurrection, which does not exclude *bodily worship*, but *only figurative carnal ordinances*.

When I have excepted the Quakers and others of the same character, I am willing to submit this interpretation to the judgment of all Christian writers.[11]

The votaries of Rome, to justify their worshipping God by images and their worshipping of angels and saints, incessantly urge upon us new-coined distinctions between supreme and subordinate, absolute and relative, terminative and transient, proper and improper, primary and secondary worship, with many others which they have contrived to puzzle the cause and delude the ignorant. I shall only observe that the nature of divine worship is so simple it will not admit these distinctions—the sacred Scripture nowhere mentions them, the common people can neither know nor observe them, and even their own learned men differ about them.[12]

I must however observe that the worship of God is by some Protestants, and I apprehend not without some propriety, distinguished into *mediate* and *immediate* worship.

---

[10] Boston, "The Distinguishing Character of Real Christians".

[11] The reader may consult Boston, Boston, "The Distinguishing Character of Real Christians"; William Ames. *Conscience with the Power and Cases Thereof*, book 4, chapter 18; Thomas Bradbury et al. *Practical Discourses concerning the Duty of Prayer: Preach'd at the Friday Evening-Lecture in Eastcheap by Several Ministers*; the ingenious Isaac Watts. *Guide to Prayer*, chapter 2, section 7; Charnock on John 4:24; John Willison. *A Treatise concerning the Sanctification of the Lord's Day*, pp. 218–220; the learned reader will find the fullest satisfaction by perusing the very accurate Witsius, *Exercitationes*, from whom I made a quotation already. I could add a great many more, but it is altogether needless in a case that is so plain and so level to a common capacity and ordinary attention.

[12] See Hughes, *Sermons Against Popery, Preached at Salters-Hall*, on Isa. 42:8, pp. 13–15.

By immediate worship they mean those acknowledgments of the divine perfections and of creature-dependence that are expressed while, in solemn addresses to the divine Being, we celebrate his praise or call upon him in the name of Christ.

Mediate worship is that which we perform in observing duly such institutions as have a peculiar fitness, in their nature or appointed use, to instruct our minds, to impress our consciences, to confirm our faith, or to direct and encourage our obedience.

Praise and supplication are duties of the first class—as reading the Scriptures, hearing the word preached, administering and receiving the sacraments, *etc.*, are duties of the second.

The Obligation on Mankind to Worship God

I proposed under the second head to represent the weighty obligations that lie on mankind to worship God. Three considerations recommend it to every man's regard: it is (1.) just; (2.) useful; and (3.) necessary. These are not vain words, they are the language of truth and soberness. Happy is the man that feareth always, from an impressed conviction of the force and weight of these most important truths upon his conscience.

1. I observed first of all that it is a *just* and *righteous thing* to worship God. This service, though performed with the highest ardors and the greatest exactness, cannot lay God under an obligation to reward it. No less is due to him on every account. His supreme majesty and boundless perfection entitle him to every divine unlimited honor:

> Forasmuch as there is none like unto thee, O LORD, thou art great, and thy name is great in might. Who would not fear thee, O King of nations? for to thee doth it appertain: forasmuch as among all the wise men of the nations, and in all their kingdoms, there is none like unto thee…the LORD is the true God, he is the living God, and an everlasting king (Jer. 10:6–7, 10).

See with what holy zeal, deep humility, and unceasing fervor the blessed angels are affected while they pay this tribute (Isa. 6:2–3). They stand in his presence and mention his name with heartfelt adoration. They well know and always consider that the infinitely high and immensely glorious Object of their lofty hallelujahs, their sweetest Hosannas, and their most ravishing melodies, humbles himself to behold even the things that are done in heaven. Who would not fear the Lord, that is a great God, and a great King above all gods? His name only is holy, fearful, and glorious, in distinction from and in opposition to every name that is named, of things in heaven, and things in earth, and things under the earth. He is worthy to receive, but who is able to give him his due? Yes, he is worthy to receive glory, and honor, and power. This is an acknowledgment to which he that wears the imperial crown and sits on the throne of glory in heaven has an indisputably rightful claim. This is his glory, and he will not give it to another; it is his praise, and he will not give it to graven images; it is the glory *due* unto his name, and therefore he will have it; "Give unto the LORD the glory due unto his name; worship the LORD in the beauty of holiness" (Ps. 29:2). It is impossible we can give him all the glory due to his name; when we have said and done our best for his honor, we are but unprofitable servants; if the God of glory pleases to take favorable notice of any mean endeavors of his creatures, to honor his holy name, it will be infinite condescension and grace; but to persevere in this exercise is their bounden duty, and in strictest equity a reasonable service.

This will appear still more evident when we consider that heaven, earth, and seas with all that they contain, are the productions of his sovereign power. This reason is given by the innumerable company of angels, and the church of the firstborn, for their worship, "Thou art worthy, O LORD, to receive glory, and honour, and power: for thou hast created all things, and for thy pleasure they are, and were created" (Rev. 4:11). The same argument is urged in Psalm 95 and in Acts 17. Nor does he intermit the exertions of his most holy, wise, and powerful providence in preserving and governing all his creatures, and all their actions, for one single moment; and therefore he ought to be worshipped (Acts 14:15–17). Above all, the redeemed of the Lord are under singular obligations to worship him. This glory is due unto his name from their hearts, lips, and daily conversation, because he chose them in Christ before the foundation of the world to be holy and to be to the praise of the glory of his grace, by *living godly* in this present world; because he redeemed them to be a peculiar people, zealous of good works; because he formed them for himself, to show forth his praise; because he is their God, and they should worship him; because he confers on them a kingdom that cannot be moved, they should have grace to serve him with reverence and godly fear.

And as it is a just and righteous thing for creatures to worship God, so his wrath will not be more terrible than just, when it is revealed from heaven against all ungodliness of men, that withhold from God the worship due to his name, or that give divine worship to any other object, "If thou wilt not observe... that thou mayst fear this glorious and fearful name, THE LORD THY GOD; then the Lord will make thy plagues wonderful," *etc.* (Deut. 28:58–68). Righteous art thou, O Lord, when thou threatenest to take such vengeance on such iniquity. And when it is executed, surely conscience, thy deputy in the devoted impious wretch, will join its suffrage with angels and holy men in pronouncing thee just, and thy throne guiltless, forever and ever (Rom. 1:20–21, 32; 2:14–15).

2. As it is just, so it is *truly and eminently useful* to worship God. Who is the better for it? I answer, it is for the profit of many. I dare not be so uncharitable as to think any of my readers will ever imagine that if we are righteous, God is the better for it. Far be the unworthy thought from us! He is over all, God blessed forever.

> Can a man be profitable unto God, as he that is wise may be profitable unto himself? Is it any pleasure to the Almighty, that thou art righteous? or is it gain to him, that thou makest thy ways perfect?... Look unto the heavens, and see, and behold the clouds which are higher than thou. If thou sinnest, what dost thou against him? or if thy transgressions be multiplied, what dost thou unto him? If thou be righteous, what givest thou him? or, what receiveth he of thine hand? Thy wickedness may hurt a man as thou art, and thy righteousness may profit the son of man (Job 22:2–3; 35:5–8).

Confess, all ye creation of God, that your goodness extendeth not unto him. But the true worshiper of the living God is profitable to *himself*, and his worshipping may profit *others*.

I say the true worshiper is profitable to himself: "Godliness is profitable unto all things, having promise of the life that now is, and of that which is to come" (1 Tim. 4:8). It is the means of producing moderation in prosperity, contentment with our lot, joy in tribulation, hope that maketh not ashamed, patience under trouble, the excusing testimony of a good conscience, and blessed experiences of the supporting, establishing, and strengthening power of the gospel. It has not only the promise of temporal and spiritual good relating to this life, but, what is still more encouraging, relating to the glory and blessedness of the better world to come. Blessed are the worshipers that dwell in the house of the Lord; they shall be filled even as with marrow and fatness. David might truly say, "It is *good for me* to draw near to God." And as it is profitable to the Christian himself to be devoted to the fear and worship of God, so his worshipping may profit others. This *holy seed* is the *substance* of the land, and the salt of the earth; for the sake of such worshipers the evil days are shortened and impending storms delayed, if not diverted; they put to shame the wicked and convince the unbelieving; they strengthen the hands and encourage the hearts of their fellow-worshipers; and they come to the innumerable company of angels, and while they join with them they produce joy in their minds and thanksgivings on their behalf.

Ho, everyone that thirsteth for substantial and satisfying happiness! Wherefore do you spend your labor for that which satisfieth not? Why do you observe lying vanities, forsaking your own mercies? One thing is needful; one thing is profitable and useful. Forsake the foolish and live, and go in the way of understanding. Incline your ear, and come unto a just and gracious God, through faith in the given Redeemer, and your souls shall live, and he will make with you an everlasting covenant, even the sure mercies of David. Seek ye the Lord while he may be found, call ye upon him while he is near. Let the wicked forsake his way, and the unrighteous man his thoughts, and let him return unto the Lord, and he will have mercy upon him, and to our God, for he will abundantly pardon. Has not experience convinced you, that the way of life must be above, or else it can be nowhere? Hast thou not heard that the ways of wisdom are ways of pleasantness, and all her paths are peace; and that she is a tree of life to them that lay hold upon her; and happy is everyone that retaineth her? O taste and see that God is good, and that his worship is an easy yoke, a light burden, and a profitable and pleasant service. Through desire separate yourselves, and intermeddle with all divine knowledge, and with all enriching satisfactions and solid happiness, in the ways of wisdom.

3. I must once more urge the obligation to worship God upon my fellow-mortals from the *absolute necessity of the thing*. To each of us God says, as Pharaoh to Joseph, thou art commanded, this do. "Thou shalt worship the Lord thy God, and him only shalt thou serve." This is the command of God, whose will is infallibly just and good; and whose authority and power are beyond control. The sense of the precept is very clear, and the obligation of it indispensible. Remember and seriously ponder the solemn thought, *he* commands, who, in creation spake and it was done, commanded and it stood fast; who speaks the raging tempest into a serene calm; who upholdeth all things by the word of his power; whose word is unchangeable truth, and eternal righteousness; it is the word of the King of kings, and must have power either to bind the conscience, or to ruin the rebel. Ruin, irrecoverable and everlasting ruin, is the dreadful sanction of this righteous law, "I…am a jealous God" (Ex. 20:5). Would you know the import of this awful name? You may read it,

> God is jealous, and the Lord revengeth; the Lord revengeth and is furious; the Lord will take vengeance on his adversaries, and he reserveth wrath for his enemies. The Lord is slow to anger, and great in power, and will not at all acquit the wicked: the Lord hath his way in the whirlwind and in the storm, and the clouds are the dust of his feet. He rebuketh the sea, and maketh it dry, and drieth up all the rivers: Bashan languisheth, and Carmel, and the flower of Lebanon languisheth. The mountains quake at him, and the hills melt, and the earth is burned at his presence, yea, the world, and all that dwell therein. Who can stand before his indignation? and who can abide in the fierceness of his anger? his fury is poured out like fire, and the rocks are thrown down by him (Nah. 1:2–6).

Consider this, all ye that forget and neglect God, lest he tear you in pieces, when none can deliver. Is it not a fearful thing to fall into the hands of the living God, that renders his rebukes with flaming fire to the wicked?

To worship God is a necessary service, moreover, if we consider the indigent and dependent nature of man. Considered in himself, he is a very helpless and a very wretched being. He is subject every moment to the greatest calamities and misfortunes. He is beset with dangers on all sides, and may become unhappy by numberless casualties which he could not foresee, nor could have prevented had he foreseen them. The man, who habitually lives in a firm reliance upon, and devotedness to God, acknowledging him in all his ways, has not the same dark and melancholy views of human nature as he who considers himself abstractedly from this relation to the supreme Being; nor such deceiving hopes as he who confides in any inferior dependence. He that daily sets God before him is powerful in *his* power, wise by *his* wisdom, happy by *his* happiness. He reaps the benefit of every divine attribute, and loses his own insufficiency in the fullness of infinite perfection.

Must mankind, so indigent, and so destitute as they are, *have a God?* and must they not, for the same reason, acknowledge the Lord, the God of heaven and earth, to be their God? Let us not hesitate to make an immediate choice while the competition is between the only living and true God, and the vanities of the nations. You are obliged by a happy necessity to make an honorable and advantageous preference of God, and his service.

The Manner of Worshipping Him Acceptably

The third head leads me to describe the *manner* of worshipping God acceptably. It is of high importance to be set right about this point—otherwise all our devotion, though directed to its proper object, will be a vain oblation, unacceptable to God, and unprofitable to ourselves. I would therefore humbly attempt to direct the right manner of performing religious worship in the following particulars.

1. God is to be worshipped only *in the way of his own appointment.* The appointments of the Deity concerning his worship are not to be gathered from the uncertain tradition of the elders, the authority of men, or the dictates of our own reason; no, they stand engrossed in the volume of *his book*, which is the *only* rule to direct us how we may glorify and enjoy him. The Holy Ghost, speaking in the Scriptures, is not only the highest judge in every controversy about the doctrines of faith, but the master of the ceremonies to introduce worshipers into the divine presence with decent propriety. He only has a right to give the whole law of worship, because it refers only to the Deity. I do not speak at present of the heathens, to whom the discoveries God has made of himself, by the light of nature, must be a rule of worship. I speak of these that have the benefit of the word of God, which gives us every necessary discovery of his mind and will, relating to the way in which he should be worshipped. Divine institutions must be

the rule of our worship, and whatever we may imagine to be useful, fit, and decent, must be examined and determined by this rule. Faith, and not fancy; the authority of God, and not the will of man, must lead the way to all our religious services. Does anyone suppose that some external representations of God by images are proper to direct or excite our devotions? God has said, "Thou shalt not make unto thee any graven image, or any likeness of any thing that is in heaven above, or that is in the earth beneath, or that is in the water under the earth, thou shalt not bow down thyself to them, nor serve them" (Ex. 20:4–5). Does another imagine that some decent ceremonious ornaments should, or may, be added to divine institutions of gospel-worship? We reply, that one step beyond institution defiles the worship. Attend to what God said about the altar he appointed to be made to him: "An altar of earth shalt thou make unto me…and if thou wilt make an altar of stone, thou shalt not build it of hewn stone; for if thou lift up thy tool upon it, thou hast polluted it" (Ex. 20:24–25). The foolishness of God in the simplicity of his institutions, is wiser than the wisdom of men, that are vain in their imaginations and with equal folly and impiety presume to improve on the appointments of JEHOVAH. Does a third person fancy it is left to human prudence to make some alterations in, or additions to, God's own appointments? He should remember that they worship him in vain, who teach for doctrines the commandments of men; and that every plant which our heavenly Father has not planted, shall be rooted up (Matt. 15:9, 13). These things have indeed a show of wisdom in will-worship and humility, and neglecting or too much esteeming the body; whereas in reality all this pretended show of wisdom has nothing worthy in itself, or truly honorable to God, but is only suited to cultivate and please the false taste of men of corrupt minds. Everybody must grant that there are some circumstances concerning the worship of God, common to human actions and societies, which are to be ordered by the light of nature and Christian prudence; but even in these the general rules of the word must be always strictly observed.

And, as we live under the gospel-dispensation, all our worship must be regulated by gospel-institution, that it may be performed according to the appointment of Christ as king of the church. Ministers should strictly adhere to the terms of their commission, *to teach men to observe and do whatsoever he has commanded*, as ever they would hope for the benefit of his promise, "lo, I am with you alway, even unto the end of the world"

(Matt. 28:20). And everyone who would serve God acceptably should keep his eye upon the divine institution, that, like Zacharias and Elisabeth, he may walk "in all the commandments and ordinances of the Lord blameless" (Luke 1:6).

2. God is to be worshipped *with the whole man*; with our bodies and spirits, which are his. Having spoken at some length on this point already, I shall only add, in the words of Dr. Guise,

> To worship God only with our bodies is *hypocrisy*; and to worship him only with our souls is partiality; they were both created by him, and for him, and are both to be devoted to him; they were both redeemed by the blood of Christ and we hope for the salvation of both in heaven, where they will be unitedly employed in everlasting hallelujahs; and therefore we should glorify God in our bodies and spirits, which are God's (1 Cor. 6:20).

3. God is to be worshipped *by the assistance of his Spirit*. When David blessed the Lord before the congregation, after they had contributed willingly and liberally towards the building of an house to his name, he expresses himself in these well-chosen words:

> Who am I, and what is my people, that we should be able to offer so willingly after this sort? for all things come of thee, and of thine own have we given thee…O Lord our God, all this store that we have prepared to build thee an house for thine holy name, cometh of thine hand, and is all thine own (1 Chron. 29:14–16).

Those that would worship the living God with acceptance ought to entertain such humble and grateful sentiments. All their just apprehensions, pure, spiritual, and holy affections, earnest desires, humble confidence, enlargedness of heart, peace and joy, freedom, fervor and propriety, and whatever else can be named, that enters into or constitutes evangelical and animated devotion; all come from the Spirit, and are all his own fruits. He must enlighten and impress the mind with suitable views of the object and nature of our adorations; incline and fix the heart in this heavenly exercise; administer boldness in entering into the holiest of all by the blood of Jesus; uphold, encourage, and assist with realizing manifestations of the truth in the conscience; and enable us to cry, *Abba, Father*; bearing witness with our spirits, that we are the children of God. Who is sufficient for these things, so essentially necessary in worshipping God? Our sufficiency is of the Holy Ghost, who is the Spirit "of power, and of love, and of a sound mind" (2 Tim. 1:7), and who is *the seven Spirits before the throne.*

4. God is to be worshipped *in the exercise of all suitable graces*, under the influence of his Spirit. Now those graces are most suitable in worshipping him, which magnify God, abase the creature, and promote that faith and love which is in Christ Jesus. As often as we go to pay the divine honors we owe him, we should consider him as on a throne, to make us keep our distance; and as on a throne of grace, to embolden our approaches. We should seriously think of his greatness and our own nothingness, of his holiness and our vileness, of his righteousness and our guilt, of his transcendent excellence and our unworthiness, of his all-sufficiency and our necessity, of his incomprehensibleness and our darkness—we should take a survey of these things to aggrandize him in our eyes, and to lay us low before him. And with what delight and gratitude should we reflect on the riches of his grace in Christ, and the various strong encouragements he has given us in him, and in the promises of his covenant, to relieve us under a sense of our multiplied discouragements in ourselves! We cannot sufficiently adore and exalt, admire and bless his glorious name, or lie sufficiently prostrate in all humility and self-abasement at his footstool. Our minds should also be possessed with awful and delightful thoughts of him, that we may fear the Lord and his goodness. When we approach to him in any act of worship, we should look by faith to an atoning Savior, and yield up ourselves to stand in his righteousness before the throne of God, and so go to him in Christ as our God, as the Father of mercies, and our almighty Friend. We should relent with brokenness of heart, with ingenuous shame, and evangelical repentance for our multiplied and aggravated offenses; and should surrender ourselves and all our concerns, for time and eternity, into our Father's hands, and be ready to do and suffer his will in all things. Our hearts should rise above this world and enter by faith, hope, desire, love and joy, into that within the veil, whither Jesus our Forerunner is entered for us; and we should be making the best of our way to that blessed world, with humble, firm dependence on God's covenant-faithfulness and love, that all things shall work together for our good; and that he will guide us by his counsel and afterwards receive us to his glory. And all this should be

done with earnestness and fervor, with integrity and uprightness of heart, that we may be sincere, and without offense, till the day of Christ.

5. God is to be worshipped *with an eye to his glory*, as our chief and highest end. "For of him, through him, and to him are all things, to whom be glory for ever. Amen." And "whether we eat or drink, or whatsoever we do, we should do all to the glory of God" (1 Cor. 10:31). He has made all things for himself. His own glory is his highest end; he cannot propose a higher to himself, for that would be to suppose he would prefer something to himself, or set something above himself. We should perform everything in religion with a reference to God, that he may be glorified. Were we to propose any end superior to his glory in our worship, we should thereby make an attempt to dethrone him, and to set up an idol of our own in his stead; but they that best know him abound most in all ascriptions of glory to him (Rev. 4:8–11). We should exalt him in our thoughts, proclaim his praises with our lips, and show forth his glory in our lives. All our views in sacred worship should be *to honor him as God*, in the most awful, cheerful, and exalted conceptions of him, and in ascribing all possible glory to him. How solemn soever our professions and appearances may be, yet if we do not habitually aim at glorifying God in our worship, it spoils the offering; or if low, mean, sinister views intermingle and govern it, they are like the dead flies, that cause the ointment of the apothecary to send forth a stinking savor. Hence we are told, that the "sacrifice of the wicked is an abomination: how much more when he brings it with a wicked mind?" (Prov. 21:27).

6. God is to be worshipped *in the name of Christ*, as our only Mediator. Whatever Christians do, in word or in deed, should be done in the name of the Lord Jesus Christ. He is the grand and only medium of all holy converse with God; we can have no safety or comfort, no liberty or success in our dealings with God in any other way, and therefore all our prayers and praises must be presented in his name; our encouragements to them, our arguments for them, and our expectations of acceptance in them, must be derived from Christ alone.

> Seeing then that we have a great high priest, that is passed into the heavens, Jesus the Son of God…let us therefore come boldly unto the throne of grace, that we may obtain mercy, and find grace to help in time of need…Having therefore, brethren, boldness to enter

into the holiest of all by the blood of Jesus, by a new and living way, which he has consecrated for us, through the veil, that is to say, his flesh; and having an high priest over the house of God; let us draw near with a true heart in full assurance of faith (Heb. 4:14, 16; 10:19–22).

There was a reference to the Messiah in the Old Testament worship, and all its acceptance depended upon him. The temple, mercy-seat, altars, sacrifices, and incense, were typical of him; and praying towards God's holy oracle was directive of Israel's faith to Christ; and to God, as propitious on a mercy-seat through him: and must we not suppose that David's thoughts turned this way when he expressed himself as he does (Ps. 138:2; 84:9; 80:17–18)? But as under the gospel dispensation, we have much clearer discoveries of Christ in his person and offices, mediation, righteousness, and grace, we are instructed and obliged more explicitly to make mention of his name, in every address to the throne of grace. We are to gather together in his name, to ask in his name, and to give thanks in his name; for this is the will of God. And in the heavenly state, everlasting hallelujahs will ring through the mansions of the redeemed, unto the God and Father of their Redeemer. This peculiar reference to Christ gives our worship the nature and form of evangelical worship; and this, together with the things before mentioned, makes it spiritual and well-pleasing in God's sight; such worship as he approves, and will smell a sweet savor in, on account of that one most perfect and most meritorious offering of Christ, by which he has forever perfected them that are sanctified (Heb. 10:14).

Is this the manner and are these the characteristics of gospel-worship? Then how must everyone, more or less, stand reproved for defects in worship! How unprofitable must our worship be unto God! And how reasonable to rejoice only in Christ Jesus!

Some Remarks concerning Liturgies

I proposed under the fourth head to offer some remarks concerning liturgies, or *forms of public service in the worship of God*. The word *liturgy*, originally *Greek*, signifies *a public service*, as everyone knows that has any skill in that language. This accounts for the very frequent use of that word in the writings of the *Greek fathers* of the Christian church. It is several times used in the New Testament, and is sometimes translated *ministra-*

tion (Luke 1:23), sometimes *ministry* (Heb. 8:6), and sometimes *service* (Phil. 2:17); and it is spoken of the *office of teaching* (Acts 13:2), of the *legal service in the temple* (Luke 1:23), of *liberality to the necessitous, by the care of church officers* (Rom. 15:27), and *of the energy of the faith of the gospel in all its public and visible demonstrations and fruits* (Phil. 2:17).

Among the *fathers* it is used sometimes in a very general sense, "to denote *all that belongs to sacred worship.*"[13]

Modern writers use this term in a sense appropriated to divine worship, and mean by it, "a form of prayers, and of other pieces of public religious devotion." My present business is to make some remarks on such forms of public service in worshipping God. That this may be executed with all possible precision, I shall attempt,

1. To declare honestly the opinion of Protestant dissenters on this head.
2. To inquire whether liturgies, in the sense of the Church of England, are authorized in the Scriptures.
3. To demonstrate, that they are unreasonable impositions.

The Opinion of Protestant Dissenters
I shall, in the first place, set down a fair representation of the opinions of *Protestant dissenters* concerning liturgies, or forms of public devotion. The reader will perceive I mean by *dissenters*, all that do not submit to *imposed forms*, as an express condition of church-communion.

They generally allow that it is not only *warrantable*, but *useful* and *expedient* that some *directory* for the better regulating all the circumstances of divine worship should be known and observed in the church, that all things may be done to edification, and without censure or offense. The *nature* of such a *directory*, and the *difference* between *it* and a *form*, may be learned from what the *assembly of divines*, which met at Westminster, *anno* 1645, say, at the close of the *introduction* to their *Directory for the Public Worship of God*, in these words:

> Wherein [namely, in their directory for all the parts of public worship, at ordinary and extraordinary times] our care hath been to hold

---

[13] The learned reader will find many examples in Johann Kaspar Suiceri. *Thesaurus Ecclesiasticus*, on Λειτουργια.

forth such things as are of divine institution in every ordinance; and other things we have endeavored to set forth according to the rules of Christian prudence, agreeable to the general rules of the word of God: our meaning therein being only that the general heads, the sense and scope of the prayers, and other parts of public worship, being known to all, there may be a consent of all the churches in these things that contain the substance of the service and worship of God; and the ministers may be hereby directed in their administrations to keep like soundness in doctrine and prayer; and may, if need be, have some help and furniture; and yet so as they become not hereby slothful and negligent in stirring up the gifts of Christ in them, but that each one, by meditation, by taking heed to himself and the flock of God committed to him, and by wise observing the ways of divine providence, may be careful to furnish his heart and tongue with further or other materials of prayer and exhortation as shall be needful upon all occasions.

Whether Liturgies are Authorized

I proposed in the next place to inquire whether liturgies, in the sense of the Church of England, are authorized by the Scriptures. The sense of this church may be gathered from the *acts of uniformity* prefixed to the Book of Common Prayer, where the constant observation of the English liturgy is positively enjoined; and "all and singular ministers in that kingdom, are commanded and bounden to say and use the mattins, even-song…and all the common and open prayer in the form prescribed," under severe penalties.[14]

The church of England does not only assert the expediency of observing some *general directory* about prayer—which is apparently very useful—she even binds a *form of words*, and an *order of sentiments* upon her members, which they must constantly use. And their conformity to this imposition is the condition of their fellowship. This is not at all countenanced in the word of God, which is *full and plain* in things of less consequence, that are agreeable to the divine will. Let us examine the high boasts of men, who pretend to find the warrant for imposing such forms

---

[14] The reader may satisfy himself on this head, by perusing at large the act, *Anno Primo Reginæ Elizabethæ*, ch. 2. entitled, "There Shall be Uniformity of Prayer, and Administration of Sacraments."

of divine worship in the oracles of God; and their glorying will appear to be vain.

1. *Before the flood* was brought upon the world of the ungodly, we have no more account of their worship than what is contained in these few words, "then began men to call upon the name of the LORD" (Gen. 4:26). This is our translation of the text. But it being very probable that public assemblies for religious offices were held long before this time, and that even when Cain and Abel offered their sacrifices their families joined with them in the worship of God, some men of great note, such as Bertram, Hackspan, and Heidegger, take it in the same sense with our marginal translation: *then began men*, that is, the children of Seth, *to call themselves by the name of the Lord*, that is, to call themselves the worshipers of the Lord, in contradistinction to the Cainites and such profane persons as had forsaken him.

It must not be dissembled however that the word הוחל, which we translate *began*, in several places of Scripture, signifies *to profane*, and upon this presumption many of the *Jewish* writers, and some of no obscure fame among us, have understood the words, as if Moses intended to intimate to us, that men began in the days of Enosh to apostatize from the worship of God, to fall into idolatry, and to apply the most holy name, which alone belongs to the great Creator of heaven and earth, to created beings and especially to the sun. But, considering that Moses is here speaking of the pious family of *Seth*, and not that of *Cain*, and that when the *Hebrew word* signifies *to profane*, it has always a noun following it, but when an affirmative mood follows, as in the passage before us, it always signifies *to begin*—considering all this, I say, we can hardly suppose that Moses is here pointing out *the origin of idolatry*, but rather *the distinction which good men began to put between themselves, and such as were openly wicked and profane*. For, that the true meaning of the expression בשם קרא, according to our marginal translation, is to *call* or *nominate by* or *after the name* of anyone, is manifest from several instances in Scripture. Thus Cain "builded a city, and called the name of the city, after the name of his son, Enoch" (Gen. 4:17); "Nobah…called it Nobah, after his own name" (Num. 32:42); "they call their lands after their own names" (Ps. 49:11). And the name of the Lord here intimated is afterwards expressly given them by Moses when he tells us, that *"the sons of God* saw *the daughters of men"*

(Gen. 6:2). Agreeable to all which is that passage, "One…shall call himself by the name of Jacob" (Isa. 44:5).

This phrase also signifies to *publish a name* by an open proclamation (Ex. 33:19; 34:5–6), and to *call on the name of the LORD by prayer* (Gen. 13:4). And in latter times the whole worship of God was comprehended under it, "and it shall come to pass, that whosoever shall *call on the name of the LORD* shall be delivered" (Joel 2:32). But to suppose, with Calmet and others, that it refers to the invention of religious rites and ceremonies in the worship of God, is an *idle dream*. It is not said they did it *by a stated form*.

2. We have no reason to suppose they had any form of prayer *from Noah to Moses*. The total silence of Scripture upon this point is enough to convince every reasonable man of it, that submits his understanding and inclinations to the authority of God.

3. Though we find Israel joining to sing God's praise, as occasions offered, in composed and (probably) inspired songs (Ex. 15; Judg. 5), and though God himself was pleased to appoint a form of blessing the children of Israel, to be used by Aaron and his sons (Num. 6:22–27), and to dictate a confession to the man that brought his first-fruits, and a solemn acknowledgment to be used by him that gave his third year's tithes (Deut. 26); yet there is no vestige of any form of prayer given by God, far less drawn up and imposed by men, for ordinary public worship, *from Moses to David*.

4. It cannot be proved that there was any form of prayer used or imposed, *from the reign of David, till the captivity of the Jews*. The texts some have urged on this head are altogether foreign to the subject. It is true, David appointed the Levites to stand every morning to praise the Lord, and likewise at even (1 Chron. 23:30). And in the days of Ezra, the priests and the Levites were set with cymbals to praise the Lord, after the ordinance of David king of Israel; and they sung together by course (Ezra 3:10–11). But these accounts of Jewish worship refer only to *praising*, they give us no light about *prayer* properly so called, nor how it was performed. But if we grant (which is too liberal a concession for anything I can see) that these places refer to prayer, I hope it will not be disputed that they only refer to *such prayers* as were given by inspiration. The difference between such prayers and any human form whatever, must be confessed to be very great. But it is plain that no hint about even an *inspired form* for that service is to be found in these texts.

5. There is no satisfying evidence that ever the Jewish church used a form of prayer, *from the captivity to Christ.* The prophets that prophesied after the captivity, or under it, are quite silent on this head, so are the sacred historians who have recorded very minutely the rebuilding of the temple and the setting up again of the worship of God in it, according to the primitive order. It is very strange that we should hear nothing of such an *improvement in their worship*, if forms of prayer had been introduced at that juncture. I know it is alleged that *Ezra and the great synagogue* composed *liturgies* for their prayers, in which are all the prescribed forms of their *synagogue-worship*, the most solemn part of their prayers being those they call *the eighteen prayers.* And the Jews say that *Rabbi Gamaliel*, a little before the destruction of Jerusalem, added to them the *nineteenth* against Christians. The learned Dr. *Prideaux* says,

> It is certain these prayers are very ancient. For mention is made of them in the *Mishna* as *old settled forms*, and no doubt is to be made but that they were used in our Savior's time—at least most of them, if not all the eighteen, and consequently that he joined in them with the rest of the Jews whenever he went into their synagogues, as he always did every Sabbath-day.[15]

But that gentleman has destroyed the force of this observation by a marginal note upon it, where he has the following words: "It must be acknowledged that *some* of these prayers seem to have been composed *after the destruction of Jerusalem*, and to have reference to it." He points to four of them in particular for examples of this. And if this be the highest seeming antiquity of *some of them*, how shall we be satisfied that the *rest are more ancient?* Does not the antiquity of the whole rest on the same evidence? Does it seem probable, nay, almost certain, that at least four of the eighteen prayers, which the Jews pretend that Ezra and others composed for synagogue worship, were drawn up after the destruction of Jerusalem, suppose by the Chaldeans? And is it certain that Ezra only reestablished the worship of God, according to divine institution, and former practice, agreeable thereunto? The just inference is that the testimony of the Jews is not at all sufficient to satisfy us about the antiquity of these prayers. But

---

[15] Humphrey Prideaux. *The Old and New Testament Connected in the History of the Jews and Neighbouring Nations*, part 1, book 6.

if *Prideaux* means that the four prayers he refers to were composed after the destruction of Jerusalem by *Vespasian*, which seems to be his meaning, the dispute is at an end and our reasoning confirmed. And this last opinion is highly probable on many accounts: for (1.) The Mishna, which contains the earliest account of these eighteen prayers, was written about 120 years after the last destruction of Jerusalem. (2.) It does not appear that the Jews had any other forms of prayer that referred to the destruction of their city and temple, more particularly than these the Doctor refers to. (3.) It is very unlikely that when the Jews composed forms of prayer for so many purposes after our Savior's time, they should not draw up something particularly relating to the crowning calamity that completed their misery. (4.) When the Mishna was composed, these prayers might well enough be called *old settled forms*, though they had never been used before the apostolic age. Their being the traditions of the elders, and generally practiced, will account for that designation being given them about 200 years after Christ, having been handed down by word of mouth from father to son, and committed to writing only by *R. Judah* in the *Mishna*. On the whole, I affirm, that there is no satisfying evidence that the Jewish church ever used, and still less that ever they imposed, *any form of prayer*, from the captivity to Christ.

6. Christ nowhere appointed a form of prayer for general public use in his church. The only thing that looks most like it, is the directions he gave on different occasions to his disciples, which are recorded in Matthew 6 and Luke 11. But this will not answer all the designs of a public stated liturgy, though it were even granted that our Lord intended it to be used as a form of prayer; besides that it does not explicitly contain a confession of sin, or thanksgiving for mercies, and is confessedly inadequate to all the ends of prayer by itself. It does not appear that Christians used precisely the very words of this prayer on any occasion in the apostolic age, though it cannot be doubted that they prayed to that import. We have many prayers in the New Testament formed on that plan, but none of them runs in the same words and order of sentiments. The words are not the same in Matthew and in Luke. And the words of the faithful and true Witness must not be *degraded* to the level of human compositions, by unequal comparisons.

7. The apostles never drew up or imposed any form of prayer on the churches. Every man of understanding and integrity is ready to grant that

the liturgies that bear the names of Matthew, Mark, Peter, and James, are mere forgeries imposed on the world. The apostles never *used forms* themselves, and, it is certain they never *imposed any forms* on others.

8. It cannot be proved that there were any set forms of prayer used in the churches during the *first three centuries*. The writers of that period do not relate anything from whence we can infer that forms of prayer were then used, but they fully convince us that it was the common practice to pray *without any regard to them.*[16]

From the whole I infer that the sense of the church of England, relative to liturgies, is unauthorized in the Holy Scriptures.

That They Are Unreasonable Impositions

I shall now endeavor to show the unreasonableness of imposing their liturgy, as an essential condition of communion in the church of England.

Besides what has been said of the want of authority in the Scriptures for such liturgies, and consequently the want of any *right* or *title* to bind any man whom God hath not bound, or wherein God hath left him free—which makes any imposition of that sort appear very absurd and unreasonable—I might offer several objections that have been frequently made against the contents of the English liturgy, which, for the satisfaction of the reader, I have thrown into the margin.[17] But there are several weighty and obvious considerations that clearly demonstrate the unreasonableness of such impositions, besides these now mentioned, which

---

[16] The reader may consult David Clarkson. *A Discourse concerning Liturgies* and Peter King. *An Inquiry into the Constitution, Discipline, Unity and Worship of the Primitive Church*, part 2, chapter 2.

[17] Edmund Calamy. *An Account of the Ministers, Lecturers, Masters, and Fellows of Colleges and Schoolmasters: Who Were Ejected or Silenced after the Restoration in 1660, by or before, the Act of Uniformity; Design'd for the Preserving to Posterity the Memory of their Names, Characters, Writings, and Sufferings*, vol. 2, pp. 814–816, tells us, that "one Mr. Smith having extravagantly commended the liturgy, as if it had been compiled by a synod or consult of archangels, and was superior even to the divinely inspired oracles; Mr. Sharp, on the contrary, drew up this short account of the liturgy:

> It is, says he, defective in necessaries, redundant in superfluities, disorderly in all, disputable in many, and dangerous in some things. That I may not, says he, as my antagonist, harangue in generals; I will give an instance in each.
>
> 1. It is defective in necessaries: (1.) In confession of sin, there is not a word of unbelief, the greatest of all actual sins. (2.) In petition, there is none for regenerating grace. (3.) In thanksgiving, there is none for faith.

deserve our attention. I shall represent them nearly in the words of an eminent writer.

1. The religion of Jesus has *no need* of *impositions*. It made its entrance into the world without their assistance, and it will be able to stand its ground without them to the last. The only weapons God would have men use in the defense of his cause and in spreading the gospel, are those

---

2. It is redundant in superfluities. Such are the ceremonies, of which there is no need in the world.

3. Disorderly in all. Neither the whole, nor any part, observing either any rules of art, or the admirable order of the Lord's prayer.

4. Disputable in many things. As, kneeling at the sacrament; substituting god-fathers in the room of parents, and giving them the charge; promiscuous admissions to the sacrament, notwithstanding the words in the exhortation, both declaring that *blasphemers*, etc., *should not presume*, and that *none should come but with a full trust and quiet conscience*, etc.

5. Dangerous in some things. As against the laws of verity, charity, unity, equity, and piety.

Against the law of *verity*, is the salvatory clause at the end of the office of baptism, *viz., It is certain by the word of God, that children which are baptized, dying before they commit actual sin, are undoubtedly saved.*

Against the law of *charity*, is the damnatory clause at the end of the *Athanasian* creed, which damns all the churches of the *Grecian* communion, who do not believe the *Filioque*; that is, who do not believe that the Holy Ghost proceedeth from the Son, as well as from the Father.

Against the law of *unity*; no church besides using it, but the schismatical *Roman*, which hath the most of it, though in another tongue.

Against the law of *equity*, in the unproportionable penalties for not using it, *viz.*, unministering and unchurching.

Against the law of *piety*; all worship of God being forbidden except by it.

All which are aggravated by enjoining *unfeigned assent and consent to all and everything contained and prescribed in it*, upon penalty of ministers being turned out of the work of their office, which they are obliged unto by the peremptory command of Christ. And whether *such a liturgy as this*, with all its circumstances, merits *high encomiums, Christ will be Judge."*

The most authentic, full, and moderate representation of the things complained of in the liturgy of the church of England, is contained in the exceptions against it drawn up by *Dr. Reynolds* (afterwards *bishop of Norwich*), *Dr. Wallis, Dr. Bates, Dr. Jacomb, Mr. Calamy, Mr. Newcomen, Mr. Clark, etc.*, which they offered to the *bishops* at the *Savoy-conference*, anno 1660. The length of it will not suffer me to insert it here. The reader will find the most material parts of it in Edmund Calamy. *An Abridgement of Mr. Baxter's History of His Life and Times*, pp. 154–158. The objections are proposed both in general and in particular instances.

which he consecrated by his appointment and blessing for this service at first: *to wit*, sound reasoning, humble entreaties, an exemplary conversation, and fervent prayer. But he has neither appointed nor allowed any *carnal weapons* in the Christian warfare (2 Cor. 10:4). The *means* are suited, in their *nature*, and *manner of working*, to the *end* they are to accomplish. This end is to *make sinners obedient to the faith*, and the way to obtain it is to commend the truths of God plainly and faithfully to every man's conscience as in the sight of God (2 Cor. 4:2). By this means, through the powerful blessing of God, the church of Christ was gathered, and by this means it will be supported in the world. Forcible impositions are *no way necessary* either to procure an establishment, or the continuance of religion, and are therefore *unreasonable*.

2. True religion will *not admit* of any impositions, which are so far from being friendly to religion that, if they do at all affect the minds of people, it is always with a *real aversion* to what they are not suffered *rationally* to choose. All that force and violence, those racks and tortures, and every instrument of cruelty that have been employed against Christianity, he who is given to be head over all things to the church could easily have engaged for it, in every age and place; but how then should the Scripture be fulfilled, or his testimony justified, "My kingdom is not of this world" (John 18:36)?

When the disciples so deeply resented the Samaritans' refusal to receive our Savior into their houses, and were immediately for commanding fire from heaven to consume them, willing to have the want of the civil magistrate's sword supplied by miraculous vengeance; our blessed Lord, far from encouraging, immediately checks the imperious and imposing humor, and tells them, "ye know not what manner of spirit ye are of" (Luke 9:51–56). Christ himself is meek and lowly, and his disciples must learn of him, and put on his temper, and not aspire at being lords over his heritage.

3. Impositions are productive of very bad effects. They are not at all calculated to promote the welfare and comfort of society, either civil or sacred; they are an endless source of uncharitableness and schism; they have a direct tendency to make men act contrary to their conscience; and they bring the conscience into bondage to men.[18]

4. No creature has any right to impose anything on mankind in what concerns the worship and service of God. If any such warrant is lodged

---

[18] See Vincent Alsop. *The Mischief of Impositions*.

in the hands of men, it is either derived from *nature*, or from *Christ's appointment*. But it is not derived from either of these sources—not from *nature*, which does indeed dictate that in the multitude of counselors there is safety; but not that every private conscience should be governed by the public one. It is true a majority ought to determine the whole in matters that are in *our own disposal*, as all those are, wherein the peace and safety of civil societies are immediately concerned, and perhaps too those circumstances of external order, that are necessary to be determined in the church. But nature did never dictate that the greater number should determine the judgment and consciences of all the rest. If it had, it would have secured *infallibility* to the majority in every country, and have afforded us proper evidence that they were in possession of it. Nor from the *appointment of Christ*, for his authority for anything of this kind cannot be produced. The Enthusiasts for impositions have frequently been challenged to produce it, but all to no purpose.

This way of reasoning has the approbation of some of the most eminent writers of the church of England. I shall give a few instances to show how far the conviction of truth prevailed over lower considerations with many of them.

Bishop Stillingfleet says, "Christ hath given the church no charter to bind men up to more than himself hath done, or to exclude those from her society who will be admitted into heaven."[19] And again, "The main inlet of all the distractions, confusions, and divisions of the Christian world, hath been by adding other conditions of church-communion, than Christ hath done."[20]

Another famous writer has the following words:

"I will take no man's liberty of judging from him, neither shall any man take mine from me. I will think no man the worse man, nor the worse Christian; I will love no man the less for differing in opinion from me. And what measure I mete to others, I expect from them again."[21]

The learned Bishop Burnet observes that "God has given us rational faculties to guide and direct us, and we must make the most of these that we can. We must *judge* with our *own reasons*, as well as *see* with our *own eyes*. Neither can we, or ought we to resign up our understandings to *any*

---

[19] Edward Stillingfleet. *Irenicum: A Weapon-Salve for the Church's Wounds*, in the *preface*.
[20] Stillingfleet, *Irenicum: A Weapon-Salve for the Church's Wounds*.
[21] William Chillingworth. *The Religion of Protestants a Safe Way to Salvation*, p. 376.

others, unless we are convinced that God has imposed this upon us, *N.B.*, by his making them infallible so that we are secured from error if we follow them."[22]

Bishop Hoadly, of precious memory to all the friends of liberty, speaking of *freedom of choice and honest use of our reason*, tells us that "it is that which alone can render the religion of a man acceptable in God's eyes."[23]

I could refer to many more if it were necessary, but these are a sufficient specimen.

---

[22] Gilbert Burnet. *An Exposition of the Thirty-Nine Articles of the Church of England*, on article 19.

[23] Benjamin Hoadly. *The Present Delusion of Many Protestants, Consider'd: Preach'd in the Parish-Church of St. Peter's Poor, in Broadstreet, November 5, 1715*, p. 11.

Gospel Worship

An ingenious writer has observed that the great differences that disturb the peace of mankind, are not about ends, but means. We have all the same natural desires, but how these desires shall be accomplished, will forever be disputed. The ultimate purpose of government is temporal, and that of religion is eternal happiness. Hitherto we agree; but here we must part, to try, according to the endless varieties of passion and understanding combined with one another, every possible form of government, and every imaginable tenet of religion.

Reason says, and revelation confirms it, that we should worship the Lord our God, and him only should we serve; and is it not equally manifest that nothing can be a sufficient, certain, and perfect rule for that end but his own will? When men have been left to bare reason, without supernatural aids, they have had very obscure notions of the one supreme God, and have run into things really inconsistent with the belief of the one Supreme, though at the same time they have been forced to own there is such a one. If we look into all the pagan nations, we shall find that a conviction of the necessity of worshipping what they reckoned to be divine, and an entire ignorance how God is to be worshipped, was the natural and unavoidable cause of all those absurd, ridiculous, cruel, and sanguinary ways of worship which they fell into, and so showed that they were without excuse, in that when they knew God from his works, they glorified him not as God, but became vain in their imaginations concerning both the object and manner of their adorations, changing the truth of God into a lie, and his reasonable service into contradiction and folly.

But blessed be God, that has made light to arise upon us in the writings of inspiration. Here we have an infallibly sure and a marvelously clear word of prophecy, unto which we do well to take heed as unto a light that hath shined in a dark place. This is the testimony bound up and the law sealed among Christ's disciples. It is equally a part of our liberty wherewith Christ hath made us free, to be delivered from the vanity of our blinded minds and from the imposed dictates of fellow-mortals, about the object and rule of divine adoration; and to be brought under an indispensable obligation to honor the word of God, making it the only rule and the highest reason of every piece of religious worship. That solemn certification which concludes the volume of God's Book is so alarming, and so reasonable, that it should stir up everyone that reads or hears it, with holy jealousy to examine every step he takes in a matter of so much weight, and so important in its consequences;

> For I testify unto every man that heareth the words of the prophecy of this book, If any man shall add unto these things, God shall add unto him the plagues that are written in this book: and if any man shall take away from the words of the book of this prophecy, God shall take away his part out of the book of life, and out of the holy city, and from the things which are written in this book. He which testifieth these things, saith, Surely I come quickly. Amen (Rev. 22:18–20).

Prepossessions are of infinite hurt and danger where the honor of God and divine institutions are any way concerned. They infallibly seduce men from the good old way of scriptural simplicity. I shall give a few instances.

1. When we give *too great respect to authority*. *Great men* are not the standard of truth; *learned men* often mistake, and many times do not discover it; and *good men*, whether seemingly such or really so, are not exempted from mistakes nor can the authority of the *multitude*, though they are generally thought to be in the right, claim our implicit regard; while we see, in things of an inferior nature, *the opinion of most men* is erroneous, we may reasonably think that in matters of the highest concern, *it* is not infallible.

2. When we *overvalue* antiquity we are in the utmost danger of being deceived. Christians, Jews, and pagans, in their turn, have all made antiquity a plea for error. All professions generally lay claim to its approbation and countenance. Few consider that the highest and oldest sanction of divine truth is the revealed will of God.

3. When we indulge an *unruly fancy* in thinking on divine things—or affect to speak of the things of God, not in the words which the Holy Ghost teacheth, but in the words which man's wisdom teacheth—we are

sure to be misled in our own apprehensions and to mislead others, as far as they pay any regard to our judgment.

4. When we *dispute and contend about divine truth*, we are many ways in hazard of being deceived. The Holy Ghost has told us, in plain terms, the tendency and the effect of such disputes (2 Tim. 2:16–17). Contentions of this sort land men in extremes, and extremes are equally opposite to truth and holiness.

5. Prejudices that arise from *education and custom* are exceedingly dangerous. How few are happy enough to open their eyes to see for themselves! And of these that do conquer these prejudices, how many run into an extreme of free-thinking, that is no less pernicious!

The reader will find these and many other causes of mistake and misapprehension about religion, explained and exposed, with great candor and good sense in a book, entitled, *A Free Discourse concerning Truth and Error, Especially in Matters of Religion* by John Edwards, D.D., a book of inestimable worth to everyone that would be impartial and successful in his inquiries after truth. I cannot help thinking it would be an eminent service to the world if some skillful hand should abridge it, and present it to the public, with proper improvements.

It is no matter of indifference whether or not we receive and observe, and keep pure and entire, all such religious worship and ordinances as God hath appointed in his word. We are commanded to do so, and it is our duty; we are encouraged to do so, and it is our honor and interest. To do otherwise must be our sin, and a sin attended with very aggravating and provoking circumstances. Sound reason and divine revelation unite their evidence and remonstrances against it, and pronounce it to be the unalienable prerogative of JEHOVAH, to prescribe the means, the manner, and the seasons of his worship; because he only knows what becomes his infinite Majesty, in the several important relations he is pleased to bear unto his creatures. And it is well known, that wherever religion was attended to among heathen nations, the *polite schemers* of the general system prudently assumed airs of consequence, to secure respect to their rites, by pretending to have express instructions from their *respective deities* for every circumstance of their worship. This pretense had the desired effect. Every punctilio was readily submitted to, and it was reckoned highly criminal to dispute the will of heaven.

May not the Lord our God raise up these heathens as witnesses against professed Christians, that have his word, authenticated with every necessary evidence of its heavenly original, in their hands? May he not say to us as he did to the Jews,

> Wherefore I will yet plead with you, saith the LORD, and with your children's children will I plead. For pass over the isles of Chittim, and see; and send unto Kedar, and consider diligently, and see if there be such a thing. Hath a nation changed their gods, which are yet no gods? but my people have changed their glory for that which doth not profit. Be astonished, O ye heavens, at this, and be horribly afraid, be ye very desolate, saith the LORD. For my people have committed two evils; they have forsaken me the fountain of living waters, and hewed them out cisterns, broken cisterns, that can hold no water (Jer. 2:9–13).

> Even from the days of your fathers, ye are gone away from mine ordinances, and have not kept them. Return unto me, and I will return unto you, saith the LORD of hosts (Mal. 3:7).

He hath written unto us the great things of his law, and therein makes known to us everything that concerns his glory and our good. Let us not then turn a deaf ear, or seem indifferent to his heavenly call recorded, "Thus saith the LORD, Stand ye in the ways, and see, and ask for the old paths, where is the good way, and walk therein, and ye shall find rest for your souls" (Jer. 6:16). Let us ask for the ordinances God hath prescribed to be means of his acceptable worship; and for the good old paths in which his people have walked, that we may be the companions of all them that fear God, in every part of instituted religious duty, which he has commanded, and to which he has annexed a promise of his gracious presence, whereby we are encouraged to expect his blessing, when we engage therein in a right manner. In this respect they are instituted means of grace and pledges of that special favor which he designs to bestow on his people.

Now those ordinances are either *solitary*, which we are obliged to observe in our closets; or *private*, in our families; or *public*, in those assemblies where God is worshipped. But as there are several offices of religious worship common to the closet, the family, and the sanctuary, with no other variation but what is occasioned by the difference of circumstances, I apprehend it is not necessary to treat of them in that order; and moreover, it would unavoidably cause a needless repetition, or oblige me to make some ill-timed references that would perplex and confound the reader.

The order that seems most natural is to treat of the several ordinances of God that belong to his worship, in so many chapters. I don't know any reason to be scrupulous about the precedency of one to another. The following arrangement is preferred, without any prejudice to a differing judgment of the reader, who, by the help of the contents, may please his own taste, and digest them in any form he thinks more proper.

I shall consider,
1. The reading of the Holy Scriptures;
2. The preaching of the gospel;
3. The hearing of the word preached;
4. Singing the praises of God;
5. Prayer to God;
6. The public blessing of the congregation;
7. The sacraments in general;
8. The sacrament of baptism;
9. The sacrament of the Lord's Supper;
10. The religious observation of the Lord's day;
11. The observation of times of thanksgiving;
12. The observation of times of solemn religious fasting;
13. Ministerial visitations of the flock;
14. Ministerial visitations of the sick;
15. Catechizing;
16. Social religious meetings;
17. Family religion;
18. The devotion of the closet, or personal religion;
19. Of liberality to the poor saints;
20. Swearing by the name of God;
21. Vowing to the Lord;
22. Casting of lots.

My design is to hold forth such things as are of divine institution in each ordinance, that we may be furnished with knowledge to discern between the appointments of heaven and the inventions of men, an attempt the more necessary, as it is evident from facts there must be mixtures, and gross mixtures too, of will-worship, where Christianity is professed. Conscious of my insufficiency for so great a service, I humbly implore the Father of lights to give me the wisdom that is profitable to direct my thoughts, to affect my heart, and to guide my pen on so important a subject, that the words may be acceptable and the things to be written may be upright, even words of truth, words that are as goads, and as nails fastened by the masters of assemblies, which are given from one shepherd.

Chapter 1
Reading the Holy Scriptures

The Bible, the Bible is the religion of Protestants, said the excellent Mr. Chillingworth. A most glorious, and a most important truth! In the *Bible* we have the only adequate rule of faith, worship, and a religious conversation. In this volume are contained the great principles of all true religion, and the charter of all our privileges and hopes, as we are men and Christians. General and constant observation will satisfy us that both the *peace* and *welfare* of *civil society* either flourish, or languish, in proportion to men's acquaintance with, and veneration for this sacred book. Look into Popish countries, where this key of knowledge is taken away, and you will see them overrun with gross ignorance, superstition, and idolatry, in the church; and with arbitrary power, oppression, and slavery in the state. To prevent these calamitous evils; and to derive upon themselves and the world, a numerous train of the richest blessings, it is the duty of all that can, to give themselves to reading the word of God with assiduity, and attention. It was recommended to Timothy, his own son in the faith, by Paul the apostle of Jesus Christ, to give attendance to reading; and every disciple of Jesus is commanded to search the Scriptures (John 5:39), and the disciples at Berea, are said to be more noble than those at Thessalonica, because they searched the Scriptures daily, that they might approve what they heard preached, upon the fullest conviction and personal knowledge of the truth (Acts 17:11).

All that is necessary to be said on this ordinance may be digested under the following heads. We shall attempt,

1. To show what God hath appointed about the reading of his holy word.
2. To prove this reading of his word to be a divine, and most excellent institution.
3. To vindicate this ordinance from some objections. And,

4. To lay down some directions for reading the Holy Scriptures with advantage and comfort.

1. What God Hath Appointed about Reading

I am first of all to show what God hath appointed about the reading of his holy word. In general, he has ordained it to be read, in churches, in families, and in the retired closet, with becoming dispositions of mind.

The dispositions of the mind that are required in this service, should be carefully attended to in performing it. Our *desires* and *hopes* should depend on God, the Father of lights, to lead us into the saving knowledge of his will, and open the eyes of our understanding, to behold the wonderful things contained in his law; we should read with *humility* and *meekness*; laying aside our pride and prejudices, and subjecting our carnal reasonings to the plain and wholesome instructions of the word, inquiring modestly and humbly into the sense of it, and then captivating every thought to the obedience of Christ; we should mix *faith* and *hope* with reading the Holy Scriptures, believing the doctrines, and hoping for the mercy and grace that are offered; for the word is no further profitable, than as it is mixed with faith in them that read or hear it; we should, in reading, receive *the love of the truth*, and delight to meditate therein both day and night; and we should, with an *unreserved subjection, obey every truth, through the Spirit.* These and such like dispositions, that glorify God, and profit ourselves, should be diligently cultivated, as often as we look into that precious book. Reading God's word, with these tempers, is a proper and necessary part of public, family, and secret worship.

1. "Reading of the word in the congregation, being part of the public worship of God (wherein we acknowledge our dependence upon him, and subjection to him), and one means, sanctified by him, for the edifying of his people, is to be performed by the pastors and teachers. All the canonical books of the Old and New Testament (but none of those which are commonly called Apocrypha), should be publicly read in the vulgar tongue, out of the best allowed translation, distinctly, that all may hear and understand. It is convenient, that ordinarily one chapter of each Testament be read at every meeting; and sometimes more, where the chapters be short, or the coherence of matter requireth it. It is requisite, that all the canonical books be read over in order, that the people may be better acquainted with the whole body of the Scriptures: and ordinarily where reading in either

Testament endeth on one Lord's day, it is to begin the next." This account you have in the Directory for the Public Worship of God, agreed upon by the Assembly of divines at Westminster, on the article of "public reading of the Holy Scriptures." That they did not mean, what is called lecturing or expounding, is evident from what is subjoined in these words, "When the minister, who readeth, shall judge it necessary to expound any part of what is read, let it not be done until the whole chapter or psalm is ended.... Beside public reading of the Holy Scriptures, every person, that can read, is to be exhorted to read the Scriptures privately."

This practice is no human invention. There is no doubt it was observed in the Jewish synagogues; and it is highly reasonable to suppose that the writings of the New, as well as the Old Testament, were designed to be read in Christian churches; and it is undeniable they were so read in the primitive churches. The church, and all the public worship that is performed therein, are founded on the doctrines contained in Scripture; and therefore everyone who would be made wise to salvation, ought to be well acquainted with it; and the public reading of it is one way of testifying the high esteem we have for it, and of further improving in the knowledge and comfort of it. We learn what was the practice of the Jews, from Acts 13:15, "And after the reading of the law and the prophets," *etc.*, where express mention is made of it. If any shall object that this was a practice *among the Jews*, and ought not, for that reason, to affect *Christians*, it is answered, by distinguishing between what was *peculiar to them*, as making a part of their ceremonial worship, and what is *common to all men*, and founded on natural reason, what was ceremonial among the Jews is abolished, and their example in such things is to be no rule to us. But *reading* of the Scriptures, being no part of that ceremonial worship, any more than *praying*, derives its obligation from a *moral reason*, besides a *positive institution* of Christ to be met with in the New Testament. So that there was nothing that obliged the Jews to read the Scriptures in their synagogues, but what does equally bind Christians to the same practice in their assemblies.

The apostle closes his first epistle to the Thessalonians with this solemn injunction, "I charge you by the Lord that this epistle be read unto all the holy brethren" (1 Thess. 5:27). Now this was to be done when they were met together for religious worship, as more evidently appears, from what the same apostle gave in charge about another epistle written to the Colossians, "When this epistle is read amongst you, cause that it be read also in the church of the Laodiceans; and that ye likewise read the epistle from Laodicea" (Col. 4:16). To read it in the church, signifies to read it when they were met together to worship God. From these passages we may reasonably gather that the other apostolical writings were also to be read in the public assemblies. This practice seems to be authorized by the example of our blessed Lord, and confirmed to be a standing part of divine public worship, for "he went into the synagogue on the sabbath-day, and stood up for to read" (Luke 4:16). In this duty we have Christ for an example.

The practice of the primitive church was exactly agreeable to this worthy pattern. Justin Martyr, describing the service in public assemblies, says, among other things, "The records of the apostles, and the writings of the prophets are read." Tertullian says, "In our public assemblies, the Scriptures are read, psalms sung, sermons preached, and prayers presented." But this is so undeniably clear, that none who knows anything of church-history will ever move a doubt about it. Cyprian, Origen, Chrysostom, Basil, and many other writers, agree in one testimony, with these now quoted.[1]

Reason, as well as divine institution, and primitive practice, may lead us to this way of thinking. The Holy Scriptures are the only rule of our faith, and of our lives; and what can be more reasonable than to publish openly, to acknowledge solemnly, and to have continually in our ears and in our memories, these words of the holy One? And what means are so proper for this purpose, as the orderly and successive reading of the books of the Old and New Testament?

I cannot forbear to transcribe a passage from Mr. Thomas Reynolds on this subject:

> Where this exercise of reading the Scriptures is omitted, it is doubtless a great defect in the public worship, which ought to be revived...and I wish it might be so, were it only for one melancholy reason, *viz.*, for the sake of those miserable people, who neither read the word of God themselves, nor have a chapter read to them from one week's end to another.

---

[1] King, *An Inquiry into the Constitution, Discipline, Unity and Worship of the Primitive Church*, part 2, chap. 1; John Edwards. *Theologia Reformata*, vol. 1. p. 622.

1. READING THE HOLY SCRIPTURES

Give me leave to add to what that gentleman has urged, that I wish it were revived, not only because our faith should always stand in the power of God, according to the Scriptures, but for this most afflicting consideration, *viz.*, for the sake of those many unhappy people, who hear very few scriptural truths from the pulpit.

2. The word is to be read, with the same gracious tempers, *in our families*, as a part of religious worship. By prayer we speak to God; in reading his word we hear God speak to us. This adds much to the solemnity of family worship, and makes the transaction more awful and serious, when it is done in a right manner; it is highly conducive to the honor of God, and the family's edification, as a useful means to instill and promote the fear of God. The strict charge God gave the Jews remains on record for our instruction,

> These words which I command thee this day, shall be in thine heart: and thou shalt teach them diligently unto thy children, and shalt talk of them when thou sittest in thine house, and when thou walkest by the way, and when thou liest down, and when thou risest up. And thou shalt bind them for a sign upon thine hand, and they shall be as frontlets between thine eyes. And thou shalt write them upon the posts of thy house, and on thy gates (Deut. 6:6–9).

No man can imagine that Christians are under less obligation to honor the word of God in their families than the Jews were to honor it in theirs. Parents are expressly called to bring up their children in the nurture and admonition of the Lord (Eph. 6:4). This, no doubt, implies, among several things else, that they should make them familiarly conversant with the Holy Scriptures, and inure them to the reading of them in family worship. It is recorded to the praise of Timothy, that from a child he had known the Scriptures (2 Tim. 3:15). Does not the example of Abraham, the friend of God, and the father of believers, deserve our imitation? "I know him," saith the Lord, "that he will command his children, and his household after him, and they shall keep the way of the LORD" (Gen. 18:19). But wherewith shall a man cleanse his way? Surely, by taking heed thereto, according to the word of God. And does not reason agree, that the most useful knowledge, which can only be learned from that precious book, should be daily cultivated in every Christian family? Is it our reasonable service, to speak unto God in family prayer and praise; and shall we not look on ourselves bound to hear what the Lord God will say to us, by his word? Should we not be swift to hear, that we may be mighty in the Scriptures, to pray and sing with our spirits, and with our understandings also? The Scripture, that is given by inspiration of God, is able to make us wise unto salvation, and therefore it has a just and reasonable right to be read and heard, in our family devotions.

3. There ought to be a *personal reading* of the Scriptures, by everyone *in private*. This ought to be done, not only occasionally, but frequently; and ought to be attended to, as one of the great businesses of life. The Scriptures were designed for every man's particular instruction and profit, wherever they are made known for the obedience of faith, and therefore the frequent reading of them should make a part of our religion in secret. No encumbrances of life, nor urgency of affairs, can be a sufficient excuse for the common neglect of this duty, because this is by far the most important of all that can possibly concern us, and is a proper means to direct us in all our other affairs. The Eunuch, under Candace queen of Ethiopia, was a man of great authority and business, and having some leisure time, as he was riding in his chariot, he improved it in reading the Scriptures; and you know, God made it a happy season for his own advantage, and hath set us an example, and given us encouragement in that history, to employ our vacant hours in the same manner. Kings and princes, who might think themselves excusable on account of the multiplicity of affairs they have often upon their hands, are notwithstanding directed to this duty. God foreseeing that, in process of time, the Jews, through their perverseness, would lust after the customs of other nations, and not content with having *him* for their *King* would set up one from among themselves; in the view of this he ordained, out of his great concern for the good of that ungrateful people, that whenever such a king should be set up, he should have a copy of the law written in a book, and that it should be with him, and he should read therein all the days of his life (Deut. 17:19). And it is mentioned as a part of the character of every real good man, that he delighteth "in the law of the LORD, and in his law doth he meditate day and night" (Ps. 1:2); that is, his strongest inclinations are to know, in a saving manner, the mind and will of God, and therefore he affectionately embraces every season and opportunity, and uses every means that may be helpful to him for this purpose. The word of Christ should dwell richly in

every Christian (Col. 3:16), to fill his *understanding* with the most useful and exalted truths; with the most sublime sentiments, just reasonings, and solid judgment about them; to fill his *will* with the most excellent and substantial goodness, to command his hearty consent, and entirely to subdue him to the obedience of Christ; to fill his *affections* with pure and spiritual pleasure, and thoroughly to possess all their powers and motions, to the exclusion of every disorderly passion and appetite; to fill his *conscience* with tenderness, light, faithfulness, and peace, and to purify it from all stupidity, rash judgment, and deceit; and to fill his *memory* with a large stock of its most important doctrines, precepts, and promises, under whatever form they are delivered to us; that he may readily call them to mind for suitable reflections and improvements, as occasions require. Thus it should take complete possession of his *whole soul*, till all his capacities of receiving this precious treasure are stored with it, that it may daily issue out of his lips, and shed its glorious virtues through his life. Now, can we hope to obtain this valuable end without an attentive, serious, frequent, personal reading of God's word? But if

> thou incline thine ear unto wisdom, and apply thine heart to understanding: yea, if thou criest after knowledge, and liftest up thy voice for understanding: if thou seekest her as silver, and searchest for her as for hid treasures: then shalt thou understand the fear of the LORD, and find the knowledge of God. For the Lord giveth wisdom: out of his mouth cometh knowledge and understanding (Prov. 2:2–6).

2. It Is a Divine and Most Excellent Institution

The second head on the reading of the Holy Scriptures, leads me to show that this is a *divine*, and a *most excellent institution*. I shall accordingly endeavor to take a view of it (1.) As God's appointment; and (2.) As an excellent and profitable service.

I. Reading of the Holy Scriptures is the appointment of God. How pertinent and striking are the following words to this purpose!

> Only be thou strong and very courageous, that thou mayest observe to do according to all the law which Moses my servant commanded thee: turn not from it to the right hand or to the left, that thou mayst

prosper whithersoever thou goest. This book of the law shall not depart out of thy mouth; but thou shalt meditate therein day and night, that thou mayst observe to do according to all that is written therein: for then thou shalt make thy way prosperous, and then thou shalt have good success (Josh. 1:7–8).

If we suppose that the divine Being has condescended to make his will and pleasure known to men; that his revealed will is not conveyed by uncertain and fallible tradition, nor dependent on human authority, nor to be collected from bold conjecture, but is written out in the Bible; that this book has every evidence of inspiration in its favor, that we could expect or reasonably wish a revelation from heaven should have; and that it is the only sufficient, sure, and perfect rule to direct us how we may glorify and enjoy God; if, I say, we suppose these things; and are they not first principles of Christianity, and things that are most firmly believed and openly owned among Christians? Then we are naturally led to these conclusions:

(1.) Not to read it is to despise God's marvelous goodness in giving us this revelation. It was justly reckoned the capital advantage that the Jews had above the Gentiles, that "unto them were committed the oracles of God" (Rom. 3:2). How inexpressibly great is our privilege even above the Jews, as we have the entire revelation of the mind of God committed to us, in its highest perfection! Now, after all this, for persons to make little or no use of their Bibles, is to pour the utmost contempt on the highest instances of divine goodness, and to bring on themselves the aggravated guilt of the basest ingratitude.

(2.) Not to read the Scriptures is to frustrate, as much as we can, the design of God in giving them to us. God proposes ends worthy of himself, in all his works; and in this, among the rest. The principal of these are the manifestation of his own glory, and the benefit of his creatures; but neither of these can be answered, where the Bible is neglected. The brightest characters of the excellent glories and infinite perfections of God are stamped upon the Scriptures, and shine forth in the works of redemption; nor is the chief good, and solid enduring happiness, represented to mankind in a true undeceiving light, except in the word of God. Therefore by neglecting carefully and constantly to make use of the Scriptures, we dishonor God, and sin against our own souls.

(3.) Not to read the Scriptures is to neglect the improvement of our capacities to the best purpose; or, more properly, it is to degrade and abuse them in mean, trifling pursuits. God hath made us wiser than the beasts of the field, and endowed us with more understanding than the fowls of heaven; but we have no solid ground to build the improvements of saving knowledge, or the refinements of spiritual tempers and heavenly affections upon, if we neglect the word of life. Without this we must wander in endless uncertainty, involve ourselves in deep perplexity, or comfort ourselves with imaginary perishing vanity; while our minds should be employed in beholding and studying his word, till we are "changed into the same image, from glory to glory, by the Spirit of the Lord" (2 Cor. 3:18).

Thus it appears that the very gift of a written revelation carries in it an implied command to read it. Though nothing in particular had been mentioned, yet considering the excellency of the Being from whom it comes, the importance of its contents, and our inferiority and subjection, what less than this can be the meaning of it? But if there are, besides this, express positive commands in the body of the revelation, to this purpose; then to read it is rendered an *act of obedience* to the best and highest authority. Here I might collect a multitude of proofs.

The word of God is addressed to all sorts of men, without distinction of character, or exception of persons. "Unto you, O men, I call; and my voice is to the sons of men" (Prov. 8:4), "Wisdom crieth without, she uttereth her voice in the streets" (Prov. 1:20).

In the New Testament, we find our Savior frequently appealing, in his discourses, to the Scriptures, for rectifying the mistakes of his hearers. How often does he put this question to them, *Have ye not read? How readest thou? Is it not written?* These forms of speech are a plain intimation, either that he took it for granted they were so well acquainted with their Bibles, that they could not be ignorant of such things; or else, they are a tacit reproof for their neglecting so necessary a duty, and carry this meaning: If you have not read, the greater is your sin, and the more your shame. He called all to search the Scriptures (John 5:39). In the parable of the rich man and Lazarus, Abraham, in his answer to the rich man's petition for his brethren, refers them to the Scriptures. "They have Moses and the prophets; let them hear them" (Luke 16:29); to wit, by a diligent perusal of, and close attention to, what they spake in their writings. We are enjoined to do all, that we may stand; and to take unto us the whole armor of God; and among other parts of it, to take the sword of the Spirit, which is the word of God (Eph. 6:17). This must imply that we should cultivate a familiar and daily acquaintance with it, that we may be able to use it with dexterity and success on every occasion.

Blessings shall be on the head of that man that meditates in the law of his God both day and night, with attention and perseverance; and that is not a forgetful hearer of the word: in keeping it he has a great reward. But they that turn away their ear from hearing the law must expect that their prayer will be an abomination; because they rebel against the words of God, and contemn the counsel of the Most High, therefore their heart shall be brought down with labor, they shall fall down, and there shall be none to help. Consider this, ye that neglect to read the word of God.

We are commanded to worship God, to believe in the name of his Son, Jesus Christ, to examine ourselves, to try the spirits, to fight the good fight of faith, to keep ourselves in the love of God, to cleanse our way, to walk in the Spirit, to live by faith, to exercise patience, and to lay hold on eternal life; with many other things, that necessarily *suppose* our previous acquaintance with the Holy Scriptures, and therefore *imply a command* to read them. I shall now go on,

II. To show, that reading the word of God is an excellent and profitable exercise. Indeed if we had no more to convince us of this, it might be *enough*, to consider that it is an ordinance of that God, "who never said to the house of Jacob, Seek ye my face, in vain." But I would, moreover, represent two things on this head.

1. It is an acceptable homage to the great God to read his word; for in that precious book, we have the only clear and satisfying discovery of his being, perfections, pleasure, and affectionate regard to unworthy men. It represents his infinite understanding, as abounding to us in all wisdom and prudence. It opens the boundless riches of his marvelous loving-kindness. It declares the sovereignty of God, together with his supreme authority over men. It holds forth these most important truths with a divine and delightful evidence. In reading it, our minds are entertained with the most solid and interesting truths, and our wills are satisfied with the most substantial goodness, while all the powers of the soul have a most extensive field for their exercise and improvement. To read the oracles of God is an acknowledgment of him in these manifestations of his glory, and in these

binding directions concerning our duty they contain and exhibit. Blessed is he that readeth these words of the Holy One! He glorifies God by abiding in his will, and shall in a little time be glorified with his God, and in his light shall see light most clearly.

2. To read the Holy Scriptures is very much to our own advantage in many respects. All Scripture is profitable for doctrine, reproof, correction, and instruction in righteousness; to make the man of God perfect, and thoroughly to furnish him unto every good work. The reading of these holy oracles is an excellent means of *filling the mind* with the most useful knowledge of the nature, will, and works of God, and of the true character of ourselves, as the creatures of God, rebels against heaven, and objects of absolutely sovereign and divine compassion; of *attaching our wills to God*, the boundless supreme Good, whose awful and amiable perfections, manifested in the face of Jesus Christ, are most endearing and desirable; of *directing us* in a regular pursuit of this satisfying portion; for if that which we hear in these lively oracles shall remain in us, we also shall continue in the Son, and in the Father; of *sanctifying our nature*, while we behold as in a glass the glory of the Lord, and are changed into the same image from glory to glory; of *fortifying our souls* against temptations; for when the word of God abideth in us, we shall overcome the wicked one; *of conquering the world*; for this is the victory that overcometh the world, even our faith; of *serving God and our generation*, according to his will; for by abiding in Christ as he is set forth in the Holy Scriptures, which testify of him, we shall bring forth much fruit; *of supporting us* under the afflictions of this life; for by the faith of the Scriptures we have access into that grace wherein believers stand, and rejoice in tribulations; yea, though now, if need be, the saints are in heaviness through manifold temptations, yet believing they rejoice, even in these afflicted circumstances, with joy unspeakable and full of glory. I shall only add that the reading of God's most holy word is an excellent means of *reconciling us* to the thoughts of death; there we are assured this last enemy is conquered and disarmed, and will shortly be entirely destroyed.

Review these glorious privileges that follow a careful perusal of the word of God, where faith is mixed with the reading of it, and say, O my soul, is it a vain thing to serve the Lord in this duty? Is it not by this that men live, and in all this is the life of their souls?

3. Vindication from Some Objections

The objections that are made against reading the word of God are as various as the systems of men's opinions which they are urged to support are different from one another. I do not insist on the objections that are taken from the supposed imposition of that book on the world. This argument has been thoroughly canvassed in Britain; and in every contest truth has been triumphant. In some hands, no doubt, the argument for the authenticity of the Scriptures, as a divine revelation, has been injured; but, I say it again, in every contest the sacred evidence of truth has been, *upon the whole*, triumphant.

It is a famous principle of the Papists "that the Scriptures should not be translated into the vulgar languages, generally used in a country where Christianity is professed." To justify this opinion, they allege several things: such as,

1. "*The Scriptures*," they pretend, "*are very obscure, and the sense of them is very difficult.*" It is well, that they dare not say, *they are useless*. But if they are useful and necessary, will the careful reading of them by men in their own tongue make them darker? Will people become more ignorant by both reading and hearing them read and explained, than they would be, if they *only* heard them explained in a familiar language, without being allowed themselves either to read, or hear the words of the holy One? *Common sense* forbids the supposition; but even *this* may probably be thought *too weak a reason* against it, as well as against *transubstantiation*; and therefore I shall suggest another, that will probably have much more weight, with the Romish church. If that supposition be admitted, it will prove that their learned men, who have (what the world would call) that *double advantage* for understanding the Scriptures, are *so much the more ignorant* for their superior advantages. Most ridiculous!

2. They tell us, "It would derogate from the majesty of the word of God, to put it into everybody's hand, that they might read it when they pleased." It must be allowed that familiarity has sometimes been abused, and become the occasion of contempt. But, if the church of Rome would give a sanction to their argument, they should forbid people to pray, to meditate on the truths of God, or ever to converse with divine things. Do they not know that the *means* of happiness are to some the *occasion* of sin and ruin? Is it reasonable to endeavor to keep people miserable, by denying them the means of being happy, in order to prevent their being guilty

of a sin, that only follows by accident from the abuse of such means? Can the majesty of God's word ever become venerable, but in its own light? Can it ever be rightly esteemed, or become truly profitable, where the contents of it are not known? God makes his sun to shine and his rain to fall on the righteous and the wicked: and though the latter abuse his goodness, the former see, enjoy, and glorify God, for these acts of his marvelous goodness.

3. They say, "The reading of the Scripture will be the occasion of great heresies." And we know that there must be heresies among Christians, as well as offenses: but how does it appear that these arise from a *candid inquiry* into the sense of God's word? Is not this the *standard* of truth? It is easy to see how heresies may spring from a neglect of the sacred oracles: but, one would think, it is most reasonable to suppose that personal knowledge of their precious contents would rather join Christians together in one judgment, while they saw the same evidence for all their principles with their own eyes. And where is the merit of being free from error, by being totally ignorant of the truth? Such orthodoxy is contemptible and pernicious. We may apply to men, who are so infatuated, that awful word, "My people are destroyed for lack of knowledge: because thou hast rejected knowledge, I will also reject thee" (Hos. 4:6). It is a disagreeable alternative, that men must either be heretics, for reading the Scriptures, or rejected and destroyed by God for their ignorance. And as a masterly writer observes,

> It cannot, to considerate men, but seem a very hard case, that there should be no salvation to be had out of the church of Rome; and yet the ordinary means of salvation, and in our Savior's judgment, the most effectual of them (*viz.*, reading the Scriptures, Luke 16:31) are not to be had in it.[2]

4. They allege, "That that which is holy is not to be given to dogs" (Matt. 7:6). This shows the regard they have for Christ's *sheep*, whom they call dogs to serve a turn. But it is not easy to account for bringing *a free access* to the familiar use of the word of God, under the predicament of giving that which is holy to dogs, without allowing that the church of Rome

---

[2] John Tillotson. *The Works of Dr. John Tillotson*, sermon 128.

stands fairly convicted of this crime in its full force, inasmuch as they allow their church's sense of these holy oracles to be delivered to all without distinction. Moreover, it is pleasant enough to see *learned linguists*, honored with the name of children or *saints*; while the *illiterate vulgar* are reputed *dogs*. A bad cause is not capable of a fair, consistent defense. Whatever plausible arguments are urged for it, yet still, in the application at least, if not in the principles of such reasoning, there remaineth falsehood. There is a striking proof of this in the popish controversy, as to the text in Matthew 7:6. The sense of it is plain and important, if we explain it by the context: *to wit*, "That counsels and reproofs are not to be unseasonably thrown away upon hardened, profane, and incorrigible sinners, who instead of taking them well, or being the better for them, would be enraged and irritated by them." While Catholics pervert this Scripture to support their sacrilegious robbery, committed upon the multitudes in their communion, that do not understand the Hebrew and Greek, or at least the Latin language, in which tongues alone they allow the Scriptures to be read; it is very plain, they exclude, under the character of *dogs and swine*, all these individuals (many, many millions of immortal souls!) who are not favored with a liberal education. On the other hand, every linguist, that is skillful in these tongues, may read what is holy, and use for himself the inspired writings. The foundation of this indulgence is laid in the *preeminence* of his character above that of dogs and swine. *Erudition* and *sanctification* seem to have the same meaning in the Antichristian creed. They have a venerable precedent, and may boast of antiquity, to countenance their opinion, the Pharisees answered the officers, "Have any of the rulers, or of the Pharisees believed on him? But this people who knoweth not the law are cursed" (John 7:48–49). That everyone may know that this is the language of Antichrist, I shall confront it with the words of the faithful and true Witness, "Jesus said, For judgment I am come into this world, that they which see not might see; and that they which see might be made blind. And some of the Pharisees which were with him, heard these words, and said unto him, *Are we blind also?* Jesus said unto them, If ye were blind, ye should have no sin: but now ye say, *We see*; therefore your sin remaineth" (John 9:39–41).

Is he not rightly called *Antichrist*, who openly contradicts and perverts this doctrine of Christ? But among other peculiarities in that church, it is probable, they have a *glossary of their own*. I hope *Protestants* do not envy them.

5. They object, "That the reading of the word of God is an infallible source of schisms and divisions, and appeal to the Protestant churches for a proof of it." But we can account for the *pretended union* of the Catholic, Popish churches, without once supposing that their ignorance of the Scriptures is the cause of it; though we allow, that this reason has a considerable influence that way. Interest, honor, pleasure, and danger, are rather too powerful motives to admit of dissensions; and when ignorance adds her influence to the whole, they operate with an almost irresistible efficacy, to secure an implicit attachment of their blinded and sensual devotees to their communion. But, if the truth is fairly stated, they are as guilty on the head of schism, as their neighbors; as may be seen in all the Protestant writers on the *unity of the church*, alleged as an infallible mark of the church of Rome being the true and only church of Christ.[3]

6. Some vindicate their neglect of the Scriptures, *because they are only a dead letter without the Spirit. They fancy that the Spirit is sufficient without the word.* I shall only observe that the Spirit is received by the hearing of faith, and acts as the Spirit of truth. Is it not very absurd then to imagine, that the Spirit who moved holy men to write the will of God, pays no regard to that book which he inspired?

The objections made against reading the Scriptures, from the want of time, multiplicity of business, hearing them read in public worship, knowledge of their contents, and the like topics, discover a bad temper of mind that does not so much need more evidence to cure it, as a powerful impression of the authority of God upon the conscience. Therefore I must refer to what has been said on the foregoing section for a sufficient answer. I proceed,

4. Some Directions for Advantage and Comfort
To lay down proper directions for reading the Holy Scriptures with advantage and comfort. We have an excellent direction on this head, "Lay apart all filthiness and superfluity of naughtiness, and receive with meekness the engrafted word, which is able to save your souls" (James 1:21). The words refer immediately to *hearing*, but may be applied also to *reading the Scrip-*

---

[3] The reader may consult Dr. Chandler's sermon on 1 Timothy 3:14–15, pp. 37–40.

tures. According to this divine example, I shall first suggest some *cautionary*, and then some *positive directions*. Under one or other of these heads, everything that is pertinent on this subject may be naturally arranged. The reader cannot expect a complete list; it is enough if the principal ones are hinted.

I. In order to read the Scriptures with benefit and comfort, it is necessary to guard against everything that may hinder our profiting by them. The following, among many instances, may be mentioned, that are extremely pernicious to our edification, and should be laid aside as much as possible.

1. Beware of *spiritual pride*, and, a *conceit of your own knowledge*. Many might have become wise and knowing, as Cicero observes, if they had not thought themselves so too soon. Alas! How many form the system of their principles before they look into their Bibles; and are already determined what to receive, before they have inquired what God has revealed! They use their Bibles, not to find what God has been pleased to make known, but to find a sanction for their own sentiments. Their imagination dictates, and God must ratify their opinions. Such pride is intolerable. Such knowledge is blindness and folly. Where this temper prevails, it prevents edification. God is righteous, when he gives up such persons to believe lies; makes their hearts fat; makes their ears heavy; and shuts their eyes. Beware of spiritual pride, which prescribes to God what he should say; or presumes to bring his word to the standard of human reason; or shows itself in the many low pretenses of cavil and objection—if ever you hope to profit by the Scriptures. For the same reason,

2. Guard against *prejudices* and *preconceived opinions*. They shut the mind against conviction, and leave a man under the power of his own fancy. If a man that is strongly prepossessed with a good or ill opinion of anything, shall happen to judge right, yet he does not found his judgment upon satisfying evidence; and how then can we call it *reasonable?* But if he is prepossessed with misapprehensions, he becomes hardened in his mistakes, and refuses to come to the light. Every man has his darling opinion, and favorite scheme, which he is tenacious of, and holds for undoubted truth; and frequently supposes that his opinion has such an important place and extensive influence in the system of revealed truth, that the whole is undermined by everyone that does not see as he sees, and do as he does. Hence comes bigotry, with her wicked brood, self-sufficiency,

vain-glorying, uncharitable judging, and despising of others. Now, because every man is easily beset with this sin, therefore we should approach the oracles of God with a mind open to instruction, and not determined by preconceived opinions. Education, conversation, and schemes may assist our inquiries; but nothing should determine us except divine evidence, nor hinder us to apprehend and submit to it whenever it is discerned. How miserably has the word of God been abused by the arts of criticism to bend it to men's apprehensions, instead of measuring their apprehensions by that rule!

3. Have a care of any *indulged lust*. To indulge any secret sin, will make us either neglect, distaste, or pervert the Scriptures. It would be a wonder indeed to see a man that loved sin reading his Bible with pleasure,

> This is the condemnation, that light is come into the world, and men loved darkness rather than light, because their deeds were evil. For every one that doeth evil hateth the light, neither cometh to the light, lest his deeds should be reproved. But he that doeth truth cometh to the light, that his deeds may be made manifest, that they are wrought in God (John 3:19–21).

The prevalence of any sin is an effectual bar to the success of the word of God, which must be received in the *love of it*; and is choked by worldly cares, and cannot dwell where sin is regarded. It is shocking to think how the Scripture has been perverted to extenuate vice, and sometimes to patronize men in sinning against heaven and before God. If we would profit by reading the inspired pages, let us lay aside all filthiness, and superfluity of naughtiness.

4. We must not read the Scriptures in a *formal, careless, and customary manner*, if we would read them with benefit. Formalities leave the mind unimpressed, and dead to any feeling of divine things. In this, as much as any other duty, we should be fervent in spirit, serving the Lord; and aim at exercising the power, as well as having the form of godliness. We should go to read the oracles of God, as the infant to suck the breast; not for amusement, or to observe a form; but to be nourished, edified, and sanctified.

To obtain real benefit then by reading the word, we must beware of spiritual pride, guard against preconceived opinions, indulge no sin, and shake off formality and sloth, rising above the customary, lifeless form of the task; to "desire, as newborn babes, the sincere milk of the word, that we may grow thereby." I shall now subjoin,

II. Some positive directions to assist in reading the Scriptures with solid advantage. This is a copious field. I shall only select a few out of many things that offer themselves to our consideration, most naturally; which may be reduced under two general heads: *to wit*, such as may enable us to read them *with understanding*; and such as may help us to read them *with affection also*. I shall very shortly collect the principal directions on each, and leave them to the reader's own reflections, without fatiguing him with a tedious illustration.

First, One great end to be proposed in reading the Scriptures is the improvement of knowledge, and an increase of wisdom. That this end may be gained, it is expedient:

1. To read them *regularly*, in a due order and proper method. Regular study is the only means of improvement in any *art or science*. He that does not observe it is superficial and vain in his knowledge, confused and inconsistent in his loose ideas, and cannot be expert in practice. The same ill consequences follow a loose, vague, immethodical reading of the Holy Scriptures; which, in a just view of their magnificent whole, their beautiful parts, and their harmonious connections, would make the man of God perfect, and furnish him throughly for every good work.

2. To *compare one Scripture with another*, and thus make the word of God its own interpreter. As Canne observes in his preface to his notes on the Bible, "Such is the fullness and perfection of the Holy Scripture, as it hath enough and sufficiency in itself for the explanation and opening the sense and meaning of it." We should diligently compare the obscure passages with the plain, the difficult with the easy, the fewer expressions with the more frequent, and the doubtful with the certain. Types, metaphors, parables, prophecies, histories, and promises should be explained by this rule. I would recommend the use of *Canne's notes on the Bible* to all, and of *Clarke's annotations and parallel Scriptures* on the whole Bible, in folio, to as many as are able to procure them, as very useful assistances.

3. To judge of Scripture by the *analogy of faith*, or by the general scope and proportion of the whole. The meaning of every part must be consistent with the design of the whole. Without this, any book would be made downright nonsense. Those that have the gift, that are called to the office

of prophesying, should prophesy according to the proportion, or analogy, of faith; *that is*, according to the main drift and governing scope of the word of faith. This is the rule of *prophesying*, and is also the rule of *reading*. Every truth has its own place in the system of revelation; when it is not kept in that place, it is like a foot out of joint, and the proportion of faith is marred and broken.

4. To *use every help* for attaining the knowledge of the Scriptures; as meditation, prayer, conversation, hearing the word preached, and reading what has been written by men to explain the sense, and bring home the force of the Scriptures. It is a crime of a grievous nature to pin our faith to any man's sleeve; while we use these means of knowledge, still let us mind *our own* importance, so far as not to suffer our judgment to become a dupe to any teacher, or writer, further than we see evidence of the mind of Christ in their doctrines. We should hear Christ, the true prophet, in all things; and honor the means of instruction which he has appointed, so far as they lead to him.

5. To consider well *the sense, connection*, and *scope of every passage*, and apply it as we believe the Holy Ghost designed it. By observing this rule, and duly considering the time, circumstances, persons, manners, *etc.*, referred to, we should acquire a deep insight into the Scriptures, and become expert in the law of God.

6. To be *willing to hear all parties in every question* about the true sense of the Scriptures. Unless this be our study, to know the truth impartially; how can we know it savingly? We should not shun to hear objections to our views of Scripture; for we are as liable to be in a mistake as others. But we should bring our own and their opinions to the clear light of the Scriptures, and receive the impartial decision of the Spirit of truth, as it is delivered in that precious book.

7. To consider *first the Scripture itself*, before we consult comments upon it; that we may judge of them by the Scripture, and not of the Scripture by them. And having thus fixed the Scripture to be the rule of judgment, we should neither *abound* in our own sense, as if none but our own sentiments were right, or as if we had no need of assistance from others; nor should we *sacrifice* our own understandings to any man, or to any number or party of men. We should neither reject what we have good evidence for, though we received it at first by education, or instruction from others; nor depend upon their opinion or authority, so as to take what they say

upon trust; but should judge for ourselves, according to the ability God has given us. This way we should prove all things, hold fast that which is good, and abstain from all appearance of evil.

Secondly, I shall now suggest some useful directions, to help us to prosecute the other great end to be proposed in reading the Scriptures, to wit, that we may be suitably affected with them, that our knowledge may become practical, and they may become effectual.

The *former* class of directions had a respect to our inquiries, as *reasonable men; this* concerns us as the meek and lowly disciples of Jesus Christ. The one sort referred to the information of our minds; the other to the edification and improvement of the heart.

That the Scriptures may powerfully and suitably affect our hearts, we should read them with attention, humility, reverence, application, frequency, delight, meditation, prayer, and desire to know and believe them, with a purpose of yielding subjection and obedience to them.

1. With *attention of mind*, taking heed to the word of God, as the delighted eye turns to the pleasant light that shines in a dark place. When Lydia's heart was opened, she attended to the things that were spoken of Paul. We should attend to the phrase, expression, connection, scope, and force of every passage. We should guard against intruding distractions that divert the mind from waiting on God in this service, and bend our whole hearts to this heavenly study: for so we are commanded, "Incline thine ear unto wisdom, and apply thine heart to understanding: seek understanding as silver; and search for her as for hid treasures."

2. With *humility*, submitting our faith and inclinations to their divine authority. We should receive with meekness the engrafted word. The good seed, in the parable of the sower, "are they, which in an honest and good heart, having heard the word, keep it, and bring forth fruit with patience" (Luke 8:15). God resisteth the proud, and revealeth the mysteries of the kingdom to those that become as little children, humble and teachable, sensible of ignorance, and disposed to receive instruction; that humbly adore the unsearchable judgments of God, and his ways that are past finding out.

3. With *reverence*, considering the Bible as the word of God. We should imagine ourselves conversing with God, while we read, as if the running title of every sentence referring to doctrine and duty were this: "God spake all these words, and said." When we read the Scriptures, we are in God's

presence, we converse with the word of life, and the rule of future judgment; we are in the greatest presence, and in the best company; the things themselves that we read are of the greatest importance, and most immediately concern our instruction for the present life, and our evidence for life eternal. The Author and the contents of this revelation demand our most profound reverence, and our best regards.

4. We should read the Holy Scriptures with *faith and self-application.* The word preached or read will not profit us, unless it be mixed with faith. We should read and know it *for our good*; remembering that he that is wise is wise *for himself.* The efficacy of divine truth arises from the application of it, by the powerful demonstration of the Holy Ghost, setting it home on the conscience with irresistible energy, realizing the word of God to the mind, while he opens the understanding to understand the Scriptures, in all the fullness of their heavenly meaning, and opens the heart to receive them in all the force of their transforming power. As we read, we should improve each particular passage according to its nature, trembling at the threatenings, yielding obedience to the commands, and embracing the promises of God for this life, and for that which is to come. Contemplating the various examples recorded in the Bible, we should use some of them as admonitory seamarks, to teach *us* to avoid the rocks of sin; use others as a conducting clue to guide *our* feet into the paths of peace; use all as incitements to awaken *our* circumspection, or quicken *our* diligence.

5. We should read the word of God *frequently*; not only to grow in the knowledge of it, but to frame our spirits more for heaven, and for gracious converse with God. Blessed is the man that meditates in the law of God both day and night (Ps. 1:1–2).

6. We should read the word of God with *unfeigned esteem and delight.* The perfections of God shine with brighter glory in his word than they do in any of his works. Its contents are infallibly true, as well as infinitely good. It well deserves to be hid in our hearts, and to dwell richly in our souls, as a means of humbling, instructing, and saving us, for by the words of truth and sound doctrine, the saints are nourished up unto eternal life. David spake the words of truth and soberness, when he expressed his love to God's law in these rapturous strains: "O how love I thy law! it is my meditation all the day" (Ps. 119:97). It is more to be desired "than gold, yea, than much fine gold: sweeter also than honey and the honeycomb" (Ps. 19:10).

7. The word of God should be read with *meditation*. The contents of it should sink into our minds. It is not the man that reads most, but that digests best, that will be mightiest in the Scriptures. The sweet singer of Israel meditated, as well as read, in the law of God, both day and night. He employed the wakeful hours of the night, as well as the leisure moments of the day, in contemplating the divine word. This is the way to become masters of our profession in every human art and science; and why should we not use the same diligence in perusing the Scriptures, that our profiting herein may appear unto all?

8. We should join *prayer* to God for his effectual blessing upon our reading. This is exemplified by the saints, "Open thou mine eyes, that I may behold wondrous things out of thy law" (Ps. 119:18). We are commanded and encouraged to do so, "If any of you lack wisdom, let him ask of God, that giveth to all men liberally, and upbraideth not; and it shall be given him" (James 1:5). "I am the Lord thy God which teacheth thee to profit, which leadeth thee by the way that thou shouldst go" (Isa. 48:17). Prayer should always accompany our reading of God's word, that the enlightening Spirit may lead us into all its truth and influence.

9. We should read the Holy Scriptures with a *desire* to know and believe them, and with a *purpose of subjection and obedience* to them. We should always open our Bibles with this fixed purpose. Whatsoever the Lord shall say unto me, I will hear and do it. In a word, let us be faithful to our present light, and persevere in further searches after more; remembering, that "if any man will do his will, he shall know of the doctrine, whether it be of God" (John 7:17).

I have been the larger on this duty of *reading the word of God* because I firmly believe, the neglect of it, and the improper manner of performing it, that prevail so much, are the principal causes of the general deadness and formality among professors, as well as of the open wickedness of the profane, in this profligate age, when fear is cast off, prayer restrained, the love of many waxed cold, and iniquity is everywhere abounding. To return to the Scriptures is the best means of a thorough reformation.

Chapter 2
Preaching the Gospel

The preaching of the cross is to them that perish, foolishness, but unto them which are saved, it is the power of God. It does not fall within my scheme to give a labored description of the nature, manner, and other circumstances, of preaching the gospel, as it is the employment of ministers. My abilities are greatly inferior to such an attempt; and besides, it is happily executed in many valuable performances on that subject that are common enough. All that comes under my consideration at present is to explain the preaching of the word, as it is an ordinance of God, and a part of his worship. In doing this, I shall observe the following order:

1. To show what is clearly contained in Scripture about the nature of preaching the word.
2. To prove that it is an ordinance of God, that is to continue in the visible church, till the end of time.
3. To inquire who may warrantably preach the gospel.
4. To vindicate this ordinance from some objections.
5. To describe the manner of preaching, in a few obvious hints.

1. The Nature

I am, in the *first* place, to show what is clearly contained in the Scripture about the *nature* of preaching the word. This office is venerable for its antiquity. Enoch, the seventh from Adam, prophesied (Jude 14), and Noah was a preacher of righteousness (2 Peter 2:5). This ordinance was of standing use in the Old Testament church, while its members continued to cleave unto the Lord. It was a divine appointment, that the priest's lips should keep knowledge, and that the people should seek the law at his mouth (Mal. 2:6–7). The Baptist, that came in the spirit and power of Elias, preached in the wilderness of Judea (Matt. 3:1). Jesus himself, after he had been tempted in the wilderness, "began to preach, and to say, Repent: for the kingdom of heaven is at hand" (Matt. 4:17). And he sent forth his disciples to preach to the lost sheep of the house of Israel (Matt. 10:6–7). And after his resurrection, they received a new and more extensive commission, "Go…and preach the gospel to every creature" (Mark 16:15).

We have several examples on record, to give us all reasonable satisfaction about the nature of their preaching. The word of God, as it referred to Christ, and testified of him, was the foundation of all their sermons, and the scope of all their ministrations. The manner of treating their subject was sometimes varied; but they still pursued the same design. The whole of their preaching consisted in a clear explication, and faithful application, of the truths of God, in a way that best suited the tenor of them, as more immediately profitable for doctrine, for reproof, for correction, or for instruction in righteousness. Sometimes they read the Scriptures, and gave the sense of them, and assisted the people to understand the reading; that is, they expounded the place which they read, and showed the true meaning of it; which is commonly called *lecturing*. This method of preaching is hinted at in Nehemiah 8:8.

I know some explain this text in a much lower sense, as signifying no more but this, "That the priests and Levites first read the book of the law in *Hebrew*, and then translated it into *Chaldee*, that the people might better understand it, being just come out of Babylon, where they had been used to the *Chaldean language*." There is no reason to exclude this sense from the words altogether; but there is as little reason for *confining* them to *this sense* only. It does not exhaust the emphasis of the various expressions, "They read in the book, in the law of God distinctly, and gave the sense, and caused the people to understand the reading" (Neh. 8:8). And again, the people "understood the words that were declared unto them" (Neh. 8:12). Do all these phrases imply no more than barely the translating of the law, and their understanding the sense of it from the translation of the original Hebrew, which was first read? When the chief of the fathers of all the people, the priests and the Levites, were gathered together unto Ezra the scribe, on the second day, *even to understand the words of the law* (Neh. 8:13), did they only come to have proper passages of the law pointed out, and translated to them?

But whatever be the meaning of this place, it is enough to my purpose if the law was sometimes *expounded* to Israel, as well as *read* in their hearing. This fact will not bear a dispute; for the priest's lips were to keep knowledge, and the people were to ask the law at his mouth; for he was the messenger of the LORD of hosts (Mal. 2:7). See also Lev. 10:11; 2 Chron. 17:8–9; Deut. 17:8–9; Ezek. 44:23–24; Hag. 2:11–14.

At other times they exhorted their hearers with earnestness to receive the great and leading truths of revelation, without observing the particular order of sentiments contained in any received passage of the oracles of God. Christ's sermon on the mount (Matt. 5–7), is an example of this. See also his discourse when he instituted the sacrament of the supper. And we have an instance of it in the apostle's speech, recorded in Acts 13.

Sometimes they pitched upon a particular point, and explained, vindicated, and enforced it, by opening a pertinent text, that was a natural foundation for the purpose they designed to prosecute. We find an example of this in Luke 4.

It would be endless to collect all the examples of preaching recorded in the book of God. Let it suffice to observe that those who were called to preach explained the prophecies of the Old Testament, opened the types, illustrated the doctrines, and divided aright the word of truth, as workmen that needed not to be ashamed. They taught, rebuked, exhorted, and comforted with all longsuffering and doctrine. They fed Christ's sheep, and his lambs.

I apprehend the whole of what belongs to this office may be summed up under the following heads.

1. The gospel-preacher is to publish and declare the truths of God, without partiality or reserve. This is made his duty by his commission, "Go into all the world, and preach [or publish] the gospel to every creature" (Mark 16:15). And this is exemplified for his imitation, where Paul told the elders of Ephesus that he had not shunned to declare unto them all the counsel of God (Acts 20:27). The ministers of Christ are commissioned officers, and are to go forth in his name and authority, to publish all that they find in their Bibles concerning him, according to the best of their understanding, just as they find it there. My meaning is, that they are not to bring their own sense to it, but to search out Christ's sense in it, and declare that to the people, by setting it forth in its own native simplicity, and inimitable glory. They are to explain the things of Christ, as far as they find them explicable; to lay things together that may strike the best light upon one another; to expatiate upon the great and copious subject, insisting most upon the most important things relating to it, by all the variety of useful representations it is capable of, and to draw out its deep and hid-

den glories, that they may be exposed with perspicuity and enlargement to open view, in their own light.

2. The gospel-preacher is to confirm and defend what is published in the Holy Scriptures. He is set for the defense and confirmation of the gospel. He is to hold fast the faithful word, as he has been taught (or rather, according to the doctrine he has received from Christ), that he may be able, by sound doctrine, both to exhort and to convince the gainsayers (Titus 1:9). The ministers of Christ are to maintain and support what they preach concerning Christ, by the light and authority of his word, by comparing Scripture with Scripture, and by just reasonings upon them, and clear deductions from them, as far as the nature of things will bear; and in this way, "earnestly contend for the faith which was once delivered unto the saints" (Jude 3).

There are difficulties to be solved, objections to be answered, seeming contradictions to be reconciled, and incomprehensibles to be contended for, as reasonable to be received, on the account of the sublimity of their own nature, and on the footing of a divine testimony. Obstinate, artful, captious, and profane gainsayers are to be reproved, convinced, or silenced; tender consciences to be assisted, relieved, and settled; honest inquirers to be satisfied; and believers to be established concerning the faith of Christ. All truths concerning him are to be proved upon solid scriptural principles, that they may maintain their ground to the honor of Christ, to the rebuke and confutation of his enemies, and to the furtherance and joy of faith, in all those that love our Lord Jesus Christ, in sincerity and truth. All this belongs to this branch of gospel-preaching.

3. To propose and recommend Christ to the acceptance of those to whom he is preaching is another part of the business of gospel-ministers. Their business is, among other things, to make known unto men that through this Savior is preached unto them the remission of sins, and by him all that believe are justified from all things from which they could not be justified by the law of Moses. As ambassadors for Christ, they are sent to beseech sinners to be reconciled unto God.

They are to preach Christ to sinners, setting him forth as a propitiation, through faith in his blood; recommending him to them in all his glorious and endearing characters, as the Son of God, and Savior of sinners; as a Prophet, Priest, and King, indispensably necessary for them, every way suitable to their wants, and altogether worthy of their acceptance; as an able, faithful, and willing Savior; as the best that could be provided, or that can be desired; and as bringing in an everlasting and complete salvation from sin and wrath, from all the evils they feel or fear, or are exposed to, and to all the blessedness they are capable of in soul and body for ever and ever. Their commission is to tell sinners to come, for all things are now ready; and to compel them to come in, that the house of God may be filled. They are to testify to all, repentance towards God, and faith towards our Lord Jesus Christ.

They are to preach to believers also, helping them who have believed through grace, that they may believe more steadfastly, rejoice more abundantly, walk more humbly, and devote themselves to God more fervently. Believers must be exhorted to cleave with purpose of heart to the Lord; and as they have received Christ Jesus the Lord, so to walk in him, rooted and built up in him, and established in the faith, as they have been taught, abounding therein with thanksgiving. The whole character of the Savior should be proposed to them to encourage their continual and increasing faith, love, hope, and joy, admiration, obedience, gratitude, and praise. All this should be attempted and enforced upon them in the name of Christ, and with an expectation of his presence and blessing, that they may know their privileges in him, and their duty toward him; and that their hearts may be comforted, strengthened, and animated in his ways, till the whole design of his grace toward them shall be perfected in glory.

Ministers are to preach Christ as an atonement for sin, and likewise as a lawgiver, whose authority binds the conscience, and who is able, and authorized, to execute all judgment, to kill and destroy, or to save alive. Faith in Christ is the effectual, powerful means of these works, by which it is made perfect; and without which faith is dead, and the highest pretensions to it an idle farce.

Thus the apostles preached, and thus the primitive Christians believed. The former determined to know nothing among their hearers, save Jesus Christ, and him crucified; and the other received these truths, as faithful sayings, and worthy of all acceptation. The word of life, thus preached and heard, is the wisdom and power of God to salvation.

2. To Continue till the End of the World

The next thing to be attempted is to prove that the preaching of the word is a divine institution that is to continue in the church, till the end of the world. Though it does not become creatures to determine what is fit for the Deity to do, it is our unquestionable duty to observe the visible impressions of his wisdom, in choosing the fittest means to obtain the end of their appointment. This is alike evident and beautiful, in the scenes of nature, and in the word of faith. We see, with wonder and delight, the harmony and dependence stamped on the natural ordinances of heaven (Job 38:33), and shall we shut our eyes against the comely, the infinitely wise design of saving them that believe by the foolishness of preaching? It pleased God to do so (1 Cor. 1:21), and he will do all his pleasure. God is absolutely sovereign. He loveth men, because it is his pleasure to love them. He "is gracious to whom he will be gracious, and hath compassion on whom he will have compassion." The *time* of manifesting his mercy is reserved in his own hand. And, is he not equally at liberty to determine by what *means*, and in what *order*, he will save them that are ordained to eternal life? We cannot, in reason, expect the favor of God, except in the way he is pleased to make it appear towards men. Our business, then, is to inquire whether the preaching of the cross is an ordinance of God for the standing use of the militant church, to convince and convert sinners, and to build up saints in their most holy faith.

It cannot be denied that this ordinance was appointed and blessed of God, both before the *Word was made flesh*, and in the *apostolic age*. The evidence of the facts is irresistibly clear and strong. The law and the prophets were until John the Baptist; and at that time the kingdom of God was preached, and every man pressed into it (Luke 16:16). And when Christ ascended up on high, he gave gifts unto men; some, prophets; and some, pastors and teachers; for the edifying of his body. Before his ascension to glory, and after he was raised from the dead, he commanded his disciples to "go ye therefore, and teach all nations, baptizing them in the name of the Father, and of the Son, and of the Holy Ghost" (Matt. 28:19–20). And to animate and encourage their persevering diligence in this noble employment, he added, "Lo, I am with you alway, even unto the end of the world." Without any force, nay, by all the laws of just interpretation, these comfortable words will bear this sense:

> Though as to my corporal presence, I am leaving this world, and going to the Father; yet while ye keep close to my commission, as God was with Moses, so am I, by my spiritual presence, with you,

and will be so at all times, wherever ye may be, to protect, counsel, assist, and succeed you; and I will continue to be present with you, and your successors in the gospel-ministry, through all ages, to the end of the world.[1]

The great design of preaching is to reveal Christ, that sinners may believe on his name, and that saints may be confirmed in the faith. That sinners may believe in him: Rom. 10:14, "How shall they call on him in whom they have not believed? and how shall they believe in him of whom they have not heard? and how shall they hear without a preacher?" That believers may be confirmed in the faith: therefore Paul and Barnabas, having preached the gospel in Derbe, and taught many, returned again to Lystra, and to Iconium, and Antioch, "confirming the souls of the disciples, and exhorting them to continue in the faith, and that we must through much tribulation enter into the kingdom of God" (Acts 14:21–22). These are the great ends of the original institution of a gospel-ministry; and there is evidently the same reason for continuing, as for instituting, this means of faith and establishment.

When the apostle describes the true doctrine of the gospel which is according to godliness, he says, "Without controversy great is the mystery of godliness: God was manifest in the flesh…preached unto the Gentiles" (1 Tim. 3:16). But how shall men preach him, except they be sent by him? (Rom. 10:15). "No man taketh this honor unto himself, but he that is called of God" to preach the word (Heb. 5:4). None may do it lawfully, safely, or with any prospect of success, but those that are called of God: and there is a full provision made in the appointments of God for this service,

> [Christ *exalted* gave] some pastors and teachers, for the perfecting of the saints, for the work of the ministry, for the edifying of the body of Christ: *till we all come* in the unity of the faith, and of the knowledge of the Son of God, unto a perfect man, unto the measure of the stature of the fullness of Christ (Eph. 4:11–16).

It cannot be said with any truth or propriety that this end was obtained fully during the apostolic age, or even at the close of it. Let any unpreju-

---

[1] John Guyse. *The Practical Expositor: An Exposition of the New Testament, in the Form of a Paraphrase.*

diced person compare Romans 11 with this passage, and he must see that, in the apostle's sense, we shall "all come in the unity of the faith, and of the knowledge" (or acknowledgment) "of the Son of God, unto a perfect man, unto the measure of the stature of the fulness of Christ," when "the fulness of the Gentiles be come in. And so all Israel shall be saved" (Rom. 11:25–26). From whence it is clear that this ordinance of heaven shall not cease till these ends are completely obtained. And it is not reasonable to suppose, that they will be fully answered, while the world allures, the flesh solicits, and the devil tempts; while iniquity abounds, and error prevails; or in other words, while the world standeth.

These arguments will receive additional light and strength when I have explained the two next sections. I shall therefore leave this point at present, and go on,

3. Who May Warrantably Preach

To inquire, who may warrantably preach the gospel. Since the preaching of the gospel is a standing appointment of heaven, some must administer the office, and fulfill the service of it. I apprehend this matter is represented in a very defensive light, in the Assembly's Larger Catechism, Quest. 158, "By whom is the word of God to be preached? Answer, The word of God is to be preached only by such as are sufficiently gifted, and also duly approved and called to that office," where two things are insisted on as necessary to a preacher.

I. He must be qualified with gifts sufficient and suitable for the work. This will not admit of any doubt, for no man is to undertake what he is not able to perform. No prudent man will begin to build, till he has first counted the cost, and upon making a just and judicious estimate, seen whether or not he is able to finish. It would be a reflection on the wisdom of a master, to employ a servant in any work he has no capacity for, or entrust him in an important affair that is like to miscarry in his hands. In like manner, we are not to suppose that God calls any to preach the gospel but those whom he has, in some measure, furnished for it. Though it is a difficult matter to determine who are sufficiently gifted for it; the work being so great, and our natural and acquired endowments very small, if compared with it; I hope the following things will be evident.

1. A sufficient degree of natural parts, and such an elocution as is necessary in those that speak to the edification of an audience, must be neces-

sary of course. Without these, all endeavors to furnish themselves for this work will be to very little purpose. Improvements suppose abilities, and elocution expresses our ideas.

2. The conversation of preachers should be, not only without offense, but exemplary. He that teaches others should teach himself, and be an example to the saints in word, in conversation, in charity, in spirit, in faith, in purity. He should be able to join with the apostle in his solemn appeal, when he says, "Ye are witnesses, and God also, how holily and justly, and unblameably we behaved ourselves among you that believe" (1 Thess. 2:10).

3. An experimental knowledge of divine truths will greatly furnish ministers to communicate the same to others, and spirit them with zeal to use their utmost endeavors, that they may be made partakers of the same faith and power of the gospel with themselves. But this is not sufficient *of itself*, for even the saints must have their pastors and teachers (Eph. 4).

4. Preachers should be apt to teach (1 Tim. 3:2). They should be well furnished with a good stock of Christian knowledge and experience, and capable of expressing their sentiments with freedom, clearness, and propriety, for the instruction of others, and for supporting and defending the truths of the gospel on all suitable occasions; and also be ready to improve all proper opportunities for it.

5. Ministers should be able rightly to divide the word of truth (2 Tim. 2:15). They must use the utmost care and good judgment in separating between truth and error, important and trifling things; and in giving to everyone a portion of God's word in due season, with a proper application of its various parts to the circumstances of their hearers.

6. The ministers of the gospel should be able, by sound doctrine, to exhort and convince gainsayers; to administer comfort to believers; and to confute the errors of all opposers, silence their cavils, and rebuke their perverseness (Titus 1:9).

To all this I may add that there are various parts of learning that may be reckoned, in some respects, ornamental, which would tend much to secure him that preaches the gospel from contempt; and others that are more immediately subservient to our understanding the Scripture, namely, a being well acquainted with those languages in which the Old and New Testament were written, and able to make critical remarks on the style and mode of expression used in each of them; and a being conversant in the writings of those, whether in our own or other languages, who have clearly and judiciously explained the doctrines of the gospel, or led us into the knowledge of those things that have a tendency to illustrate them. And inasmuch as preaching contains in it an address to the judgments and consciences of men, I cannot but reckon it a qualification necessary hereunto, that all those parts of learning that have a tendency to enlarge the reasoning faculty, or help us to see the connection or dependence of one thing upon another, should be attended to, that ministers may be hereby fitted to convey their ideas with judgment and method. These qualifications are to be acquired.

II. He that preaches the word of God must be duly approved and called to that office; as well as sufficiently qualified for it. No man is fit to be trusted to judge his own abilities. Self-love, so natural to all, is ready to blind the best, and make them form a partial judgment in their own cause. To prevent the dismal consequences that might arise from insufficient insolence this matter ought to be submitted to the judgment of others that have capacity to discern real merit, and are not under any temptation to be partial, by interested connections. I believe the apostolic charge to lay hands suddenly on no man (1 Tim. 5:22), has an express reference to this very point.[2]

The necessity of such a call to preach the gospel may be demonstrated by several proofs that are simple in their nature, and therefore the more convincing.

It may be argued from Romans 10:15, "How shall they preach, except they be sent?" In that context the apostle states a strong connection between believing, hearing, preaching, and the preacher's mission. And because it is a sending in order to preach, that men may hear, and believe, and be saved; the mission must be *ordinary* and *authoritative*. The *end* is ordinary, therefore so must the *means* be also.

The names given to the preachers of the word imply a call to their office. They are called *ambassadors for Christ* (2 Cor. 5:20), which supposes they have received their instructions and commission. They are *stewards* (Titus 1:7), who do not use to officiate without a warrant. They are *watchmen*, who watch for the good of the church (Heb. 13:17). Their commission is

---

[2] The reader may find more on this subject in Archibald Hall. *An Humble Attempt to Exhibit a Scriptural View of the Constitution, Order, Discipline, and Fellowship of the Gospel Church*, chap. 10.

much of a piece with that of Ezekiel (Ezek. 3:17), "I have made thee a watchman unto the house of Israel: therefore hear the word at my mouth, and give them warning from me." They are *angels* of the churches (Rev. 1:20), and *overseers*, or *bishops* (Acts 20:28).

Finally, the Scripture everywhere distinguishes between *gifts*, and a *call* to exercise them in the church, a distinction suggested by reason, and level to the weakest capacity to understand. Our blessed Lord called unto him his twelve apostles, and gave them *power* against unclean spirits to cast them out, and to heal all manner of diseases, and all manner of sickness (Matt. 10:1); and *then he sent them forth*, and *commanded* them to go and exert *that power* (Matt. 10:5). After he was risen from the dead, he *first* gave his disciples their *commission*, "As my Father hath sent me, even so send I you" (John 20:21), and *then* he gave them their *gifts*, "He breathed on them, and saith unto them, Receive ye the Holy Ghost" (v. 22). Indeed the wildest anarchy would inevitably follow if men that are possessed of gifts were immediately to assume the office they are capable of, especially if they were to form an estimate of their gifts by their *own* judgment, or by *their own*, and *that of a few friends*, that favor their ambitious views. We should soon see the very course of nature inverted: the servant becoming master; the common soldier becoming general; and the insolent subject claiming the throne. I would recommend a careful and attentive review of the forcible and right words contained in 1 Corinthians 12 and Romans 12 to every candid reader; and then let him say whether reason does not support and justify all that we plead for in the present argument; namely, that the word of God is to be preached only by such as are *sufficiently gifted*, and also *duly approved* and called to that office. I beg leave to add that if a man must first be proved, and then admitted to use the office of a deacon, being found blameless (1 Tim. 3:10), the argument is, at least, no less weighty for taking as cautious steps in admitting a man to the office of the ministry.

N.B., The call that I suppose every minister should have, in order to his using the office of a preacher, has been already considered in *another performance*, referred to above.

4. Vindication From Some Objections

I shall consider some of the objections that are made against this ordinance of preaching the gospel, only by such persons as I have described.

1. Some think, "That all the preaching allowed *now*, is only to *read* the Scriptures, without giving any sense of them." They fancy this notion of preaching is supported in Acts 15:21, "Moses of old time hath, in every city, them that preach him, being read in the synagogues every sabbath day." That all preaching should be founded in the word of God, has been observed; but that *preaching* and *reading it* are *the same* is far from being clear from this text, where preaching and reading Moses's writings are said to *accompany* one another, and also plainly enough *distinguished*. This refers to the service of the Jewish synagogue, where the law was read, and the people were made to understand the sense (Neh. 8:1–8; Acts 13:15). The last was called preaching, in distinction from the reading of the law, as is clear from Acts 8:35, connected with the foregoing context, from Acts 8:26, and downward.

2. It is alleged,

> That the office of a gospel-ministry was only to continue till the Spirit should be poured out, and then, according to the ancient prophecy (Joel 2:28). God would pour out his Spirit upon all flesh, and their sons and their daughters should prophesy, their old men should dream dreams, their young men should see visions; and also upon the servants and upon the handmaids, in those days, would the Lord pour out his Spirit. This prophecy was accomplished accordingly on the day of Pentecost (Acts 2:17). From all which some infer that this ordinance is now so far superseded as to become common to everyone that is possessed of the Spirit.

But plausible as this objection may appear, the conclusion is not good; for after Pentecost, we find the office of preaching was confined to a few whose business was to feed the flock of God, and preach the gospel of the kingdom. This could not be the case if all were to preach. Therefore it is plain, that passage must either refer to extraordinary gifts, and so it does not touch the present question; or, to the more ordinary gifts of the Spirit, which were then bestowed in a more plentiful measure than before, and poured upon the Gentiles as well as the Jews. Perhaps it is best to include both. And in either case, undoubted facts prove that it did not set aside preaching the word, because this was still continued after that prophecy was accomplished, as is clear from the book of the Acts, and the rest of the apostolic writings.

3. A strong objection is taken from the prophecy of Jeremiah (Jer. 31:33–34), where the Lord says,

> This shall be the covenant that I will make with the house of Israel; After those days...I will put my law in their inward parts, and write it in their hearts, and will be their God, and they shall be my people. And they shall teach no more every man his neighbour, and every man his brother, saying, Know the LORD: for they shall all know me, from the least of them unto the greatest of them, saith the LORD.

From these words it is argued that preaching is forbidden, because it is not necessary. But whatever may be the sense of these words, it is impossible to reconcile this construction of them with the practice of the apostles, who wrote to these very persons, that were made partakers, through grace, of this promise, and had an unction from the holy One, and knew all things, that they might grow in grace, and in the knowledge of our Lord and Savior Jesus Christ (see 1 John 2 throughout, particularly 1 John 2:20–28). And even when our apostle treats on this covenant (Heb. 8:11), he joins his account of it with proper instructions. Dr. Guyse, in his note upon that place, has well observed,

> that this passage must be taken, either in a *comparative* sense, as such expressions often are (see Isa. 43:18; Jer. 23:18; Matt. 9:13) or else, with reference to that *manner* of teaching, which was used, and rested in, under the obscurities of the Old Testament dispensation, and the corrupt interpretations of the Jewish doctors; or, both may be included.

And when the apostle says that the anointing of the Spirit teacheth believers all things (1 John 2:27), he evidently intimates that they have no need of being taught *new doctrines* and *revelations* by men who, under pretense of teaching the will of heaven, industriously set themselves to pervert the word of God.

4. Because it is said, that when the "Spirit of truth, is come, he will guide you" (the disciples) "into all truth" (John 16:13), some infer that the preaching of the word is unnecessary. This inference cannot be just, unless we suppose that the Spirit guides into all truth without the use of any means—a supposition that is notoriously false! (Acts 13:1–4; 8:29; 1 Cor. 2 throughout; Gal. 3:2; with many more texts that represent the word as the means by which the Spirit of God manages his work in the souls of men, and the preaching of it as having a great influence this way).

5. An argument is formed from many instances of persons preaching without being authorized. I shall pass by those of Stephen, Philip, Apollos, and some others; as they are not at all pertinent to the purpose of our objectors; their call, in everything they did, being unexceptionably clear. But there are a few cases that are thought much stronger, and deserve a particular discussion, such as, at the time of Stephen's "death there was a great persecution against the church which was at Jerusalem. And they were all scattered abroad throughout the regions of Judea and Samaria, except the apostles; and they that were scattered abroad went every where preaching the word" (Acts 8:1–4). From hence some gather that all that can may preach. I do not think the conclusion follows: for the phrases of being *all* scattered abroad, and preaching *every where*, must be understood with some limitation, as the context and the nature of the thing demonstrate; why not then also admit the same limitation concerning the *preachers?* The design of that place is not to show, how many were scattered abroad by the violence of persecution, but that the gospel made a quick and extensive spread of light and salvation in the world, and to account for the occasion and means of its doing so. And all this may be sufficiently explained, without supposing that everyone that was driven from Jerusalem, man and woman, became a preacher. But if the example is pertinent, it will prove that every church member both may and can preach. If it is alleged that there was something extraordinary in this case, and everyone was *then* able to preach, which is not to be expected *now*; but that as many as can still may do it. I would beg my friends to examine this plea well before they make any further use of it. It undermines the cause it is brought to support: for if it was extraordinary that *all* then *could* preach, why should it not be extraordinary that *all* then *might* preach? And what business have these *extraordinaries* with *ordinary* cases? They also urge: "Desire spiritual gifts, but rather that ye may prophesy.... For ye may *all* prophesy one

by one" (1 Cor. 14:1, 31). From this it is inferred that *all* may use the office of a *public teacher*. But, whether we will or not, we must take the universal term *all* in a limited sense, or else make our apostle contradict himself. He had compared the church to the human body (1 Cor. 12), and showed that different members of the church were appointed to different stations of honor and service, as the members are set in the human body; and then asks, "Are all prophets?" (1 Cor. 12:29). If all had been *prophets*, where had been the *apostles, teachers, etc.?* So that when he says, *Ye may all prophesy*, he can only be understood to speak of *all the prophets*. And this is very clearly his meaning, as will appear to anyone that examines the scope of his discourse without prejudice. They allege moreover,

"This is a true saying, If a man desire the office of a bishop, he desireth a good work" (1 Tim. 3:1). I confess they are much happier then I am, in discernment, that can see any foundation in that text for the conclusion they would draw from it, which must be to this purpose: That any man may take upon him to be an overseer of God's flock; because the apostle says, that the man that is qualified for, and inclined and called to that office, aims at a very important, useful, and honorable, though laborious post and service. Where is the connection? Let any person carefully read that whole epistle, and he will soon be satisfied that the apostle has solidly confuted the whimsical vagaries of all those teachers that take upon them a public character, without a regular call.

Thus I have mentioned and confuted the weightiest objections I have found made use of against the ordinance of preaching the gospel, by those that have a regular call to this honorable service. Of the vast many they urge, I have selected the strongest, that I might not abuse the reader's patience, by transcribing the impertinent and insolent, the confused and inconclusive harangues of these trifling scribblers. I have reason to crave the reader's pardon for insisting so long as I have done on so plain a case, and shall now proceed,

5. Describing the Manner

To describe the manner of preaching, in a few obvious hints. This is a pleasant and extensive field. Far from assuming the airs of a director, I only intend to stir up my readers, by way of remembrance, to consider how the word of God is preached, that they may answerably believe and improve by hearing it.

The design of preaching the gospel is to inform the mind, affect the heart, and impress the conscience; to reprove error, and correct vice; to awaken the secure, to convince the sinner, to convert the ungodly, and to build up saints in their most holy faith.

The intention of their office should direct and animate preachers in the most proper manner of fulfilling their ministry which they have received of the Lord Jesus. They should study to nourish their hearers in the words of faith and of good doctrine, with diligence, plainness, faithfulness, wisdom, zeal, affection, and sincerity. In doing so, they might expect a divine blessing on their labors; and that they would save themselves, and them that hear them (1 Tim. 4:16). Allowed defects, on this head, are like to prove fatal both to them that preach, and to them that hear, for the face of the Lord is set against these idol-shepherds to cut them off; and he will require the blood of his destroyed flock at their hands—an alarming consideration to every preacher.

1. In preaching the word of God, ministers should take particular care to nourish up their hearers only in the words of faith and of sound doctrine. Their commission is, like Jonah's, to preach the preaching that God bids them. They must not corrupt the word of God, nor handle it deceitfully; but by manifestation of the truth commend themselves to every man's conscience in the sight of God (2 Cor. 4:2). The doctrines they preach should be scriptural; and these should, as much as possible, be delivered, not in the words which man's wisdom teacheth, but which the Holy Ghost teacheth, comparing spiritual things with spiritual. Their doctrines should arise from, be consonant to, and proved by, the word of God. They should form their discourses on the plan of revealed truth, and take heed that they always speak only the things that become sound doctrine (Titus 2:1), that is, such doctrines and duties as are agreeable to, and put an honor upon, the solid, pure, wholesome, and healing gospel of Christ, which is a doctrine according to godliness, and lays the highest obligation to holiness and obedience upon all its professors. They ought in doctrine to show uncorruptness, gravity, sincerity; and to use sound speech, which cannot be condemned. They should not teach for doctrines the commandments of men, nor join and mix divine truths with human inventions, like them that corrupt the word of God, but as of God, in the light of God should they speak in Christ (2 Cor. 2:17). In order to answer these important purposes, they should aim at holding forth the word of life

unto their hearers in its own light, which is always the clearest, and with its own evidence, which is incomparably the most striking and convincing. It is the more necessary to preach such doctrines, because if ministers of the highest order, or an angel from heaven pervert the truth, or preach any other gospel than that which is delivered in the Scripture, he is sentenced already, let him be accursed (Gal. 1:7–8). These are the only doctrines that God will bless for the salvation of men, for they reveal unto us the true character of God, and of men, and of the Mediator between both. They are able to make the man of God perfect (2 Tim. 3:16–17).

2. Gospel-ministers should preach these heavenly truths *diligently* and *constantly, in season and out of season*, as the apostle speaks (2 Tim. 4:2), considering this as their main business of life. Hence they are commanded to *give themselves wholly to these things* (1 Tim. 4:15), making all their studies subservient to this end. They should thankfully embrace and improve all opportunities of doing good, and communicating instruction, to all among whom they minister; and be willing to lay out their whole strength, and all their abilities, for God's glory, after the heroic example of the apostle, who could say, "I will very gladly spend and be spent for you" (2 Cor. 12:15), which implies, at least, that he would cheerfully spend his time, strength, and labor, and sacrifice all his temporal ease, honor, and advantages, and would, with pleasure, wear out his life itself for the good of their souls. It is not enough to preach the word occasionally, or when leisure and inclination call for it, but this, being the business of a Christian preacher, should rule all his measures. It is the character of gospel-ministers that they watch for the souls of those to whom they minister (Heb. 13:17). The business of a watchman implies assiduity and diligent attention. This is particularly expressed in the apostolic charge, "Preach the word; be instant in season, out of season: reprove, rebuke, exhort with all longsuffering and doctrine" (2 Tim. 4:2), that is, make this the ruling concern of life, to publish and impress the word of God upon the consciences of all. Whenever there is reason to apprehend that the people are desirous to receive and hear it, ministers should be forward to preach. There are few characters more absurd than that of a slothful servant. The terms are a contradiction. It is truly said, "the desire of the slothful killeth him; for his hands refuse to labor" (Prov. 21:25). Preachers of the gospel are *the servants of the churches for Christ's sake* (2 Cor. 4:5); it cannot agree with their character to be idle and indolent; like that servant that went and hid his Lord's

talent in the earth. The sentence that will be passed on such wicked and slothful servants, who neither honor God, nor profit men, shall be equally just and dreadful: "Cast ye the unprofitable servant into outer darkness: there shall be weeping and gnashing of teeth" (Matt. 25:30). The example of Christ, and the nature of the work, demand the closest application, and the most vigorous exertion of everyone that would please God in this high calling.

3. Ministers should preach the word with all possible *plainness* and *perspicuity*. In this they have the apostle for an example, "We use great plainness of speech" (2 Cor. 3:12). It is very easy for a man of mean attainments, and of a small share of literature, to puzzle his hearers with high sounding metaphors, and great swelling words of vanity, and to work some up to a blind admiration of what they neither know nor understand; which is only amusing them, and making them lose precious time, but not instructing them. On the other hand, for anyone to speak of the deep mysterious truths of the gospel, so as not to be a barbarian to the weak, is a great difficulty; however, this is what ministers should set themselves to do. It is their work to instruct the ignorant, and to confirm those that have attained to some degree of light, as to the great truths of the gospel. This end can only be obtained, by suiting their diction to the understanding of their hearers; and not by darkening counsel by words without knowledge; or by grating their ears with expressions that have either no ideas annexed to them, or cannot convey any distinct ideas to their minds. All indelicacies of coarse expressions are to be carefully avoided, for they debase the majesty of sacred things. It is a good rule in preaching to use a style that is plain without coarseness, majestic without obscurity, grave without dullness, sprightly without affectation or levity, copied after nature, and distinguished by its ease. The style of the Holy Scriptures is incomparably the best pattern; and let me say, without offense, the savory practical writings of the Rev. Thomas Bradbury are a valuable copy. The famous story of Dr. Manton of the last century is well known, and much to my purpose.[3]

---

[3] "While he was minister at Covent-Garden, London, he was invited to preach before the Lord Mayor and court of Aldermen, and the companies of the city, upon some public occasion, at St Paul's. The doctor chose some difficult subject, in which he had opportunity of displaying his judgment and learning, and of appearing to the best advantage. He was heard with admiration and applause by the more intelligent part of the audience: and was invited to dine with my Lord Mayor, and received public thanks for his perfor-

Indeed, it is much the same to use unintelligible expressions, and to speak in an unknown tongue. The apostle's speech, and his preaching, were not with enticing words of man's wisdom, but in demonstration of the Spirit, and of power, that the faith of his hearers should not stand in the wisdom of men, but in the power of God (1 Cor. 2:4–5). Wisdom of words cannot be supposed to profit children, or the weak, foolish, and ignorant. We would justly reckon him the *greatest idiot* of the whole that would address such people in the spruce luxuriance of bombast language, and yet he is no less *absurd* that preaches the gospel to men with all the idle parade of affected pedantry, making a show of eminent skill in human learning. Besides the *absurdity* of this affectation, it is extremely *dangerous*; hence the apostle says, "Christ sent me…to preach the gospel: not with wisdom of words, lest the cross of Christ should be made of none effect" (1 Cor. 1:17). The native simplicity, majesty, and glory of the doctrine of a crucified Savior would be debased and tarnished by such pompous artificial colors as are disagreeable to its humbling nature and design, and its efficacy would be defeated by the just displeasure of God, withholding his blessing on account of this unsuitable way of preaching it. It is a rule in the Assembly's directory, under the article of the preaching of the word, that is equally obvious and just:

> To abstain from an unprofitable use of unknown tongues, strange phrases, and cadences of sounds and words, sparingly citing sentences of ecclesiastical or other human writers, ancient or modern, be they never so elegant.

I shall add the following words from a most judicious exhortation delivered to a gentleman at his ordination,

---

mance. But upon his return in the evening to Covent-Garden, a poor man following him, gently plucked him by the sleeve of his gown, and asked him, if he was the gentleman who had preached that day before my Lord Mayor. He replied, he was. Sir, says he, I came with earnest desires after the word, and hopes of getting some good to my soul, but I was greatly disappointed; for I could not understand a great deal of what you said: you was quite above me. The doctor replied, with tears in his eyes, *N.B., Friend, if I did not give you a sermon, you have given me one; and by the grace of God, I will never play the fool, to preach before the Lord Mayor in such a manner again.*" See William Harris. *Some Memoirs of the Life and Character of the Reverend and Learned Thomas Manton, D.D.*.

Study how you may, in the best manner, solve difficulties, and reconcile *seeming* contradictions, in the word of God, without starting such as are needless and unprofitable to be discussed, and without managing them with an air of controversy; and never aim at being wise above what is written: Do not *make mysteries*, where the Scripture has *made* none; nor pretend to *explain* what the Scripture has *left* as mysteries, which would soon plunge you out of your depth; but publish them to be believed upon *divine authority*, just as God has left them, though you cannot account for their *modes*, nor tell how these things can be.

And again,

Endeavor to bring your sentiments down to the lowest capacities in the assembly, as far as the nature of the thing will bear. Never entertain your auditory with cunningly devised fables, or philosophical harangues, or dry systems of mere morality, or doubtful disputations; but feed them with knowledge and understanding, like a pastor according to God's own heart (Jer. 3:15).[4]

4. Gospel-ministers should preach the word *faithfully*. They are to be accounted as "stewards of the mysteries of God. Moreover it is required in stewards, that a man be faithful" (1 Cor. 4:1–2). It is the honorable character of Epaphras, that he was to the Colossian church "a faithful minister of Christ" (Col. 1:7).

This good fidelity implies three things: That a trust is committed to them, that they are accountable for it, and that they discharge it honestly in the view of giving their account, that they may give it with joy, and not with grief. I shall just mention a few things on each of these heads. And,

(1.) Ministers have a *sacred trust* lodged in their hands. Their Master is very great, and exceeding rich; his Father hath appointed him Heir of all things; he hath loved him, and given all things into his hand; he is therefore not only rich in himself, but rich unto all them that call upon him (Rom. 10:12). Ministers of the gospel are honored to preach the unsearchable riches of Christ; they are put in trust with the gospel (1 Thess. 2:4),

---

[4] See Dr. Guyse's ministerial exhortation. John Guyse. *A Collection of Seventeen Practical Sermons*.

and the glorious gospel of the blessed God is committed to their trust (1 Tim. 1:11). This great trust is committed to them as stewards, who must use no part of the goods that are in their hands any other ways than as their Lord orders and appoints. Ministers are entrusted not to *make* a new gospel, or to *alter* the old one, in any respect whatsoever, but to *keep* it pure and entire, to support and contend for it, and to dispense and publish it. And as they have the truths of God committed to their trust, so they have the souls of men put under their care, that they may faithfully apply these truths to them for edification.

(2.) Ministers are *accountable* for the discharge of their weighty trust to God, whose stewards they are. The time will come when God will, in effect, say to each of them, *Give an account of thy stewardship; for thou mayest be no longer steward.* It is a certain determined case, that *we must every one give an account of himself unto God.*

(3.) Faithful preachers discharge their trust *honestly, in the view of giving their account.* Like faithful stewards, it is required of them, that they do not misuse and waste what is committed to their charge; as the unjust steward in the parable did, who was accused to his lord that he had wasted his goods (Luke 16:1). They should guard against all misapplication of their time, health, or studies, and give themselves wholly to the ministry (1 Tim. 4:15). And, as faithful stewards, they should use what is committed to their charge, according to the will of their Master, and to the purposes which he hath appointed. The general rule, in order to this, is, that they direct all their studies and labors to the glory of God through Jesus Christ: for "if any man speak, let him speak as the oracles of God; if any man minister, let him do it as of the ability which God giveth: that God in all things may be glorified through Jesus Christ" (1 Peter 4:11). They should, with honest intentions, search the word of God, that they may come to the knowledge of his will, and then, without regarding the favor or frowns of men, impartially declare what they find, upon careful inquiry, to be the will of God. No consideration should prevail on them to conceal the words of the Holy One, or hinder them from making an attempt to set his word fully, clearly, and powerfully home on the consciences of their hearers. They ought to state the just connection and mutual influence of privileges and duties, and never to magnify one article, at the expense of the system of divine truth. Like Paul, *They must not shun to declare unto men all the counsel of God* (Acts 20:27), if they would be accounted *faithful* to the Lord, to their own conscience, to the truth and importance of the gospel committed to them, and to the souls they minister unto, by giving to everyone his portion in due season (Luke 12:42).

5. Ministers ought to preach the word *wisely*. It is not enough that they *walk* in wisdom towards them that are without, and toward them that are within their connections of church-fellowship; they should also *preach Christ, warning every man, and teaching every man in all wisdom, that they may present every man perfect in Christ Jesus* (Col. 1:28). Wisdom and prudence ought to have a powerful influence and manifest direction in the choice of their subjects, and in suiting their discourses to the capacities and circumstances of their hearers. I say, ministers must use their prudence and wisdom,

(1.) In choosing such subjects as have the greatest tendency to promote the interest of Christ, and the general good of mankind. All Scripture doctrines are *alike true*, though not *of equal importance* to be known and attended to. They are all *profitable*, but not *alike seasonable*; therefore we read of *the present truth* (2 Peter 1:12). They are all doctrines according to godliness, but do not with the same clearness oppose particular lusts, and the dictates and concupiscence of depraved nature, and enforce obedience to the will of God. The preacher that teaches in all wisdom chiefly insists on the most important, the most seasonable, and the most practical subjects. These form, improve, and maintain the power of vital religion, and therefore he wisely gives them the first place in his ministry.

(2.) In suiting their discourses to the capacities and circumstances of their hearers. This requires singular wisdom in the ministers of Christ, who must feed babes with milk, and strong men with meat; who must teach everyone as he is able to bear, neither neglecting the instruction of any man, nor overshooting his capacity. They should seek to find out acceptable words, and carefully choose the most proper seasons to administer reproofs, counsel, or comfort. *For everything there is a time and season*; at that happy moment everything is beautiful, because then it is natural; wisdom should make just observations on the signs and appearances of the fittest times, and prudence is no less necessary in dealing with different tempers, capacities, and conditions of men to enable the preacher to speak a word in season to the weak, the wicked, the weary, the tempted, the disconsolate, the rich, the poor, the great, the small, and every other condition of men. "A word fitly spoken," that is, exactly to the point, and comes in right season, "is like apples of gold in pictures of silver. As an earring of gold, and an ornament of fine gold, so is a wise reprover upon an obedient ear" (Prov. 25:11–12). That is also a memorable observation made by Solomon, and much to the business in hand, "Without counsel, purposes are disappointed: but in the multitude of counselors they are established. A man hath joy by the answer of his mouth: and a word spoken in due season, how good is it!" (Prov. 15:22–23). That minister who is best acquainted with human nature, and is most conversant with the deep springs of action that rule the conduct of men, has a singular advantage for the prudent and successful discharge of his office: whereas the man that is destitute of this qualification, whatever proficiency he has made in studying abstracted speculations in divinity, will remain a conceited positive bigot. He cannot himself think with freedom; he cannot bear with those that differ from him; and it is morally impossible he can be a means of recovering them from the error of their way.

6. The word of God should be preached *with fervent zeal*. The apostle Paul desired the saints at Ephesus to pray for him, that utterance might be given to him, that he might open his mouth boldly, to make known the mystery of the gospel, for which he was an ambassador in bonds, that he might speak concerning it with courage, as he ought to speak (Eph. 6:18–20). And Apollos, "being fervent in spirit, he spake and taught diligently the things of the Lord" (Acts 18:25). Indeed, ministers should carefully avoid all intemperate warmth, uncharitable rancor, and unchristian bitterness; these constitute the wrath of man, and are only numbered among the fruits of the Holy Ghost by them that do not know what manner of spirits they are of. But the faithful ministers of Christ ought honestly to explain, defend, and apply the truth as it is in Jesus; and to show a greatness of mind, in despising mean and ill-natured cavils and calumnies, where they are conscious to themselves, after sufficient inquiry, that they are in the way of their duty, and preaching the truth. When they are represented as seditious, legal, antinomian, uncharitable, or what not, under the shield of conscious innocence, they may treat these ignorant or malicious accusations with a generous contempt, and unmoved by all opposition, pursue their search after truth, and without wavering represent it, as they find it has been delivered in the Scriptures to the saints. It quite unbecomes their character to use a passionate, furious address, arising from personal pique; or to expose men for their weakness; or to express any undue resent-

ment of injuries; but they ought to burn with that zeal that is consistent with, and guided by fervent love to God and the souls of men, in all their ministrations. This leads me to observe,

7. That the word of God should be preached with a *loving, affectionate regard to the glory of his excellent name*, and *the good of immortal souls*. It is as much the duty of ministers to speak the truth, as of people to receive it, in the love thereof. Love to God would make them faithful, and love to men would make them diligent in preaching the gospel. We have an illustrious example of this prevailing affection in a gospel-minister, where the apostle appeals to that church in these words: "ye know how we exhorted and comforted and charged every one of you, as a father doth his children" (1 Thess. 2:11). It is happy indeed, where a minister's heart is in his work, so that his greatest pleasure is to do his duty; while he travails, as in birth, till Christ be formed in the hearts of his hearers, and carefully waters what is planted, having no greater pleasure than to see them walking in the truth. The apostle uses one of the tenderest images to describe this amiable temper, "We were gentle among you, even as a nurse cherisheth her children" (1 Thess. 2:7–8), whom she suckles, nourishes in her bosom, bears with their weakness and frowardness, and does all she can for their ease, help, and comfort. Ministers, in like manner, should affectionately desire the edification and salvation of their people, and take great pains in imparting to them the gospel of the grace of God, and in drawing out their souls with compassion in abundant labors for them, to show that they have their dear people's spiritual and eternal concerns entirely at heart. They ought always to keep in their eye the nature of their appointment: they have no dominion over the faith of God's heritage, but are to be helpers of their joy.

8. The word of God should be preached *with sincerity*, as in the sight of God, who searcheth the heart. Ministers should singly aim at the glory of God, and the conversion, edification, and salvation of men, in the whole course of their ministry. Lower motives are unworthy of the ministers of Christ, who, under a firm persuasion of the truths of God, should deliver them, genuine and entire, just as they have received them from him; without any *additions, alterations,* or *secular views*; with an honest plain heartedness, free from craft or deceit.

To be sure, it is an appointment of God, "that they which preach the gospel, should live of the gospel" (1 Cor. 9:14).[5] But the noble aims, al-

---

[5] In the New Testament state, our Lord Jesus, by his immediate authority, has appointed

ready mentioned, ought to prevail with everyone that devotes himself to Christ Jesus the Lord, in the office of the ministry. Men act an unworthy part for themselves, as well as dishonor God, if they are determined by lower considerations. To be an *hireling in the service of Christ* is one of the vilest characters a creature can assume. Such a minister can neither be faithful to God, consistent with himself, nor careful for the souls of men. He seeks not the profit of many that they may be saved; but his own glory and wealth. *The faithful ambassador of Christ is not so.* He preaches not

---

and ordered that his servants, whom he sends forth to preach the everlasting gospel, should be maintained by those that have the benefit of their labors. This is no human contrivance, no scheme of worldly wisdom, no invention of covetous minds, for "the Lord hath ordained, that they which preach the gospel, should live of the gospel" (1 Cor. 9:14). This appointment may be vindicated and supported many ways:

1. It is founded in justice and equity, in the very nature and reason of the thing: for "Who goeth a warfare any time at his own charges? who planteth a vineyard, and eateth not of the fruit thereof? or who feedeth a flock, and eateth not of the milk of the flock?" This is the apostle's reasoning on the point (1 Cor. 9:7).

2. The divine institution of a liberal allowance to those who ministered under the Mosaic dispensation has the *same* reason still. The change of the dispensation, which must change the method of raising this contribution, has not at all weakened the force of the obligation, for, "Do ye not know that they which minister about holy things live of the things of the temple? and they which wait at the altar are partakers with the altar? *N.B. Even so hath the Lord ordained*, that they which preach the gospel, should live of the gospel" (1 Cor. 9:13–14).

3. The important nature of the ministerial work, which is enough to take up the whole of any man's time in attending to it, is an argument of no inconsiderable weight. These that preach the gospel should give themselves continually to prayer, and to the ministry of the word (Acts 6:4). This is a work that requires leisure and the most vigorous application; therefore, the apostle says to Timothy, "Meditate on these things; give thyself *wholly* to them," etc. (1 Tim. 4:15–16).

4. Our Lord's own direct appointment, than which nothing can carry with it more awful authority, may be next produced. The original unrepealed ordinance of Christ, when he gave a temporary commission to the disciples, whom he sent forth to preach the gospel, saying the kingdom of God is at hand, is expressed in these words, *N.B., The workman is worthy of his meat, and the laborer of his hire* (Matt. 10; Luke 10). We justly despise the wretched abuse of this passage and others, by *Popish zealots*, to prove their absurd opinion about *mendicant* or *begging friars*. But are these *Protestants* a great deal *better*, or, do they not go upon the same principle; who imagine, that all they *contribute* to maintain the ministers of the gospel is *mere charity*, and not a *just debt*, according to Christ's commandment?

This argument is judiciously treated in a sermon: David Rees. *The State of True Religion in All Ages, and the Charges Attending Divine Worship Consider'd.* The above thoughts are chiefly extracted from it.

himself, but Christ Jesus the Lord, and himself the servant of the churches for Jesus' sake. His highest ambition is that Christ may increase, though he himself should decrease. He has no greater joy than to see his people growing in knowledge, faith, and experience, and walking in the truth. If he is crafty, and catches men with guile, it is that he may win their souls, and save them from everlasting destruction. His conscience will not condemn him, when he adopts the words of the apostle,

> Knowing the terror of the Lord, we persuade men; but we are made manifest unto God; and I trust also are made manifest in your consciences. For we commend not ourselves again unto you, but give you occasion to glory on our behalf, that ye may have somewhat to answer them which glory in appearance, and not in heart. For whether we be beside ourselves, it is to God: or whether we be sober, it is for your cause. For the love of Christ constraineth us, *etc.* (2 Cor. 5:11–21).

Chapter 3
Hearing the Word Preached

The word of life is *preached*, that men *may hear*, and mix faith with the hearing of it; and it is a happy circumstance, when a congregation assembles under the same views, and with the same desires and expectations that brought the household and friends of Cornelius together, when Peter was to preach. We are "all here present before God," said he, "to hear all things that are commanded thee of God" (Acts 10:33). I shall take leave to represent my thoughts on this ordinance under the following heads. I shall attempt,

1. To describe that hearing of the word which God hath appointed.
2. To represent the obligations that lie upon men to honor this ordinance.
3. To show that the pretenses for neglecting to hear the gospel preached are insufficient to satisfy the conscience.
4. To lay down some directions for hearing the word preached with benefit.

1. What God Hath Appointed

I shall, first of all, describe that hearing of the word which God hath appointed for the salvation of men. It does not consist merely in using the ear, that bodily organ that is impressed with the undulating vibrations of the air; this is comprehended in the *hearing* I treat of, but is not the whole of it. There is a relation between preaching and hearing of the word: the first conveys, and the last receives through that conveyance the knowledge of salvation. Therefore, I speak of *hearing*, as it is *a religious duty* that is consecrated to the honor of God, and the service of our souls, by being employed in a religious manner; and as a religious duty that is *distinct from all other* religious duties, such as praying, praising, *etc.*, in which we join to address ourselves to God, but in hearing the word preached, we attend to the things of God, as delivered by his commandment unto us. Moreover,

I am to consider hearing as it is a branch of *public worship*, to distinguish it from bare hearing the sacred Scriptures, or any other devotional book, read in a more private way, and by persons of a private character; as well as from people's attending to useful private instructions, from parents, masters, or persons endued with edifying utterance. Now this hearing I explain may include the following things, which are either *supposed* to it, or *implied* in it.

1. An *attendance* on the ministrations of the preached gospel, as an institution of God; not chiefly from a personal respect to the preacher, but because we are convinced it is an ordinance of God, and therefore a channel of divine goodness.

2. A *diligent attention* to what is preached, in opposition to wanderings and distractions of mind, and to the admission of unsuitable and unseasonable thoughts in time of hearing. Lydia's heart being opened, she attended to the things that were spoken by Paul (Acts 16:14). We should give earnest heed to the things that are spoken, and that we have heard, lest at any time we let them slip (Heb. 2:2).

3. The exercise of the mind to *understand the sense* of what is preached is also included in hearing the gospel. Thus in the parable of the sower, our Lord prefaces the interpretation with these words, *Hear ye therefore the parable*, that is, understand the meaning of it, for otherwise they had heard it already (Matt. 13:18).

4. An *assent of the mind* to the truths preached is included likewise in hearing the word of God. The word only profits when it is mixed with faith in them than hear it (Heb. 4:2). Nothing that is said should be taken on the preacher's word, but, when his doctrine is scriptural, it should be received only as the word of God, and not as the word of man, or with any cold indifference. The sayings of God are faithful and true, and while we hear, we should be fully assured of them accordingly.

5. Since the gospel is a word of salvation sent to men, we can only be said to hear it when we *see our own concern* in what is preached, and *apply it* to ourselves, as containing words whereby we must be saved, convinced, quickened, comforted, or humbled.

6. The word is preached to affect the heart, as well as to enlighten the mind; and the hearing of it must therefore include such an exercise of *devout affections* as is suitable to the nature of the truths we hear, and our

personal concern in them. The hearts of the disciples burned within them, while Christ talked to them by the way, and opened to them the Scriptures (Luke 24:32). That knowledge of divine truths must be very superficial, which has no power to communicate life and warmth to the affections; and those affections must be very foreign to real Christianity, that spring from any other cause, besides the weight and importance of the truths that we hear.

7. Right hearing of the word takes in a *cheerful, universal subjection of soul* to its light and authority. Hence the apostle speaks *of obeying from the heart the form of doctrine delivered unto men* (Rom. 6:17). The truths of God are not given unto men for speculation, that they may be only studied as a science; but for practice, that they may purify the heart, and govern the life.

> Whosoever heareth these sayings of mine, and doeth them, I will liken him unto a wise man, that built his house upon a rock: and the rain descended, and the floods came, and the winds blew, and beat upon that house; and it fell not: for it was founded upon a rock. And every one that heareth these sayings of mine, and doeth them not, shall be likened unto a foolish man, which built his house upon the sand: and the rain descended, and the floods came, and the winds blew, and beat upon that house; and it fell: and great was the fall of it (Matt. 7:24–27).

How much must the generality of mankind err in misapprehending the nature of this duty? It is supposed to be extremely easy, but, from what has been now observed about it, we may perhaps say, with strict enough propriety, that it is no less difficult to attend on the Lord without distraction in hearing than in praying, or praising, or any other religious duty. *God must give us ears to hear*, and *hearts to understand* his truths, before *we can hear with profit*.

2. The Obligations to Honor This Ordinance

Having explained the nature of that religious hearing of the word preached which God hath appointed, I shall now try to prove the following position: That it is *the duty of those that have opportunity, and ears to hear, to hear the word of God preached*, that is, explained, and applied, *by those that are qualified, approved, and called thereunto.* This position is capable of a large compass of proof.

Every argument that was brought in the former chapter to prove that the preaching of the gospel is an ordinance of Christ, to be continued in the church till the end of time, has the same force to demonstrate the obligations that lie on men to hear it, as on ministers to preach it. I shall hint at a few topics that were not there mentioned, and leave them to the reader's serious consideration.

1. Every faculty of our souls, and power of our bodies, are to be employed for God, and used in his service. He formed the eyes to behold the evident discoveries of his glory and perfections, in his works, and especially in his word; he made our tongues to speak and sing his praise; and, for the same reason, we should apply the ears that he hath planted to hear his word. How frequently is this peremptory summons repeated, *He that hath ears to hear, let him hear what the Spirit saith unto the churches*, by whatever means, and in whatever manner he speaks! Wherever God employs *a tongue* to speak, it is but a reasonable thing that we find *an ear* to hear.

2. It is the sense of Scripture that is the word of God, rather than the letters and syllables of it. Now, since the hearing of the word is a means of understanding the sense thereof, and such a means as is fixed by divine institution, and suitable to its end every consideration that demonstrates the worthiness of the end shows the obligation to use the means of obtaining it. If we ought to know the sense of Scripture, we ought to hear the word, which is an appointed and suitable means of knowing it.

3. Homage is due to God from every reasonable creature; and the homage that is due to him is determined in his word. Worship is the acknowledgment of the divine perfections by such affections of soul, and behavior of body, and such solemnity of both, as is suitable to the perfections that are the object and ground of worship; and from these it derives both its obligation, and the respective manner of performance. Now, the infinite knowledge of God, as the Father of lights, and his authority over us, as our sovereign Lord, are properly acknowledged by hearkening to his word, that we may know his will, and do it. It is but due respect to a superior to hear what he has to say to us; and it is but the same respect continued

to use the best means to understand his meaning, where the sublimity of the matter, and the weakness of our capacity, might occasion a dangerous mistake of his will; especially if we have reason to believe, that *those means* are *a part* of his signified will, as well as *a proper way* of understanding it. All this is the real case between God and us, in reference to the hearing of his word.

4. Another argument might be drawn from the manifold infirmities of mankind. Slowness of apprehension, errors of judgment, slipperiness of memory, levity of will, rashness or tardiness in resolving, and a heaviness in acting are inseparable from mortals; and, therefore, the truths of God must be laid down in the most familiar and easy representations, and frequently inculcated. This argument deserves the most careful attention, and has the strongest establishment in the Holy Scriptures, "We have many things to say, and hard to be uttered, seeing ye are dull of hearing" (Heb. 5:11). "I myself also am persuaded of you, my brethren, that ye are full of goodness, filled with all knowledge, able also to admonish one another. Nevertheless, brethren, I have written the more boldly unto you in some sort, as putting you in mind, because of the grace that is given to me of God" (Rom. 15:14–15).

5. A bishop that preaches the gospel should be *apt to teach* (1 Tim. 3:2). And for the same reason, people should be *swift to hear* (James 1:19). The first infers the last.

6. Express and implied hints in Scripture clearly determine this point. Under the Old Testament the case is clear, "Thus saith the LORD of hosts; Ask now the priests concerning, the law" (Hag. 2:11), concerning a case in their own law, which could not be resolved, but by an exposition or comment upon it. "The priest's lips should keep knowledge, and they should seek the law at his mouth: for he is the messenger of the LORD of hosts" (Mal. 2:7). Prophets were sent by God to enforce the practice, and recover the purity of his law; and what were all their prophecies, but so many commentaries and preachings upon the law of God, as applicable to certain circumstances and occasions? After Christ came in the flesh, the same method of conveying and receiving instruction was still observed. The Old Testament was the text, upon which the ministerial instructions of Christ and his apostles were founded, "Beginning at Moses and all the prophets, he expounded unto them in all the Scriptures the things concerning him-

self" (Luke 24:27). The apostles witnessed "both to small and great, saying none other things, than those which the prophets and Moses did say should come" (Acts 26:22). This is further evident from Acts 17:2–3.

The obligation that lies on all mankind to honor this ordinance of hearing the word is clearly contained: in the command to *hear and understand* (Matt. 15:10); in the direction to *take heed how we hear* (Luke 8:18), as well as *what we hear* (Mark 4:24); in the exhortation *not to forsake the assembling of ourselves together* (Heb. 10:25); in the example of *the primitive believers, who came together on the first day of the week to break bread, and Paul preached unto them* (Acts 20:7); in the *blessing* promised to follow a due attendance on this service (Ex. 20:24; Matt. 18:20); in the denunciations of wrath upon such as *refuse or neglect to hear the* word of God (Prov. 1:24–33; Heb. 12:25); and in the great benefit of hearing *the word of God* (Ps. 119 throughout, and Acts 14:22). But this suggests,

7. Another argument, which is taken from the *unspeakable benefit* of hearing the word preached. This is, in distinction from the system of ceremonial rites, the ministration of the Spirit, and is emphatically the ministry of reconciliation. God has been pleased to stamp it with peculiar honors, that demonstrate its excellency, and demand our regard. Among other things that might be named, I shall only observe,

That the preaching and hearing of the word are the chosen means of promoting the empire of Christ upon earth. Thereby he makes "all men see what is the fellowship of the mystery from the beginning of the world, which hath been hid in God" (Eph. 3:8–9).

They are the most public arguments of the transcendent glory of our risen Savior, "All power is given unto me in heaven and in earth. Go ye therefore, and teach all nations" and preach the gospel to every creature (Matt. 28:18–19). And when Christ had ascended up on high, and led captivity captive, he received gifts for men, that the Lord God might dwell among them (Ps. 68:18–19), which the apostle gives in these words, "he gave gifts unto men…some pastors and teachers" (Eph. 4:8, 11).

They are contrived with the utmost regard both to the advantage and honor of human nature. This dispensation is every way worthy of the reason that God hath given us. Had he dealt with men on the foot of miracles, these might have confounded the senses, and carried the surprise so far as to disable the better faculties from doing their office, by bearing too hard upon the understanding, and only putting the affections into a hurry. But in this dispensation, God deals with us according to what he knows to be our frame. He gives us the firmest foundation of faith, and the plainest rules of duty, delivered in the easiest words, and supported with the strongest arguments. He informs the mind, persuades the will, and lays sacred obligations on every active power of human nature by this means, "By manifestation of the truth commending ourselves to every man's conscience in the sight of God" (2 Cor. 4:2). How fitly may such persuasions be called a *drawing with the bands of a man* (Hos. 11:4)!

Compare this method of conveying, and learning the will of God, with any other way he ever used, by appearances, visions, dreams, miracles, ceremonies, *etc.*, and it will appear to be singular and excellent; for it is more public (Mark 16:16), more lasting (Heb. 12:25–28), more full (2 Cor. 3:18), more plain (2 Cor. 3:12–14), more perfect, as all the other dispensations lead to this (1 Peter 1:11–13); in everything it has a manifest preeminence.

The personal advantages that we have by hearing the word are very excellent; for we meet with three things in the gospel, that will always be of the greatest importance to mankind; to wit: such a *knowledge* as entertains our reason, and satisfies our souls, "even the hidden wisdom that God ordained before the world unto our glory" (1 Cor. 2:6–7); such an *holiness* as makes us meet to see the Lord (1 Peter 1:23); and such *comforts* as produce joy in tribulation (1 Peter 1:5–9).

The continued opposition of Satan to the preaching and hearing of the word is no contemptible proof of their excellence; for it shows at least his envy, if not his fear of these ordinances. He hindered Paul once and again from coming unto the Thessalonians (1 Thess. 2:18). He cast some of the church of Smyrna into prison (Rev. 2:10). This wicked one cometh and catcheth away the seed of the word, which was sown in the heart (Matt. 13:19). The gospel is "hid to them that are lost: in whom the god of this world has blinded the minds of them which believe not, lest the light of the glorious gospel of Christ…should shine" into their hearts (2 Cor. 4:3–4). False apostles, evil workers, who transform themselves into the apostles of Christ, are said to be his ministers, whose end shall be according to their works (2 Cor. 11:13–15).

Finally, the preaching and hearing of the word shall have an honor put upon them in the other world. Not that they shall be continued there; for the throne of God and the Lamb is there; and there is no temple there. But by the word that we hear, we shall be judged at the last day (John 12:48).

And the great circle of the honor of the redeemed in glory is upon this foundation, that Christ shall be glorified in his saints, and admired in all them that believe; because the testimony of his servants among them was believed; and they shall be glorified in him, according to the grace of their God, and the Lord Jesus Christ (2 Thess. 1:10, 12).

This shall suffice to show, that we are under indispensable obligations to attend and reverence the hearing of the word, as it is an ordinance of the Lord Jesus Christ. I propose under the next head,

3. Pretenses for Neglecting to Hear Preaching

To show that the pretenses frequently urged, to excuse the neglect of hearing the word preached are not sufficient to satisfy the conscience. This will best appear when I have mentioned a few of them, that are thought to have the greatest weight. But in regard the neglect is chiefly owing to disaffection, we must not expect to find them supported by cogent, or even consistent arguments; the cause will not admit of them. All the objections I have met with are *superficial*, and *vague*. *Enmity* against heaven's appointment, and *indifference* to divine truths, are, by far, the best and strongest arguments the cause will allow, though they are such reasons as few have courage enough to urge, because not sufficiently hardened to dare openly to deny the God that is above. I acknowledge there are some that have quite different notions of preaching and hearing from these I have described, and yet have the most profound veneration for the word of God. I do not mean in the least to comprehend them in this censure, because I am obliged to look on them as men of another character.

1. Some excuse the neglect of hearing the word preached, because they think all is uncertain and doubtful, and that ministers impose their own imaginations, under pretense of preaching the truth. I allow this has been frequently practiced; the devil has disguised himself under the appearance of an angel of light, and his ministers commonly hide the grievous wolf under sheep's clothing. But, for this reason, the faithful minister of Christ directs his hearers to search the Scriptures, to see whether the things they hear are words that become sound doctrine; he encourages them to use their own understandings; to prove all things; to judge for themselves; and to hold fast that which is good; he scorns to be, like the old Pharisees, a blind leader of the blind, but wishes his hearers to imitate the noble Bereans, in searching the Scriptures daily, to see whether these things that they

hear be really so, or not. If what is preached and heard be not really contained in the word of God, or by just and fair consequences drawn from it, it may be despised at pleasure; but if it be, they cannot reject it but at their peril. There are treacherous dealers in commerce, quacks in physic, dunces and villains in law, bad men in power: but, I believe, no prudent man will venture to condemn these professions on their account. And yet if any man do so, he acts on the same principles, and has as good a foundation for his conclusion as our objectors.

2. Some despise preaching, and forbear hearing, under a pretense that the things they are to hear are *too high* for them; that they exceed their capacity, and are above their reach; on this account they think they cannot be obliged to attend to them. But if people would but attend to this ordinance of God, with the same application, as the industrious student does to the instructions of those that are to teach him the mysteries of trade, or matters of abstruse learning, the foundation of this objection would appear altogether insufficient to support it. Many of the doctrines of revelation are too high to be *comprehended*; but none of them too high to be *sufficiently understood*, to make us wise unto salvation.

3. Some argue that they cannot learn anything by attending to hear the preached word, because the whole is so plain and obvious. This and the last objection are as inconsistent with one another as both of them are with the truth. It is truly a hard case, that divine revelation must be either rejected as mysterious, or despised as familiar. But it is well known that confidence is a retainer to ignorance; while modesty attends upon true wisdom, and a well-furnished mind. It might justify a little indignation, to observe how boldly many conceited fools have pronounced in those matters, that have exercised the minds of the greatest men in all ages. But if nothing new is to be heard, men need to be put in mind of what they knew before, to give them, if not a further enlightening, at least a fresher savor, and a deeper and more lasting influence of the truth; for it has been long observed: that more people are undone, in reference to both worlds, for want of considering what they very well know, than for want of knowing what concerns their welfare. In the business of life, the mechanic, the accountant, and the trader become expert by *daily practice*, and not by making daily *new improvements*. It is just so in studying and hearing the word of God. Men profit by these exercises, though they do not increase in knowledge, if they receive more powerful impressions of the word of God upon their

hearts and consciences, that produce such fruits in their lives as become this immortal principle.

4. Another objection is taken from the simplicity and plainness with which the most serious and useful ministers generally preach, a manner of preaching that cannot please a hearer of taste, and a scholar. The fact is granted, and what is alleged as an objection is pled to be really a commendation of preaching. This manner of preaching should be studied upon principle and with design. We have the apostle for an example, who says, "My speech and my preaching was not with enticing words of man's wisdom, but in demonstration of the Spirit and of power: that your faith should not stand in the wisdom of men, but in the power of God" (1 Cor. 2:4–5).[1] "Which things also we speak, not in the words which man's wisdom

---

[1] "The professors of religion depart from the simplicity which is in Christ, when they relish unsound expressions, and dislike Scripture-language. When we can relish nothing, but what is from the mint and forge either of heathens or heretics, we have then no spiritual palate to taste sweetness of divine truths. The apostle Paul chose to preach, 'not with enticing words of man's wisdom' (1 Cor. 2:4). When we approve what is contrary to his choice, we shall never profit by what we hear. Titus the evangelist was to preach the truths of God, in sound speech that could not be condemned (Titus 2:8). Sound speech cannot be condemned by any, but only by such who proclaim either their own conceited ignorance, or their frontless [shameless] wickedness. This sound speech, in which we ought to speak and to hear the truths of the gospel, is the Scripture-dialect, which is preferable to all methods of elocution, which the wit of men can invent. The Scripture-style is grave where it is plain; it commands our reverence where it is most familiar; and has the greatest aptitude to bring our souls under religious impressions.

"It may with sorrow be observed, what a dark complexion things bear, with respect to the vitals of Christianity, in the national assemblies [The author is speaking of England: but is the melancholy appearance *peculiar* to them?], since the masters of them have despised, if not ridiculed, the Scripture-style, and have chosen one for themselves, which amuses their unedified hearers, and leaves them ignorant of the things which are most necessary for them to know. It will not in the least be better among them of the separation, if their guides come to be so intolerably foolish, as to choose for their patterns the aforesaid despisers of Scripture-language. They who are reputed masters of eloquence by incompetent judges, who never knew what eloquence is, must be said to be in the greatest distance from the eloquence of the heathens; and yet if they had that, it would be their deformity, and not their ornament.... The apostle's eloquence was Scripture-eloquence, and this only is subservient to the demonstration of the Spirit. To sweep the modern stage, in borrowing phrases from it, where the devil has his pulpit, to preach to his impure auditors, and to inflame their lusts, and, at the same time, to neglect the majestic eloquence of the Scriptures, is as if a chaste virgin should choose the attire of a most lewd harlot, and throw off that which becomes her modesty. Heresies and er-

teacheth, but which the Holy Ghost teacheth; comparing spiritual things with spiritual" (1 Cor. 2:13).

Coarseness of language, and homeliness of expression, cannot be justified in preaching the word of God, though they may be excused in some instances, where the circumstances of the audience may, in some degree, be an apology. If a business of importance be well done, an improper turn of speech ought, in all reason, to be forgiven.

5. It is said by many that *reading the word, and good discourses at home*, may as well, or better answer the end; and so supersede the necessity of that hearing which we plead for. Reading and hearing are both duties; and it is no sufficient objection against one ordinance that we attend upon another. They may both consist together, and there is no manner of occasion for them to interfere; or to play off one against another. Each has its proper benefit, and we cannot expect a blessing upon one, in neglect of the other. Hearing the word preached has been proved to be of divine appointment, and to object against it from equivalents and expedients is to call the great Lawgiver's wisdom or authority in question. Let me also add that if people love the word of God, they will be glad of all opportunities of being further acquainted with it, and it is to be feared that such as would be excused from *hearing* are not very diligent in *reading*.

6. Some excuse themselves from hearing, because many of the ministers are but of mean parts, and indifferently furnished for their employment. In all professions there are degrees, and everyone is not of the first rate: but there may be a competency of qualification, where there is not everything one would wish, to accomplish a man in his character. Without some measure of fitness for the work no man can be a minister; and yet God has often used the foolish things of the world to confound the wise, that no flesh should glory in his presence (1 Cor. 1:27–29) And where God is pleased to count men faithful, putting them into the ministry, and to crown their endeavors with success, it ought to be no objection that they are not perfectly accomplished. Rather we should reverence God, who perfecteth praise from the mouth of babes.

---

rors want the artificial coverings of man's contrivance; but as the sun is best seen by his own light, so gospel-truth is both most evident, and most beautiful, when it is clothed in Scripture-language. When we recede from the Scripture-style, and presume to add a varnish of our own to the truths of Christ, we then act no more wisely than a jeweler would do, if he should gild over a diamond, and so hide the luster of it, when he exposes it to sale." See Richard Taylor. *Discourses on Several Subjects*, vol. 2, pp. 274–277.

7. Many neglect to hear the gospel, because they fancy themselves *above it*. They imagine themselves superior to any service of this kind, either on account of their hoary head, high quality, great power, or eminent attainments in knowledge, and such like circumstances of worldly precedence. No doubt a peculiar respect, and a distinction, suitable to their circumstances, are due to these venerable characters. But it will be time enough to answer this objection, when it is shown that God has appointed a peculiar method for saving the superior part of mankind; for, if he has not made such a distinction, it is highly presumptuous for the creature to make it. The following text is an alarming contrast to such arrogance: "The kings of the earth, and the great men, and the rich men, and the chief captains, and the mighty, and every bondman, and every free man, hid themselves in the dens, and in the rocks of the mountains" (Rev. 6:15). The greatest of creatures must honor him that is higher than the highest.

8. Some suppose that this duty is not required of them; they are *below it*, and excused from it in consideration of their being obliged to spend most of their time in providing necessaries for the body, and the subsistence of their families. If it be allowed that the meanest have souls to be saved, and that all souls must be saved in the same way, this objection will totally lose its force, or rather will appear to be most absurd. They that have but little that is comfortable in this world are infatuated indeed, if they despise the glories of a better.

9. The last objection I shall take any notice of is this: That we are only bound to hear the testimony of Jesus, which is complete in the Holy Scripture, and therefore, what have we to do, to hear men speak their own sentiments on the word of God? It should be enough for us to hear the Holy Ghost speaking in these alone. To this I beg leave to answer that the true sense of Scripture is the word of God. Even the apostles themselves, in delivering to us what we are to own for the word of God, did not always confine themselves to the literal words spoken by Christ, when they had the sense; consequently, where the mind of God, and the certain meaning of the text is delivered, *that* is his word, so far as the true sense of the text is preserved, whether it be the syllables of it or not. Moreover, the matter will unavoidably run up to this necessity of hearing the word explained by others, or doing it, at least, ourselves; for, everyone that reads will be aiming at the sense, will attempt some paraphrase in his own mind, and be so

far a preacher to himself, as to say in himself, *the meaning of this is so or so.* He cannot avoid it; it must be so, otherwise reading the word cannot be a reasonable service; but would be all one as if it were an unknown tongue. This sense and meaning he concludes to be the mind of God, and only so far his word, as it expresses his mind. To assist such reflections is the very design of preaching.

But our opposers are self-condemned, that tell us, it is hearing enough to hear the reading of the word, and the only hearing the Scripture requires; and thereupon give us another sense of those texts we allege in proof of this duty; and accordingly state the meaning of them, and reason and argue upon them. By all this, they confute their own opinion, and demonstrate the necessity of hearing the text explained and vindicated, and the erroneous corrected. This is all we plead for: namely, to explain and apply the word for doctrine, reproof, correction, and comfort. How forcible are right words! But what doth such arguing (or more properly such ignorance, and disaffection to the evidence of truth and the force of duty) reprove? Instead of spending longer time on this head, I shall go on,

4. Directions for Hearing Preaching

To lay down such *directions* as may be profitable to assist in *hearing the word preached* with proper advantage, and saving benefit.

Our Lord gives a general direction for hearing the word, "Take heed therefore how ye hear" (Luke 8:18). The form of the expression evidently imports two things: that there is something to be avoided and guarded against; and something to be attended to, and observed by us in this matter: and accordingly, the directions on this head must be of two general sorts: some of them *cautionary*; and some of them *positive*, or proper rules for hearing the word.

I. The following cautionary directions ought to be carefully observed. A neglect of them will infallibly render men unprofitable hearers, and prevent their edification.

1. Beware of *allowed ignorance*. I call that *allowed ignorance*, when people do not use every means of knowledge with vigorous application. Such persons lose all the pains they take in hearing the word: for "when any one heareth the word of the kingdom, and understandeth it not, then cometh the wicked one, and catcheth away that which was sown in his

heart" (Matt. 13:4, 19); this is he that is represented in the parable of the sower, by the seed that fell on the wayside. The people perish for lack of knowledge (Hos. 4:6).

2. Beware of *sleep* while you should be hearing the word of God. I would not mention this circumstance, if daily observation did not clearly show the necessity of it. What makes this the more criminal and offensive is that the persons that sleep in the time of divine worship can be as lively and active in every business of life as anybody else. Does a sleepy frame suit the worship of God, who neither slumbers nor sleeps? Can a man be fervent in spirit, serving the Lord, while his eyes are closed with sleep? Must not this practice grieve the holy angels, that burn with sacred zeal in serving the Lord, give offense to the generation of the righteous, and harden the profane and infidel world? And may I not say in this case, as the apostle in another, "What? have ye not houses to eat and drink in?" (I add, *to sleep in*) but "despise ye the church of God?" (1 Cor. 11:22). Decency, reason, duty, interest, and danger, join in a common remonstrance against such an impious and profane practice. I speak freely, because the case is so common, and the evil so great.

3. Be not *careless hearers*. Life and death are set before us. These are the weightiest matters, and the greatest solemnities in the world. The attention men give to the smallest trifles, where their interest or pleasure are concerned, will rise in judgment against such as hear the word of God without a holy reverence and godly fear. God speaks, let us be all attention.

4. Be not *forgetful hearers* of the word, who do not retain what they hear, and never think of it afterwards.

> If any man be a hearer of the word, and not a doer, he is like unto a man beholding his natural face in a glass: for he beholdeth himself, and goeth his way, and straightway forgetteth what manner of man he was. But whoso looketh into the perfect law of liberty, and continueth therein, he being not a forgetful hearer, but a doer of the work, this man shall be blessed in his deed (James 1:23–25).

A word entirely forgotten cannot profit the man that heard it.

5. Beware of *worldly-mindedness* in hearing the word. In the parable of the sower, "He also that received seed among the thorns, is he that heareth the word; and the care of this world, and the deceitfulness of riches choke

the word, and he becometh unfruitful" (Matt. 13:22). The Lord charges the carnal Jews with this crime, that they came unto the prophet, as the people cometh, and they sat before him as God's people—but their heart went after their covetousness (Ezek. 33:31).

6. Be not *unbelieving hearers*, who do not receive the truth in the love of it, that they may be saved. Men may carefully attend to the word preached, and understand it very well, and yet hear it only as the word of men, and not as the word of God, while the evidence of truth has not its proper weight, and prevailing influence. It is most dangerous, as well as criminal, to hold or imprison the truth in unrighteousness (Rom. 1:18), by hindering its proper and kindly effect, and keeping that under restraint which can make men free.

7. Be not *formal and customary hearers*, who attend on the preaching of the word upon no higher principle, no better design, than education and fashion. Such persons tread a beaten path, and keep up the custom of the world, having a form of godliness, but denying the power of it; from such formalists every Christian should turn away. Formality tends only to spiritual poverty, but cannot avail to real improvement in vital religion. Men that are governed by it are in danger of the curse pronounced on the fig tree: "Never fruit grow on thee more," or, of being cut down, and cast into the fire. Customary religion is not, like the religion of Jesus, a reasonable service. The fashion gives formality all its life and action, and it is only a mere accident that has made any difference between a *Jewish, Muhammadan, pagan,* and *Christian formalist*.

8. Be not *temporary hearers*, like him that received the seed into stony places. This is "he that heareth the word, and anon with joy receiveth it; yet hath he not root in himself, but dureth for a while: for when tribulation or persecution ariseth because of the word, by and by he is offended" (Matt. 13:20–21). This is like to be the case with such professors as have the persons of men in admiration more than the doctrines of Christ, and are puffed up for one against another, that is, magnify one man's gifts, to the disparagement of another. That awful word should make everyone that hears to fear with godly jealousy,

> If after they have escaped the pollutions of the world through the knowledge of the Lord and Savior Jesus Christ, they are again entangled therein, and overcome, the latter end is worse with them

than the beginning. For it had been better for them not to have known the way of righteousness, than, after they have known it, to turn from the holy commandment delivered unto them. But it is happened unto them according to the true proverb, The dog is turned to his own vomit again; and the sow that was washed to her wallowing in the mire (2 Peter 2:20–22).

See to the same purpose, Hebrews 6:4–6.

9. Beware of thinking that it is *meritorious* in the sight of God to do barely your duty in hearing his word. We should beware of the leaven of the Pharisees, that produced this absurd prayer, "God, I thank thee, I am not as other men; for I fast twice in the week, and give alms," *etc.* When we hear the word of God, we are doing our duty; and if God shall give the increase, we are more than recompensed. Our acceptance is in the beloved Son of God.

10. Be not *curious*, or *censorious hearers*, who hear the gospel only to exercise their *wit*, or show their *spleen*; to make remarks on the exactness of the method, the closeness of the reasoning, the turns of language, or the decency and life of the delivery. Thus they turn the church of God into a theater, and go to hear his word with the same temper and design as they go to see a play; only to please a vain and curious mind. Curiosity and censure are extremely unseasonable, while men are hearing the words by which they should be saved, and by which they must be judged at last. This impertinence usually betrays more ignorance and conceit than either sound judgment or a serious turn.

II. I shall now point out some useful directions for hearing the word profitably, that may be considered as so many positive rules. I have already shown what we should studiously avoid, and now I am to show what we should carefully observe, relative to this important duty.

These positive rules may be digested into three heads as they refer to what is necessary, previous to hearing, in the time of hearing, and after we have heard the word preached. I shall mention a few directions on each.

First, Before men go to hear the word, it is highly expedient that they act with all due consideration of the nature and importance of the service they are to be employed in, and seek a divine blessing in the appointed channel; for the Lord will be sanctified in them that come nigh him (Lev. 10:3). I do not at all limit the sovereignty of divine grace, but the following things are clearly pointed out in the word of God, to direct and govern the Christian's conduct.

1. The gospel is to be heard *in a good and honest heart* (Luke 8:15), that is, a heart open to instruction, conviction, and comfort; ready to receive and improve it, and profit by it, to all the practical purposes for which it is designed.

2. A tolerable knowledge of the first principles of the oracles of God is very useful. That the soul be without knowledge is not good. Unskilfullness in the word of righteousness frequently renders the preaching of the word, even in the plainest manner, fruitless.

3. A well-chosen ministry is necessary, for we must take heed what we hear; whether it be words that become sound doctrine; and such preaching as tends to humble the sinner, exalt the Savior, and promote holiness upon evangelical principles. We should only hear such preachers as appear to be sound in the faith, exemplary in their conduct, serious in their spirits, and faithful in their work. No man acts with prudence or judgment that chooses a ministry he thinks ignorant, ungodly, unsound, unprofitable, which runs out into airy notions, or barren controversy, or, finally, that is uncharitable and censorious, which runs out in open invectives, or secret insinuations, reflecting on the conduct of others, instead of knowing only Christ and him crucified, and speaking only the words of truth and soberness, rightly dividing, and faithfully applying, the word of truth.

4. Readiness of mind to attend on the word, without prejudice of spirit, or opposition to the truth, readily embracing stated seasons, and gladly complying with every providential call, is likewise required. We have an example of it in the Bereans (Acts 17:11).

5. The mind should be previously possessed with a deep and serious concern, suitable to the nature of the work, and the greatness of the presence in which we are to stand.

6. Right ends should be proposed in hearing the word. We should study to be able to answer that question, "What went ye out for to see?" (Matt. 11:9). To obey the command of God; and to reap spiritual advantage and saving benefit to our souls; to be more thoroughly convinced of the evil of sin; more clearly enlightened in the knowledge of the divine will; more strongly impressed by divine truth; and more abundantly established in our hearts—are worthy ends in such a work.

7. We should earnestly pray for a divine blessing, to direct a suitable word with irresistible power into our souls. God giveth the increase of his word and ordinances.

8. All that design to hear the word should duly consider that it will be either the savor of life or of death unto them, "We are unto God a sweet savour of Christ, in them that are saved, and in them that perish: to the one, we are the savour of death unto death; and to the other the savour of life unto life" (2 Cor. 2:15–16).

Secondly, There are several useful rules to be observed in the time of hearing the word. Among others, I beg leave to mention the following, and leave them with my readers.

1. Hear the word with reverence and a due regard to its divine authority. Cornelius and his company professed themselves all present, to hear all things that were commanded Peter of God (Acts 10:33). And the Thessalonians heard the word which Paul and others preached, and received it, not as the word of men, but, as it is indeed, the word of God (1 Thess. 2:13).

2. Hear the word with due attention, "Set your hearts unto all the words which I testify among you this day.... For it is not a vain thing for you; because it is your life" (Deut. 32:46–47). It is said of the hearers of our Lord that all the people were very attentive to hear him (Luke 19:48). They hung upon his lips, and watched every word that fell from his mouth. And the Samaritans gave heed to the things which Philip spoke (Acts 8:6). And when the Lord opened Lydia's heart, she attended to the things which were spoken of Paul (Acts 16:14). We must rouse up the most wakeful attention, summon all the powers of our souls, and unite all the force of nature, to wait on the Lord without distraction.

3. Hear the gospel with understanding and judgment: for "he that received the seed into good ground is he that heareth the word, and understandeth it" (Matt. 13:23). If the gospel we hear be well understood, it will stick faster in the memory, and come with more power upon the conscience; it will strike with greater force upon the affections, and have the stronger influence upon the life.

4. Hear the word with application. This is implied in the reason which the apostle gives for the gospel preached to the Jews being unprofitable, it was not "mixed with faith in them that heard it" (Heb. 4:2). The word of God consists of doctrines, which are to be received; promises, to be embraced; commands, to be obeyed; threatenings, to be reverenced; and

examples for imitation, caution, or comfort. Faith must run through the whole, and mix with every part, realizing the truth and importance of every word we hear, to draw virtue from each.

5. Hear the word of God with the proper exercise of suitable affections: moved with fear at the warnings of danger; trembling at the awful threatenings; rejoicing at the precious promises; and esteeming the commandments of God concerning all things to be right.

6. In hearing receive with meekness the engrafted word (James 1:21). Perhaps it may cross the inclinations of nature, or some worldly interest, but if it bear the stamp of truth, it ought to be received without gainsaying, on the account of God, whose impression it bears. Men cannot hear with profit, except they be converted, and become as little children (Matt. 18:3), whose minds are tender and pliable, and not being swelled with a conceit of knowledge, or prejudice against the truth, are easily impressed and bent into a compliance.

7. In hearing we should seriously resolve to comply with, and be subject to the word of God, which is made known in the preaching of the gospel, among all nations, for the obedience of faith (Rom. 16:26). The churches glorified God, in behalf of the Corinthians, for their professed subjection unto the gospel of Christ (2 Cor. 9:13). The hearers of the gospel should be unfeignedly determined to hear and do whatsoever the Lord their God shall say; and firmly resolved to be doers of the word, and not hearers only, deceiving their own souls.

8. Join prayer with hearing the word. I do not mean stated addresses to heaven, that might hinder attentive hearing, or interrupt it; but ejaculations that impress the heart, and greatly help the attention. Praying hearers seldom lose their labors.

9. Project, while you hear, to retain as much as may be of every sermon. Our memories should be sacred repositories of divine truth. Like David, we should hide this precious jewel in our hearts, that they may be comforted in love, and kept from sinning against God.

Thirdly, I shall add a few directions relative to the proper exercise of these who have been hearing the word, to assist their future improvements of that ordinance.

1. Remember how you have received and heard, and hold fast (Rev. 3:3). Take the most earnest heed, lest the things that you have heard slip out of your mind (Heb. 2:1).

2. Ponder what you have heard by close and frequent meditation. If you delight in the law of God, you will meditate in it day and night (Ps. 1:2).

3. Examine the truth of what you have heard by the Holy Scripture, which is the infallible standard of truth. You must try the spirits, whether they be of God, or not (1 John 4:1).

4. Pray over the word you have been hearing, that it may be followed with a divine blessing, and may not be like water spilled on the ground, or an arrow shot in the air.

5. Converse with others about the word. When our Lord had discoursed with the two disciples, they said, "Did not our heart burn within us, while he talked with us?" (Luke 24:32).

6. Practice in your lives what you have heard and received. Knowledge in the things of God is in order to practice; therefore, our Lord says, "If ye know these things, happy are ye if ye do them" (John 13:17). And again, "Ye are my friends, if ye do whatsoever I command you" (John 15:14). Therefore look upon every word you hear as a rule of life, according to which you are to walk; and as a rule of judgment, by which you must be tried at last. The word of God is a doctrine which is according to godliness; not a mere speculation of truth, or set of notions; it is designed to form our minds, and govern our lives; to rectify the disorders sin had introduced, and restore the true order and peace of our souls, in conformity to the divine image, and in obedience to the divine will.

I shall only add that practical directions in religion, like prescriptions of art, will have no effect without being followed; and their whole virtue lies in their proper use. And, let me subjoin my earnest wish that everyone that reads these advices, may henceforth observe them. Then neither preaching nor hearing would be in vain in the Lord.

Chapter 4
Singing the Praises of God

This is a piece of religious service, that is very ancient, "Then sang Moses and the children of Israel this song unto the LORD," *etc.* (Ex. 15:1); and it will be everlasting; for in glory the redeemed shall never cease to sing the song of Moses the servant of God, and the song of the Lamb (Rev. 15:2–3). In discoursing on this ordinance of singing divine praise, I shall arrange my sentiments in the following order:
1. To explain the nature of the service.
2. To represent the obligations that lie on Christians to observe it.
3. To vindicate it against some objections.
4. To propose and answer a few questions relative to it.
5. To give some proper directions concerning the right performance of it.

1. The Nature of the Service
I shall begin with an explication of the nature of this ancient, heavenly service, as it is an ordinance of God, and constitutes a part of his worship. This is so well known among us that it may seem needless to explain it. Singing is only speaking with a tuned voice; or, it is lengthening the sound of the words by a tuneful and melodious pronunciation: for I do not speak of it in that figurative sense, in which the heavens, the earth, the mountains, and trees are said to shout and sing; or, even in that more simple sense, in which Job says, he "caused the widow's heart to sing for joy" (Job 29:13).

To sing God's praise is to speak it out musically. It supposes the exercise of the soul; for we should sing and make melody in our hearts (Col. 3:16), and sing with grace in our heart; but it does not consist wholly in the mind, it employs also the voice, "With the voice together shall they sing" (Isa. 52:8).

I think there is as much propriety in singing the praises of God in the closet, if it be managed with prudence, as in praying in secret, "Is *any* merry? let him sing psalms" (James 5:13). And it is also to be performed socially, in concert, "O come, let *us* sing unto the LORD: let *us* make a joyful noise to the rock of our salvation" (Ps. 95:1). But these things are so plain that they do not need any illustration, and therefore I shall now attempt,

2. The Obligations to Observe It

To represent the obligations that lie upon Christians to honor this ordinance, by observing it, as well as other institutions of religious worship.

A pompous collection might be drawn out of the writings of heathens, to show, that they, who, having not the written law, are a law to themselves, esteemed it as much a tribute due to the Deity to sing his praise as to call on his name. This is a strong intimation, that it is one of the works of the law written on man's heart. Among a multitude of examples of this kind, I shall select one from Arrianus, the Stoic philosopher. Says he,

> If I was a nightingale, I would do as a nightingale; and, if a swan, as a swan; but since I am a rational creature, I ought to praise God: this is my work: this I will do; nor will I desert this station to the utmost of my power; and I invite all men to the same song.

This is no contemptible proof that the duty of praising God with vocal songs is a part of natural religion; and, if natural, then it is of everlasting obligation and use, for God, as *our Maker*, giveth songs in the night.

This was a considerable part of the Jewish worship, as is plain from the whole tenor of the Old Testament; but there are many considerations of great weight that will not suffer us to *confine it to that dispensation*. I shall name a few of them.

1. It is evident that the people of God sang his praise before the law was given by Moses (Ex. 15), when they were miraculously delivered out of the hands of their cruel persecutors, by the same waves that had stood like a brazen wall, till they marched through the deep as on dry land, closing upon Pharaoh and his armed legions, "*Then* sang Moses and the children of Israel this song unto the LORD," *etc*. Now, by what law did they sing this song? It could not be by the *Levitical* law; for that was not yet given to them. It was not by any *positive* law; for there was none such in being, that

we know of. Therefore they were influenced by the *dictates of their consciences*, and perhaps, the *examples* which had been before them, by which they were as *naturally* led to *sing* his praises when they were delivered as to cry to him in their distresses.

2. Ceremonial ordinances were confined entirely to the Israelites; for to them alone pertained the giving of the law, and the service of God. The *Gentiles* were to have no part or lot in that matter, except they became *proselytes* to the *Mosaic system*. But it is a certain fact that when *psalmody* was in the most flourishing condition among the Israelites, under the direction and influence of David, the sweet psalmist of Israel, it was not confined to that people; for he exhorts all nations to be glad and sing for joy (Ps. 67:4), and all the lands to sing forth the honor of his name, and make his praise glorious (Ps. 66:1–2). This is a circumstance that cannot be accounted for if we suppose *singing* the praise of God to be *ceremonial*; but allow it to be a *moral duty*, and every difficulty is removed.

3. Singing of psalms and spiritual songs is *preferred* unto ceremonial worship and legal sacrifices, while they were in their greatest glory, and in highest esteem, "I will praise the name of God," says David, "with a song, and will magnify him with thanksgiving. This also shall please the LORD better than an ox or bullock, that hath horns and hoofs" (Ps. 69:30–31). Here the preference is fairly given to singing, on a comparison with sacrifices. The reason seems to be this: singing is a part of *moral worship*, whereas sacrifices are of *ceremonial institution*. The first may therefore be performed in a spiritual manner, but the last cannot, being a carnal commandment in the very nature of it, though subservient to a spiritual purpose.

4. This duty of singing remained in full force after the ceremonial law, with all its instituted rites, was abolished. We have a decisive proof of this in the epistles written to the churches at Ephesus and Colossae. In both these epistles the churches are asserted to be *entirely delivered* from the law of ceremonies, and yet in both of them are declared to be *under an obligation* to sing psalms, and hymns, and spiritual songs. Writing to the Ephesians, our apostle affirms that the middle wall of partition between *Jew* and *Gentile* is broken down; and that the law of commandments, contained in ordinances, is abolished (Eph. 2:14–15). And in Colossians 2:16–17, he says, "Let no man judge you in meat, or in drink…which are a

shadow of things to come; but the body is of Christ." Yet after all these strong remonstrances, he exhorts both these churches to sing the Lord's praise, "Speaking to yourselves in psalms and hymns and spiritual songs, singing and making melody in your heart to the Lord" (Eph. 5:19). "Let the word of Christ dwell in you richly in all wisdom; teaching and admonishing one another in psalms and hymns and spiritual songs, singing with grace in your hearts to the Lord" (Col. 3:16). This manifestly shows that the duty of singing is not to be thrown into the number of those services that are purely typical, because it is enjoined after the whole mass of ceremonies was abolished.

5. We are directed to this duty by examples that are recorded for our admonition, upon whom the ends of the earth are come. The histories of God's people are not a *dry record* of past facts; but they are either a *test* to discover what we are, or a *rule* to tell us what we should be. When Christ was about to leave his disciples, he parted with them in the ordinance of the supper, that should continue till his second coming, and *sung an hymn with them* (Matt. 26:30). This could not be merely in compliance with the *Jewish custom* at the passover; because he had *superseded* that solemnity by another appointment, in remembrance of himself, to be kept up till he come again. Paul and Silas sung praises to God in the stocks (Acts 16:25).The apostle, when giving directions to a Gentile church about the conduct of their public worship, says of himself as an example of the believers, "I will sing with the spirit, and I will sing with the understanding also" (1 Cor. 14:15). And the angels, that have nothing to do with ceremonial observances, are our fellow-laborers in this delightful work; for these morning-stars sang together, and all these sons of God shouted for joy, when the foundations of the earth were fastened, and when its cornerstone was laid (Job 38:6–7). And while the angel announced the birth of Christ to the shepherds, "Suddenly there was with the angel a multitude of the heavenly host praising God, and saying, Glory to God in the highest, and on earth peace, good will toward men" (Luke 2:13–14). These pure and flaming spirits will also mix their hallelujahs and songs of praise with the saints forever and ever.

6. We may say of this duty what the apostle does of charity or love (1 Cor. 13:8), *it never faileth*, though prophecies, tongues, and knowledge, as well as ceremonial shadows, shall cease; for when all the present system

of ordinances shall be changed, this will be in its greatest glory and perfection, and will continue forever. This will be the employment of saints, when they are awaked out of the dust, on the resurrection morning, in the power and virtue of the resurrection of their risen Lord. "Thy dead men shall live, together with my dead body shall they arise! Awake and sing, ye that dwell in dust: for thy dew is as the dew of herbs, and the earth shall cast out the dead" (Isa. 26:19). Their souls and bodies reunited shall come to the Zion above, with songs, and everlasting joy upon their heads (Isa. 35:14). There they shall stand, and sing in the height of it, that new song which none can learn, but those that are redeemed from the earth (Jer. 31:12; Rev. 14:3). Now, since this is the work of heaven and eternity, and we have here no continuing city, but seek one to come, let us by Christ offer the sacrifice of praise unto God continually; that is, the fruit of our lips, giving thanks unto his name (Heb. 13:14–15). And methinks there is not a more lively emblem, or affecting representation of the heavenly state upon earth, than an assembly of worshipping Christians singing the praises of God. This is just what they do in heaven, where they are forever employed in exercises of love and songs of praise. The brighter and fuller displays of divine perfections continually pouring in upon their minds will open new scenes of glory, and furnish fresh variety of matter for eternal praise. "Surely, it is good to sing praise to our God; for it is pleasant, and praise is comely." The theme is large and full; all the glories of JEHOVAH, as made known unto creatures, and all the wonders of his creating power, redeeming love, and providential care, belong to its boundless extensive grasp. The exercise is a fit means to convey instruction (Col. 3:16); to inspire heavenly affections (Ps. 57:7–8); to afford an agreeable entertainment to a holy soul (James 5:13); and to bear up and comfort the heart (Acts 16:25; Ps. 119:54).

I shall further observe a remarkable circumstance concerning this service; namely, that it is the most *disinterested* exercise, and the most *generous* service we can perform to God; for in other duties, there is a mixture of self and interest; some necessity urges to them, or some advantage is proposed by them; but here we propose only the glory of God.

On the whole, is any merry through the light of God's countenance shining upon his soul? Let him glorify God, by singing psalms, and offering praise unto him; "for with such sacrifices God is well-pleased"; and since joy is peculiarly sown for the New Testament church, it is cruel to deny her the privilege of expressing, in songs of gratitude and adoration, her sense of God's excellent loving-kindness.

3. Vindication Against Some Objections

The next thing to be attempted is to *vindicate* this ordinance from *some objections* that are made against it. Several objections will be provided against under the next section; and therefore, my present business is only to take notice of a few things that are urged against the ordinance in general, as obligatory under the New Testament dispensation. The chief of them may be reduced to the following heads: (1.) either this duty of singing is *antiquated*; or (2.) it is *needless* under the gospel; or (3.) it *unbecomes* the present afflicted state of the church. I shall reply to these objections severally, in their order.

1. It is alleged by many that this practice is antiquated, as a part of ceremonial worship that is now abolished; and they affirm that we are now to praise God only by making secret melody in the heart. Indeed, if we were as certain that it was a ceremonial rite, as we are that it was used, while the Mosaic dispensation lasted, the dispute would be at an end; but this we cannot allow. Many things enjoined upon the Jews were moral and perpetual, as, the law of the ten commandments. Every external moral service among them had certain connections or appendages with ritual and carnal duties, according to the nature of the dispensation; and when such rites were laid aside, this connection was broken, but the substance of the duty remained in full force, only it must no longer be performed in the particular form and circumstances that temporary dispensation had defined. Our reasons for thinking it a moral duty have been laid down in the foregoing section. It is, at the same time, readily granted that some circumstances in performing it were peculiar to that pompous dispensation; such as, the use of musical instruments, chosen singers, *etc.* But these are laid aside of course with the dispensation to which they belonged, as I will endeavor to show by and by; but when we allow that these are antiquated, we still insist that the ordinance itself is unaltered. If this observation were duly attended to, it would prevent all extremes, for it shows the absurdity, on one hand, of continuing these carnal appendages in New Testament worship, after the dispensation they belonged to is ceased; and, on the other hand, of setting aside the duty itself, because it is no longer to be performed

with all the same circumstances it was formerly. Our opinion strikes a just medium between both.

2. Another objection against singing is that it is *needless*; because, it is pretended, all the ends of it can be effectually obtained by prayer, and by reading and hearing the word of God. The wisdom of the flesh is enmity against God. It would be, I confess, an expeditious method to shrink religion into a thin shadow, if we were allowed to neglect everything but what our corrupt and self-indulgent nature shall think necessary. But we are not to take the measures of our duty from what we *judge* proper or needful, but only from the *will* and *command* of Christ. And, suffer me to say, it is inexpressible disingenuity to forbear, on any pretense, to exalt the name of God in any way that is lawful and possible for us, since he is daily loading us with his numberless undeserved benefits from every quarter. Most astonishing baseness! Most hateful ingratitude! Only suppose that God appointed this ordinance, and that it is fit in the nature of it to express his praise, and you will see the nakedness of the wretched evasion, *that it is needless*, in its true colors.

3. Others tell us that this joyful exercise but ill becomes the present afflicted state of the church, while she is in an evil world. No doubt a merry heart is most suitable for singing. The jovial sensualist is a shocking contradiction; for even *in his laughter, his heart is sad*. And when the children of God are made perfect in holiness and felicity, their songs will be incomparably sweeter and more elevated than while they are in this valley of sorrow. But as David's harp was useful to remove Saul's evil spirit, so are the songs of Zion to comfort the dejected soul. And many of the sacred hymns are wonderfully suitable to the lowest condition of the church of God: a circumstance that plainly enough signifies the end of their composure, and the use we should make of them. We read, indeed, that when the Jews were under the Babylonish captivity, they hung their harps upon the willows (Ps. 137:2); but the following words give us reason to believe this was upon a very singular occasion, *viz.*, when their enemies insulted over them, and in scorn required them to entertain them with some of their temple-songs. But otherwise, it is probable, they occasionally refreshed themselves with this divine music, or why should we read of their harps in that strange land? The most distressing condition in this world affords matter and encouragement enough for *songs* that are given *in the night*. "I will sing of mercy and judgment: unto thee, O LORD, will I sing" (Ps. 101:1). A man of

such a devout temper will never be indisposed, whatever be his situation, for this duty. You have a remarkable example of this, in Habakkuk 3:17–19:

> Although the fig tree shall not blossom, neither shall fruit be in the vines; the labour of the olive shall fail, and the fields shall yield no meat; the flock shall be cut off from the fold, and there shall be no herd in the stalls: yet I will rejoice in the Lord, I will joy in the God of my salvation. The Lord God is my strength, and he will make my feet like hinds' feet, and he will make me to walk upon mine high places. To the chief singer on my stringed instruments.

4. Answering a Few Questions Relative to It

In order to obtain a more extensive and exact view of this ordinance of singing God's praise, I shall propose and answer a few questions which may contribute to explain the subject and give the reasons of our practice to the public, in several instances that are connected with the service. The questions may be reduced to three general heads, which will comprehend all that is needful on the point; namely, *Who ought to sing God's praise? What should be sung?* And, *in what manner ought this service to be performed?*

I. The first question to be considered is, *Who ought to sing God's praise?* To which I answer,

1. That a *particular person* may, and every Christian ought to perform this duty by himself, in secret; "Is *any* merry? let *him* sing psalms" (James 5:13). The duty is enjoined upon a particular person in these words. In performing it, we should take care, however, not to expose religion to contempt by unguarded indiscretions and imprudencies, that might give occasion to the enemies of the Lord to blaspheme or reproach. Personal godliness should be managed in secret (Matt. 6:1–6).

2. Any *two* or *more* may join in it, as Paul and Silas did in prison, who at midnight prayed, and sang praises unto God (Acts 16:25), which is an instance of singing vocally, and in concert; and the Lord hearkened and heard, and testified his approbation with undeniable proofs.

3. Christian families should conscientiously serve God in this exercise: for "the voice of rejoicing and salvation is in the tabernacles of the righteous" (Ps. 118:15); and it is most reasonable that a church should be in each of their houses (Rom. 16:5; 1 Cor. 16:19; Col. 4:15).

4. This is a duty that should be kept up in *worshipping assemblies* and *congregations*. The reasons of this are various and cogent. (1.) It stands on record in the volume of God's book that when the Gentiles should receive the gospel, they would express their joy in the most rapturous and elevated strains of transporting satisfaction (see Isa. 35:1–10; 52:7–9; 54:1). (2.) This service is authorized by express precepts and directions concerning it (Eph. 5:19; Col. 3:16). (3.) It is recommended by several instances and examples. Our Lord sung a hymn (marg. *psalm*) with his disciples (Matt. 26:30), which was different from his giving of thanks (Matt. 26:26–27), besides that the word used in the original language (ὑμνήσαντες), does not signify *to give thanks simply*, but always denotes *a grave song of vocal praise*. The church at Corinth, in the times of the apostles, sang psalms (1 Cor. 14). It is true, there were disorders among them about this, as well as other parts of public worship, which the apostle points out, and corrects in his epistle to them: "How is it then, brethren?" (says he), "when ye come together, everyone of you *hath a psalm*, hath a doctrine, hath a tongue, hath a revelation, hath an interpretation. Let all things be done to edifying" (1 Cor. 14:26). He does not blame them for these things, more than in the 11th chapter, for eating the Lord's Supper; he only censures and guards them against their errors, that they might honor God in these duties, by observing them in the scriptural order. In the book of the Revelation, which contains a just representation of the state and condition, service and sufferings of the church of Christ on earth, in her several periods, we have frequently an account of their being concerned in this work of *singing* (see Rev. 5:9–10; 14:1, 3; 15:3; *etc.*).

From the whole it is natural enough to draw the following conclusions.

(1.) That this duty is not rightly performed by *one person only* as the mouth of the congregation, and the rest concurring by their *silent consent*; as in public prayer the minister speaks, and the congregation consents in silence. The Right Honorable Sir Peter King says, "As for the manner of the primitive singing, it was in good tune and concert, N.B., *all the people bearing a part in it.*"[1] The only plausible pretense for the contrary opinion is taken from "every one of you hath a psalm, hath a doctrine," etc. (1 Cor. 14:26), that is, as Beza observes, *one hath* a psalm, *another hath* a doctrine, etc., from whence some gather that only one person should sing

---

[1] King, *An Inquiry into the Constitution, Discipline, Unity and Worship of the Primitive Church*, part 2, chap. 1, sect. 7.

in a congregation, and the rest, as in prayer, join their consent. But let it be remembered that this passage supposes psalmody to have been a stated part of their public service, and in the present case, the occasional use of the extraordinary gifts of the Spirit in dictating a psalm is the thing our apostle means by *one having a psalm*. As doctrines were taught by the extraordinary influence of the Holy Ghost, so psalms were dictated by the same Spirit, in the same way, and all for the general edifying of the body. He that had a doctrine spake it in the hearing of the church, that they might profit by it; and he that had a psalm published it to the church, that they might glorify God in using it. I do not see that this text determines anything about the persons that *used* it; but only about the person that *had* it suggested to him. But other places of Scripture put it beyond doubt that all joined in singing (see Matt. 26:30; Eph. 5:19; Col. 3:16; in all these places we find it is the joint employment of the church).

(2.) That the obligation to sing publicly the praises of God is the *same* upon *women* and *men*. They are jointly members of his church, and heirs of his kingdom; and therefore, are equally bound to celebrate his praise. To be sure, women should keep silence in the churches: for it is not permitted unto them to speak there (1 Cor. 14:34). It is neither decent, nor allowable for them to preach, or act the proper part of the man, in any public way of speaking; for this is the meaning of the text, as is plain from "Let the woman learn in silence with all subjection. But I suffer not a woman to teach, nor to usurp authority over the man, but to be in silence" (1 Tim. 2:11–12), where he disapproves of their performing *such acts* in the church as imply *authority*; but this is no reason, why they may not bear a part in psalmody, and joining with the church to sing divine praise, since this is *no act of authority*, but a moral service, which concerns *equally* all the human species; let their glory, therefore, sing his praise.

(3.) This duty may safely and properly enough be performed in *promiscuous assemblies*. I readily confess, none can make melody to the Lord, singing with grace in their hearts, but the saints. But it would be an absurd inference that none are obliged to perform this duty but holy persons, because none else can do it aright. By such reasoning it would be easy to infer, on these very principles, that the divine moral government is confined to the saints, and consequently that all sin is confined to the saints too, if such a thing exists in the world at all; for if sinners are under no law, they cannot be transgressors. The shocking absurdity of the conclusion demonstrates the falsity of the reasoning. The obligation on all men to glorify God, by showing forth his praise, cannot be canceled. And where is the impropriety of doing it, even in *the company of the profane?* "Unto the pure all things are pure: but unto them that are defiled and unbelieving is nothing pure" (Titus 1:15). Besides, this objection is as strong against *public prayer* as against what is called *promiscuous singing*; and as strong against *promiscuous assembling*, as against *either*.

II. The next question to be discussed is, *What should be the matter of our songs?*

The answer is repeated, that we may not mistake it, where we are exhorted to sing *psalms, hymns,* and *spiritual songs* (Eph. 5:19; Col. 3:16). These characters seem to be the same with the titles prefixed to the book of Psalms, where some are called *psalms*, מזמורים, ψαλμοι (as Ps. 3–5, *etc.*); others *hymns*, תהלים, υμνοι (as Ps. 145); and others *songs*, שירים, ωδαι (as Ps. 120–134 and many others). If I confess my real ignorance about the characteristic differences of these titles, I need not blush at it. The learned reader may consult Beza, Gomarus, and Davenant on Colossians 3:16; Zanchius, Grotius, Hammond, Gill, etc., on Ephesians 5:19; with the best critics on the *words*.

I would only beg leave to observe that whereas the apostle, in his directions about singing, mentions the titles of David's Psalms, it is highly reasonable to conclude that it was his intention to give them[2] a sanction, as proper matter for this solemn service. I do not mean that the matter of our praise should be confined to these only; for, it is but reasonable, that every Scripture-song should be sung in a meter-version, as short, as simple, and as near the original, as possible. With this view, the church of Scotland has often proposed to enlarge the system of her psalmody; but, by some means or other, has never carried her design into execution.[3]

The following things are offered to manifest the propriety of using David's Psalms in singing God's praise in New Testament times.

1. They were originally written in verse. The learned Gomarus, in *Davidis lyra*, shows that this was the opinion of the ancients; and demon-

---

[2] See David Rees. *Reasons for and against Singing of Psalms, in Private or Publick Worship, Considered with Candor*, pp. 2–10.

[3] See preface from Ralph Erskine. *A Short Paraphrase upon the Lamentations of Jeremiah, Adapted to the Common Tunes*, in *Works*, vol. 2, p. 699.

strates the truth of it: and the learned labors of Bishop Hare and Dr. Grey have made it very plain.

2. They are a very rich collection of gospel-doctrines, and precious promises; a large fund of solid experience; an exhaustless mine of gospel-grace and truth; and an endless variety to suit every case, state, and condition the church of Christ can be in at any time.

3. In using them we are in no hazard of being misled into wrong apprehensions about divine truths, because they are all given by inspiration of God, and are no less useful than other parts of Scripture, for doctrine, reproof, correction, and instruction.

4. Having the Psalms among our hands for our daily study, we are furnished with peculiar assistances to sing God's praise with faith, understanding, and affection; inasmuch as we are to sing his own word, that we are daily conversant with.

These reasons have the more weight if we consider the remarkable connection which the apostle states between the word of Christ dwelling richly in Christians, and their teaching and admonishing one another in psalms, hymns, and spiritual songs (Col. 3:16). Now, can we comply with the spirit of this exhortation, with as much certainty and satisfaction, upon any other scheme of praising, as when we use only the word of God for the matter of our song?

It is, surely, more safe for Christians to use the *exactest version* of the word of Christ, in praising God, than to use any *hymn-book of human composition* whatever. Let but any man peruse a variety of such performances, and he will soon be convinced they do not agree with one another, and all of them cannot, therefore, agree with the word of Christ; he will see the spirit and temper of the man that drew them up, instead of the uniform Spirit of the living and true God, running through the whole. Being human composures, they must be subject to human infirmities. The sentiments of the author will appear in the performance; and as the best of men see but *darkly*, and sometimes *falsely*, their performances, of course, will be *imperfect*, perhaps also *erroneous*.

I may say of such performances that they are, at least *unnecessary*, and to indulge them is *dangerous*. I can refer the reader, with great pleasure, to the learned Dr. Ridgley's *Body of Divinity*[4] for a candid, sensible account

---

[4] Thomas Ridgley. *A Body of Divinity*, vol. 2, pp. 358–360.

of this matter. If he seems to be rather severe, I believe the unprejudiced reader will justify his indignation.

The ingenious and devout Dr. Watts, whose praise is in the churches, has published a book, entitled, *The Psalms of David imitated, in the language of the New Testament, and applied to the Christian state and worship*. In this imitation, he proposes to gather the meaning of the Psalms, in phrases that belong to the New Testament dispensation. I shall allow his performance all the merit its most sanguine friends can possibly wish; and yet I think Dr. Ridgley's observation is unanswerable; his words are,

> All the arguments that are brought in defense of making these alterations in the Psalms, as they are to be sung by us, will equally hold good, as applicable to the ordinance of reading them; and, it may be, will as much evidence the necessity of altering the phrase, in several other parts thereof, as well as in these.... For, it will follow from thence, that if some psalms are not to be sung by a Christian assembly, in the words in which they were at first delivered, and consequently are not to be read by them; because the phrase thereof is not agreeable to the state of the Christian church; and therefore it is to be altered, when applied to our present use; the same may be said concerning other parts of Scripture; and then the word of God, as it was at first given to us, is no more to be read, than to be sung by us.[5]

I shall dismiss this point with the following observations, that will explain and vindicate our practice in using the Psalms of David, while we sing the praises of God.

1. How Jewish soever some of the Psalms may be, yet they treated of the state of the church of God, though veiled with ceremonies. Now, we may meditate with pleasure, while we sing, on the truths contained under these shadows, and on our superior happiness, to whom it is allowed to see the clearer light of the day-spring that has visited us. And by comparing the shadow and the substance together, we may understand the subject more fully.

2. Where sacrifices are mentioned, the sacrifice of Christ is the antitype (1 Cor. 5:7).

---

[5] Ridgley, *A Body of Divinity*, vol. 2, pp. 357–358.

3. In some of the Psalms, the glory of Jewish national assemblies, in Jerusalem and on mount Zion, is set forth in bold and lively terms. This has always been, with the greatest reason, considered as applicable to New Testament churches, and a just description of their beauty.

4. Some Psalms contain histories of things done to and for the Jewish church; and surely we are bound to bless and admire the love, grace, and power of God in these instances; and hereby we are taught to consider what God, most merciful, most holy, and jealous, has done for the redemption of his church, and what he will do to accomplish her salvation from all sin and sorrow (see Ps. 136).

5. Where we find predictions of things that are to come, we should consider them either as now accomplished to us, and give God the honor of his faithfulness, or as yet to be performed in some future time, and express our hope in the word of God, that will not fall to the ground.

6. Some of the Psalms are penitential, and in singing them we are seasonably called to be affected with a sense of the vileness, treachery, and baseness of our hearts and natures.

7. As for these Psalms which contain denunciations of divine wrath, destruction, and curses upon the enemies of God and his church, we are to consider: that these expressions were dictated by the infallible Spirit of God, that the objects of them were foreseen to be irreconcilable enemies of Christ and his church, that those who sang them only applaud the equity of the doom which God has justly pronounced upon such offenders, and that they are to be sung with a full persuasion of the event, as a certain, awful, and just display of the glory and tremendous justice of JEHOVAH. I am far from approving an uncharitable spirit, a malignant temper, or ill-natured wishes; I know they are not consistent with, they are a flat contradiction to the spirit of the gospel. But there is a *false charity*, as well as a *true one*; a *sinful clemency*, as well as a *just one*. Saul would have spared Agag, whom Samuel hewed to pieces before the Lord (1 Sam. 15:9, 33); and a heavy doom was pronounced upon Ahab, for sparing Benhadad, a man whom God had appointed to utter destruction (1 Kings 20:42). Therefore, when we keep to the words and meaning of the Holy Scriptures, without maliciously applying them, out of our own heads, against particular persons and parties, we are safe in using the *sacred* and *inspired passages*, either in *prayer* or *praise*. I add, that to decline using them, out of a pretended charitable fear, is rather our sin than our duty; for, it is to think ourselves

wiser than the God of wisdom, and to make ourselves more merciful than the Father of compassions, that delighteth in mercy, and is abundant in goodness. But it is time now to proceed to,

III. The last question I proposed: *In what manner should we sing God's praise?* or, *How ought this service to be performed?* Abstracting entirely, at present, from what will come in most naturally on the head of *directions*, I beg leave to observe:

1. That it is very proper to sing *in meter*. All that is alleged to the contrary by Bishop King, in his book, entitled, *A Discourse concerning the Inventions of Men in the Worship of God,* and by others that hold his opinion, is either *weak* or *false*. I have before observed that it is more than probable the Psalms were originally written in meter; and it seems to be, in every respect, as reasonable to turn them into English meter, to sing them, as into prose to read them for instruction. See Mr. Boyse's *answer* to the bishop's performance just now referred to.

2. It is proper to sing with *artificial tunes*, that are most familiar to the assembly. This is a dictate of reason, and many ways expedient for edification.

3. There is no scriptural warrant for the *antiphonal way* of singing God's praise, by dividing it into parts, and so many singing each of them; while they sing alternately, answering one another in the song. Perhaps the Song of Solomon might have been sung in that manner, as well as Miriam's song (Ex. 15:20–21) and 24th and 118th Psalms. But, if this was the case, the matter of the song, and the difference of the persons that speak suggested the several parts, and determined the measures, of the chorus; and not the number of verses, where there is no change either of person or matter, according to the practice of chorus-singing in cathedral-worship. This is also the case in Revelation 7:9 13; 19:1–7. But nothing can be produced to make it probable that this way of alternate singing was the ordinary practice of the Christian church in the New Testament. And if anybody would see the judgment of the primitive church about it, he may consult the learned Mr. James Pierce's answer to Dr. Nichols,[6] where it is shown to be a later invention than the three first centuries.

4. We find no footsteps of using musical *instruments* in singing God's praise in the New Testament. I cannot express myself better than in the words of the forecited Mr. Boyse:

---

[6] James Pierce. *A Vindication of the Dissenters*, part 3, chapter 3.

For instruments of music, there is no question of their being used in the worship of the Jewish church. But, then it must be considered, that it is highly probable, these instruments of music belonged not to the worship of their synagogues, but only to the service of their temple. And there was a particular institution for them, as appears from Numbers 10 and Leviticus 23:24. And those other instruments of music which David appointed (1 Chron. 16:4–6), he is expressly said to have done it, upon the commandment of the Lord by his prophets (2 Chron. 29:25). And they are on that account called God's musical instruments (2 Chron. 7:6), as having the stamp of his authority. Since then instrumental music belonged to the temple-service, which was but ceremonial and typical, it must be abolished with that service; and we can have no warrant to recall it into the Christian church, without as particular an institution for it, as it had under the law; any more than we have to use other abrogated rites of the Jewish religion. Nor needs there any particular command for laying it aside, when the whole temple-service, of which it is a part, is so plainly cashiered, and it was not, that we can find, used in the worship of the synagogues, from which alone we can pretend to draw any safe pattern for evangelical worship. And it is certain, that there is no mention in Scripture of its being used in the Christian church. And indeed it seems more suitable to divine worship, when there was more of external pomp allowed in it.[7]

The use of musical instruments in the worship of God is but a modern invention. Their warmest advocates cannot pretend to find them in the Christian church before the year 660. And Thomas Aquinas, who lived about the year 1250, says, "The church does not use musical instruments to praise God, lest she should seem to judaize." Upon which place Cardinal Cajetan gives us this natural comment: "It is to be observed, the church did not use organs in Thomas Aquinas' time: whence, even to this day, the church of Rome does not use them in the Pope's presence."

And we have as severe a censure passed upon such instruments, when they are employed in this part of divine service, in the *Homilies of the Church of England*, as ever was passed upon them, perhaps, by any writer

---

[7] Boyse, *Remarks on a Late Discourse*, pp. 17, 18.

whatever. A fact that took place at the Reformation is recorded and improved in these words,

> A woman said to her neighbor Alas! gossip, what shall we now do at church, since all the saints are taken away; since all the godly sights we were wont to have are gone; since we cannot hear the like piping, singing, chanting, and playing upon the organs that we could before? But, dearly beloved, we ought greatly to rejoice and give God thanks, that our churches are delivered out of all those things, *N.B.*, which displeased God so sore, and filthily defiled his holy place, and his house of prayer.[8]

And this, as well as the rest of the homilies, is said to "contain a godly and wholesome doctrine," in the 35th article of the church of England. But I shall dismiss this, and go on to observe,

5. That I apprehend it is *most safe* in public congregations, *to read the lines severally*, as they are to be sung. I do not say, that this contributes to the propriety of the service; I think it is most becoming to sing without reading, when all that are present can join. If they can all read, have books and light, and the blessing of eyesight, they would perform this work in a more suitable manner without any interruption of reading lines, than with it. But who can be morally sure that this will generally be the case, without, at least, some exceptions? And, I cannot think it is grateful to our bountiful Benefactor to despise our more unhappy, but, perhaps, more deserving brother, because we are more highly favored with these precious mercies than he is.

The advantages of singing without the interruption of reading line by line are great and manifest. By this means the sense of what is sung will lie open to the view of the persons that engage in this service, in their Psalmbooks, and be better understood by them, than it could be by barely hearing the lines read; and there will be a more entire and continued harmony, and the affections will not be in so much danger of cooling and flattening, by the frequent pauses that are made by reading. This is the evident meaning of the Westminster assembly, in their Directory for the Public Worship of God, on the article *of singing of psalms*:

---

[8] See part 2 of "Of the Place and Time of Prayer". In *Homilies of the Church of England*.

> That the whole congregation may join herein (in singing of psalms), everyone that can read is to have a Psalm-book; and all others, not disabled by age or otherwise, are to be exhorted to learn to read. But for the present, where many in the congregation cannot read, it is convenient, that the minister, or some other fit person appointed by him and the other ruling officers, do read the psalms line by line, before the singing thereof.[9]

But yet I subjoin that the inconveniency of reading is such as should be dispensed with, where it cannot be remedied without a greater; that is, when, without this help, any part of the congregation would be debarred from joining in the ordinance. And, it is obvious, these inconveniencies I have named might be mostly prevented, if everyone that could read had a book before him, to keep the connection full in his view.

6. In the performance of this duty, there should be all the external and visible signs of reverence and devotion. Though bodily exercise profiteth little, yet God must be glorified with our bodies, as well as our souls (1 Cor. 6:20). It is highly becoming that, in this duty, the head be uncovered; the countenance composed and serious; the eye fixed, not roving and wandering; and, in a word, the whole external behavior such as, in the judgment of charity, bespeaks an engaged and devout mind and heart, and as becomes the perfections of the God we worship.

5. Directions concerning Right Performance

It remains, that I now lay down some *directions* for the right performance of this duty of singing God's praise; that we may do it with edification and comfort.

1. Reason, and the nature of the duty, plainly suggest several things, relating to the *external manner* of managing this service, which I shall barely name, such as, that some regard ought to be had to external harmony, that there may be melody made with our voices, as well as hearts. Care must be taken, that the tunes sung, and the manner of singing them, be only such as have a tendency to excite spiritual affections. In the choice of the tune, some regard should be had to the matter that is sung. And such tunes should be ordinarily sung as the generality of the worshipers can join in; for without this, the end of singing is marred.

---

[9] See "Of Singing of Psalms". In *Westminster Directory for the Publick Worship of God*.

2. Everything intended for Scripture-psalmody should be used for that purpose; but prudence should direct us, in secret, family, and public praising, to make a wise choice of what is most seasonable; and therefore, upon public *special* occasions, we ought to have regard to those *providences* of God, that his church and people are then under; whether they be *humbling* or *joyful*. Some regard should be had to the *other parts* of worship with which this duty is joined; that there may be a harmony between one duty and another. Christians, in their private families, should have regard to their family state and circumstances, and the particular providences they are under, either in a way of judgment or mercy. And private Christians may regard the particular state and present frame of their own souls. But it is a fond partiality of some people to confine all their attention to some very few psalms that hit their fancy, and to neglect the rest.

3. All the powers of the soul should be summoned to a vigorous exertion in this delightful employment. When David was to bless God, he addressed his soul in these words, "Bless the LORD, O my soul, and all that is within me, bless his holy name" (Ps. 103:1). And again, "Awake up, my glory; awake, psaltery and harp; I myself will awake early" (Ps. 57:8). Understanding, affection, and earnestness should mix in performing this heavenly work.

4. Sing praises with *understanding* (Ps. 47:7). Blind devotion cannot *please* him that dwelleth in light and glory; and it does not *become* the children of light, that are made light in the Lord. We should, like the apostle, sing with our understandings (1 Cor. 14:15), if we would honor the Father, the Word, and the Holy Ghost, who are that *one God*, who condescends to inhabit the praises of Israel.

5. Sing with the *spirit*, as well as with the understanding (1 Cor. 14:15), "God is a Spirit: and they that worship him must worship him in spirit and in truth" (John 4:24). The best of Christians have good reason to join in the prayer of the church, "Awake, O north wind; and come thou south, blow upon my garden, that the spices thereof may flow out. Let my beloved come into his garden, and eat his pleasant fruits" (Song 4:16). Exalted joy in divine praise is a fruit produced only by the Holy Ghost.

6. This service must be performed *unto the Lord*, for so he hath commanded (Col. 3:16). If it be done only to be seen, heard, or applauded by men, verily we have all our reward. We should honor this duty as a

divine institution, and aim at our own and our brethren's edification in performing it, as an act of obedience, and of homage due to God.

7. Christ, the *Mediator of the new covenant*, must be *interested* in our songs. Whatsoever we do in word or deed, we are commanded to do all in the name of our Lord Jesus Christ, giving thanks to God and the Father by him (Col. 3:17).

8. In singing praise, we should *make melody in our hearts* to the Lord (Eph. 5:19). The service is not worth the name of praise if the melody of the heart be wanting. The voice may be musical and harmonious, but God cannot be honored without it. When the heart *echoes* to the *matter* of the song, and its inmost springs of action are forcibly struck with the influence and excellency of the truth that is sung, this, I apprehend, constitutes the melody of the heart; then it sweetly chimes to the song.

9. Spiritual psalmists sing *with grace in their hearts* to the Lord (Col. 3:16). Hence their hearts are fixed, and their souls are enlarged; their minds are engaged, and their songs are invigorated. Savory and just sentiments of the grace of God are the most proper means of quickening the Christian to this honorable and delightful work. Under these views his song is swelled with transports of grateful joy, and with big, though humble, expectations of the heavenly city, whose walls are salvation, and whose gates are everlasting, adoring, and ravishing *praise*, where the cry will never cease, *Grace, Grace*—Amen, Hallelujah.

Chapter 5
Prayer

Prayer is a word of an extensive sense in Scripture, and includes not only a *request* or *petition* for mercies, but is taken for the *address* of a creature on earth to God in heaven, about *everything* that concerns his God, his neighbor, or himself, in this world, or the world to come. It is that converse which God hath allowed us to maintain with himself above, while we are here below. It is a language wherein a creature holds correspondence with his Creator; and wherein the saints often get near to God, are entertained with great delight, and, as it were, dwell with their heavenly Father for a short season, before they come to heaven. In a word, it is so great and necessary a part of religion that every attempt to assist mankind in the discharge of it is laudable, and will be acceptable to pious minds. With this view I shall endeavor:

1. To explain the nature of this duty;
2. To represent the obligations that bind us to perform it;
3. To obviate objections against it;
4. To resolve a few questions relative to it; and,
5. To lay down some plain and pertinent rules for the discharge of it.

1. The Nature of This Duty

The *nature* of *prayer* is to be considered, in the first place. It does not fall within my present design to enlarge on such metaphorical descriptions of the indigence of the brutal creation, and their dependence on God, though they are not conscious of it, as may be called *their crying to him* (Ps. 147:9); *their waiting on him* (Ps. 104:27); or *their groaning* (Joel 1:18). All that I intend is only to describe this duty, as it refers to reasonable creatures. As none but a creature may, so none but a creature endued with reason can properly pray in a religious manner. Devils have besought God for permission to do some things, and this was an acknowledgment of his supreme majesty, and incontrollable [unquestionable] dominion; but I am only concerned with prayer and supplication as it is the business of *men*.

> Prayer is an offering up of our desires to God, for things agreeable to his will, in the name of Christ, by the help of his Spirit, with a confession of our sins, and a thankful acknowledgment of his mercies.

In opening this description, I shall offer a few remarks.

1. The great God is the *alone object* of religious prayer. Because he only heareth prayer, therefore all flesh should come unto him; for with him they have to do. Idolaters have no knowledge, that set up the wood of their graven image, and pray unto a God that cannot save (Isa. 45:20). Attend, ye children of Adam, while the eternal God proclaims his character, and displays his glory, in these words of majestic, God-like import: "See now that I, even I am he, and there is no god with me: I kill, and I make alive; I wound, and I heal: neither is there any that can deliver out of my hand" (Deut. 32:39). Had not David good reason to say, "My prayer shall be unto the God of my life"? He only can hear, he only can judge, he only can answer the prayers that are made. Every perfection of Deity must adorn the matchless character of the God to whom we pray. His *majesty* must teach us to bow our knees unto him with the profoundest reverence; his *infallible knowledge*, to open our inmost wishes before him, who knows all that we desire, and our most secret groanings; his *irresistible power*, to look unto him to do for us, and in us, and to us, far above all that we can either ask, or think; and his *communicative goodness*, to encourage our souls to come boldly to his throne of grace, that we may receive mercy, and find grace to help us in the time of need, from the Father of mercies, from whom every good and perfect gift doth freely come. Here is a worthy object of humble prayer, and daily dependence.

Let the Antichristian church, that denieth the Father and the Son, by praying to creatures, and depending on their interest, as intercessors with the Deity,[1] plead what arguments, and allege what distinctions they will; we must never be induced to entertain a favorable thought of their palpable violation of the law of God, who has expressly said, "Thou shalt worship the Lord thy God, and him only shalt thou serve" (Matt. 4:10).

---

[1] See *Romanum Breviarium*.

The *one supreme God* is the *Father*, and the *Son*, and the *Holy Ghost*. We have examples in Scripture of prayer being addressed to the undivided, uncompounded *divine perfection* in each of these persons: to the Father, "I bow my knees unto the Father of our Lord Jesus Christ" *etc.* (Eph. 3:14); to the Son, "Lord Jesus, receive my spirit" (Acts 7:59); and to the Holy Ghost, "Grace be unto you...from the seven Spirits which are before the throne" (Rev. 1:4), that is, from the Holy Ghost.

I think Witsius has good reason to say, "That the warm disputes on that question, Whether Christ is the object of adoration as he is Mediator, or not? are a mere striving about words,"² since all the orthodox acknowledge his *supreme Godhead* as the *foundation* of divine worship; and his *mediation* to be the alone *channel* in which divine favors freely flow to men.

2. When we pray, we should keep our eye on the *declared will of God*, as the rule of our desires, for the Spirit "maketh intercession for the saints, *N.B.*, according to the will of God" (Rom. 8:27). The whole word of God is of use to direct us in prayer. Without this assistance we neither know what we *need*, nor what God will *give* unto us, or *do* for us; our faith has no foundation, and our confidence is marred in asking what we most of all want. The will of God declared to us in the Scriptures should direct our views, govern our choice, and invigorate our wishes. Just apprehensions, and a firm belief of God's willingness to communicate, would make us judicious and prudent in our choice, and fervent in spirit in our supplications. We know not what to pray for as we ought; but, in condescension to our infirmities, we are favored with a full and interesting account of the most proper *materials* for this service in the oracles of God. Founding our desires here, we may ask in faith, without wavering; and are allowed to believe that we already have, in the conveyance of grace, what we ask in prayer.

3. Prayer includes *invocation* of God, whereby we make mention of his name, declare our desire and design to worship him, and desire his assistance and acceptance; *Adoration*, whereby we honor him, by mentioning, with humblest reverence, his nature, attributes, works, or relations to us; *Confession* of the meanness of our nature, the vileness of our sins, our desert of punishment, and our wants and sorrows of every kind; *Petitions*, to be delivered from *all evils* of a temporal, spiritual, or eternal kind;

---

² Witsius, *Exercitationes*, sect. 21.

and to be enriched with divine blessings; *Pleading* with God, for which we shall find an almost infinite source of heavenly arguments, drawn from the greatness of our wants, dangers, and sorrows; the perfections of God; his relations to men, and especially to his people; the various and particular promises of the covenant of grace; the honor of God in the world; former experiences of ourselves and others; and especially the name and mediation of our Lord Jesus Christ; *Self-dedication*, whereby we profess our relation to God; surrender ourselves to him, profess our humble and holy resolutions to be the Lord's forever, and renounce everything that is inconsistent herewith; *Thanksgiving*, whereby we acknowledge the bounty of that hand whence we receive our blessings, and ascribe honor and praise to the power, the wisdom, and the goodness of God upon that account; and *Blessing*, while we mention the attributes and glories of God, with inward joy, satisfaction, and pleasure; and wish the glories of God may forever continue, and rejoice at the assurance of it.[3]

4. The *name of Christ* is the only ground upon which we can hope to prevail with God in prayer; and to encourage us to pray in his name, he says, "Whatsoever ye shall ask the Father in my name, he may give it you" (John 15:16).

5. The duty of prayer is managed by the *help of the Spirit*. "Because ye are sons, God hath sent forth the Spirit of his Son into your hearts, *crying*, Abba, Father" (Gal. 4:6). He is, with the same breath, called the *Spirit of grace* and of *supplications* (Zech. 12:10). He enlightens the mind, affects the heart, and inspires the Christian in his prayer with reverence, humility, confidence, hope, and holy ardor—which are all the fruits of the Spirit of God, and constitute the *life* and *power* of prayer. If these are lacking, the best composed and the most elegant prayers, however often repeated, are an abomination to the Lord.

6. Prayer may be considered in various lights, according to the condition of the person, or persons, that pray. It is performed, either (1.) *In the heart only*, without using the voice; thus, while Hannah "continued praying before the LORD...she spake in her heart; only her lips moved" (1 Sam. 1:12–13); or (2.) With the assistance of the voice, to express in words what is conceived in the heart; hence Israel are called to take with them words, and turn unto the Lord; to say unto him, "Take away all iniquity,

---

[3] See all these heads judiciously illustrated and exemplified in Watts, *Guide to Prayer*.

and receive us graciously: so will we render [unto thee] the calves of our lips" (Hos. 14:2).

Prayer may likewise be considered as *ejaculatory*, which is the *sudden flight* of sorrow, desire, or joy, that rises and goes off in a moment; this requires but little time, and hinders no other work; it is both a great sign and means of our being spiritually-minded; and it ought to be our practice upon any emergency; when Nehemiah had the king of Persia's cup in his hand, he could steal a moment for the service of a greater King, by praying to the God of heaven (Neh. 2:1, 4); or as *stated*, in more solemn, continued acts of supplication, to be managed, either *solitarily*, in our closet, when the door is shut upon us (Matt. 6:6), or *socially* in *families*, that should call upon God (Josh. 24:15; Jer. 10:25); in *societies*, that meet to converse together about the things of God (Mal. 3:16 compared with Matt. 18:19–20); and in the *public meetings of worshipping assemblies*, that "call upon the name of Jesus Christ our Lord, both theirs and ours" (1 Cor. 1:2). The house of God should be an *house of prayer* (Isa. 56:7). The great multitude that were converted at Peter's sermon continued steadfastly in prayers (Acts 2:42).

To pray unto God on *ordinary occasions* should be an ordinary, regular, frequent exercise; and when *particular occasions* call for particular earnestness and importunity, we should abound accordingly. While Peter was kept in prison, "prayer was made without ceasing of the church unto God for him" (Acts 12:5).

As no time is unfit, so no place is improper for this honorable duty. There are indeed stated times of public and private devotion; but prayers that are made in *canonical hours*, or *consecrated places*, have no greater efficacy upon that account, because Christ is, *at all times*, our *omnipresent temple*.

2. The Obligations to Pray

I have already attempted to show *what* prayer is; and I am now, by God's help, to prove *that it is a duty*. The obligation of this service may be argued many ways, for it is dictated by the light of nature, commanded by God, performed through the Spirit, accepted in Christ, encouraged in the Scriptures, exemplified in the saints, availeth much to the people of God, and many particular directions are given concerning it.

1. Prayer is a duty that is dictated by the light of nature. The notions that we may form of God, by contemplating his eternal power and Godhead, which are clearly seen by the things that he hath made, declare it to be a most proper and reasonable service. Accordingly, there is, perhaps, no heathen nation under heaven, but what acknowledges a deity by prayer. At least, there is no nation where the being of God is believed, and prayer is wholly neglected. The same principles that teach men that they live, and move, and have their being in God do as much teach them to call upon their God, and to walk in his name (Jonah 1:6; Jer. 2:10–11).

2. This is the express, repeated command of God, that we pray "always with all prayer and supplication in the Spirit, and watching thereunto with all perseverance and supplication for all saints" (Eph. 6:18). There are but few commands more frequently and pressingly urged than this is. How direct and plain is the will of God, whose pleasure is unerringly just, whose authority is indispensably binding! "In every thing by prayer and supplication with thanksgiving let your requests be made known unto God" (Phil. 4:6). The command of the great God of heaven and earth is as weighty to bind the conscience in this case as in any other branch of duty where he has been pleased to interpose his authority.

3. This duty is acceptably performed *through the Spirit* of supplication, who helpeth the infirmities of his people; and therefore they are called to pray in the Holy Ghost (Jude 20). Now, if God has promised his Holy Spirit to teach us what to pray for, and how to pray, he surely expects we should pray to him. If a prince furnishes a subject for an embassy, provides his equipage, orders him guard and convoy, and besides, instructs him how to manage, is not this equal to a formal command? Encouragement given, and all necessary assistance and supply provided, in order to a business of importance, are a sufficient signification of the ruler's will, even though there be no direct precept issued out. But the case is still plainer, where these preparations accompany a sealed commission. The force of this argument is obvious; and therefore I add,

4. Prayer appears to be the duty of Christians, because their prayers are accepted in him. This argument is alike strong and comfortable:

> Seeing then that we have a great high priest, that is passed into the heavens, Jesus the Son of God…let us therefore come boldly unto

the throne of grace, that we may obtain mercy, and find grace to help in the time of need (Heb. 4:14, 16).

The same is further prosecuted, Hebrews 10:19–22, "Having boldness" or liberty,

> to enter into the holiest by the blood of Jesus, by a new and living way, which he hath consecrated for us, through the veil, that is to say, his flesh; and having an high priest over the house of God; let us draw near with a true heart, in full assurance of faith.

One important business he manages, in his glorified state, is to offer much incense with the prayers of all saints, upon the golden altar which is before the throne; where he forever appeareth in the presence of God, as our advocate and alone intercessor (Rev. 8:3; Heb. 7:25).

5. We have many encouragements to pray. We pray to the God that heareth prayer (Ps. 65:2); to our Father, who is in heaven (Matt. 6:9); to the Father of our Lord Jesus Christ (Eph. 3:14); to the Lord, whose eyes are over the righteous, and whose ears are open to their prayers (1 Peter 3:12); to him, that will make them joyful in his house of prayer (Isa. 56:7); in a word, to him who has said,

> Ask, and it shall be given you; seek, and ye shall find; knock, and it shall be opened unto you: for every one that asketh receiveth; and he that seeketh, findeth; and to him that knocketh it shall be opened (Matt. 7:7–8).

The varied expression looks like a tautology; but, instead of reckoning it a vain repetition, let us esteem it a blessed condescension wherein God, willing most abundantly to show unto the heirs of promise the certainty of that word on which he has caused them to hope, has spoken it again and again; that we may have strong consolation in full assurance of being accepted. This argument is the stronger, as there seems to be little difference between what a superior positively commands, and what he kindly encourages.

6. We are compassed about with a great cloud of witnesses, that made conscience of this duty. The generation of the righteous has always been

the generation of them that seek God's face (Ps. 24:6). Time would fail me to mention Moses and Aaron among his priests, and Samuel among them that call upon his name; they called upon the Lord, and he answered them (Ps. 99:6). Such approved examples of fervent prayer justify our zeal for this service, as they show how *uniformly* a praying temper and exercise become the children of God. Of each of them, we may truly say "Behold, he prayeth" (Acts 9:11).

7. "The effectual fervent prayer of a righteous man availeth much" (James 5:16). Such prayer has a wonderful power with God, and prevails, as Jacob's did, when he wrestled with the Angel, and obtained the blessing (Gen. 32:28).

The miraculous effects of prayer have been wonderful. In answer to it, the sun stood still upon Gibeon, and the moon in the valley of Ajalon (Josh. 10:12–13). Yea, the sun returned ten degrees, by which it was gone down upon the sundial of Ahaz (Isa. 38:8). When Elias prayed earnestly that it might not rain, it rained not on the earth, for three years and six months; and when he prayed again, the heaven gave rain, and the earth brought forth her fruit (James 5:17–18). In answer to their prayer, the Lord granted unto his servants that with all boldness they might speak his word; he stretched forth his hand to heal, and signs and wonders were done by the name of his holy Child Jesus (Acts 4:29–33).

The common and ordinary effects and advantages of prayer are glorious, and past reckoning. Let it be carefully remembered, however, that I only consider prayer as a means of divine appointment to put us in the joyful possession of promised blessings, which God gives as freely, as he promised them (Ezek. 36:37).

Now, by prayer, all our outward circumstances are made agreeable; what we have is hereby sanctified, and what we want is supplied; our fears are scattered, and our sorrows alleviated, our minds quieted, and our hearts fixed.

By prayer we receive mercy, and find grace to help us in the time of need. In answer to it, God speaks peace to the troubled soul, quickens it when languishing under spiritual decays, and supports it when assaulted with dangerous temptations. By this means, the faith of disciples is increased, their hope fixed, their love inflamed, and their patience perfected. Hereby they are filled with the fruits of righteousness, that are by Jesus Christ to the praise and glory of God; are made perfect, established, strengthened, and settled; filled at present with the consolations of God, which are not small; and prepared for those joys and rivers of pleasures, which are at God's right hand for evermore.

Are these the blessings that accompany or follow this duty? Then how strongly does our truest interest join all its persuasive energy with our manifold obligations, to give ourselves with assiduity and zeal to the daily practice of it! Be stirred up, ye slothful and indolent; and double your diligence, all ye that seek the Lord. Abound in this work; for your labor shall not be in vain in the Lord. In doing your bounden duty, there is a great and rich reward in hand: and in a short time, what has been asked without wavering in prayer will be acknowledged in endless, rapturous praise.

8. The many particular directions we find in Scripture concerning prayer, are a clear proof that it is a binding duty. I might refer to Matthew 6 and Luke 11 and 18, where our Savior is copious and particular on this head. I shall have occasion to mention some of them in their own place. The use I make of them now is to infer the obligation that lies on us *to pray unto God*, from his having given such particular instructions to direct us to pray in a right manner. And if this argument be not sufficient to satisfy men, reason is of little use, and there needs some new method of conviction.

That which now remains is to put the reader in mind that I have been offering arguments to *prove a duty*. If I had been upon a point merely speculative, I could wish no more than to leave him convinced of the truth of what I have asserted; but my labor is lost, if those who read be not seriously resolved, under a full conviction that prayer is a duty, to set upon the diligent and constant practice of it. Those that know their Master's will, and do it not, shall be beaten with many stripes (Luke 12:47).

3. Objections Obviated

The cavils raised against this duty will give occasion to make such answers as will set the importance and obligation of it in a clearer light. And if some of them should seem plausible, we shall, nevertheless, act very unbecoming either reasonable creatures, or Christians, if we suffer ourselves to be imposed on by them, against the much greater light and evidence we have to the contrary.

1. Do they tell us that prayer is a needless and superfluous thing, as an act of homage to God, who is essentially, independently blessed; and therefore cannot need the prayers of men, and will not regard them? I reply that

this difficulty is altogether imaginary; for while we assert the necessity of praying to him who *is exalted far above all blessing and praise*, we affirm that his happiness does not at all depend on the homage of his creatures; and yet it is certain, he may be injured by his creatures in his just rights. Does he charge the Jewish nation with *robbery*, for withholding tithes and offerings, which he claimed by a positive institution; and will he hold them guiltless who deny him his natural and unalienable rights of dependence and homage, that necessarily arise from the relations he and we stand in to each other (Mal. 3)? Though God does not sustain any real hurt by withholding his due, this is not owing to the nature and tendency of the sin, but to the infinite perfections of his nature; and consequently sinners are not the less criminal upon that account.

2. Do they allege that all our sins, sorrows, wants, and dangers are in the eye of divine Omniscience, and that God is self-moved in all his ways of mercy to the children of men, and therefore it is superfluous to pray to him? I answer that we readily own, and earnestly maintain, the truth of all that is affirmed in the objection, relating to the omniscience and mercy of God, but utterly refuse the inference drawn from it. The *design of prayer* is not to inform the blessed God, or to make him more compassionate than he is in his own nature; but to affect our souls with proper convictions of the *necessity* and *sovereignty* of *divine favor*. Though God be infinitely good, yet the exercises and communications of his goodness are entirely voluntary and free. He may appoint the way and order in which he will be pleased to bestow them, and we are bound readily and thankfully to comply with it; and if his appointments about it are most honorable to himself, and most beneficial to us, they are so far from lessening that they are a new instance of his grace. Prayer has been proved to be such an appointment, and therefore the objection is altogether groundless.

3. Do they say that it is enough for us to maintain *good tempers* and to have the heart full of good desires, but there is no occasion to offer them up to God because they are always under his eye? I must observe on this head that it is absurd to pronounce a temper *good* that does not continually exert itself in a dependence upon, and devotedness to God, by desire and expectation; and where such wishes and hopes are warm and vigorous, they will not bear always to be confined within our breasts, but will sometimes unavoidably break forth by our lips; for out of the abundance of the heart the mouth speaketh, either what is *good* or *bad* (Matt. 12:34).

4. Do they pretend that we need not pray, because Christ maketh intercession for us? I allow that he does. This is a most glorious and comfortable truth; but the design of his intercession is not to supersede prayer, but to encourage it, and make way for its acceptance and audience. As our Advocate in heaven, he offers up the prayers of all the saints (Rev. 8:3), a circumstance that abundantly shows that the intercession of Christ, and the prayers of the saints, are so far from excluding one another that they go together.

5. It is objected that it is a *bold, daring*, and *presumptuous* thing for guilty and polluted creatures to speak unto the Majesty of heaven and earth. I answer, It would be *bold presumption* in us, no doubt, to rush into the divine presence uncalled; or to expect that our prayers should deserve the blessings we pray for, or procure their own acceptance. But where is the presumption, where the criminal boldness, to accept a gracious invitation, to obey a divine command, and to come to the throne of grace at God's own call? This is our warrant; this makes our interest become our duty, and our disobedience, downright rebellion.

6. Some form an objection against praying from the unchangeableness of God. His nature and counsels are immutable; how then can prayer have any efficacy, say they, when God is of one mind, and none can turn him (Job 23:13)? He will accomplish his own purposes, whether men pray or not. I allow that God's nature and purposes are immutable and fixed; and it is as certain that the effectual fervent prayer of a righteous man availeth much (James 5:16). And I firmly believe that the immutability of the divine purpose, and the efficacy of prayer, are fully consistent.[4] I shall observe, moreover, that it is both foolish and wicked to argue from things dark and intricate against those that are plain and obvious. It is a sure sign of a depraved disposition to reject that which is clear and certain, because there are other things that are past comprehension. Whatever difficulties attend the doctrine of the divine decrees, prayer is a plain commanded duty, that carries its own evidence along with it. And it is a just and weighty saying that "secret things belong unto the LORD our God: but those things

---

[4] See this argument fully treated by President Edwards, in his very masterly way: Jonathan Edwards. *A Careful and Strict Enquiry into the Modern Prevailing Notions of That Freedom of Will*. The reader may likewise consult *A Defense of Some Important Doctrines of the Gospel in Twenty Six Sermons. Most of Which were Preached in Lime-Street*, vol. 1, pp. 220–232.

which are revealed belong unto us" (Deut. 29:29). Prayer is so far from being irreconcilable, that it is entirely subservient to the divine purposes,

> I know the thoughts that I think toward you, saith the LORD, thoughts of peace, and not of evil, to give you an expected end. *N.B.* Then shall ye call upon me, and ye shall go and pray unto me, and I will hearken unto you. And ye shall seek me, and find me, when ye shall search for me with all your heart (Jer. 29:11–13).

It is truly one of the most lamentable discoveries of a hardened heart, a seared conscience, and a reprobate mind, when sinners argue in this manner, "If God have any thoughts of kindness towards them, they will be *made to pray* one time or other." What do they mean by *God's making them to pray*? Do they imagine he will offer violence to their reason and will, and force them to pray? This is not his intention in dealing with men. And let them think, what plainer calls and commands, what greater encouragements to this duty can they desire, than what they have already? To neglect it under such invitations, promises, and motives, and yet say, they expect that God should *make them pray*, is to talk *absurdities* and *contradictions.* These prayerless, presumptuous sinners are in the utmost danger of dying in their sins, and of perishing forever, and their damnation will be just and sudden.

7. Because the prayer of the wicked is an abomination to the Lord (Prov. 15:8; 28:9) some have inferred that no obligation lies upon them to perform this duty; in regard it would be provoking to God, and unprofitable to themselves, to pray before him.

To this I reply that the design of such expressions cannot be to discourage sinners from praying; for who was more vile than Simon the sorcerer, who was "in the gall of bitterness, and in the bond of iniquity" (Acts 8:23), and whose "heart is not right in the sight of God" (v. 21)? And yet the apostle calls upon him to repent of his wickedness, "and pray God, if perhaps the thought of thine heart might be forgiven thee" (v. 22). The same thing is taught us, in that singularly beautiful and encouraging passage,

> Seek ye the LORD while he may be found, call ye upon him while he is near: let the wicked forsake his way, and the unrighteous man his thoughts; and let him return unto the LORD, and he will have

mercy upon him; and to our God, for he will abundantly pardon (Isa. 55:6–7).

Now, since it is so clearly the duty, even of the wicked and ungodly, to pray unto the Lord, they ought not to sin in forbearing to do it. Their prayer is abomination before God, when they ask in hypocrisy, or when they ask amiss, that they may consume his bounty upon their lusts; but their plowing and worldly occupations are a sin, and managed to the dishonor of God, as well as their religious duties (Prov. 21:4; Ps. 10:5).

8. Some excuse themselves for the omission of prayer, because, they say, they cannot do it. This excuse is of a very criminal nature, after all the advantages we have to assist us in this duty. We have a copious variety of matter in the Holy Scriptures, which we should carefully study, as the most useful directory. We have some profitable helps to enable us to perform this service with more readiness and comfort.[5] After all, I believe, we should think it a poor excuse for a beggar, suffering himself to perish for hunger, because he could not with elegance and advantage describe his condition, and paint his misery. Should we not very naturally, and, I think, very reasonably, suppose that real indigence would supply the lack of eloquence, and should awaken him to diligence in imploring necessary relief? And shall men altogether neglect, shall they not rather cultivate, a frequent converse by prayer with that God that knoweth the secret desires of the heart, and regardeth groanings that cannot be uttered (Rom. 8:26–27)?

9. Some fancy, they are not bound to pray, except when they are moved and inclined thereunto by the Holy Ghost, who is sovereign in his grace, like the wind that bloweth where it listeth. I shall only answer in the words of Solomon,

> He that observeth the wind shall not sow; and he that regardeth the clouds shall not reap. As thou knowest not what is the way of the spirit, nor how the bones do grow in the womb of her that is with child: even so thou knowest not the works of God who maketh all. In the morning sow thy seed, and in the evening withhold not thine

---

[5] See Matthew Henry. *Method for Prayer*, a book done in the true spirit of scriptural devotion, that might be exceeding useful, if it was known, and improved according to its worth.

hand: for thou knowest not whether shall prosper, either this or that, or whether they both shall be alike good (Eccl. 11:4–6).

These are the only objections that have any appearance of weight, that I have met with. Their plea who pretend want of time and leisure for this duty, is too shameful and trifling to deserve an answer. It discovers more of a wicked heart than anything else. The Scripture addresses the reason and conscience of such profane despisers of God, with many weighty and awful considerations. I shall only say that it does not become those to speak or act in this manner, who believe a God and a providence, who know the need they stand in of his daily direction and conduct, protection and supply, and that the success of all their undertakings, together with their happiness in time and eternity, depends upon his blessing and favor. We have undoubtedly more to do with God than with the whole world. Have we time to eat, drink, and sleep in; time for our worldly business, diversions, and recreations; time for needless visits, and unprofitable conversations with our fellow-creatures; and have we—O for shame!—have we *time* for *everything*, but *prayer?* God allows us sufficient time for every duty if we are careful and skillful duly to proportion it. And, they know nothing of the nature and advantage of prayer, who think their time employed in it is lost; or that they could spend it any other way to better advantage. This part of "godliness is profitable unto all things, having promise of the life that now is, and of that which is to come" (1 Tim. 4:8).

4. Questions Concerning It

Having explained the nature, stated the obligations, and answered objections, relative to the duty of prayer, I shall now resolve a few questions about it, with a view to clear up still further the nature of this ordinance of God.

I. The first thing to be examined is, Who warrantably *may*, and who in duty *should pray* unto God? I put the question into this form because the warrant and the obligation of the duty are of the same extent, so that wherever we find the one, we may infer the other.

The answer is plain with regard to the saints, "Every one that is godly" (Ps. 32:6), shall pray unto the Lord. And as all manner of persons have need, so they are allowed to do it. We have seen the warrant and duty of wicked men already cleared up, from Acts 8:21–23 and Isaiah 55:6–7.

It is true, the Lord saith unto the wicked, "What hast thou to do to declare my statutes, or that thou shouldst take my covenant in thy mouth? Seeing thou hatest instruction, and castest my words behind thee" (Ps. 50:16–17). But though this demonstrates the inconsistency between a carnal man's profession and practice, and aggravates his sin and condemnation for breaking through every sacred obligation of light and duty, it cannot mean that there is no obligation upon him to call upon God. It only shows the absurdity of living in such sins as are mentioned, while the sinner makes a strict and high profession to the contrary. The scope of the passage shows it is designed only for conviction, reproof, and correction.

Let the poor pray, for to them God will look. Let the rich and the great pray unto the Lord, that is higher than the highest. Let the afflicted pray, that they may not perish in their troubles. Let the prosperous pray, that they may not be destroyed by their very prosperity. Let the idle pray, because they have leisure. Let the busy pray, to hallow their employments. Let the learned pray, that they may see the wonders that are in God's law. Let the ignorant pray, that they may be taught saving wisdom. Let the aged pray much, because they have but a short time to remain here. Let the dying pray as they are going out of this world, that they may enter praising into the next. Let children in their youth remember their Creator. Let the weak and feeble pray for power from on high. Let the strong and vigorous not be slothful in the work of the Lord, but do it with all their might. Let infirm Christians pray to be healed; the fallen to be recovered; the doubtful and wavering to have their faith increased; and let the faithful and established pray, that they may be thankful to God, and helpful to men, and go on to abound in the work of the Lord. Let sinners pray, if perhaps the thoughts of their hearts may be forgiven them. Let backsliders take with them words, and say in prayer, "Take away all iniquity, and receive us graciously."

II. Another question that deserves some attention is, For whom should we pray? To which I answer in the words of the apostle,

> I exhort therefore, that first of all, supplications, prayers, intercessions, and giving of thanks, be made for all men; for kings, and for all that are in authority; that we may lead a quiet and peaceable life in all godliness and honesty. For this is good and acceptable in the sight of God our Savior (1 Tim. 2:1–3).

Our prayers should extend to all men, to men of all sorts, and of all ranks and degrees, whether in higher or lower stations. And in particular, we ought to offer up to God, through Christ, supplications and prayers,

1. For the whole church of Christ upon earth. "praying always with all prayer and supplication in the Spirit, and watching thereunto with all perseverance, and supplication for all saints" (Eph. 6:18).

2. For civil magistrates, that are placed over us, as the ministers of God, as well as the ordinance of men. The apostle enjoins and presses this duty upon Christians (1 Tim. 2:1–3).

3. For ministers of the gospel, that God would open to them a door of utterance, to speak the mysteries of Christ, as they ought to speak them (Col. 4:3–4).

4. For ourselves. This, I believe, none ever was so absurd as to deny, how much soever many live in the neglect of the duty.

5. For our brethren, as well as for ourselves. The royal law is, "Thou shalt love," and consequently wish well to, "thy neighbor, as thyself." And the command is express and plain, "Confess your faults one to another, and pray one for another, that ye may be healed" (James 5:16).

6. For our enemies; for so hath Christ commanded, "Love your enemies, bless them that curse you, do good to them that hate you, and pray for them which despitefully use you" (Matt. 5:44). And since we are to pray even for our enemies and persecutors, surely our intercessions should be made for all sorts of men living on earth, whether Jews or Gentiles, pagans or Christians, sinners or saints, high or low, or of whatever character they be.

7. We are not only to pray for all sorts of men now living; but likewise for those that may live hereafter. In this respect we should earnestly desire that the interest of Christ may be propagated from generation to generation; and his kingdom and glory advanced in the world till his second coming. No less is implied in that petition, "Thy kingdom come" (Matt. 6:10).

These things are so evident, that I suppose they will be generally allowed, without any further proof. But there are two things on this question, that must be a little more particularly opened; to wit, praying for the dead, and praying for them that are known to have sinned the sin unto death.

5. PRAYER

First, I shall, in the first place, consider the case of praying for the *dead*. This practice, it must be confessed, obtained very early in the Christian church.[6] But, unless we can find its authority in the word of God, we must forbear it, upon principle, lest we fall under the deserved condemnation of those that add to his words, and incur his awful reproofs (Prov. 30:6). It must be remembered, however, that the doctrine of purgatory, to which the church of Rome has joined this practice, was not known in the world till the seventh century, when the Antichristian beast was visibly characterized as the mystery of iniquity. Then the office of praying for the dead was established by a law, on the supposition of a middle state they called *purgatory*.

> We are not indeed to pray for the dead, whose parts are done, and their final condition already determined. And it is equally idle and impertinent to pray for that which *already is*, and that which *never shall be*: that is, the bliss of those that are *blessed*; or, the salvation of those that are *lost*. Yet, O! how many senseless masses are poured out upon this account, and spilled in the air (only that the loss is not great, unless the stuff were more precious), by that church which seems to have a great deal of leisure, and little to do, to bestow so much time, in seeking to reverse what God hath already concluded. But though the *dead* can receive no manner of advantage from it; yet, like some other points of Popery, it is too gainful to the living, easily to part with it. The friends' *departed* souls can have no *feeling* out of it, but the priests' *living* bodies *feel* the comfort. And where the *pay* is so good, they are not aggrieved to spend so much breath in those kinds of prayers, that return in such *golden showers*, into their own bosoms. And so it is indeed, *N.B.*, a praying *for themselves*, though called praying for *others*.[7]

It may fully satisfy us on this point to observe that the Scripture affirms the state of the dead to be unalterable. "It is appointed unto men once to

---

[6] See Ridgley, *A Body of Divinity*, volume 2, p. 473. See Suiceri, *Thesaurus Ecclesiasticus*, on ταφη.

[7] Benjamin Jenks. *The Liberty of Prayer Asserted, and Guarded from Licentiousness*, pp. 114, 115.

die, but after this the judgment" (Heb. 9:27). Abraham said to the rich man, both of them being in the state of the dead:

> Son, remember that thou in thy lifetime receivedst thy good things, and likewise Lazarus evil things: but now he is comforted, and thou art tormented. And beside all this, between us and you there is a great gulf fixed: so that they which would pass from hence to you cannot; neither can they pass to us, that would come from thence (Luke 16:25–26).

When the servants of David said unto him, "What thing is this that thou hast done? thou didst fast and weep for the child while it was alive; but when the child was dead, thou didst rise and eat bread" he replied, "While the child was yet alive, I fasted and wept: for I said, Who can tell whether GOD will be gracious to me, that the child may live? But now he is dead, wherefore should I fast? can I bring him back again? I shall go to him, but he shall not return to me" (2 Sam. 12:21–23).

Now, if the state of the dead is unalterably fixed immediately after death, what end can be answered by praying for them? The righteous dead will not be more happy till the resurrection, nor the wicked dead less miserable forever; and therefore to pray for either the one or the other is as unnecessary as it is unwarrantable.

Secondly, I shall consider, in the next place, the praying for them that are known to have sinned the sin unto death. The rule on this head is express and plain,

> If any man see his brother sin a sin which is not unto death, he shall ask, and he shall give him life for them that sin not unto death. There is a sin unto death: I do not say that he shall pray for it (1 John 5:16).

This sin unto death is the same that our Lord calls the sin against the Holy Ghost, and says it is a species of blasphemy that shall not be forgiven, neither in this world, nor in the world that is to come (Matt. 12:31–32). It seems to consist in a malicious speaking against the clearest evidence of the miraculous operations and illuminations of the Holy Spirit, testifying unto us the will of God in the Scriptures, as if he were an evil spirit, and not the true and Holy Spirit of the living God. We should be very cautious how we impute this sin unto any individual; and it is certain, nothing less will warrant us to do so than a willful, utter apostasy from the truth, joined with a malicious reviling and contempt of what is most sacred, after it has been known and allowed to be so.

Serious souls have been frequently much distressed with the fears of having committed this unpardonable sin, because they do not attend to what the Scripture says about it. Those that have committed it are determined enemies to the cross of Christ; rejoice in iniquity; cannot be renewed to repentance for their sin; reject the word of God with a hellish delight; and hate the people of God in the same proportion as they see anything divine about them. But it is a sure sign a person has not been guilty of this sin, if he is afraid that he has committed it; if he has the least concern about his unbelief; if he has any desire of salvation through Christ; or, if he is content to be a debtor to the riches of his grace.

This sin being unpardonable according to the appointed method of saving sinners is not the spot of any of God's chosen; and therefore we are not to pray for the pardon of it, because, in doing so, we would seek God's face in vain, and could not pray in faith.

III. A third question to be resolved is, How doth the Spirit help us to pray? That he really doth assist the people of God in this duty is certain; for he is the Spirit of grace and supplication; and they pray in the Holy Ghost (Zech. 12:10; Jude 20). And, in answer to the question, I observe that we not knowing what to pray for as we ought, the Spirit helpeth our infirmities, by enabling us to understand both for whom, what, and how prayer is to be made, and by working and quickening in our hearts (although not in all persons, nor at all times, in the same measure) those apprehensions, affections, and graces, which are requisite for the right performance of this duty. There are especially these heads that are worthy of our notice here.

1. The Holy Spirit instructs the soul into the nature of its manifold wants, dangers, and provocations; as well as to discern the sufficient, suitable, and excellent provisions of the gospel. He searcheth all things, even the deep things of God; and he teacheth his people all things that are profitable for them to know, that they may not ask amiss.

2. He inclines their will to this duty, helping them against that aversion and backwardness which are so deeply rooted in their depraved nature.

He works in them both to will and to do of his good pleasure. "Where the Spirit of the Lord is, there is liberty" (2 Cor. 3:17). To will is present with such persons.

3. He powerfully encourages his people in prayer. The aggravations of their sin, the unworthiness of their persons, and the ignorance of their minds, are too great discouragements to be conquered, and discouragements that mar all confidence in prayer, unless the divine Comforter seasonably interpose, and manifest the blood of sprinkling, and the method, the freeness, and the fullness of pardoning mercy, together with the office of the prevailing Intercessor, that constantly appears in the presence of God for them.

4. He makes intercession in them, with groanings that cannot be uttered (Rom. 8:26–27). He is given to them as the Spirit of adoption, whereby they cry, Abba, Father. He indites their prayers for them, by his gracious suggestions to them, and excites and enables them to offer them up with such vehement pantings and breathings of soul, in an admirable mixture of patience and faith, importunity and hope, for all promised blessings, as exceed the power of language to express, and as sometimes melt, and sweetly overwhelm their souls, to such a degree that they cannot tell how to form them into suitable words. Prayer is so much the fruit of the Spirit, where men pray believingly, that it is not more properly they that speak than the Spirit of their Father that speaketh in them, as our Lord said in another case (Matt. 10:20). He is the Spirit of wisdom and revelation in the knowledge of the God of our Lord Jesus Christ, the Father of glory, who is the object of our prayer (Eph. 1:17). He testifies of Christ, through whom we have access to the Father (John 16:14, 24). He opens the understanding to see the truth and sublime excellency of heavenly things, and opens the heart to embrace and desire them (1 Cor. 2:9–16). Thus he opens the mouth wide to pray for promised mercies, and fills it abundantly (Ps. 81:10). He distributes the gift of praying, and he is the author of all these gracious dispositions, whereby the heart is suitably impressed in this exercise.

IV. Again it may be asked, What is it to pray in the name of Christ? This question is the more worthy of our consideration, because we are to bow our knees in this name, whenever we pray unto God. Now to pray in this name does not consist barely in making mention of it, which is too often done ignorantly, presumptuously, and inconsiderately, by those that profess to worship God by him; but this especially consists in our making a right use of what Christ has done and suffered for us, as the foundation of our hope, that God will be pleased to grant us what he has purchased thereby, which contains the sum of all that we can desire, when drawing nigh to him in prayer. Particularly, *to pray in the name of our Lord Jesus Christ*, implies that we perform this service:

1. In obedience to his command, who has said, "Ask, and ye shall receive" (John 16:24).

2. In the confidence of his encouraging promises, "If ye shall ask any thing in my name, I will do it" (John 14:13–14). He repeats the assurance in these verses, that our joy may be full.

3. By drawing all our encouragement to pray from him alone, as our great High Priest, that hath opened for us a new and living way into the holiest of all by his own blood (Heb. 10:19–22).

4. By founding all our hope of being accepted with God in prayer, upon the mediation and merits of Christ alone (Heb. 4:14–16).

5. By praying in a firm dependence on the grace of our Lord Jesus Christ to be made sufficient for us, and of his strength to be made perfect in our weakness (2 Cor. 12:9). And,

6. By resting the success of our prayers unto God entirely on the mediation of his Son Jesus Christ, as an immoveable rock of strong confidence; and quietly possessing our minds in patience and hope, waiting for an answer of peace: "And this is the confidence that we have in him, that if we ask any thing according to his will, he heareth us: and if we know that he hear us, whatsoever we ask, we know that we have the petitions that we desired of him" (1 John 5:14–15).

We are to pray in the name of Christ, and in no other name but his only, partly because our sinfulness and alienation from God are so great, that we can have no access into his presence, without a Mediator (Isa. 59:2); and partly because there is none in heaven or earth appointed to, or fit for, that glorious work of introducing us into God's favor and presence, but Christ alone; for "there is one," and but one "mediator between God and men, the man Christ Jesus" (1 Tim. 2:5). He is "the way, the truth, and the life: no man cometh unto the Father but by me" (John 14:6).

I shall only add that no peculiar reverence is due to the name *Jesus* in prayer, or any other duty, more than to the rest of the names by which that adorable person is made known to us in the Holy Scriptures. The margin of our Bibles furnishes us with a just translation, and a noble sense of that text, that *in* "the name of Jesus every knee should bow," *etc.* (Phil. 2:10); not when the *word* is named but in his name as the alone and appointed Mediator between God and men.

V. I shall, in the next place, inquire, Whether it is proper to use *stated forms* of prayer, when we call upon God?

It is generally allowed, that if set forms are sound, or agreeable to the will of God, they may be used by children, or such as are weak in knowledge. All are agreed in commending the prudence of our first reformers in England, who, by composing homilies and forms of prayer, endeavored, as much as might be, to provide a help for the doleful ignorance of the clergy. But it is humbly submitted to the impartial consideration of the intelligent and serious, whether the advantages of praying freely, without being tied to a form, are not manifest and great? A perpetual confinement to the best forms will be attended with such inconveniences as these:[8]

1. It much hinders the free exercise of our own thoughts and desires, which is the chief work and business of prayer, to wit, to express our desires unto God; and whereas our thoughts and affections should direct our words, a set form of words directs our thoughts and affections; and while we bind ourselves to these words only, we damp our inward devotion, and prevent the holy fire from kindling within us; we discourage our active powers and passions from running out on divine subjects, and check the breathings of our souls heavenward. There are secret joys, and unknown bitternesses, which the holy soul longs to spread before God, and for which it cannot find any exact and correspondent expressions in the best of prayer-books; now, must a Christian suppress all those thoughts, and forbid himself all that sweet conversation with his God, because it is not written down in the appointed form?

2. The thoughts and affections of the heart that are truly devout are wrought by the Spirit of God; and if we deny them utterance, because they are not found in prayer-books, do we not run the danger of resisting the Holy Ghost, quenching the Holy Spirit, and fighting against the kind designs of God towards us? A sin which we are expressly cautioned against, "Quench not the Spirit" (1 Thess. 5:19), and which a humble Christian trembles to think of.

---

[8] See Watts, *Guide to Prayer*, chap. 2, sect. 2.

3. A confinement to forms cramps and imprisons those powers that God hath given us for improvement and use. It silences our natural abilities, and forbids them to act; and it puts a bar upon our spiritual faculties, and prevents their growth. To satisfy ourselves with mere forms, to confine ourselves wholly to them, and neglect to stir up and improve our own gifts, is one kind of spiritual sloth, and highly to be disapproved. It is hiding a talent in the earth, which God hath given on purpose to carry on a trade with heaven. It is an abuse of our knowledge of divine things, to neglect the use of it in our converse with God. It is as if a man that had once used crutches to support him when he was feeble, would always use them; or, because he has sometimes found his own thoughts happily expressed in conversation by another person, therefore he will assent to what that other person shall always speak, and never speak his own thoughts himself again.

4. It leads us into the danger of hypocrisy, and mere lip-service. Sometimes we shall be tempted to express those things which are not the thoughts of our own souls, and so use words that are not suited to our present wants, or sorrows, or requests, because those words are put together and made ready beforehand.

5. The confinement of ourselves to a form, though it is not always attended with formality and indifference, yet it is very apt to make our spirits cold and flat, formal and indifferent in our devotion. The frequent repetition of the same words doth not always awaken the same affections in our hearts which perhaps they were well suited to do when we first heard or made use of them. When we continually use one constant road of sentences, or track of expressions, they become like an old beaten path in which we daily travel, and we are ready to walk on without particular notice of the several parts of the way; so in our daily repetition of a form, we are apt to neglect due attention to the full sense of the words. But there is certainly something more suited to awaken the attention of them in a conceived prayer, when a Christian is making his own way toward God, according to the present inclination of his soul, and urgency of his present wants.

6. The duty of prayer is very useful to discover to us the frame of our own spirits, but a constant use of forms will much hinder our knowledge of ourselves, and prevent our acquaintance with our own hearts, which is one great means of maintaining religion in the power of it. Daily observation of our own spirits would teach us what our wants are, and how

to frame our prayers before God; but if we confine ourselves to the same words always, our own observation of our hearts will be of little use, since we must speak the same expressions, let our hearts be how they will.

7. The confinement of ourselves to a form in prayer renders our converse with God very imperfect; for it is not possible that forms of prayer should be composed, that are perfectly suited to all our frames of spirit, and fitted to all our occasions in the things of this life, and the life to come. Our circumstances are always altering in this frail and mutable state. We have daily new sins to be confessed, new temptations and sorrows to be represented, new wants to be supplied. Every change of providence in the affairs of a nation, a family, or a person, requires suitable petitions and acknowledgments. And all these can never be provided for in any prescribed composition. I confess all our concerns of soul and body may be included in some large and general words of a form, which is no more suited to one time, or place, or condition, than to another; but generals are cold, and do not affect us, nor affect persons that join with us, and whose case he that speaks in prayer should particularly represent before God. It is much sweeter to our own souls, and to our fellow-worshipers, to have our fears, and doubts, and complaints, and temptations, and sorrows, and mercies, represented in such language as the soul itself feels when the words are spoken. Now, though we should often meet with prayers pre-composed, that are fitted to express our present case, yet the gift of prayer is as much better than any form, as a perfect knowledge in the art of physic is better than any number of receipts. That man that deals only in receipts shall never become a skillful physician; nor can the gift of prayer be attained by confinement to forms.

That our blessed Lord taught his disciples to pray, by giving them a general directory, is allowed; but that he ever tied them up to a form in praying cannot be proved. When he gave them a direction to pray, he said, "After this manner therefore pray ye," *etc.* (Matt. 6:9); and again, "When ye pray, say, "Our Father which art in heaven," *etc.* (Luke 11:2). It is probable enough our Lord gave these directions at different times, though the substance of them is the same. But the alteration of the words is enough to satisfy any unprejudiced mind, that he could not intend them to be used as a *stated form*. And the church of England has thought fit to differ in the words of the fifth petition from both. It is pretty clear, that the phrases *when ye pray, say* (Luke 11:2), and *after this manner pray ye* (Matt. 6:9), are precisely of the same import, and explain one another; and neither of them import that the very words which our Lord then expressed were to be constantly used, but only that the scope of them should direct us in performing this duty,

> Because the prayer which Christ taught his disciples is not only a pattern of prayer, but itself a most comprehensive prayer, we recommend it also to be used in the prayers of the church.[9]

The questions about *places* and *times* of praying do not require any particular discussion. It is as manifest that places and times are *general* and *undetermined now*; as, that they were *particularly appointed under the Old Testament*, when men were to pray *in* or *towards the temple* (1 Kings 8) and observed their *hours of prayer* (Acts 3:1). But, says the apostle, "I will therefore that men pray *every where*" (1 Tim. 2:8), and "Pray *without ceasing*" (1 Thess. 5:17). Christ, in distinction from the temple at Jerusalem, which was a figure of him that was to come, is our *omnipresent temple*; and every time is now alike holy.

5. Rules for the Discharge of It

All that remains on this subject is to give some *practical directions* about the right performance of it. I shall reduce them to the following order.

1. Premeditate what you are to pray about, before you engage in the duty. Do not rush into the divine presence, like the horse into the battle, without consideration. We have a necessary caution on this head, "Be not rash with thy mouth, and let not thine heart be hasty to utter any thing before God: for God is in heaven, and thou upon earth" (Eccl. 5:2). Ponder the occasion of prayer; digest the matter of it; affect your hearts with the awful importance of that great and dreadful name, *The Lord our God*; lay to heart your sins, wants, sorrows, unworthiness, and the marvelous riches and suitableness of the manifold grace of God, as it is manifested in our Lord Jesus Christ; and labor to feel what you are to speak. Order your speech before God by deliberate meditation, which will be attended with a double advantage, as it will contribute both to *cheerfulness* and *fervency in spirit*.

---

[9] "Of Prayer after Sermon". In *Westminster Directory for the Publick Worship of God*.

2. Pray with the spirit, "I will pray with the spirit" (1 Cor. 14:15). Whatever else may be included in that expression, it must imply that he worshipped God in the spirit, with his whole soul, in the exercise of spiritual graces, under the light and influence of the Holy Ghost, according to gospel-institution, and our blessed Lord's own direction, "the true worshipers shall worship the Father in spirit and in truth: for the Father seeketh such to worship him. God is a Spirit: and they that worship him must worship him in spirit and in truth" (John 4:23–24). Let us never forget that we have to do with the Father of spirits, who has an indisputable title to be served with our spirits, which he has made. Let us not grieve that Holy Spirit of God, whereby his people are sealed unto the day of redemption, by a piece of mere bodily service. Despise not the blood of the covenant, wherewith the people of God are bought and sprinkled, that they may glorify him in their *spirits*, as well as in their bodies, for both are his (1 Cor. 6:19–20).

3. Pray with the understanding (1 Cor. 14:15). There is the same reason for praying, as for singing praise, with understanding (Ps. 47:7). Let mystery, Babylon, that mother of abominations, say what she will in behalf of implicit faith and ignorant devotion; but let us always remember that the God of our Lord Jesus Christ, the Father of glory, must give us the Spirit of wisdom and revelation, to the right acknowledgment of himself in every duty of religious worship (Eph. 1:17). All riches of the full assurance of understanding, to see our ruined state by nature, the exceeding sinfulness of sin, our total inability to do what is spiritually good, the impurity of our hearts, the iniquity of our lives, the imperfection of our obedience, our absolute, universal need of Christ, and the rich aboundings of divine mercy streaming through the Mediator's person—would greatly contribute to our acknowledging of the mystery of God, even of the Father and of Christ, upon just apprehensions of which all prayer in the Holy Ghost is managed (Col. 2:2). Study to know what you worship (John 4:22); why you worship him (Ps. 32:6); and how you do it (Ps. 141:2–3).

4. Draw near God in prayer with a true heart (Heb. 10:22). A deceitful heart and feigned lips are abomination in the sight of that God who trieth the reins of the children of men. How can you look your Father in the face, whilst you are cherishing his enemy, the declared object of his indignation, in your hearts? Must you again be put in mind, that if you regard iniquity

in your heart, the Lord will not hear you? (Ps. 66:18); or, if your heart turn back from him, if it be not right with him, shall not God search this out (Ps. 44:18–22)? Approve yourselves *true men*, and not hypocritical dissemblers in this matter. You have to deal with the true God, who made the eye, and shall he not see? He is delighted with truth in the hidden part; and he is a jealous God, that will not be mocked. Is jealousy the rage of a man? and what less can it be than the fury of God, that is jealous; of the Lord that revengeth, and is furious; of the Lord that will take vengeance on his adversaries, and reserveth wrath for his enemies; of the Lord that is slow to anger, and great in power, and will not at all acquit the wicked; of the Lord that hath his way in the whirlwind, and in the storm, and the clouds are the dust of his feet (Nah. 1:2–3)? Draw near, therefore, with true hearts; for, otherwise you cannot escape his indignation, nor the fierceness of his anger, which will be poured out like fire.

5. Abide in Christ, and let his words abide in you, and ask what ye will, and it shall be done unto you (John 15:7). If you steadfastly cleave to Christ, and if he dwell in your hearts by faith, and by means of his word, as a principle that guides and governs, quickens and establishes you; whatsoever ye, as thus abiding in him, and depending on him, shall ask according to his will, for your own edification and fruitfulness, ye shall receive it even to the utmost of your desires and wants. "Whatsoever ye shall ask in prayer, believing, ye shall receive" (Matt. 21:22).

6. Ask in faith, without wavering: for he that wavereth is like a wave of the sea, driven of the wind, and tossed; for let not that man think that he shall receive anything of the Lord (James 1:6–7). If you would succeed in your suits to heaven, you must present them with a firm dependence on Christ, and on the wisdom, power, and faithfulness of his God, to perform his promises, without staggering at them through unbelief. He that gives way to distrusts, questionings, and sinful jealousies, whether God can or will perform his gracious promises, is as unstable as a wave of the sea, which sometimes swells upwards, and then sinks downwards, and is driven one way and another, backwards and forwards, in a tumultuous manner, by a stormy wind. Such persons flatter themselves with false hopes indeed, if they expect an answer to such requests, which dishonor, instead of glorifying God.

7. Pray with unaffected humility: for the Lord heareth the desire of the humble; he will prepare their heart, and will cause his ear to hear (Ps. 10:17).

Humble yourselves in the sight of God, who resisteth the proud, but giveth grace to the humble (James 4:6). God has said, "To this man will I look, even to him that is poor and of a contrite spirit, and trembleth at my word" (Isa. 66:2). God knoweth how to abase them that are high; but he will beautify the meek with his salvation. The proud Pharisee who insulted heaven with his impertinent, vainglorious boasting, while he pretended to pray, went away condemned; but the poor publican, who durst not come near, but stood afar off, and smote upon his breast, crying, God be propitious to me a sinner, went away justified (Luke 18:9–14). It is the will of God that no flesh should glory in his presence, either in asking, or receiving, or enjoying his favor, but that he that glorieth should glory in the Lord (1 Cor. 1:26–31).

8. Come boldly to the throne of grace by prayer, that you may receive mercy, and find grace to help you in the time of need (Heb. 4:16). This is entirely consistent with that humility I have been recommending. Open your case before God without slavish fear; for the covenant of promise gives you the best warrant to do so. The promises of it are exceedingly great, very precious, absolutely free, and inviolably sure. Never allow yourselves to forget that God is on a throne of grace, which emboldens a cheerful freedom of access to him, with holy liberty, and humble confidence in him, as the Father of mercies, and the God of salvation.

9. Be fervent in spirit, and humbly importunate, when you serve the Lord in this duty (Rom. 12:11). To encourage this fervor, our Lord spake a parable (Luke 18:1–8). When Bartimaeus heard of Jesus passing by, he began to cry out, and say, "Jesus, thou son of David, have mercy on me," and when they charged him that he should hold his peace, he cried the more a great deal, "Thou son of David, have mercy on me" (Mark 10:47–48). Moses was so importunate with God that he says to him, "Let me alone" (Ex. 32:10); and again, "Let it suffice thee; speak no more unto me of this matter" (Deut. 3:26). As if God entreated Moses to cease his importunity, it went so much against his heart to deny him. The woman of Canaan fetches an argument out of his greatest discouragements, and at last overcomes Christ with her importunity (Matt. 15:22–28). And Jacob, when he wrestled with the Angel, prayed and made supplication, saying, "I will not let thee go, except thou bless me" (Gen. 32:26).

This importunity may warrantably rise to humble peremptoriness in all things, spiritual and temporal, that have a necessary connection with our happiness; but in all temporary things, we should pray with an entire submission to the will of God, as he shall see them just or fitting for us.

10. Watch unto prayer with all perseverance (Eph. 6:18). Be assiduously careful to maintain a praying frame of spirit, and to watch for all convenient seasons for prayer, and eagerly to catch the present moment; watch against the designs of your adversaries, and for all opportunities and assistances to defeat their attempts; continue in prayer, without being weary in well-doing, and without fainting, though ye may not receive immediate answers of peace. Among many examples of this, there is none more striking than the exercise of the psalmist who cried to the Lord out of the depths, because he knew there was forgiveness with him that he might be feared; and then he adds,

> I wait for the LORD, my soul doth wait, and in his word do I hope. My soul waiteth for the Lord more than they that watch for the morning…Let Israel hope in the LORD: for with the LORD there is mercy, and with him is plenteous redemption. And he shall redeem Israel from all his iniquities (Ps. 130:5–8).

Our direction for this way of watching with perseverance unto prayer is express and plain, "Wait on the LORD: be of good courage, and he shall strengthen thine heart: wait, I say, on the LORD" (Ps. 27:14). This is also implied in that general command, to pray without ceasing (1 Thess. 5:17). *To pray always*, and *to pray without ceasing*, is to be *frequent, constant*, and *persevering*, in the duty of *prayer*; and not according to the strict sense of the words, to be continually engaged in prayer, which is impossible to human nature, and incompatible with the necessary discharge of the duties of our station. But it is to pray at all the regular and appointed times of prayer, *day* and *night*, whether in the closet, the family, or the temple. It is to pray all the days of our life, even to the end. It is to pray in and for everything; a Christian should neither begin nor end any undertaking without prayer. It is to pray constantly, never omitting or growing weary of the duty, as unavailing and ineffectual. And it is to have the heart always turned in desire to God, in an aptitude or fitness to pray, in a holy spiritual frame.

11. When you have been in prayer, look up for an answer of peace. "I will hear," says David, "what God the LORD will speak: for he will speak peace unto his people, and to his saints" (Ps. 85:8). And the prophet expresses

himself in these words, "I will look unto the LORD; I will wait for the God of my salvation: my God will hear me" (Mic. 7:7). This was the exercise of the man after God's own heart: "In the morning," says he, "will I direct my prayer unto thee, and will look up" (Ps. 5:3). This is both most reasonable, and altogether necessary, that if he grant what we ask, we may be thankful; if he deny, we may be patient; if he defer, we may continue to wait and pray, and may not faint. We should look up, as those that long to speed in their errand; we should look out, like a watchman on his tower, to see what tidings are brought us; or, as he that has shot an arrow looks to see how near it has come to the mark. We lose much of the comfort of our prayers for want of waiting to observe the returns of them. The vision may be yet for an appointed time, and that time we allow is in God's hand; but at the end it shall speak, and not lie: though it tarry, let us wait for it, because it will surely come, it will not tarry beyond the appointment of God, which is the fittest season for us (Hab. 2:3).

I shall now dismiss the subject with a few words by way of encouragement to engage and persevere in this part of divine worship. It is good for the saints to draw near unto God. It is not only good because it is their duty; but because it yields their souls a spiritual pleasure, and is also of great profit and advantage to them. Prayer is an ordinance of God, which he frequently owns for quickening the graces of his Spirit, for restraining and subduing the corruptions of the heart, and for bringing the soul into nearer communion and fellowship with himself. Satan has often felt the force and power of this piece of the spiritual armor, and it is the last which the people of God are directed to make use of (Eph. 6). Praying persons are profitable in families, neighborhoods, churches, and commonwealths; whereas prayerless persons are in a great measure useless. The believer has the utmost encouragement to this work he can desire. He may come to God, not as on a seat of judgment, but on a throne of grace; Christ is the Mediator between God and him, his way of access to God, and his Advocate with the Father; the Spirit is his guide, director, and assistant; he has many exceeding great and precious promises to plead with God; nor need he doubt of a kind reception, a gracious audience, and a proper answer, though never so mean and unworthy in himself, since the Lord will regard the prayer of the destitute, and not despise his prayer (Ps. 102:17).

Chapter 6
The Public Blessing of the Congregation

Worshiping congregations should meet in God's name, and enter into his courts with praise; they should be together in his fear, and attend upon every part of his service without distraction; and it is his pleasure that they be dismissed with *his blessing*.

This practice was authorized by a divine, unrepealed institution under the Old Testament dispensation:

> And the LORD spake unto Moses, saying, Speak unto Aaron and unto his sons, saying, On this wise ye shall bless the children of Israel, saying into them, The LORD bless thee, and keep thee: The LORD make his face shine upon thee, and be gracious unto thee: The LORD lift up his countenance upon thee, and give thee peace. And they shall put my name upon the children of Israel; and I will bless them (Num. 6:22–27).

In the New Testament we have indeed no express form of words appointed for this service; but the solemn farewell blessing subjoined to many of the inspired epistles is a sufficient warrant for this piece of public worship. These benedictions are not delivered in the same words exactly; but they come all to much the same thing. I do not see any obligation to use precisely the same words on all occasions; but neither is there any necessity to differ from that most full and comprehensive form, "The grace of the Lord Jesus Christ, and the love of God, and the communion of the Holy Ghost, be with you all. Amen" (2 Cor. 13:14). This service is used at the close of public worship, when the assembly is about to be dismissed; as the priests blessing Israel was at the close of their morning service; and the apostles blessing the churches, at the close of their epistles.

All that is necessary on this subject will fall in, while I consider two things: (1.) The importance and weight of the service; and (2.) The necessary directions about it.

1. The Importance and Weight of This Service

This is by no means a trivial, indifferent thing, however men may think of it. This will best appear from a general view of the meaning of the words appointed to be used by the Jewish priests in blessing the people; and then of the words used by the apostle in blessing the Corinthians.

I. I shall, in the first place, explain the meaning of each clause in the benediction wherewith Aaron and his sons were commanded to bless the children of Israel, as it is recorded (Num. 6:22–27). Not that there is any real darkness in it, to those who are acquainted with the Scriptures; but it is never unseasonable to stir up the pure minds of intelligent Christians, as well as to inform the ignorant, upon a matter of such infinite moment, about which we are daily conversant.

1. The first thing they were to say, when they blessed them, was, "The LORD bless thee, and keep thee" (v. 24). JEHOVAH is a name that implies existence, immutability, and eternity. It is justly paraphrased in these expressions, I AM THAT I AM (Ex. 3:14); and *which is, and which was, and which is to come* (Rev. 1:8). He is the Father of lights, and every good and perfect gift cometh from him. When Aaron and his sons blessed the people, they were to implore his blessing upon them, saying to this effect: *The LORD*, who is over all, blessed forever, all-sufficient for his own blessedness, and for making his creatures happy, and who hath blessed his people with all spiritual blessings in heavenly places in Christ Jesus, *bless you* with rich, free, and everlasting communications of all that is most excellent and desirable, most pleasant and useful, to pacify the conscience, to purify the heart, and to influence the conversation; with all saving grace here, and with an abundant entrance into the fullest enjoyment of his glory forever; and until the day break, and the shadows flee away, may he *keep you* from the evil of sin, from a present evil world, from Satan that evil one, and from an evil heart of unbelief; may he that never slumbers nor sleeps, keep you by his power through faith unto salvation, and having kept you from falling, present you faultless before the presence of his glory with exceeding joy; and may you be preserved in Christ Jesus, in whose hand are all his saints, whose care is as constant, as his love is tender, and whose unerring wisdom will guide, with the most prudent conduct, in the right way, to a city

of habitation; while his almighty power will perform all things for them most perfectly, to their everlasting comfort, and the perpetual confusion of their every enemy.

2. In blessing the people, Aaron and his sons were to say, "The LORD make his face shine upon thee, and be gracious unto thee" (Num. 6:25). What the genial warmth of the sun is to the teeming earth, or the smiles of a kind parent to a loving child, that, and abundantly more, is the free favor of God, when he is pleased to make it shine upon the souls of men; it makes their faces to shine, and their hearts to rejoice with joy unspeakable, and full of glory; it makes them strong out of weakness, and triumphant in distress. It is most reasonable, on all these accounts, that the people of God should wait to hear, with profound reverence and attention, that solemn address, wherein they are to lift up the desires of their souls unto JEHOVAH, to manifest unto them the light of the knowledge of his glory, in the face of Jesus Christ, that they may contemplate, with wonder, improvement, and delight, the cheering comforts of his marvelous kindness, and transcendently rich goodwill towards men; to arise upon them, as the Sun of righteousness, with healing in his wings, that they may go forth, and grow up as calves of the stall; and to make his grace to abound, where sin had abounded, in the most illustrious and extensive manner, in converting sinners, justifying the ungodly, pardoning the guilty, adopting the children of wrath, making his grace sufficient for his people in all their afflictions, temptations, and desertions, carrying them safe through this world, and bringing them forward to their everlasting, prepared rest.

3. When Aaron and his sons blessed the children of Israel, they were to add, "The LORD lift up his countenance upon thee, and give thee peace" (Num. 6:26). While the minds of carnal men are chiefly set upon the things of the world, the people of God are of more generous principles. Nothing but God's favor can make them happy; nothing but the light of his countenance can put gladness into their heart. They know that none but God can give quietness in the soul, and peace that passeth all understanding. Having such apprehensions, it is extremely proper to join with all that in every place call upon the name of the Lord Jesus Christ, in fervently desiring the God of all grace to indulge them with satisfying discoveries of his mercy; to give, to restore, or to continue the joys of his salvation; to uphold with his free Spirit; to give them a joyful access into his grace, and to make them stand therein, rejoicing in hope of his glory: and to bless them

with that most excellent peace which he gives and approves of; peace with himself, as their reconciling God and Father through his beloved Son, together with a sweet sense of it in their own souls; peace with all men, and especially in holy religious connections; and the peace of a sanctified heart, and of a quiet calmness of spirit with regard to all persons and things, all occasions and events; even that peace which passeth all knowledge, which exceeds all adequate conceptions of believers themselves, much more of those that have not experienced it.

This is a general account of the form of blessing, wherewith God commanded the priests, his ministers, to bless his people. And to make Israel the more sensible of the important nature of this service, he was pleased to subjoin those memorable words, "They shall put my name upon the children of Israel; and I will bless them" (Num. 6:27). By this service they were honored to have the name of God put upon them, and to be called by a designation that imported marvelous condescension on the part of God, and conferred the greatest honor upon them. The Lord promiseth to ratify and confirm the blessing (*I will bless them*), with boundless liberality, and altogether freely, without ever recalling his favor, or repenting of his love, with the greatest delight, and the most substantial blessings that will make rich, and will add no sorrow. No consideration will more effectually impress the conscience and affect the heart in religious duties than this, that a divine blessing goes along with divine institutions, and puts virtue and efficacy into them. With what humility, reverence, hope, and diligence should this inspire our minds, to make the best use of every opportunity to honor every ordinance of God! In every place where his name is recorded with such tempers, he will meet his people and bless them.

II. I shall now consider the important meaning of the apostolic benediction, recorded "The grace of the Lord Jesus Christ, and the love of God, and the communion of the Holy Ghost, be with you all. Amen" (2 Cor. 13:14). There is not one Scripture in the whole book of God more important than this, which concludeth an inspired epistle, and is very proper to be used at the dismission of worshipping assemblies. It is full of the richest comfort, and the most edifying instruction. And as we would avoid the sin of concluding the worship of God with the sacrifice of fools, this demands our most frequent attention, and careful inquiry. To assist the reader in this inquiry, I shall explain the meaning of each clause in the verse.

1. *The grace of the Lord Jesus Christ* is his free favor, his gracious presence and powerful influence, as our alone Savior, through whom, and by whose merit and mediation, all spiritual and eternal blessings are procured and conveyed. He is *full of grace*, to redeem the lost, to save sinners, to sanctify and cleanse his church, to reconcile enemies, to open the eyes of the blinded understanding, to renew the will, to quicken the dead, to purge the conscience, to heal backsliders, to lead the blind in ways they know not, to sympathize with the distressed, to comfort the dejected, to work all the works of his people, and to receive them to his glory. His grace is *with his people*, when it is savingly manifested to them, when it works efficaciously in them, and when it becomes all their dependence, and is made perfect in their weakness. Believers are complete in this grace of the Lord Jesus Christ, who is of God made unto them wisdom, and righteousness, and sanctification, and redemption.

2. *The love of God* is his immensely rich, self-moving, and infinitely free goodwill towards men. This is the original spring and source of all divine blessings. Among other illustrious characters, it is marvelous and altogether matchless for its *sovereignty, perpetuity, unchangeableness, greatness*, and *influence*. On these heads I beg leave to offer the following hints.

The love of God is *sovereign* and *free*. He is gracious to whom he will be gracious, and he hath compassion on whom he will have compassion. His love is neither deserved, constrained, nor previously desired by its highly favored objects. He loveth them, because it is the good pleasure of his own will, and according to his purpose which he purposed in himself.

It is *perpetual*. "I have loved thee with an everlasting love" (Jer. 31:3). Like God himself, it is from everlasting to everlasting; for having loved his own of old, he loveth them to the end. It prevented their everlasting ruin, by choosing them in Christ before the foundation of the world; if we love him, it is because he first loved us; and his mercy endureth forever. "The mountains shall depart, and the hills be removed; but my kindness shall not depart from thee, neither shall the covenant of my peace be removed, saith the LORD" (Isa. 54:10).

It is *unchangeable*. We have a noble attestation to this glorious truth, *I am persuaded, that neither death*, as terrible as it is; *nor life*, as desirable as it is; *nor* devils, those evil *angels*; nor their persecuting agents, though they be *principalities or powers* on earth; *nor* evil *things present*, already lying on us; *nor* evil *things to come* upon us; *nor* the *height* of worldly felicity;

nor the *depth* of worldly misery; *nor any other creature*, good or ill, *shall be able to separate us from the love of God which is in Christ Jesus our Lord* (Rom. 8:38–39).

It is *exceeding great*. No tongue can fully express it, nor any mind comprehend it. The breadth, and length, and depth, and height of it, pass knowledge (Eph. 3:18–19). The love wherewith God has loved men must be great, because God himself is love. The most extensive ideas that a finite understanding can frame about divine love are infinitely below its true nature. The heaven is not so far above the earth as the goodness of God is above the most raised conceptions we are able to form of it. It is an ocean which swells higher than all the mountains of opposition, in such as are the objects of it; it is a fountain from which flows all necessary good to those who are interested in it.

The love of God has a *powerful and extensive influence.* "The grace of God that bringeth salvation hath appeared unto all men, teaching us that, denying ungodliness and worldly lusts, we should live soberly, righteously, and godly"[1] (Titus 2:11–12). "We love him, *because* he first loved us" (1 John 4:19). "I have loved thee with an everlasting love: And *therefore with lovingkindness have I drawn thee*" (Jer. 31:3). "The love of Christ *constraineth* us" (2 Cor. 5:14). It would be easy to show, by a large induction of particulars, that grace and glory, and every perfect gift, which cometh

---

[1] "*The grace of God*, his infinitely free favor, which scorns to be shackled with conditions, or meanly dependent on human endeavors. This grace, requiring nothing of the creature, but *bringing salvation*, spiritual and eternal salvation, finished by the incarnate Creator, and free for the chiefest of sinners. This grace being revealed in the gospel, being discerned by faith, and thus appearing in luster, and with power, to *all men*, to men of every rank, every age, every character; making no difference between the servant and his master, between the ruddy stripling and the hoary sire, between the vile prostitute and the chaste vestal; but opening its inexhaustible treasures, to be received by one as well as the other—this grace does what? Cause Antinomianism, or practical ungodliness to come in with a full tide? Quite the reverse: it represses it like an immoveable barrier. It *teaches us to deny*, to renounce ungodliness, *all ungodliness*; not only external gross abominations, but *worldly lusts* also, every vicious inclination, and every irregular desire. Further, it teaches us *to live soberly*, with regard to ourselves, *righteously*, towards our neighbors, and *godly* to our great Creator. This grace, clearly manifested in the understanding, and cordially apprehended by the will, renders every duty of holiness, both practicable and pleasant; it gives us a heart, and a hand, and ability, to exercise ourselves unto universal godliness." James Hervey. *Eleven Letters from the Late Rev. Mr. Hervey, to the Rev. Mr. John Wesley*, letter 9.

down from the Father of lights, flow from the sovereign boundless love of God.

When we pray that the love of God may be with the churches, we should not wish any change in the purposes of heaven; they are secret and unalterable; our God is of one mind, and who can turn him? His love has its chosen objects, who cannot be separated from their established interest in it. But hereby we express our fervent desire that the love of God may be shed abroad in their hearts, by the Holy Ghost given unto them—that they may be rooted and grounded in the knowledge, belief and influence of it; that the Lord would direct their hearts into it; that, with all saints, they may be able to comprehend it;[2] and that their hearts may be comforted in it.

3. *The communion of the Holy Ghost* is only another phrase to signify the richest communications of the blessed Spirit of God, by whom sinners are brought into, and saints are kept in, a peculiar fellowship with the Father in his love, and with his Son Jesus Christ in the unsearchable riches of his grace. It includes the *fullness* and *impartings* of his gifts and graces, called "the supply of the Spirit of Jesus Christ" (Phil. 1:19). I am not concerned to speak of these extraordinary communications of the Spirit, which were confined to *some*, even in the earliest ages of Christianity; since the communion of the Holy Ghost, as it is common to *all Christians*, in *all ages*, is the only thing referred to, in the words under consideration.

This communion, or communication (χοινωνια) of the Holy Ghost, this supply of the Spirit of Jesus Christ, may include all his saving *operations* and blessed *fruits*. Accordingly, his work is various and powerful, and his grace abundant and full; for it is the business of the Holy Ghost

---

[2] Ephesians 3:18. *To comprehend* (καταλαβεσθαι), here, as well as Philippians 3:12, where it is translated *apprehend*, in that expression, *if that I may apprehend*, signifies, *to lay hold upon with understanding, and to realize and appropriate by believing*. If the word had been translated either *apprehend*, as it is in Philippians 3:12; or *perceive*, as Acts 10:34; or, *find* by good evidence, as Acts 25:25—any of these ways would have rendered the sense more plain, and the truth more striking. It is rather harsh to speak of *comprehending that which passeth knowledge*. But the language is as proper as the sentiment is noble, if we make the apostle's wish for the Ephesian Christians; and not for them only, but for all saints, to run in these words, *that ye may be enabled to apprehend*, or *perceive*, or *find*, by clear discernment, on the fullest evidence, *with all saints, what is the breadth, and length, and depth, and height; even to know the love of Christ, which passeth knowledge.*

to *convince* of sin, "When he is come, he will reprove[3] the world of sin" (John 16:8), to enlighten the eyes of the understanding, to know the things that are freely given us of God (Eph. 1:17–18; 1 Cor. 2:12); to renew sinners in the spirit of their minds, hence the salvation of the saints is ascribed to the washing of regeneration, and the renewing of the Holy Ghost (Titus 3:5); to comfort the saints, hence he is frequently called the Comforter (John 14–16), and their consolations are called joy in the Holy Ghost (Rom. 14:17); to crucify the flesh, with the affections and lusts thereof (Gal. 5:24); and to mortify the deeds of the body, and our members that are upon the earth (Rom. 8:13); to make intercession for the saints with groanings that cannot be uttered (Rom. 8:26–27); to testify with their spirits that they are the children of God (Rom. 8:16); to seal them to the day of redemption, as the earnest of their inheritance (Eph. 1:13–14); and to give them filial boldness in their approaches to the throne of grace; for "because ye are sons, God hath sent forth the spirit of his Son into your hearts, crying, Abba, Father" (Gal. 4:6).

The communion of the Holy Ghost be with you all, implies a fervent wish and earnest desire that they might, in the use of all proper and appointed means, be filled with the holy influences, gifts, and graces, joys and consolations of the blessed Spirit.

To express his hope and desire to be heard and accepted in this solemn benediction, the apostle subjoins his *Amen*. Our wishes should not be cold, our hearts should not waver, when we present such an important and weighty address before God. The utmost sincerity should mingle in it with the warmest affection, and both should ascend to God unitedly with lively faith and expectation.

I shall now leave it with the reader to judge in himself whether *this* is, or is not, a most interesting part of divine worship; and whether it does not merit the utmost attention. Can we say of any other, it is more weighty, and more worthy of being performed with reverence and devotion? Here we acknowledge that there are three that bear record in heaven, the Father, the Word, and the Holy Ghost, and these three distinct persons are one God; that these adorable, coequal, and coessential persons, with God-like condescension, carry on the salvation of men in a way that does honor

---

[3] ελεγξει. The word signifies, "to argue with such irresistible evidence of clear and convincing demonstration, as leaves no room for doubtful suspicion, and does not admit of any reply." Nothing can better express the work of the Holy Ghost.

to the character of God, and secures our everlasting interests; and that the redeemed of the Lord should live in a continual regard to the three persons in the Trinity, in whose name they were baptized, and in whose name they are blessed.

I could not think of any way to explain the nature, to lay out the obligations, and represent the excellency of this duty, in as just and striking a light, as by opening first the contents of the form of blessing prescribed to the priests, before the Messiah came in flesh; and then the sense of the apostolical benediction, which is used in almost every congregation of Christian people throughout the world, however divided they be in their judgments about other things.

2. Necessary Directions about It

All that remains on this ordinance is to give some *directions* concerning it. I shall dispatch this head in few words.

1. The highest decency requires that it be performed *with great reverence*. Great fear is due to God in this, as much as in any other piece of service that is done in the meeting of his saints. While ministers stand, and lift up their hands to bless[4] (Lev. 9:22–23; 1 Chron. 23:13; 1 Kings 8:54–55), the congregation should *stand up* to receive the blessing of heaven (1 Kings 8:14). Do we *in this blessing* express our desire and hope, to receive a kingdom that cannot be moved? And how can we be excused, if we have not grace, whereby we may serve him *in it*, with reverence and godly fear, since our God is a consuming fire (Heb. 12:28–29)?

An indifferent person cannot, without indignation, be a witness to that irreverence and unconcerned behavior, that are sometimes to be seen in worshipping assemblies, where people seem more engaged in preparing themselves to remove than attentive to the solemn worship in which they should be employed. Such a way of serving God is only offering him the sacrifice of fools, and is an abomination in his sight. A serious mind cannot think of it without sensible pain, that God should be thus dishonored, and his worship profaned. Such practices harden infidels, and steel their hearts against impressed convictions of the reality, power, and influence of

---

[4] It is probable enough, that the lifting up of the hands was a circumstance never omitted in blessing the church, under the Old Testament, both from the practice of Aaron (Lev. 9:22), and from the promise relating to the Gentiles, "Thus saith the Lord GOD, Behold, I will lift up mine hand to the Gentiles" (Isa. 49:22).

vital Christianity. Everything of so criminal a nature, and of so dangerous tendency, should be carefully avoided by all Christians.

2. This service should be gone about *with due consideration and judgment*. We ought to employ all the powers of our souls in meditation and reflection upon the object and the nature of our address. This would quicken our attention, and compose our minds into a temper becoming the sublimity of the work. Consideration can never be more usefully employed, judgment can never be more worthily exercised, than in hearing and receiving the blessing of the Lord that maketh rich, and addeth no sorrow.

3. We ought to join in this duty under a humbling conviction of our utter unworthiness, and of God's marvelous condescension in taking any favorable knowledge of us in our low and wretched condition; much more in making so rich, so seasonable, and so effectual provision for our necessities, as the grace of our Lord Jesus Christ, the love of God, and the communion of the Holy Ghost are. This is a source of the deepest humility, and a fountain of the most exuberant joy. Here we are led to consider creature-meanness, and divine mercy, in the most delightful and astonishing contrast.

4. We should bear in mind the *common interest* that believers have, as fellow-members of the same body, and fellow-heirs of the same inheritance, in the grace of the Lord Jesus Christ, in the love of God, and in the communion of the Holy Ghost; these are with them *all*. In this duty we should consider the relation we have to that numberless company, whom God hath chosen, whom Christ hath redeemed, and in whose hearts the Comforter will continue to make his abode forever. In this benediction, the equal regard of the adorable Trinity to all the saints is supposed, and the same disinterested care one for another is expressed.

5. Let *fervent desire* accompany the language of our lips; for in vain do we worship God in calling upon him, unless the desire of our souls be towards him, and towards the remembrance of those powerful consolations in Christ, those comforts of love, and those communications of the Spirit, that are implored, when we join in this important address to the throne of grace. There is no religious service, where every motive of duty and interest, of gratitude and affection, has a better occasion for a vigorous, powerful exertion, to excite importunity and ardor in our requests. The things

that are freely given us of God are nowhere set in a clearer, juster light, to strengthen our faith, and enkindle the most passionate desires.

6. The confidence and the rejoicing of hope should elevate our minds, and deeply possess our hearts in the whole of this service. In testimony of our assurance to be heard and accepted, we should say, *Amen.* God never called us to seek his face in vain. His effectual blessing is conveyed by his own institutions. And we dishonor the goodness, wisdom, power, and faithfulness of God if we stagger through unbelief, or abandon ourselves to hopeless discouragement, when we have such strong grounds of consolation, and of good hope through grace; together with God's most gracious promise, "In all places where I record my name, I will come unto thee, and I will bless thee" (Ex. 20:24).

The directions concerning *prayer* may also be reviewed on this head. See chapter 5, section 5.

Chapter 7

The Sacraments in General

The sacraments of baptism and the Lord's Supper fall next under our consideration; but previous to my treating particularly on each of these, I shall employ this chapter upon the sacraments in general.

I shall observe this order in treating of so copious a subject, to explain,

1. The name;
2. The nature;
3. The ends;
4. The efficacy;
5. The use;
6. The number of the sacraments, which are of divine appointment;
7. The wisdom and advantages of dealing with men by such institutions; and,
8. The persons that may warrantably dispense or administer them.

1. Their Name

The word *sacrament* is no otherwise material in handling this subject, except that it is familiar and of general use. It is not scriptural indeed; but it is harmless, and does not give any just cause of offense. And until just cause be shown, I do not see any occasion for so much complaisance, as to part with it, merely because it is not to be met with literally in the Scriptures. Although I think Jerome's observation is manly and excellent: "We are not to be solicitous about the word, when we are sure of the sense."[1] We are not to hold any doctrine that is not contained in Scripture; but what should hinder us to explain Scripture-doctrines in our own words, provided they be consonant thereunto? The Greek church knew nothing of the word *sacrament*, it being of a Latin original; but instead thereof

---

[1] "Non nobis est curae de vocabulo, cum sensus sit in tuto." Jerome. *Dialogus Adversus Luciferianos*.

used the words συμβολα (signs), τελεται (consecrations, or perfections), and most commonly μυστηρια (mysteries). They meant by all these words that there is in the sacraments, besides the outward and visible signs, some secret or hidden mystery signified thereby. The Latin church used chiefly the word *sacrament*, not only as signifying something that is sacred, but as intimating, that thereby they were bound, as with an oath, to be the Lord's. Varro and Festus say, it was an ancient practice among some nations, when any controversy arose that they could not decide, to take the following method: the contending parties deposited a sum of money, each of them, in the hand of the judge, and this pledge remained in his hand, till judgment was given in the dispute; and then the party that gained had his money restored; but the loser forfeited his deposited pledge; and this forfeit was converted to public uses, and the pledge was called by them *a sacrament*.[2]

It is certain, the word *sacrament* was used by the Romans to signify that oath which the soldiers took, to be true and faithful to their general, and to fight courageously under his banner. Tertullian, and other Christian writers, have applied it by accommodation, in this sense, not excluding the former, to this purpose: That the disciples of Christ took, as it were, an oath to him, in these ordinances, expressing their obligation not to desert his cause.

Now, since this is agreeable to the end and design of a sacrament, whatever be the first original of the use of the word, I think we have no reason to scruple the using of it, though it be not found in Scripture. Nevertheless, it is indecent, nay absurd, for Christians to contend or be angry one with another about this particular word, it being of no great importance, if we agree to adhere steadfastly to the explication given thereof in Scripture. I should be sorry to give anybody occasion to suspect that any article of Christianity was only capable of being supported by a particular set of expressions that are confessedly human.

2. Their Nature

The nature of a sacrament is to be explained in the next place. It may be described:

---

[2] John Forbes. *Instructiones Historico-Theologicæ de Doctrina Christiana*, book. 9. chap. 1. sect. 2.

7. THE SACRAMENTS IN GENERAL

A holy ordinance instituted by Christ, wherein sensible signs, that are familiar enough in their own nature, are appointed to represent, seal, and apply Christ, and the blessings of divine grace, through the belief of the truths these signs are connected with.

Sacraments represent, in a familiar and striking manner to the *eye*, the most important doctrines of the gospel, blessings of grace, and promises of the covenant, by sensible signs; whereby the understanding is instructed, faith confirmed, and the heart affected and impressed; and so Christ and his benefits are applied, by the power of the Spirit, unto the souls and consciences of true believers. I shall make the following observations concerning sacraments.

1. They are holy ordinances, instituted by Christ. The Father hath committed all judgment unto the Son, as Mediator; and the Lord Jesus Christ, as the head of his body the church, hath appointed such outward and ordinary means of communicating the benefits of redemption, as he will be pleased to bless for this purpose, both to convert sinners, and to build up his saints. These religious duties are prescribed as an *instituted method*, in which he will be worshipped, and to them he has promised his special presence; "In all places where I record my name, I will come unto thee, and I will bless thee" (Ex. 20:24). And every duty that is to be performed by divine express command, and which is designed to be a pledge of the divine presence, and a means of salvation, is a branch of religious worship, and may be styled *a holy ordinance*. It is very evident from Scripture that the sacraments are founded on Christ's institution, both in opposition to the inventions of men, and in distinction from the law of Moses; for he commanded his disciples to go, and teach all nations, baptizing them (Matt. 28:19); and to observe the Lord's Supper in remembrance of him (Matt. 26:26–27 compared with 1 Cor. 11:24–25).

Even the covenant of life, or law of works, was not without its sacraments: the tree of knowledge of good and evil being appointed to try man's allegiance, in a point that turned precisely on the will of God; and the tree of life to encourage his obedience, with the brightest hopes of inheriting eternal life. But this dispensation did not fall within the mediatorial scheme by our Lord Jesus Christ.

From the first revelation of a Redeemer in the garden of Eden, which had been the scene of a most unnatural rebellion, all along till the spiritual dispensation set up by Christ and his apostles, there have ever been some outward rites and ceremonies appointed for men, whereby God would represent the blessings of his grace, and whereby they might profess their humble acceptance of those blessings, and their correspondent obligations to duty.

But the sacraments of the New Testament are, in a peculiar manner, said to be instituted by Christ, because they are not, like the Jewish sacraments, *typical* of what is to come, but *commemorative* of what is past; and Christ himself appointed them in his own personal ministry, to remain unabolished and unalterable, till his second coming, in virtue of that fullness of power which is given him in heaven and in earth (Matt. 28:18).

2. The *parts* of a sacrament are two: the one an outward and sensible *sign*, used according to Christ's own appointment; the other an inward and spiritual *grace*, thereby signified.

The signs, and even every circumstance relative to the use of them, must be appointed by Christ, and not contrived by men; for here, as in every other duty, we must observe all things that Christ hath commanded us. It is equally presumptuous and vain to teach for doctrines the commandments or inventions of men. The signs that are used in the sacraments have a natural fitness to bring the things they represent to our mind, and a divine appointment to convey these spiritual blessings to believers.

The things signified in the sacraments are *Christ*, and the *benefits of his mediation*, or the *sure mercies* promised in the covenant of grace, wherein Christ Jesus is "of God made unto us wisdom, and righteousness, and sanctification, and redemption" (1 Cor. 1:30).

These signs may, on every occasion, bring the things they represent to the mind of a spiritual man; but they are only to be esteemed sacred when they are set apart, according to Christ's appointment, to represent such important and heavenly blessings, and to be used for the particular purposes he has commanded.

Even when these signs are sanctified by the word and prayer, they continue to be signs still. Only their use, and not their nature, is changed. Their connection with the spiritual grace which they signify is merely relative, and founded (1.) In their likeness to one another; (2.) In the appointment of Christ; and (3.) In the promise of his blessing upon the use of these signs for the purposes he has appointed.

3. The sacraments are designed only for the church; that is, they are not to be administered to all promiscuously, as the word is to be preached to every sort and degree of men, without making any difference through partiality. The word of God is an appointed means for the conversion of sinners, as well as for building up believers; and therefore all nations must be taught; but only those that are taught, and have professed their faith in Christ, and their obedience to him, must be baptized, with their household (Acts 17:14–15, 31–33). And it is plain, only such as are capable of examining themselves should be allowed to eat and to drink at the Lord's Supper (1 Cor. 11:28).

Under the Old Testament, the sacraments were administered to none but the Jews, the only people in the world that professed the true religion. Even so, under the gospel-dispensation, none have a right to sacraments but they who are therein professedly devoted to Christ, as their Lord and Savior.

4. The sacraments Christ hath appointed are to continue for stated and ordinary use in the church, till he shall deliver up the kingdom to the Father (Matt. 28:19–20; 1 Cor. 11:26). The end of the world, and the second coming of Christ, will finish this dispensation.

3. Their Ends

The ends of sacramental ordinances are, to *represent, seal, and apply* spiritual things by sensible signs, unto believers.

1. To represent them. This constitutes one difference between the word and the sacraments, that in the word divine truths are only declared; in the sacraments they are also represented by sensible signs, which have some resemblance to these truths, and are appointed to bring them to our remembrance, and to confirm our belief of them. The tree of life, and the tree of the knowledge of good and evil, were of this sort, and served this purpose to Adam, while he held fast his integrity. The bow of God set in the clouds of heaven, was designed to answer the same end to Noah, and the generations to come after him. Circumcision and the passover were ordinances of that kind to the Jews, as baptism and the Lord's Supper are to Christians.

These signs are in themselves common and familiar things; the wisdom of the flesh pronounceth them foolishness, and scoffingly asks, "What profit is there in serving the Lord by them?" But to them that are called, these things are the wisdom and the power of God, to awaken devotion, to bring to remembrance, and to promote and strengthen believing, while, in using them, they look not at things that are seen, which are temporal, but at things that are not seen, which are eternal. These signs are a standing evidence of God's faithfulness in his promises, and a clear representation of things that are invisible.

2. To seal them. Abraham received the sign of circumcision, *a seal* of the righteousness of the faith which he had, being yet uncircumcised (Rom. 4:11). The uses of signets or seals are various, such as, to ascertain property (Song 4:12; 2 Tim. 2:19); to conceal from officious and intruding eyes (Dan. 12:4, 9; Rev. 5); to imprint a character (Eph. 1:13); to ratify a commission (John 6:27); to denote consent, esteem, and approbation (John 3:33); and to confirm and assure the mind by a significant representation of something that is not so apt to strike the person with a full conviction another way, though it be as sure without that sign as with it. In this sense, I apprehend, circumcision was to Abraham a seal of the righteousness of his faith; and in the same sense we may say the sacraments are seals of the righteousness which is of faith unto us. We intend nothing else hereby but that God has added these ordinances to the promises that are given us in the word, not only to bring to mind this great doctrine, that Christ has redeemed his people by his blood, but to assure them that through believing in him, they shall be made partakers of this blessing; so that these ordinances are a pledge thereof to believers, as he thereby, in an objective way, gives them to understand that Christ and his benefits are theirs, and that he will be their covenant God forever.

In these ordinances too, the persons that submit to them signify, in an external and visible manner, their compliance with his covenant, which may be called their setting to their seal that God is true (John 3:33). This compliance is outwardly professed in these ordinances; but the profession is abominable to God, where it is not inwardly done by that faith which is of the operation of God through the gospel.

3. To exhibit and apply them. The sacramental signs are not bare representations of spiritual and invisible blessings; they are also appointed means of conveying them to believers. On this principle it is easy to account for many expressions which are otherwise unaccountable, except on the absurd scheme of transubstantiation. For example, the bread which we eat, is said to be the communion of the body of Christ; and the cup which

we bless, the communion of the blood of Christ (1 Cor. 10:16). Christ said to his disciples, "Take, eat: this is my body, which is broken for you... this cup is the new testament in my blood": drink ye all of it (1 Cor. 11:23–25). The case seems to be much the same, as if the prince invests a subject in some honorable office, by delivering to him a staff, sword, or signet, and say to him, "Take this staff, sword, or signet; this is such an office or preferment"; or, as if a father should deliver a deed for conveyance of land to his son, and say, "Take it as thy own; this is such a farm or manor." How can such expressions import less, in common sense and reason, than a present, gift, or conveyance of the offices, preferments, and lands, by and with these outward signs?[3]

These most valuable ends of sacramental ordinances recommend them to our esteem and affection. The just consideration of them would soon

---

[3] "*Forma sacramenti est unio illa*, etc., that is, The form of a sacrament is the union which is between the sign and the things signified.

This union is not corporal, and yet it is not imaginary; but it is a spiritual relation, by virtue whereof the things signified are really communicated to these that use the signs according to God's appointment.

All that partake of the signs do not receive the spiritual blessings they signify: the manner and the means of partaking of the signs, and the things they represent, are very different.

From this union follows a communication of names: thus (1.) The sign is affirmed of the thing signified; as when the sanctification of the heart is called circumcision. (2.) The thing signified is affirmed of the sign; as when circumcision is called the covenant, and the bread, the body of Christ. (3.) The effect of the thing signified is affirmed of the sign; as when baptism is said to regenerate. (4.) A property of the sign is affirmed of the thing signified; as when breaking, which agrees to the bread, is attributed to Christ. (5.) A property of the thing signified is ascribed to the sign; as when the sacramental eating and drinking is called *spiritual*.

The foundation of this relation arises (1.) From the likeness or proportion of the sign to the thing signified: for though such a similitude does not constitute a sacrament, yet it is essentially requisite among those things which make it, and is laid as a foundation to the whole. (2.) From a word of institution, which consists of a command and a promise. The command obliges us to use the creatures to that holy purpose: the promise assures us, that we shall not so use them without success. This word of institution, distinctly applied, with suitable prayers, is called the word of consecration, of blessing, of sanctification, and of separation. (3.) This relation is perfected, when the signs are used according to the appointment of Christ; and so important is this circumstance, that for want of it, that is no sacrament, to this or that person, who is either present only, or who is a receiver too, which is most effectual to others." William Ames. *The Marrow of Theology*, book 1, chap. 36. sections 26–30.

demonstrate the wisdom and grace of God, in suiting the methods of instructing and edifying his church so well to our infirmities and wants. How rich is the grace of God! How properly may he be said to abound therein towards us in all wisdom and prudence!

4. Their Efficacy

The efficacy of the sacraments is to be considered in the next place. That they are made effectual to salvation is too manifest to admit of any dispute among those that acknowledge them to be standing ordinances of God for the use of his church. The usefulness of these institutions will be represented in the next section. The present inquiry is, "From whence is the efficacy of sacraments derived, to edify and comfort the body of Christ?"

The answer must be given, first negatively, and then positively.

I. Negatively. They do not become effectual means of salvation, either by any virtue in themselves, or in him that doth administer them.

1. Not by any virtue in the ordinances themselves to answer this end. This opinion is eagerly supported by the Papists, who make the sacraments the true, immediate, and proper causes of salvation, as it respects the work of God in the soul; and affirm that the efficacy of them flows from the sacramental action of receiving the elements. Their notions go upon several false suppositions; such as, that God has inseparably connected his grace with the sacraments, or that he hath put a spiritual energy in a corporeal action, or that he has more regard to the external part of the service than to the internal. And as they build on a false foundation, so they rear a superstructure by no means agreeable to *the analogy of faith*,[4] a superstructure that disgraces every leading article of true religion. For how can

---

[4] This phrase is used by the apostle (Rom. 12:6), and translated *the proportion of faith*. By which I imagine, he meant something like what I now intend by it; namely, the mutual relation of the truths of the gospel to one another, and the harmony of the whole system in its entire connection. This analogy or proportion requires every article of faith to be kept in its own place; either as it is fundamental to weighty conclusions which arise out of it; or, as it is consequential from other truths, which it necessarily rests upon; or, as it is a confirming illustration of parallel doctrines and duties that go hand in hand with it. It seems to be a metaphor taken from arithmetical calculations, where numbers have a certain respect to one another, in a way of increasing or diminishing their value in an exact degree and order of bearing: or else, from a regular building, where the dimension of every part is planned on a judicious design, to rest upon the foundation, to support the superior fabric, to unite the contiguous parts, and to contribute to the beauty of the contrivance, and the strength and regularity of the edifice.

the virtue they ascribe to these ordinances be reconciled to the sovereignty of divine grace; or, to the influence of the Holy Ghost in the saving applications of the redemption purchased by Christ; or, to the importance of the character of Jesus Christ, in whose name alone we have salvation; or, to the nature of gospel-ordinances, which are only *means* of communicating the benefits of redemption, and not *causes*; or, to general observation and experience, which assure us, that they are the savor of death unto death to some that partake of them, as well as the savor of life unto life to others?

Do they tell us that our food has a virtue in itself to nourish our bodies? I allow it has; but this is not at all a parallel case, since no external act of religion whatever can have a tendency to nourish the soul, without the internal efficacious grace of the Spirit accompanying it (Gal. 5:16–26).

2. Not by any virtue derived from *the intention or piety of him* by whom the sacraments are administered. It is one of the ridiculous conceits of the church of Rome, "That the efficacy of these institutions depends partly upon the pious intention of the minister in consecrating them." And to complete the absurdity of their scheme, they say, "That this pious intention is absolutely necessary to make a sacrament." Ministers are stewards of the mysteries of God (1 Cor. 4:1), the administration of these being committed to them; but they have not the least power to confer divine grace, which is Christ's gift and work; thus the apostle says, "Who then is Paul, and who is Apollos, but ministers by whom ye believed, even as the Lord gave to every man?" (1 Cor. 3:5).

This impious doctrine of the Roman Catholics is a contradiction to their silly boasts about the certainty of salvation in their communion. If the intention and piety of the priest are as necessary to the very being of sacraments, as they allege, it is so far from being certain, that it is very improbable the greater part of them are baptized, and consequently that their party is a church. I shall not appeal to the living, but refer to the more faithful records of past ages for a proof of this. Do not their own writers, Baronius, Dupine, and others, acknowledge that all manner of enormities and profligacy prevailed generally among their clergy for some centuries? It is a wonderful pitch of credulity indeed, for any man to believe, against every rational evidence, that these infamous creatures had pious intentions in administering the sacraments when they were addicted to everything vicious at other times. No doubt, some will reply, the case is widely altered now; decency and purity shine forth in all their conversations in this happy age. If Protestants were to be silent on this point, I believe it will be a hard matter to persuade the kings of France, Spain, Portugal, and Naples, with the Venetians, and the dukes of Parma and Modena, as well as some others, to yield it without a contest. I do not speak of Protestants, who, I trust, will never be so unjust to truth and themselves as to come into this way of thinking. But if this plea is admitted, I must ask whether an uninterrupted succession is not a fundamental pillar of Popery? It is granted. Again, were not these profligate ages, carry them back as far, or as short way as you please, were not they so many links that connected *the past* with *the following*, and transmitted the succession down to our times? Surely. But is it probable that such impure channels could convey by their pious intentions the original institutions of heaven? For my own part, I can scarce think it possible, upon the Catholic scheme. It is very unlucky too that the ages of miracles and degeneracy were almost coeval, so that we cannot have a divine evidence of that greatest miracle of all that have been wrought in the church of Rome for upwards of 1000 years past, namely, the pure transmission of Christ's ordinances, through the *pious intention* of *impious monsters*, down to the present times. If there has been any interruption, the whole is effectually marred.

Besides, upon this principle of the absolute necessity of the concurring pious intention of the minister when he consecrates, in order to make a sacrament, no man whatsoever can be sure whether he is baptized, and the votaries for transubstantiation cannot be certain whether they worship the body of Christ, or only a bit of bread, because none but God can search the minister's heart, and really know his intention.[5]

---

[5] "Least of all can I believe that doctrine of the council of Trent, that the saving efficacy of the sacraments doth depend upon the intention of the priest that administers them: which is to say, that though the people believe and live never so well, yet they may be damned by shoals, and whole parishes together, at the pleasure of the priest; and this for no other reason, but because the priest is so cross and so cruel, that he will not intend to save them.

"Now, can any man believe this, that hath any tolerable notion either of the goodness or justice of God? May we not appeal to God in this, as Abraham did in another case? 'Wilt thou destroy the righteous with the wicked? that be far from thee to do after this manner: shall not the Judge of all the earth do right?' Much more, to destroy the righteous for the wicked, and that righteous and innocent people should lie at the mercy and will of a wicked and perverse priest, to be saved or damned by him as he thinks fit: that be far from God: 'Shall not the Judge of all the earth do right?' For, to drive the argument

It is surely the duty of him that ministers, either in the *word* or in the *sacraments*, to perform those services with pious, upright intentions. He sins, if he does not go about them in this manner; but the manner of performing his service cannot contribute to the efficacy of it, for the treasure is put into the earthen vessel, that the excellency of the power may be seen to be of God only, and not of men (2 Cor. 4:7).

II. Positively. The sacraments become effectual means of salvation only by the blessing of Christ, and the working of his Spirit in them that by faith receive them.

1. By the blessing of Christ, by whom they were instituted. This rendered all the institutions of Old Testament worship effectual; thus Christ, that was in the church in the wilderness, with the Angel that spake to Moses in the mount Sinai, and with the fathers, said, "In all places where I record my name, I will come unto thee, and I will bless thee" (Acts 7:38 compared with Ex. 20:24). And the success of New Testament institutions is owing entirely to the same cause: for Paul may plant, and Apollos water, "but God gave the increase. So then neither is he that planteth any thing, neither he that watereth; but God that giveth the increase" (1 Cor. 3:5–7).

The encouragement of Christ's ministers to labor in the gospel, and of people to attend on their ministrations, is couched in that comfortable assurance, "Lo, I am with you alway, even unto the end of the world" (Matt. 28:20). When he sends out his word, it runs powerfully, successfully, and with an evidence that triumphs over the pride and enmity of the carnal mind. Without the blessing of Christ, the purest ordinances are weak and fruitless; but with it, the weakest are efficacious. This maketh the foolish things of the world to confound the wise; the weak things of the world to confound the things which are mighty; and base things of the world, and things which are despised, yea, and things which are not, to bring to naught things that are, that no flesh should glory in his presence (1 Cor. 1:27–29). Without his blessing, wisdom is infatuated, might is impotent, and the best means unprofitable (John 15:5).

2. By the working of his Spirit in them that by faith receive the sacraments. It is the work of the Holy Ghost to search the deep things of God, and unfold the glory, fullness, and suitableness of Christ unto mankind;

---

to the head, if this be to do right, there is no possibility of doing wrong." Tillotson, *Works*, sermon 41.

and without his all-gracious influence, the veil will remain upon our hearts. But "where the Spirit of the Lord is, there is liberty" (2 Cor. 3:17). The worthy receivers of the sacraments are justly said to be all baptized by one Spirit into one body, and to have been all made to drink into one Spirit (1 Cor. 12:13).

The Holy Ghost unites the soul to Christ, and quickens it together with him; renews the whole man after the image of God; purifies the heart through the faith of the gospel; brings the man to a proper temper; excites suitable acts of faith, hope, and love; and maintains the lively impressions of divine things upon the mind; and all these have a powerful tendency to promote the work of grace in the whole conduct of the Christian life. It is the Spirit that quickeneth; for without his influence every ordinance profiteth nothing. Water-baptism profiteth nothing without the baptism of the Holy Spirit; and to come together into one place, and there to eat bread and drink wine, is not to eat the Lord's Supper, unless the communicants eat and drink into one Spirit.

O! that Christians would constantly abound in *hopes* and *wishes* of being more and more partakers of Christ in his ordinances, under a full persuasion that they are made effectual to salvation only through the blessing of Christ, and the working of his Holy Spirit. Then they would worship God in the spirit therein, they would rejoice in Christ Jesus, and have no confidence in the flesh. God would be glorified; Christ exalted; the Spirit honored; the saints comforted and confirmed; and ordinances frequented and reverenced. Under these views, we should see the primitive temper shining forth in the primitive practice of the disciples, who "continued steadfastly in the apostles' doctrine and fellowship, and in breaking of bread, and in prayers" (Acts 2:42).

5. Their Use

I shall now proceed to speak of the *uses* of *sacramental institutions*. They are profitable in many respects, and to many purposes; I shall give some instances, that will show how much a wise and gracious God consults his own glory, and our happiness, by such methods of instruction and edification.

1. Sacraments are useful to assist our meditation, while the important truths they contain are not represented in a transient manner to our ears, but presented in a figure before our eyes, that we may consider them with

more attention, and be more fully persuaded of them. The objects of sight commonly enter deeper into the mind, and leave more distinct ideas, than the objects of any other sense. The sight of the eye demands the most steadfast attention of the mind, and contributes a great deal to fix and engage it in sacred contemplation.

2. They are profitable to confirm and increase faith. Although we cannot imagine anything more worthy of being believed than the word of God; yet where he is pleased to add any sign of his most faithful promises, we should adore that wonderful grace which gives this double security to our faith. Hereby he declares more abundantly to the "heirs of promise, the immutability of his counsel…that by two immutable things" (his word, and the signs he hath appointed) "in which it was impossible for God to lie, we may have a strong consolation" (Heb. 6:17–18).

3. They are adapted to produce and enliven experience. By virtue of these ordinances, the saints anticipate the glories of heaven, and the joys of paradise, which shall in a short time be revealed without any figure, and possessed without any reserve. Here they have a clear representation of the love of God, of the grace of the Lord Jesus Christ, and of the communion of the Holy Ghost, truths that are admirably calculated, especially in the advantageous light they are here manifested, to touch the finest movements of the soul, and to strike all the inmost springs of action, with the most persuasive, the most commanding energy, and to draw out every gracious temper into a vigorous exertion of spiritual exercise. Here is every motive to a strong faith, a lively hope, an animated zeal, a holy joy, true repentance, and every other fruit of the blessed Spirit.

4. They are suited to keep just sentiments of duty upon the mind. They present the goodness of the Creator and Savior in the strongest light to our meditations, that we may see its excellency, and feel its constraining force. They are as a bridle to keep back from evil, and like a spur to excite the Christian to run his race, and finish his course with joy and diligence. Under such advantages, we should cleanse ourselves from all filthiness of the flesh and spirit, and perfect holiness in the fear of the Lord. Nothing makes duty so easy, so delightful, as the constraints of preventing love.

5. They contribute to the support and propagation of truth. They are never to be used without the word, and an explication of their nature and design (Deut. 6:20–25).

And it shall be when thy son asketh thee in time to come, saying, What is this? that thou shalt say unto him, By strength of hand the Lord brought us out from Egypt, from the house of bondage: and it came to pass, when Pharaoh would hardly let us go, that the Lord slew all the firstborn in the land of Egypt, both the firstborn of man, and the firstborn of beast: therefore I sacrifice to the Lord all that openeth the matrix, being males; but all the firstborn of my children I redeem. And it shall be for a token upon thine hand, and for frontlets between thine eyes: for by strength of hand the Lord brought us forth out of Egypt (Ex. 13:14–16).

6. They distinguish the church from the world, and form a visible character of her state and relation to Christ, whose she is, and whom she serves.

7. They are bonds of mutual love among the people of God. Those that have received such marks of being joined to Christ, who is the head of the church, ought not to disagree among themselves. They are all baptized by one Spirit into one body. When they come together to eat the Lord's Supper, one should tarry for another; because, though many in number, they are one bread, and one body, that are called in one hope of their calling. The sacraments are pledges of the communion of saints, first with Christ, and then likewise with one another.

For such valuable purposes hath Christ appointed, and with such important views should Christians observe these holy ordinances.

6. Their Number

The number of the sacraments God has appointed is to be determined in the next place.

It would be impertinent to enter upon any particular discussion of the number and nature of the sacraments of the covenant of works; or even of the sacraments belonging to the Mosaic dispensation. I shall only inquire what sacraments Christ hath instituted for continued use in the gospel-church.

We are sure that baptism and the Lord's Supper bear the stamp of heaven's authority.

And Jesus came and spake unto them, saying, All power is given unto me in heaven and in earth. Go ye therefore, and teach all nations, baptizing them in the name of the Father, and of the Son, and of the Holy Ghost (Matt. 28:18–19).

For I have received of the Lord that which also I delivered unto you, That the Lord Jesus, the same night in which he was betrayed, took bread: and when he had given thanks, he brake it, and said, Take, eat: this is my body, which is broken for you: this do in remembrance of me. After the same manner also he took the cup, when he had supped, saying, This cup is the new testament in my blood: this do ye, as oft as ye drink it, in remembrance of me. For as often as ye eat this bread, and drink this cup, ye do shew the Lord's death till he come (1 Cor. 11:23–26).

The council of Trent gives the following decision upon the question about the number of the sacraments:

If any man shall say, that the sacraments of the new law, were not all instituted by Jesus Christ our Lord; or, that they are more or fewer than seven, to wit, Baptism, confirmation, the Lord's Supper, penance, extreme unction, orders or ordination, and marriage; or even that any of these seven is not truly and properly a sacrament, let him be accursed.[6]

The first that stumbled into this opinion (as far as I can find), was Hugo de St Victore, in his work upon ecclesiastical ceremonies, sacraments, offices, and observances, about the year 1130. Peter Lombard, the famed master of the sentences, who was cotemporary with him, and wrote about ten years after him, adopted the same notion, and collected many quotations from the fathers to support it; and perhaps if he had made thirteen sacraments, instead of seven, as Scotus did, *anno* 1300, he could as easily have justified his opinion by the same kind of arguments, which rested entirely on the sound of their words, or, at most, some incautious expressions, and not on the obvious scope of their writings.

---

[6] *Acts of the Council of Trent*, sess. 7. can. 1.

This doctrine of seven sacraments received the sanction of Pope Eugenius IV in the council of Florence, 1433, for the first public ratification of it, and was finally established, as we have said, in the council of Trent, 1547, under Pope Paul III.[7] The church of Rome has no great reason to triumph, either in the antiquity of this novel opinion, which was never heard of till near the middle of the 12th century; or, in the unity of their belief of it, while their language and sentiments are so divided.[8]

And besides, they should be ashamed to impose such a number of their own sacraments, when they rob the people of half the sacrament of the Lord's Supper, which he has commanded them all to partake of, unless we suppose they have added the five to make them sufficient amends.

Their ingenious reasonings from the number of seven *sins*, and as many *virtues*, might deserve a serious answer, if they showed anything else than a desperate cause, an obstinate prejudice, and an insolent affront to Scripture and reason. Their plea from the repeated mentioning of the number *seven* in the word of God, as of seven beasts to be offered in sacrifice, of sprinkling or washing seven times, and the like, are much of a piece with the curious argument of that gentleman, who, preaching before the council of Trent, proved from the *five barley loaves, and two fishes* (John 6:9), that there were seven sacraments, no more, no fewer. From this sample, the reader may guess at the solidity of the rest.

I hope the reader will remember that the following things are necessary in every sacrament: A sensible sign, or outward element; Christ, and the benefits of salvation, represented by it; God's appointment, constituting the former a sign of the latter; and the promise of his blessing on the use of these signs, according to his institution.

Now, I affirm that the pretended sacraments of *confirmation, penance, extreme unction, ordination*, and *marriage* are essentially defective in these particulars.

1. Confirmation is defined by them,

> a sacrament of the new law, in which grace is conferred by the bishop on them that are baptized, to strengthen their soul against the as-

---

[7] Forbes, *Instructiones*, book. 9. chap. 3. Burnet, *Exposition of the Thirty-nine Articles*, article 25.

[8] Forbes, *Instructiones*, book 9. chap. 4–8. Burnet, *Exposition of the Thirty-nine Articles*, article 25.

saults of the devil, and an indelible image of the Christian warfare is impressed on them, by means of an anointing on the forehead, in the shape of a cross, made with oil mixed with balsam, and administered by a consecrated bishop, who gives them a slap on the face, using this form on the occasion… *I sign thee with the sign of the cross, and confirm thee with the chrism of salvation, in the name of the Father, Son, and Holy Ghost.*

This is a piece of will-worship, for Christ hath nowhere commanded it; the sign is of human invention; and there is no promise of a blessing upon this service. On the contrary, God has assured us that we worship him in vain if the commandments of men are our rule.

It is certain the Holy Ghost was given by the laying on of the hands of the apostles (Acts 8:15–18). But it is daring presumption to set the apostles and modern bishops on a level, as to the conferring of extraordinary gifts, which visibly accompanied the laying on of the apostles' hands, and as visibly do not attend the laying on of the hands of bishops.

Believers indeed have an unction, though not with *popish chrism*, but with *the Holy Ghost* (1 John 2:20, 27). The anointing of believers teacheth them all things; and what can this be, but the Spirit of God, who searcheth all things, even the deep things of God?

2. Penance is another of the sacraments the church of Rome hath contrived. It is said to be

> a sacrament, wherein the remission of sins committed after baptism, is conferred by priestly absolution, on such as are humbled for them, make auricular confession of them to the priest, and by their works make satisfaction for them.

Here is no visible sign that can be called sacramental. Auricular confession, which is made a part of this sacrament, is a doctrine of devils. And satisfaction for sin by the works of men is fearful blasphemy against the righteousness of the nature and law of God, and against the most meritorious, the alone sufficient merits of Christ.

3. Extreme unction is described thus by Popish writers:

A sacrament of the new law, wherein health of body is restored, if it be expedient for the soul, unto grown Christians that are dangerously ill, by the priest's anointing their eyes, ears, nose, mouth, hands, reins, and feet, with oil-olive blessed by a bishop, and pronouncing this form...*By this holy anointing, and by his divine mercy, God forgive thee, wherein thou hast done amiss by seeing, hearing, smelling, tasting, touching*: but especially the remains of all mortal sins (together with the uneasiness arising from them), for which they cannot repent in the jaws of death, are entirely blotted out.

This is a piece of will-worship invented by men, without any warrant from God. The matter and form of it are entirely human, and the success is just as good as its authority. The place in James 5:14 is nothing to their purpose. It refers to bodily healing only, and that in an extraordinary way. That miraculous restoration to health does not follow upon the Popish unction, so that they are self-condemned, while they pretend, on the authority of that text, to support a doctrine inconsistent with the letter of it. And the forgiveness of sins, mentioned in the 15th verse, follows upon prayer, and does not seem to be connected with the *anointing* spoken of (v. 14). The anointing is connected with restoration of bodily health, being joined with prayer; and the prayer of miracle-working faith having saved the sick, the Lord raised him up; but the forgiveness of his sin seems to be only an answer of prayer. The extraordinary remedy and cure, were to continue or fail together; but prayer and forgiveness will never fail. This passage will receive some light from Mark 6:13, the disciples "cast out many devils, and anointed with oil many that were sick, and healed them."[9]

Bishop Burnet very well observes that

---

[9] "Mark 6:13 *Apostoli ungebant*, etc., that is, The apostles anointed the sick, and healed them. This anointing does not favor the Papists: (1.) because it related to the curing of a bodily disease; but sacraments to the healing of the soul. (2.) The apostles healed any that were sick; but extreme unction is only applied to those that are past hope of recovery. (3.) The apostles without making any difference between them that were, or were not baptized, anointed both; but the church of Rome anoints none but the baptized. And (4.) The apostolic unction was miraculous, and for the healing of diseases; hence it is joined with the power of preaching the gospel, and casting out devils: therefore the commission was singular and temporary, and respected none but those who had received the miraculous gift of healings. In James 5:14–15 the same unction is meant, that is described in Mark: and the apostolic anointing differs widely from the Popish one; because the former refers only to the healing of the body, but the other to quite another

7. THE SACRAMENTS IN GENERAL 195

in the use of miraculous powers, those to whom that gift was given were not empowered to use it at pleasure; they were to feel an inward impulse exciting them to it, and they were obliged upon that to believe that God who had given them the impulse would not be wanting to them in the execution of it. This confidence in God was the *faith of miracles*, of which Christ said, "If ye have faith as a grain of mustard seed, ye shall say to this mountain, Remove hence to yonder place…and nothing shall be impossible unto you" (Matt. 17:20). Of this also Paul meant, when he said, *If I have all faith.* So from this we may gather the meaning of *the prayer of faith*, and *the anointing with oil*; that if the elders of the church, or such others with whom this power was lodged, felt an inward impulse moving them to call upon God, in order to a miraculous cure of a sick person, then they were to *anoint him with oil in the name of the Lord*; that is, by the authority that they had from Christ to heal all manner of diseases; and *they were to pray*, believing firmly that God would make good that inward motion which he had given them to work this inward miracle; and in that case the effect was certain, the sick person would certainly recover, for that is absolutely promised. Every one that was sick was not to be anointed, unless an authority and motion from Christ had been secretly given for doing it; but everyone that was anointed was certainly healed. Christ had promised that *whatever they should ask in his name, he would do it. His name* must be restrained to his authority, or pursuant to such secret motions as they should receive from him. This is the prayer of faith mentioned here by James; it being an earnest application to God, to join his omnipotent power to perform a wonderful work, to which a person

---

thing. James commands *any* sick persons to be anointed; but the Papists anoint only *the dying*: the end of *his* anointing was the *raising up of the sick*; but the end of *theirs* is the *fortifying of the sick against the fear of death*. In fine, here is a *command* to anoint, and a *sign*; but both of them temporary, which were to last only till the gift of healings should cease in the church." *Rissen. Compend. Theol. loc.* 17.

"The apostles used *anointing with oil* in the name of the Lord (James 5:14), as an external sign of what he would do; in that as certainly as their bodies were anointed with it their health should be restored: and this shows the vanity of Popish pretenses to the sacrament of extreme unction, which they use for the remission of the sins of dying persons, that their souls may be saved in the world they are going to; whereas the apostles used it only as a signal of restoring the sick to health." Guyse, *Paraphrase*, note on Mark 6:13.

so divinely qualified found himself inwardly moved by the Spirit of Christ. And thus the anointing mentioned by James was in order to a miraculous cure, and the cure did constantly follow it: so that it can be no precedent for an *extreme unction*, that is never given till the recovery of the person is despaired of, and by which it is not pretended that any cure is wrought.[10]

4. The next Popish sacrament is *orders*, or rather *ordination*. They give this description of it:

> It is a sacrament of the new law, wherein by the imposition of hands, and the delivering of certain instruments, to wit, a cup, and plate, or the book of the gospels, besides the accidental ceremonies of shaving and anointing, accompanied with the following words: *Take thou authority to offer up sacrifices to God, and to celebrate masses both for the living and the dead; in the name of the Father, the Son, and the Holy Ghost*. Grace necessary to discharge their office, with an impressed indelible character, is conferred on priests and deacons; and even on sub-deacons, and lower orders, though the same rites are not used about the last.[11]

The matter of this ordinance is human, as far as it respects the *ordainers*, who must be only bishops; and many of the *orders ordained*, who they allege are of seven kinds; and the *signs* and *words*, which have no Scripture-warrant; and, moreover, it is not common to Christians, which Christ intended every sacrament to be; but restrained to a part of the church.

5. The last of their pretended sacraments is *marriage*. They give the following account of it, to wit,

---

[10] Burnet, *Exposition of the Thirty-nine Articles*, article 25.
[11] That the reader's just indignation may be excited against such perverse abuses of sacred things, as well as his curiosity gratified, I shall give a specimen of their impious fooleries.
  The council of Florence, anno 1440, or thereabout, appointed "the office of priests to be conferred by delivering them a cup filled with wine, and a plate with bread...of deacons, by giving them the book of the gospels...and of sub-deacons, by delivering them an empty cup, with an empty plate laid upon it." Forbes, *Instructiones*, chap. 7. sect. 8.

That it is a sacrament of the new covenant, wherein, by the mutual consent of married Christians, expressed in words or signs, the spiritual union of Christ with the church is represented, and the grace of mutual spiritual union is bestowed on married persons.

There is no material sign appointed by Christ in this ordinance; nor is there any institution of it for such an end as they allege; nor is matrimony peculiar to Christians, being common to them and heathens; nor will they allow their priests to partake of it, any more than their laity of holy orders.

How naturally do men wrest the Scriptures! Because the apostle, speaking of the union between Christ and his church, which is illustrated by the conjugal union, says, "This is a great mystery" (Eph. 5:32), they will have it that he says, *This is a great sacrament.* And yet if anybody will believe them, when they produce their strong reasons for the celibacy of their clergy, he would think this great sacrament no better than a vile institution, inconsistent with either a good conscience, or a spiritual temper. The common saying, "That the devil has a cloven foot," is perhaps intended to describe the self-contradiction of his doctrines.

But I must ask the reader's pardon for abusing his patience with any remarks on a scheme that is absurd enough to confute itself, whenever it is mentioned.

I conclude, upon the whole, that there are only two sacraments, baptism and the Lord's Supper, given unto the New Testament church, by the authority of Jesus Christ; and that the five Popish sacraments are so called without either truth or reason.

7. The Wisdom and Advantages

The wisdom and advantages of dealing with men by sacramental ordinances are very obvious, and will not require much illustration. Human nature consists of a true body and a reasonable soul vitally united. These naturally receive mutual impressions from one another, and contribute either to the happiness or misery of mankind. Every man's experience and observation afford him the fullest evidence of this.

God knoweth well our frame, and adapts his way of dealing with men accordingly. He addresses himself to the understanding by powerful, persuasive demonstration; to the will and affections, by every advantageous, encouraging argument drawn from pleasure and profit; to the ear, by wholesome, pleasant instruction; to the eye, by assuring, confirming representations; and to all the senses, by their most proper channels to instill knowledge and affect the heart.

It does not become us to prescribe unto God what he should do; but we should wisely observe the propriety and beauty of all his appointments; "Whoso is wise, and will observe these things, even they shall understand the lovingkindness of the LORD" (Ps. 107:43).

In the sacraments we may see God's abounding wisdom, as well as his most excellent loving-kindness. He presents to our minds the most entertaining, salutary truths, in such a way as unites sense and reason, in promoting a deeper knowledge, a firmer belief, and more affecting experience of the things of God.

The bodily senses and corporeal objects are hereby entered into the service of faith; and faith is constituted governess to these handmaids, that support her throne, brighten up her evidence, and promote her exercise.

Here we learn to glorify God in his creatures, and to converse with heaven by the use of earthly things. *To mind earthly things*, by setting the heart upon them, is a character of the man who is an enemy to the cross of our Lord Jesus Christ (Phil. 3:18–19). Even as it is the honor of the saints to have their conversation in heaven, while they are conversant with things on earth (Phil. 3:20). Sacramental ordinances are well calculated to promote this most important and benevolent design. They direct our views to the sublime satisfactions of immortal blessedness; they instruct and edify the soul in spiritual mindedness; and they do both by conversing with earthly things; and while we are taught the necessary lesson of looking for the blessed hope, and the glorious appearing of the great God our Savior, we are guarded against overvaluing the means of conveying it, which are taken from this world, the fashion whereof passeth away. Here the signs are *corporeal*, and suited to our *bodies*; the things they represent, seal, and apply, are *spiritual*, and suited to our *souls*; and the happy union of the signs with the things they signify, and their mutual relation, render them every way agreeable to our complex frame.

We may apply to this dispensation of adorable wisdom and grace what the apostle says about the temporary *rejection of the Jews*, that are to be brought to the faith of Christ in the fullness of time, and the *calling of the Gentiles*, "O the depth of the riches both of the wisdom and knowledge of God! how unsearchable are his judgments, and his ways past finding out!" (Rom. 11:33).

8. The Persons That May Administer Them

I shall close this chapter on the sacraments in general by showing, *Who have authority to administer them*. This point does not require much to be said on it, after what has been already advanced on the *ordinance of preaching the gospel*. See chapter 2, section 3.

I affirm that neither of the sacraments may be dispensed by any but by a minister of the word lawfully ordained. The proofs of this assertion are plain and cogent.

1. The express declarations of Scripture put it beyond doubt, "Go ye therefore, and teach all nations, baptizing them in the name of the Father, and of the Son, and of the Holy Ghost" (Matt. 28:19); "When ye come together therefore into one place, this is not to eat the Lord's supper" (1 Cor. 11:20); "For I have received of the Lord that which also I delivered unto you, That the Lord Jesus the same night in which he was betrayed, took bread" (v. 23); "Let a man so account of us, as of the ministers of Christ, and stewards of the mysteries of God" (1 Cor. 4:1); "No man taketh this honour to himself, but he that is called of God, as was Aaron" (Heb. 5:4).

2. All that ever administered these ordinances in the apostolic age were either ordinarily or extraordinarily called. The baptism of John, Christ's forerunner, was of heaven; and so was the authority of all who ministered in these holy things. Therefore it is only bold, dangerous presumption for men to assume the exercise, without the right, of dispensing them.

And if it would be daring presumption for any man to affix the king's seal to a charter or letters-patent, unless he were a person duly authorized, and deputed by the king for that purpose, can it be thought safe or expedient for any who has not the visible evidences of the authority of Christ calling him thereunto, to administer these *seals of the righteousness of faith?*

The examples of Zipporah circumcising her son, and of Ananias, Philip, and others baptizing, are no sufficient proof that the sacraments may be administered by such as are not ministers lawfully ordained.

Zipporah circumcised her child with a sharp stone (Ex. 4:25). But this was before the settlement of the Jewish dispensation, in many of its important circumstances; and what she did either belonged to her province, and so she did her duty; or it did not, and so she did wrong; or there was no divine rule to direct who should perform this office, and so it was indifferent. But in the New Testament, we are assured that men are *sent* to baptize, as well as to preach (Matt. 28:19–20). Therefore it would be wrong for any person that is not lawfully sent to preach the gospel, to take upon him to administer this or the other sacrament.

Philip, one of the seven primitive deacons, baptized the Eunuch (Acts 8:38); but he was an evangelist as well as a deacon (Acts 21:8). And a part of the work of an evangelist was to administer the sacraments.

Ananias probably baptized Paul (Acts 9). But if he did, he was authorized by God to do so (v. 10). Besides, he was perhaps one of the seventy disciples Christ sent forth to preach and baptize; and is generally thought to have been a pastor of the Christian church at Damascus.

I defy any man to produce an example of any *private person* administering these ordinances in the apostolic churches; and it will be still harder to produce any command authorizing such a person to perform such a service. And it is certainly extremely dangerous to do anything without a clear warrant in that system of worship which owes its being, form, and success, entirely to the revealed will of God.

Chapter 8

Baptism

The ordinary sacraments of the New Testament are two, and no more: to wit, *baptism* and *the Lord's Supper*. These are authorized by our Lord's express appointment; who also consecrated them for the service of his church, by his own example; and by promising his blessing to accompany the proper use of them, according to his institution.

Baptism is my present subject; and in order to give a concise sketch of it, I shall consider the most important parts thereof in this plain easy method. I shall give some account:

1. Of the name of this holy ordinance;
2. Of its nature;
3. Of its authority and institution;
4. Of its excellency and usefulness;
5. Of the objections that are made against it;
6. Of the *persons* to whom it is to be administered;
7. Of the *manner* of performing this duty; and,
8. Of the practical directions that are profitable to be observed relative to it.

1. Its Name

Baptism, originally a Greek word, signifies *washing* (Mark 7:4, 8; Heb. 9:10). It is certain the Jews were commanded to wash the unclean, in order to *the purifying of the flesh*. A great part of their service, indeed, consisted in *divers washings*, or *baptisms*, of this sort. And it is no less evident they were to *wash* or *baptize*, as a token of *dedication to God*, "And Aaron and his sons thou shalt bring unto the door of the tabernacle of the congregation, and shalt *wash* them with water" (Ex. 29:4).

Many learned men have affirmed that long before our Savior's time, the

Jews received proselytes into their church by baptizing them.[1] And it is well known that the Jewish writers are almost universally of this opinion, as may be seen in the quotations from them in the works of those writers that were adepts in that kind of learning.

Others will have this Jewish rite to be of later date than this.[2] But they cannot deny that it is mentioned as a well known and established practice in the *Gemara*, a Jewish work, executed, as Dr. Gill thinks, about the year of our Lord 230, and near 1540 years ago.

Indeed if we consider several hints in the New Testament, the antiquity of this practice will seem at least very probable. When John the Baptist began his ministry, his most zealous opposers never asked him, *What meanest thou?* or, *What wouldst thou signify to us by this new ceremony of baptizing?* No question of this import was ever put to him. But they interrogated him about his character and authority, and about these only.

> And this is the record of John, when the Jews sent priests and Levites from Jerusalem to ask him, Who art thou? And he confessed, and denied not; but confessed, I am not the Christ. And they asked him, What then? Art thou Elias? And he saith, I am not. Art thou that prophet? And he answered, No. Then said they unto him, Who art thou? that we may give an answer to them that sent us. What sayest thou of thyself?...And they asked him, and said unto him, Why baptizest thou then, if thou be not that Christ, nor Elias, neither that prophet? (John 1:19–22, 25).

From hence Dr. Gill has observed, it appears, that the Jews expected that baptism would be administered in the times of the Messiah, and his forerunner; but I confess, it is a forced inference that he afterwards subjoins, "that no such practice had obtained before among the Jews, or they would not have been alarmed at it as they were." I should rather think it almost certain that such a practice had obtained before, and therefore the Jews were alarmed at the baptism of John, who was not authorized by the Sanhedrin; and hence they concluded he was initiating men to another system than theirs, which threatened fearful consequences to their constitution.

---

[1] Selden, Lightfoot, Spenser, Ainsworth, Witsius, Grotius, Wall, Altingius, Hammond, etc.

[2] Sir Norton Knatchbull, Stennet, Gill, etc.

8. BAPTISM

They seem to have understood the design of his baptism so well that they never inquired anything at all about the meaning of it. The apprehensions they had of the Baptist's authority and character were the only causes of their alarm. They do not so much as insinuate that there was any novelty in what he did. "There was a man of the Pharisees, named Nicodemus, a ruler of the Jews: the same came to Jesus by night, and said unto him, Rabbi, we know that thou art a Teacher come from God: for no man can do these miracles that thou doest, except God be with him. Jesus answered and said unto him, Verily, verily I say unto thee, Except a man be born again, he cannot see the kingdom of God." After an ignorant cavil, and a very gracious illustration and confirmation of the most important truth, Nicodemus, partly silenced, though not fully satisfied, said unto Christ, "How can these things be? Jesus answered and said unto him, Art thou a master of Israel, and knowest not these things?" namely, what it is to be *born again of water, and of the Spirit* (John 3:1-10).

While our Lord spake of these things, he had used a phrase that was familiar enough among the Jews, as Dr. Gill and others have observed. The Jews knew that *any Gentile* that would enter into the kingdom of God must be born again, but our Savior assures Nicodemus that *everyone*, Jew or Gentile, must be *so born*. And when Nicodemus did not apprehend his meaning, but took the words in a proper sense, our Lord speaks still plainer, and says, that *everyone* must be born of water, and of the Spirit, wondering at the same time that he, being a master of Israel, had not understood him, while he was only pointing out the obvious scope of such doctrines and services as were commonly taught, and daily practiced, in the Jewish church.

There has been much dispute about the true meaning of the word *baptism*, as it is used in this Christian ordinance, whether it signifies *immersion*, or *sprinkling*.

Some think that it only signifies the putting a person or thing into the water, whereby it is covered, or, as it were, buried in it; which is otherwise expressed by the word *dipping*, or *plunging*.

Others are of opinion that it signifies, in general, using the means of cleansing by the application of water, in whatever form that application is made, either by *pouring*, or *sprinkling*, by *plunging*, or *dipping*.

It is an extreme to be too positive in affirming that there is no right administration of this ordinance unless the person be dipped; which is the opinion of Anti-paedobaptists; and it is perhaps carrying the point too far, on the other hand, to deny that dipping is an allowable mode of administering it.

I apprehend the middle opinion is most safe, and capable of a good defense, namely, that "*dipping* the person *into* the water is *not necessary*; but baptism is *rightly administered* by *pouring*, or *sprinkling* water *upon* the person."[3]

To establish this position, I shall, first, represent the scriptural use of the word *baptize* or *baptism*; and then attempt to show that this ordinance is rightly administered by pouring or sprinkling.

1. The scriptural sense of the word *baptize* or *baptism* may be gathered from the places where it is found. Among several instances of this kind, I shall only refer to two or three.

> And when they [the Pharisees and certain of the scribes] saw some of his [Christ's] disciples eat bread with defiled, that is to say with *unwashen, hands* [ανιπτοις], they found fault. For the Pharisees, and all the Jews, except they *wash* [νιψωνται] *their hands* oft [πυγμη, *with the fist*] eat not, holding the tradition of the elders. And when they come from the market, except *they wash* [βαπτισωνται], they eat not. And many other things there be, which they have received to hold, as *the washing* [βαπτισμους] of cups, and pots, brasen vessels, and of tables [κλινων, or rather, *beds*]. Then the Pharisees and scribes asked him, Why walk not thy disciples according to the tradition of the elders, but eat bread with *unwashen hands* [ανιπτοις]?...Ye hold the tradition of men, as *the washing* [βαπτισμους] of pots and cups: and many other such like things ye do (Mark 7:2–4, 8).

Compare

> And as he [Christ] spake, a certain Pharisee besought him to dine with him: and he went in, and sat down to meat. And when the Pharisee saw it, he marvelled that he had not *first washed before dinner* [ου πρωτον εβαπτισθη] (Luke 11:37–38).

---

[3] *Westminster Confession of Faith*, chap. 28. ss 3.

From these passages the following remarks arise, without any force or straining: (1.) That the *washing of hands* (Mark 7:2–3), and *baptizing* or *washing themselves* before they ate bread, or took dinner (Luke 11:38), signify precisely the same thing. (2:) The Jews made this a daily custom, to *wash their hands*, or *baptize themselves*, before they took meat. (3.) It follows that their baptizing themselves was only by applying water to *a part* of their bodies. (4.) This water was applied in the ordinary way they used it to wash their hands, and the *manner* of doing this is clearly described, "Elisha the son of Shaphat…poured water *on the hands* of Elijah" (2 Kings 3:11). And Dr. Pocock has largely proved from the Jewish rabbis that, in later times, the Jews washed their hands in the same manner:[4] "They do not wash their hands," he says, "but with water poured on them out of a vessel." (5.) They extended their *washings* or *baptisms*, not only to *cups, pots,* and *brazen vessels*, but to *tables* or *beds* (Mark 7:4). This was one of the traditions of the elders, but none of the commandments of God. It was to be practiced by the poorest, as well as by the richest. Consequently all were furnished with opportunities for it. But burdensome as that dispensation was, this must have crowned the whole to the poor, if each family must have a laver for that purpose, and use it accordingly.

"Moreover, brethren, I would not that ye should be ignorant, how that all our fathers were under the cloud, and all passed through the sea; and were all *baptized* unto Moses in the cloud, and in the sea" (1 Cor. 10:1–2).

These words evidently refer to that astonishing interposition of the power and favor of God in behalf of Israel, when he delivered them from the land of Egypt, and out of the house of bondage, and guided them, in the greatness of his strength, by a pillar of cloud and fire, toward his holy habitation, giving them light by night, and overshadowing them by day. When they came under this conduct, to the Red sea, he divided its proud waves, and made a way for his ransomed ones to march on dry land through its mighty waters; previous to which, the cloud that had gone before them till they were enclosed by the unpassable rocks, the devouring flood, and the pursuing foe, removed, probably straight over their heads, and settled between Israel and the Egyptian host. Then, it may be, that event happened, which the psalmist records, "The clouds poured out water" (Ps. 77:17). They passed through the sea *on dry land*, while the congealed element towered aloft on the right hand, and on the left. Then *they*

---

[4] Vide Not. miscel. chap. 9. Non lavant manus nisi e vase assusa aqua. Ib.

were baptized unto Moses, that is, they were initiated into the covenant God made with them, by the ministry of Moses; and so were brought under an obligation to believe and obey the divine law of that typical mediator and deliverer: *in the cloud*, which hung over them, probably also poured out water upon them; *and in the sea*, through which they passed on dry land, while, it may be, its agitated waves scattered their gentle froth upon God's *chosen people*; but without immersing them in a common death, as they did the *army of Pharaoh*.

To pretend that the *Israelites* were, so to speak, *immersed* in the cloud, and in the sea, is neither *proper* nor *true*, according to that notion of *immersion*, which makes it signify *the putting anything or person into water, to be covered with it.* Is it most natural to think they were *put into* the cloud, or that the cloud was *brought upon* them?

When Israel was baptized in the sea, they were not put *into it*; but it was reared *over them*, and watered their host only with the dashing of its waves. Accordingly, Dr. Gill thinks, "that the cloud, when it passed over them, *let down* a plentiful rain upon them."[5] Where he yields all that we ask; that *baptism* denotes a washing, by *putting water upon* the person or thing, that is washed or baptized, as well as by *putting into water*.

"Hebrews 9:10. Which Jewish service stood only in meats and drinks, and *divers washings* [διαφοροις βαπτισμοις], and carnal ordinances, imposed on them until the time of reformation."

There were *several kinds* of *washing* used among the Jews; as *bathing, dipping*, and *sprinkling*. The reader will find many examples of this kind in the law of Moses (Num. 19:18–20; Ex. 29:4; Lev. 16:14–15, *etc.*).

And, I believe, the most part of considerate readers will be of opinion that the apostle gives some *examples* of the *baptisms* or *washings*, practiced among the Jews, in that context, as in Hebrews 9:13, "The blood of bulls and of goats, and the ashes of an heifer *sprinkling* the unclean, sanctifieth to the purifying of the flesh." Verse 19, "When Moses had spoken every precept to all the people according to the law, he took the blood of calves and of goats, with water, and scarlet wool, and hyssop, and *sprinkled* both the book, and all the people." Verse 21, "Moreover he *sprinkled* with blood both the tabernacle, and all the vessels of the ministry." Verse 22, "And almost all things are by the law *purged* with blood." Verse 23, "It was there-

---

[5] John Gill. *The Ancient Mode of Baptizing by Immersion Maintained*, p. 70.

fore necessary that the patterns of things in the heavens should be *purified* with these."

The Jewish baptisms were *divers* (διαφοροι). They are so called, not only because *many things* were washed, nor because some things were *often* washed; but the word signifies that the washings were of *different kinds*. There is a like expression used "Having then gifts *differing* [διαφορα] according to the grace that is given to us" (Rom. 12:6), where it certainly denotes a diversity both in *kind*, and in *use* (compare 1 Cor. 12 and Eph. 4). And if *these baptisms* were *really different in their kind and uses*, they must denote *washings* in general, by *dipping, bathing, pouring*, or *sprinkling*. The liquids, with which they were performed, are well known to have been *water, blood*, or *oil*.

Some have thought that even βαπτω which is a different word, and of a much stronger and more determinate meaning, does not necessarily signify *dipping*: "He [Christ] was clothed with a vesture *dipped* [βεβαμμενον] in blood" (Rev. 19:13). Dr. Owen[6] thinks it would be better rendered *stained*, by *sprinkling* blood upon it. And this sense is well supported by comparing it with that parallel text, "Wherefore art thou red in thine apparel, and thy garments, *N.B., like him that treadeth in the winefat?* I have trodden the winepress alone; and of the people there was none with me: for I will tread them in mine anger, and *N.B., their blood shall be* sprinkled upon *my garments, and I will* stain *all my raiment*" (Isa. 63:2–3). This text speaks the same language; it has the same meaning with the former. Therefore, *the vesture dipped in blood* denotes *a garment sprinkled, and raiment stained with blood*.

Now, if this word may be understood in that sense, why may not βαπτιζω, a word of far more general signification, be explained in this sense too?

2. I shall now attempt to show that the ordinance of baptism is *rightly administered* by *pouring*, or *sprinkling* of water upon the person who is baptized.

I shall take leave to represent this argument in the nervous [vigorous], well-chosen words of a late writer, who says,

> I cannot think that such prodigious numbers as came to John, could be baptized in the way of immersing their whole bodies under water;

---

[6] See John Owen. *The Complete Collection of the Sermons of John Owen*, pp. 580–581.

or that they were provided with change of raiment for it, which is nowhere intimated, nor seems to have been practicable for such vast multitudes; and yet they could not be baptized naked with modesty, nor in their wearing apparel with safety. It seems therefore to me that the people stood in ranks, near to, or just within the edge of the river; and John, passing along before them, cast water upon their heads or faces with his hands, or some proper instrument, by which means he might easily baptize many thousands in a day. And this way of pouring water upon them most naturally signified Christ's baptizing them with the Holy Ghost, and with fire, which John spoke of as prefigured by his baptizing with water (Matt. 3:11; Mark 1:8; Luke 3:16; John 1:33) and which was eminently fulfilled when the Holy Ghost sat upon the disciples *in the appearance of cloven tongues like fire*; and this is expressly called *baptizing them with the Holy Ghost*, in opposition to John's *baptizing with water*, and is spoken of as the Holy Ghost's *coming upon them*, and as God's *pouring out his Spirit*, and *shedding him forth upon them* (Acts 1:5, 8; 2:3, 17–18, 33). And with a direct reference hereunto, when the Holy Ghost *fell on* Cornelius, and his friends, Peter said; "Then remembered I the word of the Lord, how he said, John indeed baptized with water; but ye shall be baptized with the Holy Ghost" (Acts 11:15–16). The apostle Paul likewise, in a manifest allusion to baptism, speaks of God's "saving us by the washing of regeneration, and renewing of the Holy Ghost: which he shed on us abundantly, through Jesus Christ our Savior" (Titus 3:5–6). Now, whether plunging the body into water, or pouring water upon it, was the likeliest emblem of this effusion of the Spirit, let the reader judge; especially since (βαπτιζω) the word constantly used for baptizing, signifies any sort of washing, and often sprinkling; not being restrained to dipping, as its primitive (βαπτω) is; but this last word is never used to express baptizing.[7]

The arguments that are brought to prove *dipping* to be the only scriptural mode of administering this ordinance are such as these.

1. "When we read of baptism in the New Testament, the person baptized is said to *go down into the water* (εις το υδωρ); as the eunuch did

---

[7] Guyse, *Paraphrase*, note on Matthew 3:6.

(Acts 8:38), and immediately after baptism, *to come up out of the water* (εχ του υδατος) (Acts 8:39). Now, it is supposed, all this can agree to no mode of baptism, but that of *immersion.*"

Answer. The whole strength of this argument depends upon the sense that is given of the Greek particles εις and εχ, which we often render *into* and *out of.* But this argument will have no weight with anyone that knows how they are used in the New Testament. Our Savior bade Peter go (εις την θαλασσαν) to the sea, and cast a hook, *etc.* (Matt. 17:27); would it be either proper, or true, to insinuate that Peter was commanded to go *into* the sea? The queen of the south came *from* (εχ) the utmost parts of the earth, *etc.* (Luke 11:31). It is absurd to render it *out of the utmost parts of the earth*; though very proper to say that she came *from thence.* I could give abundance of more instances (Matt. 4:8; 5:1; 14:23; 15:29; *etc.*). The sense is quite easy, when the words are rendered thus, "They went down both *unto* the water, both Philip and the Eunuch; and he baptized him. And when they were come up *from* the water," *etc.* (Acts 8:38–39). And, to support this version, the two following passages may be considered, "Jesus, when he was baptized, went up straightway *from the water* [απο του υδατος]" (Matt. 3:16), not *out of it.* "John answered, saying unto them all, I indeed *baptize you with water* [υδατι βαπτιζω υμας]" (Luke 3:16), not *into it.*

2. "We are told that John was baptizing in Aenon, near to Salim, because there was much water there" (John 3:23). From which passage, it is inferred that he certainly practiced *immersion,* seeing a little water could have served as well, if he had only *sprinkled the face.*

Answer. Though the land of Canaan was a good land, of brooks of water, of fountains and deeps, that spring out of valleys and hills; yet the south part of it was but poorly watered (Judg. 1:15; Ps. 63:1). In this part John was then baptizing and preaching; and he chose it the rather because there were *many waters* (πολλα υδατα) there. The fertility of the place, in that wilderness, was a very good reason for fixing his residence there for a time, while he taught, and baptized such multitudes as flocked to him. And it will be granted, I suppose, by the most zealous pleaders for immersion, that there was some other reason for choosing Aenon, where there was *much water,* or *many waters,* than merely to get *water enough to dip* those that were baptized. It is certain, however, that *Baptists*, in latter times, commonly do their business without any large quantity of water. They generally use a cistern. And what can be a stronger evidence that they do not suppose a huge collection of waters, or a great stream, to be necessary? I must be of opinion, therefore, that the *much water* at Aenon was particularly regarded for the refreshment of the men and cattle that were brought together on the occasion. And it was for the same reason he baptized *in*, or *at* Jordan (Matt. 3:5–6).

3. An argument is taken from

> Know ye not, that so many of us as were baptized into Jesus Christ were baptized into his death? Therefore we are buried with him by baptism into death: that like as Christ was raised up from the dead by the glory of the Father, even so we also should walk in newness of life. For if we have been planted together in the likeness of his death, we shall be also in the likeness of his resurrection (Rom. 6:3–5).

This passage is supposed to imply that there is a similitude between the sign and the thing signified in baptism; and consequently, that the ordinance should be performed in such a way that, by being covered with water, there might be a resemblance of Christ's burial, and, by being lifted up out of the water, a resemblance of his resurrection.

> *Answer.* Were we to admit that the apostle, in this place, alludes to *dipping*, the most, I think, we can gather from the whole is that baptism was sometimes administered in one of these ways, and sometimes in the other; and that it cannot be said of either of these particular modes that it is essential to this ordinance; and therefore it is a pity that there should be such warm contentions as have troubled the church of Christ about so little and so disputable a thing as the external mode of its administration. But, after all, I am very much of opinion with Mr. Henry, or his continuator, Dr. Evans, who, in the exposition of this passage, says: "Why this burying in baptism should so much as allude to any custom of dipping under water in baptism, any more than our baptismal crucifixion and death should have any such reference, I confess I cannot see. It is plain that it is not the sign, but the thing signified in baptism, that the apostle here calls being buried with Christ; and the expression of burying alludes to Christ's burial: as Christ was buried, that he might rise to a new and more heavenly life; so we are in baptism buried, *i.e.*, cut off from

the life of sin, that we may rise again to a new life in faith and love." And others have thought that the reference is only to the benefits of spiritual baptism, and that nothing can be concluded about the external mode of baptism from this verse, more than from the next, which speaks of our being therein symbolically *planted together in the likeness of Christ's death*; or than from *the figure of baptism saving us*, as represented by the floating of Noah's ark, when the few that were in it *were saved by water* (1 Peter 3:20–21). But no mode of baptism can be signified by either of these.[8]

We are not warranted from Scripture to say that Christ's baptism was a burial. It is a fond conceit, more witty than solid, to call it so. By sufferings he was brought to the grave; and these sufferings are called *his baptism* (Matt. 20:22–23), or, otherwise *the shedding of his blood* (Matt. 26:28). And as the sprinkling of the blood of Jesus, that had been shed for remission of sins unto many, in order to procure their death to the law-covenant, and to sin, is represented in this ordinance of baptism, there is a striking propriety in urging this weighty consideration, to stir up believers to mortify their members that are upon the earth, and instead of continuing in sin, to live unto God.

4. It is alleged that the practice of *dipping* is supported and referred to,

> Buried with him in baptism, wherein also you are risen with him through the faith of the operation of God, who hath raised him from the dead. And you being dead in your sins and the uncircumcision of your flesh, hath he quickened together with him, having forgiven you all trespasses (Col. 2:12–13).

Answer. All sides are agreed that this passage is of the same import with Romans 6:4, and therefore, what was said on it may be compared. *Buried with Christ in baptism* (Col. 2:12) is evidently compared and contrasted with *being dead in sins* (Col. 2:13). *To be buried with Christ* has indeed a reference to *the burial of Christ*, even as *to be crucified with him* relates to *his* crucifixion; but neither of these expressions can be thought to refer to *his baptism*; and why should either the one or the other be supposed to

---

[8] Guyse, *Paraphrase*, note on Romans 6:4.

have any relation to the *mode* of our baptism? Perhaps, it will be replied, that this is implied in the text, *buried with him in baptism*. But since this is opposed to *being dead in sins*, it cannot bear a more natural interpretation than the following, which I shall give in the words of an eminent writer:

> The ordinance of baptism…is a sign of, and obligation to, all the holiness, that is, or ought to be, found…in God's covenant-people, by…being conformable to Christ's death, in utterly dying to sin, and giving full evidence of it with continuance, as he died that it might be crucified, and was manifested to be entirely dead, by his being buried and continuing some time in the grave.[9]

How much more natural and unforced is this sense than to rest the emphasis of the text on the circumstance of the mode of baptism! This sense is obvious, self-consistent, and exhibits, with force and dignity, the scope of the apostle's conclusive and irresistible reasoning.

On the whole, I conclude that the words *baptism* and *baptize* properly signify *washing*, by using the means of cleansing; either by *dipping*, *pouring*, or *sprinkling*. And it seems to me at least as probable that the divine ordinance of baptism was originally designed to be administered by *sprinkling*, or *pouring*, as by *dipping*. And, I am satisfied, it is rightly administered by *pouring*, or *sprinkling* water upon the person, without *dipping*.

I shall just add that I do not see any necessity of washing the *whole body* with water, since many things are said to have been *dipped* that were not *all over* immersed (Gen. 37:31 Ex. 12:22; Lev. 4:6, 17; John 13:26; *etc.*). It seems to answer the purpose if only *a part* of the body be washed (compare Mark 4:2–3 with Luke 11:38, also John 13:5 with John 13:8).

So much for the *name*; I shall now proceed,

2. Its Nature

To explain the *nature* of baptism. This may be gathered from its original institution in the New Testament church, "Go ye therefore, and teach all nations, baptizing them in the name of the Father, and of the Son, and of the Holy Ghost" (Matt. 28:19). "Go ye into all the world, and preach the

---

[9] Guyse, *Paraphrase*, paraphrase on the place.

gospel to every creature. He that believeth and is baptized shall be saved" (Mark 16:15–16). Where we may learn the following things.

1. This ordinance is only designed for the church of God, and none but such as are disciples have anything to do with it. It was originally appointed for them, and for none else. To baptize such as do not belong to this holy society is to mock God, and to pervert his institution. We need not ask, who hath *required* such a service? We may rather say, who hath *permitted* such a presumptuous and criminal defiance of the authority of the most high God? Shall not God most certainly, most awfully visit for such an iniquity? Shall not his soul be avenged on such daring offenders as these? He says, the nations are first to be taught, and then to be baptized; first to believe, then to be washed.

2. Baptism does not confer grace or implant any principle of divine life, as some have affirmed. According to the institution, it is obvious that men are first supposed to be disciples and believers, and then they are to be baptized. This is quite another thing than if it had been said, "baptize them, that they may become disciples and believers by that means." Baptism, as well as circumcision, is *a seal of the righteousness of faith* (Rom. 4:11). Accordingly when the apostles executed their commission which they received from the Lord Jesus, they evidently acted on very different principles from the church of Rome, or others, who, in that particular about baptismal regeneration, tread in their steps; for they never baptized any *adult* person, of whose faith and regeneration they had not some satisfying evidence before he was baptized (see Acts 2:41; 8:36–38; 10:44–48; 16:14–15; *etc.*).

It is indeed alleged that baptismal regeneration may be inferred from several texts: such as, "Repent, and be baptized every one of you in the name of Jesus Christ for the remission of sins, and ye shall receive the gift of the Holy Ghost" (Acts 2:38). But this only implies that baptism obliges to repentance, and leads our views to the righteousness of Christ, in which we are pardoned and accepted, and of which this ordinance is a seal through faith.

They likewise urge "Not by works of righteousness which we have done, but according to his mercy he saved us, by the *washing of regeneration*, and *renewing of the Holy Ghost*" (Titus 3:5). Where it is plain enough that baptism is a figure of regenerating grace, that cleanses from sin, and is effected by that renovation in the spirit of the mind, which is the special operation of the Holy Spirit; but there is no hint of the efficacy of baptism in all that are baptized, to wash them from their sins, or to save their souls.

Moreover, they quote 1 Peter 3:21, "baptism doth also now save us." I only desire the reader to connect the next words in the same verse: "(not the putting away of the filth of the flesh but the answer of a good conscience toward God,) by the resurrection of Jesus Christ,"[10] and he will immediately see the fallacy of their gloss.

But if we appeal to facts, it will be very evident that baptism does not convey an immortal principle of divine life. Simon was baptized (Acts 8:13), and yet remained in the gall of bitterness and bond of iniquity (v. 23). Many that have been baptized, both in infancy and adult age, give undeniable proofs of their continuing in the same state, and being under the same tempers. Nor can the defenders of baptismal regeneration support their opinion without renouncing the doctrine of the saints' perseverance, and every other capital point connected with it.

3. The sign to be used in this ordinance is *water*. John the Baptist, who came before our Lord's face, in the spirit and power of Elias, baptized with water (Matt. 3:11); and so did the apostles (Acts 8:36, 38; 10:47). There is no example of mixing anything in the water, or of using anything besides the water, to be a *substantial sign* in this ordinance. Anointing the person that is baptized with oil, putting salt in the mouth, and anointing the ears and nostrils with spittle, are uninstituted inventions of men that corrupt the institution of God.

4. This water is to be applied to the body, to *wash it*, or *baptize with it*. It is not to be taken in a metaphorical, but in a literal sense. Men of corrupt minds concerning the faith have wrested this ordinance in manifest contradiction to its original appointment; while some have substituted, with a slight alteration, these words of Christ, *I am the living water* (John 4:14), in the place of washing with *real water*. Others use fire instead of water, founding their opinion on Matthew 3:11. Others again dream that the person who is baptized must be whipped until his own blood overflow his body, because our Savior says, "Ye shall…indeed…be baptized with the baptism that I am baptized with" (Matt. 20:23).[11] Baptism is sometimes to be understood, by a metaphor of *sufferings*; and sometimes

---

[10] The meaning of this text will be opened afterwards, sect. 8.
[11] Johannes à Mark. *Compendium Theologiæ Christianæ Didactico Elencticum*, chap. 30, sect. 8.

by a metonymy, of conferring the extraordinary gifts of the Holy Ghost on the day of Pentecost; but the practice of the apostles, who baptized or washed with water, even after our Lord's ascension, and after the effusion of the Spirit, is an infallible commentary on the original institution of that ordinance, and clearly shows what Christ meant in that commission, "Go ye…teach all nations, *baptizing them*" (Matt. 28:19).

5. It is not every washing with water that is to be reckoned *baptizing* in a sacramental sense; even as it is not every meeting of Christians to eat bread and drink wine, that is to be reckoned *a showing of the Lord's death till he come* (1 Cor. 11:26). But washing with water is then to be esteemed a sacramental ordinance, when it is performed *in that manner*, and *for those ends*, which Christ has appointed. These will be considered afterwards.

6. The blood of sprinkling, and the Spirit of Christ, with the manifold blessings of the covenant of grace, are signified by the washing with water, in the name of the Father, and of the Son, and of the Holy Ghost, in this sacrament.

This ordinance implies some defilement, otherwise there would be no need of washing. Sin is often represented in Scripture as a matter of uncleanness, which pollutes the soul; and this it doth two ways: (1.) The principle of sin within us defaces the image of God, which was stamped upon man in his first creation; and (2.) The guilt of Adam's first sin, and of our own actual transgressions, exposes us to his punishing justice, on account of the breach of his law; for every sin is a transgression of the law of God, and the wages thereof is death. In baptism there is an implied acknowledgment of our double defilement, as we are *dead in sin*, and *condemned on account of sin*. The Jews were baptized *"confessing their sins"* (Matt. 3:6).

Baptism also sets forth the blessed provision which God hath made in his gospel, for the purification of our souls from sin, and all its defilements. (1.) He provided for the removal of our guilt, by washing away sin in the blood of Christ (1 John 1:7; Rev. 1:5). (2.) He provided for the renewing of our natures, the purifying of our hearts, and the right ordering of our conversations, by shedding on us abundantly the Holy Ghost to accomplish these glorious purposes (John 3:3, 5–6; Titus 3:5–6).

The removal of guilt, and sanctification of the Spirit, do either include or bring after them the whole train of blessedness, which consists in a covenant-interest in God, union to Christ, remission of sins, adoption, regeneration, and a joyful resurrection unto everlasting life.

Washing with water signifies the purging away of the *guilt of sin* by the blood of Jesus, "be baptized every one of you in the name of Jesus Christ for the remission of sins" (Acts 2:38); of the *defiling stain of sin* by the grace of the sanctifying Spirit, "Christ…loved the church, and gave himself for it; that he might sanctify and cleanse it with the washing of water by the word" (Eph. 5:25–26); of *both together*, "but ye are washed, but ye are sanctified, but ye are justified" (1 Cor. 6:11). *Ye are washed*, this is the general; *ye are justified, ye are sanctified*, these are the particulars included in it—*justified* in the name of our Lord Jesus Christ, *sanctified* by the Spirit of our God. And in all these texts there is an obvious reference to the spiritual signification of baptism.

7. Baptism is to be administered *in the name of the Father, and of the Son, and of the Holy Ghost.* The true reading is, *into* or *unto the name of the Father, etc.*

Here we have a glorious confession of the venerable mystery of the *Holy Trinity*; that the one JEHOVAH exists in three persons, the Father, the Son, and the Holy Ghost; and these three persons, coequal, coessential, self-existent, are one God. To be baptized *in* (or *into*, or *unto*) *their name*, implies,

(1.) That we confess the *authority* of the three-one God;

(2.) That we are devoted to his *command*;

(3.) That we adore his *perfections*;

(4.) That we profess our *homage* to him alone before all the world;

(5.) That we depend upon his *acceptance* and favor;

(6.) That from him we are to have the particular *blessings* of this ordinance;

(7.) That we would be conformed to his *image*;

(8.) That we do it with a hope of his *mercy* to eternal life;

(9.) That we are satisfied he *can* give us all this; and

(10.) That we join with the *whole number* of his devoted people.

These are *duties* comprehended in baptism, or *felicities* revealed by it; and if our souls are not employed upon them, we do but take the name of the Lord our God in vain.[12]

---

[12] All the particulars are explained by Mr. Thomas Bradbury, in his valuable sermons. Thomas Bradbury. *The Duty and Doctrine of Baptism: In Thirteen Sermons*, see his first and second sermons on Matthew 28:19. In the four last sermons on that text, he explains the relation of that ordinance to the ever-blessed Trinity, in a very comfortable light.

8. This ordinance brings everyone that is baptized under a solemn obligation *to be the Lord's*; that is, to live agreeably to the favor we receive from God, *viz.*, the pardon of our sins, and the sanctification of our souls; to watch against sin for time to come, and to abstain from all pollutions of flesh and spirit; for we are not washed with the representing sign of the blood and Spirit of Christ, that we may defile ourselves again. We engage to carry on the work of repentance and mortification of sin all our lives, as well as to live upon Christ by faith for the remission of daily rising transgressions. In short, it includes a holy resolution, through the grace of Christ, and by the aids of his Spirit, to follow every other means which God hath appointed for the rooting out of sin, with all its defilements from the soul, and restoring us to purity and holiness, and the likeness of God. Therefore our Savior, having instituted this sacrament, charged his apostles to enjoin all that they baptized to *observe all things that he had commanded them* (Matt. 28:19–20).

3. Its Authority and Institution

I shall now represent the *authority* and *institution* of *baptism*. This ordinance of the Christian church is *from heaven*, and not *of men*. Christ is the Lord and the author of it. The government is upon his shoulders, that he may give such laws, and appoint such ordinances, as are necessary for her edification. Among others he appointed *baptism*; for "the word of God came unto John the son of Zacharias in the wilderness" (Luke 3:2), and therefore John says, "he…sent me to baptize with water" (John 1:33). But this baptism of John was not a sacrament of the new dispensation, of the covenant of grace;[13] for the Baptist came to prepare the way of the Lord, by that service which referred to the kingdom of heaven, that was near, at hand, but not yet actually come (Mark 1:2–8). The baptisms of John and of Christ were not essentially different; for (1.) Both of them were from heaven; (2.) In both of them there was a washing with water; (3.) Both were performed unto the faith and confession of Christ; (4.) Both of them were signs and seals of the remission of sins; and (5.) Those that were baptized by either, were thereby laid under an obligation to bring forth fruits meet for repentance. But these baptisms differ in some circumstances: for (1.) The baptism of John was rather a preparation to the New Testament, than a

---

[13] Hermann Witsius. *De Œconomia Fœderum Dei cum Hominibus*, book 4. chap. 16. sect. 9.

sacrament of that dispensation; and (2.) The former referred to Christ, as then to come; but the latter to him as made manifest in his public character to be a Savior unto Israel.

During the personal ministry of Christ, his disciples *baptized*, as well as *taught* the people, "After these things came Jesus and his disciples into the land of Judea; and there he tarried with them, and *baptized*" (John 3:22). "When therefore the Lord knew how the Pharisees had heard that Jesus made and *baptized* more disciples than John, (though Jesus himself baptized not, but his disciples)" (John 4:1–2). This part of our Lord's ministry seems to have been confined to the Jews only. The baptism administered by the hands of his disciples was performed by *his authority* and therefore he is said to have baptized, though he did not baptize any with his own hands,[14] but by the ministry of his disciples only.

After Christ was risen from the dead, and before he ascended to his glory, he renewed the commission to his apostles, and enlarged the sphere of their ministerial labors,

> All power is given unto me in heaven and in earth. Go ye therefore, and teach all nations, baptizing them in the name of the Father, and of the Son, and of the Holy Ghost: teaching them to observe all things whatsoever I have commanded you: and, lo, I am with you alway, even unto the end of the world. Amen (Matt. 28:18–20).

Here our blessed Savior instituted this sacrament for the continued use of the gospel-church; he authorized his disciples to administer it, and consequently obliged all to whom the gospel is preached to make use of it;

---

[14] "We may suppose Christ to have taken this method, that he might maintain the dignity of his own character, as Lord of the church, and every way superior to John, who was merely a servant, and baptized only with his own hands, without commissioning others for it; as also that he might not seem to act with impropriety, and to seek his own honor, by baptizing in his own name; that he might show himself to be sent, not to baptize with water, but to the more excellent work of preaching the gospel, and baptizing with the Holy Ghost; that he might prevent disputes and emulations amongst his disciples, on account of some being baptized by himself, and others only by his commissioned servants; and that the validity and efficacy of baptism might not be supposed to depend on the worthiness of the person who administers it, but only on the authority and blessing of Christ upon the administration according to his will." Guyse, *Paraphrase*, note on John 4:2.

for it cannot be administered by the pastors of the church, unless there be some that submit to it; and, by a favor peculiar to the New Testament, these are *all nations*. So that here is a general command for the sacrament of baptism.

The *practice* of the apostles was conformable to their instructions. What they received of the Lord, that they delivered faithfully unto men; and as they preached zealously, so they received those that believed into the fellowship of the Christian church by baptism (Acts 2:38–41; 8:12–13; 9:18; 10:47–48; 16:15, 33; 18:8; 22:16; *etc.*).

It is plain, on the whole, that we have both *precept* and *example* for this service; and what more is necessary to render anything a divine ordinance? To observe it is only to *obey* a divine command, and to *follow* an approved precedent. We ought to manifest that we are the disciples of Christ, by keeping this ordinance according to his appointment, and by walking in the commendable footsteps of his flock.

4. Its Excellency and Usefulness

The fourth thing I proposed is, to display *the excellency and usefulness of Christian baptism*. But before I enter on this head, give me leave to remove some misapprehensions about the nature and design of it.

1. It is a base and carnal opinion to say it is a regenerating ordinance, that it washes away original sin, that it conveys a principle of divine life, or saves the soul. This point has been considered already.

2. It is another very dangerous and absurd opinion, that there is no salvation without baptism. This doctrine is very hard indeed; but the comfort is, it is not true. That it is *not true*, may appear from such considerations as these. (1.) Persons previous to baptism, may have all that is necessary to salvation; and if so, they must be certainly saved. Before they are baptized, they may receive the word gladly (Acts 2:41); they may have received the Holy Spirit (Acts 10:45, 47); they may fear God (Acts 10:35). (2.) The thief that was crucified together with our Lord, was saved without baptism (Luke 23:43). (3.) This is still more evident from Mark 16:16, where our Lord expressly says, "He that believeth and is baptized shall be saved; but he that believeth not shall be damned." He that believeth the report of the gospel of the grace of God, and in token of his submission to the righteousness of Immanuel, is baptized, and receives that seal of the righteousness of faith, shall inherit eternal life; but he that believeth not

with the heart unto righteousness, let his confessions be what they will; be he baptized or not baptized, he shall be damned, and shall not see life. It is very observable, he does not say, he that is not baptized shall be damned; but only he that believeth not shall be damned. If baptism had been absolutely necessary to salvation, this would have been a necessary part of that assertion. (4.) This opinion makes *means* too important, and particularly renders sacramental ordinances quite another thing than they were ever designed to be. Instead of being only *signs* of God's gracious covenant, and *seals* of the righteousness of faith, it makes them necessary *working causes* of man's salvation. (5.) Hereby the keys of the unseen world and of death,[15] are put into the hand of men, who, upon this principle, can, at their own pleasure, make passes either to heaven, or hell. But rejoice, O daughter of Zion, that thy King reigns; and there is but one that has the key of David, that opens, and no man shutteth, that shuts, and none can open. We might well say, *Woe to the earth!* if it were in the power of a selfish and peevish order of men to dispose of happiness and damnation, according to their humor.[16]

3. It is a most shameless fancy that the salvation of the baptized is owing to the *regularity* of the minister that performs the ordinance. They do not mean that the minister who is fit to baptize shall be *sober, of good behavior, apt to teach, holding fast the faithful word*; all this avails him nothing without a *lineal virtue*, which, if it did not come *from Antichrist*, certainly came *through him.* Nay, so foolish have some been in this unmannerly doctrine, as to tell us that the very *immortality* of our souls is owing to the *baptismal spirit*; which, since the apostles' days, is only conveyed through the hands of diocesan bishops. Is it not enough that these gentlemen will *confound* the *works of grace*, without *destroying* the *works of the God of nature?*

I shall now represent the *useful ends* of this heavenly institution, which are various and most important. Some of the chief of them may be represented in the following particulars.

1. Baptism is *a seal of the righteousness of faith*, as is said of circumcision (Rom. 4:11). In this ordinance we are instructed in the doctrines concern-

---

[15] "I...have the keys," etc. (Rev. 1:18).
[16] "I think there is a practice, which pays too great a compliment to this scandalous notion, about the necessity of baptism to salvation, and that is, *hurrying on the baptism of a child because it is sick*; for which I can see no show of argument, unless it springs from this root of bitterness. Baptism was never designed to be used by Protestants, as extreme unction is among the Papists." Bradbury, *The Duty and Doctrine of Baptism*

ing *original sin*, and *salvation by Christ*, in opposition to the works of the law; by believing on him, and being united to him, and not by personal worth, or our own obedience. The *righteousness of faith* denotes the obedience of Christ in all points, according to the law of works, even unto death, in the room and stead of the guilty and the wretched. This is the *righteousness of God*; for it was performed by the Son of God, and as it was required, so it was accepted by God. It is the *righteousness of the law*; for it was commensurate to all its demands in point of duty, and a compensation for all the transgressions of it, according to its penalty.

It is the *gift of righteousness*; for it is exhibited as a rich provision, to which there is free access in the declarations, offers, and promises of the gospel. And it is the righteousness of faith; for it becomes ours in possession through the belief of the truth. In baptism this everlasting righteousness is represented to our view; and by a sensible sign, our faith in it is both directed and strengthened; that we may, by a right improvement of this ordinance, become clear and strong in the faith of the grace of God, manifested in giving his Son to be a propitiation for our sins.

This may serve to throw some light on several passages of Scripture that represent the uses of this divine ordinance, such as, "as many…as have been baptized into Christ have put on Christ" (Gal. 3:27). All that are made partakers of the spiritual benefits, which are signified in the ordinance of baptism, administered in the name of Christ, have put him on, not in profession only, but in reality by faith, as the Lord their righteousness; and are, as it were, all over covered with Christ, as a man is with his garments. "Repent, and be baptized…in the name of Jesus Christ for the remission of [your] sins" (Acts 2:38). The forgiveness of sins, through faith in the name of Jesus, who is the Lord our righteousness, is held forth unto us in a figure, in the ordinance of baptism. "We are buried with him by baptism into death" (Rom. 6:4). The efficacy of the death of Christ, as the alone propitiation for our sins, is clearly represented in baptism; and everyone that believeth is made a partaker of this atonement, and has the seal of it in his baptism. Ananias said to Paul "arise, and be baptized, and wash away thy sins, calling on the name of the Lord" (Acts 22:16). It is absurd to imagine that the washing of the body can cleanse the soul from sin; but the sprinkling of the blood of Jesus covers all transgressions. This efficacious blood is signified in this holy ordinance; and to the baptized believer, this sacramental washing becomes a visible sign of the washing and cleansing of his guilty conscience.

2. The next valuable end of this ordinance is to signify and seal the conveyance of the benefits of the covenant of grace. These benefits are divinely excellent, and supremely desirable. Barely to mention them is a sufficient proof of this assertion.

A new covenant relation to God is conveyed in the promises of the covenant of grace. "This is the covenant that I will make with the house of Israel after those days, saith the Lord…I will be to them a God, and they shall be to me a people" (Heb. 8:10). This gracious promise is sealed in baptism, that we may have the clearer evidence, the stronger consolation, and the firmer confidence in believing that it shall be to us even as it hath been told us of God. "Be baptized…for *the promise* is unto you, and to your children…then they that gladly received his word were baptized" (Acts 2:38–41).

The forgiveness of sin is an inestimable blessing of the covenant of grace: "this is the covenant…I will be merciful to their unrighteousness, and their sins and their iniquities will I remember no more" (Heb. 8:10, 12). This marvelous display of divine favor is sealed in baptism unto believers, to strengthen their confidence, and to make their joy abound, "Repent, and be baptized every one of you in the name of Jesus Christ for the remission of sins" (Acts 2:38).

The adoption of sons is a blessing of the most important nature, and peculiar to the covenant of promise: "[I] will be a Father unto you, and ye shall be my sons and daughters, saith the Lord Almighty" (2 Cor. 6:18). And baptism is appointed to confirm and establish our faith concerning it, "ye are all the children of God by faith in Christ Jesus. For as many of you as have been baptized into Christ have put on Christ" (Gal. 3:26–27).

A supernatural birth into a new state of divine life is a glorious privilege that comes by the new covenant; and is of the highest necessity, as well as of the utmost importance: "Jesus answered…Verily, verily, I say unto thee, Except a man be born again, he cannot see the kingdom of God…Verily, verily, I say unto thee, Except a man be born of water and of the Spirit, he cannot enter into the kingdom of God" (John 3:3, 5). This precious blessing is promised in the word of God, and represented in baptism to our faith, that we may have strong consolation in appropriating it to ourselves. "But after that the kindness and love of God our Saviour toward man appeared, not by works of righteousness which we have done, but according to his mercy he saved us, by the washing of regeneration, and renewing of the Holy Ghost; which he shed on us abundantly through Jesus Christ our Savior" (Titus 3:4–6).

The joyful resurrection of the bodies of believers, to be reunited with their souls, and to be forever with the Lord in glory, is a most desirable event, an event that is only secured in the new covenant (1 Cor. 15 throughout). Baptism gives us a most comfortable assurance of this happy event. "We are buried with him by baptism into death: that like as Christ was raised up from the dead by the glory of the Father, even so we also should walk in newness of life. For if we have been planted together in the likeness of his death, *we shall be also in the likeness of his resurrection*" (Rom. 6:4–5). And some think we are to understand that text in this sense, "Else what shall they do which are baptized for the dead, if the dead rise not at all? why are they then baptized for the dead?" (1 Cor. 15:29).[17] When we consider the connection of the apostle's reasoning in that chapter, we must allow that whatever practice, opinion, or peculiar custom may be referred to, it clearly intimates that Christian baptism is performed in the faith and profession of the resurrection of Christ, the first-fruits of them that sleep, and of the resurrection of his saints in their order. The resurrection of Christ is an event already past; and the resurrection of all his people, though future, is most certain. The first is the sign, the pledge, and the ground of the last.

Vital saving union to Christ makes the believer a partaker of him in the power of his resurrection, and the unspeakable riches of his grace; and it is the work of the Holy Spirit to draw the soul to Christ, by clear impressed convictions of divine truth. And this supernatural, indissoluble union is

---

[17] The meaning of this passage is very happily expressed by Dr. Guyse thus: "The denial of a future state of happiness, and of the resurrection of the bodies of the saints to eternal life, subverts all the good purposes of your Christian profession, which ye entered into by baptism: for what will become of those believers, who are baptized in the name of Christ, on account of the hope they have, through him, of a blessed resurrection, after they themselves shall be numbered among the dead, and who are the rather induced thereto, by what they have seen, or heard of the faith, patience, and Christian heroism of those saints and martyrs, that have died triumphantly, in full assurance of such a resurrection? If in reality there be no rising again to eternal life, to what purpose are they baptized, for the sake of this hope and of this further inducement, relating to the dead? or, on this supposition, what good end can be answered to them by their being baptized, and so becoming professed Christians, in the stead of those believers, that are dead and gone? It is all an insignificant, trifling, and fruitless thing."

represented, and our faith concerning it confirmed, in the right use and improvement of Christian baptism, "as many of you as have been *baptized into Christ have put on Christ*" (Gal. 3:27).

We may find, by such things as these, which are more fully discovered in the gospel, that it is the proper nature and tendency of baptism to guide us to faith in Christ alone for remission of sins, holiness, and all salvation, by union and fellowship with him; and that a diligent improvement of this ordinance must needs be of great advantage to the life of faith.

3. Another excellent end of Christian baptism is to signify and seal our manifold obligations. By this ordinance we are engaged *to be the Lord's, to walk worthy of our heavenly calling*, and *to cultivate a holy, useful fellowship with the church of Christ.*

First, By this ordinance we are engaged *to be the Lord's*. This is implied in its being a dedication to God. The baptized are devoted unto God, on the warrant, and in the right, of his most gracious promise, "the promise is unto you, and to your children, and to all that are afar off, even as many as the Lord our God shall call" (Acts 2:39). They are hereby engaged to be the Lord's (1.) *Only*; in opposition to every other God: this is required in the first commandment, *Thou shalt have no other gods before me*; and it is solemnly professed in baptism. (2.) *Wholly*; in soul, spirit, and body, "ye are not your own…for ye are bought with a price: therefore glorify God in your body, and in your spirit, which are God's" (1 Cor. 6:19-20). Nor is this all the obligation that lies upon us; for even our gifts, graces, and worldly comforts should be sacred to God, and cheerfully employed in his service; and we only give him of his own, when we use them for such noble purposes. (3.) *Perseveringly*; for it is the vilest treachery, and involves us in the deepest guilt, to draw back after we have opened our mouth unto the Lord; what can be more provoking than to prove unsteadfast in his covenant? And it is as foolish as it is base to forsake the Lord, in whom we shall never find any iniquity, and to choose, in his stead, such things as shall not at all profit us; *to walk after vanity, and become vain* (Jer. 2:5-8).

Secondly, By baptism we are engaged to *walk worthy of our heavenly calling*. The apostle reasons upon this principle, "I…the prisoner of the Lord, beseech you that ye walk worthy of the vocation wherewith ye are called…there is…one baptism" (Eph. 4:1-5). Hereby we are engaged to believe the gospel; and to have a conversation becoming it, in our daily practice. The apostle sums up the whole of practical Christianity in these concise but important words, "that they may adorn the doctrine of God our Saviour in all things" (Titus 2:10).

The doctrine of the gospel of Christ, considered in itself, is most beautiful and lovely, though it has been miserably blackened, and disgraced by many, that should have given it a better treatment. Every Christian is obliged, according to his place and station, and to the utmost of his power, on every opportunity, to endeavor to wipe off these reproaches, and to retrieve the reputation of the gospel, by adorning it in all things; by living under its power, and walking conformable to its sacred obligations, encouragements, and assistances. Baptism seals the solemn obligation, "Go ye therefore, and teach all nations, baptizing them in the name of the Father, and of the Son, and of the Holy Ghost: *teaching them to observe all things whatsoever I have commanded you*" (Matt. 28:19–20).[18]

Thirdly, Baptism engages us to cultivate a holy useful fellowship with the church of God: "as the body is one, and hath many members, and all the members of that one body, being many, are one body: so also is Christ. For by one Spirit are we all baptized into one body, whether we be Jews or Gentiles, whether we be bond or free; and have been all made to drink into one Spirit. For the body is not one member, but many" (1 Cor. 12:12–14). In these verses we see (1.) That baptism binds us to have fellowship with the church as it is the visible body of Christ, not only to be *one body* with the church of the firstborn, but with the professing body; united upon the plan of gospel-truth, in visible fellowship. (2.) That this fellowship among the members of Christ, which is most intimate in its nature, and most benevolent in its blessed fruits, is a proper consequence and result of Christian baptism. And (3.) That the apostle does not there speak, either of metaphorical baptism, or of the mystical-union of the members of Christ. He is improving their baptism with water, as an argument to enforce that union, whereby they are joined together under pastors and governors (1 Cor. 12:28).

---

[18] As circumcision was the mode of entering into the Jewish church, and becoming a professed disciple of Moses, and hereby an obligation arose to perform and practice the whole Jewish law (Gal. 5:3), so by baptism we lay ourselves under a holy obligation to practice the whole religion of Christ, and to wait for all its promised blessings. Berrystreet Sermons, vol. 2, p. 179.

5. The Objections Made against It

I shall endeavor, in the next place, to remove the *objections* that are made against this ordinance of baptism.

1. Some pretend that baptizing with water is not meant in these texts; "Go ye therefore, and teach all nations, baptizing them in the name of the Father, and of the Son, and of the Holy Ghost" (Matt. 28:19). "He that believeth and is baptized shall be saved" (Mark 16:16). They allege this reason for their opinion: That though baptism is mentioned, water is not named in either of these places; and therefore it is reasonable to suppose, they say, that something else than water-baptism is originally intended.

Answer. This way of reasoning is so loose, and so apt to mislead, that if it were admitted, it would establish any fanciful opinion; and, on such pretenses, the best established article of divine revelation might be canceled. The apostles faithfully executed their Lord's commission, when they *baptized with water* such as gladly received his word. They did not go beyond the word of the Lord, to do either *less* or *more* than they were commanded. And we have already seen their practice relative to baptizing with water.[19]

2. Some allege the words of the Baptist as an unanswerable argument against the continued use of this ordinance, "I indeed baptize you with water unto repentance: but he that cometh after me...shall baptize you with the Holy Ghost, and with fire" (Matt. 3:11). From this passage they reason thus: The baptism which Christ hath instituted for continued use under the gospel is not to be administered with water, because the *baptizing with the Holy Ghost, and with fire*, is said to belong to Christ's ministry, and is distinguished from the *baptizing with water*, which is represented as peculiar to the ministry of John; and therefore, upon the coming of Christ, the last was entirely to cease, that the baptism of the Spirit only might take place.

Answer. This is the most plausible pretense, perhaps, that can be alleged against *baptism with water*. But it is certain that the *distinction* between baptizing *with water* and *with the Spirit*, that is there asserted, doth not imply that these baptisms were always separate; for this would infer that none of those whom John baptized with water had received the Holy Ghost, and if so, they were *none of Christ's* (Rom. 8:9). And it would likewise follow, upon the principles of our objectors, that none that have received the Holy

---
[19] See section 3.

Ghost should be baptized with water. The fallacy of their reasoning will appear from these two texts that refer to the New Testament dispensation, "Can any man forbid water, that these should not be baptized, which have received the Holy Ghost as well as we?" (Acts 10:47). Paul laid his hands upon those that were baptized in the name of the Lord Jesus Christ, and "the Holy Ghost came on them" (Acts 19:6), where it is evident that baptizing with water and with the Holy Ghost were *not opposed* to, but fully consistent with one another.

The obvious unforced meaning of the Baptist's words in Matthew 3:11, upon which the objection is grounded, is this: "*I*, the forerunner of the Messiah, who am sent before him to prepare his way, who will soon be manifested unto Israel, to be the end of their law for righteousness, and to abolish all their system of carnal ordinances…*I indeed baptize you with water unto repentance* [εις μετανοιαν] that you may relinquish your wrong notions concerning the Deity, and the way of access to his favor; that you may give up your carnal ordinances of divine worship, and may worship him in the spirit, not according to the oldness of the letter; but you must not imagine, that I am the author of this spiritual dispensation, though it is signified by my baptizing you, my countrymen, with water; nor must you think that this dispensation will be completed under my ministry; this honor is reserved for another. *He that cometh after me* is so much my superior in every respect, so much *mightier than I* am, that I am not fit to be employed in the very lowest post of service under him; to speak proverbially, I may truly say of him, *whose shoes I am not worthy to bear*. He, who is so mighty, and so worthy, being faithful as a Son over his own house, *shall baptize you with the Holy Ghost, and with fire*, when he sets up his kingdom, and sends his Spirit, whose extraordinary appearance will be in the form of fire; and whose operation will be enlightening, warming, powerful and purifying, like that of fire, which is the fittest emblem of his most abundant and gracious influence."

From this general view of the words it appears, that the baptism of the Spirit was not to supplant, but to crown baptism with water, as it is the thing signified by this external washing. And any other sense will never agree to the *practice* of the *apostolic church*.

3. Some have urged where Paul says, "Christ sent me not to baptize, but to preach the gospel" (1 Cor. 1:17). From which they infer that baptism is not a gospel-ordinance, or else the apostle would have been sent

to administer it. And since he was not sent to baptize, they suppose it is presumption in any other man to pretend any authority to do so.

Answer. The apostle certainly had the same commission from Christ that his fellow-apostles had. Their commission is registered in Matthew 28:19-20. The apostle speaks by way of comparison, when he says, "Christ sent me not to baptize, but to preach". His meaning must be that he was sent, commissioned by Christ, as an apostle, not to spend his time *chiefly* in that sort of service, such as baptizing, which might as well be performed by an ordinary minister; but to publish the glad tidings of salvation through Christ as a Redeemer, in all its extent and glory, wherever he came. That the apostle was also sent to baptize appears from his actually baptizing Crispus and Gaius (1 Cor. 1:14), and the household of Stephanas (1 Cor. 1:16). Moreover, he gives this reason why he baptized very few, "Lest any should say that I had baptized in mine own name" (1 Cor. 1:15).

The meaning therefore is that the *main business* of his commission was not to baptize so much as to preach the gospel unto mankind for the obedience of faith.

4. Some pretend that since there is but *one baptism* (Eph. 4:5), water-baptism cannot be the ordinance of Christ, because then there would be two baptisms, one *with water*, and another *with the Spirit.*

Answer. This objection derives all its seeming force from this fallacy, that washing with water, and baptizing with the Spirit, are *two complete, distinct baptisms*; whereas they are only *one entire baptism*, where the outward washing with water is a sign and representation of the inward cleansing by the Spirit of the living God. And this entire baptism is what the apostle speaks of, and urges upon believers, as an argument to prevail on them to endeavor to *keep the unity of the Spirit in the bond of peace.*

6. To Whom It Is to Be Administered

The next point to be settled refers to *the persons* to whom baptism is to be administered.

I have no business, in discussing this head, with the gross profanation of this ordinance by the *church of Rome*, while they administer baptism, which is appointed for spiritual purposes only, to inanimate creatures, as ships, forts, ensigns, bells, *etc.*, under a pretense of making them holy, or endowing them with certain virtues.

Neither am I to consider that opinion of *some ancient heretics*, who either administered baptism to *the dead*, or to one *substituted in the room of the deceased*, with a view to his advantage, if he died without being baptized. The laws of heaven do not allow of proxies and substitutes in the business of salvation. Their opinion arose from a mistaken view of the apostle's meaning, when he says, "Else what shall they do that are baptized for the dead, if the dead rise not?" (1 Cor. 15:29).[20]

In general, *the people of God* are to be baptized. This ordinance is designed for them in distinction from the world, "Repent and be baptized…for the promise" (I will be your God) "is unto you" (Acts 2:38–39). These are to be baptized without any *distinction of nation*, "as many of you as have been baptized into Christ have put on Christ. There is neither Jew nor Greek, there is neither bond nor free, there is neither male nor female: for ye are all one in Christ Jesus" (Gal. 3:27–28). Where the apostle sets aside all differences of *nation*, of *condition*, and of *sex*. This might be demonstrated likewise from several other texts that speak the very same language, and contain the same sentiments.

Persons that do not profess any faith in Christ ought not to be baptized. This holy ordinance should not be thrown to such swine as neither profess to know God, nor to believe the gospel. Baptism is an ordinance in which a public profession is made of the person's being devoted to God the Father, Son, and Holy Ghost; and if he be considered as *adult* (and of such we are now speaking), there is a signification, and thereby a profession made, that he gives up himself to God; and if the ordinance be rightly applied, there must be a harmony between the inward design of the person dedicating, and the true intent and meaning of the external sign thereof; which, by divine appointment, is a visible declaration of his adhering by faith to the Father, Son, and Holy Ghost, and embracing that salvation which takes its rise from them. This must be done by faith, or else it is done in hypocrisy, and will tend to God's dishonor, and the prejudice rather than the advantage of him to whom it is administered.

Moreover, it is necessary that the person who is baptized in adult years should make it appear that he is a believer by a profession of his faith; otherwise he that administers the ordinance, together with the assembly, who are present at the same time, cannot conclude that they are performing a

---

[20] Suiceri, *Thesaurus Ecclesiasticus*, on βαπτισμος.

service which is acceptable to God; therefore, for their sakes, as well as his own, the person to be baptized ought to make a profession of his faith in and subjection to Christ, as what is signified in this ordinance. This was required in order to adult baptism, by the apostles, and other ministers of Christ, in the first age of Christianity (Acts 2:38–41; 8:37–38; 16:31–33).

But the most important question concerning the *subjects* of baptism is not yet touched. It concerns the right of such infants unto baptism whose parents, or at least one of them, are members of the church, and profess their faith in Christ and obedience to him.

This point has occasioned much dispute in the Christian church, and with a great deal of warmth. I think the matter in contest is important; and yet the contest should be managed with soberness, and Christian tempers. I am fully satisfied that the children of believing baptized parents *may* and *should* be baptized. The reasons of my belief are these.

1. The covenant which God made with Abraham was the *same covenant of grace* which now subsists under the gospel. The sum of it is contained in that promise, "I will establish my covenant between me and thee and thy seed after thee in their generations for an everlasting covenant, *to be a God unto thee, and to thy seed after thee*" (Gen. 17:7). Now this is the constant style of the covenant of grace, "I will…be a God unto thee," etc., "I will be to them a God, and they shall be to me a people" (Heb. 8:10). "He that overcometh shall inherit all things; and *I will be his God*" (Rev. 21:7). "The covenant [made with Abraham], that was confirmed before of God in Christ, the law [given by Moses], which was four hundred and thirty years after, cannot disannul, that it should make the promise of none effect" (Gal. 3:17). "And if ye be Christ's, then are ye Abraham's seed, and heirs according to the promise" (Gal. 3:29), which God made to him (Gen. 17:7). Accordingly, Abraham was justified by faith (Rom. 4:3, 11, 22–25). "And the Scripture, foreseeing that God would justify the heathen through faith, preached before the gospel unto Abraham, saying, In thee shall all nations be blessed. So then *they which be of faith are blessed with faithful Abraham*" (Gal. 3:8–9). Many proofs are needless in so plain a case.

2. According to the tenor of that covenant, the *infant children of holy parents* were a part of the church of God. The express words of the covenant refer to them, "I will…be a God unto thee, and *to thy seed after thee*" (Gen. 17:7). And that the meaning might be determined beyond all possibility of mistake, the following words are added:

And God said unto Abraham, Thou shalt keep my covenant therefore, thou, and thy seed after thee in their generations. This is my covenant, which ye shall keep, between me and you and thy seed after thee; Every man child among you shall be circumcised. And ye shall circumcise the flesh of your foreskin; and it shall be a token of the covenant betwixt me and you. And *he that is eight days old* shall be circumcised among you, every man child in your generations, he that is born in the house, or bought with money of any stranger, which is not of thy seed. He that is born in thy house, and he that is bought with thy money, must needs be circumcised: and *my covenant shall be in your flesh for an everlasting covenant* (Gen. 17:9–13).

Nothing can more strongly assert the interest of infants in that covenant, and their church membership in virtue thereof. And the language of the New Testament is a confirmation of this position, "Jesus said, Suffer little children, and forbid them not, to come unto me: for of such is the kingdom of heaven" (Matt. 19:14). See also Mark 10:14 and Luke 18:16, wherein we see that *little children*, as well as *grown persons*, are *subjects of the gospel-kingdom*, which Christ came to set up in the world, and have an interest in its privileges and blessings. To use Dr. Guyse's words,

> It seems evident, that Christ's principal meaning here was not, that the subjects of the gospel-kingdom are like little children, for their temper and qualities, though he took occasion from hence to add an instruction of this nature about it (Luke 18:17). For this could be no more a reason why their children, rather than lambs or doves, should be brought to him to be blessed: but he plainly intimates, that their covenant-interest, and visible church membership, should be continued under the gospel state; and that therefore they ought to be recommended and devoted to him, which makes his reasoning on this head clear and just.

If the infants of believing parents are not supposed to be members of the gospel church now, as well as they were before the coming of Christ, their membership must be disannulled and abrogated, either (1.) By an especial *divine revocation*, as Dr. Owen expresses it; or (2.) By the *substitution of a greater privilege* in the room of it; or (3.) By introducing *a dispensation that does not admit of it.* These, I think, are the only possible cases that can be supposed. I shall in a few words examine the truth of them.

As to *the first*, I presume it is both modest and reasonable to desire to be satisfied that *God has recalled* the right of church membership, once allowed unto the children of his holy people, if it is now supposed to be disannulled. To abolish any grant of privilege, made by God unto his church, without his own express revocation of it, is to deny his sovereign authority. But I believe Dr. Owen had good reason to say that "none can do this, either directly or indirectly, in terms, or any pretense of consequence."

As to *the second supposition*, I beg leave to observe in the words of that same excellent writer.

> To say, a [spiritual] privilege so granted, may be revoked even by God himself, without the substitution of a greater privilege and mercy in the room of it, is contrary to the goodness of God, his love and care to his church, contrary to his constant course of proceeding with it from the foundation of the world, wherein he went on in the ampliation [enlarging] and increase of its privileges, until the coming of Christ; and to suppose it under the gospel, is contrary to all his promises, the honor of Christ, and a multitude of express testimonies of Scripture. Thus it was with the privileges of the temple, and worship of it granted to the Jews, they were not, they could not be taken away, without an express revocation, and the substitution of a more glorious spiritual temple and worship in their room. But now the spiritual privilege of a right to, and a participation of, the initial seal of the covenant, was granted by God to the infant seed of Abraham (Gen. 17:10).

But as he justly adds, those that oppose our sentiments about the spiritual privileges of the children of believing parents do not once pretend that they have any greater privileges conferred on them now than the infant Jews had; but "leave the seed of believers, *whilst in their infant state*, in the same condition with *those of pagans and infidels*, expressly contrary to God's covenant." He, moreover, has the following remarkable words:

All this contest is, to deprive the children of believers of a privilege once granted to them by God, never yet revoked as to the substance of it; assigning nothing in its room; which is contrary to the goodness, love, and covenant of God, especially derogatory to the honor of Jesus Christ, and the gospel.

The third supposition, of God having brought his church under a dispensation that does not admit of infants being reckoned any part of it, is as far from being true as either of the former. Besides what has been offered in opposition to this conceit already, from Matthew 19:14, I shall adduce two or three more passages, that are no less express and decisive. "For if the firstfruit be holy, the lump is also holy: and if the root be holy, so are the branches. And if some of the branches be broken off, and thou, being a wild olive tree, wert graffed in amongst them, and with them partakest of the root and fatness of the olive-tree" (Rom. 11:16–17). The sense of them is well expressed by Dr. Guyse, in these words:

> For as the offering of the first-fruits[21] sanctified the whole harvest, and the offering of a cake sanctified the whole mass of dough; so if Abraham was visibly separated to the Lord, and became federally holy by that *everlasting covenant, which he established with him, to be a God to him, and to his seed after him, in their generations* (Gen. 17:7, 19), then, in the like covenant-sense, the whole body of his descendants are holy, as a church visibly consecrated to the Lord: and as branches partake of the nature of their root; so if Abraham, who was the root of administration to the Jewish church and nation, as their natural and federal father, were relatively holy by the

---

[21] "The *first-fruits* and the *root* mean the same thing under different allusions; and signify the Jewish patriarchs, and especially Abraham, with whom the covenant was first made, from whom the whole nation sprung, and by whom it was consecrated to God, as the offering of the first-fruits sanctified the whole product of the harvest; and the offering of a cake, or of two wave-loaves, sanctified the whole lump of dough (Lev. 23:10–17; Num. 15:19–21). And it is evident from the then present state of Israel, that when the apostle speaks of the whole nation of the Jews as *holy*, it cannot be meant of a *personal* and *inherent*, but of a *relative* and *external* holiness, as persons and things, that were *separated* to the Lord, were counted *holy*; and so the whole nation of the Jews, inclusive of their seed, were commonly styled an *holy people*, in distinction from the nations, that were out of the pale of the covenant (Deut. 14:2, 21; 26:18–19; Isa. 6:13; Dan. 8:24; 12:7)."

constitution of that covenant, which was made with him and his seed; then his natural posterity, considered as springing from him, and included in that covenant, *must be relatively holy too*. And if some, yea, even the main body of the natural seed of Abraham,[22] that sprang from him, as branches from their root, are cut off from their covenant-claim for their unbelief; and if any of you, who are Gentiles, and as such were in your natural condition *strangers to the covenants of promise* (Eph. 2:12), and, like branches of a wild olive-tree, were useless and unprofitable, worthy to be rejected, and fit for burning; if nevertheless, by the wonderful kindness of God, contrary to all reasonable expectation, and to the custom of men, who use to graft the branch of a fruitful tree into a wild stock, you were incorporated into a church-state under Abraham's covenant, as his spiritual children, through faith in Christ (Gal. 3:29), together with those of his natural offspring that believe; and so are like the scion of a wild stock,[23] that is inserted, with its buds, among the natural branches of a good tree: and if, with those believing Jews, you are made partaker of all the promises and ordinances, privileges and blessings of the gracious covenant made with Abraham, as though you yourself had been one of his natural and believing descendants (Gal. 3:14 and Eph. 3:6), and so are like a graft, which derives sap from the root, and is nourished by the generous juices of

---

[22] "For understanding this, and some following verses, we are to consider, that as God's covenant was first made with Abraham and his seed, *he* is meant by the *root*; and the visible *church* of Israel, as springing from him, and from that covenant made with him, is meant by *the good olive-tree*, as it is represented under this figure (Jer. 11:16; Hos. 14:6), and by the *fatness of the olive tree*, is meant the *blessings and privileges*, which belonged to their church-state, by virtue of that covenant. Accordingly *the natural branches* signify Abraham's offspring after the flesh; and *the wild olive-tree* signifies the Gentiles; and *the grafting in of them that were cut out of the wild olive-tree,* signifies God's taking the believing Gentiles into his visible covenant; and their *partaking, with some of the natural branches, of the root and fulness of the olive tree* signifies the believing Gentiles being admitted to share, equally with the believing Jews, in all the blessings and privileges of the covenant made with Abraham and his seed, and of the church-state, into which God had brought them."

[23] "*Grafting a branch*, which is always with its *buds*, strongly intimates, as here applied to believing Gentiles, that they are brought into Abraham's covenant with their children, to partake of the same privileges, to which the children of believing Jews were entitled, and from which those of unbelievers among them were cut off together with their parents."

a good olive-tree (Rom. 11:24) to make it flourishing and fruitful. If, I say, you are thus highly favored of the Lord; "boast not against the branches: but if thou boast, thou bearest not the root, but the root thee."

"For the unbelieving husband is sanctified by the wife, and the unbelieving wife is sanctified by the husband: else were your children unclean; but now are they holy" (1 Cor. 7:14). I shall favor the reader with the excellent *paraphrase* and *note* of Dr. Guyse upon those words, who, in my humble opinion, has both represented the genuine sense of them, and solidly supported it.

For as, unto the pure, all relations and enjoyments of this life are pure (Titus 1:15), the husband, who continues an infidel, is so far sanctified or separated to a holy use in or by his believing wife (εν τη γυναικι), and by means of her credibly professed faith and holiness (they being one flesh, Matt. 19:5) as not to deprive her of the covenant-privileges, which belong to the visible people of God, and their seed (Gen. 17:7); and the unconverted wife is in like manner sanctified for covenant-use in or by her believing husband (εν τω ανδρι), and by means of his regularly professed faith and holiness, and of her conjugal relation to him: otherwise those of your children, which descend from a father and mother, one of which is a Christian, and the other not, would be in the same condition, as to the privileges and blessings that belong to the visible church, and to the external administration of the covenant, with the children of parents, both of which are heathens, and so out of the pale of the church, and strangers to the covenants of promise, and by no means to be owned as a holy seed:[24] but now, since the unbelieving

---

[24] "The terms *unclean* (ακαθας τος) and *holy* (αγιος), occur almost numberless times in the *seventy*, and in the New Testament; but I do not find that they are ever once used to signify *illegitimate*, and *legitimate*, which is the sense that some would here put upon them: and as the apostle was speaking of persons already married, and marriage is a civil ordinance of the God of nature, there was no room to doubt, whether the children of such unbelieving and believing parents were *legitimate* or not, since *that* depends entirely on the legitimacy of the *marriage*, and not at all on the *religious* character of the husband and wife, whether one, or both, or neither of them were Christians or no. Nor

parent is thus sanctified in and by the other, who believes, their offspring are externally, relatively, and federally holy, as a seed visibly separated, and appropriated to the Lord, and so entitled to all the privileges of the covenant, that they are capable of in their infancy, as much as if both father and mother were professing believers.

---

is it to be supposed, that *unclean* and *holy*, in this passage, is to be understood of *real, personal*, and *internal* uncleanness and holiness: for the children of believers are in a moral sense, as unclean by nature, as the children of other people (see Job 14:1–4; 25:4; Ps. 51:5; Eph. 2:3), and it cannot be said of *all* the children of believers, any more than of adult baptized professors, that they are renewed and sanctified by the Holy Ghost; since the event in both shows, that they are not all circumcised in heart, or that all are not Israel, which are of Israel (Rom. 2:28–29; 9:6). But *unclean* and *holy* are manifestly to be taken here, in that well known, and familiar sense, in which the church of Israel, and their seed, by virtue of their visible relation to God, as his covenant-people, were called *a holy people*, and *a holy seed*, in distinction from the heathen nations, which were styled *unclean* as being out of the pale of the church, and excluded from the privileges and blessings of God's covenant (see Deut. 7:6; Ezra 9:2; Isa. 6:13; 52:1; 62:12), and thus the parents and children of the visible church are called *holy* (Rom. 11:16), and the unconverted Gentiles are represented as *unclean*, in Peter's vision of the sheet (Acts 10:14 compared with Acts 10:28). When therefore the infants of visible believers are baptized, it is no more setting a seal to a blank, than when that ordinance is administered to persons, who never were baptized before, upon their own profession of faith and repentance, but were not really partakers of those graces: for the proper ground of baptizing one, or the other, do not lie in a *certainty*, which no minister can have, that they are really endued with the grace of God, and so *internally* in covenant with him; but in their *visible* covenant-relation to him, as that is manifested by a credible profession of faith in adult persons, and by God's promise to them and their seed; for which reason, I think, the faith and holiness of parents are to be considered, as *credibly professed* by them, in order to the entailing of a relative, federal holiness on their children, and entitling them to baptism. And as we have a reasonable ground of hope for the salvation of such professing believers, as continue, living and dying, to be visibly in covenant with God; so we have, that their seed, dying in infancy, shall be saved: for since they did not live so long, as to be capable of renouncing the gracious covenant, which God made with their parents, and with them, we may comfortably consider them, as in the hands of a *Covenant-God*, whose faithfulness engages him to continue to be so to them, that were not suffered to reject him by unbelief; and so, not to mention the great encouragement they would have to lay hold on God's covenant, were they to grow up to years of maturity, there is a vast difference between them, and the dying infants of unbelievers and heathens, which must be left to the *uncovenanted* mercy of God; and what ground of hope there is in *this*, let those Christians consider, who would set aside God's promise of being *a God to his people, and their seed*, as having no relation to *spiritual* privileges and benefits, nor *any place* under the gospel-dispensation."

"The promise is unto you, and to your children, and to all that are afar off, even as many as the Lord our God shall call" (Acts 2:39). The import of this verse may be summed up in these comprehensive words of the paraphrast so often mentioned already:

> The promise of God's covenant (Gen. 17:7), of which baptism is now to be the sign and seal, as circumcision has been heretofore, and particularly the promise of the Spirit (Isa. 44:3; 59:21), runs to you and your children: and as the blessing of Abraham is, under this new dispensation, not to be confined, as formerly, to the Jews, but is to come on the Gentiles also, who are, at present, far from God, and from his covenant (Eph. 2:12–13), even on as many of them as the Lord, our covenant-God, shall graciously call to the faith and fellowship of his Son Jesus Christ, by the gospel;[25] the same promise is to them and their children,[26] to be fulfilled in its proper season;

---

[25] "It seems too narrow to confine the promise here mentioned, to that in Joel 2, which Peter had referred to (Acts 2:16–18). For he there speaks of that promise, as then accomplished in the effusion of the Spirit only on Jews; and though he there leads our thoughts to the tenor of God's covenant, relating to his people's seed, together with themselves, as his Spirit should be poured out on their *sons and daughters*, under the gospel-dispensation, in which there is neither male nor female, but they are all one in Christ Jesus (Gal. 3:28); yet the promise here seems to look still further, to the grand promise that God made to Abraham, and his seed, in their several generations, and afterwards renewed, through the Old Testament dispensation, to Israel and their seed; and so intimates, that the gospel-dispensation would be so far from repealing this promise, that it should be established, and take effect even among believing Gentiles, as well as Jews: and it is most natural to understand this promise, as belonging in both its branches to believing Gentiles: for the same promise is said to be to them, as was to the Jews; and it can scarcely be thought, that when Gentiles came to be converted and incorporated into the same Christian body, and particular churches, as many of them were with the Jews, the Jewish members should have a right to the promise for their children, and the Gentile members should have none for theirs; nor can it easily be reconciled to that community of privileges between them, which the apostle speaks of (Rom. 11:16–17). I therefore take the sense given in the paraphrase, to be designed by the Holy Ghost, under whose inspiration Peter spoke, though Peter himself, like some of the ancient prophets (1 Peter 1:10–11) did not understand the full meaning of what he himself delivered, since he, as yet, had no distinct notion of the calling of the Gentiles."

[26] "Some suppose their adult descendants, and not their infant-offspring, are the children here intended; but of this there is not the least intimation in the text, nor does it at all agree with the scope of the apostle's argument; nay, such a construction would seem to make him speak nonsense; for then he must be understood thus, 'The promise is unto

they being thereby to be made the children of Abraham, and to be blessed with him, and so become the children of promise, even as Isaac was (Gal. 3:7, 9, 16–17, 27–29; 4:28).

These two positions, I hope, are sufficiently established, *viz.*, that the covenant made with Abraham was the same covenant of grace which now subsists under the gospel; and that the infant-children of holy believing parents, according to the tenor of that covenant, are a part of the church of God. I have largely supported the last of these assertions, because it has a great effect in determining the point in dispute. But it is time now to add a third observation, namely,

3. Circumcision was a seal of the covenant of grace, and was, by God's appointment, administered to infant-children. That it was a token, or seal of Abraham's covenant, is expressly asserted in the very institution of it (Gen. 17:9–14). And we have seen that the covenant made with Abraham was the covenant of grace; the very same covenant that now subsists. Accordingly the apostle affirms that Abraham's circumcision was a *seal of that righteousness of faith* which both Jews and Gentiles so much need, and wherein all that believe are completely justified (Rom. 4). His infant-seed were comprehended in that covenant, and this seal of their interest in it was accordingly put upon their flesh. Hence their *little ones* are particularly mentioned *among the covenant-people* (Deut. 29:10–11, and downwards to the close). The following verses are particularly striking and pertinent,

---

you, and to your children, but not to them as your children, or as sustaining any relation to you: but when they shall advance to an adult age, and be called by the ministry of the word, then the promise shall be to *them*, as well as to you,' which is no more than might be said of the children of an Ethiopian. Why then is their relation to their parents mentioned at all? and why are they joined with them, as the subjects of the promise, if after all they are to stand on their own footing as adults, as much as the children of heathens? Nor does this construction consist with the plain grammatical sense of the words; for the apostle does not say, The promise is now to you, and shall be to your children, when grown and called by the word, but, The promise is now to you, and your children: by which he very plainly intends the present privilege the Jewish children enjoy, above the present unconverted Gentiles, who are said to be afar off, and to whom he says, the promise shall belong, when called into a church-state, and to their children also." David Bostwick. *A Fair and Rational Vindication of the Right of Infants to the Ordinance of Baptism.*

Ye stand this day all of you before the LORD your God; your captains of your tribes, your elders, and your officers, with all the men of Israel, your little ones, your wives, and thy stranger that is in thy camp, from the hewer of thy wood, unto the drawer of thy water: that thou shouldst enter into covenant with the LORD thy God, and into his oath, which the LORD thy God maketh with thee this day: that he may establish thee to day for a people unto himself, and that he may be unto thee a God, as he hath said unto thee, and as he hath sworn unto thy fathers, to Abraham, to Isaac, and to Jacob… The secret things belong unto the LORD our God: but those things which are revealed belong unto us and to our children for ever, that we may do all the words of this law (Deut. 29:10–13, 29).

I grant that the man that is circumcised, upon the principles the apostle speaks of, "is a debtor to do the whole law" (Gal. 5:3). If he is circumcised with a view to establish righteousness by his works, he confesses himself a debtor to do the whole law, and makes circumcision a sacrament of the covenant of works, which is an egregious perversion of its original design. And, if any man, after faith is come, shall continue to support the doctrine and necessity of circumcision, which referred to the Messiah as still to come, he confesses himself a debtor to do everything required in the ceremonial law. But when all this is granted, it does not affect my position, that circumcision was originally designed to be a token of the covenant of grace, and an outward sign of an inward spiritual blessing, according to Deuteronomy 30:6, "And the LORD thy God will circumcise thine heart, and the heart of thy seed, to love the LORD thy God with all thine heart, and with all thy soul, that thou mayst live." "For he is not a Jew, which is one outwardly; neither is that circumcision, which is outward in the flesh: but he is a Jew, which is one inwardly; and circumcision is that of the heart, in the spirit, and not in the letter; whose praise is not of men, but of God" (Rom. 2:28–29).

4. Baptism is a seal of the same covenant made with Abraham, and instituted in the room of circumcision. This assertion is capable of several strong proofs. I might argue from Acts 2:39, where the very foundation of circumcision is urged as an argument for being baptized; and the argument would be absurd enough, unless the last ordinance succeeded in the room of the first, but I shall only insist on

Beware lest any man spoil you through philosophy and vain deceit, after the tradition of men, after the rudiments of the world, and not after Christ. For in him dwelleth all the fullness of the Godhead bodily. And ye are complete in him, which is the head of all principality and power: in whom also ye are circumcised with the circumcision made without hands, in putting off the body of the sins of the flesh, by the circumcision of Christ: buried with him in baptism, wherein also ye are risen with him through the faith of the operation of God, who hath raised him from the dead. And you, being dead in your sins and the uncircumcision of your flesh, hath he quickened together with him, having forgiven you all trespasses (Col. 2:8–13).

To explain the force of this reasoning, it is proper to observe (1.) That the apostle is there cautioning the believing Colossians against the insinuations of judaizing teachers, who insisted on the necessity of Christians, even among the Gentiles, being circumcised, and observing many of the ceremonies belonging to the law of Moses, as it was a shadow of good things to come. (2.) He affirms that Christ had all the fullness of the Godhead dwelling in him bodily (Col. 2:9), and that believers are complete in him as to every demand of the law of works, and every shadow in the law of ceremonial ordinances (v. 10). (3.) He prevents everything that can be alleged about the necessity of being circumcised "in whom also ye are circumcised with the circumcision made without hands, in putting off the body of the sins of the flesh, by the circumcision of Christ: buried with him in baptism, wherein also ye are risen with him through the faith of the operation of God, who hath raised him from the dead. And you, being dead in your sins and the uncircumcision of your flesh, hath he quickened together with him, having forgiven you all trespasses" (vv. 11–13). The sense of these words, I apprehend, is judiciously summed up in the following paraphrase:

In Christ ye are so complete, as to have no need of the ordinance of circumcision, which the Jewish zealots would impose upon you; for ye have a better circumcision of the heart, according to God's promise to his people, and their seed (Deut. 30:6), even a spiritual circumcision (Phil. 3:3), which is not effected, like that in the flesh, by the work of human hands, but by the renewing operation of the Spirit; and consists, not in cutting off the foreskin of the flesh, but in what was signified by it, even a separation of the whole body of sin, which, like the natural body, is made up of many members or parts, that spring from the corruption of nature, and are influenced, and exert themselves, by means of the fleshly body, that ye may be delivered from its guilt, power, and defilement, and at length from the very being of it, by virtue of that spiritual circumcision, which Christ is the author of.[27] And, instead of circumcision in the flesh, ye have, by his institution, the ordinance of baptism, which is of like signification, and answers the same ends, as it is a sign of, and obligation to all the holiness that is, or ought to be found in you, as God's covenant-people, by your being conformable to Christ's death, in utterly dying to sin, and giving full evidence of it with continuance, as he died that it might be crucified, and was manifested to be entirely dead, by his being buried, and continuing some time in the grave. Your privileges and obligations are likewise signified in this ordinance, as to your being quickened, and raised to a life of holiness, in conformity to the risen Savior, through that faith, which is wrought, with almighty energy in your hearts, by the same exceeding greatness of God's power (Eph. 1:19–20), which he exerted in raising

---

[27] "The circumcision of Christ cannot mean his own circumcision in the flesh, the eighth day; for that, as much as any other, was made by the hands of men; but this is said, in opposition to that sort of circumcision, to be *made without hands*, and refers to that spiritual circumcision, of which Christ is the author, and of which, as circumcision formerly was, the baptism of Christ's institution now is the sign; it signifying 'not the putting away the filth of the flesh, but the answer of a good conscience toward God' (1 Peter 3:21), and so, the signification, being the same, baptism comes in the room of circumcision, according to what is intimated in the next verse, as the Lord's Supper does of the passover. And this effectually answered the objection of Jewish zealots, as if, whatever internal privileges were pretended to, there were a defect as to *external ordinances*, for want of circumcision to signify and seal them: for the apostle herein shows, that Christ has not only provided that his people should be partakers of the thing signified by it, but has also substituted another external ordinance, of like use, signification, and design, to be continued under the gospel state, more suitable to its simplicity and spiritual nature. But if the infants of believing parents were not to be baptized, under the gospel-dispensation, a strong objection would still have remained against their being complete in Christ, as to external privileges; since the children of the Israelites, under the Mosaic dispensation, were to be circumcised, as well as themselves."

Christ from the dead; and will put forth, by virtue of his resurrection, in raising you up to eternal life (Rom. 8:11; 1 Peter 1:3). And ye, who in your unregenerate state were dead in law, under a just sentence of condemnation, on account of your trespasses; and were dead toward God, and everything that is spiritually good, in the disposition of your hearts, under the power of corrupt nature, which was signified, during the Mosaic dispensation, by your being uncircumcised in the flesh, he has now raised to a new life of grace and holiness, in order to a heavenly life of glory and blessedness, together with Christ, as your head, by quickening virtue derived from him, and in conformity to his resurrection from the dead; God having, on his account, freely forgiven you all and every one of your iniquities, whether they be original or actual, greater or lesser sins, that none of them might be imputed to you, or bind the curse of the law upon you, or be brought into judgment against you, though ye never have been literally circumcised; and therefore that ordinance cannot be necessary to your pardon and acceptance with God to eternal life.

5. Another consideration that seems to confirm the above reasoning is the remarkable manner in which the inspired historian records the doctrine and practice of the apostles. He uses the very language of the Jewish lawgiver, when he gives us an account of the solemn ratification of God's covenant with Abraham and his family. Let us first of all consult the transaction between God and Abraham, which Moses has recorded in these words,

> And God said unto Abraham…This is my covenant, which ye shall keep, between me and you and thy seed after thee; Every man child among you shall be circumcised…He that is eight days old shall be circumcised among you, every man child in your generations, he that is born in the house, or bought with money of any stranger, which is not of thy seed. He that is born in thy house, and he that is bought with thy money, must needs be circumcised…And Abraham took Ishmael his son, and all that were born in his house, and all that were bought with his money, every male among the men of Abraham's house; and circumcised the flesh of their foreskin in the selfsame day, as God had said unto him…In the selfsame day was

Abraham circumcised, and Ishmael his son. And all the men of his house…were circumcised with him (Gen. 17:9–27).

Compare with this history the account Luke has given of the families of Lydia, and the jailer,

> And a certain woman named Lydia, a seller of purple, of the city of Thyatira, which worshipped God, heard us: whose heart the Lord opened, that she attended unto the things which were spoken of Paul. And when *she was baptized, and her household…* And they said [unto the jailer] Believe on the Lord Jesus Christ, and *thou shalt be saved, and thy house.* And they spake unto him the word of the Lord, and to all that were in his house. And he took them the same hour of the night, and washed their stripes; and *was baptized, he and all his,* straightway (Acts 16:14–15, 31–33).

It is not to be supposed, that, by virtue of the jailer's own faith, all that were in his house should be effectually and eternally saved; and therefore the apostle here seems to intend that as the jailer would by faith become a true son of Abraham, so God would bring him into his covenant, in which he promised to be a God to him, and to his seed (Gen. 17:7). But it was not proper for the apostle to mention this privilege in those terms, whilst he was speaking to a heathen, who was a stranger to the Old Testament, as he afterwards did to a Gentile church (Gal. 3:7, 9, 29); and as our Lord had intimated it concerning Zacchaeus, when he said at his conversion, "This day is salvation come to this house, forsomuch as he also is a son of Abraham" (Luke 19:9).

There is no room to doubt, considering Abraham's character, but that when God first made his covenant with him and his seed, and ordered every male in his house to be circumcised, all the adult males of his family were instructed in the knowledge of God, and of his covenant, in order to their having the token of it applied to them, as well as to the children and himself, according to God's appointment (Gen. 17:7–14; 18:19). And the same may be said with respect to the Jewish proselytes and their families; since, as to this point, there was one law to the Israelites and the strangers (Ex. 12:48–49); and, if we may depend on the Jewish doctors, adult proselytes, and their houses, were to be baptized by their own consent.[28] And therefore its being said that Paul and Silas spoke the word of the Lord to the jailer, and all that were in his house (Acts 16:32), when the gospel-seal of the covenant was to be applied to him and all his, is no more an argument against his having had children that were baptized than it is that there were no male-infants in Abraham's family to be circumcised, nor any infants in the families of proselytes to be baptized, as well as circumcised; because the grown persons in both were to be instructed, before either of those rites were to be applied to them, as the grown persons in the jailer's house were first to be taught, that they might be baptized upon their own personal profession of faith, and by their own consent. And if any suppose that there were no children in his house, nor in Lydia's (Acts 16:15), they take that for granted which it is impossible to prove; but it is certain that the terms *household*, and *a man's house*, all along in the Old Testament, generally include the children of the family; and if, as is thought by many, it had been a well-known, and long-continued custom among the Jews, to admit proselytes into the church of Israel, by baptizing them and their whole families, inclusive of their infants,[29] there is a plain reference to that custom, when in this chapter it is said that *Lydia and her house*, and the *jailer and all his*, were baptized. And it is very remarkable in my account that in this history of the Acts of the apostles, God's covenant with his *people and their seed*, and the application of the New Testament seal of it to *children*, as well as grown persons, is strongly intimated, first with respect to the converted Jews, afterwards to the proselytes of the gate, and then again to the idolatrous Gentiles, in some of the first openings of the gospel dispensation among them respectively. As to the Jews, the apostle Peter called them to repent and be baptized, because *the promise was to them and to their children*, and ran in the like strain to such as should be called from among the Gentiles (Acts 2:38–39). As to the proselytes of the gate, Lydia and her household (Acts 16:15), or, as the Syriac has it, *the children of her house* were baptized; which shows at

---

[28] See Henry Ainsworth. *Annotations upon the Five Books of Moses, the Book of the Psalms, and the Song of Songs*, on Genesis 17:12.

[29] See John Lightfoot. *The Harmony of the Four Evangelists*, on John 1:25.

least, that in those early times children were deemed such parts of the household as were baptized. As to idolatrous Gentiles, the jailer and *all his* were baptized.

As my intention is only to give a reason of the hope that is in me, concerning the baptizing of the infants of such parents as profess their faith in Christ, and obedience to him, I do not think it necessary to enlarge on the answers that might be given to the arguments of Anti-paedobaptists. I shall only observe a few things cursorily concerning some of them.

(1.) They say, we have no *express command* to baptize children.

Answer. An express command is not always necessary to establish a point of duty, that follows by necessary consequence on principles that are clearly revealed; as might be shown in many instances, such as the observation of the first-day Sabbath, the apostles turning to the Gentiles on the authority of a general declaration (Acts 13:46), and several others.

(2.) They urge that there is no *express instance* of any infant being baptized in the whole Scripture. And where there is neither example nor command, any piece of divine worship that men contrive is sinful and dangerous.

Answer. We are perfectly agreed that the *appointment* or *approbation of God* is necessary to authorize everything in his worship that may be lawfully practiced. But the general assertions about the baptizing of *households*, if they do not prove that children were actually baptized, because there might *possibly* be no children in the households mentioned (and yet it is impossible to prove there really were none); yet they show that children in the households of believing parents might be baptized. We have neither an express command, nor an express example, of women showing the death of Christ in the Lord's Supper; and yet their right and obligation is not disputed by any sober person.

But for a direct answer, I beg leave to suggest these few things. (1.) There are many great truths comprehended in the Scriptures which are not *plainly* and *in so many words* asserted. (2.) Those truths which are more plainly revealed in the Old Testament are more sparingly mentioned in the New; and those which are more darkly mentioned in the Old are more clearly opened in the New. (3.) Those truths which were not controverted in the apostles' days were not so zealously pressed or defended by them, there not being any apparent reason or occasion for it. (4.) The

Scriptures which refer to the privileges of *infants* are most proper to be adduced on this argument, and not those that refer to the privileges only of *grown persons*.

(3.) They tell us, that infants can *receive no benefit* from the ordinance of baptism, because of their incapacity, and therefore ought not to be baptized.

Answer. This argument has the same weight in the case of circumcision that it has when applied to baptism; and yet the apostle says, *there is much profit of circumcision every way*; though it was performed *on the eighth day*. Infants are capable of the blessings signified in baptism; and are capable of being devoted to God in that ordinance, as much as the Jews, who, by their circumcision, became debtors to do the whole ceremonial law.

(4.) The most common objection is, that *faith and repentance* are frequently mentioned in the New Testament, as *prerequisites* of baptism; therefore it is supposed, children are incapable of baptism, because they cannot give any evidence of either of these fruits of the Spirit.

Answer. It is very true, *grown people* should first profess their faith and repentance before they can be baptized; and all the places in the New Testament where they are spoken of as requisites in the persons to be baptized refer *only* to adult people; but to suppose that a satisfying evidence of these is required in all that may be baptized, is to beg the question, and to ask more than can be granted. Might it not be said, with as much reason, that because Jewish men-children were to be circumcised on the eighth day, therefore none were to be circumcised in their *grown state*? The reasoning is frivolous and fallacious (see Josh. 5:7–8). It is certain, the Gentile proselytes must first profess their faith and repentance before they could be admitted to be circumcised, but being themselves circumcised, upon that profession all their males were immediately admitted to be circumcised also (Ex. 12:48–49). We think this is the case in baptism too, where adult unbaptized persons must first profess their faith and repentance, and then be baptized; and then their infant-seed are also to be baptized in consequence of their having received that ordinance themselves.

(5.) Some think that baptism cannot *succeed* in the room of circumcision, because it was instituted by John, and the Messiah, some time *before circumcision was abolished.*

Answer. It will follow, on the same principles, that the New Testament dispensation did not succeed in the room of the Old. Such principles as infer these conclusions cannot be solid, and no stress ought to be laid upon them.

(6.) It is supposed that infants are excepted in the original commission, which was given by Christ to his disciples, relative to baptism, "Go ye therefore, and teach all nations, baptizing them..." *etc.* (Matt. 28:19–20), where it seems they are first to be taught, and then to be baptized; and therefore infants are incapable of being baptized, because they are not capable of being previously taught.

Answer. This commission has a primary reference to the nations or Gentiles, *in order to their conversion*; and, it is certain, they were first to be taught, and then to be baptized. But I shall only quote the excellent observation of Dr. Guyse on the place, who says,

> It seems to me, that *disciple all nations* (μαθητευσατε παντα τα εθνη),[30] relates to the whole design of Christ's commission for making disciples to him; and that *baptizing*, (v. 19), and *teaching them*, (v. 20), are mentioned as particular branches of that general design, the order of which was to be determined by the circumstances of things: and these indeed made it necessary, that in discipling adult Jews and heathens, they should be taught before they were baptized; but other circumstances, in the settled state of the gospel-kingdom, made it necessary, that in discipling the children of believers, they should be first baptized, and afterwards taught, as the children of Jews, and of proselytes to their religion, were first circumcised, and when they grew up, were instructed in the faith of the God of Israel.

(7.) Some ask with an insolent triumph, why we may not as well give the sacrament of the Lord's Supper to infants as administer baptism to them?

Answer. The cases are not alike. Persons are *passive* in baptism; but *active* in the ordinance of the Lord's Supper. They *are baptized by some other*; but *themselves must take, eat, and drink*, when they show the Lord's death, and with this express design too, that they may have communion with Christ in his body and blood, in his mediation and sacrifice.

I might go over all the arguments used by Anti-paedobaptists to support their opinion, and endeavor to show that they are either inconclusive, or else they proceed on a misapprehension of the principles they assume.

---

[30] See the marginal reading in the Bible.

Infant-baptism is *no novelty*. Many learned writers have, with great industry, collected the opinions and practices of the ages following the apostolic era, and demonstrated the fact that antiquity is on its side. Several instances are referred to by Bostwick, Dr. John Edwards, Sir Peter King, Cradock, Ridgley, and others; but the curious reader will have the fullest and best conviction, by consulting the vast labors of Mr. Wall on this subject.[31] And that he may have a full view of the case, it may be proper to consult the learned Dr. Gale's *Reflections* on that history,[32] together with Mr. Wall's *Defense* of his said history against those reflections.[33]

7. The Manner of Performing This Duty

The next particular to be considered is *the manner* of performing this duty of baptism. All that I have to offer shall be summed up in these three heads: we should observe this ordinance *with simplicity, in a public congregation*, and *with a serious temper*.

1. This ordinance should be observed *with an honest simplicity*, and kept *pure and entire*, as Christ hath appointed it. The rule given us in the word of God is our directory, and we do well to take good heed to it in this duty, as much as in every other.

How grand and awful is that weighty preface to the institution of Christian baptism! "All power is given unto me in heaven and in earth. Go ye therefore, and teach all nations, baptizing them," *etc.* (Matt. 28:18–19). Who is the daring, insolent worm, that will presume to dispute the authority, or change the ordinances, of him who is given to be head over all things to the church, which is his body, the fullness of him that filleth all in all? The solemnity of this ordinance is complete, and all the great purposes of its institution are secured by the authority and blessing of Christ, who is a rock, whose work is perfect, and all his commandments are sure. His laws are not subject to any of these imperfections, which are attendants of the best contrived systems among men, and frequently need explanations, amendments, and corrections. It is most dangerous and presumptuous to add any *ceremony*, or to join any *service*, on any pretense, unto heaven's appointment. This is the most criminal rashness, and, if it is not disputing

---

[31] William Wall. *A Defence of the History of Infant-Baptism against the Reflections of Mr. Gale and Others.*
[32] John Gale. *Reflections on Mr. Wall's History of Infant Baptism.*
[33] Wall, *A Defence of the History of Infant-Baptism against the Reflections of Mr. Gale and Others.*

the authority of Christ directly, it is mingling the authority of men with the authority of him who has a name that is above every name. There are *two instances* of this corruption that I shall particularly mention.

The one is, *the sign of the cross* on the forehead of the person that is baptized. The reader will give me leave to quote the words of Mr. Thomas Bradbury,[34] on this point. Says that excellent person:

> If Christ had thought that washing with water was not sufficient without *the sign of the cross*, he would have told us, and made that supernumerary addition more ancient than it is: for *from the beginning it was not so*. We may call it *a token of fighting manfully*; but it is no token for good, nor did mankind ever find any more courage in those that have it, than in those that want it. Nor does it scatter among those that have received this mark in their foreheads, any zeal for *the doctrine of the cross*. They do not understand better than their neighbors the great article of justification, from that righteousness that was brought in by *the death of the cross*; nor do we see that it promotes the influence of the cross upon our hearts and lives, that it makes people more self-denying, and mortified to the world. In a word, it rather tends to crucify our Lord afresh, in the *honor of his authority*, and the *liberties of his people*. It has made men *schismatics*, who walk in all the statutes and commandments of the Lord blameless; and is a token of nothing so much as this, that *other lords have had dominion over us*.

Another instance of corruption in the ordinance of baptism is the appointing of *godfathers and godmothers*.[35]

> This is such an undoing of what God has established in the laws of nature, such an overruling and transferring of a *parental authority*, that it is no wonder that so little good comes of it. That it has spread perjury through the land,[36] and brought people into a habit

---

[34] Bradbury, *The Duty and Doctrine of Baptism*, sermon 2.
[35] Whoever chooses to see these points, namely, *the sign of the cross*, and *godfathers and godmothers, in baptism*, distinctly examined, may consult Pierce, *A Vindication of the Dissenters*, part 3, chapters 5, 6.
[36] These words are part of a sermon preached in London: but the case is precisely the same in *every country* where *godfathers* are used, as they are in *England*.

of promising and vowing what they never designed to perform, is not so much as denied: and what benefit may be expected to a poor child who is offered up to God, with a solemnity of so much falsehood, I cannot imagine. Solomon has given such a name to these practices, that should not make us very fond of them: *If thou vowest a vow unto the Lord, defer not to pay it; for he has no pleasure in fools.*[37]

Perhaps I shall be asked, What warrant can be alleged for parents *presenting their children*, that will not as much serve to authorize the use of godfathers and godmothers?

Answer. We think that Christian parents may dedicate their children to God by prayer, and consequently also in baptism, which we suppose infants to be capable of. We think that the parents (at least one of them) should profess their faith on this occasion, as well as their resolution, through grace, to maintain a conversation becoming the gospel of Christ, which is the fruit and evidence of an unfeigned belief of the truth; and this is requisite in the very nature of the thing, and was required in the case of the jailer (Acts 16:31–33). But the parents are not required to profess faith, and promise services, *in the name of the child, and in its stead.* Our exceptions against the manner of baptizing in the church of England are founded on these two things. (1.) By their form of baptism, parents are not suffered to present their own children, nor profess their own faith, to God. But *others must do it*, though they be strangers, and may never see the child again. Nay, they must be other persons, though the *parents* were *godly*, and the *godfathers and godmothers* were *wicked*. (2.) By their form, the *sponsors* are forced to *profess what they do not know*;[38] and to *promise what they cannot perform*.[39]

---

[37] Bradbury, *The Duty and Doctrine of Baptism*.
[38] For example, they must profess that the child to be baptized, doth "renounce the devil and all his works, the vain pomp and glory of the world, with all covetous desires of the same, and the carnal desires of the flesh." Also they must in the name of the child profess, *that it steadfastly believes all the articles of what is commonly called the Apostles' Creed*.
[39] "The godfathers and godmothers must promise, in the name of the child, that it will obediently keep God's holy will and commandments, and walk in the same all the days of its life." See *the office for the public ministration of baptism.*

2. This ordinance should be administered *in a public assembly*. John's baptism was performed in the face of multitudes; and I think the nature of the ordinance requires it to be always administered in that open public manner. Baptism is not so properly a person's *taking hold of God's covenant*, either for himself, or his child; if that is done with the soul, as it ought to be, it must be done very often in private, with greater freedom than can be used before any witnesses; but, when he does this in baptism, it is his *declaration* to the world, or at least to the people of God, that *he and his will be the Lord's*. This was plainly the case with the multitude of converts on the day of Pentecost. Peter bids them *repent and be baptized* (Acts 2:38). This repentance was a secret thing, a godly sorrow that lay within themselves; but *they gladly received the word*, and were *baptized*, about three thousand of them (Acts 2:41), and so were witnesses to one another.

The examples of the *eunuch* and *jailer* are far from concluding against this rule. As to the former, Philip was alone with him, and so preached the gospel to him, and was never like to see him more; but, however, his baptism was as public as the sermon by which he was converted, and as open as circumstances would admit. The *jailer's* case plainly turns the argument the other way, for *he was baptized with his household*, before all those that made up the auditory.

The benefits of a public administration ought to turn the scale. Certainly both ministers and people find a great deal of difference in the frame of their spirits, when they are pulled at once out of the noise of the world, and can hardly shake off the cares that hang about them; and when on *God's own day*, they have given a solemn discharge to every encumbrance of that nature. It is undoubtedly desirable in this ordinance, as well as in others, to attend on the Lord without distraction. Besides, as all things are to be done *to the use of edifying*, so whatever does most answer that end will be chosen by a man who would keep a conscience void of offense towards God. Now, as the congregation has an opportunity of being instructed about the nature and improvement of the duty, so the party baptized is received under a larger confluence of prayer.

3. Baptism is an ordinance that should be performed with the greatest measure of *seriousness*. Abraham fell on his face, when God talked with him, and gave him the covenant of circumcision (Gen. 17:17). It is indeed an awful transaction, when angels and men are called as witnesses to the

surrender that people make either of themselves or of their children. When Joshua had engaged the promise of the Israelites, that they would not forsake the Lord God of their fathers, he set up *a stone*, and told them, "this stone shall be a witness unto us; for it hath heard all the words of the LORD which he spake unto us: it shall be therefore a witness unto you, lest ye deny your God" (Josh. 24:27). The meaning is that when they saw that stone, they should remember both what God had promised, and what they had engaged unto him. But those that are baptized have many living witnesses to observe their temper on such a weighty occasion; and they will join to condemn the irreverent, careless sinner that intermeddles with holy things without consideration.

It is truly astonishing that some professors, who show much seriousness at the Lord's Supper, should make so large abatements of it in baptism. These are but two seals to the same covenant, and therefore ought to be attended to with equal reverence. Nay, if there is to be any distinction, it seems to be on the side of baptism, because that is only *once* done for a grown person, or for a particular infant; whereas we are *often* called to eat this bread, and drink this cup, and show our Lord's death till he come.

Every consideration that can demand attention, and awaken serious reflections, concurs to demonstrate that this is a very solemn and weighty transaction. In this ordinance, there is a *direct remembrance* of original sin, and a *pleasant view* of the new and living way God hath consecrated for our approach into the holiest of all.

This seriousness of temper and behavior should manifestly prevail in all that attend on that ordinance; and should be kept up and cherished when the service is ended. And here, by the way, I would observe that there is one practice, which, if it is not inconsistent with it, looks very unsuitable to it, and that is, any *sensual joys* upon the occasion of baptisms. Says Mr. Bradbury,

> What we call *a christening dinner* is but a poor attendant on our putting on the Lord Jesus Christ, and rather looks like making a provision for the flesh, to fulfill the lusts thereof. We read that Abraham made a great feast the same day that Isaac was weaned (Gen. 21:8), and that seems to be the season of life that nature itself has directed us to rejoice in; when God has preserved a child through the weakness and dangers of infancy: but to follow baptism with an excess of

riot, is turning the grace of God into wantonness. I should think, that if I had been owning the covenant for myself, or for my child, my soul would be so full of it for *one day*, that I should not have leisure for *revelings, banqueting, and abominable idolatries.*[40]

8. The Directions Relative to It

I shall conclude this chapter concerning baptism by proposing some *practical directions* to be observed relative to it. And,

1. Study to have just apprehensions of the nature, use, and design of this ordinance. A sound judgment is necessary to direct our practice, that we may do all to the glory of God, and may profit by the ordinances of the gospel. How emphatic and suitable are these words, when applied to this purpose!

> Wisdom is the principal thing; therefore get wisdom: and with all thy getting get understanding. Exalt her, and she shall promote thee: she shall bring thee to honour, when thou dost embrace her. She shall give to thine head an ornament of grace: a crown of glory shall she deliver to thee. Hear, O my son, and receive my sayings; and the years of thy life shall be many. I have taught thee in the way of wisdom; I have led thee in right paths. When thou goest, thy steps shall not be straitened; and when thou runnest, thou shalt not stumble. Take fast hold of instruction; let her not go: keep her; for she is thy life (Prov. 4:7–13).

There is one passage that deserves particular attention, and is exceedingly proper to correct and prevent misapprehensions about the nature, efficacy, and use of this ordinance, which I have reserved for this place. It is recorded, "The like figure whereunto even baptism doth also now save us (not the putting away of the filth of the flesh, but the answer of a good conscience toward God,) by the resurrection of Jesus Christ" (1 Peter 3:21). The apostle had been representing the wonderful escape of a few, that is, only eight persons, from the destroying waters of the deluge, that swallowed up the world of the ungodly. Noah and his family were saved in the ark he had prepared, which was lifted up on the surface of those collected

---

[40] Bradbury, *The Duty and Doctrine of Baptism*, sermon 2.

floods, which spread death and ruin among all the species and individuals of living creatures that were not hid in that sanctuary. And then follows the verse I have quoted, the sense whereof is judiciously expressed in the following paraphrase by Dr. Guyse.

> Answerable to this temporal salvation in the ark from the flood, by means of the waters bearing it up, we now have salvation in Christ from sin and wrath, by means of the gospel-ordinance of baptism, which in a sense may be called its antitype (αντιτυπον): not that a bare external administration of it, in applying water to the body, as though that were to wash away its defilement, is of any avail of itself for this spiritual purpose: but all its efficacy lies in what is signified by it, as the purification of the heart was by circumcision in the flesh; and as it is a solemn obligation upon conscience to return a suitable answer to its demands of obedience to God, we having been therein devoted to the Father, and the Son, and the Holy Ghost, in whose name, as the one and only true God, we were baptized (Matt. 28:19). And we are made partakers of this salvation, and thus restipulate to God, according to our baptismal engagements, through faith in the resurrection of our Savior Jesus Christ, as he was "delivered for our offenses, and was raised again for our justification" (Rom. 4:25); as also for quickening us from the death of sin to the life of righteousness in this world (Rom. 6:3–6); and raising us up, soul and body, to eternal life in the world to come, that we may live in glory with him.

Baptism does not secure salvation, by any necessity or energy; but only avails to that glorious end by the greater things that it refers to. *The washing away of the filth of the flesh* is not the thing that secures our salvation; for we have this only by *the resurrection of Jesus Christ*, who procured it. *He* made the title good, being raised again for our justification; and thus he is the author of eternal salvation to as many as obey him. This is what we profess in baptism, that our dependence for the happiness we are looking after is on him *that died for us, and rose again.* That ordinance is a seal that he hath set to his covenant, and we use it as a seal to our hopes, by which we declare them, and ratify the whole opinion that faith has of a Mediator. So that here is an honorable correspondence, a great transaction between

God and us, in the solemnity of baptism. But though this is performed by external actions, and a visible application of water, we must not suppose that the ceremonial, or the outward part is the most substantial, that draws into it all the happiness. *Baptism now saveth us.* How? By putting away the filth of the flesh, through the application of water? No, but by *the answer of a good conscience towards God.* Nothing can furnish this answer but *the everlasting righteousness* of Jesus Christ, who "died, yea rather, that is risen again, who is even at the right hand of God, who also maketh intercession for us." This enables the Christian to defy every accuser, to stop the mouth of all that would rise up in judgment to condemn him (Rom. 8:33–34).

2. Do not suppose, whether you have given up yourselves, or your infants to God in this ordinance, that you are baptized *into a party*, or *into a particular denomination*. Amidst all the varieties among Christians, as there is but "one body, and one Spirit... one hope of your calling; one Lord, one faith," so there is but "one baptism" (Eph. 4:4–6). The apostle's expostulation with the carnal factious members of the Corinthian church is spirited, and convincing throughout; particularly his general appeal to *the party* among them, that distinguished themselves by his own name, and affected to be known as his zealous friends, is noble and generous, "were ye baptized in the name of Paul?" (1 Cor. 1:13). The question implies that none is baptized into a party, according to the genuine intention of this ordinance. Christians are baptized *into one body*, and not into *these peculiarities*, that form and denominate any particular class. We cannot have a stronger proof of this than their being baptized in the name of the Father, and of the Son, and of the Holy Ghost, who have a common relation to the catholic church.

3. The needful, but much neglected duty, of improving our baptism, is to be performed by us, all our life long, especially in the time of temptation, and when we are present at the administration of it to others; by serious and thankful consideration of the nature of it, and of the ends for which Christ instituted it, the privileges and benefits conferred and sealed thereby, and our solemn vow made therein:

> Know ye not, that so many of us as were baptized into Jesus Christ were baptized into his death? Therefore we are buried with him by baptism into death: that like as Christ was raised up from the dead by the glory of the Father, even so we also should walk in newness of

life. For if we have been planted together in the likeness of his death, we shall be also in the likeness of his resurrection (Rom. 6:3–5).

By being humbled for our sinful defilement, or falling short of, and walking contrary to, the grace of baptism, and our engagements, "For it hath been declared unto me of you, my brethren, by them which are of the house of Chloe, that there are contentions among you. Now this I say, that every one of you saith, I am of Paul; and I of Apollos; and I of Cephas; and I of Christ. Is Christ divided? was Paul crucified for you? or were ye baptized in the name of Paul?" (1 Cor. 1:11–13). "God forbid. How shall we, that are dead to sin, live any longer therein? Know ye not, that so many of us as were baptized into Jesus Christ were baptized into his death?" (Rom. 6:2–3). By growing up to assurance of pardon of sin, and of all other blessings sealed to us in that sacrament, "And he received the sign of circumcision, a seal of the righteousness of the faith which he had yet being uncircumcised: that he might be the father of all them that believe, though they be not circumcised; that righteousness might be imputed unto them also: and the father of circumcision to them who are not of the circumcision only, but who also walk in the steps of that faith of our father Abraham, which he had being yet uncircumcised" (Rom. 4:11–12). "The like figure whereunto even baptism doth also now save us (not the putting away of the filth of the flesh, but the answer of a good conscience towards God,) by the resurrection of Jesus Christ" (1 Peter 3:21). By drawing strength from the death and resurrection of Christ, into whom we are baptized, for the mortifying of sin, and quickening of grace (Rom. 6:3–5). By endeavoring to live by faith, "For ye are all the children of God by faith in Christ Jesus. For as many of you as have been baptized into Christ have put on Christ" (Gal. 3:26–27). By endeavoring to have our conversation in holiness and righteousness, as those that have therein given up their names to Christ, "But now being made free from sin, and become servants to God, ye have your fruit unto holiness, and the end everlasting life" (Rom. 6:22). "Then Peter said unto them, Repent, and be baptized every one of you in the name of Jesus Christ for the remission of sins, and ye shall receive the gift of the Holy Ghost" (Acts 2:38). And by endeavoring to walk in brotherly love, as being baptized by the same Spirit into one body,[41] "For by one Spirit are we all baptized into one body, whether we

---

[41] *Westminster Larger Catechism*, q. 167.

be Jews or Gentiles, whether we be bond or free; and have been all made to drink into one Spirit...That there should be no schism in the body; but that the members should have the same care one for another. And whether one member suffer, all the members suffer with it; or one member be honored, all the members rejoice with it. Now ye are the body of Christ, and members in particular" (1 Cor. 12:13, 25–27).

4. Baptism is a duty that should be managed in the way of *looking unto Jesus*. This may be called a *general* direction that comes into every duty; but here it stands under a particular mark, for the apostle says, "baptism doth also now save us...by the resurrection of Jesus Christ: who is gone into heaven, and is on the right hand of God; angels and authorities and powers being made subject to him" (1 Peter 3:21–22). He immediately adds in the next verses, "Forasmuch then as Christ hath suffered for us in the flesh, arm yourselves likewise with the same mind: for he that hath suffered in the flesh hath ceased from sin; that he no longer should live the rest of his time in the flesh to the lusts of men, but to the will of God" (1 Peter 4:1–2). This glorious truth is fully attested by the apostle, "Buried with [Christ] in baptism, wherein also you are risen with him through the faith of the operation of God, who hath raised him from the dead. And you, being dead in your sins and the uncircumcision of your flesh hath he quickened together with him, having forgiven you all trespasses" (Col. 2:12–13).

Such a view and improvement of baptism, in its necessary relation to Christ, would have the happiest and most desirable effects. This would keep Christians to the purity of God's worship; for "if ye be dead with Christ" (as is represented in baptism) to "the rudiments of the world, why, as though living in the world, are you subject to ordinances...after the commandments and doctrines of men?" (Col. 2:20, 22). This would give a heavenliness to their conversation; for, "if ye then be risen with Christ...set your affection on things above...where Christ sitteth at the right hand of God" (Col. 3:1–2). And this would make them dare to die, knowing what consignments they have made unto them; "for ye are dead, and your life is hid with Christ in God. When Christ, who is our life, shall appear, then shall ye also appear with him in glory" (Col. 3:3–4).

I shall conclude with an extract from the judicious *Exposition of the Ten Commandments*, by the learned and laborious Mr. James Durham of Glasgow, who has suggested many very excellent directions of a practical nature, relative to the ordinance baptism, under four heads. Speaking of baptism, he says,

> We may consider, 1. The sins of those who seek it for their children; 2. The sins of those who administer it; 3. The sins of onlookers, especially of those who are called to be witnesses; 4. The sins of those who are baptized.
>
> *First*, The parents or presenters of children to baptism fail *before, in the time*, and *after* the administration of this ordinance.
>
> (1.) *Before*: by not seriously minding that which is to be done; not considering the child's condition, as needing Christ in that ordinance; nor the end of that ordinance; miskenning[42] Christ, and not going first to him, for conferring the things and blessings signified; not praying for the child, for the minister, and for a blessing on the ordinance; not blessing God that there is a covenant of grace that taketh in our children, nor offering them to be engaged and received in it; not minding the most simple and edifying way of going about it, but walking by other rules; needless delaying of it for carnal ends; and being more desirous of the sign than of the thing signified.
>
> (2.) *When we come to it, we sin*: not seeking to have our own covenant with God (by which we have this privilege of bringing our children to baptism) renewed and made sure; not considering by what right we claim it to our children; not repenting of our own breaches of covenant, nor wondering that God keepeth with us, who have often broken to him; not coming with the exercise of fear and reverence; waiting on it ofttimes without attention, or minding our duty in what is spoken; promising for the fashion when we engage for the children's education, and without either judgment or resolute purpose to perform; being ignorant of what is said or done; not concurring in prayer for the blessing; and not undertaking in Christ's strength to perform the duties called for.
>
> (3.) *After the administration of baptism*: we fail in forgetting all our engagements; in growing careless to maintain any suitable frame, and falling carnal in our mirth on such occasions; not being much in prayer for the children, nor insisting nor continuing in

---

[42] Neglecting or overlooking.

prayer for the blessing; not being faithful, according to our engagements, in educating them: in *knowledge*, that they may be so trained up as to know what God is; in *the fear of God*, pressing it upon them by frequent exhortations; in giving them *good example*; in giving them *seasonable correction* (but rather sparing them, though to their hurt), when there is cause of correction; being also unfaithful, in not seriously minding them of their engagements by baptism; much more by giving them evil example; conniving at their faults; advising them to what is sinful, or sending them where they may meet with snares, or suffering them to go there; providing for them the things of this life, without respect to that life which is to come; not enabling ourselves that we may perform our duty to them; not insisting *always* to press these things upon them that concern their souls, thinking it is enough that *sometimes* they be spoken to; never purposely stirred up and driven by that tie to see for their good; nor repenting our many shortcomings; nor lamenting for what we see sinful in them, when they follow not faithful advice. These are things that would carefully be looked unto both by fathers and mothers, and all such as engage for the Christian education of the children whom they present to that ordinance,

Secondly, In him that administereth baptism, there are ofttimes divers failings: as, when it is customarily dispensed, without respect to its end; when in prayer the child's salvation is not really and seriously aimed at, but for the fashion; when it becometh a burden to dispense it; when it is not thought much of, that Christ admitteth such into his house, or himself to be a partaker of such mercies, let it be to be a dispenser of them to others; when he followeth it not privately with a blessing; besides what failings may be in *unsuitable words*, and *human ceremonies, etc.*, and seeking himself in the words that are spoken, rather than the edification of the hearers.

Thirdly, When we are witnesses and onlookers we fail in wearying and fretting, because we are detained a while; not setting ourselves to be edified by that we see done, and hear spoken; not sympathizing with the child or its parents in prayer; not being thankful to God for such a benefit and ordinance to such a child's behoof; lightness of carriage, and in looking, speaking, or thinking in the time, as if we were not present at such an ordinance of Christ; not so seriously taken up in sympathizing with other folks' children, because they are not our own; removing and withdrawing, and not staying to countenance it; not minding the child when we are gone; not helping them as we may to be answerable to that tie they come under in baptism; not admonishing them, when we see parents and children walk unanswerably, nor testifying against them, nor mourning for the dishonor God getteth by *baptized persons' unsuitable carriage.*

Fourthly, All of us that are baptized fail wonderfully, less or more, that we never, as we ought, reckon ourselves obliged, by that tie we come under in baptism; that we neither are, nor seriously study to be, as we ought, answerable to it; that we are not thankful to God, who admitted us to that ordinance; that we do not esteem it above all carnal birthrights, how great soever; that we do not seek to have it cleared, in the extent of it, as to the privileges and benefits thereby conferred on us and our children; that we do not pursue after the blessing therein covenanted to us; that we do not improve our baptism for strengthening our faith, both in spiritual and temporal difficulties; that we are often ignorant how to make use of it; that we do not account ourselves wholly God's, as being given away to him in baptism, but live to ourselves; that we do not fight against our lusts, Satan, and the world, according to our baptismal vow; that we do not adorn our Christian profession with a holy life; that we walk and war against Christ, instead of fighting under his banner; that we do not aggravate our sins, as being committed against this tie; that we are not patient under sufferings, nor penitent and humble under all sad dispensations, notwithstanding we are by our baptism bound to take up the cross; that we do not meditate on our engagements, nor repent of our neglects; that we do not aim and endeavor to come up to the main ends of this ordinance, which are: the evidencing our regeneration and ingrafting into Christ; the giving ourselves to the Father, Son, and Spirit; sticking by Christ on the most costly and dearest terms; taking directions from him, and walking in him; seeking the things that are above, and not the things that are on earth; mortification to creatures, and to be crucified with Christ; and the improving of this tie, not only for obliging us to these, but for strengthening us in him to attain them, and to comfort ourselves in all difficulties from this ground. These things are much a-missing, alas! They are much a-missing. We lamentably neglect to draw all our strength and furniture, under all temptations, and for all duties, from Christ, by virtue of this baptismal obligation and tie. We resort but seldom to this magazine and storehouse. This precious privilege is, alas! but very little unproved by us.[43]

These are the words of that pious and sensible writer. I leave it to the reader to consider what is said, and the Lord give us understanding in all things.

---

[43] James Durham. *A Practical Exposition of the Ten Commandments.*

Chapter 9
The Lord's Supper

In discoursing of this great and solemn ordinance, which every serious Christian looks upon with a peculiar regard and veneration, because I purpose, as God shall enable me, to open as well the *doctrine*, as the *duty* of it, it will be proper enough, and, I hope, not unprofitable, to take some notice of the following things, in this order:
1. The names;
2. The Author;
3. The nature;
4. The obligation; and,
5. The excellent uses of this ordinance;
6. The objections made against it;
7. Some questions relative to it; and,
8. The practical directions that are proper to be observed about it.

1. The Names of This Ordinance

I proposed, first of all, to take some notice of *the names* by which this ordinance is described in the inspired writings. The ancient fathers of the Christian church have called it by *various names*, several of which are neither very proper, nor significant; though some of them are expressive and emphatic enough; but the most important and instructive designations of it are to be met with in the oracles of God, where it is sometimes called,

1. *The breaking of bread* (Acts 2:42; 20:7). In this ordinance bread is broken in remembrance of the death of Christ, whose body was broken for us as a sacrifice for sin, and to be the spiritual food of our souls. How improper is the Popish wafer to answer to this memorable truth! How different from our Lord's example, who took bread, and after he had blessed it, *brake it!*

2. *The Lord's table.* "Ye cannot be partakers of the Lord's table, and of the table of devils" (1 Cor. 10:21). The Lord hath furnished this table; the

flesh and blood of the Lord Jesus Christ is the spiritual provision for it, and it is sacred to his honor, to commemorate his obedience and satisfaction, whereby he hath finished transgression, and made an end of sin, and made reconciliation for iniquity, and brought in an everlasting righteousness.

3. *The cup of blessing which we bless* (1 Cor. 10:16). The reason may be, because, according to the institution and example of Christ, his servants solemnly set it apart for sacred use, by *thanksgiving* and prayer, for the spiritual benefit of the receiver; and because they who partake of it with faith, and other suitable graces, offer up their *joyful adoration, blessing, and praise* to God for a crucified Christ, and for all the great and glorious deliverances and *blessings*, which he, in his superlative, endearing love, has purchased for them by his death.

4. *The feast.* "Let us keep the feast" (1 Cor. 5:8). This ordinance may be called *a feast*, in allusion to the passover; and was very properly instituted instead of that ordinance, which was both commemorative of Israel's deliverance from the destroying angel, and pre-figurative of the death of Christ; but is now superseded by the Lord's Supper, which is a commemoration of the more glorious redemption through his blood.

5. *The New Testament in the blood of Christ* (Luke 22:20). God made a covenant with his chosen, even with his own Son, before all worlds, wherein mercy is built up for eternity. This most gracious transaction fully secures every valuable purpose. The glory of God, and the salvation of his people, are provided for, in the most effectual manner, by the obedience unto death of God our Savior. Whatever is necessary to remove our guilt, to sanctify our nature, and to save us with an everlasting salvation, is provided in this covenant, and conveyed to our enjoyment in the form of a *testament*, that we may receive it freely, and have a secure possession. This is a *new* testament, and cannot wax old, nor perish, and decay, as old things are ready to do. This New Testament is *in the blood of Christ*, who finished all that he undertook, as the surety of a better covenant, by shedding his blood for remission of sins unto many, and thereby confirmed the covenant in the whole system of its promises and privileges. Now, in the sacrament of the supper, there is a perpetual memorial of the confirmation of the new covenant by Christ's blood, as shed for the remission of our sins, instead of drinking wine at the paschal supper, in commemoration of Israel's great deliverance.

6. *The communion* (1 Cor. 10:16). In this ordinance believers have communion (1.) With the Lord Jesus Christ, in the virtue and benefits of his precious blood, and in the sufferings of his broken body, which was wounded for our transgressions; and (2.) With one another; "for we being many are one bread...for we are all partakers of that one bread" (1 Cor. 10:17).

> For as the bread, taken and eaten in that ordinance, is of one loaf, or one sort of substance, broken for us all, and is made up of many grains of corn, which are ground, and molded into one lump; so it intimates, that we, the members of the visible church, which consists of many individual Christians, are hereby in a symbolical manner considered as, and own ourselves to be united together, by faith and love, into one holy lump in conformity to Christ, and into one mystical body, of which he is the Head: for we are all partakers of that one loaf or substance, which signifies Christ, the bread of life, who came down from heaven (John 6:51); and so we have fellowship one with another, in our communion with him (the like may be said of our drinking of the wine, which is made of the juice of many grapes, and signifies the blood of Christ). And when these sacramental elements are received with faith in the object, represented by them, we have spiritual and saving communion with Christ, and communications of blessings from him, in virtue of his atoning sacrifice.[1]

7. The last of the designations given to it that I shall take any notice of, is to be found in 1 Corinthians 11:20, where it is called *the Lord's Supper*. The foundation of this name is well accounted for in the next verses, where we are told this ordinance was first instituted at *suppertime*; and from the account of its appointment in the gospels, we learn that it was observed soon after the eating of the Jewish passover. Without entering on any detail of the reasons, why it gets this name of *the Lord's Supper*, I shall only observe that the principal one is, because the Lord Jesus Christ appointed it to be a memorial of his death. Here there is a commemoration of what he has done and suffered; for we are to eat and drink in remembrance of him.

---

[1] Guyse, *Paraphrase*.

And we are to perform this service with a single regard to his glory, and in obedience to his authority. And this leads me,

2. The Author of It

To consider the *Author* of this sacred institution, which is *not of men, nor by the will of men*. The *nature* of the ordinance is a sufficient proof of this. The inventions of men in the worship of God "have a shew of [worldly] wisdom in will worship, and humility, and neglecting of the body; not in any honour to the satisfying of the flesh" (Col. 2:23). But the doctrine of the cross, which is the substantial truth in this ordinance, is a stumbling-block to the Jews; and foolishness to the Greeks. None but these that have heard and learned of the Father know the propriety, or acknowledge the wisdom of this institution.

But we have the concurring testimony of the apostles of our Lord, to assure us of its divine original. I shall quote only the words of Paul, who says "I have received of the Lord that which also I delivered unto you, That the Lord Jesus the same night in which he was betrayed took bread…this do in remembrance of me. After the same manner also he took the cup…this do ye, as oft as ye drink it, in remembrance of me" (1 Cor. 11:23–25).

But why should I spend time in proving what cannot be denied? Jesus Christ is the Author of this ordinance, for it bears his superscription, and is stamped with his name (1 Cor. 11:20). It is *the Lord's Supper*; not only observed for his honor, but observed by his appointment. To eat this supper is an *act of obedience*, as well as a *token of gratitude*. He is rightly called *the Master of the feast*, and we must not add to his words, lest he reprove us.

The two following remarks are peculiarly worthy of our regard on this subject.

1. That this ordinance is the institution of him who is every way qualified to give it both *authority* and *energy*; for he has all power in heaven and in earth. His *right* will not bear a dispute; and his *ability* and *goodwill* to give it the proper effect cannot be questioned, but at the expense of the clearest and most express declarations in the word of God.

2. That he appointed it immediately before he suffered. "Jesus the same night in which he was betrayed took bread," etc. This is a memorable circumstance, that represents the love of Christ to his church in a most endearing light. This was to him a solemn anticipation of his dying for the sins of his people, and under the weight of the wrath of God. This

institution proclaimed the ardor of his affection to them, for whom he obeyed and suffered; while it was calculated to confirm their faith, to exalt their hope, to animate their zeal, to encourage their obedience, and to strengthen them unto all patience and longsuffering with joyfulness. So boundless was his compassion, and so inviolable his attachment to the interests of his people, that, in the immediate prospect of his greatest sufferings in their stead, he left this precious memorial, this confirming pledge of his love among them, to keep up an honorable remembrance of him till he come again. Behold, how he loved them! His love is strong as death. His own dangers only showed its strength, and afforded an occasion for its triumphant and boundless exertions. "Having loved his own, he loved them to the end" (John 13:1).

3. Its Nature

I proposed, in the third place, to explain *the nature* of this ordinance.

> The Lord's Supper is a sacrament, wherein, by giving and receiving bread and wine, according to Christ's appointment, his death is showed forth; and the worthy receivers are, not after a corporal and carnal manner, but by faith, made partakers of his body and blood, with all his benefits, to their spiritual nourishment and growth in grace.[2]

In further opening the nature of this ordinance, it may be useful to consider these four things: *the outward elements*; *the things signified by them*; *the actions of our Savior*; and *the actions of his disciples.*

I. The *sensible signs* to be used in the Lord's Supper are *bread and wine*; thus it is said, "Jesus took bread…and he took the cup," which, by an usual figure, is put for the wine in the cup (Matt. 26:26–29). Here I shall observe three things that are exceeding plain in this short narrative.

1. Our Savior has appointed *bread* to be one of the signs. The warm disputes between the Greek and Latin churches, the former insisting, that *only leavened bread* should be used in this service, and the other pleading as strenuously for the use of *unleavened bread only*, seem to be of very small moment. And whether we suppose the one or the other in the right,

---

[2] *Westminster Shorter Catechism*, question 96.

as to truth, we must say, their unedifying contentions on such a point were wrong in fact. But *wafers* are most presumptuously substituted in the room of bread by the Papists, on very trifling foolish pretenses. Christ took bread, and brake it, and divided it among his disciples.

2. He used *wine* as well as bread. This is recorded for our learning and imitation. To substitute *water* in its room, as some ancient heretics have done, is a base changing of heaven's ordinances; and to *mingle the wine* on any pretense, is criminal superstition.

3. Our Lord Jesus Christ appointed *both bread and wine* to be used in this ordinance. What God hath joined together, let not man presume to put asunder. The ordinance is incomplete in its essential parts, if either of these signs be omitted. The Holy Ghost, foreseeing that the wickedness of man would be so daring, as to deny the use of the cup to the people, has entered an express caveat against it: "Drink ye all of it" (Matt. 26:27). He does not say, "Eat ye all of the bread," but he has provided against the sacrilegious encroachments of Rome, on the privileges of his church, by an express command, "Drink ye all of it." I shall now proceed to consider,

II. *The things signified* by these outward elements of bread and wine, in the Lord's Supper. Christ has explained this matter in the most precise and satisfying light, in the words of institution, for he "took bread…and said…this is my body. And he took the cup…saying…this is my blood of the new testament" (Matt. 26:26–28), where we find the bread and wine are *only representations* of the body and blood of Christ, who bare our sins in his own body on the tree, and whose blood was shed for remission of sins unto many.

If any person shall ask us what we mean by this service of eating bread and drinking wine? We reply that our Lord hath made this our duty by his dying commandment, "This do in remembrance of me." Have ye not houses to eat and to drink in, ye carnal, unthinking professors of religion, that come to this ordinance merely to eat a piece of bread, and to drink a little wine? Why then should you presume to eat and drink judgment to yourselves, not discerning the Lord's body?

"*The bread* which we break, is it not the communion of *the body of Christ?*" (1 Cor. 10:16). Yes, it brings to our remembrance the body of Christ, who, though he is God over all blessed forever, came of the fathers as concerning the flesh, and who is, and continueth to be God and man, in two distinct natures, and one person, forever. A glorious, humbling, and comfortable mystery; great without controversy; though true beyond dispute, where the testimony of the Holy Ghost is allowed a candid hearing. The suffering Jesus was really God and really man; and each nature, subsisting in one marvelous person, contributed what it could to reconcile the world unto God. In the nature of man he suffered, sorrowed, died; and the dignity of his divine person made these sorrows and sufferings meritorious, and effectual "to finish the transgression, and to make an end of sins, and to make reconciliation for iniquity, and to bring in everlasting righteousness" (Dan. 9:24). The new and living way of approach to almighty God is consecrated for us through the veil, that is, the flesh of the Son of God; and we are complete in him, who, in the body of his flesh through death, hath reconciled enemies to God, and presents them perfect in himself (Heb. 10:20; Col. 1:21–22, 28).

"*The cup of blessing* which we bless, is it not the communion of *the blood of Christ?*" (1 Cor. 10:16). It exhibits in a figure the atoning sacrifice he offered, and the precious blood of the Lamb of God, which cleanseth from all sin. We must not imagine that this blood is merely like the blood of bulls, or of goats, that it is barely comparable to choice silver or the fine gold, for God hath purchased the church with his own blood (Acts 20:28). This blood is infinitely valuable and efficacious; it is of sovereign virtue to purge the conscience from dead works, and to speak peace to the guilty soul. This is *the blood of the covenant*, which God hath made with us. This blood is the propitiation for our sins, and the ratification of the great and precious promises which are given us in him. Hence they come to be sure unto all the seed, and merely a testamentary conveyance unto us; not on the condition of our goodness, but in consideration of Christ having fulfilled all righteousness. Here we learn how God is just in justifying the ungodly; and this is the blessed point wherein the awful and amiable perfections of the Deity meet. In a suffering Jesus we see justice satisfied, the law honored, God glorified, divine wrath pacified, death destroyed, Satan vanquished, the world crucified, sin finished, and the covenant sealed.

The body and blood of Christ are only *represented and communicated to our faith* in this ordinance; but not *actually and substantially present* in it. The monstrous conceit of *transubstantiation*[3] is neither warranted in nor consistent with the word of God.

---

[3] The church of Rome maintains, that "by the consecrating of bread and wine, Jesus Christ, very God, and very man, is truly, really, and substantially contained under the

III. I shall, in the next place, take a view of *the actions of our Savior* in this ordinance. This will be most naturally done by *a short paraphrase* on

---

species of those sensible signs; and that there is a conversion of the whole substance of bread, in this holy sacrament, into the whole substance of the body of Christ; and of the whole substance of wine into his blood; which conversion is fitly called *transubstantiation*," *Acts of the Council of Trent*, Sess. 13, ch. 6. They support this opinion from the words of Christ, who said of the bread, *This is my body*, and of the cup, *This is my blood of the New Testament* (Mark 14:22–24).

But Dr. William Harris has justly observed concerning this doctrine of Rome, as it is supposed to arise out of these words:

(1.) That there is no necessity of understanding these words in this sense; because they will easily and fairly admit of another. (2.) The Romish sense is not convenient, or probable; that is, not agreeable to the subject spoken of, and the occasion of speaking them. Our Lord had been just celebrating the passover with his disciples, wherein the *angel's passing over the houses of the Israelites, when he slew all the firstborn of Egypt, was commemorated*; and having finished the passover, he took and blessed, and used some of the bread and wine that remained of the paschal-supper. He said of the bread, *This is my body*; and of the wine, *This cup is the New Testament in my blood*; that is, commemorations of both, as the Jewish paschal lamb was of the angel's passing over. (3.) The Popish sense is not consistent with the other expressions which are here used concerning this ordinance: for his body was not then broken, nor his blood then shed; nor could he command them to *do this in remembrance of him* (εις την εμην αναμνησιν), if he was corporeally and carnally present: Not to insist on the inconsistency of understanding that phrase, *This cup is the New Testament in my blood*, in a literal sense. (4.) Their sense is not reasonable: for it is contrary to the reason of our minds, and to the senses of our bodies, in the due exercise of them, and upon their proper objects and therefore is justly accounted absurd. (5.) Their sense is impossible, and cannot be true: for it implies a great deal of contradiction in it. For example; it supposes the bread to be turned into the broken body of Christ, when he himself was present with his disciples, and his body was not yet broken; that his natural body was entire and whole before their eyes, and at the same time broken in his hand; that his body was broken and not broken, and his blood was shed and not shed at the same time; that his natural body, which is but one, is at the same time many; that it is one body in heaven, and ten thousand bodies on earth, and the same body is divided and separated from itself; that in heaven his body is glorified, and on earth it is broken; that it had a being seventeen hundred years ago, and yet is made afresh every day; that is, it was in being before it began to be; that his one body may be in innumerable places at the same time; that his body is penetrable; that the accidents of bread and wine may exist without a subject—but I am wearied of such flagrant contradictions.

See William Harris. *A Discourse concerning Transubstantiation*

the circumstances mentioned by the evangelists, that give us an account of this matter, who tell us the following things about it.

He took bread: a circumstance that may reasonably bring to our remembrance the marvelous love of God to mankind, lost and ruined by sin, who chose his only begotten Son to be our surety, and laid upon him all our help. May it not remind us too, of the wonderful grace of our Lord Jesus Christ, who voluntarily took upon him our nature, to subsist eternally in his divine person? For "he took not on him the nature of angels; but…the seed of Abraham" (Heb. 2:16).

He blessed the bread, or *gave thanks*: whereby it was set apart from a common to a sacred use. He prayed that it might answer the ends of the institution, and serve as a memorial of his body, which was to be the great atonement for his church, that it might invigorate the faith of his disciples, and support their hope under the trials and sufferings they were to encounter in their way to heaven. He gave thanks to his Father, that required, admitted, and accepted a substitute, and he gave thanks, that *in himself* mercy and truth should meet together, that righteousness and peace should embrace one another. After he had blessed the bread,

He brake it: to signify the astonishing sufferings of his body; for though a bone of him was not to be broken (John 19:36), yet he was to be "wounded for our transgressions…bruised for our iniquities" (Isa. 53:5). In the garden he sweat great drops of blood. In the high-priest's hall he was scourged, spit upon, mocked by the soldiers, and had a crown of thorns put upon his head; and after he had carried his own cross to the place of execution, his hands and feet were nailed to it; and when he had been lifted up, and exposed to the reproaches of them that passed by, for six hours, his very heart's blood was let out with a spear. In this severe and self-abasing manner did the Son of God bear our griefs, and carry our sorrows, being stricken, and smitten of God, and afflicted; the sorrows of death compassed him, and the pains of hell took hold of him, insomuch, that in the article of death, he cried with a loud voice, as a person in the utmost distress, "My God, my God, why hast thou forsaken me?" (Matt. 27:46). The next action of our Savior was his distributing the bread to his disciples at the table, with these words,

Take, eat, this is my body, which is broken for you: thereby intimating that he is the *free gift* of God unto mankind for salvation and eternal life; that this ordinance is designed for the benefit of his people; and that they ought to receive and feed upon him by faith, on the warrant of his own free gift and divine command. He suffered, and his body was broken, not for *any evil he had done*; but *for the sins of his people*. And the broken bread, which he separated to a sacramental use, was a representation of his body, that has been crucified, pierced, and wounded for the iniquities of his people, as suffering in their room and stead. He enjoined them to *take and eat it* in that view; to apply Christ to themselves, and to feed upon him by a more confirmed vigorous faith, while they used this bread as *a memorial* of his sufferings, as he added,

This do in remembrance of me: as if he should say, Take and eat of this symbolical bread in a believing, humble, joyful, thankful, and obediential remembrance of my dying love; of the extremity of my sufferings on your behalf; of the deliverances and blessings which I have thereby procured for you; and of the obligations to love and duty which I have thereby laid upon you.

After the same manner also he took the cup, when he had supped, for this was an *essential part* of the ordinance, and therefore is no more to be omitted than the *taking of the bread*; and it seems to be designed for the same purposes. And although there is no notice taken of *the effusion* of the wine, probably because the Jews thought it was very immaterial, who poured it out, whether the master of the feast, or any servant; yet it must be supposed to have been done; and since the whole must be done in remembrance of Christ, this may, and should bring to our mind, his *pouring out his soul unto death*. When he had taken the cup after supper,

He gave thanks: whether he be supposed to have performed this service, when he blessed the bread, or separately after his disciples had eaten the bread, yet the performing of the service can neither be denied, nor doubted. Hence the apostle speaks of "the cup of blessing which we bless" (1 Cor. 10:16). And when he had given thanks,

He gave the cup to them: to express his marvelous love to them, and the *free gift* of himself *for them*, as an atoning sacrifice of a sweet-smelling savor unto God; and *unto them*, in the declarations of the gospel, that they might believe, possess, and be happy. He added,

Drink ye all of it: a command that warranted and obliged *all his disciples*, not *as teachers*, but as disciples, to show his death, till he come again. He delivered it to them, saying, "This cup is the new testament in my blood" (1 Cor. 11:25), or, "[this cup] is my blood of the new testament, which is shed for many for the remission of sins" (Matt. 26:28), intimating that the blood of Jesus, which was shed by divine justice to confirm the covenant of promise, and to purchase all its blessings, and particularly the forgiveness of sins unto a vast multitude of sinful men...is represented in this cup of blessing. And inasmuch as all the blessings of this covenant are to be received, enjoyed, and used, without money and without price, by virtue, and in consequence of his death, they are set before us under the notion of *a confirmed testament*, that we may have great encouragement to ask them, and strong consolation in the hope of them; for

> Christ hath redeemed us from the curse of the law, being made a curse for us: for it is written, Cursed is every one that hangeth on a tree: that the blessing of Abraham might come on the Gentiles through Jesus Christ; that we might receive the promise of the Spirit through faith. Brethren, I speak after the manner of men; though it be but a man's covenant...no man disannulleth, or addeth thereto (Gal. 3:13–15).

> And for this cause [Christ] is the mediator of the new testament, that by means of death, for the redemption of the transgressions that were under the first testament, they which are called might receive the promise of eternal inheritance. For where a testament is, there must also of necessity be the death of the testator. For a testament is of force after men are dead: otherwise it is of no strength at all while the testator liveth (Heb. 9:15–17).

Immediately after he had given them this instructive account of the cup, which is a sacramental sign, he repeated his solemn charge concerning the use of it, in these words,

This do ye, as oft as ye drink it, in remembrance of me: as if he had said, Come to my table, and drink of this cup, and as often as you drink remember *me*, your Savior and your friend; call to mind my bloody sweat, and the streams that flowed from my wounded side on the cross; remember whose blood it was, not the blood of a mere creature, but of God; consider the ends and purposes for which it was shed, to be an atonement to offended justice, and a perpetual fountain for uncleanness; and do not forget the extremity of my sufferings, that *my very soul was made an offering for sin*;

all which was of the greatest importance for your salvation; for without shedding of blood there could be no remission of sins, no reconciliation to God, nor title to the kingdom of heaven.

In this view, *our Redeemer's actions and words* are most instructive, and profitable for our direction; they explain the nature, and lead to the improvement of this ordinance. It remains, that I go on,

IV. To consider *the actions of the disciples*, which are not directly expressed, but plainly implied, in the history of this solemn service. These may be reduced to three particulars.

1. *They took the bread and the cup*: by which they declared their *belief in Christ*, and their acceptance of him, as freely given in the everlasting gospel to mankind sinners; for the elements in the Lord's Supper are witnesses between God and us; and when communicants receive them into their hands, they do solemnly declare their acceptance of Christ, and their being devoted to him, on the plan of revealed truth, where the promises of the gospel are laid as the foundation of new obedience.

2. *They did eat the bread, and drink the wine*: which was a figure of their vital union to, and participation of the Lord Jesus Christ; and represents, in a lively manner, Christ's dwelling in their hearts by the faith of the gospel. I am far from thinking that our Lord spake only, or principally of the sacrament of the supper, in the sixth chapter of John, where he enlarges on the necessity and virtue of eating his flesh and drinking his blood; but under that metaphorical description, he represents the nature, use, and advantage of such a faith, as should prevail in commemorating his death, in this holy ordinance. As by *eating and drinking* material provisions, they are digested, incorporated, and become one with the body, for the support and comfort of its present frail life; so he who by faith receives Christ, together with the benefits of his death, into his heart, is thereby united with him, as a member of his mystical body; Christ dwells in him by his Spirit, and he dwells in Christ by faith, for all the purposes of maintaining and nourishing his spiritual life, till it shall reach its utmost perfection in heaven; though in a much more sublime, effectual, and eminent sense, than his eating and drinking any corporal repasts can be for the nourishment of his mortal body.

3. *They divided the elements among themselves.* It is certain, this was the practice at the paschal-supper (Luke 22:17), and it seems to have been retained in the Lord's Supper too. Hereby the disciples of Christ express

their mutual love, and maintain their holy fellowship; they show their joint belief in one Savior, and their being *one bread*, though they are *many individuals*.

4. The Obligations to Observe It
The *obligation* that lies upon Christians to observe this duty, is the next thing to be opened. I shall represent this in three heads; and may God set home his own truths on the consciences of all that read them.

1. This is *the express command of Christ*, who said, "this do ye…in remembrance of me" (1 Cor. 11:25). Is any precept in the Bible delivered in plainer or stronger terms? And if children are obliged to obey their parents, or subjects to obey the higher powers, surely the disciples of Christ should obey their Lord and Master, who has bought them with his blood, and has therefore every right to their service. Have they given up themselves to the Lord, and declared their acceptance of him, as their Teacher and atonement, and particularly as their King and Governor, and will they dispute his authority? Are they afraid or ashamed to commemorate the sufferings of the Son of God publicly at his table? It is an alarming declaration, that Mark has recorded, "Whosoever therefore shall be ashamed of me and of my words in this sinful and adulterous generation; of him also shall the Son of man be ashamed, when he comes in the glory of his Father with his holy angels" (Mark 8:38). The *nature* of this command deserves to be particularly considered.

It is very *positive* and *express*. The meaning of it is not to be gathered by consequences; and the force of it is not to be evaded by any plausible pretenses. Nothing can be more plain than the words in which it runs, and nothing more determinate and precise than the sense they imply.

It is his *dying command*: for "the same night in which he was betrayed [he] took bread…[saying] this do in remembrance of me" (1 Cor. 11:23–24). The words of dying friends are usually esteemed very sacred, and their commands very binding, among men. Shall the dying command of the Lord Jesus be the only, or the principal exception in the reckoning of men? Shall one of the last commands with which he favored his church, and finished his testimony, before he suffered, be thought indifferent? Shall we presume to imagine that he uses his people, as the ruler of the feast, at the marriage of Cana, said men usually do on such occasions, by setting forth their good wine at the beginning, and when men have well drunk, then that which is worse? (John 2:9–10). This is a most wicked and false imputation; for the love of Christ is strong as death, and the strength of it cannot be abated.

It is a command that is *supported and enforced by a weighty reason*: for hereby we shall *show the death of Christ, till he come* (1 Cor. 11:26). This command does not proceed merely on the footing of sovereign authority, but on the most reasonable grounds. Is not the death of Christ an event that deserves to be forever remembered? Shall the songs of his ministering angels, and redeemed saints, reproach our indolence, without any effect? Shall not the united force of duty, interest, and gratitude, awaken our attention, and provoke our emulation, in this duty?

The command is *easy*. Naaman's servants reasoned with their master, that if the prophet had commanded him to do some great and difficult thing to be cured of his leprosy, he would have done it; how much more reasonable was it to follow his advice, by going to wash seven times in Jordan, and be made whole? The simplicity of the prescription was the very reason why it was slighted. If the law requires us to keep the commandments, to establish a title to eternal life, the proud legalist is willing to attempt even the impossible undertaking; but how much better adapted is the scheme of the gospel to our condition, where purchased redemption is conveyed in a promise to be enjoyed by believing? And how kind is our gracious Redeemer in appointing an ordinance, wherein we may remember his death, and rejoice in the efficacy of his sacrifice, and the fullness of his grace! He calls us to remember his death in the use of such ordinances as cannot be reckoned a *grievous yoke*. Shall Papists, under the power of strong delusions, go in pilgrimage to the (once) holy land, to visit Christ's sepulcher, or to the top of Calvary where the cross stood, in remembrance of him? And how shall we escape, if we neglect to take upon us his easy yoke, and his light burden, in order to show his death till he come? Moreover,

This is the love of God that we keep this, and the rest of his *commandments*. Herein is love, that God sent his Son to be the propitiation for our sins. This is the highest commendation, the noblest effect of the love of God to mankind. And it is the highest commendation of our love to him, to esteem Christ, whom he hath sent, to be altogether lovely. Such exalted sentiments, and such devout affections, are the blessed fruits of beholding his glory, and of being constrained by his love; for "we love him, because he first loved us" (1 John 4:19). Did love constrain the Savior to become man, and even to appear in the likeness of sinful flesh? To become obedient even unto death? To visit the grave, and sojourn for a season among the dead, and can we deny him anything he asks of us, who has done all this upon the most disinterested principles for us? Can we find a satisfying excuse for denying him this proof of our grateful obedience; a proof so little grievous and burdensome in itself, so infinitely beneficial to us?

Ingenuity, wrongly employed, may suggest what it will; but a tender conscience, that is impressed with the authority of God, will never be able to evade the force of a divine command that is recommended with so many endearments, as well as enjoined by so great a Sovereign. Still the challenge will recoil, Is this thy obedience and duty to thy Lord? Is this thy kindness to thy Friend, to slight his words, and cast his laws behind thy back?

2. Another consideration, that demonstrates the obligation upon Christians to eat the Lord's Supper, is *the many and great advantages* that are derived by believers from this ordinance. Of all divine institutions, none is so peculiarly adapted to promote their improvement in spiritual graces and comforts as this. To intend their worldly advantage, and take the sacrament only as a qualification for places of civil trust or preferment in the state,[4] is a manifest perverting the ends and designs of this ordinance; because the benefits designed to be conferred by it are purely spiritual. In

---

[4] A spirited, judicious writer of the church of England has the following remarks on this subject:

> They are excluded from any spiritual partaking of the Lord's Supper, who come merely to qualify themselves for an office. The impiety and profaneness of which is indeed past the power of words to express. What? Can worms of the earth dare trifle with the blood of the Son of God? and merely to serve their own secular concerns, pollute the altar of the Lord? Can anything be so horridly insolent, as to come evidently with this thought; "Lord, I am not come here with any view to thy glory; I am not come to remember thy death, nor expecting any benefits from it; or, at least, these are not my chief aim: I am come only to qualify myself for an office, a mere temporal business, and were it not for this, I should gladly stay away." What a language this! What spots are these at your feasts! What a hardness and stupidity of conscience is such communicating disposed to beget? This is making the blood of the covenant *common* indeed. I tremble for the consequences, knowing very well, that, though we may be deceived, God will not be mocked. To have eaten and drank in his presence thus, will doubtless send us away at the last day, with a *Depart from me, I never knew you.* And they who now thus drink of the cup of the Lord, will be found among those more deeply guilty, who shall then

the Lord's Supper we have *an exhibition of divine truths* in a clear and comfortable light; and *proper encouragements and assistances* for every spiritual temper, and for every good work.

This ordinance presents to our view *the great and substantial truths of God* in a just and comfortable light. I shall instance in a few capital articles. Here we see: how God hath loved sinners, so as to give his only begotten Son to die for them! This love must be sovereign and self-moved. How Christ hath loved the church, and given himself for her! How great the evil of sin must be, which is written in the Savior's sweat, tears, and blood! How inexorable the justice of God is, which could not suffer the cup of suffering to pass from his own Son! How fully sin is finished, Satan spoiled, the grave conquered, death destroyed, and our redemption obtained! How joyful and abundant our access into the holiest of all by the blood of Jesus is! How prevalent the intercession of Christ must be, because he is the propitiation for our sins! How solidly the promises are confirmed by the death of Jesus! How certainly they will be accomplished, in consideration of his meritorious obedience and sufferings! How God is just in justifying the ungodly that believe in Jesus Christ! And finally, how certain, glorious, and important the second coming of Christ will be! These, and many other important truths are represented with a glorious evidence to our understanding and faith in this sacrament; and they have a very close and inseparable connection with the mediation and death of Jesus Christ.

In the Lord's Supper believing receivers have *proper encouragements and assistances* for exercising every Christian temper, and for performing every good work. Where shall we find as strong motives to humility, love, patience, hope, meekness, longsuffering, joy, and new obedience, as those that arise from a just view of Christ, who died for our sins, and rose again for our justification? No argument so powerful, no consideration so irresistible as this. Compared with this, every motive is cold and ineffectual; it hath no efficacy in comparison of the virtue in the cross of Christ, which so infinitely transcends all comparison, and exceeds all that we can think. It is no excess of modesty to *rejoice in Christ Jesus*, and to *glory in his cross*.

---

drink of the wine of the wrath of God, which is poured out without mixture into the cup of his indignation.

Thomas Haweis. *The Communicant's Spiritual Companion*, p 31, 32

This is a foundation of the sublimest *hope*, and a fountain of the most exuberant *joy*. This affords matter for the deepest *humility*, and yields fuel for the most flaming *love*. Faith in our crucified Jesus is an ever-active principle of the most cheerful and exact *obedience*: is an ample and inexhaustible magazine, from which we may fetch arms to conquer, absolutely conquer, the allurements of the world, the solicitations of the flesh, and the temptations of the devil. By this a way is opened for us into the holy of holies; and what may we not venture to ask, what may we not expect to receive, who have the blood of the everlasting covenant to plead, in all our approaches to the throne of grace? Having therefore such an High Priest, having in his cross unsearchable riches, who shall make our glorying void? what shall hinder us from rejoicing, and saying, Blessed be God for these opening beauties of spring! Blessed be God for the expected fruits of autumn! Blessed be God for ten thousand thousand gifts of his indulgent providence! But above all, blessed be God for the cross of Christ.[5]

And this precious, powerful doctrine, is most clearly set before our eyes in the sacrament of the Lord's Supper, where Christ is evidently set forth crucified.

The person, whoever he be, that is unimpressed with this consideration, and unfeeling to its irresistible force, has great reason to suspect his acquaintance with the love of Christ, which passeth knowledge, or with the sublime satisfactions of vital religion.

3. The neglect of this ordinance is represented in Scripture as *a very great sin, and deserving the severest punishment.* Unless the obligation to observe it were very strict, the omission would neither be so criminal, nor so pernicious.

That this neglect is *very criminal* cannot be denied, when we remember, that it implies a variety of the greatest evils; particularly *disobedience* to the command of Christ, who requires this proof of our devotedness to him, *ingratitude* to our kindest Friend, *despising* of our own mercies, and *indifference* about the great salvation.

This neglect is *very pernicious*, as well as criminal. Shall not God punish for this sin? Shall not his soul be avenged on such offenders as these? Shall

---

[5] James Hervey. *The Cross of Christ the Christian's Glory.*

he not support the honor of his law? Shall he not vindicate the honor of his institutions? Shall he not maintain the credit of his ordinances? We need not be surprised to find the ungodly world rejecting this, and every other ordinance, but what shall we say if the people of God seem indifferent about it? Is it any wonder that clouds and darkness cover their minds, that deadness and lukewarmness chill their affections? This sinful omission is justly punished with a manifest declension in the very life and power of religion. The reasons of it are too commonly such as will not bear the examination of their own consciences; hence they are frequently under awful apprehensions, lest, as they have neglected to remember their Savior at his table on earth, he should not remember them when they appear at his tribunal.

The proof of the obligation that lies upon Christians to show forth the death of Christ in the Lord's Supper arises, then, from the command of Christ, from the unspeakable benefit of doing it in the manner he hath commanded, and from the sin and danger of neglecting it.

5. The Excellent Uses and Purposes of It

The excellent *uses* and *ends* of this holy ordinance come now under our consideration. Among many things that might be mentioned on this head, I shall confine myself to the following.

1. It is appointed to *keep up the remembrance of Christ*, who said, *This do in remembrance of me*, both after he had given the bread and the cup to his disciples; or do this *for my memorial* (εις την εμην αναμνησιν), alluding to the passover, which was a memorial of the happy deliverance of the children of Israel from the land of oppression, and from the house of bondmen in Egypt. This gracious deliverance was to be remembered by them from generation to generation; and the killing and eating of the passover-lamb was the memorial of that glorious event, "This day shall be unto you *for a memorial*; and you shall keep it a feast to the LORD throughout your generations; ye shall keep it a feast by an ordinance for ever" (Ex. 12:14). But that redemption, which God wrought for his people, and which was remembered in the Jewish passover, had no glory compared with the redemption of sinners from the curse of the law of God, by his own Son being made a curse for them, by reason of the glory that excelleth. In the Lord's Supper, Christ is remembered:

As a hearty, generous friend, whose kindness is amazingly great, and infinitely free; for while we were yet enemies, in due time he died for us. Angels are lost in wonder, while they look into the mystery of redeeming love; how then should we, to whom this love is shown, be astonished, while we are called to partake of it? With what reason may the church remember this Friend, and triumph in his favor, who, freely moved by the benignity of his own heart, and out of pure compassion to men, offered to stand in their stead! And since to save them, he must be made man, his friendship stooped to every meanness of our condition, to the likeness of sinful flesh, to the form of a servant, to the death of a slave. And where can we then be called so feelingly to remember his friendship, as at an ordinance, where all its glory is made to pass before us?

As the propitiation for our sins, who had the iniquities of all his people laid upon him, and by whose stripes they are healed. This precious truth will be forever presented to the wondering eyes of glorified saints, and forever acknowledged in their hallelujahs of enraptured praise; for as they will always behold Jesus in the midst of the throne, as a Lamb that had been slain, so they will never cease to sing, "Worthy is the Lamb that was slain" (Rev. 5:12). But while they are present in the body, and absent from the Lord, they need this ordinance to preserve the memory of it in their own souls, and to be a memorial of it in the church, as well as to transmit this truth on which the faith and hope of them that are ready to perish doth safely rest, through our age, unto the children which shall be created, that the remembrance of it may be ever fresh, and may not die in our hands. While we remember the death of Christ as the propitiation for our sins, we have every advantage to enable us to see (1.) How *exceeding sinful our sin is* in the sight of God. The cries of infants, the pains of sickness, the groans of wretchedness, the agonies of the expiring, and all the awful horrors of death, serve in some measure to tell us what an evil and bitter thing sin is, which could have occasioned such dire effects, and yet one glance at the sufferings of *Jesus* will reflect the horrid image of sin in colors infinitely darker and deeper. There we see it black indeed, when an incarnate God agonizes under its load; when horror and darkness filled his soul with intolerable anguish, and pain tortured his body, till the sweat, as great drops of blood, fell down to the ground.[6] (2.) How *just and righteous God is,*

---

[6] For the instruction and caution of some of my readers, I shall take the liberty to add a passage from a celebrated writer, that will, I trust, appear useful and pertinent.

who can by no means clear the guilty, and who spared not his own Son, but delivered him up to the death for the ungodly, that he might be just to himself in justifying the sinner that believeth in Jesus. Justice demanded righteous judgment, such as had been poured upon rebel angels, that were cast down to hell on their first transgression; and the thunderbolt of wrath was lifted up to smite us sinners to the lowest pit. In these circumstances Jesus steps between, and receives the deadly shaft in his own body on the tree, and manifests the justice of God more gloriously than could have been done by the destruction of the whole human race; by the everlasting ruin

---

When we meditate on Christ's sufferings, our faith is not to rest in, or principally be fixed on, the *grievousness* of them, as Dr. Goodwin observes (See *Christ set forth*, sect. 2, chap. 2) so that we should only endeavor hereby to have our hearts moved to a relenting, and compassion expressed towards him, and indignation against the Jews that crucified him, together with an admiring of his noble and heroical love herein; so that if persons can get their hearts thus affected, they judge and account this to be grace; whereas it is no more than what the like tragical story of some great and noble personage (full of heroical virtues and ingenuity, yet inhumanly and ungratefully used), doth usually work in ingenuous spirits, who read or hear of it; which, when it reacheth no higher, is so far from being faith, that it is but a carnal and fleshly devotion; and Christ himself, at his suffering, found fault with, as not being spiritual, when he says, *Daughters of Jerusalem, weep not for me, but for yourselves, and for your children*; that is, not so much for this, when you see me thus unworthily handled by those for whom I die, as for yourselves.

It was not the malice of the Jews, the falseness of Judas, the fearfulness of Pilate, nor the iniquity of the times he fell into, that wrought our Savior's death; God the Father had a higher design herein. And this our faith is constantly to be conversant about, considering it as the result of an eternal agreement between the Father and the Son, and of that covenant which he came into the world to fulfill; and his being made sin for us, to take away our sins by the atonement which he made hereby. And, besides this, we may add, that the highest and most affecting consideration in Christ's sufferings, ought to contain in it the idea of his being a divine person, which is the only thing that argued them sufficient to answer the great ends designed thereby, as it rendered them of infinite value; and it was upon this account, that his condescension expressed herein might be truly said to be infinite. These things, I say, we are principally to rest in, when we meditate on Christ's sufferings, in this ordinance; though the others, which are exceedingly moving and affecting in their kind, are not to be passed over; since the Holy Ghost has, for this end given a particular account thereof in the gospels, not barely as a historical relation of what was done to him, but as a convincing evidence of the greatness of his love to us.

Ridgley, *A Body of Divinity*, vol. 2, p. 431.

of millions and millions of created worlds. (3.) How *boldly we may approach the throne of grace*; because sin is finished, justice is satisfied, and Satan, the world, death, and hell, are conquered by the death of Christ. He is to be remembered also,
As an absent friend of ours.

> It is a common ceremony of friendship, to lay up something in remembrance of a friend we have valued, which, we say, *we keep for his sake*, when he is gone, or is at a distance: as it is usual likewise to drink to one another, *remembering such a friend that is absent*. Jesus Christ is our beloved and *our friend*; the best friend that ever souls had: he is *now absent*, he hath left the world, and is gone to the Father, and the heavens must contain him till the time of the restitution of all things. Now, this ordinance is appointed for the remembrance of him. We observe it in token of this, that though the blessed Jesus be *out of sight*, he is not *out of mind*.[7]

And this ordinance should always bring him to our remembrance.

As our Lord that will come again in the clouds of heaven. Though he is gone to heaven now, yet he hath promised us he will return, and receive his servants to be forever with himself. *I go*, says he, *to prepare a mansion for you.* When we see him in the symbols of bread and wine, we should think how quickly we shall see the sign of the Son of man in the clouds; how soon we shall in our flesh see God our Savior, and with our eyes behold him, in that very body which the nails tore, and the spear pierced; shall see him, but now brighter than the sun when it shineth in its strength, coming to be glorified in his saints, and to be admired of all that believe.

This *remembering of Christ* supposes some *knowledge* of him, and some *acquaintance* with him. We cannot be said to remember one we never knew. It implies *a fixed contemplation* of him, as the propitiation for our sins. It produces *a powerful impression* of the truth upon the conscience, and *the joyful experience* of its benign influence upon the whole soul, so as to work it into a fellowship with, and conformity to Christ in his sufferings.

2. The Lord's Supper is appointed, that Christians may therein "shew the Lord's death till he come," as the apostle expresses it (1 Cor. 11:26).

---

[7] Matthew Henry. *The Communicant's Companion*, chap. 2.

The cross of Christ is a stumbling-block to the Jews, and foolishness to the Greeks; but to them that believe, whether Jews or Greeks, Christ crucified is the wisdom and the power of God to salvation. And as he does not conceal his righteousness, but sends the doctrine of his cross, as a word of salvation unto men; so he would have this truth believed with the heart unto righteousness, and confessed with the mouth, and in our actions, unto salvation. With this view, *the eating of bread, and drinking of wine*, according to Christ's appointment, is made the duty of Christians, that they may, by this service, *show his death*; that is, may *openly profess their esteem of it, their dependence on it, their rejoicing in it, their obligations unto it*, and *their expectations from it.*

By this service believers openly profess their value and esteem for Christ, who died for them. Such are the fruits, the purchases, the victories, the triumphs, of his cross, that we have the utmost reason to call it by the most honorable name, to esteem it *our crown of glory*, and *diadem of beauty.* Hereby we solemnly declare that we do not reckon it *the least reproach* to Christianity, and that we are so far from being ashamed of it that, whatever constructions an unbelieving world may put upon it, to us it is *the wisdom of God, and the power of God*; that it is all our salvation, and all our desire; that we think never the worse of Christ, and his holy religion, for his ignominious death, because we see in it God is glorified, by it man is saved. Then is the offense of the cross ceased; then is the reproach of it rolled away forever. Blessed is he whosoever shall not be offended in a crucified Jesus!

Hereby believers profess their dependence upon the death of Christ. We have no reason to be afraid to venture our souls and their eternal salvation with him who is able to save to the uttermost all that come to God by him. In this solemn ordinance God declares himself well pleased in his Son; and by our receiving it, we declare our confidence in the favor of God through him, and that we trust in him alone for the remission of all our sins, believing that in him we have redemption through his blood, the forgiveness of our sins, according to the riches of the grace of God.

By this service they profess their rejoicing in his death. And nothing is so reasonable as to *glory in the cross of Christ*, and to *joy in God through our Lord Jesus Christ, by whom we have now received the atonement.* The learned Greeks may glory in their wisdom, the carnal Jews in the strictness of their life, and formal Christians in their profession of religion; but these that are justified in the Lord will glory in him only. His death will warrant their most confident boasting; and he that believeth in him shall not be ashamed.

In this ordinance believers profess their obligations unto a crucified Jesus, who by the grace of God tasted death for all the chosen heirs of salvation. "Forasmuch then as the children are partakers of flesh and blood, he also himself likewise took part of the same; that through death he might destroy him that had the power of death, that is, the devil; and deliver them who through fear of death were all their lifetime subject to bondage" (Heb. 2:14–15). Had not he tasted death in our stead, we could never have looked with the smallest hope towards God; had not he become our ransom, we must have gone down to the pit of everlasting ruin; what thankfulness is due to him because he died for us? How much greater thankfulness is due, since he bare our sins, which is more than death? Those that worship in this ordinance practically say, "the love of Christ constraineth us; because we thus judge, that if one died for all, then were all dead: and that he died for all, that they which live should not henceforth live unto themselves, but unto him which died for them, and rose again" (2 Cor. 5:14–15). And finally,

Believers hereby do openly profess their expectations from the death of Christ. Their expectations are very great; the powers of language cannot express them; and even the most enlarged thoughts cannot comprehend them. They expect that God will do unto them, and in them, and for them, exceeding abundantly above all that they can ask or think. The promises of God are the measure, as well as the ground of their expectations; and these promises have a glorious establishment in the death of Christ, according to that expression,

> And for this cause he is the Mediator of the new testament, that by means of death, for the redemption of the transgressions that were under the first testament, they which are called might receive the promise of eternal inheritance. For where a testament is, there must also of necessity be the death of the testator. For a testament is of force after men are dead: otherwise it is of no strength at all while the testator liveth (Heb. 9:15–17).

Our Lord expresses the same truth in the institution of his supper, saying, *This cup is the new testament in my blood, which is shed for remission of sins unto many* (Matt. 26:28). Blessed be God for his confirmed promises in Christ Jesus! Blessed is the happy soul, whom a gracious God causeth to take them for a ground of sure, sublime, and undeceiving hope!

3. The Lord's Supper is appointed to be *a public testimony of believers' communion with Christ.* "The cup of blessing which we bless, is it not the communion of the blood of Christ? The bread which we break, is it not the communion of the body of Christ?" (1 Cor. 10:16). This ordinance is not duly honored, unless we observe it under a persuasion that *his body was broken for us*, that *his blood is the blood of the new testament*, and that *it was shed for us.* The end of the service is to assure us that when we truly believe on him, he is as really and closely united to us by his Spirit, through the belief of the truth, as the food which we eat and drink is united to our bodies. For this sacrament doth not only put us in mind of the spiritual blessings wherewith we are blessed in Christ, and of our enjoyment of them by faith; but also it is a means and instrument, whereby God doth really exhibit and give forth Christ and his salvation to true believers. By using this ordinance according to God's appointment, his people both *receive* and *give* a public testimony of their marvelous and mutual union and fellowship; they show that *he dwelleth in them, and they in him.*

4. This ordinance is instituted in order to *strengthen and comfort the fruits of the Spirit in believers.* Here we have the blood of Christ, that pacifies the conscience, and administers humble boldness towards God, represented in the clearest light; also we see in this institution a plentiful provision made for all our wants, and the rich supplies of the Spirit for the wilderness-state of believers, both to subdue their corruptions and to strengthen their graces. Here we may draw water with joy out of the wells of salvation, and, like Elijah traveling to the mount of Horeb, may receive from time to time our provision, in the refreshment of which we may hold on our way, and wax stronger and stronger, till we come to the heavenly Horeb, the mount Zion, the Jerusalem which is above. If our corruptions are strong, here is grace to mortify them; here we are taught, and do receive, humility to supplant pride, heavenly-mindedness instead of worldliness, and purity instead of pollution. The example before us, as well as the grace ministered, powerfully calls upon us to learn of him to be meek and lowly of heart; not to be of the world, even as he was not of the world; to walk in holiness, as he also walked. Are our graces all feeble and weak? Where shall we blow the smoking flax into a flame, if not here, where everything conspires to confirm our faith, to enliven our hopes, to

kindle our warmest affections, to enlarge our charity, to inspire our zeal, to sharpen our repentance, to constrain our obedience, to teach us meekness, to quicken our languor, to encourage our perseverance, to excite our thankfulness; in short, to work in us every divine temper and disposition? This blessed ordinance is designed to strengthen us mightily in the inner-man, to support us under all discouragements without, and fears within, that we might go on from strength to strength, from grace to grace, till we come to the blessed place where we shall go from glory to glory.

5. The Lord's Supper is appointed *to promote the fellowship of saints in the sacred bonds of truth and love.* "We being many are one bread" (1 Cor. 10:17). Here it is implied, that there is a *communion of saints.* They live in different periods, they are situated in distant places, and they have different apprehensions about some lesser things; but they are all united together, and thus united they constitute the body of Christ: "Now ye are the body of Christ, and members in particular" (1 Cor. 12:27). And here it is affirmed that those who partake of the sacrament of the Lord's Supper, *declare and avouch* themselves to be of this communion; *for they are one bread,* signifying that *they are one body.* They receive the *sign,* and wear the *badge,* of the society in this ordinance; and thereby declare (1.) That they are no more of the communion of the world, which lieth in wickedness; (2.) That they will not henceforth be indifferent about the honor and interests of the body of Christ; and (3.) That, by his grace, they will be companions of them that serve the Lord Christ, and will cultivate a holy communion with them in all that concerns their duties and comforts, strengthening and comforting one another in the fear and love of God. The Lord's Supper reminds Christians of these obligations, and strengthens them to fulfill them with zeal and pleasure.

These are some of the very important ends of this holy institution. To approach God in it, without a view to them, is presumption; and to approach him in it, with other views, is to pervert the nature of the duty altogether.

6. Objections against It Removed

I proposed, in the sixth place, to *resolve the objections* made against this ordinance. I apprehend the most material and plausible ones are the following, which have a respect either to the *erroneous,* or to the *profane,* to the *careless,* or to the *scrupulous.* I shall consider the objections of each.

1. *The erroneous and deluded enthusiast* objects against this ordinance, that it is now antiquated and out of date, since the Holy Ghost was given; because it was only to continue till that period.

Answer. This objection arises from a mistaken notion about the ordinances of Christ, as if they were *purely* for the employ of the mind, without *any regard* to bodily exercise. A notion that has been considered and confuted in *the introductory discourse*, where the *nature of gospel-worship* was explained. The objectors might be asked, Whether the church of God is more spiritual now than it was in the apostolic age, when this ordinance was instituted and actually observed? Also, Where they have any intimation in the word of God that this ordinance was to cease? The apostle expressly saith, "as *often* as ye eat this bread, and drink this cup, ye do shew the Lord's death *till he come*" (1 Cor. 11:26). This text is plain and peremptory. It affirms that this ordinance is to be administered while the world stands; for hereby we are openly and solemnly to show Christ's death till he come the second time, without sin unto the salvation of his people, which he will do at the judgment of the great day.

The ridiculous fancy, that *the coming of Christ by his Spirit* is there intended, deserves very little regard; for (1.) The Spirit was *then* given; (2.) Upon this principle, the ordinance was only intended for the unregenerate; and (3.) Whenever persons come to be fit for receiving it, they must waive it. An opinion that is so objectionable ought not to be received among Christians.

2. *The profane and debauched* object that they neither value, nor will mind any such service. The whole they affect to represent as a piece of whimsical preciseness.

Answer. "These speak evil of those things which they know not: but what they know naturally, as brute beasts, in those things they corrupt themselves." They despise divine institutions, "foaming out their own shame; wandering stars, to whom is reserved the blackness of darkness forever" (Jude 10, 13).

3. *The careless and slothful man* objects that there is no reason to be so forward about this duty; it may be very well deferred to a more convenient season.

Answer. "Whatsoever thy hand findeth to do, do it with thy might; for there is no work, nor device, nor knowledge, nor wisdom, in the grave, whither thou goest" (Eccl. 9:10). The command of Christ has a present, constant obligation. A careless neglect of duty is a sin, as well as a profane transgression of any of the divine precepts. Indolence is one of the most detestable, ruining follies in human life; it exposes a man to shame, and clothes him with rags. But the folly of it is comparatively innocent, where it does not affect our duty towards God, and the happiness of our immortal souls. Carelessness in this case has every criminal aggravation; it is the madness of folly; for it implies contempt and hatred of God, and such a sinner despiseth his own soul, and makes light of the greatest mercies. Indulgence to carnal ease is a certain source of manifold calamities to men. "Go to the ant, thou sluggard; consider her ways, and be wise" (Prov. 6:6). Look up to heaven, look down to hell, look about you in the world, and blush to think that you, O indolent, careless sinner, should be the only exceptions to general industry and action in the whole compass of creation! And even you are wise and forward enough to do evil, though to do that which is good you have neither knowledge nor inclination. Confess the truth, and thereby give glory to God, and answer this question to your own conscience: Do not you love darkness rather than light, *because you know your deeds are evil?* Are not the commandments of God grievous to your carnal minds, which are not subject to the authority of his law?

4. *The scrupulous and doubting soul* objects against *his observing* this ordinance, because it is such a grievous sin, such a fearful thing, to eat and drink unworthily: "he that eateth and drinketh unworthily, eateth and drinketh judgment to himself, not discerning the Lord's body" (1 Cor. 11:29).

Answer. In order to state this point in the clearest light I can, I beg leave to observe (1.) That the apostle is there speaking of one that was *a church member*, who, he supposes, may eat and drink unworthily; and the effects of this sin at Corinth clearly showed that many of the saints there had been guilty of it (1 Cor. 11:30). (2.) To eat and drink unworthily is to eat and drink in an ignorant and irreverent, factious and uncharitable, carnal and sensual manner. (3.) The sad effect of this eating and drinking unworthily is an eating and drinking *judgment* (κρίμα) to one's self. This is the proper and primary signification of the word which we translate *damnation*. It is often used for *temporal judgment*, as in 1 Peter 4:17; and from the circumstances in the text, it must be so understood here, and not of *eternal damnation*, as many honest and truly gracious souls have taken it, to the terrifying of their spirits, and discouraging their approaches to the Lord's table; for the apostle explains his meaning in the next verse, where he instances in *temporal judgments* which had befallen many of the Corinthians for their abuses of that sacred ordinance; and tells them that when they were thus judged, they were chastened of the Lord, that they should not be condemned with the world (1 Cor. 11:32). This opposes *judgment* to *final condemnation*; and intimates that some of them, at least, who were visited with those temporal judgments, were the children of God, and would be eternally saved. (4.) The ground of this punishment, and the demonstration of this guilt, is *their not discerning the Lord's body*; that is, not considering the death of Christ, with a religious regard to it, as represented in this ordinance; nor making a *difference* between these sacred symbols of the Lord's body and blood for spiritual purposes, and common food for the refreshment of animal nature. Not to discern the Lord's body, according to the letter of the text, and the circumstances of the context, is to receive this holy supper without a due regard to the *object* presented in it, which is the broken body of the Lord; for, in this ordinance, Jesus Christ is evidently set forth crucified among them that partake of it (Gal. 3:1). And *these that do not discern*, are such as do not distinguish or consider that crucified Savior, who offered himself, once for all, a perfect sacrifice to divine justice, as he is brought to our remembrance in this duty; who do not exercise their spiritual senses and graces on this holy mystery, or who do not regard, with their best affection, the love, sufferings, and death of Jesus; which some may, through ignorance or carelessness, and others through sensual indulgence, render themselves incapable of, as these Corinthians did.

On the whole, it is plain that this alarming passage is intended for our *caution, excitement,* and *direction*, in a duty of the greatest consequence; but not to discourage *the true circumcision*, as the apostle calls believers in Christ, who "worship God in the spirit, and rejoice in Christ Jesus, and have no confidence in the flesh" (Phil. 3:3). These he invites, and pronounces heartily welcome, saying, "Eat, O friends; drink, yea, drink abundantly, O beloved" (Song 5:1).

7. Some Questions Relative to It Answered

There are several *inquiries* relative to this ordinance, that demand some consideration. They will, no doubt, appear in different lights to different readers; and perhaps to many they will appear, for the most part, unnecessary and superfluous. All the apology I shall make is, that they have all some connection with my subject, and every one of them has been matter of dispute is the Christian church.

Question 1. May this sacrament be administered to persons that are not baptized?

Answer. It may not; for all that drink into one body in this ordinance are supposed to have been *previously* baptized into one Spirit (1 Cor. 12:13). And these that heard the word of the Lord preached by Peter on the day of Pentecost were *first* baptized, and *then* they continued steadfastly in the breaking of the sacramental bread (Acts 2). And, finally, the uncircumcised males in Israel were not to eat of the passover.

Question 2. May this sacrament be given to baptized children?

Answer. It must be confessed that the practice of giving it to children was both ancient and general. It was common in the western churches in the end of the third, and during the fourth century, as it is to this day in the eastern or Greek churches. But it has no countenance in the word of God. The words Christ hath chosen in the institution of this ordinance are expressly against it; for infants cannot *take bread*, nor *eat it*; but must be fed with milk, and not with strong meat; they can neither *examine* themselves, nor *discern* the Lord's body, nor *show* the Lord's death, and therefore ought not to have this sacrament given them, or he that does it, will have the greater sin.

Question 3. May any who profess the faith, and desire to come to the Lord's Supper, be kept from it?

Answer. "Such as are found to be *ignorant* or *scandalous*, notwithstanding their profession of the faith, and desire to come to the Lord's Supper, may, and ought to be kept from that sacrament, by the power Christ hath left in his church, until they receive instruction, and manifest their reformation."[8] (1.) The *ignorant* should be kept from it; because they know not God, and obey not the gospel of Christ, they cannot discern the Lord's body, nor eat and drink to his glory. (2.) The *scandalous* too must be refused admission; for the rule is as plain as it is express on this head: "But now I have written unto you not to keep company, if any man that is called a brother be a fornicator, or covetous, or an idolater, or a railer, or a drunkard, or an extortioner; with such an one no not to eat...put away from

---

[8] *Westminster Larger Catechism*, question 173.

among yourselves that wicked person" (1 Cor. 5:11, 13). Such persons evidently discover a temper of mind that is a contradiction to the character of these saints, who are putting on the Lord Jesus Christ, and walking in him. They profess to know God, but in works they deny him.

Question 4. Who may warrantably and worthily partake of the Lord's Supper?

Answer. None but these *that are in the faith, and that have Christ in them the hope of glory.* "Examine yourselves, whether ye be in the faith; prove your own selves. Know ye not your own selves, how that Jesus Christ is in you, except ye be *disapproved* [αδοχιμος]"[9] (2 Cor. 13:5). Compared with 1 Corinthians 11:28, "Let a man examine himself, and so let him eat of that bread, and drink of that cup." Every one that may, with a good conscience, approach unto the Lord's table should previously examine *himself*, to discover his state and real character. In making this inquiry, he should proceed by *the word of God*, as the only infallible means of apprehending the truth, and manifesting him in a just light to his own conscience. His principal business is to know whether *he is in the faith*, and whether *Jesus Christ be in him*; that is, whether he rightly understands, and truly believes the doctrines of divine revelation in their amiable connection and dependencies; and whether Christ dwells in his heart, with powerful influence and dominion there, by the faith of them, bringing his conscience, tempers, and conduct into a willing, universal subjection to his authority and revealed will.

What is further necessary on this point will naturally fall in among *the directions* in the next section; and therefore passing this, I shall go on to,

Question 5. Whether or not is a full assurance that we are the children of God necessary to clear our right and duty to partake of the Lord's Supper?

Answer. None have a right to the Lord's table but his children; but many of these blessed persons cannot assert their own character, or claim their privileges belonging to it. These that fear the Lord sometimes walk in darkness, and have no light; and in such a case they should trust in the

---

[9] This is the exact, proper meaning of the word rendered *reprobates*, in our translation. It is an allusion to *metals*, that are tried by the touchstone, or same other way, to prove, whether they be good and pure, or not; and *upon trial*, are found to be *spurious*. Such metals are *rejected* and *disapproved*; and, in like manner, there is a generation of hypocrites in the church that are disallowed, and disapproved of God, because they are not in the faith, and Jesus Christ is not really in them through the belief of the Scriptures.

name of the Lord, and stay upon their God, as the only means to have present peace, and to clear up their way to present duty.[10]

Question 6. Is this ordinance of the Lord's Supper appointed for the conversion of sinners?

Answer. The nature and design of this service clearly show that it is only appointed for the use of such as have believed through grace. The person that is dead in trespasses and sins cannot remember Christ, with confidence in his name, and love to his service; he cannot show his death in the joyful hope of his coming, nor have communion with the saints. And while all that eat of the bread, and drink of the cup in the sacrament, are called to examine themselves, it is implied that the unconverted have no business to engage in the service: "let a man *examine himself*, and so *let him eat*," etc. (1 Cor. 11:28). This ordinance, being appointed for spiritual nourishment and growth in grace, supposes that the receivers are living Christians; and that which is appointed as a means of health and strength to the living cannot be thought to give life to the dead. Sacramental bread and wine are not given to enliven a soul that is dead in trespasses and sins, but to nourish and strengthen one that is alive. There can no nourishment be intended without a supposition of life. It is *the communion of Christ's body*, and therefore supposeth union to him by faith. It is for the friends of Christ, who have received the atonement, and for them only to be feasted at his table.[11]

---

[10] "One who doubteth of his being in Christ, or of his due preparation to the sacrament of the Lord's Supper, may have true interest in Christ, though he be not yet assured thereof; and in God's account hath it, if he be duly affected with the apprehension of the want of it, and unfeignedly desires to be found to Christ, and to depart from iniquity: in which case (because promises are made, and this sacrament is appointed for the relief even of weak and doubting Christians), he is to bewail his unbelief, and labor to have his doubts resolved; and so doing, he may, and ought to come to the Lord's Supper, that he may be further strengthened." *Westminster Larger Catechism*, question 172.

[11] "I grant, there is so much of the word of God recited, and made use of in the administration of the ordinance, that it may prove the means of the conversion of a hypocrite. This is possible, and more than possible, with reference to some spectators who come; or to some hypocrites who communicate. I grant likewise, that many have been awakened to serious impressions—by the fears of unworthy receiving.

"But however that may have sometimes been *the event*; it will not follow, that it was *the design of Christ* in the institution: for then it would have been the duty of ministers to give *infidels* the Lord's Supper, and to give it to the most *notoriously profane*, as a means of their conversion, even to such as make no profession of saving faith and repentance.

Question 7. How is Christ present in the sacrament of the supper?

Answer. We are not to suppose that he is present in a corporal sense. Neither is his very body and blood there present in the Popish, nor in the Lutheran sense; that is, neither by *transubstantiation* nor *consubstantiation*. The Papists would have us believe that there is no substance of bread and wine after the consecration of the elements; and to account for several scriptural expressions, as well as to impose the belief of this position on the world, who can only see, taste, and handle bread and wine, they are forced to allow that this body and blood of Christ, for the substance of them, have the accidents of bread and wine adhering to them still.[12] The Lutherans maintain that the bread and the wine continue to be bread and wine after consecration; that they have both the substance and accidents of bread and wine; but in virtue of the consecration, the body and blood of Christ come to be really and corporally present in, with, and under these elements. This

---

The preaching of the word is appointed to turn men from darkness to light, and from the power of Satan unto God, and therefore *all should hear*: and if the Lord's Supper be instituted for that purpose, *all should communicate*. We may look for such an effect from the preaching of the word, because of God's institution of it to that end; but this cannot be said as to the Lord's Supper. It is not, as the word preached, *the seed* of the *new-birth*; but *the food* of the *newborn*. We must be born before we eat, and feed before we be nourished. It is appointed for spiritual nourishment and growth in grace. Though it may prove an [occasional] means, it doth not appear, it was instituted for that purpose. A minister may be converted at his ordination; yet the laying on of hands is not instituted for the conversion of ministers.

"There have been many other things besides this sacrament, have been the means of conversion unto some; the holy lives, and patient sufferings, and courageous deaths of good men, fervent prayer of near relations, God's terrible judgments on some notorious sinners, and many other things. I have read of one who gave a young prodigal a ring with a *death's-head* on it, upon this condition, he should spend one hour every day looking on that ring, thinking on it, which produced a mighty change in his life. And yet who will say, *these are converting ordinances, and so intended by God!* Our own sickness, or the sickness of a friend, by the grace of God, may be instrumental to convert a man; yea, falling by temptation into heinous sin, hath affrighted some to leave their sins: but there are not means to be chosen, or used to such an end. No, nor is the Lord's Supper to be used by infidels, and impenitent ungodly people, as a means to convert them. They are not allowed to claim it, nor are ministers allowed to give it them. It cannot be given them without impiety; much less should force be used to constrain them to take it: though it may accidentally prove the means of their conversion—as a thief may steal a Bible, or sermon-book, and be reformed by it. But this is not the end of this sacrament." John Shower. *Sacramental Discourses*, part 2, pp. 70–73

[12] This impious notion is solidly confuted by Barrow, Tillotson, Edwards, etc.

opinion goes upon a mistaken notion about the nature of a sacrament; it supposes the ubiquity of Christ's body, or that it is omnipresent; and it implies that two bodies may occupy one place at the same time.

Some have chosen another way of representing their sentiments on this subject. According to them, "the bread and wine, after consecration, are truly and really the body and blood of Christ, though not after a carnal, but after a spiritual manner." A grave writer[13] says, this is but the same nonsense which the divines of Rome put upon us on the like occasion, when they tell us that the blood of Christ is really sacrificed and shed in the sacrament, and then add, by way of gloss, that it is done *unbloodily*. By the like analogy they may tell us, if they please, that the body of Christ is there incorporated *unbodily*, and *flesh not carnally* may pass the press jointly in the next edition of the book of bulls. To confute these unscriptural extravagances, it may suffice to observe the following things: (1.) In the communion there is nothing given but bread and wine. (2.) The bread and wine are signs of Christ's having given himself a sacrifice for us, of a sweet-smelling savor unto God. (3.) Nothing is eaten but bread, and nothing is drunk but wine in this ordinance; and these are eaten and drunk truly and properly. (4.) The *spiritual* eating of Christ's flesh, and drinking of his blood, is common to all believers, in every place, and at every time, as well as when they eat the Lord's Supper.

Therefore we say that *Christ himself* is present in this ordinance to our faith, in believing on his name through his own word, as an estate is present in the *title-deeds*, or some valuable legacy in the confirmed *will* of a deceased person. He is only present to them who discern his body and blood, or his person and sacrifice, represented to their minds in words and significant signs. Any other presence is fanciful and absurd; but this is most real, and full of everlasting consolation; it is agreeable to all that we can conceive about a sacramental token, and is suited to make the most deep and lasting impressions of his death on our minds; it strengthens our belief of God's word, and produces the corresponding fruits of the Spirit.

Question 8. In what posture should the Lord's Supper be received?

Answer. In such a posture as we use at a feast, where we *sit*. The church of Rome is zealous for the *kneeling* posture, because they suppose the real body and blood of Christ are present. The church of England, and

---

[13] Mr. Hales of Eaton.

the Protestants in Poland, use the same posture, to testify their reverence and their belief of the divinity of the Redeemer. The churches of Helvetia use *sitting* or *standing* indifferently, though their ministers always stand. The reformed churches in France enjoined *standing*. Some have taken the sacrament *walking*, being persuaded that the Jews did eat their passover (from which this ordinance was borrowed) in *a walking posture*, from "thus shall ye eat it; with your loins girded, your shoes on your feet, and your staff in your hand" (Ex. 12:11). The churches of Holland, Germany, Geneva, Scotland, *etc.*, that are commonly called Calvinists, use *sitting*. This *last opinion* seems to be the most proper and scriptural. It may be supported several ways. (1.) This was the posture used by the disciples, when Christ instituted this sacrament: "And as they *sat and did eat,* Jesus said," *etc.* "And as they did eat [the passover], Jesus took bread, and blessed, and brake it, and gave to them, and said, Take, eat: this is my body. And he took the cup, and when he had given thanks, he gave it to them: and they all drank of it" (Mark 14:18–25 see also Matt. 26:20–29 and Luke 22:14–20). (2.) The sitting posture is most agreeable to the nature of this ordinance, as it is *a feast upon the sacrifice of Christ*, our passover, that is sacrificed for us. It is certain that the Jewish feasts upon a sacrifice were all observed in this posture, of which many undeniable proofs might be collected. When Israel built an altar before the golden calf, and made proclamation, saying, Tomorrow is a feast to the Lord, or to Jehovah, we are told, they rose up early in the morning, and offered burnt-offerings, and brought peace-offerings, and the people *sat down to eat and to drink*, and rose up to play (Ex. 32:5–6). The reader may also consult 1 Samuel 9:12–13,22, where we find those that were bidden to the feast, which was kept upon a sacrifice, *sat*, while they were eating it. When Samuel went to Bethlehem to sacrifice unto the Lord (1 Sam. 16:5), he afterwards *sat* at the feast upon it; and therefore he was commanded to *arise* and anoint David as soon as he was brought in, (v. 12), which supposes that he was *sitting* before. (3.) This posture seems most fit to signify *the honor* God admits his people to, in virtue of the sacrifice of Christ. He uses them as his friends and children, with every confirming token of familiarity and affection, in this ordinance; and if our Savior had not thought this posture reverend enough, he would certainly have forbid it, or appointed another. (4.) Even reason itself closes with the scriptural institution upon this head; for what posture so well *becomes a feast*, as that we plead for? Does not nature teach us to sit at table, and neither to stand nor kneel? We should thus present our bodies before God in this duty, because it is our most *reasonable service*.[14]

Question 9. May the people, as well as the minister, receive this sacrament in both kinds?

Answer. When the church of Rome had contrived the doctrine of transubstantiation, she declared that both the body and the blood of Christ were comprehended under the species of bread, and upon that pretense took the cup from the people, because it was no way necessary. But upon their own principles, it would be more consistent to lay aside the use of the cup altogether, than to appropriate it to their clergy, who may be supposed most intelligent, and therefore best qualified to discern many substances under one species. If the cup is not necessary, their clergy need not use it; if it is necessary, the people should have it. Christ gave both the bread and the cup to his disciples, not under the notion of their being *apostles*, but *disciples*. This is plain from "let *a man* examine himself, and so let him eat of that bread, and *drink of that cup*" (1 Cor. 11:28). He has given more express commandment concerning the participation of the cup than of the bread: "Drink ye all of it" (Matt. 26:27). If the church of Rome had paid any regard to the form of Scripture-words, they might have continued the sacramental cup, and refused the bread, to the people, with as much plausibility. Their rebellion against the words of the holy One would have been more concealed in the one case than in the other. But Antichrist "opposeth and exalteth himself above all that is called God, or that is worshipped" (2 Thess. 2:4).

Question 10. Is the Lord's Supper a real propitiatory sacrifice for sin?

Answer. When the Papists present the host (*so they call the consecrated bread*) upon the altar (*which is the name they give the communion-table*), they pretend to offer up the true and very body and blood of Christ, as a proper atonement for those persons on whose account the mass is celebrated; and therefore their priests are much employed in saying masses, not only for the living, but the dead. The doctrine of *transubstantiation* misleads their judgment about the nature of *the sacrament*. Hence they put

---

[14] Besides that we read of *the table of the Lord* (1 Cor. 10:21), even reason seems to suggest the decency and propriety of communicants joining in *a table posture*, rather than sitting in separate *pews* or *seats*, that have not the least appearance of a *feast*. This circumstance may not be thought very important, but neither is it unworthy of some regard, since *all things should be done decently, and in order*.

sacrifice in the place of sacrament, and fancy Christ is sacrificed as often as he is sacramentally represented in this ordinance. But to affirm there is any real propitiatory sacrifice for sin here is contrary to the very words of the apostle, who says, "we are sanctified through the offering of the body of Jesus Christ once for all.... For by one offering he hath perfected for ever them that are sanctified" (Heb. 10:10, 14). The single sacrifice of Christ without the gates of Jerusalem is a sufficient propitiation for the sins of Jews and Gentiles; every other is superfluous, the very supposition of any other is false and abominable.

Question 11. *May the Lord's Supper be administered in private?*

Answer. It must be confessed that the private administration of this ordinance was pretty early introduced, and has been too generally practiced. Many have supposed it lawful and profitable to celebrate this ordinance privately, as occasions offer, in the times of persecution. It is not my business to inquire what may be expedient in particular exigencies; but it seems to be a perversion of this ordinance to administer it *privately*, that is, not in public assemblies, in either of these two cases: either (1.) To *please* them that are able to attend in public, but will not; for this ordinance was originally planned to manifest and promote *the communion of saints*; and therefore communicants, *as a church*, are supposed to *come together to break bread* (Acts 20:7), and to *come together into one place to eat the Lord's Supper* (1 Cor. 11:20). As the passover might not be eaten except in Jerusalem, so the Lord's Supper can only be eaten regularly in church-meetings. Or (2.) To oblige *the sick* or *the dying*; for this looks like making it *a passport* for a sinner to heaven; by this means it is often administered to persons that have no right to it; and hereby the consciences of men are quieted upon a false foundation. In both cases the original intention of the ordinance is perverted. But who can forbear expressing the warmest indignation against the ignorant zeal of a multitude of professing Christians, who fancy their everlasting welfare depends on the ordinance? Such unthinking persons despise and reject the Savior, in the same degree as they overrate the means that should lead them to him, and build them up in the knowledge of him.

Question 12. *How often should this ordinance be administered and received?*

Answer. It is beyond all doubt that the primitive church celebrated this service very frequently. It seems to have been one main design of their coming together on the first day of the week, that they might *break bread*, in commemoration of Christ's death (Acts 20:7). In later times this practice has been changed, but the appointments of heaven should be sacred with everyone that calleth Christ his Master.[15]

8. Practical Directions concerning It

All that remains now to be considered on this ordinance is to lay down the necessary and proper *directions* relative to it. These are commonly, and I think with much reason, classed under three heads, as they refer to the Christian's behavior *before* he engages in this duty, *while* he is employed in it, and *after* he has been at the Lord's table.

I. The duties that demand, in a particular manner, the consideration of Christians *before* they eat the Lord's Supper, may be reduced to these four particulars; viz., *Self examination, meditation, prayer*, and *being filled with the Spirit*. I shall explain these weighty points as briefly as I can.

1. In order to our worthy receiving of the Lord's Supper, *let us examine ourselves* (1 Cor. 11:28). The reason of this branch of our preparation is obvious. All that profess religion are not really what they appear to be. Every man has most reason to be suspicious of himself, both because he can best discern his own character, and because his particular concern in the part he is to act is greatest, and the consequences of his conduct are most important to himself. The most attentive consideration is necessary in a point of such unutterable moment; and prudence will naturally suggest that every advantageous circumstance for accomplishing a diligent search should be sought and embraced. Three things will greatly favor such a duty, and we should carefully study them, if we would be faithful to ourselves, and successful in our trial.

Retirement from the hurries and encumbrances of the world, that we may be disengaged from distracting thoughts, which are a great hindrance in a careful inquiry into the state of our souls.

Impartiality, in attending to what really makes *against us*, as well as what is *in our favor*. This is the more worthy of our serious attention, because we are under strong temptations to flatter ourselves, out of love to our honor and present ease. And,

---

[15] Whoever would see this question properly examined may find some useful assistance in John Erskine. *Theological Dissertations*, dissert. 5, on *frequent communicating*; and Stephen Charnock. *Works*, vol. 2, pp. 480–485.

Acquaintance with the word of God, which will be the rule of the future judgment, and must be the rule of our judgment about ourselves at present. Every other rule of self-judging is deceitful, and at best uncertain. But peace shall be on as many as walk according to this rule, and on all the Israel of God. This is the test of truth, and the discerner of the thoughts and intents of the heart, which cannot escape its judgment, however deep or secret they be.

As every heavenly blessing is conveyed in the Scriptures, to be enjoyed through the faith of them; and every gracious temper, and truly Christian experience, is the fruit of the incorruptible seed of the word of Christ dwelling richly in the soul; it is a necessary consequence that the grand object of self-inquiry is *whether we are in the faith?* (2 Cor. 13:5).

Every other question we should propose to our consciences refers to this, and must be answered only by the evidence we have, or have not, that the word of Christ dwelleth in us. The solid grounds upon which believers discern that they are in Christ, know their sins and wants, and form a safe judgment concerning the truth and measure of their knowledge, faith, repentance, love to God and the brethren, charity to all men, forgiving those that have done them wrong, desires after Christ, and new obedience—are closely connected with this. And our inquiries about these things should be conducted with a view to discover whether the pretensions we make unto these sublime attainments are well founded; or, in other words, whether it is *the faith of revealed truth* that produces these desirable fruits. Something not unlike these appearances may be found in persons who have never tasted that the Lord is gracious; and the genuine evidence that these are unfeigned fruits of the Spirit, and that they prevail in our minds, must arise, not so much from the circumstances, manner, and effects of these gracious tempers, as from *the influence of the word upon the mind* in forming, improving, and directing them. If we are really *in Christ*, it is through the word of Christ dwelling richly in us in all wisdom; if we are really *convinced of sin*, it is by the holy spiritual law dwelling in our conscience with approbation; if we are acquainted with *our wants* it is by the word discovering what the soul stands in need of to fill it, what is provided for our numberless wants in the new covenant, and the suitableness of this provision to our manifold necessities; if *our knowledge* is sound and sufficient, it arises from the Scriptures which are able to make us wise unto salvation; if *our faith* is precious and unfeigned, it is the belief of the truth, which is the doctrine that is after godliness; if *our repentance* is unto life, it is produced by seeing the glory of the Lord, as it is manifested in his word; if *we love God*, we will keep his commandments; if *we love the brethren*, it is for the truth's sake which dwelleth in them; if *we have charity, or love to all men*, it is the effect of a realizing belief of the love of God to us while we were enemies to him; if *we forgive them that have done us wrong*, it is because we are forgiven ourselves by God; if we have *desires after Christ*, it is the effect of a saving apprehension of his name and revealed character, as every way precious and desirable; if *our obedience is new*, it arises from the incorruptible seed of the word dwelling richly in us, and springing up, and bearing fruit, in some a hundredfold, and in some sixty-fold, and in some thirty-fold. This observation might be illustrated in all the genuine fruits of the Spirit, which, as they demonstrate the reality and prevalence of a divine principle of the word of Christ dwelling richly in the soul, so they are only unfeigned and distinguishing characters, as far as they are connected with the word of Christ. Everything unconnected with this is *hypocrisy, and mere appearance*.

2. Another duty that is no less necessary before we eat the Lord's Supper is *meditation*. Experience can attest the great advantage of being frequent and deliberate in this employment. Superficial thinking is generally rather hurtful than truly profitable. Meditation fixes the attention, and increases knowledge, while it also inflames and affects the heart. Hereby divine truths become practical principles in the mind, and impress upon it a prevailing sense of their evidence and importance, and of our concern in them. Meditation is many ways necessary, and on many accounts profitable. It is recommended by the most illustrious examples, and urged by the weightiest arguments. To engage in any important business of life without consideration is both imprudent and unreasonable; but to approach God in the ordinances of religion without it, is impious and profane. Israel brought many oblations, and delighted in approaching to God, while their oblations were *vain*, because *they did not consider* (Isa. 58:2; 1:3–13).

Previous meditation is particularly necessary when we are to commemorate the death of Christ in the Lord's Supper, that the mind may be impressed with the great and interesting truths that are referred to by the sacramental signs. To collect the proper materials for this employment of our thoughts on such occasions would require a good deal of attention.

However, it would be seasonable to have our thoughts fixed and affected by the serious consideration of the nature of sin; of the depravity of our nature, and misery of our fallen state; of the glory of God's attributes in man's redemption; of the marvelous person of our Redeemer; of his kind and benevolent undertakings in the council of peace; of the nature, necessity, and design of his sufferings; of his glorious exaltation; of his important character in the new covenant; of the unsearchable riches and free conveyance of his grace; of the communion of the Holy Ghost; of the fellowship of believers; and of the happiness of heaven.

These are important subjects, and must be considered in the light they are presented to our faith in the oracles of God, lest we become vain in our imagination concerning them, and our foolish heart be darkened. By such meditations, mixed with faith, the saints approach, with an awful reverence and holy joy, unto the God of our Lord Jesus Christ in this duty, their souls are humbled and comforted, are quickened and encouraged to walk in the truth. Hereby they are built up in their most holy faith, and are kept in the love of God.

3. *Prayer* is a third duty that should employ the most serious attention of the saints, before they receive the Lord's Supper. This is principally necessary for two reasons: both because the preparation of the heart cometh only from the Lord, and because the success of gospel-institutions depends wholly on his blessing. In all our ways we should acknowledge him, that he may bring them to pass; but in religious duties we should be eminently careful to ask of the Lord the way wherein we should go, and to implore his presence to go with us, and to give us rest. God has engaged to supply all our need, and to fulfill all our believing petitions. Let us therefore open our mouth wide, that he may fill it. Let us ask and receive, that our joy may be full. In everything that respects this ordinance we ought, by prayer and supplication, with thanksgiving, to make our requests known unto God, that he may convince us of sin, humble us under a heartfelt conviction of our undone estate, manifest unto us his own glory, reveal his Son in us, establish his covenant with us, fill us with his Spirit, unite our hearts in the love of his people, and make us more and more partakers of Christ in the power of his resurrection, in the fellowship of his sufferings, and in conformity to his death. The *matter* of prayer is as various and extensive as the connections of this ordinance with the truths of God, and the duties of religion. The *necessity* of prayer is so great that for all things he will

be inquired of. And the *encouragements* to pray are so many that we may come with boldness to the throne of grace, to receive mercy, and to find grace to help us in the time of need.

4. We should be *filled with the Spirit*, when we show the death of Christ. He is the Spirit of wisdom and revelation, that takes of the things of Christ, and shows them unto men. The supplies of the Spirit of Jesus are received by the hearing of faith, and not by the works of the law. One of the sublime descriptions of the gospel is expressed in these words, where it is called *the ministration of the Spirit* (2 Cor. 3:8). The Holy Ghost is *the Spirit of grace* (Heb. 10:29; Zech. 12:10).

Those that are filled with the Spirit of Christ are actually partakers of his influences and fruits in a very plentiful measure. This comes to be more or less men's character, in the following respects: As they come to have *every power and faculty of their souls* more subject to the Spirit's authority, and under the influence proper to it; as they grow on to experience his operations in all *the several kinds of them*; as his agency comes to be *more constant and stated* in them; as his energy becomes more mighty, and operative in them, so as actually to produce its proper and genuine effects; and finally, as they taste so much delight in his truths and ways that they reach forward with the greater ardor toward perfection. Where these things are and abound, they will make Christians active, zealous, and self-denied, in the ways of religion. Then will the soul be disposed to say with Job, "Oh that I knew where I might find him!" (Job 23:3) or with David, "As the hart panteth after the water brooks, so panteth my soul after thee, O God. My soul thirsteth for God, for the living God: when shall I come and appear before God?" (Ps. 42:1–2).

II. I shall now proceed to *the directions* that are proper to be observed by Christians *while they eat end drink the sacramental bread and cup*.

It is required of them that receive the Lord's Supper that, during the time of the administration of it, with all holy reverence and attention they wait upon God in that ordinance; for, "this is it that the Lord spake, saying, I will be sanctified in them that come nigh me, and before all the people I will be glorified" (Lev. 10:3). That they diligently observe the sacramental elements and actions; for these point out the proper matter of our meditation on that important service. That they carefully discern the Lord's body and blood, which are evidently set forth under the significant elements; for these eat and drink unworthily, that do not discern the Lord's body (1 Cor. 11:29). That they affectionately meditate on his sufferings and death, as they are the price of our redemption, the sacrifice of atonement for our souls, and the punishment of our sins, for here his body is represented as broken for us, and his blood as shed for the remission of our sins (Matt. 26:26–28). That they stir themselves up to a vigorous exercise of those graces which the nature of this ordinance requires. Many particulars might be mentioned to illustrate this direction; the reader may take the following for so many examples, and may enlarge the catalog from such other instances as will occur to his own reflection.

1. Communicants should look on sin as an offense against heaven, that is most exemplarily condemned in the flesh of the Son of God, who was made sin and a curse for us, whose soul was made an offering for our sins, and who was bruised for our iniquities, who bore our griefs, and carried our sorrows, and who was delivered for our offenses.

2. They should judge themselves, by acknowledging their transgressions, and by accusing, condemning, and passing sentence against themselves, as sinful wretched creatures, that have plunged themselves into the utmost depths of ruin, in which they should have continued forever, had not Christ redeemed them by his blood.

3. They should look upon Christ whom they have pierced, and mourn after a godly sort. The motives to that repentance which is unto life, can only arise from a united view of the majesty, authority, justice, and mercy of God; and these attributes of the Deity shine with luster and harmony only in the face of Jesus Christ, who is evidently set forth crucified before our eyes in this ordinance.

4. They should hunger and thirst after righteousness. Christ is the end of the law for that righteousness which it demands, as the essential condition of our entering into life. To improve the excellency of the knowledge of Christ is an important branch of practical godliness, and a principal end of the Lord's Supper.

5. They should feed on Christ as the true bread that came down from heaven. His person, offices, and grace are represented in the gospel as a rich entertainment to satisfy all our desires, and to supply all our wants. By the full assurance of faith confiding in, and depending upon him, as freely given to us, and giving all things with himself, we feed upon him, and grow up into him as our head.

6. They should rejoice in the love of Christ, which is so great that he gave himself for his church, and washed them from their sins in his own blood, and now he ever liveth to make intercession for them; having loved his own, he loved them to the end. Behold, how he loved them!

7. They should exercise gratitude and thankfulness, while they remember what Christ has done, and look forward with hope to what he has laid up for them that love his appearing. Who that considers these things with any attention can forbear to join in the common acclamation, "thanks be unto God for his unspeakable gift" (2 Cor. 9:15)?

8. They should renew their covenant with God; that is, they should declare anew that they acquiesce in the covenant of grace as made with Christ; and in so doing surrender themselves to the Lord, to be wholly his, trusting that he will keep them by his power through faith unto salvation (Isa. 44:5; 1 Peter 1:5).

9. They should renew and exercise their love to all the saints, by breathing out the secret and habitual desires of their souls before him, that all the saints, as well as themselves, may receive abundantly out of the fullness of Christ; that they may keep themselves in the love of God, looking for the mercy of our Lord Jesus Christ unto eternal life; and that they may be edified and joined together in love. Though this expression of their love be more immediately and directly manifested to the society that joins with them in solemn communion, yet it is not to be confined within such narrow limits, but includes in it the highest esteem for all that are sanctified in Christ Jesus, called to be saints, though their place of abode be remote from ours, though they walk not with us; and though they be not known to us in the flesh. This love is the bond of perfectness in the body of Christ; it prevents many disorders, and is the happy means of producing very many desirable effects.

I have endeavored to avoid such general directions as are not peculiar to this ordinance, and have confined myself to these that arise from the nature of the Lord's Supper, as it is *a distinct institution* of the Lord Jesus, for promoting the faith, holiness, and joy of his church. The reader must judge for himself; and if they are conducive to his improvement, let God have the praise. It is proper now to add,

III. A third class of *directions*, relative to the behavior of Christians *after they have been at the Lord's table*. In general, I might observe that *a conver-*

sation becoming the gospel of Christ should be the great aim of all that have been showing the death of Christ (Phil. 1:27). Now this conversation that becometh the gospel is,

1. A behavior in the world and towards fellow-Christians that is *suitable to their church-state and character*, walking without offense to them that are without, and edifying one another in love. We have a bright example of this in the primitive Christians, who "continued steadfastly in the apostles' doctrine and fellowship, and in breaking of bread, and in prayers" (Acts 2:42); and who "were of one heart and of one soul" and were liberal, generous, and communicative with the most cheerful open frankness (Acts 4:32).

2. A conversation becoming *the doctrines of the gospel*. These are not a system for speculation, nor designed to amuse and entertain the fancy with ingenious notions. They are *incorruptible seed*, and wherever they are truly understood, received, and kept, they bring forth the fruits of righteousness with patience and perseverance (Luke 8:15). They are truly called "the doctrine which is according to godliness" (1 Tim. 6:3). They have a natural tendency to promote and advance powerful practical religion.[16]

3. A conversation that flows from *gospel principles*; from the *faith* and *love* of *revealed truth* dwelling richly in the soul. It is not enough that our behavior be agreeable to the letter of the word; but it must be a course of conscientious cheerful obedience to the authority and will of God. "Whatsoever is not of faith is sin."

4. A conversation becoming *the ordinances of the gospel*. These represent unto us the authority of God, and lay us under an obligation to be holy, as he is holy. "holiness becometh thine house, O Lord, for ever" (Ps. 93:5). Let everyone that nameth the name of Christ in them depart from all iniquity. God forbid we should provoke divine jealousy, and mock the Most High, by walking contrary to the intention and scope of these ordinances, which we profess to receive and observe, in obedience to their Author.

5. A conversation that becomes *the great ends of the gospel*, which are to abase the creature; to make the Savior precious; to establish the righteousness, honor, and authority of the law; and to promote the union and comfort of the saints.

---

[16] See Dr. Gill's sermon on 1 Timothy 6:3. John Gill. *The Doctrine of Grace Cleared from the Charge of Licentiousness.*

6. A conversation that becomes *the grace of God manifested in the gospel.* This teacheth us to deny all ungodliness and worldly lusts, and to live soberly, righteously, and godly in this present world (Titus 2:11–12). These who are holy and without blame before God in love are to the praise of the glory of his grace, wherein he hath made them accepted in the beloved (Eph. 1:4, 6).

7. A conversation that becomes *the sublime hopes and expectations of the gospel.* He that is begotten to a lively hope by the resurrection of Jesus Christ from the dead purifieth himself from all filthiness of flesh and spirit, and perfecteth holiness in the fear of God. These glorious hopes are fixed within the veil, whither the Forerunner is for us entered, and where no unclean thing can be admitted. To indulge sin, or to neglect duty, cannot be reconciled with the exercise of this blessed hope, which is sanctifying and operative.

8. A conversation *in heaven* (Phil. 3:20). They should be guided by heavenly views and aims, and should principally mind heavenly things. With affections set on the things that are above, at the right hand of God, they ought to esteem themselves only strangers and pilgrims on this earth; and, as such, are under every obligation to abstain from fleshly lusts, which seek gratification in the enjoyment of riches, pleasures, or honors.

9. A conversation *becoming the blood of the covenant*, that immensely valuable price wherewith they are bought. "What? know ye not that your body is the temple of the Holy Ghost which is in you, which ye have of God, and ye are not your own? For ye are bought with a price: therefore glorify God in your body, and in your spirit, which are God's" (1 Cor. 6:19–20).

10. A conversation that may *adorn the doctrine of God their Savior in all things* (Titus 2:10). The doctrine of the gospel of Christ, considered in itself, is a most beauteous and lovely doctrine, though it has been miserably blackened and blemished by these that should have given it a better treatment. Whoever professeth this doctrine is obliged to wash off that reproach and dirt which have been cast upon it; and, in their respective places and stations, to endeavor, as far as in them lies, to restore religion to its primitive luster and splendor, and so to retrieve the reputation of it. They ought to *adorn the doctrine of God their Savior in all things*; that is: *in civil* as well as *sacred things*; for religion must command and direct even our recreations, our diversions, our converses, and our particular callings,

to consecrate our common employments. *In duties of the second table*, as well as in those of the *first*; for the same God who sees and observes the temper of our minds in dealing with himself observes it also in our dealings with men; and the second commandment, "Thou shalt love thy neighbor as thyself," is like unto the first. *In good works* as well as *in holy words*, for it is only *well doing* that wipes off the reproach which is cast upon our holy profession, "so is the will of God, that with well-doing ye may put to silence the ignorance of foolish men" (1 Peter 2:15). To judge of *a Pharisee* by the ear, and not by the eye, he must appear an excellent saint; for that sort of men "say, and do not" (Matt. 23:3). *In suffering* according to the will of God, with Christian fortitude, patience, submission, and resignation; as well in making the divine law a rule to our practice. *In a more narrow and private*, as well as in a more *public and enlarged capacity*; for in every station we have certain talents, and if they are few and small, we should be more faithful in using, more diligent in improving them. *In doing well*, as well as *in ceasing to do evil*, for the law of God does not only forbid us to commit sin, but commands us to do the will of the Lord, and a religion made up of mere negative characters may well enough suit a self-righteous Pharisee (Luke 18), and doubtless many of that stamp will be found among the goats on the left hand of the Judge at the last day (Matt. 25). *In all companies*, both *holy* and *profane*; there is not so great danger in the company of the saints, but it is a very nice point to know how to act in the presence of the wicked. Prudence will advise us to be *wise as serpents*, and a good conscience will oblige us to keep ourselves *innocent as doves*, that our unseasonable rashness may not expose us to the fury of men, nor our temporizing compliance to the displeasure of God. David had studied this case with great care, "I will keep my mouth with a bridle, while the wicked is before me. I was dumb with silence, I held my peace, even from good; and my sorrow was stirred. My heart was hot within me, while I was musing the fire burned: then spake I with my tongue" (Ps. 39:1–3). Here was a notable conflict in David's soul betwixt his *prudence* and his *zeal*, while the wicked were before him. Prudence advised *silence*; zeal prompted *speech*; the case was desperate, and there seemed to be no hope of doing good. *Prudence* prevailed, and he was silent; but as soon as there appeared to be a fair probability of doing more good than harm, or rather of doing some good, and no harm, then zeal opened his lips, and he spake with his tongue. A modest word in season, even amongst the profane, has proved a seed of

God in the mind, which divine grace in due time has awakened to conversion. *In all relations* wherein the wisdom and goodness of God have placed us, as superiors, inferiors, or equals. And finally *in all the various conditions of life*, with respect either to plenty or want, sickness or health, good report or evil report, liberty or restraint. In all these, or in any other condition that shall fall to our lot, the gospel of Christ should be regarded and adorned in all things; because it allows of no dispensation, and it gives no indulgence to do evil that good may come of it.

Thus I have attempted to represent the Christian life in a variety of lights; but itself is one simple and uniform thing, that is very properly called "a conversation becoming the gospel of Christ." It should be the daily persevering business of the saints to maintain such a conversation, as the proper fruit of their engaging in this ordinance, and as the best evidence of their having profited by it.

I entirely agree with a late writer, who says:

> That there are a multitude of tracts already on the nature and preparation for the *sacrament*, is certain; but it is as certain, that too many of them serve only to mislead and deceive. The most I have seen tend to establish a self-righteous spirit, to counteract the very intention of the ordinance, and destroy the life and benefit of it. They set persons on an *external preparation*, and substitute the *form of godliness* for the *power* of it. The consequence of which is, that instead of being the better for communicating, many grow more hardened, proud, and self-sufficient; counting themselves righteous, though unawakened to a sense of sin, ignorant of God's righteousness, and strangers to all true spirituality of temper. The *Week's Preparations*, whether *new* or *old*, may be especially reckoned among this number. *Treatises* which, so far from preparing for an appearance at the *Lord's table*, blind the eyes and harden the heart, set up a false standard, and under the name of *Christ*, establish the kingdom of *Satan*, by leading men to trust upon their own works, their prayers, humiliations, fastings, and sacraments, *etc.*, instead of directing them as corrupt, sinful, guilty, and perishing creatures, to rely upon the blood and righteousness of *Jesus Christ* for all their salvation.[17]

---

[17] Haweis, *The Communicant's Spiritual Companion*, Preface.

The same, I apprehend, may be said of *those writings* that are so full and large in setting forth some peculiarity of circumspection, zeal, and diligence, as a duty immediately incumbent on communicants after they have been showing the Lord's death. Their *design* is *good*, but the *use* that is made of such excitements to extraordinary occasional activity and holiness is too often *bad*. The *temper* of a worthy communicant should not be *occasional*, but *habitual*; and their conversation should not be less strict on every other occasion, than for a few days after they have been eating and drinking in the sacrament of the supper. No good reason can be given why Christians should be more *fervent in spirit* the *first week* after they have been at the Lord's table, than *through their whole life*. Real *Christianity* implies all that belongs to the character and behavior of a *worthy communicant*; and there is nothing in Christianity that may, at any time, or on any pretense, be dispensed with. *Communicating* is not *an addition* to the Christian character, but *a branch* of it, and an *appointed means* of promoting the life and power of godliness.

If, instead of perusing many other treatises on the *nature, use, and ends of this sacrament*, people were to consider with attention and judgment the excellent description of it in the *Assembly's Larger Catechism*, questions 168–178 with the Scriptures annexed, it might, through the divine blessing, be a happy means of making them intelligent, conscientious, and profitable receivers of the ordinance.

Chapter 10

The Observation of the Lord's Day

All that we are, and all that we enjoy, are under every obligation to be sacred unto the service and honor of the Lord our God. Our *time*, as much as everything else, should be consecrated to his glory and pleasure. He is the only worthy Object of our faith, obedience, and worship; and we should have no other gods before him. His authority must prescribe the duties and manner of that worship which glorifies him, and which becomes us to perform. And his right extends even to *the seasons* of his worship; both to such seasons as return at *stated* periods, and to such as are pointed out by certain *occasional* occurrences. The *Sabbath* is an appointment of the *first* sort; and *times of humiliation and thanksgiving* are of the *last*. The Sabbath is to be kept at the return of the time appointed at all events; but times of solemn humiliation and thanksgiving are to be gathered from a careful attention to our condition, and a just comparison between it and the appointments of God relative to these duties.

My business in this chapter is to explain *the observation of the Lord's day*, as it is an ordinance of divine appointment, referring to the worship of God. Several preliminary disquisitions are connected with this point, which, for greater perspicuity, must be considered, in order to explain and urge *the practical part* of the subject, which is my principal design. I shall digest my thoughts under the following heads, *viz.*,

1. To consider the names;
2. The original institution;
3. The nature;
4. The obligations;
5. The proper employments of *the Lord's day*;
6. The directions necessary to be observed relative to the sanctification of it; and,
7. The motives that should engage our regard to it.

1. The Names Given to This Day

The *names* given to this sacred day are *various*. To overlook the names it has got from men, who have used a needless freedom in their ingenious inventions, I shall only take notice of these four *scriptural* designations; *viz., the Sabbath-day, the seventh day, the first day of the week*, and *the Lord's day*.

1. It is frequently called *the Sabbath-day*, or *the day of rest*. The occasion of this name may be learned from "And God blessed the seventh day, and sanctified it: because that in it he had *rested* [or kept a Sabbath] from all his work" (Gen. 2:3). And as he rested on that day from creating any new species of beings, so he sanctified and consecrated this day to be holy to his honor and service, that men should *rest* upon it from all servile work, except such as is manifestly a work of necessity or mercy.

2. It is called *the seventh day* in Genesis 2:3, where we are told the reason of that name; because it was the seventh day from the creation. This name is very common in the Old Testament; but it is nowhere to be found in the New. The reason of this will appear in considering the next head.

3. It is called *the first day of the week*. This name is very familiar in the New Testament, but never found in the Old. On the *first day* of the week Christ rose from the dead, and appeared to his disciples; on the *first day* of the week they came together to break bread; on the *first day* of the week they are to collect for the necessities of the poor.

4. It is called *the Lord's day*, "I was in the Spirit on *the Lord's day*" (Rev. 1:10), where we find it is represented as a day that the Lord Jesus Christ hath a peculiar claim to have observed, in obedience to his authority, and in honor of his name. Wherever God is said to lay claim to things in Scripture, it is implied that these things are of his appointment, and for his glory. Thus *the bread and wine* in that ordinance, which Christ has appointed in remembrance of his death, are called *the Lord's Supper* (1 Cor. 11:20), denoting that it is an ordinance of his own appointment. In like manner, *the Lord's day* may be fitly so called for this reason, because it is instituted *by him*, and designed to perpetuate the remembrance of his resurrection from the dead. This designation is never given to the Jewish Sabbath, but is appropriated wholly to the Christian dispensation.[1]

---

[1] The reader will find a judicious inquiry concerning *the names* of this day of sacred rest in John Owen. *A Treatise on the Sabbath*; *first exercitation*, sections 9–15, to which he is referred for his full satisfaction on the point.

2. Its Original Institution

The *original institution* of the Lord's day claims our attention, in the next place. Without entering into the controversies that have been moved on this subject, I shall deliver my own opinion in the following propositions.

1. Though the same light that discovers the being of God demonstrates the reasonableness of worshipping him, yet it is impossible mankind could ever fix the just proportion of their time, that should be employed in that service with any reason, unless they had been directed by the authority and will of God. Men could not absolutely determine whether some part of every day be sufficient and most proper for that purpose, or whether they should separate on that account one whole day out of five or ten, seven or seventeen. They could not assign the just medium between too much and too little. Human prudence indeed would teach us in the main, that since social worship should be performed, it seems to be more convenient, that a whole day should be separated now and then, rather than to make perpetual interruptions of the business of life, by separating a small part of every day for this purpose; and prudence will also convince us that this day must be publicly known and appointed, at least, by common consent. But it is obvious, there would be endless differences of opinion what day this should be, and how often it should return, if it were left merely to the fancies, conveniences, and agreements of men.

2. To guard against all these inconveniences, as soon as God had made man, and set him to labor in the garden of Eden, he appointed him one day in seven to be a day of rest from labor, and to be a season of religious worship: "God blessed the seventh day, and sanctified it: because that in it he had rested from all his work" (Gen. 2:3).

By this express appointment, our first parents were secured from all mistakes about the most proper seasons of their social solemn worship; and had this institution been faithfully observed by their posterity, it would have secured mankind from many doubts and contentions on this subject. Every circumstance is precisely determined, and no room is left for ambiguity or evasion. The example and institution of God are clear and express.

I know it is alleged that Moses only mentions in the history of Adam a certain Sabbath, by way of *anticipation*, which should be instituted in time to come among the Jews. But it might be proper to consider the following objections to this opinion. (1.) Can it be imagined that, in so short a history of the creation of the world, Moses should take such particular notice of a certain day, as blessed and sanctified by the Creator, which should not be sanctified and blessed till two thousand and four hundred years afterwards? (2.) Are not the finishing of the creation, and the institution of a Sabbath, joined in close connection in the Mosaic history? And why should we not then believe that when God rested on the seventh day from all his work, he *then* blessed this seventh day, and sanctified it, *at that very time?* (Gen. 2:1–3; Ex. 20:11). (3.) Did he bless and sanctify this day only for himself, and for his own rest? No, surely; but for the rest of man, "The sabbath was made for man" (Mark 2:27). And the reason given to man for the appointment of a Sabbath, *viz., God's resting from all his works of creation*, is expressed the same way in Exodus 20:11 as it is in Genesis 2. And why then should we doubt whether the ordinance of the Sabbath was given by *God* to Adam, as well as by Moses to the Jews?[2]

3. It is very probable that the pious patriarchs, in the beginning of the world, actually kept *a weekly Sabbath*; though there be no very plain and particular account thereof in the writings of Moses, whose history of the patriarchal age is brief and concise. Critics fancy they find this actually hinted in Genesis 4:3, where it is said, "*In process of time* it came to past, that Cain brought of the fruit of the ground an offering unto the Lord," which was doubtless an instance of public worship. We render the words, *in process of time*; but they may, with equal justice, be rendered, as it is observed in the margin, *at the end of days*; that is, at the end of *some period*, which was at that time well known; and perhaps at the end of *the week*, which was a famous period in the days of Noah (Gen. 8:10–12), and in the days of Jacob (Gen. 29:18–28). If it be thought to refer to the end of *the year*, rather than to the end of *the week*, yet still the expression implies that there were *certain stated seasons of public worship*, observed religiously by the patriarchs in that period. This goes a great way to prove all that I affirm. Another passage in the book of Job, who, I suppose, was a real man, and that he lived long before Moses,[3] which is supposed to imply the same truth, is found in chapter 1:6, where we are told, "there was *a day* when

---

[2] The *proleptic sense* of that passage in Genesis 2 is solidly confuted by Owen, *A Treatise on the Sabbath*; John Brown (of Wamphray). *De Causa Dei Contra Antisabbatarios*; Witsius, *Œconomia Fœderum*; John Edwards. *A Complete History or Survey of all the Dispensations and Methods of Religion*, chap. 1.

[3] Vide Dr. Grey's letter to Warburton.

the sons of God came to present themselves before the LORD." It seems to be plain enough that *the sons of God* denote *religious men*, and that their *presenting themselves before the Lord* refers to their *public worship*. The only thing that is any way doubtful is *what day is there spoken of*, whether it was the weekly Sabbath, or some other solemn season of divine worship; but whether it was the one or the other, it is undeniable that there were *certain stated times* of religious people assembling together to worship God in that age.

As Dr. Watts has observed,

> But suppose the Bible were entirely silent on this subject; yet it may be justly remarked here, that as there is *an express institution* of a Sabbath in the beginning of the Bible, without any plain and uncontested *example* of *the practice* in the *patriarchal ages*; so in the first *Christian age*, there are several plain *examples* of *the practice* of keeping the Lord's day, without any *express institution* of it in the New Testament. But as from such *Christian examples*, we reasonably infer *an institution*, so from the *ancient institution*, we as reasonably infer that there were some *patriarchal examples* of the practice.

4. As soon as God formed Israel into a church-state, he made known his will unto them, concerning the observation of one day in seven for a day of holy rest, and of public worship. If the day of sacred rest was utterly lost among the slaveries of Egypt, which some think is not improbable, this loss was made up immediately after they were brought into the wilderness, when Moses spake unto them in these words, "This is that which the LORD hath said, To morrow is the rest of the holy sabbath unto the Lord...Six days ye shall gather it; but on the seventh day, which is the sabbath, in it there shall be none" (Ex. 16:23, 26). In these verses the Sabbath is mentioned, not as a new institution, but with a particular view to point out the precise day that should be observed. And this duty received a still more explicit explication and establishment on mount Sinai,

> Remember the sabbath day, to keep it holy. Six days shalt thou labour, and do all thy work: but the seventh day is the Sabbath of the LORD thy God: in it thou shalt not do any work, thou, nor thy son, nor thy daughter, thy manservant, nor thy maidservant, nor thy

cattle, nor thy stranger that is within thy gates: for in six days the LORD made heaven and earth, the sea, and all that in them is, and rested the seventh day: wherefore the LORD blessed the sabbath day, and hallowed it (Ex. 20:8–11).

5. The seventh-day Sabbath was to be observed, by divine appointment, till Christ rose from the dead. That most glorious event was to put a period to the observation of the Jewish institutions; but it is plain, the law concerning the seventh-day Sabbath was in force always, until he who is the end of the law finished his works of obedience and satisfaction, and rose again from the dead to enter into his glory. This will be more evident, when I have observed:

6. That the Sabbath was changed, by *divine authority*, from the *seventh* to the *first day of the week, at the resurrection of Christ*. Some have attempted to show that the Christian Sabbath is observed now on the same day of the week that was kept from Adam to Moses,[4] but all must agree that the first and seventh days are not the same. The only thing to be proven is that *divine authority* has *substituted* the first day of the week in the room of the seventh, in virtue of the resurrection of Christ. I can only suggest the heads of argument that might be used on this point, without much illustration. (1.) The Sabbath is *an everlasting appointment*, for it was instituted in a state of innocency, and then enjoined unto our first parents. The original reason for observing it seems to confirm the perpetuity thereof, *viz.*, God's own rest from his work of creating the world in six days. The place which this command of the Sabbath holds in the law of God, in the midst of other precepts that are confessedly moral, is a further argument. The continued observation of the Sabbath in the apostolic age is still a further proof. And the reasonableness, if not the necessity, of such an appointment in the world, both for the honor of God, and for the good of men, strongly establishes the perpetuity of the Sabbath. (2.) Jewish sabbatisms are *abolished* since Christ rose from the dead. This is the evident meaning of these texts wherein Christians are forbidden to subject themselves to the bondage of Jewish rites: "we, when we were children, were in

---

[4] See Arthur Bedford. *The Scripture Chronology*; John Kennedy. *A Complete System of Astronomical Chronology*; Guyse, *Paraphrase*, note on Colossians 2:16; Owen, *A Treatise on the Sabbath*

bondage under the elements of the world" that is, under the Jewish dispensation. "But now, after that ye have known God, or rather are known of God, how turn ye again to the weak and beggarly elements, whereunto ye desire again to be in bondage? Ye observe days, and months, and times, and years" (Gal. 4:3, 9–10) that is, the Mosaical appointments concerning all their Sabbath-days, and new moons, and sabbatical years, which were given to the Jews. The apostle had good reason for his godly jealousy concerning such as fell into this course; and to say, "I am afraid of you, lest I have bestowed upon you labour in vain" (Gal. 4:11). To the same purpose we read in Colossians 2:16–17 that no man should judge, that is, censure or condemn, Christians, in meat, or in drink, or in respect of a holy-day, or of *the Sabbath-days*, to wit, of *the seventh-day Sabbaths*, because these sacred times are a shadow of good things to come; but the body, or substance, is of Christ. (3.) Notwithstanding the abolition of Jewish Sabbaths, the general law of the Sabbath *still remains* in as much force as ever. Accordingly the first Christians conscientiously observed a weekly Sabbath. (4.) The apostolic church observed *the first day of the week* for holy rest, and for religious worship. The evidences which persuade us of this are such as these: Christ rose from the dead on the first day of the week. On the very day of his resurrection, the disciples being assembled, perhaps for worship, with the doors shut for fear of the Jews, Jesus came and stood in the midst of them (John 20:19); and having pronounced his peace upon them, he repeated his commission to them, and breathed on them, saying, Receive ye the Holy Ghost. The very next first day of the week, he appeared unto them again, Thomas being with them, and gave them clearer proofs of his resurrection, when they were all met together. "When the day of Pentecost was fully come, [the disciples] were all with one accord in one place...And they were all filled with the Holy Ghost" (Acts 2:1, 4). Now, by an easy computation, it is plain that the day of Pentecost was on the first day of the week. Upon the first day of the week, the disciples came together at Troas to break bread, and Paul preached unto them (Acts 20:7). Paul gives orders concerning a collection for the saints upon the first day of the week, directing everyone to lay by him in store according as God had prospered him: and he says, he gave the same order to the churches of Galatia (1 Cor. 16:1–2). And, to add no more proofs in so clear a case, the religious observation of the first day of the week among Christians was so generally and so early known, that in the days of the apostle John, it acquired an honorable title, and was called *the Lord's day* (Rev. 1:10). (5.) The observation of *the first day of the week* for the Christian Sabbath is founded upon, and commenced at, *the resurrection* of Christ. This position is very evident from the apostolic history (John 20), and from Hebrews 4:9–10, "There remaineth therefore a rest to the people of God. For he that is entered into his rest, he also hath ceased from his own works, as God did from his." The *rest* mentioned (v. 9), is truly rendered in the marginal reading, *a keeping of a Sabbath*. The reader may consult Dr. Owen on the place;[5] together with his treatise on the Sabbath where he will find this point judiciously explained and vindicated.[6]

7. The appointment concerning the first-day Sabbath is of *perpetual force until Christ's second coming*. The proofs of this assertion will be laid before the reader, when I come to represent *the obligations* that lie upon Christians to observe the Lord's day, which is the business allotted to the *fourth* section.

I cheerfully acknowledge my obligations to Dr. Watts.[7] The greatest part of this section may be considered as an abridgment of his first discourse. The reader will find his account too, in consulting Dr. Owen's *Second Exercitation on the Sabbath*.[8]

3. Its Nature

I shall now proceed to explain *the nature* of this institution concerning the Lord's day, by showing (1.) What *sort* of an appointment it is; and (2.) For what *ends* it is instituted. The consideration of these two things will sufficiently open the nature of it, and lead us, with judgment and prudence, to comply with the design thereof.

I. I am, in the first place, to consider *what sort of an appointment the Sabbath is*. In general, it is *a divine*, *a holy*, and *a benevolent institution*. (1.) It is *a divine ordinance*. In how many places do we find God claiming an interest in it, and calling it *his Sabbath*? He is the author, director, and end thereof. It is God who said, "Ye shall keep my sabbaths" (Lev. 19:30) and again, "Keep the sabbath day to sanctify it, as the LORD thy God hath commanded thee" (Deut. 5:12). The employment of our bodies and minds

---

[5] John Owen. *An Exposition of the Epistle to the Hebrews.*
[6] Owen, *A Treatise on the Sabbath.*
[7] Isaac Watts. *The Holiness of Times, Places, and People.*
[8] Owen, *A Treatise on the Sabbath.*

on the whole of that day is prescribed under the direction and authority of JEHOVAH, who commands us to turn away our foot from the sabbath, from doing our pleasure on his holy day, and to call the Sabbath a delight, the holy of the LORD, honorable, and to honor him, not doing our own ways, not finding our own pleasures, nor speaking our own words (Isa. 58:13:.) And this ordinance is evidently designed for the honor of God, that we may thereupon show forth his praise, and record his marvelous works. Our regard to this duty should be an act of willing obedience to divine authority, and an expression of unfeigned zeal for the glory of God. (2.) The Sabbath is *a holy ordinance*. The Lord calls it *his holy day*, and commands us to *call it the holy of the LORD* (Isa. 58:13), and *to keep it holy* (Ex. 20:8). This day is separated from the rest of the days of the week, that it may be unalienably sacred to the honor and worship of that God, who is *glorious in holiness*. Nothing that is *common* or *worldly* in its nature or design becomes that *holy day*, or should be allowed to mingle in its holy services. The purity of spiritual devotion is most suitable to a holy Sabbath. (3.) It is *a most benevolent ordinance*; as our Lord has told us in the defense he made for his disciples, who, passing in a footpath through a cornfield on the Sabbath-day, plucked the ears of corn, and did eat, rubbing them in their hands. The Pharisees caviled against their practice, and affected to represent it as a breach of the Sabbath-day. Christ vindicated his disciples against the unjust imputation, by putting the objectors in mind of the example of David, and those that were with him, who, being hungry, did eat the showbread, which was not lawful, in ordinary cases, for any to do but the priests alone (Luke 6:1–4). And he said to the self-righteous, censorious Pharisees, at the same time, "The sabbath was made for man, and not man for the sabbath: therefore the Son of man is Lord also of the sabbath" (Mark 2:27–28). The sense of these verses is thus expressed by Dr. Guyse:

> A great part of the morality of the Sabbath lay in its being made for *the good of man*; chiefly for the spiritual benefit of the soul, that it may be at liberty to serve God, and have holy communion with him; and partly for the relief of the body, that it may have rest from the fatiguing labor of the week: and, it is plain, that as man was created the day before the institution of the Sabbath, he was not made for the Sabbath, nor could be bound by its law to abstain from what is necessary for the support of his life. The Messiah has therefore

undoubtedly a divine right to order what he thinks for the good of man, in subservience to the great design of a Sabbath; and my disciples are not to be blamed for using the liberty which I gave them, to eat a little corn, for the refreshment of the body, and fitting it for the holy services of the day.

How kind is this institution even to the laborious cattle, and much more to mankind! It is a seasonable relaxation to the wearied body, and a blessed opportunity to the immortal soul. I proceed, in the next place,

II. To inquire *for what ends the Sabbath is appointed.* Here I might observe (1.) That the Sabbath in the state of innocency was intended to be *an instructive* and *a confirming sign* in many respects; for thereby our first parents were taught to look for a *better state* than that they were then placed in, though that was very comfortable; and were encouraged to expect it, as a sure and incorruptible possession; it reminded them of their dependence upon God, while it directed their attention above the world, and assured them of being forever happy in a continued persevering obedience to their Maker. (2.) The Sabbath was unto the Jews *a sign between God and them* (Ex. 31:17). It was a sign to bring to remembrance their deliverance out of the land of Egypt, and to lead forward their views to the more glorious redemption, which was to be wrought by the Messiah. Perhaps it was a sign that the system of ceremonial observances was to have an end; but it was surely a sign that a better rest than that of the earthly Canaan was prepared for the people of God. (3.) The Christian Sabbath, supposing it to be a moral institution, is ordained for such purposes as these: to display *the sovereignty of God*, whose universal dominion is acknowledged in a command that binds all the world, in one day from week to week to lay aside their own business, and to attend to his worship. To preserve *a sense and profession of religion* in the world, which are not a little promoted by this public and social service. To refresh *the fatigued bodies of men*, with such rest and care as are necessary for their preservation and comfort. To keep up *lively impressions* of the great truths of Christianity in our memories; particularly, *the creation of the world, the fall of man, the incarnation of Christ, his death and resurrection.* To lead forward our views to *the rest that remaineth for the people of God* (Heb. 4:9). To call off our attention from temporal to spiritual objects. And to afford us *a lively emblem* of heaven, and of the conversation of the glorified saints in celebrating their eternal Sabbath, in the general assembly and church of the firstborn, who rest from all their worldly toilsome labors (Rev. 14:13).

This shall suffice for a general account of *the nature* of the Sabbath, since the reader may now understand, in some degree, what sort of an ordinance it is, and for what purposes it was ordained.

4. The Obligations to Observe It

The next point to be considered is *the obligation* that lies on men to observe the Sabbath-day. Previous to this it will be proper to show, how far it is a *moral duty*, and in what sense we maintain its *moral obligation*. This will be plain enough from the following positions. (1.) This duty is not, like many of the works of the moral law, written upon the heart of mankind, and manifest by the light of reason. The precise period of its revolution can neither be discovered, nor accounted for, on the principles of reason. Let it be supposed that men, unassisted by supernatural revelation, are led into the knowledge of the being and government of God; they might give a good reason for many of the duties that are required in the moral law; but they could never satisfy either their own minds, or the minds of others, about the proportion of their time which should be dedicated to the worship of the Deity, however reasonable it is to allow that some part of time should be separated for that exercise. But whether it should be the half or the fourth, the seventh or the tenth, is more than any man's reason could determine. Upon this account the fourth commandment is said to be *a moral-positive*, and not *a moral-natural institution*. (2.) There is a great difference betwixt these two propositions, which seem to be at first view not unlike one another, *viz.*, That *the seventh-day Sabbath is moral*, and that *a seventh-day Sabbath is moral*. To observe one day in seven is a moral duty; but to observe the seventh or the first day in that weekly period is not so. From the beginning to the end of the world, one day in seven has always been sacred, by divine appointment, for bodily rest, and for religious worship, among the people of God, and will be so to the end of time. But the determination of the precise day is an *occasional* appointment. (3.) There were several *ceremonial appendages* to this institution among the Jews, which expired with their system. On the Sabbath they were to offer double sacrifices, and to keep it in remembrance of the deliverance from slavery, and bondage. But whatever was ceremonial, or peculiar to the Jews, in their observation of the Sabbath, was so far from interrupting, that it rather cooperated, in their circumstances, with the original design of this moral duty. (4.) What I affirm then is that *the observation of one day in seven, by a holy resting all that day, and spending the whole time in the public and private exercises of God's worship, except so much of it as is to be taken up in the works of necessity and mercy, is a moral duty*; and *that God only has a right to determine which day he will have observed for that purpose.* The *proofs* of this proposition will represent the force of our *obligations* to *keep the Sabbath holy.*

The following preliminaries may be profitably attended to, in order to represent the arguments to be adduced in a proper light. (1.) It is a branch of the moral law, that God should be worshipped. (2.) We are obliged by that same law to perform *social* worship. (3.) Reason tells us that social worship must be occasional, and cannot be persevered in without interruption. (4.) The advantages of having some determined season fixed for that purpose are too evident to be denied, or even disputed. (5.) No authority can be acknowledged, with any propriety, in fixing a precise time, but that of JEHOVAH.

These observations are self-evident; and a due regard to them would put an end to the dispute concerning *the morality of the Sabbath*, because they are equally applicable to every place, and to every people, in every age. But to set the force of this sacred obligation in a proper view, I shall propose the following considerations.

1. The Sabbath was instituted *in paradise*, while our first parents continued to stand in their original integrity (Gen. 2). Upon this account it cannot be a ceremonial ordinance, because it was ordained *before* any of the types that prefigured Christ to come in the flesh, or that had any respect to an atonement for sin.

2. It was originally ordained upon a *foundation* that is *equally* good at all times, and in every age and place. The Wisdom of God saw it meet for his own glory, and needful for man's good, that man should have one day in the week separated for more immediate and special converse with God. It would not have been good for Adam before his fall to be without such an appointment; for though there could be no interruption of his happiness and fellowship with God, when he was dressing the garden, because he was *upright*, yet, being only *a finite creature*, and engaged in worldly business, his mind could not be so intense upon the duties of immediate worship every day, as it would be on a day set apart for that purpose. And if Adam

in *innocence* needed a Sabbath, for the more immediate service and solemn worship of God, much more do we, who are *sinful creatures*, and deeply immersed in worldly cares, need such a day.

3. The obligation to keep the Sabbath-day holy, may be strongly inferred from *the place it holds in the ten commandments.* It is enjoined in the midst of *the ten words* God spake at mount Sinai, and therefore must be of the same nature and kind with them. It was spoken, with the rest of the moral precepts, by the mouth of God, in the hearing of all Israel; it was written with the finger of God upon tables of stone; it was lodged within the ark along with them; and had every equal mark of honor stamped on it that the rest had. Why then should men suppose it to be a temporary institution, and the rest to be of moral obligation?

4. The *reasons* of this commandment are all of them moral and perpetual, and therefore such is the obligation of it to us. The ceremonial law was enforced by arguments drawn from the peculiarity of the Jewish dispensation, and therefore the law itself was local and temporary. But the reasons of resting one day in seven, which are annexed to the fourth commandment, are drawn from the principles of eternal truth, without any respect to temporal or local circumstances. They are expressed in these words, "in six days the LORD made heaven and earth, the sea, and all that in them is, and rested the seventh day: wherefore the LORD blessed the sabbath day, and hallowed it" (Ex. 20:11). Now, if these were sufficient reasons, why the Jews should observe a particular Sabbath, they are still as cogent and forcible with us. Hence our Lord says, "The sabbath was made *for man*" (Mark 2:27); not for *the Jews*, as such; nor for *Christians*, as such; but for *men, as men.*

5. *Christ came not to destroy the law, but to fulfill it* (Matt. 5:17). He severely threatened those who would seek to invalidate the obligation of *the least* of the commandments of the law (Matt. 5:18–19); and, in confirmation hereof, said to his disciples, "pray ye that your flight be not…on the sabbath day" (Matt. 24:20). This he recommended unto them with a view to the destruction of Jerusalem by Vespasian; an event that was to happen about forty years after the death of Christ, when all Jewish ceremonies were abolished, together with the Jewish Sabbath. And yet he intimates that his disciples would lie under an obligation to observe a Sabbath-day, and that it would be a heavy addition to their affliction, if they should be forced to take their flight on the Sabbath, when they ought, and de-

sired to be employed in the spiritual exercise of devotion, and holy duties proper to that day.

Some think that our Lord in that passage (Matt. 24:20), intends only the *Jewish*, or *seventh-day Sabbath*, and that he consulted the edification of his own people among the Jews, some of whom would, for a season, be kept in bondage to the law of ceremonies, and make conscience of observing the seventh day still, through their ignorance of their liberty by the coming of Christ. I shall reply in the words of Dr. Owen,

> Many things on the other side are *certain* and indubitable, which render this conjecture altogether improbable: for (1.) All real obligation unto Judaical institutions was *then* absolutely taken away; and it is not to be supposed, that our Lord Jesus Christ would beforehand lay in provision for the edification of his church in *error*. (2.) Before that time came, they were sufficiently instructed *doctrinally* in the dissolution of all obligation in ceremonial institutions. This was done principally by St Paul in all his epistles; especially in that unto the Hebrews themselves at Jerusalem. (3.) Those who may be supposed to have continued a conscientious respect unto the *Judaical Sabbath*, could be no otherwise persuaded of it, than were the Jews in those days. But they all accounted themselves absolved in conscience from the law of the Sabbath, upon eminent danger in time of war, so that they might either *fight* or *fly*, as their safety did require. This is evident from the decree made by them under the Hasmonaeans. And such imminent danger is now supposed by our Savior; for he exhorts them to forego all consideration of their enjoyments, and to shift merely for their lives. There was not therefore any danger *in point of conscience*, with respect unto the *Judaical Sabbath*, to be then feared or prevented. But in general, those in whose hearts are the ways of God, do know what an addition it is to the greatest of their earthly troubles, if they befall them in such seasons, as to deprive them of the opportunity of *the sacred ordinances* of God's worship, and indispensably engage them in ways and works quite of another nature, then, when they stand in most need of them.[9]

---

[9] Owen, *A Treatise on the Sabbath*, pp. 194, 195.

6. It must be remembered too that Christians, who are bound to observe all things whatsoever their Lord has commanded them, without adding to his law, or diminishing from it, in anything that concerns their faith, worship, and obedience, observed the first day of the week ever after the resurrection of Christ. So that in the matter of the Sabbath, they showed themselves to be not without law to God, but under law to Christ. This might be proved by a large induction of particular proofs, such as John 20:19–20, 26; Acts 2:1–2 and 20:7; 1 Cor. 16:1–2; Rev. 1:10.[10] Now, what reason can be given for the disciples assembling for divine worship on the first day of the week, so statedly as they did, besides this which we affirm to be the true one, that the authority of God made it their duty to do so? This reason will account for their conduct, and nothing else will give us satisfying light into a practice that obtained so universally in the Christian church.

If all these considerations be put together, they will amount to a satisfying proof that the observation of the Sabbath is *a moral duty*, and of *perpetual obligation*, ever since man was upon earth, and will be a standing ordinance till the consummation of all things. Some of the most plausible *objections* against this opinion are not unworthy of a slight remark, before we proceed to another head.

Objection 1. "The Christian life in general ought to be a Sabbath, or a holy rest from sin, from a vain world, and from the labor of enslaving ceremonies; and therefore there is no need of a set day."

Answer. It is absurd to reason against facts, which are not at all changed by ingenious arguments. The objection would be stronger against the appointment of a Sabbath unto Adam before his fall, than it can possibly be in the case of Christians. And yet we are sure it would be against incontestable facts to attempt to prove that man in his creation-state had no such ordinance. Christians should be in the fear of God all the day long; and yet they must labor in an honest calling with industry, to provide for themselves and families. And as they cannot, they ought not, to retire wholly from the busy scenes of life; so they have great occasion for Sabbath-opportunities.

Objection 2. "The apostle condemns the observation of any particular days under the New Testament, 'Ye observe days, and months, and times,

---

[10] The argument from each of these texts is judiciously opened, urged, and vindicated in Ridgley, *A Body of Divinity*, vol. 2, pp. 272–274.

and years. I am afraid of you, lest I have bestowed upon you labour in vain' (Gal. 4:10–11)."

Answer. The apostle could not intend to include *the Lord's day* among these periods, because this would be a flat contradiction to his uniform doctrine, "Now concerning the collection for the saints, as I have given order to the *churches of Galatia*, even so do ye. Upon *the first day* of the week let every one of you lay by him in store, as God hath prospered him" (1 Cor. 16:1–2). The same may be said of Colossians 2:16–17, where the apostle speaks only of *Jewish Sabbaths*, as is evident from his joining them with *holy-days* and *new-moons*.

Objection 3. "The Sabbath was given to the Jews as *a sign*; and therefore it was ceremonial, and is of course abolished."

Answer. It was undoubtedly *a sign*, between the Lord and the people of Israel (Ezek. 20:12). But there are some signs that are not typical, such as the rainbow, the signs of the weather, and even the moral law is called a sign (Deut. 6:8). The Sabbath was to the Jews, and it is to Christians, a sign of the dominion of God, of his favor to his people, of an eternal rest he has prepared for them, and of their being a holy people to him.

Objection 4. "There is no holiness in days, and one is as good as another; and no preference should be given to one day above another."

Answer. This way of talking will as much disprove the Mosaic appointments concerning the Sabbaths, new-moons, and other solemn days that Israel was commanded to observe, as it will invalidate the Christian Sabbath. We believe it is separated by divine authority, from the rest of the days of the week, and therefore dare not use it to any other purpose than he has appointed.

Objection 5. "God doth not require us to be more holy at one time than another."

Answer. I readily allow that he doth not; for he requires us to be holy in all manner of conversation, as he is holy (1 Peter 1:15). But he has appointed *a season for every purpose* (Eccl. 3). Holiness should show itself in the whole compass of our natural, civil, and religious conduct; while wisdom and prudence should arrange the whole in the comeliest order, and should choose the fittest seasons for more close application to each of them. Upon this principle, it is no less reasonable that we set apart some determined proportion of our time for the worship of God than that we fix our seasons of eating, sleeping, or business; but we ought to be holy in them all.

Objection 6. "We have no express command in the Scripture to observe the Sabbath under the New Testament."

Answer. Our obligation to do so is everywhere supposed; the manner of observing it is described; and the services of it are explained. All these circumstances taken together are tantamount to an express command; they imply no less; and their obligation is as clear and strong as if the duty had been prescribed in the most positive terms. Besides, there was no need of an express command to recommend a moral duty, that does not rest upon a positive institution. The authority and ground of the Sabbath are invariable.

5. The Proper Employments of It

The proper employments of the *Lord's day* are now to be explained. Here it is expedient to show (1.) What we ought not to do; and (2.) What we may and should do, on that holy day.

I. The things which we ought not to do on the Lord's day may be comprehended under two heads, *viz.*,

1. *Things that are in themselves sinful.* These are criminal at any time, but much more so on the Sabbath; for hereby we contract double guilt, not only in committing the sin, but in breaking the Sabbath. Such sins are for the most part presumptuously committed, and have a great tendency to harden the heart; they do not only hinder the efficacy of ordinances, but if they be indulged and persisted in, they are a fearful step to apostasy from the faith and profession of the gospel.

2. To engage either in *worldly employments*, or *recreations*, that are lawful on other days, is inconsistent with the sanctification of the Sabbath. Because these particulars are important and exceedingly ensnaring, I hope to be excused by the serious reader if I consider them severally.

(1.) Worldly employments are by no means to be engaged in upon the Lord's day. We are expressly commanded to lay aside, and wholly to abstain from, everything of that kind on the Sabbath, "in it thou shalt not do any work" (Ex. 20:10). To enter on particulars would not consist with the bounds I must confine myself to in this discourse. And yet there are some instances that must be mentioned, because they are become so common that they are supposed to be matters of *indifference*, if not of *duty*, such as *buying and selling*, or *encouraging* those who do so. Nehemiah has recorded a noble instance of heroic zeal in this matter. His words are these,

> In those days saw I in Judah some treading wine presses on the sabbath, and bringing in sheaves, and lading asses; as also wine, grapes, and figs, and all manner of burdens, which they brought into Jerusalem on the sabbath day: and I testified against them in the day wherein they sold victuals. There dwelt men of Tyre also therein, which brought fish, and all manner of ware, and sold on the sabbath unto the children of Judah, and in Jerusalem. Then I contended with the nobles of Judah, and said unto them, What evil thing is this that ye do, and profane the sabbath day? (Neh. 13:15–17).

That passage is no less remarkable,

> Thus said the LORD unto me; Go and stand in the gate of the children of the people, whereby the kings of Judah come in, and by the which they go out, and in all the gates of Jerusalem; and say unto them, Hear ye the word of the LORD, ye kings of Judah, and all Judah, and all the inhabitants of Jerusalem, that enter in by these gates: thus saith the LORD; Take heed to yourselves, and bear no burden on the sabbath day, nor bring it in by the gates of Jerusalem; Neither carry forth a burden out of your houses on the sabbath day, neither do ye any work, but hallow ye the sabbath day, as I commanded your fathers (Jer. 17:19–22).

These express remonstrances reprove those tradesmen, who post their books, state their accounts, or prepare their goods, which are to be exposed to sale on the following day. And if we do not run all these lengths in profaning the Sabbath, yet we become highly guilty, when our thoughts and discourse run upon business. This is in effect, to join with those that said, "When will the new moon be gone, that we may sell corn? and the sabbath, that we may set forth wheat?" (Amos 8:5). Such people are severely reproved by the Lord, when he says, "they come unto thee as the people cometh, and they sit before thee as my people, and they hear thy words, but they will not do them: for with their mouth they shew much love, but their heart goeth after their covetousness" (Ezek. 33:31).

(2.) Recreations that are lawful on other days of the week are not lawful on the Sabbath-day, and therefore must not be indulged. Accordingly these that *sanctify the Sabbath* are represented as turning away their foot from doing their pleasure on God's holy day, and calling the Sabbath a delight, the holy of the Lord, honorable, honoring him, not doing their own ways, nor finding *their own pleasure,* nor speaking their own words (Isa. 58:13). Among the many ways of profaning this holy day by unhallowed recreations, I shall only mention a few instances. Every reader's own reflection will enable him to add many more. *Unnecessary visits* should be carefully abstained from, for by these the worship of God in families is interrupted, the minds of men are perverted, and filled with vanity, the motions of the Spirit are quenched, heavenly-mindedness is prevented, and the advantage of public worship is greatly hindered, if not wholly lost. *Social festivity and mirth* should be refrained, for that tends to encourage and strengthen a carnal mind, and to indispose us for the spiritual services of this holy day. *Walking in the fields* for pleasure is a criminal recreation on the Lord's day, because it diverts the mind from useful meditations on the word of God, and engages our eyes in beholding vanity. The taking *unnecessary journies* is another recreation that cannot be reconciled with the exact regard we should have to the honor of the Sabbath. *Talking of news,* or *of common affairs,* is another sin that should be forborne on the Sabbath-day, for such kind of discourse does not only hurt our own souls, but encourages others to break the Sabbath as well as ourselves. Finally, *all manner of sports* are sinful on the Lord's day. A sensible writer of the church of England expresses himself upon this subject in this manner.

> It is sad on this occasion to recount, that *a declaration* for liberty of *sports* and *recreations* on the Lord's day was heretofore published among us. It must needs be a sin of a high nature, when not only the *civil,* but *ecclesiastical rulers,* agreed to countenance and promote such a disorder. The judgment of God followed them for this heinous offense, and I fear will light upon those at this day, who are desirous to see *those declarations* retrieved. For it is observable, that some of those men who are most zealous for those things for which there is *no express command* from God, are despisers of the *Lord's day,* which is of *divine institution,* and they are forward to do anything on that day. But they should remember, that *sports and pas-*

times are unfit entertainments at such a time; because they dispose the mind to undue mirth, they render us incapable of attending on God, they take off our thoughts from what is serious and solemn.[11]

II. The *positive duties* to be performed on the Lord's day are now to be represented. The subject is very extensive. The reader that wishes to see it judiciously and largely explained will find an excellent gratification in the pious Mr. Willison of Dundee's treatise.[12] I shall, as briefly as possible, collect into one view the duties of this day that are of a *public, private,* and *personal nature.*

1. The *public duties* of the Lord's day are such as these: *Singing God's praise* in the congregations of his people. We should bless God at all times; but our thanksgivings should be more abundant and more public in the assemblies of his saints. His courts should be entered with praise. The walls of his church are salvation; and therefore her gates ought to be praise. The title of the ninety-second psalm is, "A Psalm or Song for the sabbath day." It is the proper duty of this day to rejoice in God's works, both of *creation* and *redemption,* and in the illustrious displays of his glory in both. *Prayer* and *supplication* is another branch of the public service of the Sabbath. The saints are a people that seek the Lord's face, and that call upon his name. They assemble in his "house of prayer" (Isa. 56:7). The house of God shall be called a "house of prayer" while the sun and moon endure before him (Matt. 21:13). *Hearing the word* publicly read and preached is another part of our employment on the Lord's day. When

---

[11] Edwards, *Theologia Reformata*, vol. 2, p. 450. That author refers to "the king's majesty's *declaration* to his subjects concerning lawful sports to be used," first published by King James, in the year 1618, and confirmed in the year 1619, by King Charles I under the direction of Dr. Laud. I shall gratify the curiosity of the reader with an extract from that infamous paper. Speaking of the observation of the Sabbath, his majesty says, "As for our good people's recreation, our pleasure...is, that, after the end of divine service, our good people be not disturbed, letted [hindered], or discouraged, from any lawful recreation, such as, *dancing*, either men or women, *archery* for men, *leaping, vaulting,* or *any other such harmless recreation,* nor from having of *may-games, whitson-ales,* and *morris-dances,* and the setting up of *may-poles,* and *other sports therewith used*; so as the same be had in due and convenient time; without impediment or neglect of divine service: and that women shall have leave to carry rushes to the church for the decoring of it according to their old custom." pp. 10, 11.

[12] Willison, *A Treatise concerning the Sanctification of the Lord's Day.*

the disciples came together on the first day of the week at Troas in Macedonia, Paul preached unto them (Acts 20:7). *The administration of the sacraments* is likewise a proper branch of public worship on that holy day. On the first day of the week the primitive disciples *came together* to break bread (Acts 20:7). It would seem to have been their practice at the commencement of every week. To *make public collections* for charitable uses, is expressly commanded, as another duty of Christians when they meet to worship God, "Upon the first day of the week let every one of you lay by him in store, as God hath prospered him" (1 Cor. 16:1–2).

These are some of the public services which every Christian should attend to on the Sabbath, as he has an opportunity. They are suitable to the dignity of the institution. They bring the resurrection of Christ to remembrance, and they anticipate the felicities of that rest which remains for the people of God.

2. The *private* or *domestic duties of the Sabbath* are very important and necessary. The command concerning the Sabbath is immediately given to masters of families, and other superiors. This is evident from the tenor of it. "in it thou shalt not do any work, thou, nor thy son, nor thy daughter, thy manservant, nor thy maidservant, nor thy cattle, nor thy stranger that is within thy gates" (Ex. 20:10). This command is directed to them for obvious reasons. They are not only bound to keep it themselves, but to see that it be observed by all that are under their charge. They ought to recommend by their example too all that they command by authority; and they are prone ofttimes to hinder them, by employing their servants on the Sabbath to promote their own ends. Now, governors of families should employ their families in serving the Lord upon that day in such duties as these, *viz., family worship*, which is a reasonable acknowledgment of dependence upon God, and of gratitude unto him. As families are bound to forbear all manner of servile work on the Sabbath-day; so also to keep it holy in *a family capacity*, which, without all doubt, implies the worshipping of God upon it, by singing his praise, by reading his word, and by calling on him in prayer. *Family catechizing and instruction* is another branch of domestic duty on the Lord's day. Then should children be trained up in the way they should go (Prov. 22:6), and educated in the nurture and admonition of the Lord (Eph. 6:4). The master of the family should be in a particular manner earnest on this holy day to command his children and his household after him to keep the way of the Lord (Gen. 18:19). *Godly conference* is

also a proper part of family religion on the Lord's day. Our speech should then be with grace, and our lips like those of the righteous that feed many. These that fear the Lord will speak often one to another; and their conferences are approved of God, and crowned with his blessing; for he hearkens and hears it, and a book of remembrance is written before him for them that fear the Lord, and that think upon his name (Mal. 3:16). In a word, every duty of domestic religion should be attended to with great zeal and diligence on the Lord's day, which is set apart on purpose for immediate converse and communion with God.

3. The duties of *personal godliness* should employ their own part of this day which is dedicated to holy rest, and to the worship of God: *Secret prayer* addressed to the God of our Lord Jesus Christ. *Reading* of the Scriptures, and of other books, that may enlighten our minds in the knowledge of their precious contents. *Meditation* upon divine subjects. *Self-examination* concerning our state, temper, and practice. *Comparing* what we hear from men with what is delivered in the lively oracles of God; and every other duty whereby we may testify our reverence of God, and wherein we may enjoy communion with him—are proper services in the closet upon this holy day. So much for the *work* and employment of the Sabbath.

I have already hinted that works of *necessity* and *mercy* are allowed exceptions from the duties that are of a religious nature on the Lord's day. I shall particularly explain my meaning concerning *these*, before I leave this head, because they are much misrepresented, if not misunderstood.

First, Works of necessity that may be done on the Sabbath are such as could not be foreseen or provided against the day *before*, and could not be delayed till the day *after* the Sabbath. Some things are necessary, as they tend to the *support* of nature, as eating and drinking; and other things are necessary, as they are subservient to the worship of God; as going to a place of worship, and attending there, perhaps with some bodily fatigue; while others are no less necessary for providing against such dangers as are otherwise unavoidable; such as flying from enemies, or defending ourselves against them, quenching of fire, and the like.

Secondly, Works of mercy that are lawful on the Sabbath are such as proceed from humanity and compassion both to the souls and bodies of men, and even to the very beasts; as visiting and relieving the sick, supplying the poor, providing food and water for cattle, and many similar cases. Our

Lord vindicates the propriety of doing works of this kind on the Sabbath, "What man shall there be among you, that shall have one sheep, and if it fall into a pit on the sabbath day, will he not lay hold on it, and lift it out? How much then is a man better than a sheep? Wherefore it is lawful to do well on the sabbath days" (Matt. 12:11–12).

However, when we maintain the lawfulness of performing works of necessity and mercy on the Sabbath-day, the following cautions ought to be attended to. (1.) Let the necessity be *real*, not pretended. (2.) If we think that we have a necessary call to omit any duty on the Sabbath-day, let us take heed that this necessity do not arise from some sin we have committed; and if it come in the course of providence, we should rather submit to the impediment than be pleased with it. (3.) If necessity obliges us to engage in secular employments on the Lord's day, as in the instances of those whose business is to provide physic for the sick, let us, nevertheless, labor after a spiritual frame becoming the holiness of the day, so far as may consist with what we are immediately called to do. (4.) As we ought to see that the work we are engaged in is necessary, so we must not spend more time therein than what is needful. And (5.) If we have a necessary call to engage in worldly matters, whereby we are detained from public ordinances, we must endeavor to *satisfy others*, that we are obliged thereunto by the providence of God; that so we may neither give them offense, nor set a temptation before them to follow their own employments, without just reason, which would be a sin unto them against God, and the generation of the righteous. Under these restrictions, we affirm, that *works of necessity and mercy* not only *may*, but *ought* to be done; are not only *allowed*, but *commanded*.[13]

6. Directions for the Sanctification of It

The *directions* relative to the right observation of the Lord's day may be chiefly summed up under these particulars.

1. Guard against the sins that profane the Sabbath, such as vain thoughts, indulged ignorance, earthly-mindedness, forgetfulness of God, aversion to duty, hardness of heart, hypocrisy, formality, wanderings of heart, weariness of duty, prejudice at the preachers of the word, despising the great salvation, allowed drowsiness in time of divine worship, idle

---

[13] Ridgley, *A Body of Divinity*, vol. 2, p. 282.

conversation, gaudiness of apparel, encroachments upon the length of the day, by rising late and going early to bed, doing servile work on it, neglecting secret or family duties, performing them in a superficial manner, and a thousand other sins, that profane the Sabbath. Take heed, lest there be in any of you an evil heart of unbelief, departing from the living God, in any of these cases. These who do not, in such instances, depart from evil, cannot sanctify the Sabbath, because these sins are contrary to the very design of its appointment.

2. Prepare for the approach of the Sabbath. The words of the commandment relative to it are very express on this point: "*Remember* the Sabbath-day" (Ex. 20:8). This is a holy spiritual institution, and therefore ought to be seriously considered before we engage in the services of it. The business of the week should be ordered with such dispatch and prudence, that it may not hinder or disturb us on the Sabbath-day. We should timeously [in good time] leave off work the night before, and go seasonably to rest, that our bodies may be refreshed with sleep, and that we may rise early on the Sabbath-morning, and continue wakeful and lively through the day. It is a criminal encroachment on the duties of this holy day that some are guilty of, while they sit up later and work longer on *Saturday-night*, than any other night in the week, because they intend to lie much longer a-bed on Sabbath-morning; or else go sooner to bed on Sabbath night than any other night, that they may rise sooner on Monday than any other day of the week. Under the law, the later part of the day, that preceded the Sabbath, was called *the preparation for the Sabbath* (Luke 23:54), intimating that it is our duty to prepare on the foregoing day for the Sabbath. Nehemiah, that godly prince, ordered the gates of Jerusalem to be shut, when it began to grow dark before the Sabbath (Neh. 13:19).

Serious meditation is a good means of fixing the heart on the duties of this holy day. The subjects of meditation are various, and in the highest degree important; such as the holiness of God, our dependence on him for life, and for all things that pertain to life and godliness, the obedience and death of Christ, his resurrection from the dead, his ascension to glory, the rest that remains for his people in the presence of God, the ground of our present hope, and our future joy. By such meditations, accompanied with prayer, and dedication of our souls and bodies, of our time and talents unto the service of the Lord, we should prepare to meet our God in the sanctification of his holy day.

3. Study to be *in the Spirit on the Lord's day* (Rev. 1:10). This is a most comprehensive expression, and a noble pattern for our imitation. Perhaps the apostle was favored with an *unusual ecstasy* when he said, "I was in the Spirit on the Lord's day." Leaving what was extraordinary in this manifestation of the glory of the Redeemer, which had such an extraordinary effect on the mind of the beloved disciple, on that particular occasion, I shall only observe, that there is a sense in which it is the common duty and privilege of the saints to be in the Spirit on that holy day. Our thoughts and conversation should then be abstracted from the things of the world, in order to converse with God; our worship should be performed in spirit and in truth, our intentions should be to improve in spiritual mindedness upon the Lord's day; a heavenly temper, arising from the attentive consideration of the dying love of Christ, and of his resurrection from the dead, should prevail in our souls; and we should be filled with the Spirit, and cheerfully engage in the performances of Sabbath duties, with a frame of mind becoming the freedom and spirituality of the New Testament dispensation, which is eminently the ministration of the Spirit (2 Cor. 3:8).

4. Keep in your eye the great *ends* of the Sabbath, which have been mentioned in *the third section*. Wrong ends in religious duties entirely mar and pervert the very nature of them. The form of godliness is the same in a *formalist* and in a *real Christian*, but the principles and ends of these two characters constitute an essential difference between them. The legal self-righteous Pharisee, who sought to establish his own righteousness, kept many of the commandments of that very law, in the letter of it, which the people of God desire to observe with their whole heart, but their ends and motives are essentially different. This being the case in general, we should take heed to our ends in every religious duty. In sanctifying the Lord's day, we should aim at the honor of God, and comfortable fellowship with him through Christ, in the several duties of religious worship that are instituted thereupon to record his name, and to enjoy the comforts of his favor and presence.

5. Delight in the Lord's day as a high privilege bestowed upon you. Make it the matter of your holy joy. Give thanks to God your Creator, who has not suffered you to spend all your time in the drudgeries of this world, but has appointed one day in seven for your release from the business of earth, and for your employment in the work of heaven. Give thanks to Jesus your Redeemer, who on this day finished the work of your redemp-

tion, and arose from the dead; and as those which are risen with Christ, set your affections on things that are above, where he is at the right hand of God. Do not say with the carnal Jews, concerning the duties of divine worship on the Sabbath, "what a weariness is it!" (Mal. 1:13), "When will the…sabbath be gone, that we may set forth wheat…[and] sell corn?" (Amos 8:5). Do not so much inquire what earthly business you may do on this day without sin, as what you can omit, and be excused from doing till tomorrow. "Call the Sabbath…the holy of the LORD, honourable" (Isa. 58:13).

6. Take care you do not lose, amidst the *labors* or the *pleasures* of the following week, any of the spiritual advantages and improvements you have made on the Lord's day. "Look to yourselves, that we lose not those things which we have wrought" (2 John 8), that is, that ministers may not lose their labors in preaching, nor the people lose theirs in hearing. Treasure up something on every Christian Sabbath that may add to your spiritual riches, to your knowledge, your faith, your love, your zeal, your hope. It is a day appointed for the enriching of your souls; let not the cares of the world rob you of those divine treasures. You are employed about heavenly truths on that day, and see that you be not drawn back again by the allurements, or the toils, of this mortal state. Maintain that favor and relish of divine things, while employed in the business of life, which you had while you were attending upon the ordinances of the sanctuary. Thus you will be holy even in managing your earthly affairs, and you will walk with God in them all.

7. I would add, in the last place, that every Lord's day should lead our meditations, our faith, hope, and desire, onward to the eternal rest in heaven, and the glorious worship of that world. Amidst all the cares and fatigues of this life, amidst all the interruptions you feel in your devotions here, and the inroads that are made upon your religious employments and joys, even on God's own day, yet still rejoice in the view and hope of that state where you shall find everlasting rest, a Sabbath which never ends, and be forever employed in divine exercises, without the weariness or infirmities of flesh or spirit. Alas, how soon are our souls tired, and our flesh wearied with spiritual duties! How do our hearts wander on every occasion from God and his worship! But in that state of joyful rest, which remains for the people of God, they shall behold, with a steady fixedness of soul, the great God who created all things in six days, and shall give him

the honor of that creation in an endless Sabbath; there they shall see the blessed Jesus, who rose from the dead on the first Christian Sabbath, and who fulfilled all the righteousness of the law, to redeem them from worse than Egyptian bondage, and laid the foundation of a new creation, even of new heavens and a new earth, wherein dwelleth righteousness. There they shall find complete and perpetual rest from all that is sinful, and from all their sorrows; there too, they shall enjoy a day of glorious and blissful worship, in communion with the holy and happy inhabitants of that world; and it must be an everlasting day, for *there is no night there.*

7. Motives to Engage Our Regard to It

I shall now represent the *motives* that should constrain us to sanctify the Lord's day. These reasons are annexed to the commandment concerning this duty; and they are numerous, but each of them weighty and binding.

1. The first is taken from *the equity* of the institution. God allows us six days of seven for our own affairs, and reserves but one for himself. "Six days shalt thou labour, and do all thy work" (Ex. 20:9). This supposes that we ought to engage in secular callings on other days. To be indulged six days in seven for our own employments is a very large allowance. If he had claimed six days in seven, he must be obeyed, because he is Lord of our time, and may dispose of it as he pleases, but how much more when he says, "Six days shalt thou labour, and do all thy work: but the seventh day is the sabbath" (Ex. 20:9–10)? Let no temptation prevail on any man who calls himself a Christian to break through this merciful institution. Do not begin to say within your hearts that your family obliges you to work on the Sabbath; for man doth not live by bread alone, but by every word that proceedeth out of the mouth of God. Do not make any merchandise [commerce] on the Sabbath, because it is gainful; for what is gotten in the way of presumptuous rebellion against God is not like to prosper. Unjust gain is an abomination in the sight of the Most High, and his curse is in their store.

2. Another reason is taken from *God's challenging a special propriety in the Sabbath-day.* Thus it is called "the sabbath of the LORD thy God" (Ex. 20:10). He has consecrated or separated this day to himself, and so claims a particular right to it, as *his own day.* Therefore it is no less than sacrilege, or a robbing of God, to employ it otherwise than he has commanded. A servant's time is his master's property, who is entitled to the

disposal of it in a lawful manner, during the daily period of labor; and the Lord's day should be held sacred, and devoted wholly to the honor and service of his glorious and fearful name who is *the Lord our God*.

3. God sets *his own example* before us, to bind us to our duty by imitating so noble a pattern. Thus it is said, "in six days the LORD made heaven and earth, the sea, and all that in them is, and rested the seventh day" (Ex. 20:11). Though *six days* were employed in creating the world, the Almighty God could have made all things with the same degree of beauty and perfection they have ever appeared in, *at one instant*; but he performed this work by degrees, to teach us that whatever our hand finds to do, we should do it in the proper season allotted for it; and as he ceased from his work on the seventh day, he requires us to rest from ours, in conformity to his own example.

4. The last reason assigned in the fourth commandment, for our sanctifying the Sabbath, is taken from God's having "blessed the sabbath day, and hallowed it" (Ex. 20:11). *To bless a day* is to give it to us as a particular blessing and privilege; accordingly we ought to reckon the Sabbath a great instance of God's care and compassion to men, and a very great privilege, which should be highly esteemed of them. God sanctifies a day, when he sets it apart from a common to a special use; and thus we ought to reckon the Sabbath as a day signalized above all others, with the character of *God's holy day*; and as such, it should be employed in holy duties, answerable to the end of its institution; and thereupon we should worship him in the beauties of holiness, in the humble expectation of his gracious blessing that maketh rich.[14]

---

[14] I beg leave to transcribe a passage from Dr. Owen *on the Sabbath*, that must be agreeable to every serious reader. It runs in these words: "Let men, in whose hearts are the ways of God, seriously consider the use that hath been made, under the blessing of God, of the *conscientious observation of the Lord's day*, in the past and present age, unto the promotion of holiness, righteousness, and religion, universally in the power of it; and if they are not under invincible prejudices, it will be very difficult for them to judge, that it is a plant which our heavenly Father hath not planted. For my part, I must not only say, but plead, whilst I live in this world, and leave this testimony to the *present and future ages*, if these papers see the light, and do survive, that if I have ever seen anything in the ways and worship of God, wherein the power of religion or godliness hath been expressed; anything that hath represented the holiness of the gospel, and the author of it; anything that hath looked like a *praeludium* [an introduction] unto the everlasting Sabbath and rest with God, which we aim through grace to come unto, it hath been

Since we are under so many obligations to sanctify the Sabbaths of the Lord our God, let us not be so presumptuous as to break the divine law, to rob God of his own day, to bid defiance to his example, and to despise his blessing. The angel said to the women that went to the sepulcher, "Come, see the place where the Lord lay" (Matt. 28:6). May it not be said to Christians, Come, observe the day upon which he rose from that place? O! that our hearts might reply, "This is the day which the Lord hath made; we will rejoice and be glad in it" (Ps. 118:24). One such day is better than a thousand.

To sanctify the Sabbath is a blessed means of great advantage to ourselves; as indeed, "These that seek the Lord shall not want any good thing." But the happiness that accompanies and follows *the conscientious observation of this day* is distinguished with peculiar expressions of eminence and grandeur. The two following passages, among many others, that are no less clear and emphatic, will sufficiently demonstrate the great benefit of this duty.

> Thus saith the Lord, Keep ye judgment, and do justice: for my salvation is near to come, and my righteousness to be revealed. Blessed is the man that doeth this, and the son of man that layeth hold on it; that keepeth the sabbath from polluting it, and keepeth his hand from doing any evil. Neither let the son of the stranger, that hath joined himself to the Lord, speak, saying, The Lord hath utterly separated me from his people: neither let the eunuch say, Behold, I am a dry tree. For thus saith the Lord unto the eunuchs that keep my sabbaths, and choose the things that please me, and take hold of my covenant; even unto them will I give in mine house and within my walls a place and a name better than of sons and of daughters:

---

there, and with them, where, and among whom, *the Lord's day* hath been had in highest esteem, and a strict observation of it attended to, as an ordinance of our Lord Jesus Christ. The remembrance of their ministry, their walking and conversation, their faith and love, who in this nation have most zealously pleaded for, and have been in their persons, families, and churches, or parishes, the most strict observers of *this day*, will be precious with them that fear the Lord, whilst the sun and moon endure. Their doctrine also in this matter, with the blessing that attended it, was that which multitudes, now at rest, do bless God for; and many which are yet alive do greatly rejoice in. Let these things be despised by those who are otherwise minded, *to me* they are of great weight and importance." Owen, *A Treatise on the Sabbath*, pp. 397, 398.

I will give them an everlasting name, that shall not be cut off. Also the sons of the stranger, that join themselves to the Lord, to serve him, and to love the name of the Lord, to be his servants, every one that keepeth the sabbath from polluting it, and taketh hold of my covenant; even them will I bring to my holy mountain, and make them joyful in my house of prayer: their burnt offerings and their sacrifices shall be accepted upon mine altar; for mine house shall be called an house of prayer for all people (Isa. 56:1–7).

If thou turn away thy foot from the sabbath, from doing thy pleasure on my holy day; and call the sabbath a delight, the holy of the Lord, honourable; and shalt honour him, not doing thine own ways, nor finding thine own pleasure, nor speaking thine own words: then shalt thou delight thyself in the Lord; and I will cause thee to ride upon the high places of the earth, and feed thee with the heritage of Jacob thy father: for the mouth of the Lord hath spoken it (Isa. 58:13–14).

Chapter 11
The Observation of Times of Thanksgiving

The Sabbath is a *stated season* for holy rest, and for religious duties. The first day of every returning week should be set apart for the holy purposes of its institution. But besides that *fixed* appointment concerning the periodical revolution of a day that is sacred to religious duties, there are particular providences, and particular occasions and circumstances, that demand particular attention, and loudly call upon us to be employed in *extraordinary services* of *joy*, or of *humiliation*. I shall begin with the extraordinary duties of *joy* and *gratitude*, which are the proper employment of Christians on *times of thanksgiving*. Upon this subject, I shall attempt to do five things.

1. To explain the nature of religious thanksgiving, as it is an extraordinary service.
2. To show the reasonableness thereof.
3. To represent the ends of it.
4. To answer a few questions relative to it. And,
5. To offer some directions about the manner of performing it.

1. The Nature of the Duty

The first head is, to explain the *nature* of religious thanksgiving, as it is an *extraordinary service*; I say, *as it is an extraordinary service*, to distinguish it from the *daily* thanksgivings of the saints, who ought in everything by prayer and supplication, *with thanksgiving*, to make their requests known unto God (Phil. 4:6). In everything we should give thanks, for this is the will of God, and a reasonable acknowledgment of his undeserved goodness. But there are some *special occasions* that call for particular expressions of gratitude and thankfulness. Concerning such occasions, I would make these few remarks.

1. The foundation of this duty is laid in the sovereign goodness of God, who doth good to all. The mercies he confers are the ground of the praises

he expects and demands. Therefore, while sun and moon endure, all nations shall have reason to call him blessed; his works shall praise him, and his saints shall bless him. The obligation to this duty will continue as long as he exerciseth patience, and loads men with his mercies, either of a *common*, or of a *special* kind. Yet,

2. The seasons of *extraordinary* thankfulness are only *occasional*. They are not determinable by the revolution of the sun. The providence of God appearing for us, to work our deliverance from distress or danger, and to open a pleasant prospect of future comfort and happiness, in circumstances that clearly show his hand in the dispensation, points out the *time* and the *matter* of our extraordinary service. The particulars of this kind are so many that I cannot pretend to make any satisfying account of them: Every creature of God, for the nourishment of our bodies, is good, and nothing to be refused, if it be received with thanksgiving (1 Tim. 4:4). It is of the Lord's mercies we are not consumed (Lam. 3:22). We are less than the least of his mercies (Gen. 32:10). When the Lord hears the voice of our supplication, we should take the cup of salvation, and call upon his name (Ps. 116:1, 13). Singular manifestations of divine favor call for extraordinary expressions of humble gratitude (2 Sam. 7; Ps. 103).

The savory words of Mr. McEwen are pertinent to this purpose:

> The thankful Christian in every condition, writes himself *a debtor to the Almighty.* Him he regards as his principal benefactor; him, as the fountain of his life, and joy, and comfort; the creatures as the conduits through which they are conveyed. If he is refreshed by the kindly visits of an agreeable friend; it is God who comforts him: for he sees his face as the face of God. If, by prudent counsel, he is prevented from carrying any unworthy projects into execution; such is the language of his heart, "Blessed be the Lord God of Israel, which sent thee this day to meet me; and blessed be thou; and blessed be thy advice, which kept me back." If the gifts of ministers have been edifying and refreshing to his soul; he adores him who put the treasure into these earthen vessels: Solomon must have a thousand; the keeper of the vineyard but two hundred. He does not bury the former loving-kindnesses of the Lord in the grave of a bad memory, as though the oldness of their date canceled his obligations; but every renewed mercy he regards as a new indenture, and

says, "Bless the Lord, O my soul, and forget not all his benefits." Is he in prosperity? he rejoices; for it is God who comforts him. Is he in adversity? he rejoices; for it is God who corrects him. Afflictions he considers as blessings in disguise; as mercies, which God vouchsafes him, even against his will. Is he punished for his sins? he is thankful; for God punishes less than his iniquities deserve. Is he chastened? he is thankful; for it is that he may not be condemned with the world. Is he persecuted for righteousness sake? he is thankful; for it is given him in the behalf of Christ, not only to believe in his name, but also to suffer for his sake. To enhance divine favor the more, he sets a peculiar mark on the endearing circumstances that attend them. Such a mercy was bestowed, when I was going on frowardly in the way of my own heart; and might rather have expected tribulation and anguish. Such a blessing was conferred when I was reduced to the greatest extremity, and in the utmost article of danger. For *this* I solicited the throne of grace, and he heard me out of his holy temple. With *that* he prevented my supplication; and before I called, he did answer. Such are the sentiments wherewith his heart is only touched, for all those good and perfect gifts that come down from above. But chiefly for spiritual blessings in Christ Jesus; for thine unspeakable gift, O God! and for that mercy which is from everlasting to everlasting.[1]

That agreeable writer is, indeed, only considering the general temper of a thankful Christian, and the ordinary expressions of his heartfelt gratitude; but when the degrees or circumstances of ordinary mercies are *unusual*, the mercies become *extraordinary*; and, that our thankfulness may be proportioned to our mercies, it must *on such occasions* be *extraordinary* too.

3. A prudent regard to the nature, season, and other circumstances of God's mercies should determine the manner, place, length, and other external circumstances of our service, in regard to occasional and extraordinary thanksgiving. These are not indifferent things in any religious duty; and it is the business of a prudent man to choose them with judgment, and to improve them with diligence, both in order to his own profiting

---

[1] William McEwen. *A Select Set of Essays, Doctrinal and Practical*, vol. 2, pp. 149–153.

the more in the ways of God, and in order to his setting them in the more advantageous light before the world. Unexpected mercies require immediate and eminent acknowledgments. Mercies that flow in daily upon us should be daily acknowledged. Public mercies ought to be followed with public praise. Personal or family mercies should be matter of personal or family thankfulness. The circumstances of our mercies should be a directory and obligation to corresponding circumstances in the expressions of our unfeigned gratitude. The *time* may be lengthened, or shortened, according to the occasion and case. It would be highly improper to enlarge in giving thanks for the refreshments of our bodies every time we eat or drink, in the same manner, as when we show the Lord's death. The same fervor and seriousness should prevail in our minds upon both occasions; but a prudent man will consider these exercises in a very different light in other respects.

4. In occasional thanksgiving we may consider *the mercies* for which we give thanks; the *impression* made by these mercies on our minds; and the *external acknowledgment* of the divine favor in these bestowments. These things are distinct in their nature, and yet must all cooperate in this solemn service. When God's mercies duly impress the mind, they produce "the sacrifice of praise to God continually, that is, the fruit of our lips, giving thanks to his name" (Heb. 13:15). Unless the words of our lips proceed from the convictions of our conscience, they must be detestable in the sight of the all-seeing, holy, and jealous God.

5. This duty may be considered, either as it is *personal*; thus David went in and continued before the Lord, while he poured out his soul in pious gratitude (2 Sam. 7); or, as it respects *a family*, who may, and should, like the prodigal's family, rejoice before the Lord on particular occasions (Luke 15); or, as it refers to *a society* of the people of God, who may be glad *together* in his fear, like Daniel and his fellows (Dan. 2); or, as it concerns *the church* at large; and so in the midst of the congregation of assembled elders we should show forth his praise (Ps. 22). But in whatever light it be viewed, the substance of the duty is the same; accidental circumstances can have no material effect upon that.

2. Showing the Reasonableness Thereof

I shall now attempt to demonstrate *the reasonableness* of observing *times of religious and solemn thanksgiving*. I shall briefly mention the following heads of argument, and recommend them to the reader's consideration.

1. The *instinct* of every creature leads it to such expressions of gratitude to its benefactors as render ungrateful men altogether inexcusable, and show them to be extremely wicked; for the ox knoweth his owner, and the ass his master's crib, and both are obsequious in their way to their masters; and particular indulgences even to the brutes make evident impressions on them. Shall not Israel then know; shall not God's people consider? Shall the beasts of the field be unsuccessful teachers of mankind now, and swift witnesses against them at last? May God, who hath endued us with more understanding, prevent it!

2. This is the *command* of God, who has made it our duty to *be thankful* (Col. 3:15), and to *offer unto God thanksgiving* (Ps. 50:14; Heb. 13:15); and the practice of the saints shows that this law, this way of God, is in their hearts.

3. One great design of God, in conferring his favor upon us, is that we may give thanks unto his holy name, and triumph in his praise, as it is nobly expressed (Ps. 106:47). We should not frustrate[2] the grace of God.

4. Unless we are thankful for the blessings we receive, we provoke God either to withdraw them, or to curse us in the continued enjoyment of them.

> For she did not know [that is, did not acknowledge] that I gave her corn, and wine, and oil, and multiplied her silver and gold...Therefore will I return, and take away my corn in the time thereof, and my wine in the season thereof, and will recover my wool and my flax (Hos. 2:8–9).

---

[2] The expression referred to is found in "I do not *frustrate* the grace of God" (Gal. 2:21). These words do not imply that the purposes of divine grace may be defeated, or that the operations of the Spirit of grace may be resisted: for *his counsel shall stand, and he will do all his pleasure*. But men frustrate the grace of God, when they either *reject the gospel of the grace of God* which bringeth salvation, or *do not bring forth fruits* in their conversation, that become its sublime privileges and obligations. I suppose the *last sense* is most agreeable to the apostle's scope; and it is in this sense I use the phrase.

The earth which drinketh in the rain that cometh oft upon it, and bringeth forth herbs meet for them by whom it is dressed, receiveth blessing from God: but that which beareth thorns and briers is rejected, and is nigh unto cursing; whose end is to be burned (Heb. 6:7–8).

5. This is a duty that eminently ascribes unto God the glory due unto his name. The ten lepers "lifted up their voices, and said, Jesus, Master, have mercy on us" (Luke 17:13), but only one of the ten, who were all cured, is said to *glorify God* (v. 15), and this is explained in the next verse by *giving him thanks*.

Perhaps it will be alleged that these arguments only show the propriety of gratitude, as a general temper, that is highly becoming and ornamental in daily life. And suffer me to say that every proof of this point goes far to establish my position; for if daily mercies oblige us to daily gratitude, then extraordinary appearances of divine favor bind us to express our gratitude in an extraordinary manner. The manner and occasions of our giving God thanks, should be proportioned to the manner and circumstances of receiving our comforts. And where the *special calls* of providence are not attended to with particular and solemn attention, there is reason to fear, that the ordinary calls of it will in time be despised and forgot. "To every thing there is a season, and a time to every purpose under the heaven" (Eccl. 3:1), "and a wise man's heart discerneth both time and judgment" (Eccl. 8:5).

3. Representing the Ends of It

The third branch of my method is to represent *the ends* for which we should observe *extraordinary times* of religious thanksgiving. Here it is proper to observe that men take their aim vastly too low, when they intend by this service to acquit themselves of all obligations for the mercies they have received; and accordingly say, at the close of it, "This day I have performed my vows." A just view of divine favor would represent them in such a light as far exceeds our most affectionate expressions of gratitude and praise. If we are less than all God's mercies, then surely our praises cannot be at all profitable to him. But in giving thanks, our end should be,

1. *To glorify God*: "Whoso offereth praise glorifieth me" (Ps. 50:23). He is worthy to receive the highest, the warmest expressions of *honor, and*

glory, and blessing; and is infinitely exalted above all the blessing and praise of the most glorious and excellent of his creatures. Glorious and happy in himself, he should be acknowledged as the Author of being and happiness to all his creatures. In recording his benefits, we should give him the praise of his power and mercy, of his patience and veracity, and of his condescension and liberality. It is the height of impiety to suppose that we can add anything to his honor or blessedness; but it is extremely unkind and unreasonable to forbear due acknowledgments of both, especially when his bounty challenges our observation and admiration of both. This tribute is due to his name, and we hereby only acknowledge an obligation that we can never dissolve. That is a sublime expression which we find in Psalm 150:2, "Praise him for his mighty acts: praise him according to his excellent greatness." Not that our praises can bear any proportion to God's greatness, for it is infinite; but because he is greater than we can conceive or express, we must raise our conceptions and expressions to the highest; and when we have done our utmost, we must own that though we have praised him *in consideration of his excellent greatness,* yet not *in proportion to it.*

2. *For our own good,* which is promoted by this means in several respects, for: hereby our minds come to be more deeply affected with divine blessings, which make a more lasting impression when they are commemorated in a way of solemn grateful praise. Examples of this are to be found in many places of holy writ, especially in the book of Psalms. Hereby our obedience becomes more liberal and generous. While we remember the Lord's loving-kindness, and the acts of his mercy, the soul is constrained to say, "What shall I render to the Lord for all his benefits?" Hereby we will be more effectually fortified against dejection, as David was,

> Why art thou cast down, O my soul? and why art thou disquieted in me? hope thou in God: for I shall yet praise him for the help of his countenance. O my God, my soul is cast down within me: [*N.B.*] therefore will I remember thee from the land of Jordan, and of the Hermonites, from the hill Mizar (Ps. 42:5–6).

And hereby we will be more confirmed in the hope of eternal life, which God that cannot lie promised before the world began; because the mercies we have received will not only appear valuable *for themselves,* in the reckoning of a thankful Christian, but chiefly because they are *a door of hope* concerning future enjoyments: "Who delivered us from so great a death, and doth deliver: in whom we trust that he will yet deliver us" (2 Cor. 1:10).

> Notwithstanding the Lord stood with me, and strengthened me; that by me the preaching might be fully known, and that all the Gentiles might hear: and I was delivered out of the mouth of the lion. And the Lord shall deliver me from every evil work, and will preserve me unto his heavenly kingdom: to whom be glory for ever and ever. Amen (2 Tim. 4:17–18).

> Therefore, behold, I will allure her, and bring her into the wilderness, and speak comfortably unto her. And I will give her her vineyards from thence, and the valley of Achor for a door of hope: and she shall sing there, as in the days of her youth, and as in the day when she came up out of the land of Egypt (Hos. 2:14–15).

3. *For the credit of religion*, which is honored by the thankfulness of its professors. One of the capital objections which has been made against religion in all ages, namely, that they are full of gloom and melancholy, is prevented, when Christians abound in thanksgiving. By this means the ways of wisdom are manifested to be what they really are, ways of pleasantness, and paths of peace (Prov. 3:17). It is our duty to adorn the doctrine of Christ in all things (Titus 2:10). To aim at this glorious end, is worthy of such as are begotten with the word of truth, and made a kind of first-fruits unto God. This is "a good work that is truly profitable unto men."

4. Answering Some Questions Relative to It

The next head on this subject was to answer a few *questions* relative to it. The following seem to be most important.

Question 1. Is there a *clear warrant* for observing times of solemn religious thanksgiving, under the New Testament dispensation?

Answer. There is no ground of suspicion about such observances under the Old Testament. The fact is clear beyond exception. All the Jewish feasts are so many examples of it. Since the resurrection of Christ, the obligation of ceremonial appointments is happily superseded. But as the foundation of solemn duties of gratitude on special occasions is laid in the moral law, it is impossible that the duty itself can be set aside, though particular circumstances that are suited to particular conditions may be changed. Upon these principles we maintain that the warrant for this duty is as clear and firm now as ever it was; and when the duties of fasting, praying, and all others that belong to our present imperfect state shall cease, the work of thanksgiving will remain, and will be the everlasting employment of the saints.

Question 2. To whom does it belong to appoint the times of religious thanksgiving?

Answer. As the solemn services of such times are merely *occasional*, and are *regulated by the occurrences of providence*, the *determining* of the precise day, hour, or place, for the performance of them, is but a circumstance. The *authority and obligation* of the duty are *of God*, and not *of men*. "Also that day they offered great sacrifices, and rejoiced: for *God had made them rejoice with great joy*" (Neh. 12:43). But it will not admit of any dispute, whether *every man* has, or has not, a right to point out the precise time for this service. None but such as are *vested with authority* can, with any propriety or success, determine this. And therefore (1.) Every *individual* has a right to judge *for himself*, and ought to judge accordingly, in choosing such a time, and so much time, as will not encroach upon the duties he owes to God and man, to express his thankfulness for divine benefits. (2.) Every *master of a family* has a right, for the same reason, to command his children, and his household after him, to keep the way of the Lord, in solemn thanksgiving for family comforts. (3.) The *rulers in every particular congregation*, upon the same principle, ought to set apart a proper time, when there is occasion, for peculiar expressions of gratitude for special mercies, that more immediately respect that congregation. (4.) These that have the *rule over the churches* have a right, upon the same account, to call them to general and public thanksgiving, for such blessings as are of general concern to the body of Christ. (5.) It seems evidently to be the province of *civil rulers* to call their subjects to express their joy before the Lord for *national mercies*. None but they have authority to command or enforce a duty of such universal concern. The church can only judge them that are within her communion; and therefore her authority cannot reach as wide as the influence of a general blessing, and consequently cannot be adequate to the occasion of extraordinary gratitude, which the ways of providence demand from a nation or people as such. The only objection this reasoning is liable to arises from a supposition that the duty of religious solemn thanksgiving is to be performed *only* by the people of God. It is granted that only the saints can bless God; but it is no less evident that *men, as such*, ought to be called to praise the Lord for his wonderful works (see Ps. 107; Acts 17:22–31).

Question 3. Is *feasting* proper or suitable on a thanksgiving-day?

Answer. In all ages, feasting and convivial mirth have generally accompanied warm expressions of joy. Even the seasons of extraordinary gladness appointed to the Jews are called *the feasts of the Lord* (Lev. 23:2). And a cheerful moderate use of the comforts of life seems to be agreeable enough to the nature and design of such observances. We are not left to walk at random, and without rule, however, in this case. Our directory is recorded, "be not drunk with wine, wherein is excess; but be filled with the Spirit; speaking to yourselves in psalms and hymns and spiritual songs, singing and making melody in your heart to the Lord; giving thanks always for all things unto God and the Father in the name of our Lord Jesus Christ" (Eph. 5:18–20).

Question 4. Is it warrantable to keep *periodical seasons* of extraordinary thanksgiving, suppose *weekly*, or *monthly*, or *yearly?*

Answer. Extraordinary events are but occasional in their nature, and therefore it is improper to commemorate them on stated periodical revolutions. Such *stated festivals* would have too much the appearance of being moral unalterable institutions; and besides, it is not competent for men to set apart their time for any purpose they please. Unless when Providence clearly points out the necessity of observing a day to the Lord, we are as much bound by the divine law to do the business of life on the six common days of the week as to keep a seventh day holy. At the same time, I think that any extraordinary mercy that has delivered us from some dreadful calamity, and that has secured *a continued succession of blessings*, may be properly enough remembered *annually* with extraordinary praise; especially, if we be threatened with the *same alarming calamity* from which we were beyond expectation delivered. Perhaps the Jewish feast of *Purim*, and of the *dedication*, may be accounted for upon this principle (Est. 9:26–32; John 10:22). And for the same reason, many worthy persons have thought it their duty to commemorate the deliverance from the gunpowder plot, the glorious revolution in Britain 1688, and the happy accession of the illustrious Brunswick family to the British throne, in days of *anniversary* gratitude. But in this view, they are only occasional duties, and are designed to be observed only as long as particular circumstances render the observation of them expedient; and to be laid aside, when these circumstances are altered.

Question 5. What is the best way to judge of *the frequency* of those solemn services of thanksgiving to the Most High?

Answer. The best rule is *to observe the ways of divine providence towards us*; and whatever is new and various in its merciful course ought to be suitably acknowledged in the exercise of praise. Thus new refreshments of the body with food, drink, or sleep; new opportunities of attending divine ordinances; new accessions to former possessions; new deliverances from imminent dangers; or new manifestations of divine favor—are a call to *new expressions* of particular gratitude. The case is precisely the same, whether these or the like things respect a person, a family, a society, a congregation, a country, or nation, only allowing for circumstances that must necessarily differ. Perhaps some will be ready to imagine that there is nothing extraordinary in giving thanks for our food, and rest, and success in labor or business. But this, I fear, proceeds from their inattention to the importance of these mercies, or from their formality in the duty. *These* are only occasional and extraordinary services. It would be our sin to omit them; and it would become our sin to employ the whole of our time in them.[3]

5. Directions concerning Its Performance

The *directions* I would offer concerning the observation of times of religious thanksgiving are these.

1. Everything *inconsistent* with the nature and design of the service must be laid aside, and guarded against; such as (1.) An opinion that there is an

---

[3] Many people err greatly in their notions about *the solemnity* of the ordinances of God. Nothing is solemn with some but what is *long*; and nothing is solemn with others but what is *seldom*. Both do err, not knowing, nor considering the Scriptures. *The solemnity of any ordinance lies only in our worshipping God therein, according to his own appointment, in spirit and in truth, in that season, manner, and length of the service, which best agree with the nature of the duty.* And therefore, if we speak with the Scriptures, there should be *as much solemnity* in one duty as in another. I do not mean that every duty should be of equal length, and performed with the same circumstances; or that every duty is of the same importance in itself, or in its consequences; but what I affirm is that every religious duty has *no other solemnity* than what arises from its being *agreeable to divine institution*. And as the whole of the law is briefly summed up in *love*, so the scriptural solemnity of every ordinance consists in its *conformity to revealed truth* (Matt. 28:20; John 15:10, 14).

intrinsic holiness in some days or times above others, which is a fond notion of some ignorant, though perhaps well-meaning people. Hence they give a guilty preference to one season of the year, or to one day of the week, before the rest, for the work of extraordinary thanksgiving. It is certainly right to choose the most convenient times for it, and if a man's engagements in life shut him up to one day in a week, he ought to employ that day in that exercise; but not because it is such or such a day of the week, rather, because it is a season when he can wait upon the Lord with the least outward distraction. (2.) All *carnal mirth* that tends to dissipation, and carnal joy, is improper while we are employed in the duty of thanksgiving. We should rejoice before God, who is a Spirit, in such worship as becomes his perfections and will; and therefore should worship him in spirit and in truth. "I will sing with the spirit, and I will sing with the understanding also" (1 Cor. 14:15). (3.) *Formality* should not be indulged in this duty; for it is not the setting of so much time apart, or the performance of such a course of duties, that constitute the nature of religious thanksgiving. Our heart, and all its powers, must be stirred up with unfeigned ardor in blessing the Lord our God (Ps. 103:1–2). (4.) We would not consider occasional thanksgiving as a sufficient acknowledgment of divine mercies; but should order our conversation aright, as becometh the gospel of Christ, and the bounties of Providence (Ps. 50:23; Phil. 1:27). Far less should we imagine that our acknowledgments are any recompense for our blessings; for hereby we only confess obligations that can never be canceled. And (5.) Such times should neither be observed, in obedience to the authority of men, nor in compliance with custom; but only in obedience to God, and with a single regard to his glory, "One man esteemeth one day above another: another esteemeth every day alike. Let every man be fully persuaded in his own mind. He that regardeth the day, regardeth it unto the Lord; and he that regardeth not the day, to the Lord he doth not regard it" (Rom. 14:5–6).[4]

---

[4] I do not suppose the apostle is there treating directly of either *religious fasts* or *thanksgivings*, far less of *the Lord's day*. I apprehend he is only speaking of "Jewish festivals, so far forth as they were of a ceremonial and typical nature, but *N. B.* were still thought to be obligatory, by many of the believing Jews, while the Gentile Christians took them to be abolished." See Guyse, *Paraphrase*, note on the place. But *the light* in which he represents these believing Jews who observed such ceremonial days, and those believing Gentiles who did not observe them, is *moral*; and teaches us, that obedience to the authority, and concern for the glory of God, should guide our consciences, and direct our views in the observation of such times as we set apart for his worship.

2. We should take heed to the *manner* of performing this duty. Thanksgiving is a good work; but the *right performance* of the duty is necessary, that God may be honored by it. I shall only mention the following particulars on this direction. (1.) We must praise God *with our whole heart*, like Mary, who said, "My soul doth magnify the Lord, and my spirit hath rejoiced in God my Saviour" (Luke 1:46–47). All the powers of our souls should unite in this holy joy before the Lord; which will be the case, whenever the ways of God's kind and merciful providences, whether they respect temporal or spiritual blessings, as the immediate ground of our gratitude, are in our heart. An heartfelt sense of divine bounty is an essential branch of the duty; and without it, every profession profiteth little. (2.) We should bless God with *ardent zeal*. We have a striking example of this recorded in the solemn thanksgiving of Deborah and Barak, on the day that God delivered the Canaanites that had mightily oppressed Israel for twenty years, into their hand; "Awake, awake, Deborah: awake, awake, utter a song: arise, Barak, and lead thy captivity captive, thou son of Abinoam" (Judg. 5:12). The expressions are repeated, to signify the greatest vehemence and warmth of vigorous affection and delight in the work of giving thanks to the Most High. (3.) We should bless the Lord *with cheerfulness*. At best, our gratitude must fall far short of the value of his good and precious gifts. There is no expression more commonly made use of to describe this exercise than that of *rejoicing*; because gladness and cheerfulness are essential to the right performance of it. (4.) We should give thanks *in the name of Christ*; for this is the will of God, "Giving thanks always for all things unto God and the Father in the name of our Lord Jesus Christ" (Eph. 5:20), "do all in the name of the Lord Jesus, giving thanks to God and the Father by him" (Col. 3:17). In his name every knee must bow, to give thanks, as well as to pray; for he is that golden altar which sanctifieth all our services. He is the head of that covenant, in which all saving blessings flow to us, and in which a kind provision is made both for the performance, and for the acceptance, of such duties as are well-pleasing to God. (5.) We should rejoice before God *with holy reverence, and godly fear*, while we give him thanks. Levity of mind or behavior is most unbecoming on such solemn occasions. Our God is a consuming fire, and therefore we should join trembling with our mirth (Heb. 12:28–29; Ps. 2:11). (6.) This, as well as every other piece of worship, should be performed *in the beauty of holiness*. "Praise is comely for the upright" (Ps. 33:1). It waits for

the Lord in Zion, the mountain of holiness, and best becomes the lips of a holy people, "All thy works shall praise thee, O Lord; and thy saints shall bless thee" (Ps. 145:10). Without this ornament, our thanks must be an abomination to the Lord, as much as the prayer of the wicked. Where the people of God are most improved in holiness, they will always be most enlarged in uttering the memory of his great goodness, and in singing of his righteousness. And (7.) *With due consideration* of the nature and circumstances of God's manifold mercies. Whoso is wise, and will carefully observe and consider the various instances of God's kind and gracious providential conduct, even he shall see and confess the loving-kindness of the Lord (Ps. 107:43). The most careful observers of the works of God are most thankful; because attentive consideration discovers free, abundant, and everlasting mercy, even under common appearances, and in ordinary events (see Ps. 136 throughout). The greatest mercies make no impression on the thoughtless; while the wise in heart enjoy and praise God, in all his ways of providence and grace towards them (Ps. 107 throughout).

3. We should take heed to *our behavior* after we have been engaged in this heavenly and delightful work. That is a remarkable passage to this purpose, which we find in 1 Chronicles 29:10–18:

> Wherefore David blessed the Lord before all the congregation: and David said, Blessed be thou, Lord God of Israel our father, for ever and ever. Thine, O Lord, is the greatness, and the power, and the glory, and the victory, and the majesty: for all that is in the heaven and in the earth is thine; thine is the kingdom, O Lord, and thou art exalted as head above all. Both riches and honour come of thee, and thou reignest over all; and in thine hand is power and might; and in thine hand it is to make great, and to give strength unto all. Now therefore, our God, we thank thee, and praise thy glorious name. But who am I, and what is my people, that we should be able to offer so willingly after this sort? for all things come of thee, and of thine own have we given thee. For we are strangers before thee, and sojourners, as were all our fathers: our days on the earth are as a shadow, and there is none abiding. O Lord our God, all this store that we have prepared to build thee an house for thine holy name cometh of thine hand, and is all thine own. I know also, my God, that thou triest the heart, and hast pleasure in uprightness. As for

me, in the uprightness of mine heart I have willingly offered all these things: and now have I seen with joy thy people, which are present here, to offer willingly unto thee. O Lord God of Abraham, Isaac, and of Israel, our fathers, keep this for ever in the imagination of the thoughts of the heart of thy people, and prepare their heart unto thee.

The remark of Mr. Henry on the 18th verse is this:

For the people David prays, that what good God had put into their minds, he would always keep there, that they might never be worse than they were now; might never lose the convictions they were now under, nor cool in their affections to the house of God; but always have the same thoughts of things they now seemed to have. It is of great consequence to us, what is innermost, and what uppermost in the imagination of the thoughts of our heart; what we aim at, and what we love to think of: if any good have got possession of our hearts, or the hearts of our friends, it is good by prayer to commit the custody of it to the grace of God: Lord, keep it there; keep it there forever.

Another example, to the same purpose, is recorded in Psalm 116:12–19,

What shall I render unto the Lord for all his benefits toward me? I will take the cup of salvation, and call upon the name of the Lord. I will pay my vows unto the Lord now in the presence of all his people. Precious in the sight of the Lord is the death of his saints. O Lord, truly I am thy servant; I am thy servant, and the son of thine handmaid: thou hast loosed my bonds. I will offer to thee the sacrifice of thanksgiving, and will call upon the name of the Lord. I will pay my vows unto the Lord now in the presence of all his people, in the courts of the Lord's house, in the midst of thee, O Jerusalem. Praise ye the Lord.

The psalmist resolves to express his gratitude in a course of humble, exact obedience. The Lord had shown him what was good, and he is determined to walk humbly with him.

The pious resolution of Hezekiah too is on record for our learning. When the Lord had miraculously recovered him from a mortal disease, that was incurable by human means, and had added fifteen years to his life; that *godly prince* remembered with thanksgiving the kindness of God; and, among other warm expressions of gratitude, the following words are truly noble and exemplary, "What shall I say? he hath both spoken unto me, and himself hath done it: *I shall go softly all my years in the bitterness of my soul*" (Isa. 38:15). Let us go and do likewise, in a constant dependence on the grace that is in our Lord Jesus Christ.

Chapter 12
The Observation of Religious Fasts

Fasting is an occasional duty, as well as thanksgiving, only the causes of it are of a different kind. In explaining it, I shall observe this order:
1. To consider the nature of a religious fast;
2. To prove that it is a divine institution;
3. To point out the ends to which this exercise should be directed;
4. To answer some questions relative to it;
5. To give some practical directions concerning the observation thereof; and,
6. To recommend this duty, by proposing some encouragements to the performance of it.

1. The Nature of a Religious Fast Considered

I am, in the first place, to consider *the true nature* of *religious fasting*. The general notion of fasting, as it denotes *an abstinence from food*, is too well understood to need any description. The *causes* of that abstinence constitute the *only difference* between one kind of it and another. The *sick* fast because they loath food; the *poor*, because sometimes they cannot get what their soul desireth; the *glutton*, because he would strengthen his appetite; the *man of business*, because he is not at leisure to take his repast; the *miser*, because he would spare his money; an *afflicted patient*, either to recover his health, or to prevent a disease; and so in other cases. But the *saints*, upon particular occasions, abstain totally from all food (unless bodily weakness do manifestly disable them from holding out till the fast be ended, in which case, somewhat may be taken, yet very sparingly, to support nature, when ready to faint), and also from all worldly labor, discourses, and thoughts, and from all bodily delights, in order to dispose their souls for such spiritual exercises as are suitable to their condition and circumstances. Concerning this kind of fasting, which is of a religious nature, I would observe:

1. That *mere abstinence* from food is not properly in itself *any part* of religious worship, any more than bowing the knee is a part of prayer, or melodious music a part of praise. Bodily fasting is only a *means* of divine appointment, to fit us for spiritual exercises.

2. The *degree* of abstinence from meat and drink, when people fast, ought not to be *equally* bound upon all. *Fasting* is not a *part* of worship, but a *means* to dispose us for extraordinary worshipping; and therefore should be used only so far as it may be an *help* to that end; and it is certain that the measure which would be helpful to some for that end would be hurtful to others. *Total abstinence* might as much indispose some weakly persons for duty as it would assist others of a more confirmed constitution. In every part of religious duty, we should mind that God desires "mercy, and not sacrifice" (Hos. 6:6), where severer regards unto circumstances would hinder people from observing what is essential in any ordinance. Yet in such a case they ought not to indulge the use of meat and drink with the same freedom as at other times; but to abstain *in part*, altering the *quantity* or *quality* of them, or *both*, that they may be thereby *afflicted* (Lev. 23:29), as Daniel did, who, in his mourning, "ate no pleasant bread, neither came flesh nor wine into [his] mouth" (Dan. 10:3).

3. Fasting is a duty that may and should be performed when there is a call to it, either: by *individual persons* in secret, of which we have many examples on record, as of David (2 Sam. 12:16); of Anna (Luke 2:36–37); of Daniel (Dan. 10:2–3); of Cornelius (Acts 10:30); and of several others; and our Lord gives particular directions concerning such fasts (Matt. 6:16–18). Or by *families*, as is plain from Zechariah 12:12–14. Or by *societies*, whether they be *larger* or *smaller*; for there is the same reason for this duty in these societies, that there is in a family; and we find examples of the observation of it accordingly, both under the Old Testament (Ex. 33:4) and under the New (1 Cor. 5:2 compared with 2 Cor. 7:7).

4. Fasting is an *occasional* duty; and therefore unless the occasions for it still continue, and the calls for it recur, it is improper to make it *periodical*, so many times a-year, or on such and such months, weeks, or days. Where there is a present providential call, there can be no doubt about the seasonableness of the duty; but to fix the times of fasting, *on any other principle*, is an egregious perversion of the ordinance.

5. There is no fixed rule to determine the *precise length of time* to be

employed in this duty. The time should be regulated by circumstances, as best suits the persons that are engaged in it.

> We find the saints, in Scripture, ordinarily kept their fasts *by day*: but we have an instance of a personal fast kept *by night*, "David fasted, and went in, and lay *all night* upon the earth" (2 Sam. 12:16). It is recorded to the honor of Anna too, that she served God with fastings and prayers *night and day* (Luke 2:36–37). The fast of Esther with her maidens, observed also by all the Jews in Shushan, lasted *three days* (Est. 4:16). We read of the *fasting-day* (Jer. 36:6). Sometimes, it would seem, it was but a *part of a day* that was spent in such exercise; as in Cornelius his fast, which seems to have been over before the ninth hour, that is, before three o'clock in the afternoon, "Four days ago," says he, "I was fasting *until this hour;* and at the ninth hour I prayed in my house" (Acts 10:30). Much about that time of the day, Daniel got the answer of his prayers, made in his personal fast, namely, about the time of the evening-oblation, or the ninth hour (Dan. 9:21). And the people being assembled with fasting, they read in the book of the law one fourth part of the day, and another fourth part they confessed and worshipped (Neh. 9:1, 3). So they continued in the work six hours; that is, from the time of the morning-sacrifice to the evening-sacrifice, with which the work seems to have been closed. Wherefore none are to be solicitous as to what *quantity of time*, more or less, they spend in these exercises, so that the *work* of the time be done. Men lay a snare for themselves in tying themselves to a *certain quantity* of time in such cases. It is sufficient to resolve, that, according to our abilities, we will take as much time as the work shall be found to require.[1]

6. Bodily fasting is in order to such *spiritual exercises* as the providence of God calls to on a particular occasion. Those employments of the *mind* to which we are called, on occasion of a religious fast, are *meditation, humiliation, confession of sin, repentance, covenanting,* and *extraordinary prayer*. Where these are omitted, the Lord may well say: is this the fast that I have chosen? (Isa. 58:5). They are *essential* to the right observation of a

---

[1] See Thomas Boston. *A Memorial concerning Personal and Family Fasting*.

religious fast; and will naturally fall under our consideration afterwards. I shall therefore proceed,

2. That It Is a Divine Institution Proved

To prove that *fasting on a religious account* is a *divine institution*. The arguments on this head may be drawn from such topics as these.

1. We find it has been *occasionally practiced*, almost in every civilized country. Wherever Christianity is professed, this duty has been practiced. Among the deluded *followers of Muhammad*, it is rigorously enjoined and observed. The *Indian pagans* have several remarkable fasts.[2] When the prophet had intimated the displeasure of God against Nineveh, *the heathen king*, undesired by Jonah, proclaimed a fast (Jonah 3:5–8). Perhaps *religious fasting* and *sacrificing* have spread equally wide in the heathen world; and it is not improbable they have been propagated through the same channel, to wit, an imperfect *tradition* relating to what was *originally* an *ordinance of God*.

2. God has *expressly and frequently commanded* his people to humble themselves before him with fasting and prayer. The Jews were to afflict their souls by fasting on the tenth day of the seventh month, by an ordinance that should remain in force as long as their dispensation lasted (Lev. 23:27 compared with Isa. 58:5). It was made the duty of a sinning people to turn to the Lord "with fasting, and with weeping, and with mourning" (Joel 2:12). And these commands are not abolished by the coming of Christ; for the apostles use the same language, they require the same thing, in substance, that Moses and the prophets did, "Be afflicted, and mourn, and weep" (James 4:9).

3. God has *promised his Spirit* to cause his people to walk in *this*, as well as in *all his other* commandments and ordinances blameless, "I will pour upon the house of David, and upon the inhabitants of Jerusalem, the Spirit of grace and of supplications… And the land shall mourn, every family apart… and their wives apart" (Zech. 12:10, 12). Those that are most filled with the spirit of grace and supplication are most frequent and most earnest in this self-abasing work, which is so far from being inconsistent with the liberty of the gospel state that it is one of the ends of the coming of the blessed Comforter to produce it.

---

[2] Thomas Broughton. *An Historical Dictionary of All Religions*.

4. The *directions* concerning it, both in the Old and New Testament, *suppose* the obligation of the duty; because it is unworthy of God to give any directions concerning *such worship* as he never appointed, and consequently can never accept. Among many directions of this sort, I shall refer to one passage in the writings of the prophets,

> Blow the trumpet in Zion, sanctify a fast, call a solemn assembly: gather the people, sanctify the congregation, assemble the elders, gather the children, and those that suck the breasts: let the bridegroom go forth of his chamber, and the bride out of her closet. Let the priests, the ministers of the LORD, weep between the porch and the altar, and let them say, Spare thy people, O LORD, and give not thine heritage to reproach, that the heathen should rule over them: wherefore should they say among the people, Where is their God? (Joel 2:15–17).

And to another in Matthew 6:16-18, where our Lord gives the following advices concerning the management of this duty:

> When ye fast, be not, as the hypocrites, of a sad countenance: for they disfigure their faces, that they may appear unto men to fast. Verily I say unto you, They have their reward. But thou, when thou fastest, anoint thine head, and wash thy face; that thou appear not unto men to fast, but unto thy Father which is in secret: and thy Father, which seeth in secret, shall reward thee openly.

5. Another argument arises from the *connection of this duty with prayer*, in many places of the New Testament, as "this kind goeth not out but by *fasting and prayer*" (Matt. 17:21). "When they had *fasted and prayed*, and laid their hands on them, they sent them away" (Acts 13:3). "When they...had *prayed with fasting*" (Acts 14:23). "Give yourselves to *fasting and prayer*" (1 Cor. 7:5). Now, since prayer is allowed to be a moral duty, and fasting is so closely joined with it, it seems to arise from the same principle, and to be of the same obligation.

6. We have the prophets, the apostles, and the martyrs of our Lord for *examples*, to direct our practice, and to animate our zeal in this duty.

David was a man after God's own heart, and he was often in religious fasting (2 Sam. 12:16; Ps. 35:13). Daniel was a man greatly beloved of his God, and he fasted frequently (Dan. 9:3; 10:2–3). The centurion was a devout man, and this was one important branch of his devotion (Acts 10:30). Paul was not behind the very chief of the apostles, and he was in fastings often (2 Cor. 11:27). Our blessed Lord has left us an example of this duty too, though many of the causes and ends of our fasting could not affect him (Matt. 4:2). Time would fail me to make up the list of the excellent persons, whose names are recorded with immortal honor, that have considered this duty as an essential part of their religion.

7. The *success* of this work is a strong mark of divine approbation. Shall I refer to the case of Ahab, whose humiliation was temporary and partial, and yet the Lord would not, on account of it, bring the threatened evil in his days, notwithstanding his grievous sins? (1 Kings 21); or, the success of Esther's fast? (Est. 4–7); or, of the fast which the Ninevites observed? (Jonah 3); or, of Cornelius? (Acts 10); of Moses? (Ex. 34); of Daniel? (Dan. 9); of Ezra and the Jews? (Ezra 9); of Jehoshaphat? (2 Chron. 20); of Israel? (Judg. 20). These, and many more, had all the seal of God's good pleasure with their work, set upon the duty, in the blessings, either temporal or spiritual, that attended it. And, as it is our duty to go forth by the footsteps of the flock, so we ought to expect the like success that they found through grace.

These arguments have the greater force when it is considered that our Savior has pointed out *the observation of religious fasts* as a proper exercise to his disciples and followers, after he should go unto the Father, "Jesus said unto them, Can the children of the bridechamber mourn, as long as the bridegroom is with them? but the days will come, when the bridegroom shall be taken from them, and then shall they fast" (Matt. 9:15).

3. The Ends to Which This Exercise Should Be Directed

The great and important *ends*, to which our religious fasting should be directed, merit our next attention. Woe to many professed Christians for their misapprehensions about the proper ends of this ordinance! Fasting was never intended to procure the favor of God, or to strengthen that innate pride which dictated the Pharisee's prayer, "God, I thank thee, that I am not as other men…I fast twice in the week" (Luke 18:11–12). Such as imagine their fasting is an atonement for their offenses, are farther from the kingdom of heaven than the openly profane.

The Jews are severely censured for *fasting to themselves*, and *not to the Lord* (Zech. 7:5–6). This error was not peculiar to them. Others are no less guilty on that head than they were. When men fast to be seen of men, or to deserve good from God, to pretend a grief that does not affect their heart, or to desire mercies merely for their own pleasure, to consume them on their lusts—in such cases they but fast to themselves, and not to the Lord; and is this the fast that the Lord hath chosen? Shall not divine jealousy flame against such presumptuous offenders? But if we would sanctify a fast unto the Lord, we must observe it for these purposes.

1. To *bewail our unworthiness before God*, against whom we have sinned, and in whose sight we have forfeited every desirable enjoyment. The expressions of such self-loathing are various and strong; but the inward temper of the real penitent goes beyond every external token of it. "God be propitious to me a sinner" is a noble representation of heartfelt sorrow. Mercy, the exceeding riches of the mercy of God, is all the encouragement of an enlightened sinner. As an object of sovereign mercy, he confesses his guilt and wretchedness, that he deserves nothing, and lives by indulgence, that his life is forfeited into the hand of provoked justice, and himself a monument of forbearing affronted patience. In these circumstances, his abstinence from worldly comforts is a fit means of impressing deeper on his mind the humbling, yet seasonable truth.

2. As the leading end of all religious duties is *the glory of God*, so it is our duty to *fast unto the Lord, even to the Lord* (Zech. 7:5). To fast unto the Lord is to observe his call in this duty, to be determined by his authority, and to comply with the ends of its institution, in returning to God from whom we have departed by our iniquity, and in cleaving to him with purpose of heart. We have to do with God in fasting, and it will strike the hypocritical professor speechless, when he shall be interrogated in these positive terms, *Hast thou at all fasted unto me, even unto me?* He shall be muzzled, and unable to find any reply. The glory due to God in this duty includes an acknowledgment of his patience, submission to his sovereignty, and confidence in his favor, as our God, who is pacified notwithstanding all that we have done.

3. Fasting is appointed to be a means of *keeping under the body* (as the apostle expresses it, 1 Cor. 9:27), and of *bringing it into subjection*; lest, like

a proud rebel, it should claim and exercise dominion over the soul, which was originally designed to bear rule. *Sin* is called *flesh*, not only because it is base and earthly in its nature and propensities, but because it works by the members of the body; hence the apostle speaks of "the deeds of the body" (Rom. 8:13). Now, the deeds of the body must be mortified, and the body itself must be kept under, and brought into subjection; the flesh, with the affections and lusts thereof, must be crucified; and fasting is ordained with great propriety to be a means, through the Spirit, of accomplishing this design, to the praise of God, and to the happiness of the saints. Hereby their thoughts and connections are fixed for another world, which flesh and blood cannot inherit in their present state.

4. Another end of religious fasting, is to *increase the fervor of devotion, and the earnestness of our prayers*: to this it hath always been found highly instrumental: then the soul soars highest, when it is least fettered and encumbered with the flesh; and then God hath been pleased to manifest himself most to the soul, when the body hath been most subjected to it. Times of *fasting and prayer* have been eminently blessed with his favor, which, with the duty of *alms-giving*, are three handmaids that should never be separated. A goodly three! *prayer, fasting* and *alms-giving*, which, like the mistresses whom they serve, *faith, hope*, and *charity*, or *love*, should not be put asunder. And,

5. Fasting is appointed to be a means of *bringing us to God in Christ, as the precious rest of our immortal souls*, "turn ye even to me…with fasting" (Joel 2:12). A day of solemn fasting is not only intended to loose the bands of wickedness, but to take hold of God's covenant, according to Jeremiah 50:4–5: "going and weeping: they shall go, and seek the Lord their God…saying, Come, and let us join ourselves to the Lord in a perpetual covenant that shall not be forgotten." So much for the ends to which our fasting should be directed.

4. Some Questions Relative to It Answered

I shall now propose and answer some *questions* relative to this ordinance, such as,

Question 1. What may be judged *a sufficient call* to the observation of this duty?

Answer. The call to this duty must be determined by the circumstances in which we are, because providence must clear it up. These circumstances may affect *ourselves* immediately, or *others* we are related to; and, in *either of these cases*, it may become our duty to fast unto the Lord. Our own or our brother's situation may be considered in a *fourfold light*, and in any, or all of them, our call to fasting is undeniably plain. Either,

1. God is *manifestly dishonored* by some sin, which is an occasion of much offense to the generation of the righteous, and of insolent triumph to the profane world; and then the *offending sinner* ought to do as Israel did at Mizpeh, "they…fasted on that day, and said there, We have sinned against the LORD" (1 Sam. 7:6). Surely it is meet, in such a case, to say unto God, "I have done iniquity, I will do no more" (Job 34:32). If God is dishonored by our fellow-professors, although our own conversation should be without blame in the eyes of the world, the call to extraordinary fasting and prayer is very clear. The apostle censures the Corinthian church for their very culpable neglect to *mourn*, that the incestuous person might be taken away from among them (1 Cor. 5:2). If, therefore, such sins are to be found with us, or with our connections, as bring guilt on the conscience, and scandal on the ways of religion, we are certainly called to "be afflicted, and mourn, and weep" (James 4:9). Or,

2. The tokens of God's high displeasure appear in *afflicting providences*; and then it is very expedient for us to roll ourselves in the dust, and so to accommodate our spirit and way to the dispensation, by humbling ourselves under God's mighty hand with *fasting*. If the calamity is *personal*, I suppose it will be readily allowed that the call is plain; for those that are afflicted ought to pray with extraordinary fervor and perseverance (James 5:13). If the distress affects our neighbors, we should join with David in humbling our soul with fasting; for if we are not heard in their behalf, our prayer shall return into our own bosom (Ps. 35:13). If desolating judgments lie upon the church, we ought to imitate the noble example of Nehemiah, who sat down, and wept, and fasted, after he had heard that "the remnant that are left of the captivity there in the province are in great affliction and reproach: the wall of Jerusalem also is broken down, and the gates thereof are burned with fire" (Neh. 1:3–4). Or,

3. Some *awful judgment is threatened*, and hangs over our own head, or the head of such as we are related to; and then we are called, by the providence of God, to humble ourselves before him with *fasting*. The men of Nineveh, who complied with such a call, will rise up in judgment against those inconsiderate people who regard not the doing of the Lord, nor the

operations of his hand; for, being told that *yet forty days and Nineveh should be destroyed*, they called a fast, and humbled themselves before God (Jonah 3:4–9). When God *threatened* the death of the child born to David by Bathsheba, that holy man "besought God for the child, and…*fasted*" (2 Sam. 12:16). The example of Ahab, who *fasted*, when he heard the heavy tidings sent unto him from God, by Elijah, and was heard and approved for so doing, is also much to the present purpose (1 Kings 21:27). When the lion roareth, the beasts of the forest tremble; and when God's hand is lifted up, and he appears to be about to strike some awful decisive blow upon our persons, or upon our relations, upon our country, or upon the church, it is *high time* for us to strip ourselves of our ornaments, and to lie in sackcloth and ashes. Or,

4. Some *special mercy* is to be desired of the Lord; and then it is our duty to implore it with *fasting*. When Daniel prayed with peculiar earnestness and perseverance, for the return of the Jews from their seventy years' captivity, he *kept a fast*, on the solemn occasion (Dan. 9:1–3). When ministers, elders, or deacons, are separated to their office, it should be performed with *prayer and fasting* (Acts 6:6 compared with 13:2–3 and 14:23). Christians, if rightly exercised unto godliness, will have many occasions of this kind to go unto the throne of grace, to receive mercy, and to find grace to help them in the time of need. The same God who makes some mercies fall into the lap of others, without their being at much pains about them, will give his own children many an errand to himself for them, before he is pleased to grant the desire of their hearts. As the bounties of God come to his people from the hand of a promising God, so for all the blessings of his covenant he will "be enquired of by the house of Israel" (Ezek. 36:37).

In any of these cases the call to this duty is clear, and demands our cheerful compliance without delay. The call is from God, and our compliance becomes a matter of duty. To fast without a call from God is *presumption*; and to neglect the observation of this duty, when providence gives an evident call, is *rebellion*. "Happy is the man that feareth alway" (Prov. 28:14)!

Question 2. Who have authority to appoint the observation of solemn fasts?

Answer. Since fasting is an occasional duty, and since divine providence points out the occasions which the law of God makes it our duty to observe, the authority of men in *the appointment of fasts* can only extend to

12. THE OBSERVATION OF RELIGIOUS FASTS 367

such *circumstances of time, place, and order* as conveniency and decency render expedient. Human authority is only *a declaration*, in such a case, of the call of God manifested in a compared view of his word and providences. The import of the question, therefore, comes to this: *Who has a right to declare, in particular circumstances, the call of God to this duty?* This question is not so puzzling as some have imagined. According to the different lights in which we consider mankind, we must acknowledge *the right* to be invested in different hands (although only in the hands of *superiors* of one kind or other); and therefore, I observe (1.) That *every individual* is to judge for himself about the call to *personal fasting*; because his own conscience is his only *human guide* in whatever concerns his own conduct. I say, his *human guide*, for the will of God is the guide, even to his conscience, but his conscience is not under any human authority whatever, being subject only to *the Judge of all*. (2.) None can so properly declare the duty of a family as to the *season of fasting*, as the *head* of the family which is called to that exercise. To suppose that the right to judge of a call to family fasting is in any other hand would destroy all that order and subordination which constitute the happy preference of a well-regulated society, to mere confusion. (3.) It will not be denied that the *rulers in a particular congregation* are entitled to judge of the special calls of the congregation unto this duty. They ought to watch for the good of the flock; and it is their province to consider what Israel is called to do. (4.) On the same principles, it follows, that *the church, in her public capacity*, ought to judge *when* the Lord is calling his people in general to this duty, and to determine accordingly. Some causes of fasting are of such a nature as to belong *only* to the judgment of the church; such as, *error, divisions, apostasy*, and *formality* of professors; *unsuccessfulness of the gospel, death of the godly*, and *alarming appearances of God's leaving a people; ordination of church officers*; and the like. Many of these may affect the church at large, and consequently fall under the consideration of her representatives, as a seasonable call to *general fasting*. In such a case, the province of declaring the mind of God belongs to her representatives, who are called to watch for her public welfare. (5.) If a *people* or *country* be called to humble themselves before the Lord, either by some national calamity, or by some threatened stroke, or by some enterprise of national concern, wherein the favor of God is visibly necessary, it is the province of the *civil rulers* to call the nation to the seasonable duty of *fasting*. Whatever may be pretended for or against *na-*

tional churches, it is absurd to say that *the church in a particular nation, and the nation itself, are of the same extent*. Experience has always shown the contrary. But we may suppose many cases, such as, the commencement of war; general national calamities, by the sword of an invading enemy, by famine, or by the pestilence, and many more, which convey *a common call*, in the providence of God, to *a nation as such*, to seek the Lord by fasting and prayer; and, if we do not allow the authority of the civil magistrate to *declare the duty* of his subjects in such national affairs, we shall never find any sufficient means of carrying the duty into practice, in its full extent. Not only are Christians of every distinct communion, that live in such a country, called to this duty, but even the profane and secure, who would not reverence any church authority, are to be commanded to join in humiliation, as a duty of general concern. Can human wisdom imagine any tolerable expedient for this purpose, if the magistrate's right be refused? To acknowledge God by fasting and prayer, in the supposed circumstances, is a moral duty, incumbent on the subjects, as they are *sinful, afflicted*, or *dependent men*. Christians will, no doubt, aim at performing this duty upon *Christian principles*; so they will *every other duty* that has its foundation in the light of nature, as well as *this*, which arises from the dictates of a natural conscience, as much as any part of natural religion.[3] I beg leave to make one observation before I proceed, concerning the Jewish church,

---

[3] "Men use to signify the violent passions of their soul, by forbearing the repast and delights of the body. Is it a passion of *grief* one is oppressed with? you will see him oft forsake his food: thus, David, 'My heart is smitten and withered like grass, so that I forget to eat my bread.' Is it *fear* that possesseth the heart, with the apprehension of some great danger impending or approaching? you will have such a one refuse his wonted repast: so the mariners did in the sea-storm (Acts 27). Is it *anger* that vexeth the man? Ahab was deep in his passion upon the denial of Naboth's vineyard, and he throws himself upon his bed, and will not eat. Is it *desire* of compassing any great design that the head and heart are taken up and transported with? Such a one will not allow himself time for his meal: 'Cursed be he (saith Saul), that eateth any bread till evening, that I may be avenged of mine enemies:' we find the smith in the prophet so earnest at his idolatrous work, that he pincheth himself with hunger; and he will not eat, though his strength faileth, nor drink, though he be ready to faint. Now, in extraordinary prayer and *fasting*, the Christian is to have *all those affections*, in a spiritual and holy manner, wound up to the highest key possible. He is to have a deep *sorrow* for sin, *fear and trembling* at the judgments of God dreaded to come for it, a holy *anger* and *indignation* against sin, with a violent *desire* to be revenged on it, for the dishonor it hath cast upon God. Now, because the excess of natural passions discovers itself this way, even to afflict their very bodies, and makes them deny themselves that which nature most exacts; therefore God

and their fasts; namely, that *every Jew was a church member, as well as a civil subject*; and therefore, the priests, the ministers of the Lord, had as *extensive a province* as the magistrate; consequently their authority could affect that holy nation in the same extent as that of the prince; but the case is *quite otherwise* in every nation besides theirs. Therefore though it is readily granted that the fasts appointed among that people, by the *authority of the church*, might be observed *nationally*, yet it is as plain, it cannot be so in any nation since. Besides, it cannot be denied that, even under that dispensation, *the magistrates* in Israel called them to the exercise of *fasting*, as Samuel at Mizpeh (1 Sam. 7:5–6); Jehoshaphat (2 Chron. 20:3); Ezra, at the river Ahava (Ezra 8:21) and others. These were *judges, kings*, or *governors*; and whatever *other* character they had, it is clear they proclaimed these fasts in virtue of their *princely authority alone*; and, as the *causes* were *ordinary*, so the *duties* of their fasts were *ordinary* too. It is plain, they were *good princes*; but there is no reason to suppose that their *personal goodness* entitled their proclamations to the regard of their subjects, who only complied with them, because they were attended with a *providential call* to the duty as seasonable, and because they were issued by *lawful authority*. These are the only reasons that can be assigned, with any decent regard to either probability or truth; and no indulgence is due to men's inventions, when they are employed to support any favorite unscriptural notion.

Question 3. What are those substantial duties which constitute the essential part of a religious fast?

Answer. A fast cannot be sanctified to the Lord in an acceptable manner without the following things (1.) *Serious consideration of our ways* (Hag. 1:5). Such times are set apart from conversing with the world, that we may more diligently review our past life, and may carefully search and try our ways. Our inquiries on this occasion should extend to the *circumstances* of our sins, as well as to the sins *themselves*. We should consider the light, love, mercies, and warnings we have sinned against; and should trace up the whole to the corruption of our nature, that empoisoned fountain from whence they have all proceeded. (2.) *Deep humiliation of soul before the Lord*, which was signified by the sackcloth and ashes used, on such occasions, under the law. The consideration of our ways is to be pursued till

---

will have his people, in their extraordinary humiliations, do the like, *N. B., that nature may not put grace to shame.*" William Gurnall. *The Christian in Complete Armour*, on Ephesians 6:18.

our soul be humbled within us, and our heart rent, not only with *remorse* for sin, but with *regret* and kindly sorrow for it, as an offense to a gracious and merciful God (Joel 2:12–13). (3.) *Free and open confession of sin*, without reserve, is a very material part of the duty incumbent on us in religious fasting. The *consideration* and *humiliation* just now mentioned natively produce *extraordinary confession of sin*; an exercise most suitable on such an occasion (Neh. 9:3; Dan. 9:20–21). (4.) *Repentance towards God*, in turning from sin unto him both in heart and life, is also included in the duty of fasting unto the Lord (Joel 2:12). We fast to no purpose, unless we *hate sin* with a perfect hatred, and *long* for entire deliverance from it. (5.) *Earnest persevering prayer* for such mercies as our condition requires, is included in the service of a solemn fast, as we see in every account of any extraordinary exercise of this kind (Ezra 8; 9; Neh. 9; Dan. 9). (6.) *Solemn covenanting with God* is implied among the rest of the duties of fasting (Jer. 50:4–5; Neh. 9:38). *This lies in the solemn, express, declared resolution of the mind, to cleave unto the Lord's truths and ways; and to depart from all iniquity in principle and practice* (Deut. 26:17–18; Isa. 56:6; Ps. 116:16–19).

Question 4. What is to be thought of *Lent-fasts*, and others of the Popish church, that recur periodically?

Answer. They are entirely a piece of *will-worship*; and, instead of glorifying, they dishonor God. They are merely human inventions; and, in the observation of them, there is a show, and but a show of mortification. Fish, with the richest sauces, is an allowed dish on such an occasion; and perhaps few will reckon it a great hardship to be confined to such delicacies, as the Romish canons, mitigated by connivance, allow their votaries to use. These may be called *fasts* in the same sense as *Croesus might be called poor*, or *gluttony* be called *temperance*. But, if they were observed with the strictest decorum the case will admit, it is both sinful and dangerous to countenance them, for we must not add to God's appointments, lest he reprove us (Prov. 30:6); and the curses written in the Scriptures shall be added to the presumptuous offender that adds anything to their contents (Rev. 22:18).

5. Directions concerning Its Observation

I shall now give some *directions* about the observation of a *religious fast*. These may be reduced to three heads, as they refer either to our *preparation* for it; or to our *management* in it; or to our *behavior* after it.

I. We should be *prepared* for this duty, in order to our engaging successfully in it; and here several things are necessary *previous* to the duty, such as:

1. *A full evidence* that we have *a clear call* to it; for without this we cannot fast in faith, and *whatever is not of faith, is sin.* To obtain a satisfying evidence of this, we should carefully attend unto the circumstances of our lot, and the dispensations of providence, that, by comparing both with the word of God, we may know what is *the good and acceptable will of God* in regard to *present duty.*

2. *Ordering our worldly affairs* beforehand, with such prudence that we may have no interruptions in the duty from any occurrences that prudent foresight might have provided against. How can we justify ourselves to our own consciences if we are hindered in this exercise by such impediments as we might have prevented? If things we could neither foresee nor prevent shall intervene, to hinder us, the case is different, and we may then lament that as *our misfortune,* which we cannot reflect upon as *our crime.*

3. A just consideration of the *nature* and *object* of the duty is previously necessary, in order to our giving glory to God in this work. If we have wrong notions of its *nature,* we must err in the performance of it; and our error must be the greater, and perhaps the more dangerous, the more strictly we adhere to our erroneous views. If we suppose it consists merely in hanging down the head, or in abstinence from bodily comforts, or in a form of religious duties, our fasting must be an abomination to the Lord. We ought likewise to consider the *object* unto whom we approach, when we sanctify a fast upon Christian principles. We are not to fast to *ourselves,* to please our own humors; nor to *men,* whether they are in office in church or state; but unto the *Lord our God,* for the sins we bewail have been committed against him, and the mercies we implore must come from him. Here God must be considered, not only as a *Lawgiver,* whom we have dishonored, but as *our God,* pacified and well-pleased in his Son, notwithstanding all that we have done against him. Then would our expressions of *grief* and *hatred of sin* be unfeigned and heart-affecting, and our requests would ascend with humble assurance, as well as fervent desire of being heard. We should be *exceeding vile in our own eyes,* if we saw *the Lord to be our exceeding joy.*

4. Previous to our engaging in this work, we should shun, with the utmost care, everything that might indispose us for the duty, such as *carnal*

mirth, sensual delights, rich meats or drinks, much sleep, and things of that sort. *These* might affect our spirits with a *levity* or a *dullness*, that are highly improper for such an occasion. The priests were commanded to "lie all night in sackcloth" (Joel 1:13). If the *literal austerity* of this command is superseded, the *moral* couched in it is still in force, and will be as long as there is any occasion for this exercise.

II. *In managing the duty of fasting*, it may be proper to observe the following general directions.

1. Let us have *no dependence* upon any previous preparations for this duty. When we have done all that God commands us, we are but *unprofitable servants*, and only do our indispensable duty. But who is the presumptuous man that dare say to God concerning *any branch* of his duty that it is *perfect?* None of the human race can safely venture any risk on such a bottom; for if the Lord enter into judgment with us, no flesh living can be justified in his sight.

2. We should proceed in the exercise *by the rules of the word.* The footsteps of the flock are, in a very particular manner, recorded in Nehemiah 9:2–3:

> The seed of Israel separated themselves from all strangers, and stood and confessed their sins, and the iniquities of their fathers. And they stood up in their place, and *read* in the book of the law of the Lord their God one fourth part of the day; and another fourth part they *confessed,* and *worshipped* the Lord their God.

Here we have an excellent *directory* for fasting, which should be performed: by *reading* such passages of Scripture as are peculiarly suitable for the occasion of the fast; by *confessing* our sins before God; and by fervent, persevering *prayer.*

3. *Humiliation for sin* being the essential business of the fast, we ought to *examine ourselves*, with the most jealous attention, as to our *state, temper*, and *conversation.* The whole word of God is of use to direct us in this work; but particular passages, that are most adapted to answer this purpose, ought to be selected on the occasion, that our minds may be more affected with sin, and we may see more and more a happy necessity of being reconciled to God by the death of his Son, and of being saved by his life. Among all the collections to favor this design that the Christian world

has been blessed with, there is perhaps none equal, I do not fear, however, to say, there is none better, than the *Westminster Assembly's Larger Catechism on the commandments,* in the answers to the questions, *What is required?* and, *What is forbidden?* especially the latter. By the assistance of these, many new discoveries will be brought into the conscience, both in the articles of *sin* and *duty*; and the whole represented in *a scriptural light,* which is incomparably the *clearest* and most *affecting*. We must search our ways, in order to *mourn* over them, and to *mourn after a godly sort*; that, under a persuasion of the mercy of God in Christ, we may look on them with abhorrence and grief, and may turn our feet unto the testimonies of the Lord our God, with full purpose of, and endeavor after new obedience.

4. Let us recognize all the solemn obligations that the *grace* and *authority of God* lay upon us to be *his*, and to *walk in newness of life,*

> Therefore we are buried with him by baptism into death: that like as Christ was raised up from the dead by the glory of the Father, even so we also should walk in newness of life. For if we have been planted together in the likeness of his death, we shall be also in the likeness of his resurrection: knowing this, that our old man is crucified with him, that the body of sin might be destroyed, that henceforth we should not serve sin. For he that is dead is freed from sin. Now if we be dead with Christ, we believe that we shall also live with him: knowing that Christ being raised from the dead dieth no more; death hath no more dominion over him. For in that he died, he died unto sin once: but in that he liveth, he liveth unto God. Likewise reckon ye also yourselves to be dead indeed unto sin, but alive unto God through Jesus Christ our Lord…What fruit had ye then in those things whereof ye are now ashamed? for the end of those things is death. But now being made free from sin, and become servants to God, ye have your fruit unto holiness, and the end everlasting life. For the wages of sin is death; but the gift of God is eternal life through Jesus Christ our Lord (Rom. 6:4–11, 21–23).

5. Let us study to be *without guile*, because we have to do with an omniscient jealous God, who cannot be imposed on by *false pretenses,*

Moreover when ye fast, be not, as the hypocrites, of a sad countenance: for they disfigure their faces, that they may appear unto men to fast. Verily I say unto you, They have their reward. But thou, when thou fastest, anoint thine head, and wash thy face; that thou appear not unto men to fast, but unto thy Father which is in secret: and thy Father, which seeth in secret, shall reward thee openly. (Matt. 6:16–18).

6. We should learn caution from the Jews, whose abuse of this ordinance is recorded and reproved in

Wherefore have we fasted, say they, and thou seest not? wherefore have we afflicted our soul, and thou takest no knowledge? Behold, in the day of your fast ye find pleasure, and exact all your labours. Behold, ye fast for strife and debate, and to smite with the fist of wickedness: ye shall not fast as ye do this day, to make your voice to be heard on high. Is it such a fast that I have chosen? a day for a man to afflict his soul? is it to bow down his head as a bulrush, and to spread sackcloth and ashes under him? wilt thou call this a fast, and an acceptable day to the LORD? Is not this the fast that I have chosen? to loose the bands of wickedness, to undo the heavy burdens, and to let the oppressed go free, and that ye break every yoke? Is it not to deal thy bread to the hungry, and that thou bring the poor that are cast out to thy house? when thou seest the naked, that thou cover him; and that thou hide not thyself from thine own flesh? (Isa. 58:3–7).

In these verses we see the *sin of the Jews* in their fasting, which is largely represented for a warning to us. They fasted indeed; but their fasts were an abomination; for (1.) *In the day of their fast they found pleasure* (v. 3), which was quite opposite to the intention of the duty, namely, to afflict their souls. Perhaps they indulged to bodily recreations; but they undoubtedly found a malicious pleasure in gratifying their envy, malice, and pride. (2.) Though they fasted they were covetous and unmerciful, *they exacted all their labors* (v. 3). They were severe on their servants, and rigorous to their insolvent debtors. When they fasted they pretended to ask mercy from God; but never once practiced any mercy to men, from a principle of duty to their God. (3.) *They fasted for strife and debate* (v. 4), everyone accusing his neighbor, and pretending to fast for the sins of others. When the Lord hearkened and heard, they spake not aright; no man repented him of his wickedness, saying, "What have I done?" (Jer. 8:6). Alas! how visibly do professors in our day err in this point! how very little regard is paid to our Lord's advice, "cast out first the *beam* out of thine own eye, and then shalt thou see clearly to pull out the *mote* that is in thy brother's" (Luke 6:42)! (4.) *They smote with the fist of wickedness* (Isa. 58:4). Which refers either to the *barbarous murders* that they committed, under a pretense of zeal for God; as in the case of Naboth, who was falsely accused and condemned in the day of Jezebel's fast (1 Kings 21); or, to the *persecutions* of such as would not conform to the prevailing spirit, and measures of the times. (5.) *They fasted to make their voice to be heard on high* (Isa. 58:4); either in the heat of their clamor one against another; or in the public open manner of their devotions, which they performed so as to be taken notice of, and they might get the applause of men. And (6.) They satisfied themselves with the *bare externals* of fasting, and thought they did enough, if *they hanged down their head as a bulrush, and spread sackcloth and ashes under them* (v. 5). But will ye, Jews or Christians! will ye be so partial and blind, when ye consider such a scene as this, to call it *a fast, an acceptable day to the Lord?* God hath said, *we shall not fast so* (v. 4). We should not do it, for it is our sin; and we shall not be suffered to persist in such vile insults upon his authority and honor.

The right observation of the fast that the Lord hath chosen implies (1.) *Our doing justly*, by *loosing the bands of wickedness*; that is, every sinful obligation our dependents are under to us; by *undoing the heavy burdens*; that is, every species of oppression; by *letting the oppressed go free* from these miseries that made his life bitter; and by *breaking every yoke* of bondage and slavery, whereby life was rendered miserable. (2.) *Our loving mercy*, by *dealing our bread to the hungry* to feed them; by *bringing the poor that are cast out to our house* to lodge them, by *covering the naked, when we see them*, with clothes; and by every act of generous friendship to our relations, especially those of our own house, *not hiding ourselves from our own flesh* (see vv. 6–7). But, since we are not to do all these things *in the time* of our solemn fast, we certainly ought to have a disposition for such friendly, humane, and Christian offices, while we are humbling ourselves before the Lord, and to manifest it on every proper occasion.

7. I shall only add, in the last place, that we ought, *in fasting*, to cultivate the excellent tempers that prevailed among the Corinthians, when they *mourned* on account of the incestuous person, as the apostle describes them, "For behold this selfsame thing, that ye sorrowed after a godly sort, what carefulness it wrought in you," about the one thing needful! "yea, what clearing of yourselves," only upon the ground of the righteousness of Immanuel! "yea, what indignation," against sin! "yea, what fear," of your heavenly Father! "yea, what vehement desire" to be like God! "yea, what zeal," for his glory! "yea, what revenge," against sin in your souls! (2 Cor. 7:11). Let us seek to be filled with the Spirit of grace and supplication, that we also may mourn after this godly sort.

III. The directions relative to *our behavior after* we have finished the more immediate duties of a solemn fast may be reduced to these general heads.

1. Beware of *spiritual pride*. Have no confidence in the flesh. Leave that arrogant prayer ("God, I thank thee, that I am not as other men are…I fast") to the proud Pharisee. When you have fasted, still continue to use the dialect of the publican: "God be merciful to me a sinner" (Luke 18:11–13). Take heed and beware of pride, which never makes more bold and dangerous advances than when we have been employed in the duties of religion. The opinion of the merit of good works is very erroneous and absurd; but the natural bias of the human heart easily goes into it; and there is so much of the *old man* in the best, that they are too apt to think highly of their religious performances. "Wherefore have we fasted," said the Jews, "and thou seest not?" (Isa. 58:3).

2. *Beware of carnal security*. Nothing is more hurtful than security and indolence, and yet nothing is more common among Christians. We cannot be enough on our guard against its advances, because they are extremely insinuating and plausible. There is no duty more frequently recommended in the book of God than *watchfulness*. To affect our minds with just apprehensions of its nature, and with a proper attention to the obligation and practice of it, our Lord spake many parables; but, instead of observing these, how naturally do we imitate Micah, who said, "Now know I that the LORD will do me good, seeing I have a Levite to my priest" (Judg. 17:13). But when he was saying that he should have peace, though he walked in the imagination of his own heart, destruction from the hand of the Danites was very near; and such will be the fearful end of all that confide in their

duties, and become secure after they have been engaged in them. If they are his own people, the Lord will not make a full end; yet will he not leave them altogether unpunished. A secure Christian is in a deplorable situation. We should never forget that we have been purged from our old sins; and should constantly watch and pray that we do not enter into future temptations.

3. *Bear in mind the causes of the fast*, after the duties of it are finished. These should be remembered in our ordinary addresses to God: I will "direct my prayer unto thee, and will look up" for an answer (Ps. 5:3). The Lord frequently accepts the prayers of his people, when he does not immediately grant the mercies they ask of him; therefore, as we ought to continue in prayer, we should also wait to hear what the Lord God will say in a favorable return to our supplications, and persevere, in the meantime, in the use of the *appointed means*, to obtain this desirable *end*. But in waiting for light, whatever the sovereign Lord may do, let us not look for *impressions*, far less for *voices*, nor *extraordinary revelations* of any kind, or in any way, to discover our duty in particular cases (2 Peter 1:18–19); but, having laid ourselves fairly open to the divine determination, and made humble and earnest supplication unto God for light in our particular case, we ought to believe that we shall be guided, taught, and directed by him, according to his promise (Prov. 3:6; Ps. 25:9). In the confidence of this, we should, depending on God, weigh the matter, and the circumstances of the case, in the balance of sanctified reason, according to the general directions of the word, such as "whatsoever things are true, whatsoever things are honest, whatsoever things are just, whatsoever things are pure, whatsoever things are lovely, whatsoever things are of good report; if there be any virtue, and if there be any praise, think on these things" (Phil. 4:8). The conduct and motions of *providence*, with reference to it, should also be carefully observed and compared with the *word of God*. In pursuing the *ends of fasting* in such a course, we shall see the *faithfulness* of God, in *guiding us with his eye*; and his *favor*, in *showing us a token for good*.

4. *Bring forth fruits meet for a religious fast*, in the whole course of your future conversation (Acts 26:20). Every tree is known by its fruits: a corrupt tree cannot bring forth good fruit; and no more doth a good tree bring forth corrupt fruit. This natural case is *an image* of moral things. The saints are *new creatures*, the workmanship of God created in Christ Jesus *unto good works*. There are certain fruits that are meet for every branch

of the Christian system, and when these are viewed as *one whole*, they constitute *a good conversation*, as the apostle speaks (James 3:13). Now, the *fruits*, or the *works*, that are *meet for fasting*, are: *temperance* in using the mercies of providence; *abasing thoughts* of ourselves; *daily crucifying* of the flesh, with the affections and lusts thereof; *new obedience* upon gospel-principles; and *heavenly-mindedness*, setting our affections, not upon the things that are below, but upon the things that are above, where Christ is at the right hand of God (Col. 3:1–2). We confess our obligation to all this when we sanctify a fast; and we ought each day to perform our vows. Having opened our mouths to the Lord, we cannot *practically* go back, without the vilest ingratitude and rebellion. Only let your conversation be as it becometh the gospel of Christ; and justify your professions by your practice, that you may not fall under the dreadful character of these, who "profess that they know God, but in works they deny him" (Titus 1:16).

6. Encouragements to This Service Proposed

I shall conclude this subject with a few *encouragements* to the *practice* of fasting. I am not writing to heathens that are without any Scripture revelation of the nature of God, or of the good pleasure of his will; but to such as have the word of salvation sent unto them, and therefore must be without excuse, if they continue ignorant of its interesting contents. We, my dear fellow-sinners, have the most powerful inducements; we have the most inviting considerations, proposed in the oracles of God, to encourage us to this duty. For,

1. We are called to fast *unto the Lord*, who was in Christ reconciling the world to himself; and what can be a more engaging motive than this? We are not compelled by authority, nor driven by terror; but drawn by love. Who can resist a call, where *majesty* and *mercy* so harmoniously mingle their influence? If we approach God aright in this duty, our sorrow will be the fruit of joy in God through our Lord Jesus Christ, by whom we have now received the atonement; love will sweetly constrain us to every expression of godly zeal that enters into a religious fast.

2. Godly sorrow in religious fasting "worketh repentance to salvation not to be repented of" (2 Cor. 7:10). If there was any room to apprehend the real tendency of the exercise to be unto the ruin of our souls, it might, with good reason, be thought improper and unpleasant; but, having so strong assurances that spiritual grief and contrition of soul, on account

of our offenses committed against God, has the happiest tendencies and effects, we have the greatest reason to embrace every call to the duty with unfeigned pleasure.

3. Fasting is called *an acceptable day to the Lord* (Isa. 58:5). He is pleased to assure us that we give glory to him in this duty; and has declared that he is well pleased with such a service. Wonderful condescension! Shall we not reckon it our duty and honor to worship God in a way that he is pleased so eminently to honor with distinguishing marks of his favor? *A day* that is *acceptable to the Lord* must be *an accepted time*, and *a day of salvation* to men. That such a day is highly acceptable to the Lord is largely explained,

> Then shall thy light break forth as the morning, and thine health shall spring forth speedily: and thy righteousness shall go before thee; the glory of the LORD shall be thy rereward. Then shalt thou call, and the LORD shall answer; thou shalt cry, and he shall say, Here I am. If thou take away from the midst of thee the yoke, the putting forth of the finger, and speaking vanity; and if thou draw out thy soul to the hungry, and satisfy the afflicted soul; then shall thy light rise in obscurity, and thy darkness be as the noonday: and the LORD shall guide thee continually, and satisfy thy soul in drought, and make fat thy bones: and thou shalt be like a watered garden, and like a spring of water, whose waters fail not. And they that shall be of thee shall build the old waste places: thou shalt raise up the foundations of many generations; and thou shalt be called, The repairer of the breach, The restorer of paths to dwell in (Isa. 58:8–12).

4. Another *encouragement* to observe this duty arises from the *success* of it. The Holy Ghost has left many examples of its marvelous success upon record, as we have observed on the second section. Now, what has been so successful in many cases, as *a means* of taking away the fearful tokens of God's wrath, of deriving the most important blessings upon men, and of mortifying sin through the energy of the sanctifying Spirit—must be highly worthy of our warmest regards. The Lord's hand is not shortened that it cannot save, his ear is not heavy that it cannot hear; and therefore, let us come with boldness to the throne of grace in this, as well as in every other duty of divine appointment, expecting the same benefit that others have experienced; for our God changeth not, but is the same yesterday, today,

and forever. The history of ages past stands on record for the learning of generations to come, that through patience and comfort of the Scriptures we might have hope (Rom. 15:4). It is no guilty presumption, but a very reasonable expectation, that we shall find the same benefit in the ways of religion that others have received,

> Why sayest thou, O Jacob, and speakest, O Israel, My way is hid from the LORD, and my judgment is passed over from my God? Hast thou not known? hast thou not heard, that the everlasting God, the LORD, the Creator of the ends of the earth, fainteth not, neither is weary? there is no searching of his understanding. He giveth power to the faint; and to them that have no might he increaseth strength. Even the youths shall faint and be weary, and the young men shall utterly fall: but they that wait upon the LORD shall renew their strength; they shall mount up with wings as eagles; they shall run, and not be weary; and they shall walk, and not faint (Isa. 40:27–31).

Chapter 13
Ministerial Visitations of the Flock

All that labor in the word and doctrine, are bound to preach the gospel *publicly*, and to teach in the chief places of concourse. This is a *part*, but not the *whole*, of the ministry they have received of the Lord, and which they ought daily to *fulfill* in the churches, as they have an opportunity. Like their divine Master, they should *go about doing good*. Like his apostle, they should *teach from house to house* (Acts 20:20). In the course of his ministry, Paul taught *both publicly and from house to house*. His *example* has all the *weight of a command*, to oblige us to imitate his method of teaching *both ways*; for, besides his being a skillful workman, that needed not to be ashamed, rightly dividing the word of truth, it is reasonable to think that many happy effects will follow on family and personal instructions from the ministers of Christ. The people have no opportunity, nor would it be proper they should propose many cases, wherein prudent consultation with their pastor might be useful, *on public occasions*; and therefore, they ought to have an opportunity, and to be encouraged, to propose them *in private*. And private instructions, being *more personal*, are apt to make a deeper and more lasting impression. Moreover, the case of individuals may be more particularly touched by those instructions than in a public discourse. Several considerations of this sort have determined the churches of Christ, to make this a branch of *standing ministration* in the dispensation of the gospel. The rules prescribed for managing it in the *church of Scotland* are well calculated to promote the cause of *religion and virtue*.[1] All that I shall attempt on this head is only to give a few examples of such instructions, as are not improper to be urged upon the serious consideration of people, in the course of ministerial visitation of families and persons.

But before I enter on them, I beg leave to lay down these preliminary remarks. (1.) That I do not pretend to offer *a finished draft* of such a service;

---

[1] Church of Scotland. *The Principal Acts of the General Assembly, 1708*, p. 17.

but only to give *a general sketch*, that Christians, for whose use this performance is more immediately intended, may be stirred up to remember how they have received and heard, and to hold fast, and repent. (2.) That the faithful minister of Christ must be supposed to *know the state of his flock*, and to adapt his method of address accordingly. (3.) That he ought not so much to regard the *number of topics* he inculcates, as the *weight* and *seasonableness*, the *earnestness* and *evidence* of his address, according to his opinion of the temper, circumstances, stations, and dangers, of the persons he instructs; and all this should be managed with a particular view to their several capacities; because an increase of knowledge, reformation, and holiness, are the great objects of the duty.

Having premised these particulars, I shall now proceed to give *a rude draft* of some hints, that may be usefully suggested, through a divine blessing, in teaching from house to house.

1. General Principles

I. It may be proper to begin with a concise but instructive account of the *first principles of the oracles of God*, putting them in mind of the foundation-truths of our holy religion. The following specimen may serve for an example: Man is a reasonable being; his understanding is superior to that of the beasts of the field; and, as he is capable of more noble actions, so he is conscious of sublimer desires than they are. Our chiefest end should be to *glorify God*, who is the Author of our being, who preserveth us in life; and who daily loadeth us plenteously with his undeserved benefits. To *enjoy him forever* constitutes the only true happiness of the immortal soul. The glory of God, and our everlasting enjoyment of him, are objects of the most exalted nature, and demand our most earnest attention. Human sagacity cannot find out the acceptable way of ascribing to our Maker the glory which is due to his name; nor discover the method of enjoying him as our portion. Our duty and happiness cannot be separated, because much of our happiness consists in doing our duty. But what *reason*, with all its improvements, could never imagine, is clearly revealed in *the Holy Scriptures* of the Old and New Testament; which are a sufficient, plain, and complete guide in every article of truth and duty, that refer to our everlasting happiness; for they are able to make the man of God "perfect, thoroughly furnished unto all good works" (2 Tim. 3:16–17). Yea, let me not leave room for an unworthy comparison of anything else that human pride would set up in derogation from their dignity, *they are the* only *rule to direct us how we may glorify and enjoy God.* They are the fountain of all saving knowledge, the ground of the faith of God's elect, and the only reason and rule of all acceptable obedience. From that source of infallible truth, we learn that there is but one living and true God, who is infinite, eternal, and unchangeable in his being, wisdom, power, holiness, justice, goodness, and truth; that there are three persons in the Godhead, the Father, the Son, and the Holy Ghost, and that these three distinct, divine, and coequal persons are one God, the same in substance or nature, and equal in power and glory; and that he foreordained, according to the counsel of his will, before the beginning of time, whatsoever comes to pass in the works of creation and providence, which are copied from his eternal purpose, without the smallest deviation from his all-perfect plan. From the same oracles we learn that the worlds were made by the word of God, who spake and it was done, who commanded and it stood fast; and that man was made upright, after the image of God, in knowledge, righteousness, and holiness, with dominion over the creatures on the earth, and in the air and sea. In this holy and happy state, his Maker honored man with a wonderful instance of his favor, by entering into a covenant of life with Adam, as the common representative of all his posterity, that should descend from him by ordinary generation, wherein he promised the continuance and consummation of happiness to mankind, upon condition of persevering, perfect obedience; declaring, at the same time, that *the wages of sin is death.* This covenant was manifestly calculated to display the goodness of God, and to secure the obedience and felicity of man. But man, though placed in all this honor, did not abide in it. By the deceiving arts of Satan, he was enticed and ruined. Sin separated us from the favor of God, and robbed us of his image; it cast us out of his sight, and subjected us to his wrath and curse. Sin is the abominable thing a holy God detests; it is the accursed thing a just God will punish. We have all "sinned, and come short of the glory of God" (Rom. 3:23). We are dead in trespasses and sins. We have destroyed ourselves. The wrath of God abideth upon us. Woe, woe to the world, because of our offenses against heaven! These very deplorable circumstances of guilt and perdition, into which we plunged ourselves, by sinning against God, gave occasion for that most astonishing *scene* of benevolence and mercy, that swallows up all expression, and even thought itself is lost in wonder and joy. Behold, what manner of love is this that God hath showed to us! He "so loved the world, that he gave his only begotten Son, that whosoever believeth in him should not perish, but have everlasting life" (John 3:16). We could do nothing to expiate our guilt, or atone for our offenses, to subdue our sins, or return to God, to save our souls, or even to prepare them for that salvation; and, behold, *then* the kindness and love of God towards guilty, lost, and miserable men appeared. *Then* the decrees of sovereign mercy to a ruined world brought forth, and the Dayspring from on high visited our earth. God's only begotten Son was provided in the counsels of eternity, and revealed in time, to put away our sin, and to bring us back unto God. The expedient was wonderful, but none else could answer[2] the exigency of our case. He has accomplished the work of our redemption, by putting himself into our *law-place*, by taking upon him our iniquities, by uniting our nature forever to his person, by obeying the law, and suffering all it threatens in our stead, by rising from the dead, and ascending on high, and by improving his recovered life, as an Advocate and King, for the most beneficent purposes. The testimony God hath given us of himself is that he is *the God of peace*, who brought again from the dead our Lord Jesus Christ, the great Shepherd of the sheep, by the blood of the everlasting covenant; and that he was in Christ reconciling the world to himself, not imputing their trespasses unto them. The testimony he hath given of his Son is that he is *the true God and eternal life*; that he is a Child born unto sinful men, and a Son given unto them; that he is of God made unto a perishing world, by gracious appointment, wisdom, and righteousness, and sanctification, and redemption; that whosoever cometh unto him, shall in no wise be cast out; and that whosoever believeth in him, shall never perish, but hath everlasting life. The testimony he hath given of the Holy Ghost is that he is one with the Father and the Son; that he is freely received by the hearing of faith; that it is his office to quicken the dead, to convert sinners, to open the understanding, to change the will, to testify of Christ, and to dwell in believers now, and to raise them up at the last day; and that he is the author and worker of every gracious temper, as well as the dispenser of all extraordinary gifts.

---

[2] *Could answer*—Does the language seem harsh, or the sentiment doubtful? To some it may; but I dare not retract it. The reader will find all I have said, affirmed by an inspired writer, who tells us, "There is no other name under heaven given among men, whereby *we must be saved* [εν ω δει σωθηναι ημας]" (Acts 4:12). The expression is remarkable: *by which it is fit*, or *meet*, or *becoming*, and *worthy, that we be saved*.

The Scriptures largely show us that until we are brought into a new state of reconciliation to God by Jesus Christ, we remain in our sins; and being in the flesh we cannot please God; that all attempts, therefore, to make ourselves meet for salvation, and more deserving of divine favor, are both *foolish* and *wicked*; that *faith in Jesus Christ*, given to sinners in the record of the gospel, is the *first step* of practical religion; because without faith it is impossible to please God; that an *appropriating persuasion* of the testimony of God concerning the Redeemer, in the declarations, promises, offers, and invitations of the gospel, is the only means of furnishing the soul with effectual principles of true holiness; that there is no preparation, no prerequisite, no entitling qualification, required *previous* to our receiving and resting upon Christ alone, for the whole of our salvation, as he is freely given to us in the gospel; and that this faith, which receives Christ, and rests on him alone for salvation, is the free *gift of God*, and is, in distinction from all works, the alone *means of salvation*, "by grace are ye saved through faith; and that not of yourselves: it is the gift of God: not of works, lest any man should boast" (Eph. 2:8–9).[3]

As no man can obey the law in any point, until he has actually received Christ himself, with all his fullness, and is thereby begotten unto the hope of eternal life by him, so it is the greatest absurdity, and the most dangerous presumption for any to flatter himself that he is in a state of favor with God, if he continues to live in the *habitual neglect* of commanded duty, or if his conversation be after the *course of this world*. Faith without works is dead; it is altogether detestable unto God, and wholly unprofitable unto men. A loathsome dead carcass is not more offensive to living men than

---

[3] "*Ye are saved*, says the apostle. Ye are delivered from wrath, reconciled to God, and made heirs of his kingdom. How? *By grace, through faith*. Grace, like a magnificent sovereign, from the riches of his own bounty, and without any respect to human worthiness, confers the glorious gift. *Faith*, like an indigent petitioner, with an empty hand, and without any pretense to personal desert, receives the heavenly blessing. Both grace and faith stand in direct opposition to *works; all works* whatever: whether they be works of the law, or works of the gospel; exercises of the heart, or actions of the life; done in a state of nature, or done under the influences of grace; they are all and every one of them, *equally* set aside in this great affair. That the bill of exclusion is thus extensive, or rather quite *unlimited*, appears from the reason assigned: *lest any man should boast*; that all pretense of glorying may be cut off from fallen creatures; that the whole honor of obtaining salvation may be appropriated to *him*, who hid not his face from shame and spitting. And is he not worthy, unspeakably and infinitely worthy, to receive this unrivaled honor, as a recompense for his unparalleled humiliation?" James Hervey. *Theron and Aspasio*, dial. 7.

an unfruitful profession of faith is to the living and true God; and it is not more capable of any of the functions of natural life than such speculative believers are of bringing forth the fruits of righteousness to the glory and praise of God. The *formal professor* and the *careless liver* speak the same language, and are guilty of the same presumption, when they impiously glory in the *Christian name*, and impudently pretend to *faith* and *hope*; but their pretensions are only *vain words*; for their faith does not work by love, and their hope does not purify their hearts, and produce a heavenly conversation.

The *faith of the gospel* is manifested in such *exercises of the heart*, and in such *actions of the life*, as prove it to be *unfeigned*, and diffuse a powerful evidence of its energy and influence in the world.

The Savior of the world having opened the eyes of a man that had been blind from his birth, the Pharisees, hardened in unbelief and enmity against the clearest demonstration of the Messiah's character, which appeared with irresistible evidence in that miracle, cast out the poor man from their communion, because he would not join with them in reviling his Benefactor: "Jesus heard that they had cast him out; and when he had found him, he said unto him, *dost thou believe on the Son of God?*" (John 9:35). The question was *personal*; but the Holy Ghost, by recording it in the Scriptures, has given a sufficient intimation that it is as *really addressed to us* as it was to that man. The searcher of hearts, whose eyes are as a flame of fire, says unto us, *Do ye believe on the Son of God?* Do ye see your *absolute need* of him? Are you convinced of the *defects* of your own purposes and endeavors? Are you wearied out of all your false refuges? emptied of all hope in yourselves? and brought to see and feel the danger of your state by nature? Do you see the *incomparable worth* of the precious Savior? Do ye breathe with ardent desire after him? Do ye confide in him as the only foundation of your hope? and, Do ye rejoice in Christ Jesus, having no confidence in the flesh? Is the blessed Redeemer, and his glorious salvation, the object of your frequent, delightful, and serious *contemplation?* Do you *value an interest in Christ* above all the world? And are you in earnest to have and maintain good evidence, that your hope in Christ is well founded? Do the *favor of God*, and the *concerns of the unseen and eternal world*, appear of greater importance than everything else to you? Do you *trust* in Christ, as he is proposed in the gospel, to give you a clear, sensible, and experimental acquaintance with the great things of your eternal peace? to be the alone Propitiation for your sins, and to recommend you to divine favor in his imputed righteousness? and, to sanctify you, by saving manifestations of his glory? Do you *love the saints*, for the sake of the truth that dwelleth in them? Is your love to them disinterested and beneficent? Do you *walk by faith?* Do you aim daily at living by the faith of the Son of God, as your righteousness and strength? Does the faith of the promises keep you from sinking; and the faith of the commandments and threatenings of the law, when viewed in their amiable connection with the mercies of the gospel, keep you from sinning with deliberate pleasure? Does the faith of *forgiveness with God* lead you with confidence to the throne of grace, to receive mercy, and to find grace to help you in the time of need? Consider what answer ye will give; for *you have to do with God*, who understandeth the secrets of the heart. Evasive *arts* will serve no other purpose than to aggravate your crime, and to render your hearts more obdurate, and your condemnation more fearful.

2. General Duties

II. After such a general view of the *principles* of Christianity, the *general duties* incumbent upon all that *name the name of Christ* deserve our next attention. The divine law, which is the rule of them, is exceeding broad; and the duties of it are exceeding numerous. I shall select the following, while many others of equal importance have as strong a claim to our regard. (1.) Make the *word of God your daily companion.* Read it frequently and attentively. Meditate in it day and night. Study, by reason of familiar use, to have your senses exercised to discern good and evil. You do well to take heed to it, as unto a light that hath shined in a dark place. Use it, as you would a lantern, to enable you to make a safe choice of every step in a dark night, on a dangerous road. Search the Scriptures daily, to see whether your own opinions are just, whether the books you read, and the sermons you hear, are sound and spiritual; and whether your practice becomes the gospel or not. Never say to *the word of the holy One*, out of compliment to any book of genius and taste, or of pleasure or science, or out of regard to the business and cares of the world, as the Christians, spoken of by James, said to the poor man, "Stand thou there, or sit here under my footstool" (James 2:3). Whatever engagements you have on your hands, remember this is *one*, and an *indispensable one* too—to hear God address himself to your consciences from day to day by his word.[4] (2.) Study to *know yourselves*. This is a very extensive branch of useful knowledge. Do not trust your own opinion of yourself; lest self-love deceive you. Do not judge of yourself, by comparing what you are now, with what you were formerly, or with what others are; for this is not wise. Come *with openness* to the light of the Scripture, to be convinced and humbled, or comforted and directed, by its instructions, as the case shall require. Study to know the depravity of your natures, the deceitfulness of sin, the vanity of the world, your wants and dangers, and the end and measure of your days. The duties of your station, and the design of particular providences, with your carriage under them, are necessary pieces of *self-knowledge*. (3.) Endeavor to obtain and keep up a deep impression of this important truth, *that you have but* one business *to do*; and that *every* affair and conduct in human life must be calculated for, and subservient to, *that one great end of your being*. God has made us for himself; to glorify and enjoy him. We are but pilgrims and strangers upon earth; and have here no continuing city. There is another state before us, a state of our everlasting residence, a state where we must be unspeakably and inconceivably happy or miserable, to all eternity. Our whole work therefore is to be pressing toward the mark for the prize of our high calling; to be looking to, and preparing for another and better country, even a heavenly. This is our whole business; and therefore, not to be enterprised as a secondary concern; not to be crowded into a corner, to make room for more agreeable entertainments; nor to be attended only at our vacant hours, when disencumbered from worldly business and sensual gratifications. *To fear God, and keep his commandments, is the whole of man* (Eccl. 12:13). I do not mean to inculcate the necessity of a *recluse life*, wholly taken up in devotion, and wholly separated from the common business and society of the world. No; I only recommend a *due sense* of the obligations we are under, in point of duty and interest, *to serve and enjoy God, as well at one time as another; as much in one business of life as another; and as much in our secular affairs, domestic concerns, company, and diversions, as in the special duties of religion and devotion.* Though *these* call for the more solemn engagement of the whole soul in their performance, being immediately directed to God himself; yet *the other* also

---

[4] The reader will find this duty explained and urged in Chapter 1, *On Reading the Scriptures*; which he may turn to for a fuller view of it.

are to be done in obedience to God, and with an eye to his glory. So that Christians have but *one business*; though they have *a great many duties of various kinds* belonging to it. Resolve then to engage in every affair of common life, and endeavor to manage it, out of duty to God, with a spiritual frame of soul, and from a hearty desire therein, to *show yourselves approved unto God*. (4.) Honor *the ordinances of God*, and wait upon God in them *all*, without any reserve. Let every duty, whether of the closet, of the family, or of public worship, be diligently and constantly maintained, each in its proper season. Live in the omission of none of them; nor let any ordinary occurrence or excuse divert and put you by, when the proper season and opportunity call for your attendance on them. You are under the *same* obligations at *all times*, as at *any time*, to honor divine institutions; and to observe them *all*, as to observe *any* of them; for they are *all* enjoined by the *same authority*; and to be performed to the *same object*; and for the *same end*. Therefore he who lives in the willful neglect of any known duty, relating to the ordinances of God, does thereby turn his back upon God and salvation. Be careful, then, to *prove*, to know and do, *what is the good, and perfect, and acceptable will of God*, concerning your duty in this matter. (5.) *Remember the Sabbath-day to keep it holy*. Sanctify it by a holy resting all that day, even from such worldly employments and recreations as are lawful on other days; and spending the whole time in the public and private exercises of God's worship, except so much as is to be taken up in the works of necessity and mercy.[5] (6.) *Abstain from all appearances of evil* (1 Thess. 5:22). Keep at the farthest distance possible from all error and sin of every kind, under what specious appearances soever they be presented to you; and even from everything that you suspect to be false, or sinful, or tending to draw yourselves, or others, into any sin or error. A prudent man foreseeth the evil, and hideth himself from the enemy that would rob him of his peace, or endanger the purity of his soul. Watch and pray, that ye enter not into temptation. Go not into the way of the wicked; stand not in the council of the ungodly; forsake the way of lies; and hate evil, all ye that love the Lord. You are not able to turn away the face of the least of the enemies of your souls, who are both artful and malicious. If sinners entice you, consent ye not. Evil communications corrupt good manners. Can a man take fire in his bosom, and not be burnt? or, Can we venture on temptations without being soiled? Our only safety is to have no fellowship with

---

[5] This point is largely handled in chap. 10, *Of the observation of the Lord's day*.

the unfruitful works of darkness, but rather to reprove them. (7.) *Walk by rule, in an exact observance of stated devotions.* The man that would live godly in a present evil world must walk circumspectly, redeeming the time. He must always abound in the work of the Lord, doing the duty of every day in its day, and of every season in its season. Common discretion teaches people to manage the business of life, upon this principle; and Christian prudence will as much direct us to time religious duties upon some plan; if we would perform them, with any prospect of advantage to ourselves, or with any view of recommending them to the esteem and approbation of the world. We are counseled to be in the fear of the Lord all the day long; to pray without ceasing; and to meditate in God's law day and night. But how can we comply with the mind of God in these things, unless we reduce to order and rule the system of our devotion, in the closet, family, and public assemblies? The quotation[6] on the margin contains an easy plain draft

---

[6] "You should begin the day with God. When you wake in the morning, let God have your first thoughts. Lift up our heart to him, with thankfulness for the preservations of the night; and in supplication to him for his presence with you, in the duties of the succeeding day. After such ejaculations, before you rise from bed, you will do well to consider with yourself, what are the duties before you this day, whereby God may be most glorified, your spiritual interests best subserved, and you most useful in your generation. Whilst arising from bed, and dressing yourself, entertain meditations upon subjects suited to the occasion, such as the necessity of your resurrection from spiritual death, or the certainty and consequences of the final resurrection at the great day of Christ's appearing and kingdom; the necessity of your being clothed with the righteousness of Christ; or the glorious livery, in which you hope to appear before the tribunal of your Judge, when you shall shine as the firmament, and as the stars forever and ever. These, or such like meditations, a variety whereof will readily offer to your mind, may be an excellent means to put your soul into a proper frame for the duties before you.

"When risen from bed, retire as soon as you conveniently can into your closet. Read some portion of the word of God; mixing it with faith, giving a close attention, making devout reflections and occasional ejaculations of prayer and praise, according to the subject-matter you are entertained with. After reading, pause a while, and endeavor to affect your mind, with lively impressions of the infinite perfections of the glorious Majesty, before whom you are approaching. Lift up your eyes to God, with fervent aspirations after the influences of his blessed Spirit, to help your infirmities, to teach you to pray, as you ought; and to make intercessions for you, with groanings which cannot be uttered. Thus, in the name of Christ, bow your knees before God, with an awful sense of the infinite distance between him and you, and of your entire unworthiness of his favor; yet with a humble hope and confidence in his infinite grace and mercy in Christ; and keep up a strict and continual guard over your thoughts and affections, that they do not wander from the business before you, and render the duty a mere superficial lip-service.

of a regular useful, and practicable system of Christian devotion. (8.) *Ob-*

"From your closet proceed to the duties of *family worship.* Call your whole household together; let none be absent. Read a chapter in the sacred Bible: and I would advise you commonly to read in course, that the whole word of God may be read in your family. Perhaps it may be an agreeable practice, and most for edification, to read in the Old Testament one part of the day, and in the New Testament the other. I would advise you to sing part of a psalm, and then pray with your family. Which done, gravely dismiss them, to their respective secular occasions.

"Having thus carried yourself and family through the morning-sacrifices, do not suppose, that you are now discharged from all religious and spiritual concerns, until the return of the stated times of divine worship, but keep your soul diligently, study to preserve and cherish still a spiritual frame. Intermix frequent occasional meditations and ejaculations, with all the business you are engaged in. After dinner, I would advise you to retire again into your closet for some exercises of devotion. Imitate David and Daniel in the frequency of your secret retirements; and make it your stated rule, at evening, in the morning, and at noon, to pray, and to let God hear your voice.

"Choose some convenient time every day for religious meditation, and solemn reflection. Daily spend half an hour, at least, in this useful and delightful employment; and more when your circumstances will allow it. Let the time be stated; and let no ordinary avocations prevent your duly attending upon this exercise, at the return of the appointed season. Perhaps experience will teach you, with the patriarch Isaac, to choose the evening for this service. But this depends upon the respective business and circumstances of life, and dispositions of mind, of each particular person. The whole word of God will afford you matter for your meditation; that you have a large field before you, enough to keep you happily employed to all eternity: but the perfections of the divine nature, the astonishing work of redemption by Jesus Christ, the glorious excellency of his person, and the wonderful benefits of his salvation, the incomparable glories of the heavenly world, the preciousness of your soul, with its various wants, and the like, should be the most common, as they are the most important subjects of your contemplation. Engage in this business as in the presence of God, call in your thoughts from every foreign concern, and keep them closely engaged. Deeply muse, until the fire burns: meditate on divine and eternal things, till they become real and visible to the eyes of your mind; even till your soul is brought (if it pleases God) to the top of Pisgah, and to a view of the heavenly Canaan. But I need not insist upon the methods of performing this duty. By a faithful and steady attendance upon it, your experience will quickly teach you the best manner of its performance.

"And now being brought to the close of the day, end it as you began it, with respect to the duties both of your closet and family. And when you betake yourself to your rest, review the conduct of the day past; and consider what matter of repentance, or of thanksgiving, is thereby before you. Solemnly interrogate yourself, whether you are fit to die; and what your state is like to prove, if you this night should awake in the eternal world. Your answer to this momentous question, must either excite your diligence to flee from the wrath to come; or animate your love and gratitude to God, and your zeal for his service, in hope of the glory to be revealed. To conclude, endeavor to improve your waking minutes on your bed (whether before you first fall asleep, or when you

serve carefully the dispensations of providence. This is an important branch of Christian duty, and verily hath its reward; for "Whoso is wise, and will observe these things, even they shall understand the lovingkindness of the LORD" (Ps. 107:43). No sooner does religion take place in the soul, and men are brought under the influence and power of it, by an effectual touch from the divine Spirit, but their eyes are open toward God, and fixed upon him; and as religion prevails in the soul, a sense of God prevails also. They eye his authority, own his providence, and endeavor to converse with him therein; and, according as this temper is more or less predominant, they are more or less religious. Therefore adore his hand in the affairs of daily providence, relative to your food and raiment, your health and strength, your protection and refreshment. Own his providence in the success of your affairs, and the countenance of your friends. Acknowledge his hand in your *adversities*, which are not casual productions, nor accidental events, but the appointments of a wise and merciful God. Own his providence in the severest strokes of it; if he gives a thorn in the flesh, sends a messenger of Satan to buffet you, or takes away any of your dearest enjoyments, submit to his will, and say, *Good is the word of the Lord.* Reverence his providence in *public affairs* that concern the nations of the world, in all their changes and revolutions; consider them as conducted by a wise and steady hand, as answering the purposes of the great *Lord of all*, and as constituting part of his glorious scheme in the government of the world. Own

---

shall awake in the night) in religious and divine meditation. So when you wake and rise in the morning, still be with God.

"Thus I have set before you a method of filling up your time with duty; with such duties, as will every one of them tend to promote your progress to eternal bliss. And I need now only further put you in mind, that besides these daily exercises of religion, there are seasons wherein the whole day should be taken up in the immediate service of God: excepting when we are called off by works of necessity and mercy. Such is the Lord's day, which ought to be so strictly sanctified that we should not so much as allow ourselves to think our own thoughts, or to speak our own words. Such are likewise occasional days of humiliation and thanksgiving, which the Scripture calls our Sabbaths. The frequent and devout celebration of these days may prove of eminent usefulness to promote the life and power of godliness. The Scriptures do not indeed direct how often these should be attended. They are a free-will offering: and the state of your soul, with the dispensations of providence towards yourself, your family, or the church of God; and the respective business, whether temporal or spiritual, which you have before you, will be a sufficient direction, as to the time and manner of performing these duties." See Jonathan Dickinson. *Familiar Letters to a Gentleman upon a Variety of Seasonable and Important Subjects in Religion*, pp. 370–374.

his providence in your *religious affairs*: observe daily your heart, temper, and frame, your miscarriages and unworthiness, discouragements and infirmities, darkness and fears, comforts and assistances—that you may join trembling with your mirth before him. Thus walk with God, and maintain a daily intercourse with him in *all his providences*; in stated, common providences; and in special, occasional providences; exercising under *both* such graces as answer the several dispensations of God towards you. *Trust in the Lord*, whose kingdom of providence ruleth over all; trust in him as thy covenant-God, "with all thine heart; and lean not unto thine own understanding. In all thy ways acknowledge him, and he shall direct thy paths" (Prov. 3:5–6).

N.B., Having urged these *general duties*, it may be expedient to descend to such *particulars* as are adapted to the several situations and circumstances of the persons to be dealt with, in respect of *temper, stations, relations, age, employment*, and *condition*. In writing on the subject, I am obliged to make a much fuller enumeration than can be supposed to be either necessary or seasonable, on any particular occasion; and also to *detach* these instructions and duties that might be laid down with more propriety, in a *running connection*. I therefore proceed,

3. Particular Duties of Christians Recommended
III. To suggest some of the particular duties that ought to be proposed to the consideration of people, and pressed home on their conscience, according to that *six-fold view* of their character, situation, and circumstances I have mentioned just now.

To the Tempers of People
First, When we consider mankind at large, we are amazed at *the variety of tempers* among them, which arise from their different constitutions, education, or callings. Every temper of the human mind is an instrument of unrighteousness unto sin, and exposes a person to the power of some well-laid temptation. Who can understand his errors? The heart is deceitful above all things, and desperately wicked. Out of the heart proceed evil thoughts, murders, adulteries, etc., and these are the things that defile a man; while a deceived heart, working by his *spirit* or *temper*, leads everyone away from God, and turns him to *his own way*, in opposition to *the way of godliness*. The general rule is, carefully to *keep ourselves from our*

iniquity (Ps. 18:23), and to "lay aside...the sin which doth so easily beset us" (Heb. 12:1).

1. *Take heed and beware of a covetous temper*; for it is *idolatry* in the sight of God, it is evil in its nature, and pernicious in its consequences; it is inconsistent with the love of the Father, and cannot be subject to the divine law; it is *the root of all evil*, and destroys much good. Let your conversation be without covetousness, and be content with such things as you have; for God hath said, I will never leave you, nor forsake you. Give glory to God, by choosing him as your *exceeding great reward*. Wherefore should you dishonor God, and ruin your souls, by giving a foolish and guilty preference to *lying vanities*, when a gracious God demands your heart, and promises you happiness in his favor and presence?

2. *Be angry, and sin not; neither let the sun go down upon your wrath.* Causeless and immoderate anger proceeds from a proud and haughty temper; and is contrary to gospel-meekness, which is of great price in the sight of God. Learn of Christ, who was meek and lowly. Remember that every passionate tongue is set on fire by hell. No one has offended us so often as we have offended God; and therefore our anger should be against our own sins. Let all bitterness, and wrath, and anger be put away. In patience possess ye your souls. There is no passion in heaven, and there should be none in a heavenly mind. Put on, as the elect of God, holy and beloved, bowels of mercies, kindness, humbleness of mind, meekness, longsuffering; forbearing one another, and forgiving one another, if any man have a quarrel against any; even as Christ forgave you, so also do ye.

3. *Lay aside all guile and hypocrisies.* What purpose can they serve, while Omniscience is your witness, and will open the book of his remembrance at your judgment? All things are naked and opened unto him with whom we have to do. Study to be sincere in your professions of love to God and men. The honorable character of Nathanael, an *Israelite indeed, in whom there was no guile*, is left on record for our imitation; as a brand of infamy has marked the odious character of a set of people, *who professed much love with their mouth, while their heart went after their idols*. The man that shall be honored to abide in the tabernacle of God, and to dwell in his holy hill, must walk uprightly, and *speak the truth in his heart*. We should daily pray that the Lord would deliver our soul from lying lips, and from a deceitful tongue; but if we practice them, while we pray against them, we curse ourselves. Guard against all deceit, both in your dealings with God

and men. Cursed be the deceiver, and the mouth of liars shall be stopped. Show yourselves valiant for the truth, and open without craftiness.

4. *Be clothed with humility*; for God resisteth the proud; but he giveth grace to the humble. Pride is a sure sign of a little mind, and a haughty spirit goeth before a fall. Self-conceit resteth only in the bosom of fools. In the catalog of these things which the Lord hateth, and which are an abomination in his sight, we find *a proud look* occupies the first place (Prov. 6:16–19). These that are puffed up with pride are in the high way to fall into the condemnation of the devil. Behold, his soul which is lifted up is not upright in him. Be kindly affectioned one to another; with brotherly love, in honor preferring one another. Pride ever must, and ever will, provoke contempt. Gifts of knowledge, utterance, prudence, or mental endowments of any kind; as well as health, strength, riches, and honors, are *talents*, with which God has put us in trust, and for which we must give an account—a consideration that should make us both humble and active in making use of them.

5. *Mortify your members which are upon the earth; fornication, uncleanness, inordinate affection, and evil concupiscence*, for which things' sake the wrath of God cometh on the children of disobedience. Remember that the Lord our God and Redeemer hath said, "Thou shalt not commit adultery" (Ex. 20:14). An infallible commentator hath assured us that this commandment implies, "that whosoever looketh on a woman to lust after her hath committed adultery with her already in his heart" (Matt. 5:27–28).

> Know ye not that your bodies are the members of Christ? shall I then take the members of Christ, and make them the members of an harlot? God forbid. What? know ye not that he which is joined to an harlot is one body? for two, saith he, shall be one flesh. But he that is joined unto the Lord is one spirit. Flee fornication. Every sin that a man doeth is without the body; but he that committeth fornication sinneth against his own body. What? know ye not that your body is the temple of the Holy Ghost which is in you, which ye have of God, and ye are not your own? For ye are bought with a price: therefore glorify God in your body, and in your spirit, which are God's (1 Cor. 6:15–20).

This is the will of God, even your sanctification, that ye should abstain from fornication: that every one of you should know how to possess his vessel in sanctification and honour; not in the lust of concupiscence, even as the Gentiles which know not God (1 Thess. 4:3–5).

The *fear of God*, ruling in your heart, would preserve you from sinful compliances with enticements to this sin, and make you act on the principles of Joseph, who repelled the temptation of his mistress, saying, *How shall I do this great wickedness, and sin against God?* Let not filthiness, and foolish talking, and jesting that is not convenient, be once named amongst you, as becometh saints. Avoid all dangerous familiarities, that may endanger the purity of your minds; and be temperate in using the refreshments of nature.

6. *Swear not at all* in your daily discourse. "Thou shalt not," at any time, or on any provocation, "take the name of the LORD thy God in vain; for the LORD will not hold him guiltless that taketh his name in vain" (Ex. 20:7). None is so ignorant as not to know that *swearing* is a profanation of that glorious and fearful name, *the Lord our God*. He that lives in the fear of God is so far from being capable of it, that it shocks him to hear others offending this way. We should daily pray that *God's name may be hallowed* (Matt. 6:9); and therefore ought not to blaspheme it. Angels praise, and devils tremble at that name, which is wantonly profaned by the profligate swearer. The wickedness of this sin is so transcendent, so unprovoked, so unprofitable, that I shall only leave that dreadful passage, to the consideration of those who dare be guilty of it, "As he," speaking more immediately of Judas, though not confined to him only, "loved cursing, so let it come unto him: as he delighted not in blessing, so let it be far from him. As he clothed himself with cursing like as with his garment, so let it come into his bowels like water, and like oil into his bones" (Ps. 109:17–19).

7. *Take heed, lest at any time your hearts be overcharged with surfeiting and drunkenness* (Luke 21:34). Let your moderation in eating and drinking be known to all men; for the Lord is at hand. Gluttony and drunkenness are the works of the flesh; and the practicers of them are *sensual persons, not having the Spirit* of God. Excess in eating or drinking is most wicked and shameful, being not only a sin against God, but a reproach and an injury to ourselves. Whether we eat or drink, we should do all to the glory of

God; but this is impossible, where men prostitute these precious bounties of heaven, to the base purpose of making their belly their god. It is high time to awake out of sleep; the night is far spent, the day is at hand; let us therefore cast off the works of darkness, and let us put on the armor of light. Let us walk honestly as in the day; not in rioting and drunkenness: but put ye on the Lord Jesus Christ, and make not provision for the flesh, to fulfill the lusts thereof.

8. *Slander, calumny, backbiting,* and *tale-bearing* are a black list of unmanly, as well as unchristian vices. They are the result of the *meanest pride, malice,* and *cowardice.* All that are guilty of them proclaim themselves to be the servants of their father the devil; for their temper is his very image, and they do his works. "He that uttereth a slander, is *a fool*" (Prov. 10:18), that is, a very wicked person; for he neither feareth God, nor regardeth man. That memorable passage should continually dwell on our minds, wherein God addresses himself to the wicked in these words,

> What hast thou to do to declare my statutes, or that thou shouldest take my covenant in thy mouth? seeing thou hatest instruction, and castest my words behind thee... Thou givest thy mouth to evil, and thy tongue frameth deceit. Thou sittest and speakest against thy brother; thou slanderest thine own mother's son. These things hast thou done, and I kept silence; thou thoughtest that I was altogether such an one as thyself: but I will reprove thee, and set them in order before thine eyes. Now consider this, ye that forget God, lest I tear you in pieces, and there be none to deliver. Whoso offereth praise glorifieth me: and to him that ordereth his conversation aright will I shew the salvation of God (Ps. 50:16–23).

Grievous revolters from God will naturally choose to *walk with slanders* against men; *they are brass and iron,* without either shame or remorse; *they are all corrupters* (Jer. 6:28). It is quite contrary to the genius of true Christianity for a man to go up and down as a tale-bearer among his people, saying, Report, and I will report it; such poor creatures cannot rest until they do mischief, and their sleep is taken away, unless they can propagate some malicious report, to make some envied character fall. They should be detested by all the world; for they will *reveal* the most important *secrets* (Prov. 11:13); their *words are as wounds* that affect the reputation, and tend to the ruin of society (Prov. 18:8); and where there are none of that vile cast, *strife ceaseth* (Prov. 26:20). Even heathens know, by the light of nature, that *backbiters are worthy of death*, as a deserved judgment of God (Rom. 1:30, 32). The man that shall abide in the tabernacle of God, and who shall dwell in his holy hill, backbiteth not with his tongue, nor doth evil to his neighbor, nor taketh up a reproach against his neighbor (Ps. 15:1, 3).

9. *Be not slothful, but be ye followers of them, who through faith and patience inherit the promises* (Heb. 6:12). To be slothful in the business of this life is criminal; but to be slothful in what concerns a future state is a great folly, as well as a grievous sin. Give the utmost diligence in the use of every appointed means of salvation; for the case is of the highest importance to the everlasting welfare of your souls. Let us not give occasion for any to reproach us with lukewarmness in the service of God. The laborious ant, the busy world, the unceasing exertions of the power and providence of God, and even the assiduity of the devil, who goeth about continually, seeking whom he may devour, as well as the never-intermitted services performed by angels, and the spirits of just men made perfect, before the throne, concur with every obligation of duty, and every regard to our own interest, to provoke our emulation. Let us constantly and vigorously press toward the mark, for the prize of the high calling of God in Christ Jesus. Never was ambition so well directed as toward this mark; and never did so many powerful motives concur to excite all our diligence, and to engage all our powers of body and mind, as in this noblest cause.

10. *Do not rest in a lifeless form of religion*, without experiencing its power. Do not suppose you are Christians, merely because you have been born in (what is called) a Christian land, because you were baptized in the name of Christ, because you have been favored with a Christian education, and because you keep up the form of godliness. All this may be in your case, and yet you may have no more but *a name that you live*. You should not only consider what you profess *to be* and *to do*; but aim at being *really* what you would have the world think you to be. You should not only consider what you do in the duties of religion; but from what *motives* you act, and what *ends* you propose. A mere form of knowledge in the truths of religion, and of obedience in the practice of it, may be easily acquired; but what will it profit a man, when he has got it? For he is not a Christian, that is one outwardly; neither does God reckon that to be religious wor-

ship, which implies only bodily service; but the true circumcision worship God in the spirit, and have no confidence in the flesh. Rise nobly above the influence of *custom, example, education,* and *form*. Yield yourselves to the Lord, in obedience to his commandments, and study to approve yourselves to him, in every branch of vital godliness, as these that are alive from the dead. In serving God, we should never forget with whom we have to do; and that no worship becomes him, except what is performed in spirit and in truth.

11. Do not *confide in your religious performances*. Though we ought to *do righteousness* in our daily practice; yet not to *go about to establish a righteousness of our own*. If you think to be received into, or continued in, the favor of God, on account of your works, you make void the law of God, by reducing it to your own standard; you deny the grace of God; you lay a foundation for boasting; you make the cross of Christ of none effect. It is not according to our works that we are accepted; for God justifieth the ungodly through faith in Christ, who was made under the law, to redeem us that are under the law. We have the instructive example of the apostle of the Gentiles for our directory in this matter,

> But what things were gain to me, those I counted loss for Christ. Yea doubtless, and I count all things but loss for the excellency of the knowledge of Christ Jesus my Lord: for whom I have suffered the loss of all things, and do count them but dung, that I may win Christ, and be found in him, not having mine own righteousness, which is of the law, but that which is through the faith of Christ, the righteousness which is of God by faith: that I may know him, and the power of his resurrection, and the fellowship of his sufferings, being made conformable unto his death (Phil. 3:7–10).

12. *Be not mockers, lest your bands be made strong* (Isa. 28:22); "The eye that mocketh at his father, and despiseth to obey his mother, the ravens of the valley shall pick it out, and the young eagles shall eat it" (Prov. 30:17). This shall be the punishment of an unnatural son to an earthly parent. How much more shall a righteous God severely punish these presumptuous sinners that *delight in their scorning* at his Son and Spirit, his word and ordinances, his people and Sabbaths? These alarming words should be engraven on our hearts, and frequently in our thoughts,

Because I have called, and ye refused; I have stretched out my hand, and no man regarded; but ye have set at nought all my counsel, and would none of my reproof: I also will laugh at your calamity; I will mock when your fear cometh; when your fear cometh as desolation, and your destruction cometh as a whirlwind; when distress and anguish cometh upon you. Then shall they call upon me, but I will not answer; they shall seek me early, but they shall not find me: for that they hated knowledge, and did not choose the fear of the LORD: they would none of my counsel: they despised all my reproof. Therefore shall they eat of the fruit of their own way, and be filled with their own devices. For the turning away of the simple shall slay them, and the prosperity of fools shall destroy them. But whoso hearkeneth unto me shall dwell safely, and shall be quiet from fear of evil (Prov. 1:24–33).

13. *Take heed lest ye be overcharged with the cares of this world*, for they choke the word of God, and render professors unfruitful. Who, by taking the greatest thought, can add one cubit to his stature? or, make one hair of his head white or black? Cast all your cares upon the Lord, for he careth for you. Be anxiously careful for nothing; but in everything by prayer and supplication, with thanksgiving, make your requests known unto God. The cares of the world become dangerous to us, either from a distrust of the care of God about us, or through a sinful delight in the enjoyments of sense. Our ambition should not aspire to great things in the world. Daily bread from day to day is all that our Redeemer taught his disciples to pray for. Our treasures are to be laid up in heaven; and where the treasure is, there will the heart be also. Consider your circumstances; and never give place to proud ambition, which would carry you above a station, where you might live in ease and credit, to aim at grasping an empty bubble of imaginary happiness, that will pierce you through with many sorrows.

This I say, brethren, the time is short: it remaineth, that both they that have wives be as though they had none; and they that weep, as though they wept not; and they that rejoice, as though they rejoiced not; and they that buy, as though they possessed not; they that use this world, as not abusing it: for the fashion of this world passeth away. But I would have you without carefulness (1 Cor. 7:29–32).

14. *Be not lovers of pleasures, more than lovers of God.* The poor unsatisfying delights of the world entirely disappoint our wishes. An immortal soul can taste no real joy from the low gratifications of a beast, however refined. Look into your own hearts, and say, what happiness all your pleasures have brought you. Have you not been commonly disappointed in their possession, and grasped a shadow, where you thought to embrace a substance? Your heart beat high in the prospect of some delightful scene; but when it came, it palled upon your taste, and disgusted more than it delighted you; and in an hour of retirement, when reflection returned, and the delusions of imagination gave way to the just remonstrances of conscience, how sensibly have you felt that you chased a phantom of happiness, which proved to be real *vanity and vexation of spirit!* No pleasures are solid and lasting, but these that are to be found in the ways of wisdom. The pleasures of this life (including the *excess of lawful pleasures*, as well as those things that are *only pleasant to the corruption of our nature*) enter in, and choke the word of God (Luke 8:14).

15. *Ponder well the path of thy feet.* Consult reason and prudence, in regard to the expediency and seasonableness of every undertaking. All things are lawful, but all things are not expedient. Be ye "wise as serpents, and harmless as doves" (Matt. 10:16). Vain babbling does not become the disciples of Christ; and it is still more unworthy of them to let corrupt communication proceed out of their mouth. The whole book of Proverbs is an excellent directory on this point. I shall only mention one passage,

> Keep thy heart with all diligence; for out of it are the issues of life. Put away from thee a froward mouth, and perverse lips put far from thee. Let thine eyes look right on, and let thine eyelids look straight before thee. Ponder the path of thy feet, and let all thy ways be established. Turn not to the right hand nor to the left: remove thy foot from evil (Prov. 4:23–27).

Be not *rash* in your resolutions; be not hasty in making promises, or in pronouncing threats, in complimentary panegyrics, or in severe censures; for he that is hasty, in these things, with his mouth, sinneth. Do not lay a foundation for some strong temptation to future sin, or else for bitter sorrow, by some inconsiderate rash step, in any important business of life. In every enterprise, set the Lord before you, and choose such a course as will be attended with fewest trials to the peace and purity of a good conscience.

16. *Take heed, brethren, lest there be in any of you an evil heart of unbelief in departing from the living God* (Heb. 3:12). Believe with your heart what you know of the being, perfections, and word of God. Do not doubt, far less deny, his veracity. Consider *his commandments*, as eternal righteousness; *his threatenings*, as a revelation of his wrath against all your ungodliness and unrighteousness; *his doctrines*, as unchangeable truth; *his promises*, as unconditional declarations of his goodwill towards men, and as yea and amen in Christ; *his counsels and invitations*, as opening a door of access into the enjoyment of his favor in Christ; and *his providences*, as holy, just, and wise. And believe all these, with a particular view to your own duty and interest; that you may be comforted, and kept, through the faith of them, unto salvation, by the power of God.

17. *Be strong and of a good courage*, in everything that concerns *your duty* and *comfort*. Be not afraid of the discouragements that attend the way of your duty. Cleave to God with purpose of heart; and on no consideration suffer the fear of man to be your snare. Fear the Lord your God only; for he is able to destroy both soul and body in hell (Matt. 10:28). Do not yield to the suggestions of despair, but build your comfort upon everlasting grounds, that will bear you up under every kind of events. That you may be fortified with prudent Christian courage against every occurrence, on the best principles, you must go in the strength of the Lord your God, and make mention of his righteousness, even of his only. Consider your everlasting interests, as secured on the bottom of the everlasting covenant, which is ordered in all things and sure; and consider your temporal concerns, as under the direction of his providence, who is the God of all grace, and your own God. Such views will inspire you with a modest courage; and will greatly contribute to keep your minds in perfect peace, by staying them on the Lord.[7]

To Their Stations
Secondly, Mankind, according to their *several stations*, may be considered either as *superiors*, or as *inferiors*, or as *equals*. The same person, viewed in different lights, may perhaps be a superior in one respect, an inferior

---

[7] I could add many more examples, but *these* may serve to show what may be offered on similar cases.

in another, and an equal in a third; but if he is considered in one view and comparison, he cannot, in the same respect, be both a superior and an inferior, or an inferior and an equal. The supposition of such a thing is a contradiction in terms. The different stations of mankind have duties proper to the stations respectively annexed to them. I shall give a few instances to guide you, through the blessing of God, to the proper discharge of the duties of your stations.

1. It is incumbent on *superiors* to carry in a becoming manner toward all that are below them; to maintain the dignity of their own character, by a prudent moderate use of their authority; and to give an example of the duties they require, so far as may consist with their station. Generosity and soberness, in their eminent places, will greatly adorn their own character, and will best secure a due respect to all their commands. Superior stations call for great circumspection, and a peculiar eminence in holiness, diligence, and usefulness.

2. It is the duty of *inferiors* to acknowledge those that are over them in the Lord, and to honor them; to regard their persons and obey their lawful commands; to pray for them, as God hath commanded; and to imitate their graces and virtues.

3. *Equals* ought to carry with all openness, meekness, and condescension to one another; to forbear every disgustful appearance of affecting to be haughty, ambitious, and assuming; to provoke emulation, by prudent counsel, and a holy example; and to take the words and actions of their equals in the most favorable light, if there happens to be any ground for an unkind construction.

To Their Manifold Relations

Thirdly, Another light in which we may view the world is taken from *the manifold relations*, whereby mankind are tied to one another, according to the *nature* of the relation, and the *share* of every individual in the particular connection. What may be said on this head will probably be thought *unnecessary* by some; others will perhaps reckon it *foreign* to my purpose; and it is possible some will say they are *hard sayings*. I am prepared for every censure. Bishop Hopkins expresses himself entirely to my satisfaction on this point, in the following words:

As there is nothing wherein the life and power of godliness, and the very life of religion, is more concerned, than in *a conscientious performance of relative duties*; so there is nothing that grates and jars more upon the spirits of men, than to be put in mind of, and reproved about, *these duties*, which are of such common and daily occurrence in the whole course of our lives.[8]

Upon this principle, I shall despise censure, while I endeavor, in the meantime, not to give any offense that would merit it; and proceed to set before you as concise and just an account of *relative duties* as I am able. They may be classed under these divisions, as they refer (1.) To *magistrates* and *subjects*; (2.) To *husband* and *wife*; (3.) To *parents* and *children*; (4.) To *masters* and *servants*; (5.) To *neighbors*; Or (6.) To *friends*.

To Magistrates and Subjects
1. The *right behavior of magistrates and subjects to each other*, is to be explained in the first place. *Magistrates* are the ordinance of God, and his ministers unto men for good. The authority, with which they are invested, is originally in, and derived from the King of kings, and Lord of lords. Their *empires* are but so many *provinces* of his universal kingdom of nature. Their kingdoms are *only* of this world; nor are they authorized to claim any power in what pertains *merely* to the conscience. To reform the church of Christ, and to establish the system of her order and fellowship, belong to *another province*.[9] But it pertains to their office, and is their duty, to provide a system of wholesome, useful laws; to appoint men of approved ability and integrity to be in trust, for the execution of these laws, under them; to distribute justice impartially, and particularly to maintain the cause of the oppressed poor, and to restrain the insolence of their proud oppressors; and to be most exemplary for virtue and religion. In a word, they ought to fear God above all, to be prudent in their designs, courageous in their performances, faithful in their promises, wise in their counsels, careful observers of their own laws, zealous for their subjects' welfare, merciful

---
[8] Ezekiel Hopkins. *Works*, p. 133.
[9] "I despair of seeing due love among church members restored, as long as the church among us is so mixed with, and so little separated from the world, and until the church be more distinguished from the nation, for as fond as we have been of *a national church*." See Thomas Boston. *Works*, p. 303.

to the oppressed, favorable to the good, terrible to the evil, and just to all. They ought to remember that *they are gods*, and therefore should rule and govern, as they judge God himself would do, were he visible here upon earth; and also that *they are men*, and therefore must give an account unto the great God of all that trust he hath reposed in them.

Subjects owe reciprocal duties to magistrates; particularly, they ought to submit "to every ordinance of man for the Lord's sake" (1 Peter 2:13–14). We find the apostle instructing Titus, to put those to whom he ministered "in mind to be subject to principalities and powers, to obey magistrates" (Titus 3:1). Indeed, if anything be enjoined that is contrary to religion, it is a plain case that they ought to obey God rather than men; but in every other case, they ought to be subject to the higher powers. Subjects should *honor* magistrates. Their exalted stations entitle them to esteem and reverence. Disrespect, showed to their persons, tends to weaken their power, and to hinder the good effect of their administration. The apostle reckons that they, who were not afraid to speak evil of dignities, despised government (2 Peter 2:10). The Jews were expressly forbid to "revile the gods," that is, their governors (Ex. 22:28). *Subjects should pay to their governors that tribute and custom* which the law appoints. What can be more reasonable than that they should contribute with cheerfulness toward the support of the government, who are protected by it in the possession of their rights? The apostle, speaking of the duty of subjects to pay tribute to their rulers, presses the performance of it with this consideration, that they are taken up with the common concerns, "For for this cause pay ye tribute also: for they are God's ministers, attending continually upon this very thing" (Rom. 13:6). Subjects ought to *pray for those that are in authority*. We find the apostle laying a great stress upon this, " I exhort therefore, that, first of all, supplications, prayers, intercessions, and giving of thanks, be made for all men; for kings, and for all that are in authority; that we may lead a quiet and peaceable life in all godliness and honesty" (1 Tim. 2:1–2). A good magistrate is a great blessing; and the higher his station is, the greater is his usefulness. It is very reasonable that those who share in the benefits of his government should give thanks for him unto God, by whom kings reign, and princes decree justice; and put up fervent requests for the preservation of his life, and the success of his undertakings. The welfare of many is concerned in the right management of rulers; and therefore we should be earnest in our addresses to the King of kings, that he would give them that wisdom which is profitable to direct; that they may use their power to restrain the vicious, and to encourage virtue and religion.

To Husbands and Wives
2. The duties of *the conjugal relation* are to be considered, in the next place. The relation betwixt husband and wife is the most intimate of all others; and comprehends all the sweets and endearments of the strictest friendship; especially where it obtains between discreet, virtuous, and worthy persons. A certain superiority of one of the parties in it, is so tempered with an equality between both, by reason of the near union of their persons and interests, that it founds and requires duties *common* on both sides, as well as some that are *distinct* and *peculiar* to each.

The duties that are *equally* incumbent on both husband and wife are chiefly the following, *viz.*, *Love to each other's persons*: for what true conjugal happiness can there be without a mutual strong affection? and how without it can the many careful and difficult offices of a married life be duly discharged? The fairest, civilest, kindest usage cannot be an equivalent for the want of cordial love, where it is perceived to be absent. *A strict care about maintaining peace* is another *common* conjugal duty. An hearty mutual love is a promising and hopeful means to this end; nor can it be reasonably expected, where this is wanting. Both parties should habituate themselves to soft and kind expressions and actions, looking on all words of bitterness and disdain, especially of the grosser kind, as monstrous, and in the highest degree unsuitable. They should also watch against *taking offense*, by making all reasonable allowances for difference of sentiments and temper, as well as for various discomposing accidents; and by the practice of much mutual forbearance, without narrowly criticizing every unguarded word and step that may proceed from surprises, or easily admitting jealousies and suspicions of unkindness. And whenever any impressions of uneasiness, or displeasure, are made on either party, let them speedily be removed by suitable condescensions on the other, instead of eagerly vindicating the thing that has given the offense. *The inviolable preservation of conjugal fidelity and chastity* is a bond of equal obligation on both the husband and the wife. By the marriage-contract they pass over their right in themselves to their partners, and become each other's property; a property of the most nice and tender sort, which cannot be alienated, without the highest injustice done to the party injured, and such a wrong as is not to be repaired. And finally, *endeavors must be used by both parties to promote each other's interest as one common interest.* In their worldly concerns they must rise and fall together; and the indolence or extravagance of either will greatly affect them both. With regard to their spiritual interest, if married persons have any just sense of it at all, they will readily acknowledge a strong obligation on them, jointly to pursue it in their own souls, as well as in their family. With these views they ought to come together; and with these they should dwell together, as *heirs of the grace of life,* in the united exercises of religion and virtue, praying with and for each other, frequently conferring on divine things, strengthening one another's hands, in works of piety and goodness, and attending to every religious duty with so much the more exactness and diligence, that these their prayers and religious endeavors may not be hindered.

The duties that are particularly incumbent on *the husband* in the conjugal state, may be summed up in his *loving his wife as himself* (Eph. 5:33). To *rule his wife* is not made in Scripture the distinguishing province of the husband. This is left implied in the prescription to her of being subject; nor is it so proper to call the governing party to the exercise of his power, which he is generally ready enough for of himself, as to regulate it. *Love* therefore, is fitly and only recommended to the husband, who being the superior, may be most likely to think himself dispensed with in it; and that hereby he may recompense, and render more easy, the submission of the wife. Love also, on the husband's part, has some particular measures of condescension in it; and where it is strong, and managed with prudence, it will secure his doing his whole part well. Now, this must be shown in the management of his authority. His authority must not be sunk in a *fond love*; and no more must his love be lost in an *overbearing authority*; but they should temper and correct the one the other. By no means should he affect to make a show of his superiority at all times, even on the most trifling occasions; but for the most part, he should content himself to desire rather than to enjoin, and try to gain over reason and consent by proper arguments, rather than arbitrarily exact a compliance with his will. He should also support his wife's dignity and authority in the family, as next to his own, and secure unto her her proper share of government over children and servants. He ought to make the best reasonable provision for her he can, both during his own life, and in case of his prior decease. In a word, his behavior must be full of tenderness, condescension, and forbearance, for all this is implied in that command, *Husbands, love your wives, and be not bitter against them*. They ought neither to speak nor act anything toward them with a design, or which has a tendency to exasperate or grieve them; but should be as much superior in love as in authority, and in many instances *do honor to the wife as to the weaker vessel*, and because she is such.

The duties of *the wife* are *obedience* and *submission* to her husband. The man is the head of the woman (1 Cor. 11:3). Hence wives are called to submit themselves, and to be in subjection, to their own husbands (Eph. 5:22–23; 1 Peter 3:1); to see that they reverence them, even as Sarah obeyed Abraham, calling him *lord* (Eph. 5:33; 1 Peter 3:6). Paul says "I suffer not a woman to teach, nor to usurp authority over the man" (1 Tim. 2:11–12). All her deportment should be so ordered as to confess the *headship* of her husband. Her desires and advices should be urged with the law of kindness in her mouth. No point must be attempted to be gained by authority and clamor. And methinks, when nature has formed the sex with such advantages for persuasion, in a soft and gentle way, it is as imprudent as it is unnatural to leave it for that of imperiousness, violence, and vociferation; and to exchange *the graces*, which nature has made of her train, for *the furies*. Moreover, she ought to be an *help meet for her husband* in everything, that pertains to his body and soul, his estate and reputation. Her domestic character is admirably well described in that beautiful passage (Prov. 31:10–31).

To Parents and Children
3. The duties of *parents and children* respectively, are now to be represented. And here I shall begin with the duties incumbent on parents toward their children.

The sum of *parental duties* is laid down by Paul, "ye fathers, provoke not your children to wrath; but bring them up in the nurture and admonition of the Lord" (Eph. 6:4). Here is a restraint laid upon parents, as to the exercise of their authority over their children: *Fathers, provoke not your children to wrath*. This does not mean that they must spare the rod, or withhold necessary correction, when their children are in a fault; for that is, in some cases, highly necessary for their good, and is recommended in Scripture, as one means of a good education, *The rod and reproof give wisdom* (Prov. 29:15). But the charge to parents, not to provoke their children to wrath, must be understood in this limited sense: "Do not use undue and unreasonable severity against them; and give them no just occasion to be angry with you, for any tyrannical exertion of your power and authority." As the horse which is bridled in too strait, grows impatient of the reins; so when children are restrained with too much severity, they are apt to grow impatient of their parents' authority, and to fly out into wild licentiousness. Let parents therefore be as much on their guard against cruel severity toward their children on the one hand, as against a foolish and fond indulgence of them on the other. Unreasonable severity is the way to discourage them, and to alienate both their *love* and their *fear* from their parents. If you would have them love you, and profit by your instructions, you must not provoke their hatred, but endeavor to secure their affection; you must strive to soften them with kindness, and not harden them by cruelty. The example of our *heavenly Father*, who is slow to wrath, and plenteous in mercy, who never afflicts willingly, nor grieves his children but for their profit, is a pattern to human fathers. It is their duty to *bring them up*, to nurse them in their infancy, to feed and clothe them, to watch over them, and protect them in their helpless age; and also to provide, as well as they can, for their comfortable subsistence in the world, when they grow up to years of maturity. Parents should lay up for their children (2 Cor. 12:14). Or, if they cannot leave them estates, they ought to provide them with *trades*, by which they may get a livelihood. Poor parents, who can lay up nothing for their children, should bring them up to *labor*, and inure them to *industry*, which sometimes proves a better portion than an estate of inheritance. "If any provide not for his own, and specially for those of his own house, he hath denied the faith, and is worse than an infidel" (1 Tim. 5:8). They should bring up their children in *human knowledge and literature*, and endeavor to polish their minds by as liberal an education as their circumstances will afford to give them. It is as much their duty to cultivate their minds as to nourish their bodies; and to form them for usefulness in civil life, as to feed and clothe them, till they grow to be men and women. But their duty is not confined to this; for they are under the most solemn obligation to bring them up in the *knowledge and fear of the Lord*. Give them a religious education, by making them familiarly conversant with the Holy Scriptures betimes, and adding catechetical instructions to assist their understandings from their childhood up; as also by prudent discipline and moderate corrections, when necessary and seasonable; and by your own regular example, and daily prayers with and for them. In this manner, as a nurse cherishes her children, nourish them up "in the words of faith and of good doctrine" (1 Tim. 4:6), according to the commandment of the Lord; that, by his grace, they may learn to fear him, and reverence their superiors, and may know the way to eternal life through Jesus Christ. Watch over and restrain the first appearances of pride and passion, vanity and deceit, and all the buddings of corrupt nature in them. Warn them against youthful sins and errors, that would be destructive to their comfort, reputation, and usefulness in this world, and to their eternal happiness in the next. Exert your parental authority, like faithful Abraham (Gen. 18:19), to regulate their outward behavior; and inure them to public, family, and secret worship. Do all that in you lies, in a humble dependence upon the Lord for his blessing, to cultivate their minds, morals, and religion; and to train them up in the way they should go, in hope, that when they are old, they will not depart from it (Prov. 22:6). And pray to God to make all your endeavors successful. You may perhaps command your children's ears so far as to oblige them to hear you, but their hearts are out of your reach and power, and can only be renewed by almighty grace. Beg this blessing of him for your dear children; wrestle with him earnestly for the life of their souls; bear their everlasting interests upon your minds, both in your family and in your closet devotions. Give them the clearest proofs that you have a vast concern for them, by the earnestness of your prayers in their behalf.

The *duties of children* to their parents, are summarily comprehended in *the honor* they are commanded to give them. "Honour thy father and thy mother" (Ex. 20:12). This is a precept of very great consequence; the apostle calls it "the first commandment with promise" (Eph. 6:2), because it is the only commandment about second table duties, that is backed with the promise of a blessing; and it is indeed the only one in the whole system of the moral law that has any particular promise annexed peculiar to itself; that in the second commandment being of a more general nature, and relating to them that love God, and keep, not only this, but all his commandments. The Scripture often presses upon children the discharge of their duties to parents; and there is great reason for it; for, I believe it may be said that, if persons are undutiful to their parents, they seldom prove good in any other relation. The honor which children are required to give to their father and their mother includes in it these four capital branches of filial duty, *love, reverence, obedience*, and *relief*. Children, *love* your parents, who have been, under God, the means of your being; and to whom you are obliged for many, many benefits, in your helpless years. They have watched with pleasure for your sake; they have sympathizingly wept in your afflictions; and have reckoned your comfort a remarkable accession to their own joys. Your love to them is on every account become a debt which can never be discharged. *Reverence* is no less due to your parents than *love*. "Ye shall fear every man his mother, and his father" (Lev. 19:3). There is hardly a worse sign of a bad temper than a contempt of parents. He that was guilty of this under the Mosaic constitution was pronounced *accursed* in a very solemn manner, to deter persons from so horrid a crime. "Cursed be he that setteth light by his father or his mother. And all the people shall say, Amen" (Deut. 27:3). Ye should not only show them respect, when they are benevolent and indulging, but even when they correct you, ye should give them reverence. It is the duty of children to be *obedient* to their parents according to the flesh; for *this is right*, even according to the law of nature, much more upon the principles of divine revelation. Hearken to their counsels and commands in all lawful things; and yield a submissive, cheerful, and ready obedience to them, as is meet in the Lord. "Children, obey your parents in all things: for this is well pleasing unto the Lord" (Col. 3:20). As the command of God has made this your duty, so the Lord Jesus Christ, who was *subject* to his supposed father and real mother, has left you an example of filial obedience (Luke 2:51). And finally, it is the duty of children to *relieve and support* their parents, if they need their help. It is a thing in itself most equitable, and the word of God informs us, it is *acceptable before him, that children requite their parents* (1 Tim. 5:4). Gratitude binds it upon you as a duty to make every suitable return for all their trouble, tenderness, care and pains, love and solicitude, kindness and expense, in bringing you up, and conducting you through all the exercising follies and dangers of your childhood and youth. And you may expect that, by the favor of God, which ordinarily adds the blessings of providence to dutiful children, you may be happy and prosperous in your temporal affairs, through all the circumstances of this life, as far as it may be for God's glory, and your own good.

To Masters and Servants
4. I come now to the relative duties of *masters and servants*, who ought, by the law of Christ, to live in the fear of the Lord. The duties of *masters and*

mistress towards their servants are compendiously expressed in these short precepts, "Masters, give unto your servants that which is just and equal; knowing that ye also have a Master in heaven" (Col. 4:1). "Ye masters, do the same things unto [your servants], forbearing threatening: knowing that your Master also is in heaven; neither is there respect of persons with him" (Eph. 6:9). Here their duty is plainly enjoined them, in the several branches of it; as *to give unto their servants that which is just and equal*, that is, to provide for them, and to pay them their wages, according to their agreement with them, or with their parents and friends on their behalf, lest the hire of the laborer and servant, kept back by fraud, make a loud cry in the ears of the Lord of hosts, and the God of justice avenge their wrongs (James 5:4). *To forbear threatening their servants* is equally reasonable. Do not rage and storm at them, as some passionate masters are wont to do; nor treat them with haughty contempt and insult, but with mildness and lenity [gentleness], as becomes the disciples of Christ, who, even when he was reviled, reviled not again, and when he suffered, he threatened not. You also are but servants of the great God, and are only fellow-servants with them that serve you. You likewise need forgiveness from your Master in heaven, and therefore should not be unwilling to practice it towards your servants, when they happen to offend you. *There is no respect of persons with God*, who will not give a partial preference to the master. Your servants are your fellow-creatures; they are made of the same blood; and their natures are as noble as yours; and, if they are truly religious, they are as high in the favor of God, and may wear as glorious a crown in heaven as yourselves. *To endeavor to promote the spiritual welfare of their servants*, by persuading them to fear God, and by an exemplary behavior in their families, whereby the doctrine of God our Savior may be adorned in all things. Encourage *religion*, as well as *industry*, in your family and servants; for as their industry tends to promote your interest, so their religion tends to the glory of God, and the good of their souls. Instruct your servants in the knowledge of the principles and duties of Christianity; and allow them *sufficient time* for religious duties, even, if needful, out of that time wherein they would otherwise be employed in your service. Let your eyes too be upon the faithful of the land, that they may dwell with you; and let these be preferably chosen to serve you, who walk in a perfect way (Ps. 101:6–7). For the sake of your servants, and for the sake of Christ, for the sake of your souls, and for the sake of your interest, and for the sake of your children, whom you would be sorry to find corrupted by wicked servants—be earnest for the spiritual welfare of your servants; for they are now your charge, and you must give an account concerning them at last.

The principal duties that *servants* owe to their masters and mistresses may be reduced to these heads: "Let as many servants as are under the yoke count their own masters worthy of all honour" (1 Tim. 6:1). A meek and humble deportment, in a special manner, becomes their low station in life; and they are far from being contemptible, when their temper and behavior are conformable to their circumstances; but they make a very despicable figure, when they are assuming and haughty. *In Christ Jesus there is neither bond nor free*, in respect of spiritual gospel-privileges; but the spiritual advantages of Christianity do not impair, but strengthen the obligations of the saints, to discharge the duties of civil life. The apostle was aware that Christian servants were in danger of deriving encouragement from the honor which the gospel puts upon them, to act disagreeably to their condition in the world, and wisely guards them against such a temptation, "They that have believing masters, let them not despise them, because they are brethren; but rather do them service, because they are faithful and beloved, partakers of the benefit" (1 Tim. 6:2). Let servants be "obedient unto their own masters, and to please them well in all things" (Titus 2:9). Behave in such a way as shall win the favor of your masters, and give them pleasure in seeing all their just and reasonable commands executed. Attend cheerfully to the duties of your station, without murmuring or disputing against them, or returning rude and saucy answers, when they require anything you do not like, or reprove you for your faults. Your obedience ought to be cheerful, and without grumbling. Mind therefore to be "obedient to them...with good will doing service, as to the Lord, and not to men; knowing that whatsoever good thing any man doeth, the same shall he receive of the Lord, whether he be *bond* or free" (Eph. 6:5–8). "And whatsoever ye do, do it heartily, as to the Lord, and not unto men; knowing that of the Lord ye shall receive the reward of the inheritance: for ye serve the Lord Christ" (Col. 3:23–24). Servants should be "obedient unto their own masters...not purloining, but shewing all good fidelity" (Titus 2:9–10). Be careful to manage your master's affairs, that are committed to your trust, to the best advantage for his profit. You must neither defraud your master, by wasting, secreting, or embezzling his goods; nor suffer him, either knowingly, or by negligence, to be wronged. Beware of too narrow a notion of a *servant's honesty*. Everybody will allow that it is dishonest to rob a master; but you must consider it as dishonest to waste his goods, or to spend your time in sloth and idleness. Your services must be fulfilled with constancy, not merely while his eye is upon you, to observe your behavior, but in every case you must obey "as the servants of Christ, doing the will of God from the heart" (Eph. 6:6). "Obey in all things your masters according to the flesh; not with eyeservice, as menpleasers; but in singleness of heart, fearing God" (Col. 3:22). Dare you not be remiss and sluggish in the sight of our *fellow-creatures?* Surely the consideration of your being ever under the eye of the *great God* should excite you to follow your work with industry, when no other beholds you. Be conscientious and faithful in every trust, that you "may adorn the doctrine of God our Saviour in all things" (Titus 2:10).

To Neighbors

5. The mutual duties of *neighbors*, that live near one another, and whose connections arise from the settled bounds of their habitations, shall be briefly touched in the next place. In a large sense, *all mankind are our neighbors* (Luke 10:27–37). But I speak of our neighbors, at present, in a more confined sense of the word, as having a peculiar respect to such as are *near each other in situation of life, business, or dwelling.*

We are not obliged to make such neighbors our *intimate companions*, and familiar friends. It is quite against all the dictates of prudence, or sound policy, to do so, unless we find in them the requisites of useful friendship, and the principles that found reasonable expectations of reaping the agreeable fruits of improvement and pleasure. But, least of all, must we suffer ourselves, in conformity with the manners of those among whom we live, to become partners with them in any unlawful courses, whom we ought rather to reprove than to imitate and countenance therein. It is a necessary and important part of our duty to arm ourselves with a sacred resolution and circumspection, that we may not be drawn into sinful practices, and neglects, after the example, and by the influence of those who are about us. Rather than to do this, and so to sin against God, and wound our consciences, we must be content to bear patiently the censure of being unneighborly and unmannerly, and sacrifice some conveniences and comforts of the social life, to the greater obligation of maintaining our integrity, when the former cannot be had but at the expense of the latter.

And, by the way, we should avoid, as far as we can, settling in such places where profane and profligate sinners abound; and where we can find few or no religious people to associate with.

Neighbors should *live in peace*, and promote it with the utmost zeal, among themselves. For this purpose, they should each mind his own affairs, and not officiously pry into, or intermeddle with the affairs of other persons or families; nor hastily take up, or spread, much less raise, reports prejudicial to their neighbors.

They should be *courteous, affable, and obliging*, to one another, when they have any occasion of conversing together, treating each other with the accustomed forms of civility, and forbearing a supercilious, stiff, and distant manner. Civil respect is an easy, cheap price for the manifold advantages it produces among neighbors.

They should be ready to *do and return those good offices* which tend to mutual safety and accommodation; and should not be backward to join, in proportion to their leisure or ability, in all reasonable and practicable undertakings, for the common good of the whole neighborhood.

They should be ready to *assist with their counsel, advice, and protection*, as far as their own necessary affairs and obligations will admit, those about them who may need and desire it. *He that hath friends, must show himself friendly.* They should reserve some portion, at least, of their voluntary charities, to be distributed among the poor of the place where they dwell; even though the larger measures of it should be pre-engaged elsewhere. It is the property of a good man to *disperse abroad, and give to the poor* (Ps. 112:9); and it seems but reasonable that a channel which lies so open to his hand and so near his own door should not be wholly overlooked by him.

To this may be added that neighbors should be suffered to *reap some secular advantage* at one another's hand, by providing themselves from among them with, at least, some of the necessaries and conveniences of life; and not for the sake purely of small savings, without necessity for such frugality, to procure them all from places at a distance.

Finally, They should strive all they can to *promote religion and virtue* in the places of their respective residence, to reform the immoral and profane; and for this end to improve all the influence they can make over them by kindness and service. The people of God should mourn over those sins they see or hear of among their neighbors, which they cannot prevent;

and while they pray for both their spiritual and temporal welfare, should set them an example of goodness, in their daily conversation (1 Peter 3:16; Phil. 4:8).

To Friends
6. I shall only add a few thoughts on the relative duties of *friendship*. This forms a relation of much greater intimacy than neighborhood, and so establishes an obligation to a higher sort or degree of kind affections and actions. When I speak of *friends*, I mean persons, in other respects independent, who voluntarily agree to cultivate a familiar correspondence together. Here Scripture and reason come in to regulate our conduct, in order to render these friendships really profitable. The following rules may be attended to on this subject.

Do not give your friends reason to think that you will do more for them than you intend to do. It is a very heinous fault, which some people allow themselves in, that they make large professions of friendship and kindness to others, which they never design or care to make good. They are friends to all who apply to them, as far as fine promises and fair unmeaning words will go. But this is so egregious trifling with the sacred name of friendship, and such an outrage on all integrity and fidelity, that a truly conscientious person will not be guilty of it, but will rather choose to declare less than he intends, and to do more than he has declared, than to profess more, and do less.

On the other hand, do not indulge too high expectations from your friends. This weakness will create disappointment and uneasiness to yourselves, and make you become troublesome, nay, and injurious also, to others, by complaints of hard measures, whenever your unreasonable hopes and wishes are not gratified.

Use your utmost endeavors to answer the confidence you have suffered your friends to repose in you. Preserve inviolably in religious silence the secrets of your friend, which he has committed to you under the seal of friendly confidence, which you would show yourself utterly unworthy of, if, through indiscretion, importunity, or a talkative humor, and much more through any bad design, you are drawn to disclose them. Carefully keep, and cheerfully restore, your friend's property, deposited in your

13. MINISTERIAL VISITATIONS OF THE FLOCK

hand for safe custody. Prosecute the business your friend has committed to your care, and which you have undertaken for him, with the same diligence and activity as if it were your own. "Confidence in an unfaithful man…is like a broken tooth, and a foot out of joint" (Prov. 25:19).

Observe a decency and respectfulness in your language and behavior to your friends, together with a candid interpretation of their words and actions. Never put their temper to the trial; lest the proof weaken the grounds, and diminish the confidence of your friendship. Avoid everything that would make your friend contemptible to others, or uneasy in himself. Forbear the sallies of refined satire, and witty raillery against your friends; for however innocently and pleasantly they may be meant, they are generally construed to have a real tendency to make them appear in a ridiculous light; and their temper may dispose them to receive grating impressions from them.

Utterly renounce all backbiting, severe invectives, or sly insinuations, and secret practices, against those you have owned as friends; and even the malicious pleasure of publishing their real faults and infirmities. These things are a flat contradiction to the very show of friendship, and prove all the professions of it to be hollow and hypocritical. And as you must be cautious not to blemish the reputation, or disturb the repose, of your friends yourselves, so you should be ready to patronize and defend them against the reflections and injurious treatment they may meet with from others. Far from basely taking a part in, or even patiently observing, a popular cry against them, and an *unjust run* on their good name, it becomes you manfully to withstand it. And as to their *real faults* (which who is without?), it is the part of friendship, first to veil them from public notice as far as possible; and then, if they happen to get abroad, to offer all the alleviations and extenuations in their favor which the truth of things will allow, and particular circumstances, with the general frailty of human nature, suggest.

Guard against *jealousy*, the great bane of friendship. Put the most favorable construction on circumstances that look unkind and suspicious. When your expectations are not answered, suppose that equal or superior obligations and engagements elsewhere, some accidental reasons, or human infirmities, rather than any falsehood or ill design have occasioned it. You should demur for some time on reports, to the prejudice of your friends, till you have an opportunity of knowing the certain truth; and even be ready to pass by offenses of a slighter nature.

Banish all *flattery* from your friendship, as entirely inconsistent with the true notion and laudable end of it. Flattery can never serve your friend. It may, and probably it will do him a great deal of harm, by cherishing his pride and vanity, and countenancing him in sin. But it certainly betrays, in those who are guilty of it, a sordid design of serving some private interest of their own, by the weakness of others. Counsel, admonition, and reproof are useful parts of friendship, and a proof of disinterested love. "Faithful are the wounds of a friend; but the kisses of an enemy are deceitful" (Prov. 27:6). And such a faithful, friendly love will dictate the doing this unpleasant, though necessary office, with that prudence and judicious choice of proper seasons and proper faults, and with such gentleness and tenderness, that it may appear *a kindness* in the design of the reprover, not proceeding from any affected superiority or censoriousness, and may become in effect *a kindness* to the reproved, who ought to take it well, and seek to profit by it.

Be forward to serve your friends, even with some self-denial, and without a nice and scrupulous balancing of favor given and received, which carries a very unfriendly aspect.

Thankfully acknowledge the favor conferred on you, without denying or diminishing them, because your desires are not always gratified; and be forward to oblige, in your turn, and within your power, those who have first and most obliged you. Such friendly offices must be mutual, or they cannot be lasting.

Maintain *a common sense* of joys and sorrows with your friends, in their prosperity and adversity.

Be constant to your engagements, so as not to break with them through fickleness and levity of spirit, on slight and trifling occasions; especially do not withdraw from them in a time of adversity. And, finally,

Improve all friendships and familiarities of converse, for the mutual promoting of religion and virtue; that you may not only help one another in the things of life, but encourage each other in the ways of the Lord. Thus "a man that hath friends must shew himself friendly" (Prov. 18:24).

To Their Age

Fourthly, Mankind may be viewed according to their different *ages*; and so they may be reduced to these three classes: *children, grown men*, and *old people*. The first includes such as are not come to the vigor of manhood; the second comprehends all that are come to the stature and strength of perfect men; and the last takes in those who have passed that period, and begin to stoop under the infirmities of age and declining life.

1. *Come, ye children, hearken unto me: I will teach you the fear of the Lord* (Ps. 34:11). Know ye that the Lord he is God; it is he that hath made you, and not you yourselves. Remember your Creator in the days of your youth, while the evil days of age and affliction come not, nor the years draw nigh, when you shall say, we have no pleasure in them. While you are yet young, begin to seek the Lord, by reading his word very often, and with great care and diligence, and by asking in prayer from God, in the name of Christ, whatever you want. If you would cleanse your way, and purify your conversation from folly and vice, you must take good heed to it, according to the word of God. Fear the Lord from your youth, as Obadiah did (1 Kings 18:12). It is recorded of Timothy that from a child he had known the Scriptures, which were able to make him wise unto salvation (2 Tim. 3:15). It is, my dear young friends, your duty, your honor, and your very life, to *know the Scriptures*. In them you will find a rich store of all useful knowledge. *There* you are informed that God in the beginning created the heaven and the earth; that he upholdeth all things by the word of his power; that he made the first man and woman, Adam and Eve, very good, after his own image, in knowledge, righteousness, and true holiness; that he commanded them to keep all his commandments, and particularly not to eat of the fruit of one of the trees in Eden, called *the tree of the knowledge of good and evil*; that our first parents, and all their posterity, would have been perfectly happy, and have lived forever, if they had not sinned against God, by doing what he hated and expressly forbade them to do; that the devil, entering into a serpent, deceived our first parents, who sinned against God by eating of the tree of the knowledge of good and evil; that, as we would have been happy, if our first parents had continued to obey God, so all mankind were ruined by their sin; that the wages of sin is death and everlasting misery; that we cannot endure this punishment; that God will not forgive our sin without a full satisfaction for it; that the only begotten Son of God became man, obeyed, died, and rose again from the dead, as-

cended up to heaven, sitteth at the right hand of God, and ever liveth to make intercession for poor guilty, perishing sinners; that there is no name under heaven given among men whereby we must be saved, besides the name of Jesus Christ; that he is both able and willing to save you; that you are ignorant, guilty, weak creatures; that you are in absolute need of the Lord Jesus Christ: as *a prophet*, to teach you heavenly wisdom; as *a priest*, to atone for all your many, many sins; as *a king*, to subdue your iniquities, write his laws in your hearts, and make you, in all your conversation, holy; that this almighty gracious Savior is freely given unto you in the declarations and promises of the gospel, that you may believe that testimony God hath given you concerning him, and by believing it, may rejoice in the possession of Christ, as the rock of your salvation, and the fountain of your hopes; that the way of holiness is pleasant, plain, and honorable; that sin is both ruining and shameful; that your soul shall not die with your body, and even your bodies shall be raised out of the grave at the last day; that you must give an account unto God in that day for all your thoughts, and words, and actions; that the righteous shall be saved with an everlasting salvation; that the wicked shall go away into everlasting punishment; that the Lord, with whom you have to do, is always present with you, and a witness to all that you think, and wish, and say, and do; and that these who seek him early, shall find him to be merciful, and gracious, longsuffering, and abundant in goodness and truth. These are but a few instances of the precious things you will find in the Holy Scriptures. O search, search them with care, my dear friends; for in them you have eternal life, and they testify of the blessed Jesus.

Walk in the truth, as you have received a commandment from the Father (2 John 4). You reverence the will of your earthly parents and masters; and this is but doing your duty. Oh then do not the abominable thing that your heavenly Father hates. "Fear God, and keep his commandments: for this is the whole duty of man" (Eccl. 12:13).

Little children, *be sober-minded* (Titus 2:6). You did not receive your being from the hand of your Creator, to play the fool, and to riot in madness; and you are not fit to guide yourselves in the world. You do not know its vanity, and the vexation of spirit that is in it. Therefore be not hasty, and rash, forward, proud, passionate, and self-willed.

Dear children, *flee also youthful lust* (2 Tim. 2:22). These defile the body, and destroy the soul; they are your shame, and will be your grief sooner or later. Shun all appearance of evil; and if your wicked companions entice you to sin, do not consent. Do not tell lies; for the God of truth hates a lying tongue. Do not swear by the name of God; for it is glorious, holy, and fearful. Do not covet anything that is your neighbor's; for the Lord has said that covetousness is idolatry. Do not steal; for thieves shall not inherit the kingdom of God. Do not mock your parents, or masters, nor disobey their lawful commands; for by honoring thy father and mother, thy days shall be long upon the land which the Lord thy God giveth thee. Do not wish ill to any person, far less scold or beat them; for God has commanded you to love your neighbor as yourselves, and even to love, and bless, and pray for your enemies. Avoid all bawdy, obscene talk, and much more all indecent, light, and lewd behavior; for whoremongers and adulterers God will judge. Do not profane the Sabbath-day by foolish jesting, and sinful recreations; for it is the Lord's day, and he has commanded us to keep it holy. Do not follow a multitude to do evil. Be not companions of the wicked, of the licentious and profane. Do not flatter yourselves with the foolish hopes of living to a good old age, and of having time enough to be religious afterwards; for how can you do this with any reason? You see your brethren, or sisters, or neighbors, dying as young, perhaps younger, as you are; and what reason have you to think that you shall all be old people then? Do not imagine that you will at last be religious, though you were to live long, if you are careless about all that is good now.

Let me beseech you, in the days of your youth, to make *prayer to God* your pleasant and daily business. You have many, many inducements to do so, for he is your Maker, and the fountain of your comfort and happiness. Nothing should hinder or divert you from praying to God in the name of Christ, at least every morning and evening. You ask your parents for what you want, and they answer your reasonable demands; should you not much more make your requests known to God in everything, by prayer and supplication, with thanksgiving? Yes, my dear young ones, ask, and you shall receive; seek, and you shall find; knock, and it shall be opened unto you. Come boldly, come frequently to the throne of grace, that you may receive mercy, and find grace to help you in the time of need. Turn not away your ear from him who says to you, as he did to the Jews of old, "Wilt thou not from this time cry unto me, My father, thou art the guide of my youth?" (Jer. 3:4). "My son, give me thine heart" (Prov. 23:26).

One thing is needful. O choose that good part which shall never be taken from you. Know the Lord as your God and Redeemer, and serve him with a perfect heart, and with a willing mind. Worship and glorify him, as the only true God, and your God. Receive and observe, keep pure and entire all such religious worship and ordinances as God hath appointed in his word. Use all God's names, titles, attributes, ordinances, words, and works, with a holy reverence. Spend the whole of the Lord's day in the public and private exercises of his worship, except so much as is to be taken up in works of necessity and mercy. Preserve the honor due to everyone in their several places and relations, and perform the duties you owe them. Use all lawful endeavors to preserve your own lives, and the lives of others. Preserve your own and your neighbor's chastity in heart, speech, and behavior. Employ all lawful means to preserve and increase your own and your neighbor's wealth and outward estate. Maintain and promote truth between man and man; and support your own and your neighbor's good name, especially if you are called to bear witness in any court. Be content with your own condition; and do not envy your neighbor's, even though it seem to be better than yours.

Be careful to *improve in your education.* Honor your teachers. Receive their instructions with pleasure; and submit to be told of your faults with patience. Get your memories stored with the *Assembly's Shorter Catechism*, that most valuable compend [summary] of revealed truth; and make yourselves masters of it, that you may be able to repeat it with exactness. Be not ashamed to revive it in your memories, by often reading it over, that you may have it very distinct. It is most ridiculous to hum and ha, and stammer from one question to another, from one subject to another. You would be ashamed to blunder in such a manner in the business of life. Be diligent in this, and every other duty of religion, and the Lord be with you.

2. To these that have arrived at, but not exceeded that period of human life which is the common *center* between the extremes of childhood and old age, and are *grown men*, I shall suggest the following things.

When you are become men and women, put away childish things (1 Cor. 13:11). Rise nobly above the little follies of youth, and throw off the silly trifling ways of thinking and speaking, which well enough become that period of life, but would be a disgrace in riper years. *Be not children in understanding; howbeit in malice,* and every sinful corrupt temper, *be chil-*

dren still; that is, grow in spiritual knowledge, but continue still ignorant of, and indifferent about, nay averse to, the unfruitful works of darkness.

Do not neglect *the principles of your religious education.* Carry these through life with you; let them have a due place in your consideration; preserve them in your memories; correct every error you can perceive in your education principles, relative to religion, by impartial and free inquiry, now that you are advanced to maturer judgment; and remember how you have received and heard, and hold fast that which you have, that no man take your crown. You have more knowledge, and it may be more convictions, than many others; take heed you do not act against your knowledge, nor stifle your convictions. This would highly aggravate your guilt and condemnation. You know who hath said, "that servant which knew his lord's will, and prepared not himself, neither did according to his will, shall be beaten with many stripes" (Luke 12:47).

Do not plunge too deep in *the cares of the world,* lest they choke the word of God, and render you unfruitful. What would you be profited, though you should gain the whole world, if you lose your own souls? And what comfort can you expect to have in such a bustle, as puts it out of your power to enjoy yourselves, or to wait upon God in the way of his own appointment? Be not entangled with foolish and distracting cares, which only disquiet the mind, and dishonor God.

Do not forget God in *the hurry of your business.* The ox knoweth his owner, and the ass his master's crib; and should *you,* on any pretense, be unmindful of God? O base ingratitude! O folly and madness! Can you forget to take your victuals and sleep? I believe not; how can you then forget to acknowledge the Lord, who is your Father, your Maker, and your Savior? Hath he not made you, and established you? And should you thus requite the Lord, to prefer your own low interests to his glory? Remember it is the Lord that strengthens you for labor, and gives you power both to get wealth, and to use it; therefore acknowledge him in all your ways, that he may direct your steps.

Still bear in mind *your infirmity and weakness.* All flesh is grass, and all the glory of man, even in the prime of life, is as the flower of grass; and you know the grass withereth, and the flower thereof falleth away. Be careful then so to number your days, that you may apply your hearts unto wisdom. In your best condition prepare for *the days of darkness,* for they shall be many. Happy is the man, that feareth always.

Finally, *Be good and faithful stewards of your Lord's talents.* Occupy till he come. Consider your youth, your health and strength, your vigor of body and mind, as so many precious talents, which God has committed to your keeping, that you may glorify his name, promote his interest, and serve your generation by his will, in a faithful diligent improvement of them. Blessed is that servant whom his Lord, when he cometh, shall find so doing.

3. Allow me now to bespeak the attention of *old people*, who are visibly on the decline of life. Your hoary head shows how near you are to the mansions of the dead, and that your days are almost numbered. I have no intention to depart from that *decent respect*, which is a just tribute to your advanced age, while I present a few important considerations to your most serious thoughts.

Look back on *the kindness of God* to you in the former part of your life. Have not goodness and mercy followed you all the days of your life? Have you not been borne by him from the belly, and carried from the womb? Has he not taught you from your youth? Be stirred up to bless the Lord for his past mercies, and do not bury his goodness in ungrateful oblivion.

Review *your own ways.* You find your memories much more retentive of youthful occurrences than of later events. Often think of *the sins of your youth.* Adopt the psalmist's prayer in reference to them: "Remember not the sins of my youth, nor my transgressions: according to thy mercy remember thou me for thy goodness' sake, O Lord" (Ps. 25:7). It is a most dreadful case, when the iniquities of youth come to be confirmed principles in old age.

Lift up your eyes to behold *the solemn train attendant on death*, which is making a quick approach to cut you off out of the land of the living. A delightful heaven, or a terrible hell, everlasting punishment, or eternal life, are the immediate consequences of your dissolution. Can you reckon it an indifferent thing, whether you shall inherit the kingdom, which the Father of our Lord Jesus Christ prepared before the foundation of the world; or, if you shall depart, with the curse of the King of kings, into everlasting fire, prepared for the devil and his angels? Seriously consider these most weighty and interesting truths; and do not flatter yourselves with a foolish hope, where the case is so infinitely important, and where a false step may be so fatal. O be wise, and lay to heart your latter end. Converse with eternal things in your meditations; and make them familiar to your daily thoughts. This will gradually wean your affections from this present evil world, and strengthen your faith in realizing views and expectations of a better world. This will make you live as strangers and pilgrims on this earth, and to seek a better country, that is, a heavenly.

The Holy Ghost has delineated the character that should adorn your advanced years, when he charges Titus to speak "the things which become sound doctrine: that the *aged men* be sober, grave, temperate, sound in faith, in charity, in patience. The *aged women* likewise, that they be in behaviour as becometh holiness, not false accusers, not given to much wine, teachers of good things" (Titus 2:1–3). Here we have a sum of the principal duties incumbent on old people, to make their deportment both amiable and useful in the world. *The aged men must be sober*, very watchful, circumspect, and sedate in their temper and carriage; they ought to be *grave*, observing a due decorum in their dress, mien, and air, and in all that they say and do—they should be *temperate* in eating and drinking, and prudent in their conduct; they must be *sound in faith*, uncorrupt as to the doctrines of faith, and sincere in believing them, and careful to live answerable to them; *sound in charity*, or *love*, abounding in love to God, in cordial affection to all the saints, and in Christian benevolence to people of all nations, ranks, and characters, as fellow-creatures; and *sound in patience*, which ought to be exercised in bearing tribulations and offenses, and in subduing their own peevish passions, and in bearing with the infirmities of others. *The aged women likewise must be in behavior*, in dress, and in all regular deportment, *as becometh holiness*; they must *not be false accusers*, slanderers, or backbiters of others, to the injury of their reputation; they should *not be given to much wine*, or any other intoxicating liquors, under pretense of recruiting the strength and spirits of decaying nature; and they ought, instead of amusing young people with old wives fables, to be *teachers* of good things, to entertain them with profitable discourse, and to recommend, by counsel and example, everything that is good and laudable, as to speech, apparel, and behavior. "The hoary head is a crown of glory," when it is thus found in the way of righteousness (Prov. 16:31).

Do not repine at your present circumstance, nor be fretful in your condition, though attended with various infirmities, and much weariness and pain. Encourage yourselves in God, who, though your outward man perish, can renew your inward man day by day. Trust in him, who has hitherto helped you, to be assisted by his grace unto the end. Run with patience the race set before you, until you fully receive the end of your faith, even the everlasting salvation of your souls. Bring forth fruit in old age, that you may convince the world, and have more and more the comfort of it in your own souls, that the Lord is upright, and your rock.

Are you grown old in *the service of Satan?* Have you hitherto wrought the will of the flesh? and do you remain in a state of alienation from the life of God, and strangers to the power of godliness? O, my poor fellow-sinners! how deplorable and dangerous is your most wretched condition! "The sinner being an hundred years old shall be accursed" (Isa. 65:20). God speaks of Ephraim as grossly stupid, because he was so little apprehensive of the signs of his own case, "gray hairs are here and there upon him, yet he knoweth it not" (Hos. 7:9). Do these, my aged friends, appear in a literal sense upon you; and should you not consider what they are the forerunners of? Or, can you consider this, and not be concerned, to be ready for the hour of your departure, which is at hand? But though your case is bad, it is not desperate. "Behold, now is the accepted time; behold, now is the day of salvation" (2 Cor. 6:2). Therefore he saith, "To day, after so long a time…if ye will hear his voice, harden not your hearts" (Heb. 4:7). After much patience, this is the voice of the compassionate Redeemer, "Behold, I stand at the door, and knock: if any man hear my voice, and open the door, I will come in to him, and will sup with him, and he with me" (Rev. 3:20).

To Their Employments in Life
Fifthly, I shall next consider mankind in reference to their *employments in life.* This might be branched out into many heads. I shall only propose the following things, that deserve some regard.

1. *Let none be idle and unemployed in some lawful business.* Before the fall, Adam had a calling appointed him by his Maker, who put him into the garden of Eden to dress it, and to keep it (Gen. 2:15). And since mankind sinned, the decree of heaven is that they shall eat their bread with the sweat of their face, till they return to the earth (Gen. 3:19). *Industry* is the way to prosperity; for the hand of the diligent maketh rich, and *the Lord blesses the work of our hands*; whereas, *idleness* exposes a man to many sins, and many punishments. The *slothful* servant is a *wicked* servant (Matt. 25:26).

2. Those who are *looking out for an employment,* ought to pray earnestly to God, to guide them in their choice, by his infinite wisdom. He only knows what kind of business will be best for you; in what family or neigh-

borhood you will have the most helps and encouragements to holiness; and where you will be most exposed to temptations, to evil company, and to an early corruption. In all your ways acknowledge him, and he will direct your paths. Beseech the all-wise God to go before you in this weighty undertaking, and to lead you to such a master, and to settle in such a place, where you may most advantageously work out your own salvation.

3. Having entered upon business, *follow it with diligence.* Take pleasure in it, and attend thereunto with delight. Embrace all proper opportunities of doing business with advantage. Every excess of care and diligence is an extreme, which is both sinful and hurtful; but diligence is a duty we owe to God, and to ourselves. Indolence and slothfulness clothe a man with rags. The sluggard is brother to him that is a great waster.

4. *Undertake no more business than you can well manage with ease* in your own minds, and *with honor and justice* among men. Consider your ability of mind and circumstances, and proportion your schemes in life to these, after making proper allowances for some unforeseen possible accidents. If a man lays in a larger stock than he has occasion for, or overtrades himself, or runs into many branches of trade, or ventures too far with the substance of others, he is certainly overbuilding his foundation, and by grasping at too much, is in hazard of being undone. A man that tries to carry more than his strength is answerable to, must strain and hurt himself. Ambition ought to be laid under prudent restraints.

5. *Be frugal*, and do not suffer your expenses to go beyond your income. Do not make it your rule to do as others do, but *as your circumstances will allow.* Consider your substance, your trade, and the number of your family, and regulate your expenses accordingly. Always make it a principle to provide for yourselves and families, without being unjust to the world. If men call you *covetous*, merely because you do not copy the fashionable luxurious taste for dress, furniture, and delicacies of meat and drink, be not shaken from your purpose by their imputation; it is better to have their censures and thrive, than their applauses, and become bankrupt and a beggar.

6. *Be very careful and circumspect in managing your affairs.* Have your eyes upon your own business; and do not trust it wholly to servants. Even the most faithful servants have need of the master's inspection; and how much more should you watch over strangers? Be cautious, who you have dealings with, and upon what terms you give them credit. Do not trust

your memories, but make entries of things in proper books, which will prevent disputes with your friends, and exhibit a true authentic state of your affairs. At proper times inspect your affairs, that you may know the state of them, and how to regulate your future conduct. Avoid suretiship; and be careful how you run bold ventures with money or goods belonging to others, without the consent and approbation of the proprietors. Consider you have them only as *a trust*; and it is required in a steward that he be found faithful.

7. *Be strictly honest and honorable in all your dealings*, observing punctually the rules of equity, honor, and justice, in all your commerce. *Honesty is the best policy.* Have a just weight, a just balance, and a just measure. Do not impose on the weak or the ignorant. Be content with moderate profits. Be faithful to all your promises. Let your *justice* be tempered with *clemency* towards your solvent debtors. Manage your affairs so as your conscience may not reproach you, nor the world cry shame of you, should they know your whole conduct. Keep close to that golden rule of doing to men as you would that they should do to you in the same circumstances. And do not encroach upon the business of others, especially if it is out of your proper way of dealing; for this is contrary to the rule just now mentioned, and if it be not dishonest to interfere with the business of others, it can never be reconciled with either true honor or humanity.

8. *Do not make haste to be rich*: for "the thoughts of the diligent tend only to plenteousness; but of every one that is hasty, only to want" (Prov. 21:5). Those that are rash and inconsiderate in their affairs, and do not take time to think, are in the road to poverty and disappointment.

> They that *will be rich* [without considering the measures they take] fall into temptation and a snare, and into many foolish and hurtful lusts, which drown men in destruction and perdition. For the love of money is the root of all evil: which while some coveted after, they have erred from the faith, and pierced themselves through with many sorrows. But thou, O man of God, flee these things (1 Tim. 6:9–11).

Follow providence, wherever it seems to open a prospect of success to lawful moderate industry; but do not attempt to force it. In arduous undertakings do not grasp too much in your ambitious desires, and then you will prevent much anxiety, and all the train of grievous consequences that ensue on fatal disappointments. Plants and fruits that are most forward are soonest blasted, and seldom come to anything. The slowest growth is usually most substantial. Therefore, avoid all hastiness that would put you upon methods which God, and conscience, and prudence, would join to disapprove.

Suffer the word of exhortation, which I have to subjoin to all that has been said on the *various employments of human life*, in the words of the apostle,

> But this I say, brethren, the time is short: it remaineth, that both they that have wives be as though they had none; and they that weep, as though they wept not; and they that rejoice, as though they rejoiced not; and they that buy, as though they possessed not; and they that use this world, as not abusing it: for the fashion of this world passeth away. But I would have you without carefulness (1 Cor. 7:29–32).

To Their Several Conditions
Sixthly, Mankind may be viewed with respect to their *several conditions*; and so they are either in a *state of prosperity* or *adversity*.

1. *A prosperous condition* may be considered in as many lights as the various and manifold benefits that constitute the comfort of the person's situation and circumstances, who is in such a case. I shall give a few examples drawn from daily life.

Are you *rich in worldly possessions?* Beware you do not deny God, and say with profane scoffers, *Who is the Lord?* Do not wickedly rob God of his glory, as the bountiful Father of your mercies, saying in your heart, My power, and the might of my hand, hath gotten me this wealth; but thou shalt remember the Lord thy God; for it is he that giveth thee power to get wealth. When you are waxed rich, do not forget God, nor lightly esteem the Rock of your salvation. Your promotion has neither come from the east, nor from the west, nor from the south; but God is judge; he setteth up one, and putteth down another. *Walk humbly with the Lord*, whose blessing has made you rich and prosperous. You are only *stewards* of a larger share of your Lord's substance, whose is the earth, and the fullness thereof, and who says, "The silver is mine, and the gold is mine" (Hag. 2:8).

They that trust in their wealth, and boast themselves in the multitude of their riches, yet none of them can by any means redeem his brother, nor give unto God a ransom for him. If riches increase, set not your heart upon them; for they profit not in the day of wrath. Seriously consider the duties of your condition, as they are drawn out in the strict and awful command of Paul to Timothy,

> Charge them that are rich in this world, that they be not highminded, nor trust in uncertain riches, but in the living God, who giveth us richly all things to enjoy; that they do good, that they be rich in good works, ready to distribute, willing to communicate; laying up in store for themselves a good foundation against the time to come, that they may lay hold on eternal life (1 Tim. 6:17–19).

These are most important and necessary branches of your duty, both towards God and man. *Be not high-minded*, nor lifted up with pride, self-sufficiency, and contempt of others, on account of any distinctions a bountiful Providence has made in your favor. *Do not trust in uncertain riches*, by setting your hearts upon, or placing your confidence in your earthly possessions, which are all precarious and fleeting, and, when least expected, may make themselves wings, and flee away. *Trust in the living God, who giveth us richly all things to enjoy*; put your entire trust in the only living and true God, who daily loads us with his benefits, and who, in the riches of his mercy and goodness, gives us everything for necessity, and many things for delight, yea, all things that we enjoy for present support and comfort, pertaining to life and godliness, through the knowledge of him that hath called us to glory and virtue. *Do good* with your riches, to the utmost of your power, instead of abusing them to hurt others, or misspending them lavishly upon yourselves. *Be rich in good works*, which your affluence obliges you to, and makes you capable of. *Be ready to distribute* of that abundance, which the Lord of the universe has committed to you in trust. *Be willing to communicate*, of your own accord, on all proper occasions, for promoting every good cause, and to help the necessities of the poor, especially of the household of faith. Thus you will *lay up for yourselves a good foundation*, not of hope and dependence, but of comfortable evidence, *against the time to come*, when the riches and fashion of the world shall pass away; and by so doing you will finish your course with more joy to yourself, and with more honor to your profession. This exhortation is faithful and plain; but it becomes the minister of Jesus to be open, and to use great plainness of speech, where the glory of God, and the good of men, are concerned. *Charge them that are rich*, says the apostle, instead of concealing their vices for fear of offense, or flattering them in their follies, to gain their favor. *Charge them* to eschew sin, and do good.

Have you *a good state of bodily health?* Remember that this is the gift of God, who favors you above many. Cast your eyes around you, and see the condition of mankind at large; one is distracted, another blind, a third lame, and thousands of other cases will present themselves to your observation, which render life a continual burden, and embitter its every comfort. Who maketh you to differ from these distressed objects? Be stirred up to honor God, and to work out your own salvation, and to do good to others, while it is yet today with you. Consider that evil days are coming, wherein you shall say, *We have no pleasure in them*.

Are you happy in having *comfortable families?* Do your children fear God; and do your servants serve the Lord? Confess that it is the Lord who has made your lines to fall in pleasant places, and has given you such agreeable connections. Behave yourselves wisely in a perfect way; and walk within your house with a perfect heart. Daily maintain all the branches of family religion among your amiable offspring and domestics.

Do your souls prosper? O! let your thanksgivings be frequent, and your conversation circumspect and tender. Grow in grace, and in the knowledge of our Lord Jesus Christ. Abstain from fleshly lusts, which war against the soul. Press towards the mark for the prize of the high calling of God in Christ Jesus. Fight the good fight of faith, and lay hold on eternal life. Abide in Christ, and let his word abide in you. Hold fast that which you have, that no man take your crown. Be frequent in the duties of religion, and so your profiting shall appear to yourselves, and to all men.

I might mention several other views of *a comfortable condition*, which demand corresponding duties; but, instead of enlarging on this topic, shall go on to consider mankind in another light, as involved in distresses and calamities, which constitute *a state of adversity*, which God hath set over against the former.

2. *The afflictions of the righteous are many; but the Lord delivereth him out of them all* (Ps. 34:19). I cannot pretend to reckon them up; for they are more in *number and kind*, than the hairs of their head. I shall only name a few examples.

Are you *the poor of this world?* Observe and justify the hand of Providence in your lot. Be as poor in spirit, as you are in circumstances. Be content with such things as you have, and let your conversation be without covetousness. Cast not away your hope and confidence on account of your discouragements. Be rich in that faith, which embraces the promises of God for eternal life. Trust in the Lord, and do good, so shalt thou dwell in the land, and verily thou shalt be fed. Delight thyself also in the Lord; and he shall give thee the desires of thy heart. Commit thy way unto the Lord; trust also in him, and he shall bring it to pass.

Are you *sickly, and infirm in body?* Consider this as coming forth from the Lord of hosts, who is wonderful in counsel, and excellent in working. See that you call on God by prayer and supplication, with thanksgiving. Rejoice in Christ Jesus, having no confidence in the flesh, but making mention of his everlasting righteousness and atoning sacrifice, by which the sting is taken out of every affliction, and the believer is enabled to rejoice in tribulation. Make the Lord's testimonies your songs in the house of your pilgrimage. Look, and long, and hasten towards that heavenly country, where the inhabitant shall not say, *I am sick*; and where there shall be no more curse, nor weeping, nor sorrow. O blessed place! O desirable period, where and when, songs of deliverance shall crown the head, and joy unspeakable and full of glory shall fill the heart, and rapturous praise shall employ the tongue, world without end.

Are you *uncomfortably joined in your relative connections?* Think how necessary and solid the friendship of Christ is to his people; he is a friend born for adversity; he is our true Noah, that shall comfort us concerning our toils, and cares, and griefs. Carry with prudence and humanity towards them, who are undutiful and unkind to you. Examine carefully whether you have not provoked them to be undutiful to you. Imitate our blessed Redeemer, who, when he was reviled, reviled not again. Do not render evil for evil, but commit your cause to him that judgeth righteously; and continually labor to overcome evil with good. Reverence the hand of God in your relative trials; and come boldly, and frequently, to the throne of his grace, that you may receive mercy, and find grace to help you in the

13. MINISTERIAL VISITATIONS OF THE FLOCK 433

time of need, that your behavior in difficult circumstances may adorn the gospel of Christ.

Is your *soul lean, and dead, and dark, tossed with temptation, and crushed by overwhelming sorrows?* Trust in the name of the Lord, and stay upon your God. Wait on the Lord; be of good courage, and he shall strengthen your heart; wait, I say, on the Lord. Says not the faithful and true Witness unto you, *If ye would believe, ye should see the glory of God?* Allow me to put you in mind of that precious passage, recorded in 2 Peter 1:2–11,

> Grace and peace be multiplied unto you through the knowledge of God, and of Jesus our Lord, according as his divine power hath given unto us all things that pertain unto life and godliness, through the knowledge of him that hath called us to glory and virtue: whereby are given unto us exceeding great and precious promises: that by these ye might be partakers of the divine nature, having escaped the corruption that is in the world through lust. And beside this, giving all diligence, add to your faith virtue; and to virtue knowledge; and to knowledge temperance; and to temperance patience; and to patience godliness; and to godliness brotherly kindness; and to brotherly kindness charity. For if these things be in you, and abound, they make you that ye shall neither be barren nor unfruitful in the knowledge of our Lord Jesus Christ. But he that lacketh these things is blind, and cannot see afar off, and hath forgotten that he was purged from his old sins. Wherefore the rather, brethren, give diligence to make your calling and election sure: for if ye do these things, ye shall never fall: for so an entrance shall be ministered unto you abundantly into the everlasting kingdom of our Lord and Saviour Jesus Christ.

I would earnestly recommend to the most serious consideration of such as are bowed down under any distress, in body or mind, in circumstances or relative connections, that precious treatise of Mr. Boston of Ettrick, entitled, *The Sovereignty of God in Afflictions*, commonly known by the name of *The Crook in the Lot*.[10]

---

[10] Thomas Boston. *The Crook in the Lot*.
 N. B. I have not taken any notice of *catechetical instruction*, which may be very usefully

4. Conclusion with Solemn Prayer

IV. Because every ordinance, as well as every creature of God, is sanctified by *prayer*; it is proper that the minister conclude this service with *solemn prayer*; wherein he should endeavor to be as particular in confessions, thanksgivings, and supplications, as the different conditions of families and persons require. Two happy effects may be expected to follow upon such particular enumerations of sins, wants, mercies, and dangers.

1. This will more deeply impress the minds of the persons concerned, when they hear the instructions delivered to them in a way of doctrine, reproof, caution, or exhortation, recapitulated in prayer. This is a hopeful means of convincing them that their pastor earnestly wishes their salvation, of inducing them to lay these things more to heart, of fixing them deeper in their memories, and of directing their thoughts to God in Christ for pardon, grace, and glory. And,

2. Hereby they will be furnished with an example of that kind of religious exercise, which they had been exhorted to practice; which will obviate one of the most common objections some people make against a hearty compliance with their duty, that they know not how to go about it. But in this part of the service I am recommending, they will have an example of confessing sin before God in the name of Christ, who is our advocate with the Father, and the propitiation for our iniquities; of praying for the destruction of the body of sin in our souls; of asking on the account of the Mediator of the new covenant, these things that are agreeable to the will of God; of giving thanks for mercies we have received; and of representing the case of others, as well as their own, before the Lord.

---

practiced sometimes, especially in dealing with children, nor of the questions concerning personal and family religion, that may be found in the *directions* of the *general assembly*, referred to at the beginning of the chapter. I shall only add that I never meant that the *whole substance* or *contents of this chapter* should be repeated in every family—that would be manifestly absurd. All I intend is only to explain the system of practical religion, at large, that particular persons or families may find their duty pointed out, and urged upon their conscience, in some part of the whole. The minister of Jesus ought to consider what branch of truth and duty is most seasonable, when he deals with different people; and to adapt his instructions accordingly, confining himself chiefly to one head, or, at most, to a few.

I make this remark for the sake of some inconsiderate persons who might censure this account of *ministerial visitations of their flocks*, for being *tedious and large*; or, who might fancy the duty was *superficially performed*, unless it was drawn out to such a length, and enlarged to such a variety, as the scheme I have represented.

I shall only add that such a conclusion of this solemn service is highly proper, because the success of it depends entirely on the divine blessing, and therefore should be fervently asked by prayer and supplication, "Who then is Paul, and who is Apollos, but ministers by whom ye believed, even as the Lord gave to every man? I have planted, Apollos watered; but God gave the increase. So then neither is he that planteth any thing, neither he that watereth; but God that giveth the increase" (1 Cor. 3:5–7). "Thus saith the Lord God, I will yet for this be inquired of by the house of Israel, to do it for them, I will increase them with men like a flock" (Ezek. 36:37).

Now, may *God*, who hath chosen the foolish things of the world, to confound the wise; the weak things of the world, to confound the things which are mighty; and base things of the world, and things which are despised, yea, and things which are not, to bring to naught things that are—may *He* accompany this *feeble essay* upon so important an ordinance, with the efficacious power of his Holy Spirit, for promoting the interests of real religion!

Chapter 14
Ministerial Visitation of the Sick

In the day of trouble, people should call on God *for themselves*. This is both their allowed privilege, and their bounden duty. *Christian friends and acquaintances* should visit the afflicted, and call upon God in their presence, and on their behalf. Reason suggests the propriety, and the word of God enforces the obligation upon the saints to do so. The Lord Jesus Christ will make honorable mention at the last day of these who *visited his sick*, and had compassion on his afflicted *members* (Matt. 25). "The effectual fervent prayer of the righteous availeth much" (James 5:16). When David's neighbors, and even his enemies, were sick, he mourned in sackcloth, and poured out his soul in prayer for them (Ps. 35). The advantages of united social prayer in that condition are great and many. But God willing more abundantly to show the exceeding riches of his grace, and the marvelous regard he has for the comfort of his people, has made it their duty to *call for the elders of the church*, when they are afflicted; and has made it *one branch of the ministerial work* to exhort, direct, encourage, or alarm, as the case of the sick person seems to require, and to pray over them (James 5:14). My present business is to treat of this duty, as it belongs to the pastoral office; and in doing this, I shall arrange my thoughts under these heads.

1. To represent the obligations that lie both upon *Christians* and *elders* to observe it.
2. To give an account of the manner of *elders* performing it. And,
3. To lay down some directions concerning the use *Christians* should make of it.

1. Obligations upon Christians and Elders

I shall endeavor, in the first place, to represent *the obligations* on both *Christians and elders* to observe this duty. The topics I might enlarge on for this purpose are chiefly these three: *it is a reasonable service, God has appointed it*, and *the church has all along carefully and comfortably walked in it.*

1. It is *a reasonable service* for sick people to call for the elders of the church, and for the elders, when they are called, to visit them, embracing that opportunity to instruct, and exhort, and pray over them. The *wants* of mankind place them in a state of dependence upon one another; and as no man can acquire a tolerable degree of expertness in every branch of useful knowledge and business, because his capacity is so limited, and his life is so short; an all-wise providence has so equally overruled men's genius and taste, that there are students in every science, and practicers in every employment, who apply their minds and hands for the public good; while, perhaps, they are conscious to themselves of no higher motives than their own pleasure and interest. It is a parallel case in the church, where an exalted Savior has poured down his gifts among men, in great abundance and variety; but all these gifts do not center in one person; for one Christian excels in one of them, and another person in another. Hence their order is beautiful, and their edification is promoted, when they severally keep their place in the body of Christ, and use their several gifts for general good. But God having set pastors and rulers in his church, who are particularly called by their office to attend to reading, meditation, prayer, and conversation, that their profiting may appear unto all, and that they may be able to *speak a word in season*; it is most reasonable for sick people to employ them, with a fair prospect of being benefited by their discourses, and of having their hearts more affected, while their case is represented in prayer before God. So that this duty has a foundation in the light of nature, and the circumstances mankind are placed in. But the force of this reason for the observation of it will be greater and clearer, when I have showed,

2. That *God has appointed this ordinance* for the edification of his church; and, therefore, we may confidently expect his presence and blessing in it. God said to Abimelech, "restore [Abraham] his wife; for he is a prophet, and he shall pray for thee, and thou shalt live" (Gen. 20:7). And speaking to Job's friends, he said, "my servant Job shall pray for you: for him will I accept: lest I deal with you after your folly" (Job 42:8). It was represented as a mark of *true prophets*, with whom was the word of the Lord, that *they made intercession to the Lord of hosts for others*, under the Old Testament (Jer. 27:18; Joel 2:17). And the will of God is declared, in the most precise and express terms, in James 5:14, "Is any sick among you? let him

call for the elders of the church; and let them pray over him." This fixes the rule for the New Testament dispensation; and prevents all dispute about the obligation of the duty.[1]

3. The obligation of this duty may be further illustrated from this consideration, that the church of Christ has carefully and comfortably walked in it, from age to age. In observing it, we "go forth by the footsteps of the flock" (Song 1:8), and do not walk in any new untrodden path. Job observes that "to him that is afflicted pity should be shewed from his friend" (Job 6:14). The apostle commands Christians to bear "one another's burdens, and so fulfil the law of Christ" (Gal. 6:2). Wherever humanity prevails, Job's observation is exemplified; and the apostolic precept is cheerfully obeyed, wherever the Spirit of Christ really dwells. When "one told Joseph, Behold, thy father is sick," he immediately went to see him (Gen. 48:1). When Hezekiah was sick unto death, the prophet Isaiah came unto him, and faithfully told him the will of God (2 Kings 20:1). When Job was grievously distressed, his three friends came together to mourn with him, and to comfort him (Job 2:11). When Lazarus died, "many of the Jews came to Martha and Mary, to comfort them concerning their brother" (John 11:19). Even Jesus himself, being informed that Lazarus, whom he loved, was sick, went at last to that house of mourning.

This duty, founded in humanity, is made *a religious service*, by the special appointment of heaven; and the *reward* attending it is very great, for "it is better to go to the house of mourning, than to go to the house of feasting" (Eccl. 7:2). The benefit of a friendly Christian visit, to the persons that are pained in body, or grieved in spirit, is obvious, and confessedly great; and the advantage of it, to the persons that go on this business, is also very considerable; for hereby they see *what is the end of all men*, and are admonished to *lay it to heart*. And who can describe the exalted pleasure a spiritual mind finds, in suggesting a word in season, and approaching the God

---

[1] The apostle joins *the elders anointing of the sick person with oil in the name of the Lord Jesus*, with their *praying over him*; but this is no objection against the continuance of *the last part* of the primitive service; as it affords no foundation for practicing *the first*, now that miraculous gifts are ceased, being no longer necessary for the confirmation of the gospel. *Anointing with oil* was, in the earliest age of Christianity, an ordinance for the *miraculous cure* of sick persons (Mark 6:13). But *prayer*, in behalf of the sick, was *never* considered in that light. Therefore we retain *the one*; and reject with abhorrence the Popish sacrament of *extreme unction*, whereby they pretend to perpetuate *the other*. See chap. 7, sect. 6.

of all grace through Christ, in the presence and behalf of a poor distressed fellow-mortal? There is a secret and remarkable joy in this sorrowful work.

The ministers of Christ, being set to watch for the souls of men, ought, like their divine Master, to wait on teaching and prayer, with a peculiar respect to the various cases of the diseased in body, or troubled in mind; like him, they should make every application, in their behalf, welcome; and embrace every opportunity that offers, to reprove, rebuke, and exhort with all longsuffering and doctrine. This has been the practice of the servants of Christ in all generations; and they have the best reason to say that they have served a good Master, and their labors have not been altogether in vain in the Lord. The liberal soul has frequently been made fat; and they have sometimes been watered themselves, while they have been watering others.

The afflicted can tell, and their friends can bear witness, that such visits have been accompanied with much comfort, in many cases, to their souls. The words that have been fitly spoken have awakened their consciences, removed their fears, resolved their doubts, and been helpful to their joy. Surely it is good, profitable, and pleasant to observe this ordinance with a conscientious zeal, expecting the blessing of God upon his own appointment, because he has promised to come and bless his people, while they record his name.

2. An Account of the Manner of Elders Performing It

I shall now proceed to consider *the manner* of *elders* performing this duty of visiting the sick. Several things that might be largely explained on this head shall be slightly touched, as they are only *circumstances*, which do not essentially affect the performance of the duty, such as, that they should *cheerfully* embrace every call from the sick; *faithfully* declare unto them the counsel of God; *feelingly* compassionate their condition; *prudently* inquire into their case; *seasonably* administer to their conviction and comfort; and *earnestly* study to promote their true interest. These are necessary and important circumstances, but they are only circumstances, in *visiting the sick*.

Man is born to trouble, and *all flesh is grass*, the *rich* and the *poor*, the *wise* and the *foolish*, the *righteous* and the *wicked*, the *dejected* and the *joyful in spirit*, the *tempted* and the *comforted*, the *doubting* and the *confirmed*, the *young* and the *old*, the *teacher* and the *scholar*—*all meet on a sickbed*, as well as *in the grave*. Hence the province of the elders of the church, in visiting the sick, is very extensive, and very difficult. How much do they stand in need of *the wisdom that is profitable to direct them*, that they may acquit themselves with a good conscience, and answer the end of the duty! Our only comfort and dependence should be that *the residue of the Spirit is with the Lord*. This part of the ministerial work should, therefore, be managed with a single eye to the only wise and almighty God; that he may direct to what is seasonable, and accompany his truths with efficacious power.

1. It is proper to suggest some general instructions to sick people, which have an extensive effect, through a divine blessing, upon the temper and exercise that are particularly requisite in their circumstances, such as, that *God, who is above*, ruleth in the world, and his kingdom of providence is over all his creatures, insomuch that one hair of our head cannot fall to the ground without his appointment and influence; that afflictions are the bitter fruits of sin, and entered into the world as a punishment of it; that all the miseries of this life cannot atone for the least of our numberless offenses; that infinite punishment is the deserved wages of that accursed thing; that the bitterest repentance cannot obtain forgiveness, since it is only a confession of our guilt; that the blood of Jesus Christ, the Son of God, cleanseth us from all sin; that our only sanctuary, as guilty, perishing sinners, is in Christ, the end of the law for righteousness to all that believe; that our access unto God in him by one Spirit, is open in the gospel; that believing in him, we shall have eternal life through his name; that every dispensation of mercy and affliction shall operate, under divine influence, to promote the present and everlasting good of the saints; that afflictions are not, of themselves, any sure evidence, either of the love, or displeasure, of God; that diseases come not by chance, or by distempers of body only, but by the wise and orderly guidance of the good hand of God, to every particular person smitten by them; that they are a proof and earnest of mortality; and that God, whose voice should be heard, and whose name is written, on every chastening rod, is the alone Physician, that can sanctify our trials, and deliver out of trouble. These are useful hints, and ought to be familiar to the minds of such as are groaning under bodily trouble.

2. There are particular duties too, which should not be neglected on this occasion. The ministers of Christ do not go beyond their commission, when they admonish the sick, as there shall be cause, to *set his house in order* (2 Kings 20:1), by a proper settlement of his affairs, by taking care for the payment of his debts, and by making restitution or satisfaction, if

he hath done any wrong. They should exhort him to be reconciled to those with whom he hath been at variance; and fully to forgive all men their trespasses against him, as he expects forgiveness, at the hand of God (Matt. 6). They should recommend to him, the important concerns of *a future state*; and to *prepare to meet God*, by justifying him in his greatest distresses, acknowledging, that *the Lord is righteous* (Lam. 1:18); by maintaining a sense of the hand of God under his heaviest afflictions, still remembering, that *it is the doing of the Lord*; by trusting in an afflicting God, saying, *Though he slay me, yet will I trust in him*; by bearing with patience the load of trouble that the Lord appoints for him, saying, *I will bear the indignation of the Lord, because I have sinned against him*; and by *waiting patiently* till he see the end of the Lord, without murmuring, or fretfulness, on account of the prosperity of others, or anything he may think singular in his case.

3. The instructions, delivered to the sick, should be *adapted*, as much as can be, *to their particular tempers and conditions*. A few examples will explain my meaning on this point.

If the elders suspect the sick person of *ignorance*, they should examine and instruct him in the principles of the Christian faith; representing, in the most easy and affecting light, the doctrines which relate to the majesty of God, his glorious holiness, and tremendous inexorable justice, his dominion, and his unbounded compassions; to the fall of man, his guilty, ruined, and impotent condition; to the insufficiency of his own works, and the unavailableness of all his tears, to obtain the forgiveness of sins, or instate himself in the favor of God; to the adored person of Christ, and the manifold riches of his grace, which flow upon men from the execution of his offices; to the free and merciful exhibition of this Savior unto him, as a lost and perishing sinner; to the warrant he has, and the obligation he is under, to trust in Christ, as the propitiation for his sin, and his righteousness before God; to the safe and honorable enjoyment of the favor of God through that Savior, who died for his sins, and rose again for his justification, that being reconciled by the death of Christ, he might be saved by his life; and to the nature, use, excellency, and necessity of faith, repentance, hope, love, and new obedience.

If they apprehend him to be *secure and slothful*, they ought to stir him up to consider his ways, and examine himself, whether he be in the faith. *Prudence* forbids security, and demands the most careful, jealous attention to the state of our souls, when we are visited with afflictions, which, for anything we know, may put an end to our stewardship, and day of merciful visitation. The omniscience and jealousy, the holiness and justice, the patience and mercy of God, with whom we have to do; the importance of salvation, and the worth of our souls; the dying love of Christ, and the glories that have followed his sufferings; the joys of heaven, and the terrors of the wrath to come—*all these* powerful motives should be mentioned, urged, and reinforced, with earnestness and zeal, to induce him to awake from his slumber, to rouse himself from his bed of sloth, and to consider, with the most serious attention, the great and everlasting interests of his immortal soul.

If the sick person shall *declare any scruple, doubt, or temptation*, that hang upon his mind, they should endeavor to resolve and settle him, by faithfully declaring the mind of God concerning that case. Does he allege, that *he fears the day of his merciful visitation is over?* He should be informed that this is a dangerous mistake; for God says, *Today if ye will hear his voice*, as a God of mercy, *harden not your hearts*. Does he insinuate, that *he has sinned the sin unto death?* He must be told that *it is impossible to renew such* obstinate, malicious, and determined *enemies* to the truths of the gospel, and to the people of God, *unto repentance*; and therefore their very apprehensions about that sin, are a clear proof they are not guilty of it. *Does he express his fearful thoughts about death, that king of terrors?* He must be directed to confide and rejoice in Christ, who gives the victory over that formidable enemy, by the merit of his cross, and the abundant supplies of his Spirit. *Does Satan accuse him of the vilest crimes, and fright him with terrifying apprehensions?* He should be put in mind of the never-failing rock of the sinner's dependence, even Jesus, the surety of the covenant, who took our guilt upon him, and bore our sins in his own body on the tree. *Does the law denounce its curse against him, as a transgressor?* Let him be taught to appeal to him, who hung on the accursed tree, on purpose that all the nations of the earth might be blessed in him. *Does hell open its jaws, and demand its prey?* He must be encouraged to look up to that gracious Being, who says, "Deliver him from going down to the pit: I have found a ransom" (Job 33:24). *Does his vileness make him not only ashamed, but afraid; because no unclean thing can enter into heaven?* He must be put in mind, that the blood of Christ cleanseth from all sin; and though his sins be as scarlet, they shall, through this blood, be as white as snow. *Do all his duties and religious performances, appear to his view in a very humbling light?* He must be told that these are not his righteousness, and therefore must be renounced; for he must be complete only in Christ. *Does he complain, that he has no right to the promises?*[2] They should convince him, that all the promises were made to Christ in the first place; that he is the heir of them all; that they are revealed to mankind in the Scripture, without any exception of persons or characters, that *whosoever will* may believe and plead them, and enjoy, through faith, all the blessings contained in them. These, and many other distressing cases should be heard, and resolved, with the utmost tenderness and zeal; and the elders of the church should, on such occasions, be very careful to lead the thoughts, the dependence, and the joys of the afflicted, entirely out of themselves unto Jesus Christ, revealed in the Scriptures, as the alone ordinance of God, for the salvation of sinners, and for the consolation of believers.

If the elders find the sick person *wavering and unsettled* in his mind; because he knows not what judgment to form about his *state*, whether he is in the faith, or not; they should cheerfully contribute all they are able, to assist him in a case of such near concern for the glory of God, and his comfort. It is very proper to remark, on this occasion, the fatal error of many, who would build their hopes upon their religious duties, and righteous deeds; and that such a building must unavoidably be shaken by every temptation, and sapped by every working of corruption. An humble, well-grounded assurance of our reconciliation to God, is a most precious blessing, and rises fullest and strongest from these comfortable Scriptures, that tell us, "the Son of the Most High came into the world to save sinners; that he died, the just for the unjust, that he might bring us to God; that he poured out his soul for transgressors." The faith of these declarations will be a means, both of humbling and exalting us, of filling us with shame, and filling us with hope, that we may abhor ourselves, and yet rejoice in God our Savior. He should be informed of the unspeakable danger of resting

---

[2] *No right to the promises.* This way of speaking is become familiar to many, who certainly do either not understand, or do not consider the meaning of the phrase. What is meant by *a right to the promises*, but a right or warrant to believe that it shall be to us even as it hath been spoken to us of the Lord because he is faithful that hath promised? And what *conveys this right*, or *contains this warrant*, but the authority and grace of God in the declarations, offers, invitations, and commands of the Scripture; which demonstrate, that it is our allowed privilege, and bounden duty, to believe the promises; and that unbelief will prove the greatest sin, and just condemnation, of everyone that rejects the counsel of God against himself?

upon mistaken notions, and false evidences of Christianity. The genuine characters of a real believer should be pointed out, that by a careful attention to them, he may judge whether he be in the faith, *viz.*, that he hates every sin, because it is offensive to God; that he unfeignedly desires to love Christ above all things; that he wishes to be an eternal debtor to the free grace of God, reigning through the righteousness of Christ; and that he is zealous of good works, and one that rejoices in the prosperity of pure and undefiled religion.

If the sick person is *joyful in his tribulation*, they ought to assist and improve his joys, by encouraging him to *rejoice always in the Lord* (Phil. 4:4). They should be helpers of his joy, by directing it to the love of God, the priesthood and righteousness of Christ, the covenant of promise, and these immutable things, in which it is impossible for God to lie. They should admonish him to be strong only in the grace that is in the Lord Jesus Christ; because God hath set the day of prosperity and of adversity over against one another; and he that now lifts them up, may soon cast them down again. Their most agreeable tempers and their best dispositions are liable to manifold interruptions and changes; but *the joy of the Lord shall be our strength*, in the hour of temptation, and in every time of need.

If the person is, through mercy, *recovered*, or *recovering* from his affliction, he should be exhorted to stir up his soul to bless and love the Lord, who has healed all his diseases, and redeemed his life from destruction; to walk worthy of the kindness of God unto all pleasing; to pay his vows which he made unto the Lord in the time of trouble; to wait with hope and patience upon him in future trials, from the experience he has had of divine goodness in his past deliverances; and to testify a grateful sense of the mercies of God, by a conversation adorned with meekness of wisdom, humility, and prudence.

More examples might be named, and each of these that have been touched might have been enlarged on; but this would be foreign to my purpose, and therefore I shall add,

4. That elders in visiting the sick should, if desired, *pray with him, and for him*. The season most proper for this part of the service should be prudently chosen, when the sick person is best composed, and may be least disturbed in joining, and when other necessary offices about him may be least hindered. In prayer, it is proper to enlarge upon these topics that are most suitable to the person's condition; for these are most likely to engage

the attention, and affect the heart, of the patient. And because God has not given absolute promises concerning bodily health and comfort, nor are these a real blessing, except in so far as they are sanctified; therefore our desires of them should be limited by the sovereign will of God, while ardor and importunity for the blessing of God upon the afflicting providence, and for the everlasting salvation of the soul, should employ our chief attention.[3]

5. *Before*, or *after* prayer, they may take an opportunity from the present occasion, to exhort *those about the sick person*, to consider their own mortality; to number their days so as to apply their hearts unto wisdom; to return unto the Lord by faith in Christ; to take hold of the Lord's strength, that they may make peace with him, and they shall make peace with him;[4] in health to prepare to meet their God in sickness, death, and judgment; and all the days of their appointed time to wait till their change come; that when Christ, who is our life, shall appear, they may also appear with him in glory.

6. If the elders of the church are called to visit *a person, or family, which God has chastened with some afflicting breach*, by taking away the head or

---

[3] The heads of prayer, in general, for such an occasion, are to be found in "Of Visitation of the Sick". In *Westminster Directory for the Publick Worship of God*.

[4] *Make peace with him*. The passage I refer to is recorded in Isaiah 27:5. The Scripture-sense of this expression is quite another thing than is commonly meant by people, who talk of *making their peace with God* on a sick-bed, or in the near prospects of an eternal world. The prophet speaks of making peace with God, by *believing* on the name of his Son Jesus Christ, who has made peace by the blood of his cross; and is a Child born *unto us*, and a Son *given to us* in the testimony of God, and whose name is the Prince of peace. But all that is commonly understood by these inconsiderate people, who speak of *making their peace with God* in the views of death, amounts barely to this: that they entertain a notion of his character, which is borrowed from the ideas of what is called *a good-natured man*, who is not easily provoked, but will overlook many offenses against himself, before he is raised to a passion; and when he is so provoked, is soon brought into temper again, by a humble acknowledgment of the fault. Such a good-natured man as this is often imposed on; his nearest dependents frequently impose on him, and say, "If we act ever so contrary to his mind in such an affair, when we have gained our point, as he is a good-natured person, we shall easily make it up again." I believe the consciences of many will bear witness that they consider God in this very light, when they talk so freely of *making their peace with him*; and that they have no view to *him*, "whom God hath set forth to be the propitiation, through faith in his blood, to declare his righteousness for the remission of sins that are past, that he might be just, and the justifier of him which believeth in Jesus" (Rom. 3:25–26).

the members of it, they ought to embrace the call in providence, and to endeavor to make their visit as useful as possible. The conversation should turn upon the most seasonable and improving subjects, such as, the eternity of God, who is from everlasting to everlasting; the vanity and shortness of human life, which is like a vapor, that appeareth for a little, and vanisheth away; the certainty of a future state; the unutterable joys of heaven, and the inconceivable sorrows of hell; the death and resurrection of the Redeemer; the glorious, indissoluble union of Christ and his people; the absurdity and danger of being carnally minded; and the blessedness and advantage of being spiritually minded, which is life and peace. These are instructive and affecting points; and the providence of God calls us to consider them, as the source of our joy, and the rule of our conduct, when he has taken away our dear and intimate friends and relatives. *Such conversation*, accompanied with *suitable prayer*, might make it *better to be in the house of mourning, than in the house of mirth* (Eccl. 7:2).

3. Directions to Christians Concerning the Use of It

I proposed, in the last place, to lay down *some directions concerning the use Christians should make* of ministerial visits to the sick; and especially concerning the use which sick people should make of them *themselves*. To this purpose it is proper to observe,

1. That *the sick should send for the elders of the church* (James 5:14). It is their duty to inform the elders of their condition, and to desire their instructions and prayers. If this rule were duly attended to, it might be a happy means of preventing unreasonable offenses against ministers, for not making visits to the sick sometimes, when it is seasonable, and they would incline to do it; but being ignorant of their case, cannot perform this service. And as the sick should call for the elders of the church, so they ought to desire their visits before their strength and understanding fail them. If their bodily strength is gone, and their understanding impaired, one end of the visit is lost.

2. When elders are called to visit the sick, they should only be considered, *as ministers*, by whom, as they bring glad tidings of great joy to their fellow-sinners, people believe, as the Lord giveth to every man. How absurdly and ignorantly do many talk of a minister's visit and prayers! As if they contributed to the sick man's happiness by *some power* in themselves, and by *some efficacy* in their devotions. Among many of the abominations

derived from Rome, this is one, that the ministers of religion can open and shut, by their importunity, the gates of heaven and hell. Truly, in vain is salvation looked for from the hills, or from the multitude of mountains; from the number of duties, or from the persons employed in performing them; except in so far as these are *instituted means*, through which a God of sovereign mercy is pleased to manifest his undeserved favor to men.

3. Before they send for the elders of the church, they should *pray to God for his blessing* to accompany the visit they solicit. The blessing of God sanctifies every enjoyment, and should therefore be fervently implored upon it. Paul might plant, and Apollos water, but God must give the increase. It is proper that elders call on God for direction and assistance, when they are to go on such visits; and it is no less reasonable that the persons to be visited call on the Father of lights for a blessing on his own ordinance.

4. The sick person should *receive with attention* the instructions that are administered to him from the word of God, considering the messengers of them in this light, that they are only reporters of the will of God unto men. His faith of the alarming, encouraging, or searching truths, which are reported unto him, in the name of God, and agreeable to his word, should rest, not on the credit and veracity of the instrument that has declared them, but on the authority of God himself, who cannot lie. God's word is the only foundation of faith and hope, concerning the things that are not seen. It is imprudent to risk our everlasting concerns upon the credit of any man; and it is the more absurd, because we have access to *the sure word of prophecy*, to satisfy ourselves concerning every point of our faith and obedience.

5. Let the sick endeavor to *profit* by the instructions of their elders. Let them remember how they have received and heard, and hold fast, and repent. They should remember that their privileges are accountable talents; and that they shall be judged, they know not how soon, concerning their merciful enjoyments. Let them consider the fearful condition of that servant, who knew his Lord's will, but did not obey it. *If ye know these things*, says Christ, *happy are ye, if ye do them.* God, and their own consciences, and faithful ministers, will witness against such persons, as have sent for the elders of the church to visit them, in the time of their distress, and

have treated their visits as a mere compliment, without laying up in their hearts, and practicing in their lives, the precious truths they have heard on such a solemn occasion.

Chapter 15
Catechizing

Among the methods that have been successfully attempted for promoting the knowledge of the Scriptures, it is well known that *catechizing* has been of eminent service. In treating of this duty, I shall endeavor to do six things, *viz.*,

1. To explain the *nature* of the duty, and show what is meant by catechizing.
2. To show in what *manner* it should be performed.
3. To consider the *matter* it is conversant about.
4. To prove the *obligation* we are under to observe it.
5. To propose and answer a few *questions* relative to it. And,
6. To give some practical *directions* concerning it.

1. The Nature of the Duty Represented

The *nature* of the duty of *catechizing* will be evident enough from the following description of it: namely, that *it is a plain, clear, and familiar way of instructing people in the principles of the Christian religion, by proposing such questions concerning them, as are adapted to their capacities and improvements.*

This notion of *catechizing* supposes that the truths contained in the oracles of God may be summed up, and digested into *a system*, in a judicious abridgment, conceived in human words. And, upon this principle, *articles of faith, creeds, confessions,* and *catechisms* have been *always* used in the Christian church, as everyone acquainted with her history must know. I am sensible that *systematical divinity* has been greatly abused; and, in this fashionable age of refinement, it is zealously decried; but abuses only call for *reformation*, not for the *abolishing*, of what is good in itself. Moreover, it should be considered that the best things are liable to the greatest corruptions and abuse; and those who declaim with greatest warmth against systems are commonly obliged to take this course, in order to discredit a method of inquiry which would soonest detect some of their principles that cannot bear the light of it.

Though all Scripture is given by inspiration of God, and is profitable for doctrine, for reproof, for correction, and for instruction in righteousness, yet some particular passages are more eminently useful for these purposes than others; accordingly, we have several most valuable and concise systems of doctrine and duty in the Scriptures themselves. *The ten commandments, with their preface* (Ex. 20). *The Lord's prayer*, as it is commonly called (Matt. 6). *The mystery of godliness*, in its several branches (1 Tim. 3:16). And many more examples might be referred to, for the proof of this.

At present I suppose that *such composures are warrantable;*[1] and that *just consequences, drawn from the express words of Scripture, ought to be considered as a part of the system of revealed truth.*[2] These are positions of considerable weight in treating on this subject; but my plan does not permit me to enlarge on the evidences of them. The reader that wants the fullest satisfaction may consult the books referred to in the footnotes.

Catechizing, which implies the using of *catechisms*, is a mode of conveying instruction that is very natural and easy; it fixes the attention, and engages all the active powers of the soul in the subject. The most effectual means, and the most proper seasons, should be preferred for this business, which is of great importance for increasing knowledge, for affecting the heart, and directing the practice.

2. The Manner of Performing the Duty Considered

I proposed, in the second place, to show in what *manner* this duty of *catechizing* should be performed. And,

1. It should be performed *with a strict regard to the capacities and improvements* of the person to be catechized, that he may edify in knowledge. If the questions put to him are far above his capacity, he cannot understand them; if they directly contradict his received sentiments, he will be ready to detest them; and if they are beneath his more advanced understanding, he will probably despise them and the teacher too. Our Lord taught his

---

[1] This sentiment is well supported in William Dunlop. *A Preface to an Edition of the Westminster Confession*; and in the introduction to John Gill. *Body of Doctrinal Divinity*.

[2] This point is judiciously treated by the learned John Cumming. *Dissertation concerning the Authority of Scripture-Consequences*.

disciples as they were able to bear, and not as he was able to teach them. It requires some consideration to enable a faithful teacher to execute this part of his work prudently and successfully.

2. It ought to be managed *with upright intentions*; not to display the superior abilities of the person that catechizes; nor meanly to expose, or triumph over the weaknesses of those who are catechized.

3. Catechizing should not be confined to one or a few heads of the system of revealed truth. First principles must be first laid; but Christians, leaving these, must go on unto perfection. All things that God hath revealed must be taught, as well as all things that he hath commanded must be carefully observed.

4. It should be *regular and methodical*. Some order must be observed, if any success is expected to attend it. This will as much help the memories, and fix the attention of them that are taught, as it will assist the teacher. And in this kind of teaching, there should be a progression from such fundamental points, as are plain and obvious, to those that are more improving to the mind. The harmony of Scripture-truth should be steadfastly maintained, and carefully explained, in a manner that will tend to throw the clearest light on the whole, and manifest the dependence of the parts with most advantage.

3. The Matter of It

I shall now consider the *matter* of this duty, or what it is conversant about, when men use it according to divine appointment.

1. It is a base prostitution of this ordinance when it is employed to prepossess the mind, and bias the heart, in favor of unprofitable and frivolous *traditions*, relative to religion, which are handed down, with great art and industry, especially in the church of Rome, from one age to another.[3] No doubt, the events of providence, recorded in the faithful historian's page, deserve the attention of mankind; and whoso is wise will certainly observe them, because they come forth from the Lord of hosts, who is wonderful in counsel, and excellent in working; but *traditions about religious doc-*

---

[3] I said, *especially in the church of Rome*; because the system of traditional opinions and observances is considered in that church, as a particular and important branch of *professed study*. But is the case greatly altered in these Protestant communions, where *long practice* is supposed to give prescription, and venerable antiquity is urged to forbid candid inquiry? Perhaps some will think that *both err on the same principle*.

trines, worship, and practices, make void the word of God, and ruin the souls of men.

2. It is against the very intention of this ordinance to use it as *an engine of wit*, and to make catechizing only *a slave to curious and speculative knowledge*. All this amounts only to impertinent trifling in the most weighty and serious matters; and it is certainly most unseasonable, when the honor of God, and the good of precious souls, are so nearly concerned. Neither should the teacher affect mysterious language, nor propose nice and critical questions, with a view to puzzle them he catechizes, or to be thought very knowing and profound. Such questions will have a very bad effect on many, who will take the hint to pursue speculative inquiries in religion, to gratify their vanity, to the neglect of vital, powerful godliness. And who can tell what numberless bad consequences may follow in other respects? Perhaps the hearers, after all that the teacher says upon these points, are not able to understand them, and then they are in danger of falling into erroneous notions; perhaps they find eminent writers that resolve these questions another way, and so they either despise their living teachers, or become prejudiced against these writers; or, perhaps they are divided among themselves, and, instead of useful conversation, on points wherein they are of one mind, their discourse turns, even on the Lord's day, upon abstracted notions which they cannot well understand, and which, if they could understand, they would derive very little benefit from, as to the advancement either of their holiness or joy. Teachers should consider themselves, in catechizing, as acting in the stead of Christ, who hath the tongue of the learned, to speak a word in season to him that is weary. Judge impartially, *ye subtle metaphysical catechists!* and then say, whether your instructions carry any marks of conformity to his, or not; and whether you are really skillful workmen that need not be ashamed, rightly dividing the word of truth. I speak as to wise men, judge ye what I have said.

3. Catechizing should not be confined to *party-principles*, as I may call them. One may long seek after instruction upon such a scheme, before he can tolerably satisfy his own mind, that his notions are solid. The wisdom that arises from the frequent inculcating of the distinguishing, characteristic sentiments of any party, has seldom any of the genuine marks of "the wisdom that is from above," which is "first pure, then peaceable, gentle, and easy to be intreated, full of mercy and good fruits, without partiality, and without hypocrisy;" but it is commonly stamped with every feature

of that wisdom which "'is earthly, sensual, devilish;" and produces such "envying and strife" as are attended with "confusion and every evil work" (James 3:15–17). It is a much stronger evidence of *a warm eager temper*, than of *candor and good sense*, in a teacher, if he labors to hang the whole system of Scripture-truth upon *the peculiarities* of his own, and his party's opinions. Whether we account for this, by reckoning the person *weak in judgment*, or deeply *prejudiced*, it is certain, his way of managing the cause he favors must expose himself, and perhaps his party also, to the censure of the malevolent, and to the contempt of all sober men; unless they are blessed with more consideration than such forward bigots, to allow for the goodness of the cause, while they pity the advocates that plead it. How much has religion suffered in the world through such weakness and prejudice! Let not the teachers of the church contribute to its misfortunes, by making their party-sentiments *a principal part* of their catechetical instructions; for while this would strengthen spiritual pride in the people whom they teach, as well as make them despise and judge those that do not walk with them, it will render themselves odious in the eyes of such as do not approve their way. Suppose every denomination of Christians were to take this course, and the consequence must be, as in the days of the apostle, that everyone would say, "I am of Paul; and I of Apollos; and I of Cephas; and I of Christ" (1 Cor. 1:12). Where this is the language of professors, I am not afraid to risk an appeal to every man's conscience concerning *every party*, but *his own—are they not carnal?*

4. The *subject-matter of catechizing* should be both *confined* and *extended* to *all the chief heads of the Christian religion, contained in the word of God. To the law, and to the testimony* of the God of heaven, should be the constant appeal of Christian teachers; for this is the alone rule of faith and practice.

Many excellent attempts have been made, by different hands, upon this subject; and I believe their well-meant labors have been approved of God, and, through his blessing, have been useful to many, many precious souls. But of all the performances of this nature, perhaps none has equaled *the Assembly's Shorter Catechism*,[4] which sets forth the principles of Christianity in the most excellent method and order.

---

[4] *Westminster Shorter Catechism.*

It would be tedious to give a particular division of the several heads of divinity, according to the order of the Catechism: but, in general, the *method* thereof may be taken up under these four comprehensive articles; namely, the *chief end*, the *only rule*, the *glorious object*, and the *great subject*... of the *Christian religion*.

The *chief end* of the Christian religion is the *glorifying* of God, and the *enjoying* him forever (question 1).

We have the *only rule* of the Christian religion described (1.) In its *matter*; which is the *word* of God, contained in the Scriptures of the Old and New Testament (question 2). (2.) In its *principal parts*; which are, first, what man is to *believe* concerning God; and then, what *duty* God requires of man (question 3).

The *glorious object* is *God*, considered (1.) *Essentially*, in his spiritual nature and infinite perfections, and in his most perfect unity and simplicity (questions 4, 5). (2.) *Relatively* or *personally*, in the three distinct persons of the Godhead, and in the consubstantiality and absolute equality of these persons (question 6). (3.) *Efficiently*, in his acts and operations, which are either immanent and essential, as his *decrees*; or transient and external, as his *works of creation and providence*, wherein he executes his decrees (questions 7–12).

The *great subject* of the Christian religion is *man*, considered (1.) In his *state of innocency*, where the covenant of works is opened, question 12. (2.) In his *state of nature*, together with the sinfulness and misery of that state (questions 13–20). (3.) In his *state of grace*, or begun recovery; where the Catechism treats of the *nature* of the covenant of grace (question 20); of the *Mediator* of the covenant, who is described in his person, offices, humiliation, exaltation, and in the application of his purchased redemption by the *Holy Spirit* (questions 21–32); of the *benefits* of the covenant, in this life, at death, at the resurrection, and through all eternity (questions 32–39); of the *duties*, whereby we evidence our covenant-relation and gratitude to God, in the *ten commandments*, as connected with their *preface* (questions 39–82); of man's utter *inability* to obey the law in this life (question 82); of the *aggravation* and *desert* of sin (questions 83, 84); and of the *means* whereby our salvation is carried on, and perfected at death: the internal means, *faith* and *repentance*; and the external means, *the word, sacraments,* and *prayer* (questions 85 to the end).[5]

But whether *that catechism,* or *another,* shall be preferred, is a point that will depend greatly on the taste and education, the connections and circumstances, of the teachers. Only they must remember to hold fast the form of sound words; and to consent to wholesome words, even the words of the Lord Jesus Christ, and to the doctrine which is according to godliness; holding forth the *Word of Life,* in this branch of their ministry, with all faithfulness, and keeping it invariably in their eye.

4. The Obligation on Christians to Observe It

The *obligation* upon Christians to observe the ordinance of *catechizing* may be proved from several considerations. It is an *excellent, ancient, necessary, useful,* and *easy* method of instruction. I shall attempt a brief illustration of these particulars.

1. Catechizing is a very *excellent method* of instructing people in the knowledge of the doctrines and duties of Christianity. Far from being *a base and beggarly exercise,* as some have represented it; it has the highest marks of *honor and respect* put upon it in the oracles of God, and has been always held in *great esteem* among the saints. Common sense has approved similar methods of initiating mankind into arts and sciences; and it has been thought no less honorable for *learners* to submit to such instructions, than for *teachers* to open their understanding to useful knowledge by such means. None despise this way of education but the *ignorant* part of mankind, who are blind to their own interest, and therefore are prejudiced against the best means of promoting it; and their folly and pride render them objects both of pity and contempt, in the eyes of all prudent men. The *excellency of catechizing* is manifest; for it is the *fittest means* of alluring and engaging all the powers of the soul to the study and practice of divine truth; which it naturally tends to do, by enlightening and enlarging the understanding, by strengthening and storing the memory, by awakening diligence and application in the pursuit of useful knowledge, and by rewarding careful inquiries with adequate satisfactions. It is even an honorable testimony in its favor, that none despise this ordinance, but such as

---

[5] See Messrs. Ebenezer Erskine and Fisher's *preface* to *The Assembly's Shorter Catechism Explained by way of Question and Answer.*

are under the power of bad tempers, and show an aversion to the authority of Christ in other manifest branches of religious duty.

2. Catechizing is *an ancient method* of instructing mankind. Some think that Enoch, the seventh from Adam, who prophesied of the coming of the Lord to judge the world, was called by that name, to keep up the remembrance of this exercise; his name signifying *one dedicated*, or *instructed*. Perhaps this is too nice a refinement; and therefore, though I have mentioned it, I do not rest the proof of the position upon so weak a foundation. It seems more reasonable to suppose that this ordinance is referred to, in Genesis 14:14, where we read, that Abram "armed his trained servants," to pursue the four kings who had carried Lot captive. These *trained* servants were *instructed* in the knowledge of the only true God, and *dedicated* to his service; hence we find God saying of Abraham, "I know him, that he will command his children and his household after him, and they shall keep the way of the LORD, to do justice and judgment" (Gen. 18:19). This explains the meaning of their being *trained* in the former passage, though it would be too narrow to exclude their being *formed to military discipline* from the sense of the place altogether.

After the Lord had given Israel his statutes and judgments, he subjoined the following charge, "these words, which I command thee this day, shall be in thine heart: and thou shalt *teach them diligently* unto thy children, and shalt talk of them when thou sittest in thine house, and when thou walkest by the way, and when thou liest down, and when thou risest up" (Deut. 6:6–7). The expression in the original is, *Thou shalt sharpen*, or *whet*, or *grind them*, instead of, *thou shalt teach them diligently*; and the harmonious sense of the Jewish Rabbis, who all understand it of *catechetical instruction*, is quite natural and obvious. That exhortation, "Train up a child in the way he should go" (Prov. 22:6), is of the same import; accordingly the marginal reading is, *Catechize a child in his way*. And Solomon has recorded his father's pious care, to instruct him in the ways of wisdom, "He taught me also, and said unto me, Let thine heart retain my words" (Prov. 4:4).

If we believe the rabbinical writers (and why should we not in *such a point?*) there were never fewer than four hundred schools for catechizing in Jerusalem, from the time of Antiochus Epiphanes, when they made a decree, that their children should be put to catechizing at thirteen years of age. The apostle seems to allude to this practice when he speaks of the Jews as *instructed*, or *catechized out of the law* (Rom. 2:18).

All antiquity in *the Christian church* is entirely in favor of this service. Not only the ages which succeeded the apostles, but the apostolic age itself, contain many demonstrative proofs that this was a part of the daily *ministration* among the disciples. The practice of the church, after the apostles were taken from their labors on earth, is recorded in the writings of the *ancient fathers*;[6] and the New Testament gives us sufficient light into the practice of the apostolic church, for there we find that Theophilus and Apollos had been *instructed*, or *catechized* (Luke 1:4; Acts 18:25); and that ministers of the gospel are called *teachers*, or *catechizers*, "Let him that is *taught* [or *catechized*]...communicate unto him that teacheth [or *catechizeth*] in all good things" (Gal. 6:6, see also 1 Cor. 14:19).

Perhaps it may be alleged that these passages do not amount to a clear proof of *that method of teaching*, by asking questions, and receiving answers, which is commonly called *catechizing*; because the word I have translated *catechize* is sometimes taken in *another sense*, as in Acts 21:21, where Paul is told that the believing *Jews were informed*[7] of several things concerning him, that gave them offense. The answer to this shall be in two particulars: (1.) There is nothing more common than to *propagate calumny* by question and answer; but (2.) I do not confine catechetical teaching to that *precise mode* of asking questions, and receiving answers; but include also *the summing up* of the heads of Christian doctrine and duty, in a concise and easy light. They are the same in *substance*, and only differ in *a point of form*. Either the one, or the other, may be used, as prudence shall direct. But if it be granted that *any of these ways* of initiating men to the knowledge of divine things has been commonly practiced, under the Old and New Testament, all that I affirm is yielded. I shall only add that he must be an incurable skeptic who can allow himself to hesitate whether he should allow that *both of them* might be occasionally practiced, as circumstances should direct, after he has attended to the full evidence contained in the Scripture on this point.

---

[6] Suiceri, *Thesaurus Ecclesiasticus*, on κατηχεω.

[7] *Informed*. The original word is *catechized* (κατηχηθησαν), which may refer to the *manner* of obtaining their information, by the *answers made to their inquiries* concerning his doctrine.

3. Catechizing is *a necessary method* of leading people to the knowledge and practice of true religion. The necessity of it is strongly implied in that remarkable passage,

> For when for the time ye ought to be teachers, ye have need that one teach you again which be the first principles of the oracles of God; and are become such as have need of milk, and not of strong meat. For every one that useth milk is unskilful in the word of righteousness: for he is a babe. But strong meat belongeth to them that are of full age, even those who by reason of use have their senses exercised to discern both good and evil. Therefore leaving the principles of the doctrine of Christ, let us go on unto perfection; not laying again the foundation of repentance from dead works, and of faith toward God, of the doctrine of baptisms, and of laying on of hands, and of resurrection of the dead, and of eternal judgment (Hebrews 5:12–6:2).

Here the apostle supposes that there are *two sorts* of Christians; some are but *babes*, while others are *of full age*; that the word of God contains suitable entertainment for both of them; the principles of the oracles of God being as *milk* to the babes, and the more important doctrines of divine revelation, as *strong meat* to them that are of full age; and that the former must be taught which be the first principles of the oracles of God, while the last must be carried on unto perfection, in higher advances of Christian knowledge. These are the grounds of the reproof and exhortation he gives the Hebrews, which are entered on record for our learning; and clearly show the necessity of continuing this exercise in the Christian church. *Ye have need that one teach you*, is the apostle's expression.

4. Catechizing is a very *profitable method* of promoting the interests of religion. The benefits of it are every way great, and are not confined to the present age, but descend unto posterity in a happy train of blessings. By this means, the purity of religion is preserved and spread in the world; the knowledge of it is transmitted to posterity; the understanding is most naturally opened to receive the things of God; the memory is best helped to retain them; the mind is guarded against error and false doctrine; people are enabled to receive more profit by the public ministry of the word; a holy useful conversation, as becometh saints, is promoted; the peace of

the church is greatly secured; and the amiable excellencies of vital religion are rendered more conspicuous, while the love of Christians abounds, "yet more and more in knowledge and in all judgment; that [they] may approve things that are excellent; that [they] may be sincere and without offense till the day of Christ; being filled with the fruits of righteousness, which are by Jesus Christ, unto the glory and praise of God" (Phil. 1:9–11).

The advantages of instructing mankind by way of *question and answer* are so striking that this method has been used by the greatest masters of arts and sciences, with amazing success. The question suggests some article that demands and fixes the attention; and at the same time contains some hint, either in its bosom, or in its connection, that helps the scholar to a pertinent answer; it gives full employment to his own thoughts; and yet does not exclude the assistance of his teacher. It furnishes his mind with useful knowledge, and animates him to industry in his searches after truth.

5. Catechetical instructions are *an easy path* to learning. They suit themselves to different capacities; and deduce conclusions less obvious at first view, by an easy progression from principles that are generally known and confessed; they state the doctrines of revelation in a perspicuous light; and open their connections, dependence, and influence; they imprint them on the memory; and inspire the learner with the pleasant hope of obtaining the object of his studies; instead of leaving him bewildered in a maze of confusion and uncertainty, they point out his way, and encourage his attempts in seeking for the knowledge of the Lord.

Method is a great friend to improvement. How much more easy is a judicious system of regular education than the blundering, ill-directed labors of one that gives application indeed, but without any rule or art? All the world acknowledge the superior advantages of the former above the other. If any call them in question, they show their ignorance of the subject they pretend to judge of, and provoke the scorn of all who know it. Men of discernment decline such unqualified judges; and submit the cause to common sense, and the experience of ages past and present, secure of a hearty approbation from these impartial tribunals.

In a word, if *that system* of improvement in Christian knowledge is *most easy*, which is *plainest*, and *shortest*, and *safest*, and most *successful*, then catechizing ought to be preferred to every other. The rest are proper means to gain several important ends; but this is the most natural way to enlighten the mind, and promote the increase of Scripture-knowledge.

Thus I have showed *the obligation*, both in point of duty and interest, of honor and pleasure, that lies upon mankind, to observe the ordinance of catechizing; which is *an excellent, ancient, necessary, useful*, and *easy method* of teaching the mysteries of the kingdom of heaven.[8]

5. A Few Questions Relative to It Answered

I shall now collect come miscellaneous thoughts upon this subject, in a few *questions and answers*, which I could not so well digest under the rest of the heads.

Question 1. Who are authorized to perform this duty?

Answer. It falls chiefly upon *heads of families, teachers of youth*, and *ministers of the gospel*.

1. *Heads of families* ought to catechize and instruct their *children* and *servants*. They should catechize their *children*; training them up in the way they should go (Prov. 22:6). Early instruction in the principles of religion is a duty they owe unto their children, as well as to provide for them the necessaries of life; hence they are commanded to "bring them up in the nurture and admonition of the Lord" (Eph. 6:4). Very observable to this purpose are those words of the prophet, "Whom shall he teach knowledge? and whom shall he make to understand doctrine? them that are weaned from the milk, and drawn from the breasts. For precept must be upon precept, precept upon precept; line upon line, line upon line; here a little, and there a little" (Isa. 28:9-10). So must parents teach their children, by suiting their instructions to their capacities, and frequently repeating them; endeavoring to throw light into their minds, as well as putting words and phrases in their mouths. They ought also to instruct their *servants* catechetically, even as Abraham did, who has this honorable testimony, from the faithful Witness, that *he commanded his household to keep the way of the Lord* (Gen. 18:19). Masters cannot be faithful to God, who has put them in trust with the charge of a household, unless they show them *the way of the Lord* wherein they should walk, and command them to *keep* it. Abraham,

---

[8] I have purposely omitted the objections that are usually made against submitting to this ordinance, not because they are too formidable to admit of a satisfying answer; rather because they are generally *empty cavils*, that deserve but little regard. The reader will find the most plausible of them, fully answered in the London ministers' *Vindication of the Presbyterial Government and Ministry*, pp. 142-152; and in Crofton's treatise: Zachary Crofton. *Catechizing, God's Ordinance*, pp. 105-122.

in the steps of whose faith they must walk, if they are his seed, and heirs according to the promise, has set them an example of their duty in both these branches of it; as it refers to *parents* and *masters*; and as it includes *instruction* and *precept*.

2. The duty of catechizing is incumbent on *the teachers of youth*, that have the care and oversight of their education; as *schoolmasters and mistresses*, who should improve the opportunity they have, of instilling into their minds and memories the great truths and duties of religion, as they are capable of receiving them. *The tribe of Levi* received no inheritance in the land of Canaan; because their business was to minister before the Lord, in offering sacrifice, and making intercession for the people; and to minister among the tribes, as teachers of their youth; whose lips should keep knowledge, and at whose mouth the people were to seek the law (Mal. 2:7). Accordingly, the forty-eight cities, appointed for them, were scattered through all the country, that there might be an equal opportunity for all to profit by their instructions, at public schools, wherein the Levites presided, and taught the knowledge of the law of God. And under the New Testament, such institutions were early set up, and greatly encouraged for the propagation of Christianity. But there is no occasion to enumerate particular examples in this or that period, among this or that party; for, *in every country*, the teachers of the youth have *always* been considered as persons authorized, in virtue of their office, to form the minds of their pupils unto the knowledge and study of *their religion*, whether that was *Jewish, Christian, Muhammadan*, or *pagan*.

3. *Ministers of the gospel* should instruct and catechize their *flocks*. They are commanded both to *feed Christ's lambs and his sheep* (John 21). They must fulfill the different services of that ministry they have received from the Lord, by feeding *the babes* with milk, or initiating them to a familiar acquaintance with the first principles of the Christian faith; and by feeding *those that are of full age* with strong meat, or leading them on to higher and more enlarged views of the scheme of heavenly truth. By this exercise, ministers come to know the state of their people; and consequently are enabled to form a better judgment about the doctrines that are most necessary to be insisted on in the course of their public ministry; and to judge with more certainty of their *fitness* in point of knowledge, for being admitted to the Lord's table. And as this ordinance is, in these respects, profitable to ministers, so it is many ways useful to their people, who are

improved in knowledge, and perhaps corrected in some of their mistaken notions, by a clear representation of the connection and dependence of particular points in *the chain of divine truth*.

Question 2. Should *grown people*, who have made good advances in sound learning, be *publicly catechized?*

Answer. Catechizing seems to be chiefly designed for the benefit of *young persons*, and such as are *weak in knowledge*; but should *not be confined* to them. Judicious Christians, conscious to their own imperfections, will always be most forward to support the honor, and promote the credit of this duty, by attending on it; they will choose to be hearers, even when they know they are not to be called to answer; and they will encourage all that fear the Lord to take the same course. Now, if such persons of reputation are publicly catechized, their example will have a very happy effect in two things.

1. Then the *offense* of the duty will cease; and it will no longer be considered as a service for children, or as a brand of infamy upon ignorance. Pride infatuates mankind, and shuts their eyes against both their duty and interest. When once they suspect that *their honor before the people* is at stake, their self-love is alarmed; and immediately they begin to be offended at the ordinances of heaven; and will find a thousand pretenses to justify their neglects of such duties, as they apprehend to be dangerous to their reputation. Every cause of stumbling, on this account, should be carefully avoided; and, in the present case, the way of preventing all offense is plain: *Let both the weak and the strong be catechized.* And,

2. *The example of the strong will stir up the weak to emulation.* To provoke to zeal by living examples, is a very successful method of exciting mankind to useful actions; and is a motive which has its own weight, and ought to be urged in the duties of religion (2 Cor. 8–9). When sensible and experienced Christians give their answers, concerning the doctrines and duties of revealed truth, the ignorant will be edified by what they hear, and will be convinced, by this means, that they have not attained, neither are already perfect in knowledge; which superficial scholars are too willing to suppose in their own favor; and will be excited to diligence and assiduity in using the means God has appointed for their growth in grace, and in the knowledge of our Lord Jesus Christ.

Upon these considerations, which are grounded on the general rule, "Let all things be done unto edifying" (1 Cor. 14:26), I apprehend that catechizing should be practiced in *congregations, societies,* and *families,* without any other difference than what arises from the different *capacities and ages* of the persons to be so instructed.

Question 3. On what *particular occasions* should this duty be performed?

Answer. It is hard to determine these with any certainty or exactness; only the following observations may be considered.

1. Parents should be *very frequent,* as well as earnest in the *teaching of their children*; hence they are commanded to *teach them, when they sit in the house, and when they walk by the way, and when they lie down, and when they rise up* (Deut. 6:7). They have many opportunities to converse with them; and their discourses should be managed with a view to promote the good of their souls, and to train them up in the way they should go.

2. Masters of families should choose *proper seasons* for instructing their households, allotting some particular time for this business; lest, if it be left to be determined by conveniency, and a conjuncture of favorable circumstances, it be much neglected, if not wholly dropped. The *Lord's-day evening* seems to be a fit season for this work; which is an employment every way suitable to the nature of Sabbath-sanctification, and will engage the attention of the family to the duties of religion, and prevent improper discourse.

3. Before persons are received into church-fellowship, and admitted to partake of the Lord's Supper, they should be required to make a profession of their faith, and submit an account of their knowledge unto the rulers in the congregation where they are to join. The purity and knowledge which should adorn *the church, which is the house of the living God,* are a sufficient proof of this; for (1.) It is the will of Jesus Christ, that no grossly ignorant, or scandalous person, should come to the sacrament; (2.) That, if those who are grossly ignorant or scandalous offer to come, they should be *kept back* by the officers of the church; (3.) That church-governors have some *sufficient means* to find out who are such ignorant and scandalous persons, that they may be kept away; and (4.) That a proper *examination* into their knowledge and practice, is the proper method of making such a discovery: "But sanctify the Lord God in your hearts: and be ready always to give an answer to every man that asketh you a reason of the hope that is in you with meekness and fear" (1 Peter 3:15). "I know thy works, and thy labour, and thy patience, and how thou canst not bear them which are evil: and thou

hast tried them which say they are apostles, and are not, and hast found them liars" (Rev. 2:2).

4. Ministers should allot a *suitable proportion* of their public labors, in the work of the gospel, to the catechizing of their congregations. I say *a suitable proportion*, because there is certainly a just medium between the extremes of being too frequent, and too seldom, in that work. There is *a proportion of faith*, which makes the word of God beautiful and harmonious; and there is also *a proportion of service*, which makes the labors of a minister or Christian respectable and useful.

Question 4. Wherein doth catechizing differ from preaching?

Answer. Both of them are ordinances of the living God, and both of them are conversant about his revealed will; yet they have distinct provinces; for (1.) Catechizing lays the foundation of knowledge, and preaching carries on the building. (2.) Catechizing compendiously sums up the articles of the Christian faith, to render them easy to the understanding; preaching represents them severally in such points of view as may most deeply affect the heart. (3.) Catechizing has a more particular respect to the *theory*, and preaching to the *practice* of religion. And (4.) Catechizing has its effect when Christians become intelligent, sound in the faith, and able readily to give unto every man that asketh them, a satisfying reason of the hope that is in them; preaching has its effect, when they are holy, and walk in Christ, rooted and built up in him, and stablished in the faith as they have been taught, abounding therein with thanksgiving (Col. 2:7).

6. Directions concerning It

It remains now that I finish what I proposed on this subject, by giving some *directions* concerning catechizing. These naturally fall under two heads; as they refer either to them that catechize, or to them that are catechized.

To Teachers

First, I might offer some *directions* to *teachers* who catechize others; whether they be parents, or heads of families, or schoolmasters.

1. Consider what you may *reasonably expect* from them you instruct. If you do not attend to their capacity, your pains must be lost, and your labor vain; you will fret yourself, but cannot profit them.

2. Endeavor to be as *plain* as possible. Do not use any words that are above the most ordinary capacity to understand. Avoid all pompous ele-

gance of diction, and all the curious distinctions of art, in stating the question. The greatest merit of a catechist is to be concise and plain in proposing the questions he asks. This will render him useful to the weakest; and establish his character, as a man of discernment, with all sensible judges.

3. Govern well your *temper*, and forbear every token of passion and wrath, if you are disappointed in your expectations from individuals. The wrath of man worketh not the righteousness of God, in any case; in this exercise it must confound your pupils; and probably will leave a panic fear upon their minds, that will recur whenever you enter on that duty, and so may defeat every attempt you make for their future good.

4. *Sympathize* with the modest and bashful. Encourage their timorous minds, not by unseasonable commendations, but by helping them to such hints as will furnish an answer. Do not take any advantage from their hesitating answers to expose their weakness; but, as much as you can, keep them in countenance, and, if possible, without letting them know that you are giving them any assistance. This will have a good effect, to inspire them with modest courage, and will be an excellent means of their improvement.

5. Pursue some *regular, digested plan* in catechizing. This will be of great service to yourselves; and will be a good help to the instruction of these you teach. This will enable you to speak with more clearness, and propriety, on the several heads of Christian doctrine. Your work will hereby become more pleasant to yourselves, and more useful to your pupils.

6. Remember to direct *their faith* unto the word of God. Encourage and assist their searches into that fountain of unerring wisdom, that their belief may not stand in the wisdom of men, but in the plain and powerful evidence of the authority of God.

7. Do not *seek*, nor *improve any advantages* against them, by puzzling them with perplexing questions, or urging upon them such objections as subtle adversaries have used against the truth, and reinforcing these difficulties, in order to confound them. Examine your own breasts, and tell me, does not such a method of managing this duty proceed from some bad temper? If you triumph in the success of such mean arts, is your glorying good? At best, I might say of your proceeding in this way that *ye know not what manner of spirit ye are of.*

8. Study to make your catechetical instructions subservient to the great interests of *practical and experimental religion*; that they may not only un-

derstand the theory of Christianity, but improve its principles, as doctrines which are according to godliness. Christ stated this connection in a very strong light to his disciples, "If ye know these things, happy are ye if ye do them" (John 13:17).

To Those That Are Taught
Secondly, The directions I would recommend to *these that are taught* may be reduced to these particulars.

1. Choose *a proper system* of the principles of religion, to assist you in pursuing the knowledge of the Scriptures. I cannot forbear to congratulate the happiness of such as have been initiated to the study of the inspired volumes, by the help of the *Assembly's Confession of faith, and Catechisms.*[9] The intrinsic merit of these composures has been generally acknowledged

---

[9] "I may be bold to assert, that everyone who has read and attended to what has been offered, cannot but be convinced, that the plan upon which this Catechism is formed, is peculiarly methodical; every doctrine in it digested and posited in the proper situation; the questions and answers rising one after another in such an order, as happily to show the relation and dependence of one truth upon another. Here the truths of the gospel are not cast together in a confused heap, but are all so connected together as to make one golden chain, or one uninterrupted scale of spiritual truths; yea, so exact and comprehensive is the method of it, that a person who desires to study this important science more distinctly and minutely, cannot proceed in his studies upon a more regular plan, nor range his thoughts in a more exact order, nor pursue his inquiries into the truth in a more direct way, and to greater advantage, than by going through the body of divinity in this train of thought. By pursuing the science after this manner, the student will be conducted, step by step, into the scheme, and will be prevented from missing any important branch of divinity in his progress: for, besides the exactness of the method, there is a peculiar copiousness in the plan, as it presents us with a fullness of matter, by introducing all the sweet and important truths of the ever-blessed gospel, in such a manner as tends to enliven, confirm, and illustrate every sentiment contained in it. I need not here say how much this Catechism outshines, in all these respects, other Catechisms that have been put forth to the world in competition with it, or in opposition to it; for, besides the confusion in their method, there are some very apparent and important defects; perhaps not one word concerning the Trinity of persons, concerning the divine decrees, concerning the corruption of our nature, concerning the work of the Spirit, or concerning effectual calling, justification, adoption, or sanctification, by the grace and Spirit of God. When things of this sweet or important nature are omitted in any plan of divinity, shall we not say, that these must be very inexcusable deficiencies? And there is reason to fear, that a set of principles which excludes these things out of it, must be very erroneous, and such as would leave us short of the saving blessings and comforts of the gospel.

"But I must mention another excellency attending this body of divinity, which is

among sensible, serious people; and their usefulness has been represented by the ablest pens of every denomination. Their praise is so great and so general in the churches, that it would be inexcusable presumption in me to attempt an addition to what has been so oft and so well said on this subject. Allow me, however, to propose to the scholar, who thirsts after the knowledge of the Scriptures, that, along with the assistance of these excellent performances, he also peruse some concise, judicious comment on them; such as the labors of Vincent, Henry, Brown, or others, that have explained the *Shorter Catechism*, and taken whatever is most material in the *Confession of faith*, or *Larger Catechism*, into their explications; but the most copious and useful help on this head, may be found in a performance, entitled, *The Assembly's Shorter Catechism explained, by way of question and answer: by some ministers of the gospel*.[10]

2. Having chosen your companion and guide, *study it carefully*, and make that system your own. He that skips from one book to another is distracted, instead of being helped, by that variety, which, for want of digesting, turns to corruption; and, as he can never advance beyond the outlines of true learning, so he is in the utmost hazard of falling into error, and being puffed up with a conceit of his knowledge, which will prevent all future improvements.

3. Guard against *the fear of man*, which causeth a snare. Slavish fear is an enemy to the peace of your minds, and will greatly prevent your prof-

---

thus: it all along pays a special regard to, and discovers a happy reverence for the whole word of God; as it owns the *Bible*, which is the religion of Protestants, for its only standard; as the whole of it is extracted and reduced from thence; and as it is ready to stand or fall with revelation. A great variety of proofs are brought and referred to, in both the Larger and Shorter Catechisms, to which a multitude of others may be added. Those that embrace this system of principles, are always ready to appeal to the Scripture-test, its obvious meaning, and its evident consequences. It is our professed principle, *To the law and to the testimony: if they speak not according to this word, it is because they have no light in them.*

"Let it therefore be still remembered, that while we speak in such commending strains of the Catechism, we do not intend that the compilers of it were divinely inspired, though we cannot but apprehend they were eminently assisted in this work; and every word we say in praise of the doctrines in it, we design as an encomium upon the sacred oracles, that invaluable treasure of gospel-knowledge, that excellent mine of gospel-doctrine, and that unerring standard of spiritual truth, to which is owing all the true and certain knowledge we have of spiritual things." Samuel Pike. *A Form of Sound Words*, pp. 75–77.

[10] *The Assembly's Shorter Catechism Explained by way of Question and Answer.*

iting by the instructions you hear. Consider the majesty of God, in whose presence you are; and that your teachers are but your fellow-mortals, appointed to be helpers of your knowledge and joy by this service. Modesty is a virtue you should diligently cultivate; but to be afraid of man is a sin that punishes itself, and is followed with many bad consequences.

4. Do not affect *the applause of men*, as the reward of acquitting yourselves tolerably well, when you are catechized. It is a grievous perversion of this work, when people render it a slave to the gratification of their pride. An error too common in the world! Consider the deep mysteries you are conversant about, with proper attention; and you will see reason to be humbled for your ignorance, instead of being puffed up with an opinion of your knowledge, which has no proportion to them, though it may go beyond some of your fellow-Christians. The person that is ambitious of the honor which depends on the breath of fame, cannot receive the truths of God in the love of them, nor relish their distinguishing pleasures and beauties, which constitute what the apostle calls "the simplicity that is in [or *toward*] Christ" (2 Cor. 11:3).

5. Be not *opinionated* in your own sentiments; but lie open to conviction, even in points where you have some reason to think your opinion right. Perhaps you have only had a very imperfect information; or, it may be, have not impartially examined the strength of the arguments on the other side. Prepossessions are extremely dangerous; for they keep men in chains of ignorance, and defeat the best means for their instruction. On this principle, the Jews remain in unbelief, pagans in idolatry, Papists under strong delusions, and every erroneous sect in their mistakes. I am far from intending that you should implicitly submit to your teacher's sentiments; but I would have your ears open to his instructions, that you may hear them without prejudice, and, after examining impartially what he has offered in support of an opinion differing from yours, may retain or change your former opinion, as the force and evidence of truth shall determine your minds.

6. Give an account of your faith with *reverence and modesty*. Consider every answer as a confession of your faith concerning the point you were interrogated on. Great fear is due unto the Lord in the meetings of his saints; for his name is glorious and fearful; and he is holy, just, and jealous. The ground of this duty is recorded, "sanctify the Lord God in your hearts:

and be ready always to give an answer to every man that asketh you a reason of the hope that is in you with *meekness and fear*" (1 Peter 3:15).

7. Last of all, seek an increase of knowledge in the doctrine of Christ, with a view to the practice of holiness; that having learned what is that good and acceptable will of the Lord, you may walk in his truths. I shall take the liberty to suggest three things on this point, that deserve most serious consideration. (1.) The great end of all our knowledge in religion is to practice what we know. The knowledge of God and of our duty hath so essential a respect to practice, that the Scripture will hardly allow it to be properly called knowledge, unless it have an influence upon our lives, "hereby we do know that we know him, if we keep his commandments. He that saith, I know him, and keepeth not his commandments, is a liar, and the truth is not in him" (1 John 2:3–4). (2.) Practice is the best way to increase and perfect our knowledge. Knowledge directs us to practice; but practice confirms and increaseth our knowledge, "If any man will do [God's] will, he shall know of the doctrine, whether it be of God" (John 7:17). (3.) Without the practice of religion, our knowledge will be so far from being any furtherance and advantage to our happiness that it will be one of the unhappiest aggravations of our misery. He that is ignorant of his duty, hath some excuse to pretend for himself; but he that understands the Christian religion, and does not live according to it, hath no cloak for his sin, "that servant, which knew his lord's will, and prepared not himself, neither did according to his will, shall be beaten with many stripes.... For unto whomsoever much is given, of him shall be much required" (Luke 12:47–48).

Chapter 16
Social Religious Meetings

Man is a creature made for *society*. His joys are tasteless, while he has no friend to whom he can communicate them; and his sorrows become greater than he can bear, without the relieving alleviations of sympathy and compassion. Solitude commonly fatigues and weakens his mind, while agreeable company administers the most sensible ease under his pains, and gives a peculiar relish to all his pleasures. This social principle, which operates with such extensive energy, was, no doubt, implanted in human nature, for purposes worthy of the wisdom and goodness of the Creator; and seems to be calculated for the improvement and happiness of mankind. The benefit of it to men in *civil life* is soon perceived, and universally confessed; and the advantages of it in *religion* are neither less nor fewer, though seldom reflected on, and therefore neither acknowledged nor improved as they ought to be. This prevailing bias in the breast of man to society is under the direction of his *will*; and hence the world is unanimous in forming their opinion of men's character and disposition from their company; and except *when art or design offer violence to nature*, this way of estimating characters and dispositions must always prove just and decisive. The wicked assemble in their troops; and the saints are companions of all them that fear God.

It is neither my present business to consider the communion of saints at large, nor their more restricted fellowship in congregations; but to delineate that fellowship of a still more private nature, which Christians should cultivate among themselves in *select societies*. In treating on this subject, I shall attempt to do five things.

  1. To give some account of the nature of these religious societies.
  2. To establish the warrant from Scripture for such meetings.
  3. To inquire for what purposes they should be formed and kept up.
  4. To show in what manner they should be conducted, in order to answer their end. And,

5. To stir up Christians to manifest proper regards to them.

1. The Nature of These Meetings Considered

The *nature* of religious social meetings may be gathered from this short account of them: *viz.*, "They are regular societies of Christians, who have voluntarily agreed to assemble together, at stated times and places of meeting, for obtaining, and communicating, the useful purposes of holy friendship one with another."

The persons concerned in them are supposed to be *Christians*, in distinction from the men of the world; and their practice proclaims the character they choose to be called by.

These societies differ from *occasional* meetings of the saints; for they have their *fixed times and places of meeting*; and their assembling together is a *stated* exercise.

They do not meet on worldly business, nor with interested views; but *for obtaining and communicating the useful purposes of holy friendship one with another.* These are their professed intentions; and charity, which thinketh no evil without sufficient evidence, obliges every member to believe these are the governing motives with his brethren, and to cooperate with them for answering these noble ends.

These societies are *voluntary*, inasmuch as their members, though not exempted from the authority and obligation of the law of Christ in this point, are to show that they are hearty and cheerful in the duty; not constrained by the authority of men, nor forced by the influence of example; but induced by a holy regard to the authority of God, and an ardent zeal to profit by the gifts and graces of fellow-believers. They are a voluntary society in the same sense that the Christian church is so denominated.

They are *regular* societies, conducted by rule, and not left to the humor and discretion of every member, who may take it in his head to dictate or prescribe to them the nature of their employment, or the manner of performing their social services. Our God is not the author of such confusion, but of peace, as in all churches of the saints; therefore let all things be done decently, and in order. I shall now go on,

2. Their Warrant from Scripture

To establish the *warrant from Scripture* for such meetings. No doubt, the argument, in their favor, drawn from *the reasonableness of the service*, is clear and satisfactory; for, if the common sense of mankind prompts them to social connections for their common benefit and pleasure, which is evidently the case, we may be sure this instinctive propensity will operate with no less efficacy in sanctified minds, to induce them to promote their mutual happiness in social intercourse; nay, in proportion as this cause is more important and interesting than any worldly concern, their solicitude about it should be greater. This proof of the obligation that lies upon Christians to seek their own good, and to indulge the propensities of their renewed nature is clear to the weakest capacity, and shows that every one of them is, in this point, *a law to himself*. But God, who knew that his people would, notwithstanding all this evidence, deal very treacherously, and be transgressors from the womb, has not left us without many convincing proofs of the warrant and obligation of religious social meetings, in his word, where *line is laid upon line, and precept upon precept*, in every form that can bind the conscience, or affect the heart. For,

1. The Scripture represents the people of God as standing in such *dear and intimate relations to each other* as necessarily imply an obligation upon them to maintain the most intimate fellowship and correspondence with one another their respective circumstances and situation can admit of. Thus they are represented as *fellow-citizens*, who have the same privileges, and the same interests (Eph. 2:19); as *fellow-soldiers*, who have the same enemies, allies, and warfare (Phil. 2:25); as *fellow-servants*, who have one Master, one work, and one reward (Rev. 6:11); as *children of the same Father* (Gal. 3:26) and *heirs of the same inheritance* (Rom. 8:17); as *brethren in the same family* (Matt. 23:8); and as *members of the same body, and every one members one of another* (1 Cor. 12:12; Rom. 12:5). This being the case, I must be excused, if I am much bold, in behalf of Christ, to enjoin, and press upon them, a duty so becoming these relations they stand in to one another. Everybody allows it to be a wise and reasonable thing that *people of the same civil profession*, who are engaged in the same studies, business, or trade, should form themselves into societies, in order to inform one another of what may be for their common interests; and to consult together for rectifying what may be amiss, or for improving their joint benefit. But is it not still more reasonable and wise that *Christians*, united by such intimate relations, whose interests and dangers are so much the same, should associate together, in order to instruct, to admonish, to comfort and encourage each other; in a word, to employ themselves in such exercises as

may promote their best interests, and may tend to the immediate benefit of every individual? I would not say that they cannot *at all* perform the duties, belonging to the relations I have named, without such engagements as these proposed; but I think it may be safely affirmed that such engagements are the most proper, the most direct, and the most effectual methods for this end, as to several of them.

2. The Scriptures assure us that with this service *God is well pleased.* That remarkable passage is a sufficient proof of this,

> Then they that feared the LORD spake often one to another: and the LORD hearkened, and heard it, and a book of remembrance was written before him for them that feared the LORD, and that thought upon his name. And they shall be mine, saith the LORD of hosts, in that day when I make up my jewels; and I will spare them, as a man spareth his own son that serveth him (Mal. 3:16–17).

I cannot understand this text of any conversation about the things of God, but what was of a *private* nature. It describes the employment of the godly, at a time when religion was openly despised, and vice avowedly encouraged by the generality, who said, *It is vain to serve the Lord*, and called *the proud happy; yea, they that wrought wickedness were set up. Then they that feared the Lord, spake often one to another*; they sought each other out, they often met, they often conversed together; consulting how they might escape the pollutions of the world, how they might establish and support one another against the prevailing vices of that age, and how they might encourage each other in the ways of righteousness. It is evident, at first sight, that this does not refer to their assemblies for public worship; but to their private meetings for the purpose of mutual free conversation. The period which the prophet speaks of was *an evil time*, when the prudent man kept silence as to any public appearance; but the Lord was a little sanctuary to his people in their sorrowful condition, by honoring their private assemblies with his presence and approbation; for *he hearkened and heard* their pious discourses; *and a book of remembrance was written before him for them that feared the Lord, and thought upon his name*, which is an expression taken from the manner of men, who, partly to provide against the treachery of a weak memory, and partly to prevent the extinction of much useful knowledge by death, the common lot of mortals, enter things into a journal; and it implies that God, who condescends to favor these religious conversations with his blessing now, will abundantly reward his people, who have persevered in these courses, at last; which is most comfortably expressed in the following words, *They shall be mine, saith the Lord of hosts, in that day when I make up my jewels; and I will spare them, as a man spareth his son that serveth him.* And if this duty is so advantageous in a time of prevailing iniquity, why should it be thought improper at other times? These that fear the Lord will never want abundance of matter, and frequent enough calls, to speak one to another; and "his ear is not heavy that it cannot hear." Having therefore so many occasions, and so great encouragements, to abound in this work of the Lord, let not Christians neglect their duty, and despise their true interest.

3. The Scripture recommends social religious meetings as *excellent helps in the ways of God*. That encomium on society by Solomon's pen is sublime and striking,

> Two are better than one; because they have a good reward for their labour. For if they fall, the one will lift up his fellow: but woe to him that is alone when he falleth; for he hath not another to help him up. Again, if two lie together, then they have heat: but how can one be warm alone? And if one prevail against him, two shall withstand him; and a threefold cord is not quickly broken (Eccl. 4:9–12).

From these verses we see that even in the enjoyments of life, which are immediately suited to our senses, we need assistance of social friendship; and the argument acquires new force, when we consider that the mysteries of religion, which faith is conversant with, are *things not seen*. The benefit of friendly reproof, seasonable comfort, and prudent counsel, is both great and necessary, in order to our holding on our way, and being strong in the Lord. These are commanded duties, and the performance of them is encouraged by many precious blessings they derive upon the saints,

> Let the word of Christ dwell in you richly in all wisdom; teaching and admonishing one another in psalms and hymns and spiritual songs, singing with grace in your hearts to the Lord (Col. 3:16).

Bear ye one another's burdens, and so fulfil the law of Christ (Gal. 6:2).

Again I say unto you, That if two of you shall agree on earth as touching any thing that they shall ask, it shall be done for them of my Father which is in heaven. For where two or three are gathered together in my name, there am I in the midst of them (Matt. 18:19–20).

But exhort one another daily, while it is called To day; lest any of you be hardened through the deceitfulness of sin (Heb. 3:13).

And let us consider one another to provoke unto love and to good works: forsaking the assembling of ourselves together, as the manner of some is; but exhorting one another: and so much the more, as ye see the day approaching (Heb. 10:24–25).

4. The Scripture has recorded many *examples* of such meetings, both in the *Old and New Testaments*, which may sufficiently convince us, they are not to be thought a piece of *will-worship*. In some cases that are not clearly defined in the word of God, it is our duty, and a safe course, to go forth "by the footsteps of the flock" (Song 1:8). We have the plainest examples of them that fear the Lord to direct our way in this duty: David made the saints *his equals, his guides, and his familiar friends*. He and they took counsel together, and went unto the house of God in company (Ps. 55:13–14), and unto them he says, "Come and hear…and I will declare what [God] hath done for my soul" (Ps. 66:16). Perhaps the correspondence which this man after God's heart had with the godly was only *occasional*; but I presume these texts clearly show that he engaged himself in *some* correspondence with them; and in *such* a correspondence too, as answered the end proposed by religious societies. The *devout Jews*, during their captivity in Babylon, used to assemble on the banks of the river; there they sat down, yea, they wept, when they remembered Zion; and they hanged their "harps upon the willows in the midst thereof" (Ps. 137:1–2). *Daniel and his companions* joined in fervent supplication to the God of heaven, desiring mercies of him concerning the king's secret (Dan. 2:17–18). *Esther and her virgins* joined in fasting to implore the Lord, who has

the heart of kings in his hand, to grant the queen favor, when she was to approach the royal presence without the king's desire (Est. 4:16).

But the examples in the *New Testament* are still more encouraging; for here we are compassed about with a great cloud of witnesses. All the evangelists inform us of the frequent and familiar intercourse, that passed in their retirements, between *Christ and his disciples*. After our Lord's resurrection, we find *the disciples* meeting together on the first day of the week, in a private capacity, until they were furnished, on the day of Pentecost, for more public services (John 20:19, 26). *Many were gathered together, and prayed, in the house of Mary the mother of John* (Acts 12:12). And we read of a society, accustomed to meet by a riverside, out of the city of Philippi, "where prayer was wont to be made" (Acts 16:13). Perhaps something of this sort is implied in these passages that give us an account of churches in particular houses; as in the house of *Aquila and Priscilla* (1 Cor. 16:19); of *Nymphas* (Col. 4:15); and of *Philemon* (Philemon 2). But if that character, *a church in a house*, is to be understood of *a religious family*, which I shall not dispute, yet the force of the argument from such examples is not wholly enervated; for (1.) Though family religion is lovely, useful, and necessary (as we shall show in the next chapter), yet that intimate religious correspondence proposed by fellowship-meetings, and the benefits to be obtained thereby, are seldom, if ever, attainable by the exercise of family religion alone. How rarely can we find a family, of which all, or even the greater part, are either qualified or disposed for religious conversation! How oft is a sincere and active Christian classed in a family whose other members are absolutely averse to religious exercises! And would it not be exceeding hard to shut up such an one from religious intimacies? But (2.) Let us even suppose a whole family disposed to religious correspondence with one another, yet I see no reason why such correspondence should be confined to the family; on the contrary, since Christians are commanded to make their *light shine before men* (Matt. 5:16), and "as every man hath received the gift, even so minister the same one to another" (1 Peter 4:10), it seems to be highly reasonable, and even the duty of the members of a well disposed family, to enter into fellowship-meetings with neighboring Christians, in order to attain these valuable purposes.[1]

---

[1] Perhaps it may be thought that all that has been said on the proof for social religious meetings does not amount to a positive evidence that these societies should be *stated*,

On the whole, I presume it appears evident that the Scriptures, and the reasonableness of the thing itself, give us a real and encouraging warrant for such social engagements as these we propose, and that we ought therefore to regard *society-meetings* as a wise and excellent method, which, by a concurrence with that strong turn our minds have to society, has a noble influence to secure us against the fatal dangers we are exposed to, by correspondence with persons of vicious principles, or immoral practices; and, at the same time, has an immediate powerful tendency to procure us that satisfaction and improvement, and all these advantages, which are the *ultimate ends* of the *social temper*.

3. The End and Design of Them Shown

Social religious meetings should be formed, and kept up among the people of God, for such *purposes* as they are directly and effectually calculated to obtain and promote. Among others, I shall consider the following, which have a peculiar claim to the attention of Christians.

1. One important design of these societies is to *promote and increase the knowledge of the truths, ordinances, and works of God*: of *his truths*, that they may be better understood, more firmly believed, more steadfastly adhered to, and more powerfully efficacious upon the heart and life, "Let the word of Christ dwell in you richly, in all wisdom; teaching and admonishing one another in psalms, and hymns, and, spiritual songs" (Col. 3:16); of *his ordinances*, that the nature, use, and ends of them may be more distinctly known, and more carefully attended to in practice; that with one heart and one mouth they may glorify God, in the way of his own appointment; and of *his works*, both of providence and redemption, which are full

---

and not merely *occasional*. But though I were to allow that it does not directly prove the *stated and determined times and places of meeting*, which yet I think are plain enough, at least in Acts 16:13, "And on the sabbath we went out of the city by *a river side, where prayer was wont to be made*"; I say, though I were to allow that *no direct proof is*, or *can be* adduced from Scripture, to show that these meetings ought to be so observed, the affection, *that they should be observed at stated times, and places*, would still remain as evidently confirmed, as the proof concerning the obligation upon Christians to observe them at all, was clear. For if what has been suggested on the subject is a proof that such societies should be established, and kept up, with a view to the important purposes mentioned in *the next section*; it will follow, upon the principles of common sense and of daily experience that there *must be* stated times and places for meeting; or else these important purposes must be defeated. Common prudence is sufficient for everybody's conviction and direction on this point.

of instruction, and excellent helps towards the improvement of faith and experience. All that are wise in heart will observe the doings of the Lord, and the operations of his hand; and will say, *What hath God wrought?* The truths of religion will be very imperfectly understood, and but superficially practiced, where the study of the works of God is not made a branch of the Christian's daily employment, both in his closet, and in social life, "The works of the LORD are great, sought out of all them that have pleasure therein" (Ps. 111:2). This object of our studies *as men*, and *as Christians*, is important and interesting, incomprehensible and entertaining. It enriches the mind with useful knowledge, and promotes an abounding in every fruit of the Holy Spirit; as the dispensations of divine providence furnish us with all the means, seasons, opportunities, and advantages of faith and obedience.

2. Another great object to be pursued in these societies is to express and exercise *mutual Christian sympathy* among the members. There they can open their breasts, and tell their sorrows, their temptations, their weaknesses, and griefs, to their Christian friends, with more freedom than to others, and with greater hopes of being assisted with seasonable comforts and cautions, examples and counsels, which may, through the divine blessing, defeat the temptation, relieve the mind, and encourage against dejection. The command of God has made what is our interest to become our duty, on this head; for "We then that are strong ought to bear the infirmities of the weak, and not to please ourselves. Let every one of us please his neighbour for his good to edification" (Rom. 15:1–2). This is also enjoined in "Bear ye one another's burdens" (Gal. 6:2). The intimate union, and mutual sympathy, of the members of our body invariably produce a communication of pain or injury from every single member to the rest; so that they are afflicted with it, and ready to do what in them lies for its relief. This is a proper representation of the people of God, who are under the strongest obligations to consult one another's comfort under every distress, by helping to exhibit, in the clearest light, the sovereignty of the grace and providence of God, the alone ground of hope in the atonement of a risen Savior, the office and work of the Spirit, the stability of the covenant of promise, the nature and evidences of vital religion, and the manner of God's dealing with other Christians. And the expressions of their sympathy should not be confined to these offices of brotherly kindness; they ought to shine in a more enlarged sphere, in their joint addresses at the

throne of grace, in behalf of such as are grieved in spirit, and whose soul is bowed down in them. This is a noble branch of social intercession, and an eminent testimony of feeling benevolence.

3. Such society is further intended for the *mutual encouragement of the saints* in the ways of godliness, that they may *provoke one another unto love and to good works.* By considering their respective wants and dangers, infirmities and temptations, on one hand; and the grounds of hope and encouragement, that are in Christ, and in the promises, on the other; the members of Christian societies are excited to use all proper means, by example, exhortations, and cautions, to stir up one another, with fervency and faithfulness, to the love of God, and of Christ, and of the truths of the gospel; and to an affectionate union and communion one with another; and so to love as brethren, and to excite each other to every evangelical and moral duty, and to everything that is truly excellent, and worthy their Christian character. To this purpose the apostle says, "let us consider one another to provoke unto love and to good works: not forsaking the assembling of ourselves together, as the manner of some is; but exhorting one another: and so much the more, as ye see the day approaching" (Heb. 10:24–25). While the godly walk together in the fear of the Lord, they commonly walk in the comforts of the Holy Ghost, and are edified. Like fellow-travelers, they entertain and hearten one another; and their joy becomes more complete, by their Christian intimacies. Like fellow-members in the body, they give vigor and spirits to one another; and their courage is strengthened by the combination of prudent efforts for their common good. This is beautifully expressed in

> But speaking the truth in love, may grow up into him in all things, which is the head, even Christ: from whom the whole body fitly joined together and compacted by that which every joint supplieth, according to the effectual working in the measure of every part, maketh increase of the body unto the edifying of itself in love (Eph. 4:15–16).

Here is a manifest allusion to the *human body*, which is composed of different joints and members, knit together by various ligaments, and furnished with nerves, tendons, and other vessels of communication from the head to every part of the body, which, by these means, is nourished, actuated, and invigorated, and arrives to its full strength and stature. In like manner, Christians, who are duly and orderly adapted one to another, and cemented together in fellowship, like joint to joint, and all of whom are united to Christ, the head, by that energy which is communicated from him, through *this* and every other ordinance of the church, and through *every member* in its place and sphere of action, according to the efficacious operation of his Spirit, exerted in the proportion that is suited to the state, condition, and exigence of every part—improve and build themselves up in all the love, which every member ought to have, and by which he affectionately acts towards the head and fellow-members, and towards the whole church, till he and they be perfected in the other world.

4. Another end of Christians' meeting in fellowship-societies is that they may *communicate their gifts and graces* to each other's edification. Hence is that command of the apostle, "As every man hath received the gift, even so minister the same one to another, as good stewards of the manifold grace of God" (1 Peter 4:10). All *talents for public offices* are the gifts of an exalted Savior; and these that have received them should occupy with them for the honor of the Lord Jesus, till he come; but there is no evidence that the apostle only, or even principally, intended *such talents* in that passage. All the *private capacities* for usefulness in the church, as well as abilities for public offices in it, are the free gift of God; for to everyone is given "grace according to the measure of the gift of Christ" (Eph. 4:7). Now, the will of God is that everyone, who is favored with such capacities and talents, should carefully employ them, in proportion to what he has received, for the advantage and edification of his fellow-Christians, as persons entrusted with, and accountable to their great Lord and Master, for the various gifts and endowments, which he has graciously bestowed upon them, that they may manage them with wisdom and faithfulness, like honorable stewards, for the good of the church, for which he gave them. And, in order to render their ministering their respective gifts more useful to others, and that they may profit the more by the gifts conferred on their brethren, it is expedient and necessary that such societies as I am treating of should be carefully maintained; and such a communication of gifts and graces as I have mentioned should be considered as one important object of them, "For the perfecting of the saints…till we all come in the unity of the faith, and of the knowledge of the Son of God, unto a perfect man, unto the measure of the stature of the fulness of Christ" (Eph. 4:12–13).

5. These religious associations give the best opportunities for Christians to act the part of *kind monitors to one another*; and thus to fulfill that branch of social duty which is recommended in these important precepts, "Now we exhort you, brethren, warn them that are unruly, comfort the feebleminded, support the weak" (1 Thess. 5:14). "Exhort one another daily, while it is called To day; lest any of you be hardened through the deceitfulness of sin" (Heb. 3:13). All that know their own weakness, and consider their dangerous situation in a present evil world, will easily believe that it is not good for them to stand *single*; if they can have the benefit of religious friendship, to correct their errors, and point out their duty and comforts. This consideration will be a powerful inducement to enter into Christian fellowship, and to improve that fellowship with a view to that purpose. There is no contradiction in the saints being *brethren* one to another, and their being also *keepers* one of another; for their brotherly love, and zeal for the honor of their common Father, should prompt and dictate every admonition, reproof, or advice, to their brethren, whom they ought to watch over, not with a censorious eye, nor with affected airs of insolence and superiority; but with such unfeigned affection, as every member is tender of the comfort of the body, and labors to protect and succor all the rest of the members. The plan of religious meetings should be formed with a view to encourage and promote such an useful point of social exercise. It is not enough that it be not excluded; it should have a place in the daily services of Christian societies, if an opportunity offers to put it in practice.

6. One of the most valuable ends of fellowship-meetings is that Christians may *join together in prayer and praises, and other spiritual exercises.* There is a most encouraging motive to this part of their employment, in these words of our Lord to his disciples, "Again I say unto you, That if two of you shall agree on earth as touching any thing that they shall ask, it shall be done for them of my Father which is in heaven. For where two or three are gathered together in my name, there am I in the midst of them" (Matt. 18:19–20). Good words, and comfortable words! O that they might dwell richly in believers! Then they would delight in drawing nigh to God, by the better hope which the gospel has brought in; then they would take a holy pleasure in admonishing one another in psalms, and hymns, and spiritual songs; and then their united prayers and praises would be followed with establishment in the faith, with joy and peace in believing, and with a rich increase in every good word and work.

I have been the larger in representing *the designs* of Christian religious societies, for two reasons: (1.) Because right apprehensions about these have a great effect in fixing the rules, by which they are to be conducted, in regard the manner of improving them must be subservient to the purposes intended by them; and (2.) Because I suspect the designs of social meetings are generally too confined; for instead of aiming at the extensive purposes I have named, some societies propose only to handle *theological questions*; some confine their inquiries wholly to *cases of conscience*; and others devote them wholly to *narratives of Christian experience*; in a word, some pursue one part of the scheme, and some another; but there are few instances of societies endeavoring to obtain *unitedly* all the great ends of this duty.

The *scope* of divine revelation is to set the two infinitely distant characters of *God* and *man* in their true and proper light; and to evince and exhibit the grand connections, dependence, and obligations, as to every ground of hope or fear, on the part of man to the great God, resulting from the characters of the Deity there revealed, in a manner exactly suited to the powers and affections of the human mind; hence the word of God carries our dependence back to the divine character, and leads forward in obedience to the divine will. The *dispensations* of divine providence, viewed in connection with the Scriptures, cooperate with the knowledge a person has of God and himself, to excite love or enmity, hope or fear, according to his notions of a personal interest in the favor of God, or of his being a child of wrath. And, consequently, the *word and providences* of God, which are immediately subservient to faith and practice ought to be studied, in their connection, by every Christian; and to be the subject of conversation among the saints in their social meetings; that they may grow in the knowledge of Christ; sympathize in each other's sorrows; encourage one another in the ways of God; have communion in their gifts and graces; exhort one another; and pray and praise together.

4. The Manner of Conducting Them

The next point to be considered is *the manner* of conducting these societies, that the foregoing ends may be effectually obtained in them.

Attempts have been made this way by many eminent hands, who have pointed out the most proper regulations for preventing the inconveniences and evils which are most pernicious to these societies, and for the most effectual obtaining the valuable purposes of religious fellowship.[2] All that

---

[2] See Walter Smith and John Hepburn. *Directory; or Rules and Directions for Fellowship*

I can propose is only to mention some general rules on this head, referring the reader to these who have employed their labors on the subject at greater length.

1. As the sole design of these societies is to promote Christian knowledge and real holiness in heart and life, every member of them is to have this continually in view, trusting in the divine power, and gracious conduct of the Holy Spirit, through our Lord Jesus Christ, to excite, advance, and perfect all good in him. Where the eye is single, the whole body will be full of light.

2. In order to the being of *one heart and one mind*, and to prevent all things which gender strifes, as well as to remove all occasion of offense from being taken against the society, no person is to be admitted a member, or to be allowed to continue such, who is not sound in the faith, and holy in all manner of conversation; and as family and closet religion, morning and evening, and a regular attendance upon public ordinances, are important branches of Christian duty, it is requisite that all the members diligently and constantly maintain these duties, each in its proper season; and that they attend on the ministrations of the gospel in the same connections of church-fellowship.[3]

3. Such societies being formed by *choice*, and supported by *affection*, it is expedient that no person be admitted a member but upon the rec-

---

Meetings; and *An Inquiry into the Nature, Obligation, and Advantages of Religious Fellowship: Together with an Attempt to Direct in the Proper Exercise of It*; and James Hervey. *Rules and Orders of a Religious Society*: Edinburgh edit. of his works, vol. 5, pp. 256, etc.

[3] I have long lamented what I cannot help reckoning an abuse in private Christian societies—that the terms of admission to them are so confined as to exclude from these associations a great many of their fellow-Christians, with whom they can cheerfully join at the *Lord's table*. I can easily allow their intentions are good; but cannot grant that their zeal is according to knowledge, and worthy of praise. You will not pretend, my Christian friends, that this hedge is set so close about your societies by God; or, if you do, it is necessary you point to the institution of Christ upon the head; and as little can it be pretended, that the limitations, which exclude your fellow communicants, are warranted by reason, unless you suppose the *communion* in your society to be *more solemn* than in the Lord's Supper. But I must go still further, and declare my opinion, in the words of that judicious and godly man, Mr. Alexander Shiells: "I think some ignorant creatures, that desire to be instructed, should be admitted to your Christian fellowships to hear, where conveniency will allow, though not to be employed." He gives this reason for his opinion, that some, *who were not baptized*, among whom was Lydia, resorted to the river-side at Philippi, where prayer was wont to be made (Acts 16:13). See Alexander Shields. *A Letter concerning the Due Boundaries of Christian Fellowship*, p. 21.

ommendation of some of the members, who are acquainted with, or at least certified of the inoffensive and orderly conversation of the person applying—with the consent of the major part of the society present.

4. To prevent confusion, and defeat the dark schemes of malice or prejudice, it is convenient that no person be removed from the society, but at a full meeting, after all due pains has been used, in the spirit of meekness, to reclaim the offending member from the error he has adopted, or the immorality he has been guilty of, to the hurt of his own soul, the discredit of religion, and the just offense of the society. *N.B., Errors* relating to the Trinity, original sin, imputed righteousness, the sovereignty of the grace of God, the obligation of his law, etc., and *a disorderly carriage*,[4] or a proud, contentious, haughty, disputing temper (the greatest adversary to Christian love and peace), shall be *sufficient grounds* for such removal.

5. All the members of such societies should heedfully keep themselves from all things which may dishonor the name of God, bring a scandal upon religion, give occasion to the enemies of the cross of Christ to speak evil of the truth, or mar the advancement of religion in their own souls, such as: pride, in a conceit of their knowledge, wisdom, or prudence; valuing themselves upon any distinction, in station, riches, or family; sinking into a carnal, worldly frame; practicing fraud or dishonesty, or conniving at the dishonesty of others; making compliances against the light of conscience, to avoid shame, or to promote worldly interest; becoming lukewarm and indifferent about the concerns of God's glory, the advancement of true religion, and the interest of their own souls; forgetting their first love to God, to Christ, to the truth, and to their neighbor; profaning the Sabbath-day, or any part of it, in unedifying discourse;[5] or keeping such company as may endanger the peace and purity of the soul.

---

[4] By a *disorderly carriage* is meant, not only the gross commission of scandalous sins, but also what are esteemed matters of little moment in the eyes of the world; such as: a light use of the words, *Lord, God, Jesus, faith, conscience,* etc., in common conversation; the doing needless business on the Lord's day; the frequenting alehouses or taverns, without necessary business; and things of that sort, which cannot but be interpreted as an evidence of the want of God's presence in the heart, and of the want of the fear of God before the eyes.

[5] By *unedifying discourse on the Sabbath-day*, I mean, not only all conversing on low, earthly, temporal matters, but all trifling contentions and unprofitable disputes about religion, instead of conversing on these sublime and heavenly subjects, which have a direct tendency to build up the soul in knowledge, to establish it in faith, and to prepare it for the everlasting rest.

6. Every member should consider himself as peculiarly obliged to live in an inoffensive and orderly manner, to the glory of God, and the edifying his neighbors; and ought to study the advancement, in himself and others, of faith in our Lord Jesus Christ, repentance unto life, love to God, gospel-humility, new obedience, and every fruit of the Spirit; for herein Christian edification consists.

7. The members of a society should watch over one another in love; should be willing to hear of their faults, and of the fears or suspicions of these their friends concerning them; should guard against every disgust to one another; and if any arises, should tell the party, not in a rash, reproaching, ill-natured way, but in such a winning, inoffensive manner, that the offender cannot choose to be irritated, as though there was a design to insult over him, or to act the part of an enemy under the color of discharging this friendly duty; but if this method is unsuccessful, the society must be told; they should desire the prayers of one another, and should pray for one another; and they should confirm upon their own hearts, by serious consideration, the deep obligations they lie under to one another, as members of a religious society; who have given themselves up to walk together in love and union, in the fear of God.

8. In all their prayers and conversations, the members of such societies should study all clearness, plainness, and brevity, and to stick close to the plain and obvious sense of the Holy Scriptures, carefully avoiding all niceties and refinements upon them; and should carefully forbear every word or expression, even though they be scriptural, which they do not understand.

9. No doubt, there may be escapes in the expressions of members, both in prayer and conference; and therefore they should beware of judging hastily, or making a man an offender for a word; but if any member shall use expressions which are either unintelligible, or favoring of error, or such as any of the meeting scruple to join in, he should be prudently asked to explain them, or, in the spirit of meekness, desired to forbear to use them.

10. The members of such societies should have stated times and places of meeting; and it is proper these should be once a week, and chosen with a view to their own conveniency, that none of the duties of their business, or in their families, may suffer any neglect.

11. Every member should give constant attendance, and endeavor to be present at the appointed hour of meeting precisely; and whoever ab-

sents himself four meetings together, without giving a satisfactory account to the society, should be looked upon as disaffected to it. Every member should often ask his own heart, *whether he has a desire to come to the meeting? And if not, why? And whether his awakened conscience will stand to the reason of his aversion, when he stands before the judgment seat of Christ?* And finally, *whether he should not be afraid to admit a reason now, that he will be ashamed of in that day?*

12. The members of these societies should meekly, humbly, and devoutly join together, in the following exercises of religious duty and improvement. (1.) They should begin with singing the praises of God; and then should read some peculiarly instructive portion of his word; after which, with great seriousness and profound reverence, they should bow their knees before God, and offer up their united prayers to him, through Christ, the only acceptable and all-sufficient Mediator, under the influence, and by the direction and assistance, of the Holy Spirit. *N.B.*, Every part of the prayer, and of the chapter, is to be pronounced with that deliberate slowness which may command attention, and create awe. (2.) Such subjects of conference should then be proposed, as may best answer the ends of their association. Different systems of education naturally lead Christians into different methods of managing this part of their work; and perhaps every one of these methods has some advantages, as well as disadvantages. Among so great diversity, I shall take the liberty to propose the following scheme, allowing such as prefer another, the liberty of following their own opinion. Let a chapter, or entire article, in some orthodox, clear, and concise summary of divine truth be read with distinctness and deliberation together with such texts of Scripture as evince the foundation of that chapter or article in the word of God; and then let such a question or questions be proposed from it, as will lead the members to give their opinion severally, on the point of truth or duty, which is the scope of the passage; each endeavoring to consider it as profitable for doctrine, for reproof, for correction, and for instruction in righteousness. When a certain proportion of the time devoted to social conference (not exceeding the half of it however), has been spent this way, part of a psalm might be sung by another member, and supplications presented at the throne of grace, if time will permit. The person, who officiated in praising, reading, and praying, at the beginning of the exercise, and who, for order's sake, may preside all the time the society is met, may then ask, whether any of the members

have any question to propose, about any case of conscience? or if there be anything in the state of their mind, about which they want the advice of the society? Also, whether anything has cast up to any of them, in the course of their experience, or of God's providence towards them, which may be either edifying, confirming, or comforting, or which may afford matter for praise, or may require their mutual sympathy in prayer before God?[6] This service being ended (3.) A third member shall conclude the solemn services of that meeting by prayer and singing,

13. When the duties of the occasion are finished, the societies should, as they may have a call, or an opportunity, deal with their members that are irregular, or consider any other business that concerns their associations, as to the admission or excluding of members.

---

[6] Everything which tends to nourish spiritual pride, or tempts to hypocrisy or affectation, which discourages Christians of lesser abilities and lower attainments, or leads to enthusiasm, should certainly be avoided with the utmost care. But some *experiences* are in themselves confirming evidences of the truth of Christianity in general, and of practical godliness in particular, such as remarkable returns of prayer, signal deliverances from temptations, or afflictions, or dangers of any kind, special benefits received in the use of ordinances, etc. To communicate such experiences to Christian friends is highly reasonable, and on many accounts very expedient. It was practiced by David, "Come and hear, all ye that fear God, and I will declare what he hath done for my soul" (Ps. 66:16). The advantages of this sort of social converse are excellently represented in Robert Fleming. *The Fulfilling of the Scripture*.

To mention the inmost secrets of one's heart in an open meeting, is no doubt a great weakness, and highly imprudent. It would expose to the censure of some, and to the indiscretion of others, who might probably make a bad use of what is communicated to them. And to require every member, in their turn, to communicate what they have experienced of the same, or like nature, is still more dangerous and unreasonable. But if, instead of these irregular hazardous ways, it be left to everyone's self to propose whatever he wants the opinion of the society about, as *a possible case*, by asking what advice they would give in such a case, and, at the same time, members are left at liberty to speak on the subject, or to be silent, as each inclines; the dangers of abusing such communications would be effectually prevented.

To neglect this kind of conversation altogether in societies, on account of these abuses, would be very wrong, and would defeat some of the most important purposes of religious fellowship; for how can we comfort the feeble-minded, and support the weak? how can we edify and provoke one another to love, and to good works? How can we assist and strengthen one another against the mistakes, errors, and failings, we are naturally liable to? Or how can we encourage one another in the ways of religion; and yet be utterly unacquainted with the state of each other's souls; or denied the privilege and opportunity of supposing such cases, and asking such questions, as may give some insinuation of the state of our minds, or, at least, may procure the advice and opinion of our brethren concerning these things?

14. As it is not for edification that the number of members be very large, so it is most absurd that any of them should publish what is said or done in the society.

15. Because the regulations for the society describe the character and behavior of the members, and show both what they *should be*, and what they *should do*, it is expedient, they should be read, at least, four times a year, openly in the presence of the full meeting, in order to put the brethren in remembrance of their duty.

These seem to be the most important rules for the profitable management of religious societies. Every essential circumstance, I presume, will be found to be implied in them. But in order to give the fullest satisfaction to my readers, I shall refer them to the careful perusal of that valuable performance, which I have mentioned already, entitled, *An inquiry into the nature, obligations, and advantages of religious fellowship.*

5. Christians Excited to This Duty

All that now remains on this subject is to stir up Christians to manifest *proper regards* to this duty, by joining themselves to private religious societies, and behaving in them as becometh saints.

All the *arguments* by which the obligation of the duty has been established, and all the interesting and important *ends* to be pursued in it, might be reviewed, in order to excite the people of God to testify a holy zeal in this cause. I submit the most careful review of them to the reader's consideration, and address them to his conscience, wherein I heartily with the Spirit of God may give them a deep and abiding efficacy. I shall only add a few more considerations to the same effect.

1. Religious intimacies are the *best preservatives* against the infections, which arise from our communication with persons of vicious principles and ungodly lives. Such is the inclination mankind have to society, that the most of people think *any* company is better than *none;* and hence they readily enter into such correspondence with those who are nearest them, as soon grows up to familiarity. If the mind be not solidly established in the principles of the doctrine of Christ, and in a holy society with those that are sound in the faith, and holy in their conversation, what hazard does a person run of being debauched, both in principles and morals, by the influence of such companions as he takes up at random? Their bad opinions are likely to steal in upon his mind; and if they are not entirely ap-

proved, they will not, however, seem very dangerous to his view; thus evil communications will corrupt sound principles and good manners. How necessary is it then, that everyone who fears the Lord, should cautiously avoid this dangerous infection, by prudently entering into intimacies, and forming the closest friendships, with those only, whose conversation and example may establish him in the faith of Christ, and confirm him in the good ways of the Lord? This is one of the means which God hath appointed, and will bless, for keeping his people in a present evil world; that they may shine as lights, in sound sentiments, and purity of manners, following that which is good, and mutually helping each other forward in the paths of righteousness.

2. Religious fellowship appears to be attended with all *the advantages* which a reasonable man can propose to himself by any kind of intimacies. Such familiar friends as he takes counsel with in the duties of religion will be of great service to furnish and impress his mind with such sentiments, divine and moral, as form the soul to true devotion and unfeigned holiness. The very constitution of such societies gives one the prospect of having a number of true friends, that will be particularly concerned for his interest, who will encourage him in things that are worthy, and be so singularly kind, as to tell him of his faults, and advise him how to correct them. And an easy relaxation of mind, mixed with innocent cheerfulness and joy, may be expected in the most rational and least dangerous way, among chosen religious companions, who know how to rejoice in the fear of God.

3. The benefits arising to Christians in these societies are *mutual;* every member has the same access to them, and may enjoy them in the same measure, with his brethren. While one is edified, his companions are instructed; while he is comforted, they are refreshed; and thus private and personal improvements become diffusively useful, while everyone ministers to another the gifts he has received from a gracious God.

4. Religious societies, duly formed, and properly exercised, are likely means of doing much good to all around them. There is something in the character of a real Christian, so lovely and desirable, that even persons who will not imitate are obliged to esteem and approve of him. What may we not expect then from a society of such persons, whose holy and useful labors of love are a standing evidence of the power and truth of godliness, and are witnesses against a loose age? Their example would put their accusers to shame, and allure many that feared the Lord to join in the same employment.

5. Religious fellowship in Christian societies puts us in mind of, and tends to prepare us for, that sublime, holy, and honorable society of the church of the firstborn, who are assembled on high, where everlasting beauty, order, peace, and holiness, are maintained in the presence of Jesus our common Lord. Whether we reap all the pleasures and satisfactions we desire and expect, or if we meet with some little inconveniences, uneasiness, and contest, in any Christian society on earth, let us point our thoughts and hopes still upward to that divine fellowship of the saints, and the spirits of just men made perfect, where those joys will be full, and these contentions and disorders can have no place. In the exercise of this hope, let us wait with patience for the manifestation of the sons of God, "Not forsaking the assembling of ourselves together... but exhorting one another: and so much the more, as ye see [that glorious] day approaching" (Heb. 10:24–25).

In a word, the regard we owe to the command of God, to the institution of Christ, to the edification of his people, to the good of mankind, and to the improvement of our own soul in knowledge, love, and obedience; and the duty we owe to the blessed Spirit, who has distributed his gifts to every man severally as he willeth, that these may be ministered by the saints one to another—these considerations combine their weight and evidence to stir up Christians to join in this duty.

I have the mortifying apprehension to fear that this attempt to excite the people of God to join in the much neglected duty of *social religious meetings* will be forgot when it has been read. Perhaps some will admit the reasonableness of the duty; but, on some pretense or other, they excuse the neglect of it; while others appoint some distant period for setting about that work, but before it come, they find the conviction abated, and their conscience easy; and so they persevere in their neglect. I have only one thing to comfort me under these mortifications—that I have honestly declared, what I take to be the will of God, unto my readers, and particularly to the members of my own congregation; and having done so, I have delivered my own soul; and the guilt of despisers must rest on their own heads (Ezek. 33). A consideration that is equally encouraging to a faithful monitor, and dreadful to such as will not profit by his instructions, drawn from the word of God!

Chapter 17
Family Religion

The great Author of our nature, who has made us sociable creatures, has instituted various societies among mankind, both civil and religious, and joined them together by various bonds of relation. The first and radical society is that of *a family*, which is the nursery both of the church and state. It is therefore of the greatest importance to religion and civil society that families be under proper regulations, that they may produce proper plants for church and state, and especially for the eternal world, in which all the temporary associations of mortals in this world finally terminate, and to which they refer.

The method I would observe in treating on the great and useful duty of *family religion* is the following:

1. To mention the various parts of it;
2. To prove it to be a duty;
3. To show in what seasons it should be statedly performed;
4. To consider what particular obligations the heads of families lie under, and what authority they are invested with, to maintain religion in their houses;
5. To inquire into the causes of the general neglect of it;
6. To press the performance of the duty upon the heads of families by some arguments;
7. To answer some of the most common objections made against it; and then,
8. To give some practical directions about it.

1. The Various Parts of It Considered

I proposed, in the first place, to consider *the various parts of family religion*; especially under the view of their belonging to the province of the head of the family; and they may be reduced to these four: to wit, religious instruction, worship, discipline, and example.

1. A very considerable part of this duty consists in parents and masters *instructing* those committed to their charge, in the fundamental principles, and in the careful practice, of the necessary duties of religion; instilling them into children in their tender years, as they are capable of them, *line upon line*, and *precept upon precept, here a little, and there a little* (Isa. 28:10); and into those that are more grown up, by proper and suitable means of instruction, and by furnishing them with such books as are most proper to teach them those things in religion, which are most necessary for all to believe and practice.

And in order hereunto, they should take care that those under their charge, their children and servants, should be taught to read; because this will make the business of instruction much easier; so that, if they are diligent, and well-disposed, they may, after having been taught the first principles of religion, by reading the Holy Scriptures, and other books, greatly improve themselves, so as to be prepared to receive much greater benefit and advantage from the public teaching of their ministers.

And in this work of instruction, their care should be chiefly to inform their children and servants of those principles of religion which are most fundamental and necessary; and are like to have the most lasting and powerful influence upon their whole lives: that, being grounded in the principles of the doctrine of Christ, they may go on to perfection in the higher improvements of knowledge and holiness.

This work of instruction of families, as it ought not to be neglected at other times, so it is more peculiarly seasonable on *the Lord's day*. The public exercises of divine worship are a capital branch of the duties of that day; and religious parents and masters should take care that their children and servants observe them; but when the public worship of that day is over, there is still an important branch of private duties remaining, which every head of a family ought to see performed. The work of instruction of children and servants is one of them; and it may be managed, either by reading the Scriptures, and other good books, or by catechizing, or by conference, as a prudent regard to circumstances may require. Care likewise should be taken that they use the means of acquiring knowledge themselves, on that day particularly; this being the chief opportunity that many servants have to apply their minds without disturbance to that delightful study.

2. Another part of family religion is the *worshipping of God*. This is so necessary to keep alive and to maintain a sense of God and religion upon

the minds of men, that, where it is neglected, I do not see how any family can in reason be esteemed a family of Christians, or indeed to have any religion at all.

Heads of families must not only teach those under their care, but must go before them in offering up, in their name, and in their presence, the spiritual sacrifices of the family, before the Lord continually, both on ordinary and extraordinary occasions. The ordinary services in family worship are these three: solemn *praises*, which is a part of daily worship, wherein we not only give glory to God, but teach and admonish "one another in psalms and hymns and spiritual songs, singing with grace in [our] hearts to the Lord"; solemn *reading of the word of God*, that "the word of Christ [may] dwell in [us] richly in all wisdom" (Col. 3:16); and solemn *invocation of the name of God by prayer*, in such acknowledgments, requests, and thanksgivings, as are particularly suited to the situation of the family, and to the concerns of those that join in their family capacity. The obligation that lies on the people of God to this branch of family worship is strongly implied in that alarming passage, "Pour out thy fury upon the heathen that know thee not, and upon the families that call not on thy name" (Jer. 10:25).

One thing I must by no means omit, because it is in many families already gone, and in others going out of fashion; I mean, a solemn acknowledgment of God, by *begging his blessing* at our meals, upon his good creatures provided for our use, and by *returning thanks* to him for the benefit and refreshment of them. This is a piece of natural religion, owned and practiced in all ages, and in most places of the world, but never so shamefully and scandalously neglected, and I fear by many slighted and despised, as it is amongst us at this day; and, alas! most neglected where there is greatest reason for the doing of it; I mean, at the most plentiful tables, and among those of highest quality; as if persons were ashamed, or thought scorn to own from whence these blessings come; like the nation of the Jews, of whom God complains in the prophet, "she did not know," that is, she would not acknowledge, "that I gave her corn, and wine, and oil, and multiplied her silver and gold" (Hos. 2:8). Shall not God visit for this horrible ingratitude? and shall not his soul be avenged on such a perverse nation as this? *Hear, O heavens, and be horribly astonished at this!*

3. Family-religion implies the exercise of an *holy government* or *discipline* in the family. Reason teacheth us that "every man should bear rule in his own house" (Est. 1:22); and, since *that*, as well as other *power, is of*

God, it ought to be employed *for God*; and they that so rule, must be *just, ruling in his fear*.

The authority God hath given heads of families over their children and servants is principally designed for this end, that they may thereby engage them for God and religion. In order to this, they ought (1.) To *command* their families, children and servants, to walk in the ways of the Lord, as Abraham did, who thereupon received this honorable testimony: "I know him," saith the Lord, "that he will command his children and his household after him, and they shall keep the way of the Lord" (Gen. 18:19). (2.) To oblige, by their reproofs, admonitions, and corrections, such as are in the family, to abandon sinful and scandalous vices:

> Then Jacob said unto his household, and to all that were with him, Put away the strange gods that are among you, and be clean, and change your garments: and let us arise, and go up to Bethel; and I will make there an altar unto God, who answered me in the day of my distress, and was with me in the way which I went (Gen. 35:2–3).

And (3.) To expel such out of their family as persist, notwithstanding the use of means for their reformation, in walking contrary to God. David's resolution on this head is recorded for our imitation,

> I will behave myself wisely in a perfect way. O when wilt thou come unto me? I will walk within my house with a perfect heart. I will set no wicked thing before mine eyes: I hate the work of them that turn aside; it shall not cleave to me. A froward heart shall depart from me: I will not know a wicked person. Whoso privily slandereth his neighbour, him will I cut off: him that hath an high look and a proud heart will not I suffer. Mine eyes shall be upon the faithful of the land, that they may dwell with me: he that walketh in a perfect way, he shall serve me. He that worketh deceit shall not dwell within my house: he that telleth lies shall not tarry in my sight (Ps. 101:2–7).

In the government of a religious family, the heads of it should make it appear that they are more jealous for the honor of God than for their own authority and interest; and more displeased at that which offends God than at that which is only an affront or damage to themselves.

4. Another principal part of this duty consists in parents and masters giving *a good example* to their families, in a constant and devout serving of God, and in a sober, prudent, and unblameable conversation. Without this, their best instructions will signify but very little, and the main force and efficacy of them will be lost. The want of this must weaken the authority of all their good counsel; and make them appear quite contemptible, while they recommend practices which they do not observe themselves.

2. Arguments Proving It to Be a Duty

Having mentioned the *various parts* of family religion, I shall now proceed to *prove it to be a duty* for Christian families thus to worship and serve the Lord. The arguments that demonstrate this may be drawn both from the light of *nature* and of *Scripture*.

First, Family-religion appears to be our duty from *the light of nature*, several ways; for,

1. It is a just debt to the supreme Being, upon account of his perfections, and the relation he sustains to us as families; and therefore it is our duty to maintain it. God is the most *excellent* of beings, and therefore worthy of homage in every capacity from his reasonable creatures. It is the supreme excellency of the Deity that renders him the object of personal devotion, and the same reason extends to family religion; for such is his excellency, that he is entitled to all the worship which we can give him; and after all, "he is exalted above all our blessing and praise," that is, he still deserves more blessing and praise than we can give him. In whatever capacity we are that admits of service to him, we are bound to serve him in that capacity; because he justly deserves it all; now we are capable of serving and worshipping him *as a family*; for family devotion is a thing possible in itself, and therefore we ought to worship him in that capacity. Moreover, God is the author of our *sociable* natures, and as such is entitled to our *social services*, particularly in our families, these being the first kind of societies that ever were instituted, and the radical societies from which all others are derived. And finally, God is the *proprietor, supporter*, and *benefactor* of our families, as well as of our persons; and therefore our families as such should pay him homage.

2. Family-religion was the principal *design of the institution* of families; and therefore we are indispensably bound to observe it. Can it be thought that God would unite a number of immortal creatures together, in the

most intimate bonds, in this world, without any reference to their future state? Were families made for *this world* only, or for the *next?* If for the next, then religion must be maintained in them, and those who omit this duty live in families in direct opposition to the first end of their institution.

3. Family-religion tends to the *greatest advantage* of these families where it is observed. The advantage of being religious is generally confessed, however rarely it is practiced; for the godly are under the blessing and guardianship of heaven; they are restrained from those practices which may be ruinous to them in time and eternity; they are not enslaved to their self-tormenting passions; and they possess the most refined and substantial joys. Let me now appeal to the consciences of the most inconsiderate of my readers, whether it be not more probable that the members in a family will be religious, if the head of it solemnly worships God with them, and instructs them, than that they would be so, if he neglected these duties? How can he expect that his children and servants will become worshipers of the God of heaven, if they have been educated in the neglect of family religion? Surely these, who love their children; who would make some amends to their servants for all the service they do to them; who wish the blessing of heaven to rest upon their families; who would have their children to make their houses the receptacles of religion, when they set up in life for themselves; who would have religion survive in the world, and to be conveyed from age to age; and who would deliver their own souls—are under every obligation to observe family religion, as the most likely means of obtaining these purposes.

4. Family-religion is *an inestimable privilege*, as well as a duty. How great is the privilege, to hold a daily intercourse with heaven in our dwellings! to have our houses converted into temples for that adorable Deity, whom the heaven, and the heaven of heavens cannot contain! to mention our domestic wants before him with the encouraging hope of a supply! to vent the overflowings of gratitude! to spread the favor of his knowledge, and talk of him whom angels celebrate upon their golden harps, and in anthems of praise! and to have our families devoted to him, while others live estranged from the God of their life! If all this does not appear the highest privilege to men, it is because they are astonishingly disaffected to the best of beings, and stupidly insensible of their own mercies.

5. Even the practice of *heathens* and *idolaters*, who observed some sort

of family religion, and accordingly had their *household gods*,[1] confirms the obligation upon *Christians* to worship and serve the only living and true God. Will they not blush, that heathens should exceed them; and that they should be *worse than infidels?* Must they not tremble, lest heathens should rise up in judgment against them, and condemn them? Laban had his family gods, which Rachel stole from him (Gen. 31), and Micah had his, which the Danites took away (Judg. 17–18). These indeed were but *idols*; but being substituted in the place of the true God, they received the homage of the family. The design of revealed truth is to turn mankind from this darkness to light, and from these dead idols to serve the living God.

Secondly, Our obligation to family religion may be argued from *the Scriptures*, where this duty is recommended to us, in a variety of lights.

1. God has *commanded it* in several precepts, which, either directly or consequentially, refer to the whole, or to some branch of family religion. After the apostle Paul had given various directions about relative duties in families, he subjoins, "Continue in prayer, and watch in the same with thanksgiving" (Col. 4:2). Peter exhorts husbands to dwell with their wives according to knowledge, etc., that *their prayers* be not hindered (1 Peter 3:7), which undoubtedly implies that they should pray together. Moreover, the saints are enjoined to pray "always with *all prayer* and supplication" (Eph. 6:18); and surely *family prayer* must be included in these comprehensive terms.

2. We have the brightest *examples*, to encourage our regards to this duty. Good examples infer an obligation upon us to imitate them; and when they are transmitted down to posterity with honor in the sacred records, they are proposed to our imitation, and as *really* bind us to the duty as express precepts. On this head, we are surrounded with a glorious cloud of witnesses. Even before the introduction of the clearer dispensation of the gospel, we find that the saints carefully maintained family religion. On this account, Abraham was admitted into such intimacy with God that he imparted unto him his secrets. "And the LORD said, Shall I hide from Abraham that thing which I do?... For I know him, that he will command his children and his household after him, and they shall keep the way of the LORD" (Gen. 18:17–19). We find Isaac and Jacob follow

---

[1] See Broughton, *Dictionary*, on the word, *lares*.

the same practice. They, as well as he, *built an altar to the Lord*, wherever they pitched their tents; an altar being then a necessary utensil for divine worship. This circumstance is repeatedly taken notice of, in the short history we have of these patriarchs (Gen. 26:25; 33:20; 35:1, 3). Job was so intent upon family devotion, that he rose early in the morning, and offered burnt-offerings; and thus he did, not upon extraordinary occasions only, but continually (Job 1:5). When David had spent the day in the glad solemnity of bringing the ark to its place, he returned home "to bless his household" (2 Sam. 6:20).

In the New Testament, we often find our blessed Lord in prayer and instructive conference with his family, the disciples. Paul thrice mentions *a church in a* private *house* (Rom. 16:5; 1 Cor. 16:19; Col. 4:15), by which he probably means the religious families of Nymphas, and of that pious pair Priscilla and Aquila. And Cornelius is an instance peculiarly observable, he "feared God with all his house…and prayed to God alway" (Acts 10:2), that is, at all proper seasons; and when the angel of God came to direct him to send for Peter, *Cornelius was praying in his house* (v. 30), that is, with his domestics, as the phrase often signifies; and the context seems to determine this to be the sense here (see v. 33). After such authentic examples as these, it is of less weight, though still it is proper to add, that, in every age, *persons of piety* have been exemplary in family religion; and, if we look around us, we will find that by how much the more religious persons are, by so much the more conscientious they are in this duty. The voice of praise and supplication is in the tabernacles of the righteous.

3. As we learn from the Scriptures, that the Lord will bless the houses of his people, where he is worshipped (Ps. 30), so we are assured, by the same authority, that divine fury will be poured out on the families which call not on his name (Jer. 10:25).

Thus I have endeavored to represent, in the most advantageous light, the arguments from reason and revelation, which demonstrate the obligation of the several services of family religion[2] and now go on,

---

[2] The argument for the obligation of family religion is very judiciously stated, and prosecuted, in Durham, *A Practical Exposition of the Ten Commandments*, on the fourth commandment, which the reader is desired to consult.

3. The Seasons of Family Duties

To show *in what seasons*, or *how frequently*, the duties of family religion should be performed. This can only be determined by considering the nature of these duties, which belong to the system of it. An holy conversation and pious *example* are necessary at all times; for no indulgence should be given, for a moment, to any temper or behavior that do not become the gospel of Christ. *Family-instruction* is a duty of such a nature that it must be limited to some particular season; and, as I have already observed, the evening of the Lord's day seems to be most convenient for that purpose, not excluding such other opportunities as shall occur in providence. The exercise of *family government*, in order to promote the great ends of religion in the family, should only appear on particular occasions, and should be guided wholly by occurrences; for a constant show of authority renders it contemptible, and defeats its own purpose. And it is more than intimated in Scripture that *family worship* should be performed *every day*, and particularly *morning and evening*. Thus the sacrifices under the law, which were attended with prayer and praise, were offered daily, morning and evening. To this the psalmist alludes, "Let my prayer be set forth before thee as incense," which was offered in the morning, "and the lifting up of my hands as the evening sacrifice" (Ps. 141:2). That passage is express to this purpose, "It is a good thing...to show forth thy lovingkindness in the morning, and thy faithfulness every night" (Ps. 92:1–2).

Even *reason* directs us to *morning* and *evening*, as the proper seasons for family worship. Can you, who have the charge of a family, venture them out into the world all the day, without committing them to the care of Providence in the morning? Is it proper to employ them in your secular business, without imploring the divine blessing upon them? As to the evening, how can you venture to sleep, without committing yourselves and families to the divine protection; and returning God thanks for the mercies of the day? How can you neglect so reasonable a service? And finally,

The very *course of nature* seems to direct us to these seasons for our life is parceled out into so many days, and every day is a kind of life, and sleep a kind of death. Now, should we enter, as it were, upon life in the morning, without acknowledging the Author of our life? Or should we, as it were, die in the evening, and not commend our spirits into his hand? The morning introduces all the honest labors and agreeable enjoyments of life, with new advantage; it restores mankind to the busy scenes of industry and action, with fresh vigor and pleasure; and night is a kind of pause, or stop in the progress of life. The consideration of both should kindle in us a devout temper towards our divine Benefactor and Preserver. I shall only add that passage, wherein the prophet hints that we should worship the Lord, as the author of the revolutions of day and night, "Seek him that…turneth the shadow of death into the morning, and maketh the day dark with night" (Amos 5:8). Now, what time is so proper for this, as the morning and the evening of every day?

4. The Obligations on Heads of Families

I proposed, in the next place, to consider what obligations *the heads of families* lie under, and *what authority* they are invested with, to maintain religion in their houses.

However mankind may reason in speculation, it is undeniable in fact, that in all societies there must be a subordination, and particularly in families; and that it is the province of the head of such societies to rule and direct them. Upon that obvious principle it follows that the head of a family, when there is no fitter person present, whom he can safely and honorably employ, ought to perform worship in it, and to cause all his domestics to attend upon it. In order to procure the attendance of all his domestics, the gentler methods of persuasion ought to be used, where they will succeed; but when it becomes unavoidable, compulsive measures may be taken to oblige all his domestics to an attendance. I allow that the consciences of all, bond and free, are subject to God only, and that no man ought to compel another to that as a duty which is against his conscience. But this is not the case here; domestics may plead a great many excuses for not joining in family worship, but they will hardly plead that it is against their conscience; that is, they will hardly say that they believe they would sin against God in so doing.[3] Here then he may use his authority, and perhaps some word they hear may touch their hearts. And in common cases, he should cause

---

[3] Family-religion is not the *peculiarity of any party* of Christians, but is generally owned to be obligatory by all them that call upon the name of the Lord Jesus; and therefore Christians of every denomination should conscientiously observe it, if they would act consistently with their own principles. The only *lawful excuse*, which inferiors, children or servants, can have for not joining in the duties of religion, in the families they belong to, must arise from some *essential corruption* in the *matter*, or *manner*, of the worship; or else from the *notoriously bad character* of the person who performs that duty, as openly maintaining fundamental-errors, or living in gross and known sin. But

them all to attend on all the services of family worship; because he is invested with this authority, in order to edify his family in the fear of God; and therefore should use it as a good steward of the manifold grace of God, by promoting religion among all that are within his gates.

That masters of families are authorized and obliged to all this, is evident: from God's commending Abraham for commanding his children and his household, that they should keep the way of the Lord (Gen. 18:19); from Joshua's resolving that not only *he*, but also *his house*, should serve the Lord; a resolution he could not perform, unless he had authority over his house to compel them, at least externally, to serve the Lord (Josh. 24:15); and from the superiority they have over their domestics, which gives a right to command them in this case, as well as in their own affairs.

5. Causes of Its Neglect

Among all *the causes of the neglect* of family religion that have contributed to the decay of godliness in the hearts and houses of such as call themselves

---

for persons to break up fellowship in the duties of family religion, with those who are not of their way of thinking, in regard to church-communion, is a most extravagant instance of madness, ignorance, and pride. *A tree is known by its fruits*; and if we examine this practice by its fruits, we shall immediately discover the *quality* of the tree. Now, the necessary consequence of this practice, in many thousand cases, must be the *total neglect of family religion*. It is, I might say, the easiest thing to conceive, but I rather say, the commonest thing to be seen, that in many families, the husband, parent, or master, is of one opinion, and the wife, children, or servants, are of another, in regard to church-communion; and where this is the case, what method must be taken in order to support family worship? Shall it be said that these who are *of one mind* should join in that duty? But in how many cases shall we find that the master of the family has none within his gates, that is of his sentiments? The absurdity of this way of doing might be represented in a variety of other lights: but, instead of enlarging on these, I shall finish this note with the following observation: that ever since the everlasting gospel was preached to all nations, for the obedience of faith, an all-wise Providence hath disposed the lot of Christians in such a manner that they have been connected in every relation of life, and with every sort of people; with Jews and Gentiles; with bond and free; with heretics and ungodly men; with such as they approved to be brethren in church-communion; and with such as they esteemed brethren in Christ, though they could not unite with them in church-fellowship. This is an undeniable *fact*, confirmed by history, observation, and experience; and, I apprehend, it may be accounted for by observing the *happy effects* of this situation of the people of God, whose light is made hereby to shine more extensively; and who are hereby knit together in a more diffused love to the whole body of Christ, from the daily opportunities they have of observing the holiness and uprightness of such as differ from them in their sentiments, upon principle, in lesser points.

by the name of the Lord, it is certain that the want of a saving knowledge, unfeigned belief, and real love of the truth, has the greatest and most dangerous influence. The *subordinate causes* of this criminal neglect I apprehend to be such as these.

1. The *ill constitution of families* at the first, by unsuitable marriages and relations. The *Israelites* were early cautioned not to mix with the idolatrous nations, "Neither shalt thou make marriages with them; thy daughter thou shalt not give unto his son, nor his daughter shalt thou take unto thy son" (Deut. 7:3). The apostle's advice to *Christians* is likewise much to the same purpose, "Be ye not unequally yoked together with unbelievers: for what fellowship hath righteousness with unrighteousness? and what communion hath light with darkness? and what concord hath Christ with Belial? or what part hath he that believeth with an infidel?" (2 Cor. 6:14–15). An *unsuitable* is ever like to prove an *unhappy match;* and what can be more unsuitable than to join the pious and the profane? the well-educated and well-disposed person, with the loose and profligate? *Worldly views*, it is to be feared, often overrule the choice of young people, and of their parents or guardians, in regard to marriage; but surely such conduct is not to be justified; nay, it is extremely criminal. Is the reputation of family connections, or the advancement of an estate, a valuable consideration, to induce any person to hazard the loss of family religion, with all the train of sins and calamities attendant on such a loss?

Do you indeed expect to teach such relations the fear of God; and thereby make an acquisition to the church of Christ from the world that lieth in wickedness? Ah! presumptuous, ignorant mortal! you have more reason to fear they will turn away your heart from following the Lord than to hope you will prevail on them. Besides, there is no person can truly say that his *motives are pure and religious*, in forming marriage-connections, with such as do *not seem to profess religion upon principle.* It is a contradiction to common sense, and daily experience, to pretend any such thing; and proves *the pretender* to be either *a fool* or *a cheat*. Upon the whole, I would recommend the apostle's caution in this case, "she is at liberty to be married to whom she will; [*N.B.*] *only in the Lord*" (1 Cor. 7:39). The rule is the same for men and for women; and the contempt of this rule is one sad cause of the neglect of family religion among many who profess godliness.

2. *Omitting of family religion at first setting out in the world* is another cause of the continued neglect of it. Would young persons begin with

God, and use themselves to family worship from the first, they would be likely to proceed with ease and comfort; whereas, a neglect at the first discourages a future attempt; and the longer the duty has been neglected, the more backward people usually are to return to it. It is therefore necessary that young persons should dedicate their houses to the Lord, by setting up his worship in them, *as soon* as they commence masters of families; and having begun in the Spirit, let them not end in the flesh; but go forward in the ways of God, until they appear before him in Zion.

3. *Excess of modesty, and bashfulness of mind* furnish us with another view of the sources of that fatal *neglect* of family religion, which is so common. To neglect the worship of God in the family on this account may sometimes be *a temptation*; but it is always *a fault.* All the ability God hath given a man, whether great or small, should be cheerfully employed in his service; and, "to him that hath shall be given."

4. *The decay of serious religion*, and *the abatement of zeal for the honor of God*, in the heads of families, is another cause of this lamentable neglect. Too often they are in company when they ought to be at home; and if they are abroad till some of the family be in bed, and all of them have need to be there, it is no wonder that there is no family worship. Such a practice certainly deserves a warm reproof. It is ill in *young persons* to be abroad at night, when they ought to be under the roof and eye of their masters, or parents; but for *elderly persons*, heads of families especially, to be thus employed, is still worse. Such an evil example is of very extensive influence, besides the aggravated sin of the practice.

5. *Multiplicity of worldly affairs, and inordinate regards to worldly good*, are the last of the causes of neglecting family religion I shall mention; but though I have named them last, they ought to be esteemed the most dangerous and destructive sources of that wretched indifference to practical religion, in the family, and everywhere else, that prevails so generally among professors of Christianity. Surely worldly affairs might be so adjusted, and should be so pursued, as to leave room for both personal and family religion. Wise men will order their affairs with discretion; that the fervor of their spirit in serving the Lord may not be impaired, nor their services diminished, by their engagements in business. Christians ought to look at things unseen; for the body is more than meat, but the soul is more than both. The *hurries of business* can be no good excuse for this neglect, unless one fault can be supposed to be a proper excuse for another; but

there is reason to fear that this is often made an excuse, when it might be easily prevented. There is a love of this world inconsistent with the love of God, and the friendship of it is enmity with God. An eager pursuit of this world, and its pleasures, honors, and riches, was always dangerous, and is ever likely to prove ruinous to religion, and fatal to the souls of men.

I have enumerated these causes of the prevailing neglect of family religion, with a view to the benefit of *two sorts* of persons. (1.) To point out the most dangerous springs of this dreadful complicated sin, to such as have been hitherto enabled to cleave to the Lord with purpose of heart, that they may the better shun the first appearances of evil, and escape the first temptations that prepare the way to open apostasy. (2.) To direct such as have never attempted, or have given over their first attempts to set and keep up family religion, to consider the shameful causes of their sinful neglect; that, upon a view of their odious nature, they may be ashamed of a practical neglect of so important and so reasonable a service, when they discern the sources of such base ingratitude to that God who sets the solitary in families.

6. Arguments Pressing the Observation of It

The arguments I would use to press the performance of all the parts of family religion upon masters of families, generally go upon a supposition of the confessed obligation of the duty which has already been considered in the second section of this chapter. These arguments may be reduced to the following heads.

1. Consider the dreadful *consequences* of neglecting this duty. It were not strange if a disorder in your temporal affairs should follow hereupon. The blessing of God is absolutely necessary to success in business, notwithstanding all your prudence and industry. Now, what if this should cease with the other? But on the other hand, what if you are successful, but not in answer to your prayers, nor with a distinguishing blessing; will that be any real advantage to you? To get the world with a curse should be dreaded; and yet it will be so, if God is not acknowledged in getting it.

Again, this neglect may very probably have ill effects upon your families. The constant worship of God in a house serves to keep everything orderly and peaceful; it unites the hearts of all the inhabitants in the love of God, and of one another; the natural effects of it are harmony, peace, and love; it will therefore be no wonder, if the neglect of this spoil the beauty of your society, and stain its glory; and if sensuality, pride, and discord, should enter in at that door, where family worship is shut out. If you do not perform your duty to God, why should you wonder if inferiors perform not theirs to you? Should friends prove less tender, children less dutiful, and servants disorderly or unfaithful, you may but too justly say, "This comes of laying down, and neglecting the worship of God in my family."

But however this be, the neglect must have an ill effect upon your own souls. It is more than probable that it will breed ill habits of mind, and lay too sure a foundation for many after-miscarriages of life. One wrong step is usually followed with another. Having yielded thus far, Satan and the world have a great advantage, and you are laid open to the temptations and snares of both. Who can tell, but that in a little while you will be as seldom in the duties of your closet, as now you are in these of your family? And this will naturally draw after it a carelessness and formality in public worship, and perhaps end in a total neglect of it. Nay more, what I am now warning you of affects *the world*, as well as *the church*, and tends to the general corruption of manners in all the relations of life. Religious families will be good in every capacity; but irreligious ones in none. Consider therefore, I beseech you, this great evil; and let the ill influence it has upon the nation, and the church of God amongst us, upon relations and families, and your own souls, move you to sober reflections hereupon. Remember I am addressing myself to *you*, who stand under solemn engagements to God, by your baptismal dedication, and the bonds of a visible profession, and the relation of church-fellowship; *you* must therefore be chargeable with *great unfaithfulness*, if you neglect a duty you are under so many obligations to perform.

2. Consider the *infinite advantage* of maintaining religious worship in your families. This is the best and surest foundation of the duties of all relations, and the best security for the true discharge and performance of them. Abraham, who, by the testimony of God himself, was so eminent an example of this kind, both of a good father, and of a good master of a family, found the good success of his religious care in the happy effects of it, both upon his son Isaac, and upon his chief servant and steward of his house, Eliezer of Damascus.

What an unexampled instance of the most profound respect and obedience to the commands of his father did Isaac give, when, without the least murmuring or reluctance, he submitted to be bound, and laid upon the altar, and to have been slain for a sacrifice, if God had not immediately interposed to prevent it? (Gen. 22).

What an admirable servant to Abraham was the steward of his house, Eliezer of Damascus? He was diligent and faithful in his master's service, who trusted him in his greatest concernments, and with all that he had. When he employed him in that great affair of the marriage of his son Isaac, what pains did he take! what prudence did he use! and what fidelity did he show, in the discharge of that great trust, giving himself no rest till he had accomplished the business he was sent about! God seems to have left these instances purposely upon record in Scripture, to encourage fathers and masters of families to a religious care of their children and servants.

And to show the power of religion to oblige men to their duty, I will add one instance more. How did the fear of God secure Joseph's fidelity to his master, in a very great and violent temptation? When there was nothing else to restrain him from so lewd and wicked an act, and to which he was so powerfully tempted, the consideration of the great trust his master reposed in him, and the sense of his duty to him, but, above all, the fear of God, preserved him from consenting to so vile and wicked an action: "how then can I do this great wickedness, and sin against God?" (Gen. 39:9). So that, in prudence, and from a wise consideration of the great benefit which will thereby redound to you, you ought, with the greatest care, to instill the principles of religion into those that belong to you, and to go before them in the duties of family worship.

3. Masters of families should consider that to keep up the worship of God in their families, is the way to leave them with comfort, when they come to die. When Christ was about to leave the world, it was with no little satisfaction that he appealed to his Father concerning the faithful discharge of his duty in his own family: "I have manifested thy name unto the men which thou gavest me out of the world...I have given unto them the words which thou gavest me; and they have received them" (John 17:6–8); and then, with assured hope, he recommends them to his Father's care and blessing: "Father, keep through thine own name those whom thou hast given me" (v. 11). Even so may a pious master of a family recommend his children, and his household, to the blessing of God, when he is going to be parted from them; and he may reasonably hope it shall fare the better with them, through the many prayers he has offered up to heaven *for*

them, and *with them;* for "What man is he that feareth the LORD?...His soul shall dwell at ease; and his seed shall inherit the earth" (Ps. 25:12–13).

4. Consider the account you must give of your family duties at the appearing of our Lord Jesus Christ. How severely does the Scripture speak of those who neglect to provide for their own, and them of their own house! *They have denied the faith, and are worse than infidels* (1 Tim. 5:8). Here let me ask you, Are your domestics, your wives, children, and servants, nothing but *material bodies?* If so, I grant your duty is fulfilled by providing for their bodies; if they are only formed for this world, and have no concern with a future, then it is enough for you to make provision for them in the present state. But are you so absurd as to indulge such a thought? Are you not fully convinced that your domestics were made for eternity, are endued with immortal souls, and have the greatest concern with the eternal world? If so, can you think it sufficient that you provide for their bodies and their temporal subsistence? I appeal to yourselves, is there not as much reason for your taking care of their immortal spirits as of their perishing bodies? Ought you not to be as regardful, and as laborious for their comfortable subsistence in eternity, as in time? Nay, is not your obligation to family religion as much more strong as an immortal spirit is more important than a machine of animated clay; and the interests of eternity exceed those of this transitory world? If then he that does not provide for his domestics a competency of the necessaries of life *has denied the faith, and is worse than an infidel*, what shall we say of him that neglects their souls, and takes no pains about their everlasting welfare? Surely he must be worse still than *one that is worse than an infidel*; and how extremely bad then must he be? He has *more* than denied the faith in practice, however confidently he may profess it.

As God has set *ministers* to be as *watchmen* in his *churches*, so he has set *you* in your own *houses;* and if any *souls perish* there through your neglect, *their blood will be required at your hands* (Ezek. 3:17 18). Should God demand of you, in the great day, as he demanded of Cain, *Where is thy brother?* (Gen. 4:9). "Where are those children, and those servants, which I gave you in charge, to bring up for me? Did you diligently instruct them in the knowledge of God? Did you set them good examples of piety and devotion? Did you praise and pray for them, and with them; and so lead them the way to the throne of grace?" What will you that neglect to worship God in your families, answer to the Judge? Will you presume to say with Cain, *I know not; am I their keeper?* Prepare yourselves then for his reply, ye arrogant sinners! *What have ye done? the voice of your children's and servant's blood crieth unto me from the earth: and now ye are cursed* (Gen. 4:10–11). Nay, how will ye answer for this neglect to those of your own household? It will surely be a sad parting from your prayerless families, when you come to die, unless your consciences be altogether asleep. And what can you expect but to hear them curse you to your face another day, for your very sinful neglects? Such are the sad prospects which the head of a prayerless family may reasonably have of a judgment-day, and of another world! And lastly,

5. Consider the *sin* and *danger* of omitting this duty. The *sin* of this omission is evident; for although it might be very consistent with a tender conscience to omit it, for want of being instructed about its obligation, because nothing would be necessary to bring such to the practice, but to convince them it is their duty, yet the omission of family religion, where people are convinced in their judgment of its obligation, discovers such a stupid indifferency about religion, or so inveterate an aversion to it, as renders the sin *exceedingly sinful*. The *danger* is proportioned to the sin; for the artillery of heaven is discharged against the criminal neglecters of this ordinance, in that dreadful imprecation, which, as dictated by inspiration, is equivalent to a prediction or denunciation, "Pour out thy fury upon the heathen that know thee not, and upon the families that call not on thy name" (Jer. 10:25). Observe here that *you* are ranked with *heathens* that know not God; and that the *divine fury* is imprecated upon you; and it shall fall, it shall certainly and speedily fall, upon your devoted heads, and your prayerless families, unless you fly out of its reach, by flying to the Lord in earnest supplications in your houses.

Let me once more entreat and beseech you, *in the bowels of the Lord Jesus Christ*, for your *family's* sake, for the *nation's* sake, and for your *own soul's* sake, that the worship of God may be set up, and religion may be seriously attended to, in your families, without any more delay. But I must now leave the matter to God and your own consciences; and go on,

7. Objections against It Answered

To answer some of the most common *objections* people raise against their performing this duty of family religion, in any or all the branches of it. I grant, it would be more honest for people frankly to own that they have no heart to it, and that *this* is the real cause of their neglecting it, and not any valid objection they have against the duty; but since they will torture their invention to discover some pleas to excuse themselves for the neglect of the duty, their pretenses must be examined and answered; and I submit to this part of my work with the more pleasure, because I always find that opposition to truth and duty tends to the establishment of both.

1. Some pretend, they have no time, and their secular business would suffer by family religion.

Answer. If you were formed only for this world, there would be some force in this objection; but how strange does such an objection sound in the mouth of an heir of eternity? Pray, what is your time given to you for? Is it not principally with a view to the great affairs of another world? and will you say that you have no time for what is the great business of your lives? Why do you not plead too that you have no time for your daily meals? Is food more necessary for your bodies, than religion for your souls? If you think so, what is become of your understandings? Besides, let me ask, what employment do you follow? It is either lawful, or unlawful. If *unlawful*, then renounce it immediately; if *lawful*, then it will admit of the exercise of family religion, for God cannot command contradictions; and since he has commanded you to maintain his worship in your houses, this is a sufficient proof that every calling which he allows you to follow will afford time for it. Moreover, may you not redeem as much time from idle conversation, from trifling, or even from your sleep, as may be sufficient for family religion? May you not order your family devotion so as that your domestics may attend upon it, either before they go out to their work, or when they come to their meals?

I fear this is but *a mere excuse* with most persons that make it. However, let your worldly business be what it will, surely God's business, and the business of your own and your family's souls, deserves to be first minded. And besides, this is but an improvident way of employing your time, to lay it all out on your worldly business, to the neglect of God and his worship; because he can blast your best endeavors, and bring them all to nothing; and it is only *his blessing* upon your endeavors that *can make you rich*.

2. The excuse which is most commonly made by those who have no heart to this duty is, they have no gifts for it; they are too ignorant to perform it with any credit or advantage.

Answer. It is very remarkable that this is almost the only case in which people are apt to express a mean opinion of their own abilities. But certainly this is not the language of *Christian humility.* If you had a proper sense of your wants, this pretense would not hinder you. Did you ever hear a beggar, however ignorant, make this objection? No; a sense of his necessities is an unfailing fountain of eloquence. But how strange does this objection sound from *you,* who have enjoyed Bibles, preaching, and useful books so long; and yet do not blush to say, *you cannot worship God in your families!* Alas! what have you been doing? However, you must confess that neglecting these duties of religion is not the way to improve your minds in knowledge, and to qualify you to perform them better. And that the duty may not be wholly omitted, it might be proper to use some judicious *catechism,* for the instruction of your children and servants, and to use some well-composed *forms of prayer,* as persons that are weak in their limbs do their crutches, till you can lay them aside. It is only bigotry that will say, you should neglect *the substance* of the duty, unless you can also perform *every circumstance* of it in the best manner. But as I believe no *form* can be found that will suit all the various cases and circumstances of your families at all times, I propose this only as an expedient for the present, that family prayer may not be neglected upon the account of your insufficiency.

3. Some allege, they are ashamed to engage in the duties of family religion.

Answer. Some put darkness for light, and light for darkness; they call evil good, and good evil; such are these objectors, whose shame makes them despise their true glory. How comes it that you are not ashamed to be like the heathens who know not God? Do you suppose it is indeed a shame to worship the God of heaven, and to share in the employment of angels? Are sinners ashamed to serve their master, though their service is sin, and their wages death? Why then should you be ashamed of a service so holy, so pleasant, and honorable? A little practice will free you from all this difficulty.

4. Some neglect family religion, because they know not how to begin it.

Answer. It is your honor to own that you have been hitherto mistaken; and that you will rather reform than persist obstinately in the omission of an evident duty. Confess your sin in neglecting it hitherto, and turn from it unto God in Christ, with grief and hatred, with fixed purpose of, and present endeavors after new obedience.

5. Some excuse their neglect by pleading that their family will not join with them.

Answer. How do they know that? Have they tried it? Are they not masters of their own families? They may and should exert that authority in *this*, which they claim in *other* cases.

6. Others fancy, they would be ridiculed and laughed at, if they observed the duties of family religion.

Answer. It is against all reason to be more afraid of a laugh or a jeer than of the displeasure of God; and to study to please men rather than God. These who are resolved never to become religious, till they can obtain the applause of the wicked for being so (for they only will ridicule family religion), will never be religious at all. It is a most serious consideration, and deserves to be thought on by these who are so jealous of their honor, that the neglect of this duty will be treated with *the contempt* of the Judge, and of the whole universe, at last.

Therefore, dismissing your foolish excuses, which only make you more ridiculous, and more wicked, let me beseech you for Christ's sake, with the greatest importunity and affection, that wherever you have your habitations, JEHOVAH may there have an altar, and prayers and praises may there be presented before the Lord in their returning seasons continually, till you be called to worship him in his temple above, where your prayers shall be swallowed up in everlasting praise[4].

8. Directions Relative to It

The most important *directions*, relative to family religion, are the following, which concern both the *masters* and the *members*, of Christian families.

To Masters and Heads of Families

First, I would offer some *directions to the masters of families*, concerning the duties of religion they ought to perform in their families.

---

[4] The reader will find many excellent thoughts to this purpose, in Philip Doddridge. *A Plain and Serious Address to the Master of a Family: On the Important Subject of Family Religion*, wherein the author considers and confutes *all the pretenses* of Christians to excuse their neglect of so necessary and useful a duty, as that of family worship is shown to be.

1. Choose *proper times and seasons* for family worship, when you can be most at liberty from your worldly business, and when you, and those who worship with you, will probably be in the best frame to attend on this duty; as in *the morning pretty early*, before your thoughts are too far engaged in the business of the day; and in *the evening before it be too late*, and the family grows drowsy and sleepy. It would be prudent in most families to fix certain stated hours for worship, and to keep to them as much as possible; for we seldom want leisure for what we are used to do at *certain times*, as eating and sleeping; and no more should we *ordinarily* want time for prayer, did we but, with the same prudence, fix the hours for it, as we do for our bodily refreshments.

2. Let this duty be performed *constantly*, for so hath God commanded, "Continue in prayer, and watch in the same with thanksgiving" (Col. 4:2). Guard against interruptions and intermissions of this duty. Let not worldly business hinder you any day from that which is a greater duty, and of more serious importance to you than any mere worldly affair ever can be. If you would have God's presence continued with your families, let them continue to call upon him, who taketh pleasure in the dwellings of Jacob.

3. Let the religious duties of the family be performed with *great seriousness*. Take heed that they do not degenerate into *mere form* and *custom*. To worship the God of glory is always a very solemn thing, whether it be done in the church, or in the family. Consider always *with whom you have to do*.

4. Make conscience of performing *all the parts* of family religion, which have been described in the *first section* of this chapter. The *torn* and the *maimed* among the flocks, the herds, or the goats, were expressly forbidden to be offered in sacrifice by the Jews (Mal. 1). Our spiritual sacrifices of religious duties should be complete, or else they cannot be acceptable to God by Jesus Christ.

5. Convene your *whole family*, when you would worship God in the daily services of morning and evening religion; for otherwise you mock God, and injure such of your children or servants as you neglect to call together to join in your addresses to God. Remember that *you and your house should serve the Lord*; not *you and a few of them*; but *you and all that are within your gates* (Josh. 24:15).

6. Take heed to your daily conversation, lest you give occasion to the world to say that you make religion a cloak to cover your sin from the censure it deserves, and to impose upon the unwary. Do not render the wor-

ship of God base to the thoughts of your family by any practice that might cause them to abhor and despise the sacrifices of the Lord.

7. Preserve peace and good agreement in your families, as much as possible, that *your prayers be not hindered.* Grieve not the Spirit of grace and supplication by ungodly contentions, which hinder the Spirit of prayer, and cannot work the righteousness of God. And finally,

8. Be careful whom you admit into your family. Choose such domestics as you have reason to think will cheerfully help you forward in the religious duties of the family. David's resolution is remarkably worthy of your imitation on this head, "Mine eyes shall be upon the faithful of the land, that they may dwell with me: he that walketh in a perfect way, he shall serve me. He that worketh deceit shall not dwell within my house: he that telleth lies shall not tarry in my sight" (Ps. 101:6–7). Then will the music be sweet in family duties, when there is a holy concert of godly people in the house.

To Members of Them
Secondly, I shall offer some *directions to the members of Christian families,* whether they be wives, or children, or servants.

1. Bless the Lord who has ordered your lines to fall in pleasant places. Acknowledge the appointment of your happy situation to be the doing of the Lord. The queen of Sheba counted them happy that stood before Solomon, not so much because they saw his magnificence and glory, though that was extraordinary, but because they heard his wisdom. Happy also are ye, if you are wise to know your privilege, that you serve a godly master, are under gracious parents, or married to a pious husband, from whose prayers and counsels, and Christian examples, you may gain more, than if they could confer on you all the wealth, delicacies, and preferments of Solomon's court.

2. Improve the advantages of your happy situation, or else it will go worse with you than others. Rebellious Israel is threatened in these terms, they "shall know that there hath been a prophet among them" (Ezek. 2:5); the meaning is, they shall know it to their sorrow and cost; and so shall those that have lived in families, under governors, who went before them by their godly example in the ways of religion, and lamented over their precious souls so oft with prayers and tears; if they are unprofitable under such enjoyments, they shall know to their terror what families they once lived in, though they had not a heart to improve their mercies. Your case will be

fearful indeed, if you shall find the way to hell out of such doors, and force your way to damnation through such means afforded you to prevent it.

3. If you that fear the Lord are shut up by necessity, against your own inclination, to fix your abode in families, where God is not acknowledged in the duties of religion, I would recommend to you the following things: mourn over your loss as a great affliction; as David did when he lived in Saul's wicked family, whose court and family, for irreligion and impiety, he compareth to the barbarous Arabians and profane Ishmaelites, lamenting that he was shut up with such, whom, by his relation he could not well leave, and for their wickedness he could worse bear: "Woe is me, that I sojourn in Mesech, that I dwell in the tents of Kedar!" (Ps. 120:5). Again, be the more frequent and fervent in the secret duties of religion, because you have no opportunity of joining in such services in the family. Last of all, adorn in all things the doctrine of God your Savior by a faithful performance of every branch of your duty to your relations in the family, though they be not as religious as you would wish them to be. Consider the duties of your station, and fulfill them in the fear of God with judgment, prudence, and persevering attention. Then your practice will bring up a good report on the ways of the Lord; and even your enemies will be constrained to confess that the whole of man is to "fear God, and keep his commandments" (Eccl. 12:13).

This shall suffice for an account of *family religion*, which has been considered, chiefly with a view to the *daily and ordinary services* of it, in *this chapter*. For *other branches* of it, that are *occasional*, the reader must be referred to *these chapters*, where they have been professedly treated of. For example, he will find *family fasting* considered (chapter 12); *Family-thanksgiving* (chapter 11); *Family-catechizing* (chapter 15); *Family-sanctification of the Sabbath* (chapter 10); and he will also find some useful hints concerning *family reading of the Scriptures, prayer, praise*, and *conference*, in chapters 1, 4, 5, and 16.

Chapter 18
Personal Religion

Vital religion is rooted in the heart, and stands opposed to what the apostle calls *the form* or *appearance of godliness* (2 Tim. 3:5), which, like the picture of a man, may represent his shape and likeness, though destitute of life and motion; but undefiled religion arises from a settled principle, which produces a cheerful and uniform regard to all the divine laws. The saints, being the epistle of Christ, have put on the new man, which, after God, is created in knowledge, righteousness, and true holiness; and therefore follow holiness in all manner of conversation. Even their behavior among men, in the affairs of common and civil life, is conducted upon the sublime principles of an unfeigned faith of the word of God, and of a supreme view to his glory. And all their personal concerns with heaven are managed upon the same noble principles, which carry them as much above the world, in spiritual converses with their God, in the way of his own appointment, as *the God that is above* is greater than men, and things below. I believe I speak the sense of all real Christians, when I say, this is, at least, their *desire*, and their daily *endeavor*. In order to assist *them*, and to direct *others*, in what concerns these holy and immediate approaches through Christ to his God and their God, to his Father and their Father, I shall attempt to do the following things.

1. To explain the nature and particular branches of personal religion.
2. To prove that it is the duty of Christians thus to worship God.
3. To show in what seasons the duties of it should be performed.
4. To press upon the conscience serious and just regards to this service, by some arguments.
5. To expose the weakness and absurdity of the objections commonly made against it. And,
6. To give some practical directions about it.

1. The Nature and Particular Branches of It

I shall, in the first place, attempt to explain *the nature*, and *particular branches*, of *personal religion*, which is proper to the closet, and a fit employment for our hours of sacred retirement.

1. As to the *nature of personal religion* and *secret worship*, there is some circumstantial difference betwixt this and that which is social and more public; for instance: this is to be performed in some place of retirement, as far removed from the observation of the rest of mankind as possible; it is to be performed by a single person, in the presence of none but God; it is not subject to the same confining limitations of time, continuance, order, gesture, and other circumstances, as social worship; and it takes in all that devotion which is suitable to the state, situation, temper, hopes or fears, joys or sorrows, of any particular person.

2. The *particular branches of personal religion*, are chiefly the following, *viz.*, Reading the Scriptures, meditation upon them, self-examination, prayer, and praise.

Reading the Scriptures is one part of the duty of the closet, and a very important branch it is; for hereby the mind is enlightened, the conscience is awakened, the heart is affected, the Spirit is received, the soul is comforted, the conversation is directed, and practical religion is powerfully promoted. The propriety of this part of secret worship will not admit of the slightest suspicion, if the very letter of the Scriptures be attended to; for *the man is blessed, who meditates in the law of God, day and night* (Ps. 1:1–2).

Meditation upon the word of God is another branch of closet-religion, which every Christian should daily abound in. It is *the duty* of the saints to *meditate on the word of God*, and to commune with their hearts concerning it, in order to raise their affections, and impress their consciences, "This book of the law shall not depart out of thy mouth; but thou shalt meditate therein day and night, that thou mayest observe to do according to all that is written therein: for then thou shalt make thy way prosperous, and then thou shalt have good success" (Josh. 1:8). And this has been their *practice* in all ages, and in all circumstances,

> I will meditate in thy precepts, and have respect unto thy ways.... Princes also did sit and speak against me: but thy servant did meditate in thy statutes.... My hands also will I lift up unto thy

commandments, which I have loved; and I will meditate in thy statutes.... Let the proud be ashamed; for they dealt perversely with me without a cause: but I will meditate in thy precepts.... O how love I thy law! it is my meditation all the day.... Mine eyes prevent the night watches, that I might meditate in thy word (Ps. 119:15, 23, 48, 78, 97, 148).

He that is truly wise unto salvation will not only consider the *word*, but the *works* of God; he will dwell with holy pleasure in the devout contemplation of his works of creation and daily providence, which exhibit the occasions, means, and opportunities, of remarking his eternal power and Godhead, his wisdom and sovereignty, his faithfulness and mercy; and of performing the services, which become these operations of his hand (see Ps. 104 and 107).

Self-examination according to the word is also a part of the service Christians ought to perform in their most secret retirements, "Examine yourselves, whether ye be in the faith; prove your own selves. Know ye not your own selves, how that Jesus Christ is in you, except ye be reprobates?" (2 Cor. 13:5). They should examine themselves in order to discover their state, temper, and conduct, that the discovery may direct them how to carry towards God, in point of joy or sorrow, upon a review of what he has wrought *in* them, and *for* them. Their design in this inquiry should not be to find a ground of hope in themselves; but to discover the particular and important occasions they have for the most useful improvements of the hope set before them, to strengthen the things that are ready to die, to crucify the world, to mortify the deeds of the body, or to abound in prayer with thanksgiving.[1] I fear many are guilty of too much neglect on this head,

---

[1] The gospel-method of *examining ourselves*, together with the too common abuse of this service, are represented in an advantageous easy light by Walter Marshall. *The Gospel-Mystery of Sanctification Opened in Sundry Practical Directions: Suited Especially to the Case of Those Who Labour under the Guilt and Power of In-Dwelling Sin. To Which Is Added, a Sermon on Justification*, direction 13, which the reader is earnestly desired to peruse with great attention, as suggesting the *most useful scheme* for this duty that is to be found, perhaps, in any book that has ever been written on the subject. Without the clue that valuable writer puts into his hand, the reader may as soon be misled on this head, as on any point of practical Christianity; but with that assistance, he may escape the dangers he is otherwise exposed to, in reading many pious writings, and may even convert their unguarded and perplexing representations of this duty, to his own comfort and advantage.

while they consider self-examination merely as a work of preparation for sitting down at the Lord's table. No doubt, all who eat and drink in remembrance of Christ, are previously to examine themselves (1 Cor. 11:28). But this no way weakens the general obligation that lies upon Christians to be employed frequently in this exercise.

Prayer is likewise a principal part of personal religion in our retirements from the world. How particular and express are the directions Christ hath given concerning it, on several occasions! He has taught us both the *matter* and the *manner* of performing this service (Matt. 6; Luke 11). *Ejaculatory* prayer, even in the midst of the businesses of life, by secret and sudden liftings up of the soul to God, is many ways useful; but does not interfere with the obligations upon single persons, to pour out their hearts before him, in a more solemn and continued manner or method. There is nothing that renders these ways of praying inconsistent; and the persons who are most conscientious in the first, will be most frequent and fervent in the last. And finally,

Praise is a capital branch of closet-devotion. I do not mean only such expressions of thanksgiving and blessing as are proper to be used in our prayers to God; but *the singing of psalms*. Perhaps some will reckon this piece of secret worship *a novelty*; and others may reckon it *a contradiction*, to worship God in secret, and yet sing psalms, which must subject them to be overheard. Indeed there is too much reason to suspect that singing of psalms is not the *general practice* of Christians in our day, and the bare proposal of it has the appearance of *novelty* to these unwise people who measure their duty by their own practice; but it was no novelty with the first professors of the Christian religion, and obtained very much in the primitive church, when their zeal and devotion were warmest. All antiquity agrees with the observation of a learned man, who says, "Psalmody made up a very great part of the Christian's devotions, both in the public assembly, and more privately in the family, *in their retirements in the closet*, and in their waking beds."[2] There is no contradiction in supposing that we may *sing God's praise in secret*, with a low, suppressed voice, by which we may go through all the notes of a tune, with as much advantage as if we sung never so loud; as anybody may be fully satisfied by making the easy experiment. The most plausible objection against using this piece of secret

---

[2] Preface to Henry Hammond. *A Paraphrase and Annotations upon the Books of the Psalms.*

worship is its being *impracticable* to a multitude of Christians, who cannot get their Bibles used at all in their retirements, for want of conveniency and means of perusing them; but this difficulty is not insuperable in our age, more than in the primitive times; nay, our advantages are unspeakably greater than theirs. Let Christians then imitate these worthies who committed, some of them the whole, and all of them at least a part of the Psalms to their memory, that they might use them in worshipping the Lord.

Thus I have enumerated the *several parts* of the religious worship that belongs more especially to the closet, and have given some account of the duties we should perform in our secret retirements from the world. I shall not take upon me to determine *in what order* they should be performed; it is left undetermined in the word of God, as far as I have observed; and therefore everyone may judge and choose as he finds most expedient.

2. Obligations on Christians to Practice It

I shall now endeavor to prove that it is *the duty* of Christians to worship God personally, in their most secret retirements. It would be a very easy task, if there were occasion for it, to show that it is the duty of everyone to read the Scriptures in secret, to meditate in secret, to examine himself in secret, to pray in secret, and to sing the praises of God in secret. But I shall only consider the duty *in general*, and prove the obligation that is upon us *to retire and converse with God in secret.* And the arguments I would use on this head are rather intended to awaken the conscience, and engage the heart to the practice of the duty, than *strictly* to demonstrate the obligation of it; for the foundation of the duty is so deeply laid in the necessary dependence of the reasonable creature upon his Maker, that it is nowhere represented in the word of God as *a new institution*; but wherever it is at all mentioned, the obligation of the duty is always supposed, and some precept, rule, example, or motive, is all that we shall find in the Scripture about it, and these referring chiefly, or only, to the matter, seasons, or manner of discharging it.

1. The obligation of worshipping God in secret is clearly implied in all the *commandments concerning social worship*; for all the obligations, relative to divine worship, fall first upon single persons, before they can affect families or churches, which are made up of individuals.

2. The *example of Christ* is left on record for our imitation on this head; and his example hath all the force of a law in things that pertain to the wor-

ship of God; for as his word is our rule, so his practice is our pattern. Now we often read that Christ prayed *alone*; and if we would act like Christians, we should follow his steps, "And in the morning, rising up a great while before day, he went out, and departed into a solitary place, and there prayed" (Mark 1:35). "And it came to pass in those days, that he went out into a mountain to pray, and continued all night in prayer to God" (Luke 6:12). "And when he had sent the multitudes away, he went up into a mountain apart to pray: and when the evening was come, he was there alone" (Matt. 14:23). Christ took all occasions for secret intercourse with God; and they that have the Spirit of Christ will pursue the same course.

3. An argument may be drawn from the great *end of sending the Holy Ghost*, according to that remarkable promise,

> And I will pour upon the house of David, and upon the inhabitants of Jerusalem, the spirit of grace and of supplications: and they shall look upon me whom they have pierced, and they shall mourn for him, as one mourneth for his only son, and shall be in bitterness for him, as one that is in bitterness for his firstborn. In that day shall there be a great mourning in Jerusalem, as the mourning of Hadadrimmon in the valley of Megiddon. And the land shall mourn, every family apart; the family of the house of David apart, and their wives apart; the family of the house of Nathan apart, and their wives apart; the family of the house of Levi apart, and their wives apart; the family of Shimei apart, and their wives apart; all the families that remain, every family apart, and their wives apart (Zech. 12:10–14).

When the Spirit is poured out, he becomes the *Spirit of grace and supplication* in everyone he sanctifies; and such persons as partake of the Spirit, worship God in the spirit, not only in *the gates of Zion*, and in *the dwellings of Jacob*, but each person *apart*.

4. The concurring *practice of all the saints*, who are a praying people, is a clear evidence of the obligation of the duty, and of the true genius of vital religion. They are called, "the generation of them that seek [the LORD]" (Ps. 24:6). Their history throws light on this branch of their character, as we see in the case of Daniel (Dan. 6:10), of David (Ps. 119:164), of Saul (Acts 9:11), of Cornelius (Acts 10:2), and many others.

5. The *personal wants, sins, and enjoyments of mankind* show the necessity of their secret converse with God, the author of every good and perfect gift, with whom there is forgiveness that he may be feared, and for whom praise waiteth in Zion.

I shall shut up this head, in the words of a late writer,

> The duties I have been recommending, are not only part of the homage we owe to God, as his creatures; but part of the necessary care we owe to ourselves: and as we are *new creatures*, may be placed among the principles of self-preservation. To neglect them, is to neglect the means of our safety and spiritual life; and indeed if the neglect be total, it argues us destitute of life. A Christian without his oratory, without converse with heaven, is but the image of a Christian: he is like a man in arras, a poor, meager, lifeless thing. So that this argument may be reckoned conclusive, and I shall close the head with it: that we ought to maintain intercourse with God in retirement, because that is our strength and our life.[3]

3. The Seasons of Personal Religion

The *third thing* I proposed to do on this subject was to show *in what seasons* the duties of personal religion should be performed, by entering into our closet, and conversing with God in the manner he has prescribed.

I do not apprehend there are any particular *hours* appointed by God for devotions, that are *divinely canonical*; that is, there is no precise hour, or hours in the day, set apart by God for this service, so that it is expected we should retire at that time rather than any other; much less any sacred hours, when our devotion will be more acceptable than at another time. The Jews, indeed, had their stated hours of prayer; particularly, the third, sixth, and ninth hours of their day, answering nearly to our nine o'clock in the morning, midday, and three in the afternoon. David seems to refer to these hours of devotion, when he says, "Evening, and morning, and at noon, will I pray" (Ps. 55:17). The *original* of these observances is altogether uncertain. But as the Christian dispensation was introduced by its teachers becoming all things to all men, and bearing one another's burdens, and so fulfilling the law of Christ, we need not be surprised to hear that Peter and

---

[3] Benjamin Bennet. *The Christian Oratory*, p. 669.

John went up into the temple to pray, about "the hour of prayer, being the ninth hour" (Acts 3:1); even though such hours of worship are not bound upon the disciples of Christ. Besides, these services they went up to perform in the temple seem rather to be *social* than *personal*. However, this practice of establishing hours of prayer was soon taken up in the *Christian* church, from a humor that pretty early prevailed, of modeling their worship according to the manner of the *Jewish* church; hence we find the primitive writers frequently mention *the hours of prayer*,[4] which at length were multiplied and diversified, as their inclinations led them; some making *six*, others *seven*, of these *canonical hours*; which are not only accounted sacred by the *Papists*, but have been had in veneration by *some Protestants*, who have written books to accommodate the devotion of them.[5] But I need not stand to argue with impartial men that all this is an arbitrary service, and can plead no higher authority than what we call *ecclesiastical*; nor can I look upon it as anything else than one of the common shifts men have invented to keep up the *form* of devotion, when the *spirit* of it was very much lost. But passing this, I go on to observe,

1. The Scripture sufficiently intimates that we should be *frequent* in the duties of secret worship. This is the least that can be intended by those texts, wherein we are exhorted to "Pray without ceasing" (1 Thess. 5:17), to pray "always with all prayer and supplication" (Eph. 6:18), "always to pray, and not to faint" (Luke 18:1), and to "watch unto prayer" (1 Peter 4:7). The meaning is not that prayer should engross all our religion, much less that it should employ all our time; but surely they import that we should be *frequent* in the duties of religion.

2. The Scripture directs us to worship our heavenly Father *daily*. This may very clearly be gathered from the *Lord's prayer*, which I take to be *a plan* designed to instruct us in the matter, method, and order of our requests at the throne of grace. Now, among other admonitions it affords us touching the discharge of the important duty of closet-prayer, one is that we are *every day* to be employed in it; for thus it runs: "Give us *this day* our *daily* bread" (Matt. 6:11); or, "Give us *day by day* our *daily* bread. *And* forgive us our sins" (Luke 11:3–4). So that he who doth not pray at least *daily* doth not act as a disciple of Christ, and cannot justly call him Master. And the voice of all nature calls us to serve God *daily* in the immediate

---

[4] Suiceri, *Thesaurus Ecclesiasticus*, on ευχη.
[5] See Broughton, *Dictionary*, on the word *service*. See Hicks's *Appendix to his letters*.

duties of religious worship; for "Day unto day uttereth speech, and night unto night sheweth knowledge" (Ps. 19:2). If men whom God hath set over the works of his hands on earth are silent for one day concerning his praise, the heavens and the earth must bear witness against their ingratitude.

3. We may further conclude from Scripture-hints that every Christian ought to worship God, not only *daily*, but *twice every day*. The Jews had their *continual burnt-offering*, which was offered before the Lord every morning and evening (Num. 28:24, 31). And some have thought the apostolic command to "Pray without ceasing" (1 Thess. 5:17), refers to this Jewish practice; and binds us to worship God in the morning and evening of each day. We are to have our morning and evening sacrifice, and to offer them up in the name of Christ continually. We should not suffer the daily sacrifice to cease. And methinks there is something of *a natural fitness* in it, that we should thus begin and close the day with God. How reasonable is it that in the *morning* we should look up to, and adore the hand which has protected us through the night, committing ourselves to the conduct thereof through the day! And it is equally reasonable we should do the same at *night*, reviewing the past day, owning the providence of God in it, and making acknowledgments answerable to our occasions. It is a good thing to show forth the lovingkindness of the Lord in *the morning*, and his faithfulness *every night* (Ps. 92:1–2). This practice is in every respect a good thing; for it is acceptable to God, suitable to our circumstances, and profitable for us, and therefore it should not be neglected among the saints.

4. The examples of the people of God, recorded in Scripture, seem to carry the matter still higher, and recommend *three times* as proper to be observed in the course of *daily devotion*. Thus David, "Evening, and morning, and at noon, will I pray" (Ps. 55:17). And Daniel "kneeled upon his knees *three times a day*, and prayed, and gave thanks before his God," which, it seems, was his daily custom, for it is added, "as he did aforetime" (Dan. 6:10). And no doubt the Christian may find his account in the like zeal. A short retirement *at noon*, when circumstances will admit of it, may be a repast in the midst of the hurries, business, and company of the day; may help to revive good impressions made by the morning-devotion; may recover the mind out of the world; and may give it a happy bias towards divine objects, and so may dispose it, not only for the remaining duties of the day, but for more solemn converse with God at night. Thus, the sacred

fire of heavenly devotion would be kept in, and the soul would be in the fear of the Lord, all the day long.

5. Besides the *stated* ordinary times of retirement, there are special occasions of *more solemn devotion*. When Christ commissioned his disciples to the high and difficult office they were to be employed in, he spent a whole night in prayer (Luke 6:12–13). The Christian will have many of these extraordinary occasions, in the course of his life; nor will he neglect them, if he be duly attentive. But as I have mentioned several of these *mercies* and *judgments*, which demand peculiar attention, and direct us to come with extraordinary importunity and perseverance to the throne of grace, in the exercise of praise or humiliation, when I considered the ordinances of *thanksgiving* and *fasting* (chapter 11 and 12), the reader may review what has been delivered on these heads, which will save me the trouble of repetition.

What has been already noticed concerning the *several branches* of closet-religion, and the *seasons* of performing it, gives occasion for the following *inquiry*, which must be discussed before I leave this head, *viz.*,

Question. "Is it necessary for *every Christian* to go through *all the work* that has been prescribed, *every time* he retires for secret worship, by *reading the Scripture, meditating upon it, examining himself by it, praying, and praising*? Can it be expected from the main body of Christians that they should have time and capacity for so much, and such manner of work, in their constant closet-devotion?"

This question is important, and attended with difficulties, whatever answer we give to it. Some will be discouraged, if we answer in the affirmative; and some would catch at an answer in the negative as an excuse for criminal and allowed neglects of several branches of secret worship.

The answer I would give shall be comprehended in the following particulars. (1.) I allow that there are some Christians who are *not qualified* to perform some parts of this service, with any great profit or advantage, *at any time*; such as *meditation* and *self-examination*; though no doubt a willing mind, and a warm heart, would supply several defects of the head, and remove, in a course of time and practice, many difficulties that seem at first insuperable. (2.) There are others who can but *seldom* go through all this service in their closets. This is the case of many servants, whose business and severer masters challenge almost the whole of the time they can spare out of their beds. (3.) There is none that can *always* be supposed to have that measure of health, and that easy situation in life, which would enable him to go through the whole service proposed, every time he retires to his closet. (4.) Though there are some that can *never* go through all this work to any great purpose, others that can but *seldom*, and none that can *always* do it, yet I believe there are others that may *often* attend the whole of it ordinarily *once every day* at least, if it be not their own fault. (5.) I apprehend, there can be no reasonable excuse made for totally omitting to *sing* one or more verses, in the manner before mentioned; and to *read*, or at least call to remembrance, some passage of God's word; and to pour out our souls before the Lord in *prayer*, every morning and evening. And *the meditation* upon that, or other passages, may be continued for a longer or shorter time, as occasion may serve, even while people are engaged in the business of life. And (6.) Let some stated times be set apart for performing these duties *with more deliberation*, at such intervals as the particular circumstances of different persons will best admit; and yet not so distant as to allow the sense of religion to wear off the mind; suppose then that these who can, should devote an hour every night to the foresaid exercises; and these who cannot conveniently spare as much time from the business of an imperious master or mistress, should set apart at least two or three nights each week for *more continued* reading, meditation, self-trial, prayer and praise; still, however, worshipping God in secret, by singing, reading, or repeating some passage of his word, and praying, every morning and evening at least; though not at so great length, as it is proposed they should do on the occasions I am directing them more particularly to observe, for obtaining all the purposes of personal devotion. If anybody is so ignorant, or so prejudiced, as to imagine that all this will only tend to make people *formal*, or else induce them to *trust in themselves*, I would have them consider that the very same objections may be made, and with the same reason too, against *family worship*, and *public ordinances*, and indeed against *all social religion*.

4. The Duty Pressed by Several Arguments

I shall now proceed to press upon the consciences of Christians *serious and just regards* to the duties of personal religion, by some arguments. Many things might be urged on this head, to awaken the conscience, to excite diligence, to interest our fears and hopes, our joys and wishes, in *a service* which is both *honorable*, and *pleasant*, and *advantageous*; whereas *the neglect* of it is both *sinful*, and *shameful*, and *ruining*.

First, I would recommend personal religion to your esteem and affectionate practical regards, by representing the dignity, satisfaction, and profit which accompany or flow from it.

1. Personal religion is truly *honorable*. Nothing is honorable that is out of character. A rich miser, and a beautiful harlot, are mean and disgraceful things. A swine is not honored by a jewel of fine gold fixed on its snout, which it will employ, on the first opportunity, to plow the dunghill, and wallow in the mire. A rebel is not honored by a numerous train of eager followers, risen up in arms against their rightful sovereign without a just cause. But these are deservedly esteemed honorable persons whose mind and behavior are just what their character requires. Our moral character is by far the most honorable in this lower world. The branches of it are comprehended in two commandments,

> Jesus said unto him, Thou shalt love the Lord thy God with all thy heart, and with all thy soul, and with all thy mind. This is the first and great commandment. And the second is like unto it, Thou shalt love thy neighbour as thyself. On these two commandments hang all the law and the prophets (Matt. 22:37–40).

To be *godly*, *righteous*, and *sober*, is the sum of what the law requires, and of what *the grace of God teaches us* (Titus 2:11–12). The man who is of this character is truly honorable, and possessed of the honor which cometh from God, who has put his laws into his mind, and written them on his heart. He is in the fear of the Lord all the day. Caesar cannot confer, and money cannot purchase, this inestimable honor, which the Lord puts upon them that honor him (1 Sam. 2:30). The highest pinnacle of human glory is infinitely more beneath the honor of being the Lord's servant than the earth is distant from the remotest star. What connections are so great and honorable as these of the saints, who, in the duties of religion, have their fellowship with the Father, and with his Son Jesus Christ? *They find favor in his sight.* An honor more enduring than the foundations of the earth. An honor which secures their happiness, when all below threatens to destroy it. An honor that makes the possessor of it superior to all human disgrace, unmoved at reproach, satisfied under oppression, and willing to take up or bear the cross of Christ with all its ignominy, "And they departed from the presence of the council, rejoicing that they were counted worthy to suffer shame for his name" (Acts 5:41).

> By faith Moses, when he was come to years, refused to be called the son of Pharaoh's daughter; choosing rather to suffer affliction with the people of God, than to enjoy the pleasures of sin for a season; esteeming the reproach of Christ greater riches than the treasures in Egypt: for he had respect unto the recompence of the reward. By faith he forsook Egypt, not fearing the wrath of the king: for he endured, as seeing him who is invisible (Heb. 11:24–27).

2. Personal religion is *a pleasant* employment, as well as an honorable one. *Peace and joy* are among the first-fruits of the Spirit of grace and supplication which believers receive. They that have believed do enter into rest; and begin to find, in their comfortable experience, that it is good for them to draw near to God. They are made to know that the kingdom of God is righteousness, and peace, and joy in the Holy Ghost. It is true, to a pleasure-loving soul, these, like objects seen by a jaundiced eye, are ever misrepresented. The way to them through the strait gate, and in the narrow way, that leadeth unto life, looks forbidding; and a life of self-denial, and mortification of our members which are upon the earth, seems to promise nothing but wretchedness. But they who make the trial, find the difference, and are ready to set their seal to God's truth; and to declare that they have not been disappointed of their hopes. Each step taken in Christ's ways brings pleasantness and peace. The very mournings of the soul, returning to its rest in him, are delightful; and none knows the joy of the tears of penitence but those who drop them. Rough as the way appears, it is but as the gloomy avenue, not in itself destitute of pleasure, which opens to some delightful prospect; and these sweet sorrows are quickly followed by *peace and joy in believing*. Nor for a time only, but all life through, the prospect brightens, the pleasure is heightened. The intercourse of the believing soul with God in secret meditation, the communion maintained with him in prayer and praise, the consolation of the Scriptures, and the growing conformity of the soul to his image, together with the reviving hope of, and eager looking for that glory, which shall be revealed in the saints, when, from drinking of the streams below, they shall go to drink

at the fountainhead above—*these* are accompanied with solid, substantial, rational pleasures, as much superior to the poor joys of sense, as the mild sunshine and genial warmth of a long and temperate summer exceed the suddenly expiring and crackling blaze of thorns.

3. Personal religion is highly *advantageous*. *Their souls shall live that seek the Lord* in the duties of it. Therefore, O sinner, "acquaint now thyself with him, and be at peace: thereby good shall come unto thee" (Job 22:21).

> Trust in the Lord, [O believer!] and do good; so shalt thou dwell in the land, and verily thou shalt be fed. Delight thyself also in the Lord; and he shall give thee the desires of thine heart. Commit thy way unto the Lord; trust also in him; and he shall bring it to pass. And he shall bring forth thy righteousness as the light, and thy judgment as the noonday. Rest in the Lord, and wait patiently for him…Mark the perfect man, and behold the upright: for the end of that man is peace (Ps. 37:3–7, 37).

The advantages of closet-devotion are many; for,

Christians have *greater freedom*, and may be more particular in their addresses to God in secret, than when they pray with others, even with their own families. The Christian has many things to say to his God, when alone, which would not be proper to mention in the hearing of any fellow-mortal. There are peculiar sins, and peculiar mercies, peculiar blessings, and cares, and sorrows, which are fit to have a place only in our closet-devotions. That we may *enter into our closet, and shut the door* upon us, and shut out the world, and every creature, and there speak to our heavenly Father alone, and tell him all that is in our heart, is such a privilege as no Christian can be without, and which no good person will make light of.

Again, secret worship is an excellent means *to preserve a lively sense of religion in the soul*, and *to prevent a decay of the divine life*. The confession of your most secret sins to God, and prayer for help and strength against your secret temptations, with the other acts of devotion which are proper for the closet, will necessarily lead you into an acquaintance with yourselves, and keep you from being strangers to your own hearts. It will put you on a frequent review of the tempers of your minds. It will help you to take notice of your first declensions, and to prevent the progress of them. Hereby, in a word, you will be daily improving in the divine life, in your acquaintance and communion with God; and so, by this means, you will be sensibly ripening every day, for the enjoyment of his immediate presence, and for the heavenly life of eternal glory.

Moreover, the constant and conscientious performance of the duties of secret religion is *one of the best evidences of Christian sincerity*; and without it, it cannot be supposed that our *hearts are right with God.* Many worldly motives, such as custom, example, and reputation, may prevail with a person to attend public worship, and even to pray in his family; but take a man alone in his closet, and there he will follow his real inclination. The *Pharisees* prayed in the *synagogues*, and in the *corners of streets*, on purpose *to be seen of men*; which was a clear proof of their *hypocrisy.* But these who make conscience of the duties of secret religion, when no eye sees them, either to applaud or censure them, go beyond the highest aim of such hypocrites, who take pains only for *the name* of being religious, without any nobler purpose. That soul appears to be born from above which loves to converse with God, alone, unseen, and unheard by all the world. Closet-devotion is the delight of the saints, who do not court the praise of men, but seek the honor that cometh from God only. Hence their perseverance in it comes to be a distinguishing part of the character of real Christians, who worship God in the spirit.

Secondly, Another class of impelling motives to engage Christians to have just regards to personal and closet-religion arises from a consideration of *the sin, the shame, and danger of neglecting it.*

1. It is *an heinous sin* to omit the religious duties of the closet; or even to perform them in a careless and superficial manner. This sin is a *robbing of God*, who demands the homage of his reasonable creatures in secret; and expects to be acknowledged as their Fear and the Object of their worship, not only in public assemblies, but in their most private retirements. And these who do not give unto the Lord the glory which is due unto his name, in their secret devotions, *sin against their own souls*, as well as rob God; for by this neglect their heart becomes hard, and their conscience seared, their mind is blinded, and their affections become carnal. Can you that profess the religion of Jesus allow yourselves to indulge a neglect so injurious to God and to your own souls? Can you make a light matter, or ever a mock of this sin, which robs God, and wrongs your own souls? If you can thus deny God, and despise your souls, your heart is certainly hardened through the deceitfulness of sin, and the god of this world has blinded your eyes; or

else you could never be easy under such a crime, nor secure in so dangerous a situation.

2. To neglect the secret worship of God is most *shameful*, as well as criminal. Do not many, who run on in the omission of this service from day to day, confess as much; while they studiously affect the appearance of devout persons, in order to establish their reputation for being such among their fellow-professors? Would not these persons blush at a detection of their secret practice, which they take all possible care to conceal? Such despisers of closet-devotion are witnesses, on the behalf of God, that their way is shameful and scandalous. But although some should become so hardened in this sin as to publish it with airs of triumph, and should acquire all the impudence of a whore's forehead, and refuse to be ashamed, still I must insist that *the sin they boast of is most shameful.* It would be less absurd for a man to rejoice that his foot is out of joint, or that he is a rebel against every social obligation, and an enemy to common sense, than to boast of his *injustice, ingratitude*, and *contempt of reason and conscience*, manifested in his *casting off fear, and restraining prayer before God*. What can be so *unjust*, as for a creature to withhold the proper expressions of his allegiance to, and dependence upon, his Maker and Preserver? What is so *ingrateful* as a creature that lives, and moves, and has its being in God, and yet refuses its acknowledgments of his power and patience, of his wisdom, care, and goodness? What is to be found in the whole circle of creation to parallel *the contempt of reason and conscience* such atheists are chargeable with? Doth not the ox acknowledge his owner? and doth not the ass know his master's crib? But these brutish fools are void of understanding; they do not consider, neither do they know their honor and interest. Their odious character is painted with black, but proper colorings, by the inspired pencil, in

> The fool hath said in his heart, There is no God. They are corrupt, they have done abominable works, there is none that doeth good. The LORD looked down from heaven upon the children of men, to see if there were any that did understand, and seek God. They are all gone aside, they are all together become filthy: there is none that doeth good, no, not one. Have all the workers of iniquity no knowledge? who eat up my people as they eat bread, and call not upon the LORD (Ps. 14:1–4).

Perhaps some contemptible *atheist* may be found, who will make a merit of throwing off all pretensions to a religious character, and fancy himself the more honorable for treating it with ridicule. We need not, however, attempt any excuse for having affirmed that *such an impious boast is shameful*. It is only one instance of men *glorying in their shame* (Phil. 3:19). What would the world be entitled to think of a man who should *pretend it was honorable* for children to be disobedient to their parents; for servants to be unfaithful to their masters; for subjects to rebel against lawful authority; and for mankind to be unnatural and undutiful in every relation? Would not this doctrine be esteemed abominable and odious? and would not the teacher of it deserve the punishment of *an enemy to mankind*, and of *a traitor against society*; unless he should rather in compassion be indulged the privilege of *a lunatic?* But is he a better man, or are his principles really less odious, who would endeavor to persuade the world that it is their honor *to be without God?* Shocking, shameful impiety! O, do not this abominable thing!

3. The neglect of secret worship is not only sinful and shameful, but it *ruins* the poor infatuated sinner who despises it. His case is far from being either hopeful or safe, who has thrown off the care, and lost the conscience of this duty. Though there should be nothing scandalous upon his name, yet the very *withholding of prayer* is enough to ruin him; and this itself is a dreadful prognostic of destruction, when he has neither power nor heart so much as to cry for *deliverance from the wrath to come.* Horrible is like to be the end of the generation that will not call upon the name of the Lord. Such as will not seek his face in the day of his merciful visitation shall in vain cry to him in the day of his wrath; and shall find him then as deaf to their idle entreaties as before they had been dumb in praises and supplication. Their dreadful condition is represented in that alarming description of it,

> Because I have called, and ye refused; I have stretched out my hand, and no man regarded; but ye have set at nought all my counsel, and would none of my reproof: I also will laugh at your calamity; I will mock when your fear cometh; when your fear cometh as desolation, and your destruction cometh as a whirlwind; when distress and anguish cometh upon you. Then shall they call upon me, but I will not answer; they shall seek me early, but they shall not find me:

for that they hated knowledge, and did not choose the fear of the LORD: they would none of my counsel: they despised all my reproof. Therefore shall they eat of the fruit of their own way, and be filled with their own devices (Prov. 1:24–31).

Consider this, ye that forget God, lest he tear you in pieces, and there be none to deliver.

Thus I have set before you, my dear fellow-men! both life and death, blessing and cursing; and have endeavored to engage your affectionate practical regards to the duties of secret personal religion; by representing them as honorable, pleasant, and advantageous; and by setting forth the neglect of them as sinful, shameful, and ruining. I must now commend what has been offered on these points to the Lord the Spirit, to give the increase, in my own, and in the conscience of every reader.

5. Objections against It Answered

I am now to consider *the objections* some pretend to make against the devotion of the closet. I say, *pretend to make*, because I reckon them rather excuses for sloth and disaffection than real conscientious reasons, even in the opinion of the objectors. The most usual of them are the following.

1. Some allege, they *cannot* pray, though they allow it is very right for these that can to do it.

Answer. If you cannot pray as you would, I advise you rather to read some *form of prayer* than altogether to omit the duty. Use crutches (as Dr. Gouge expresses it), till you are able to go alone; only do not content yourselves therewith, but labor in your own words to pour out your souls unto God in prayer. And for your better help therein, take these directions. (1.) Carefully observe the prayers of others, their order and method. (2.) Study your own heart and ways. Look back into your life, calling to mind your past sins, with the aggravating circumstances of them; and, at the same time, consider your spiritual wants; and observe the particular blessings God bestows on you. Confess your sins, and beg the pardon of them; pray for a supply of your wants; and do not forget to bless God for his mercies. (3.) Acquaint yourselves with the word of God, that you may be furnished with proper matter for secret prayer. (4.) Be frequent in the exercise of prayer; for this is the best way to increase in the liberty and comfort of the duty. (5.) Be not over-nice about your words and expressions; for God who seeth in secret, regards not so much the expressions of your tongue as the earnestness of your hearts. And (6.) Do not neglect the constant reading of some part of the Scriptures, and singing God's praise, in your closet-devotion; for you cannot pretend that the objection of inability can excuse you from these, except in the case of these who cannot read.

2. Others object that the house or room in which they live is so small, and so full, that they cannot find any convenient *place* to retire into.

Answer. He that does not want a heart to the duty, will find a place for the performance of it. We can find a place to sin so secretly that none can see us; and had we as great a desire to pray in secret, we would find a convenient place for the same. But to the objectors I would say, Can you really think that this pretense will excuse you at the judgment-seat of Christ for living like heathens, without performing the duties of secret religion? Perhaps the house is so small, and so full as you allege; but is there no out-house, nor garden, nor field, nor retired corner, into which you may withdraw yourselves? Isaac, we read, went out into the field to meditate and pray; Peter, to the top of the house; Christ, into a mountain; and certainly, did you take delight in conversing with God in secret, you would find some convenient place, either within doors or without.

3. Others say, they want *time* on account of the multitude of their affairs, which cannot be neglected.

Answer. The more and greater your affairs are, the more call you have to call upon God to endue you with prudence, and to crown your enterprises with success. Time spent in seasonable devotion will prove no hindrance, but rather a furtherance to your business. Oh! that prayerless worldlings would seriously consider these words of our Savior, "what shall it profit a man, if he shall gain the whole world, and lose his own soul?" (Mark 8:36). Besides, you ought to consider that if you neglect the duties of religion, that you may increase your wealth, by continuing your labor *in the time* when God requires your attendance on himself, the wealth is cursed which is thus gotten; and that substance, which is *the price of your prayers and praises*, may, for what you know, be *the price of the blood of your own soul, and of the souls of others* you involve in your sin. Moreover, what business can you have of so great importance as the glorifying of God, and the enjoying of him forever? For shame then, let not these things, which concern your chief end, and your everlasting happiness, give way to your worldly employments; or, to speak more properly, let not the most substantial and everlasting realities be despised, in order to pursue a vanishing shadow. Rather borrow time from your sleep and food, if you cannot have it otherwise, than omit this necessary duty. Jesus Christ has set us an example of thus redeeming our time, "in the morning, *rising a great while before day*, he went out, and departed into a solitary place, and there prayed" (Mark 1:35).

4. Some may perhaps object against these stated services of the closet, that they are not so *necessary* as is pretended; a man may get to heaven without so much ado, or walking in so narrow a road.

Answer. Although I would not expect such language from the lips of one that had any tolerable notion of the principles of Christianity, yet I fear some such opinion is secretly harbored in their minds, or else it might be expected they would be more zealous in serving the Lord. But surely, such an opinion ill becomes Christians that profess to believe for eternity, and to make religion their business in time. It ill becomes those that are so keen about the world, and ready to run over one another in pursuit of it. And, I must add, that these who can easily satisfy themselves with but little of religion have good reason to suspect they have none at all.

Lastly, Some may object that this service savors of *legalism*, and tends to bring the soul into bondage.

Answer. I am indeed ashamed to mention this as an objection, though some may be found that pervert the gospel of Christ, and the scheme of the Christian religion, so far as to make it. No doubt, *we are saved by grace, through faith* (Eph. 2:8). But "the grace of God that bringeth salvation" teaches to deny *all ungodliness*, and worldly lusts; and "to live soberly, righteously, and *godly* in this present world" (Titus 2:11–12). The gospel is the highest dispensation; it establishes the law, and affords the strongest motives and greatest encouragements to practice all the branches of vital godliness and good works,

> That he would grant unto us, that we being delivered out of the hand of our enemies might serve him without fear, in holiness and righteousness before him, all the days of our life (Luke 1:74–75).

> I beseech you therefore, brethren, by the mercies of God, that ye present your bodies a living sacrifice, holy, acceptable unto God, which is your reasonable service. And be not conformed to this

world: but be ye transformed by the renewing of your mind, that ye may prove what is that good, and acceptable, and perfect, will of God (Rom. 12:1–2).

This is a faithful saying, and these things I will that thou affirm constantly, that they which have believed in God might be careful to maintain good works. These things are good and profitable unto men (Titus 3:8).

From these texts it is evident that the unfeigned belief of the sovereignty of divine grace works by love to every part of Christian duty; and that, to say we hope to be saved by Christ, and thereupon take up with a low groveling state of religion, is to disgrace our profession as Christians. But it is high time to dismiss these trifling objections, which I should not have insisted on so largely, if at all made mention of them, had it not been with a view further to illustrate and enforce the noble and everlasting *obligations and excellencies* of personal religion. I shall now subjoin,

6. Practical Directions respecting It

Some *practical directions* concerning the duties of *personal religion* and *closet-devotion*, that they may be performed with more regularity, advantage, and comfort.

1. When you come before the Lord, study to possess your mind with a firm belief of the perfections and presence of that God you profess to worship. Remember he is a God of terrible majesty, who hates all the workers of iniquity, and to whom all things, and all hearts, are naked and open; a God of infinite discernment, that cannot be deceived, and that will not be mocked; a jealous God, who will be sanctified by all that approach to worship him; and a God in Christ, who showeth mercy, and giveth grace to help in the time of need. These thoughts of God in your secret retirements will be of great service, to strike your souls with a holy reverence, to embolden your confidence, to make you vile in your own eyes, and to make the Mediator of the new covenant appear necessary in all his important characters.

2. Behave in your closets *as dying persons*, fully assured that it will not be long till you must bid an endless farewell to this world, and all its concerns. Look upon your closet as your antechamber to the mansions of glory. For-

getfulness of this is the cause of all our trifling in the service of God, and in the concerns of our souls. With what attention should you read the word of God in your retirements, since it will be the rule of your judgment at last? With what grace in your heart should you make melody to the Lord, while you sing his praise? And with what fervor should you put up your prayers to God? How intense would your thoughts be in divine meditation? How accurate your searches into your state and character? And how strict your watch over your thoughts, words, and conduct *if you really set the eternal world before you*? Then you would be no less careful about *the manner* of performing religious duties than to perform them; and would principally endeavor in the whole to approve yourselves to your Judge, whose approbation alone will be of any service in that awful situation.

3. Be *constant and regular* in performing the services of the closet. Consult prudently the most convenient *times* and *hours* for them. I suppose, it is generally a good rule for morning-devotion, *the sooner the better*; however, if possible, before you engage your thoughts and labors about any worldly business. In the evening you are more at liberty; only let not the worship of the closet be delayed till you grow drowsy, and unfit for anything but sleep. A very warm devotion will hardly admit so large an interval as twelve, fourteen, or sixteen hours, betwixt the seasons of sacred retirement; but these intervening periods of secret worship must be fixed by persons in the most prudent way their circumstances and employments will permit.

In order to your being more constant in secret religion, you will find it necessary to guard against everything that would interfere with it, such as sloth, ease, excess of worldly business, diversions, pleasures, company, etc., and even the conversation of your friends, that most agreeable enjoyment, must be used with caution. *Self-denial* must be exercised in these and other matters; and an *holy resolution* put on, if we would be steady and persevering in this exercise. In short, make this employment your chief comfort, and then you will not admit every trifling excuse to produce a neglect, or at best a careless performance of the duty.

4. Let your *outward conversation* in the world be answerable to such a course of holy walking with God *in secret*; and make the devotion of the closet subservient to a holy life, as a means of promoting and advancing it, in all the branches thereof. If, notwithstanding your religious observances, you are proud, censorious, uncharitable, sour, and unsociable; ready to

justify yourselves, and despise others, saying to them, "Stand by thyself, I am holier than thou"; much more if you take encouragement from thence to acts of injustice, fraud, or fleshly indulgence—your devotion is false, and looks like the sacrifice of the wicked, which is an abomination to the Lord. The frequent reviews you take of your hearts and lives in your closets should be in order to correct the irregularities and indecencies thereof. You should converse with God and yourselves there, that you may be the fitter to converse with the world. The devotion of the closet should appear in its good effects upon your conduct out of it; in the integrity, candor, and usefulness of your conversation; in the serenity of your minds, and cheerfulness of your behavior; and in every temper and action which become the gospel of Christ. In this manner go from strength to strength, daily conversing with God in secret, and showing openly to the world *whose you are*, and *whom you serve*; not by imprudent babbling about religious experience to everybody you meet with, but by a good conversation in Christ, which will be an authentic voucher for the reality of vital religion to the world around you, and will be the most effectual confutation of these who falsely accuse you on the score of religion.

Chapter 19
Liberality to the Poor Saints

From the beginning, a disposition to *take care of ourselves* was planted within us, without which we must have been indifferent about our safety, improvement, and comfort, or even life itself. It was therefore the first impression God made upon our minds; and we may observe too, that to this principle, revelation makes its first addresses, in order to excite us to think of redemption. A principle in itself most useful, and if attended to, productive of the best effects; while, by neglecting or acting contrary to its dictates, through indolence, or the service of divers lusts, we render ourselves no less guilty than when we violate her sister-principle, *love and goodwill to others*, by indulging what is more commonly allowed to be criminal selfishness.

Whenever the soul is made a partaker of a divine nature, according to the mercy and truth of the gospel of Christ, in regeneration, the spirit of corrupted selfishness, and its concomitant evils, begin to pass away; and the lost image of God, with all its happy fruits, are restored. In consequence of which, the person who has tasted that the Lord is gracious seeks not his own worldly profit, but the profit of many, that they may be saved. He then begins to consider the nature, and to discharge the duties of his stewardship, as one that is put in trust with the things of this life, in order to serve a public good, by showing mercy to the poor, and especially to the poor saints, that are of the household of faith:

> But whoso hath this world's good, and seeth his brother have need, and shutteth up his bowels of compassion from him, how dwelleth the love of God in him? My little children, let us not love in word, neither in tongue; but in deed and in truth (1 John 3:17–18).

In treating on the subject of liberal contributions to assist needy Christians, I shall attempt to do five things,

1. To explain the nature of this service.
2. To state the obligations that lie upon the saints to perform it.
3. To inquire whence this duty comes to be so much neglected.
4. To give some directions concerning the objects, measure, manner, and season of it. And,
5. To press upon the conscience a serious and practical regard to the duty, by some arguments.

1. An Account of the Nature of the Duty

I shall begin with some account of *the nature* of that *liberality to poor saints*, which is the subject of the present chapter.

If we believe a providence, we must own that God interests himself in the affairs of this life, to the enlarging of some, and lessening of others, as his infinite wisdom sees best. Even a heathen prince was brought, by God's awful dealings with him, to such a conviction, that "the most High ruleth in the kingdom of men, and giveth it to whomsoever he will," as to be constrained to acknowledge that "he doeth according to his will in the army of heaven, and among the inhabitants of the earth: and none can stay his hand, or say unto him, What doest thou?" (Dan. 4:32, 35). And this is the current doctrine of inspired writers, with respect to all ranks and degrees of men,

> The LORD maketh poor, and maketh rich: he bringeth low, and lifteth up. He raiseth up the poor out of the dust, and lifteth up the beggar from the dunghill, to set them among princes, and to make them inherit the throne of glory: for the pillars of the earth are the LORD's, and he hath set the world upon them (1 Sam. 2:7-8).

> For promotion cometh neither from the east, nor from the west, nor from the south. But God is the judge: he putteth down one, and setteth up another (Ps. 75:6-7).

> He poureth contempt upon princes, and causeth them to wander in the wilderness, where there is no way. Yet setteth he the poor on high from affliction, and maketh him families like a flock (Ps. 107:40-41).

This being the case, whoso is wise will observe these things; and, while he discerns a happy preference in his situation to that of his neighbor, will thankfully ascribe the praise of it to the love and kindness of the Lord. And because he well knows that the earth, and the fullness of it, is the Lord's, and that he hath given the enjoyment of it to the children of men, therefore he desires to honor the bountiful Giver of all his mercies, with that substance which the Lord hath given him, by *dispersing it abroad*, and *doing good as he hath opportunity, to all men, especially unto them who are of the household of faith* (Gal. 6:10).

Barely to distribute one's temporal substance, for the most useful purposes, and to the most worthy objects, does not deserve the glorious name of *Christian liberality*, unless it be accompanied with the following essential circumstances, *viz.*,

1. It must be *voluntary and cheerful*, without the compulsions of shame or fear. This is very clear from the repeated express directions about it: be "ready to...communicate" (1 Tim. 6:18). "He that sheweth mercy, with cheerfulness...distributing to the necessity of saints; given to hospitality" (Rom. 12:8, 13). "Every man according as he purposeth in his heart, so let him give; not grudgingly" etc. (2 Cor. 9:7).

2. It must be performed *as unto the Lord*; in obedience to his authority, and with a single view to his glory. This duty is called "pure religion, and undefiled before God and the Father" (James 1:27), which would be a wrong description, if it were not to be considered as a branch of holy worship, and to be performed out of respect to God. When it is practiced upon these principles, it becomes *a sacrifice with which God is well pleased* (Heb. 13:16).

3. What is done for the comfort of the saints must be done for them *in the name of Christ*, and on his account,

> He that receiveth you receiveth me, and he that receiveth me receiveth him that sent me. He that receiveth a prophet in the name of a prophet shall receive a prophet's reward; and he that receiveth a righteous man in the name of a righteous man shall receive a righteous man's reward. And whosoever shall give to drink unto one of these little ones a cup of cold water only in the name of a disciple, verily I say unto you, he shall in no wise lose his reward (Matt. 10:40–42).

They should be considered as sustaining the place of Christ himself; and entitled, in his behalf, to whatever we would reckon ourselves bound to do for him, in like circumstances. In as much as any office of humanity and love, the necessity of the saints requires, is done, upon these principles, to them, Christ reckons it to be done to himself (Matt. 25).

Where these circumstances concur, the *mercy* showed to the saints becomes an act of truly sincere and uncorrupted *worship*;[1] and it is approved and accepted of God in Christ. I shall now proceed,

2. The Obligations on Christians to It

To state *the obligations* that lie upon the saints to show mercy to the poor; and especially to their brethren in Christ. The arguments to prove this obligation are of several kinds; as,

1. The *pleasure* which God expresses in a compassionate spirit, or in giving to the poor, manifests it to be a duty exceedingly acceptable to God. God, who himself is mercy, delights in his own image, and therefore in the mercy exercised by his creatures. Doing good, and communicating, are sacrifices in which God is said to be well pleased. Charitable donations are an odor of sweet smell, a sacrifice acceptable and well-pleasing unto God. He is so infinitely delighted with charity, and so nearly concerned in it, that he tells us, "He that hath pity on the poor lendeth unto the LORD" (Prov. 19:17). God is equally pleased, as if himself received the charity at your hands. Our glorified Redeemer in heaven, and his poor members on earth, are joined together in so close, intimate, and indissoluble a union that what is done to his poor is actually and truly done to him, and as such he makes his estimation of it. *You have fed me*, will he say, *you have clothed me, you have visited me: inasmuch as you have done it to one of the least of these my little ones, you have done it to me: Come ye blessed of my Father.* And the blessings pronounced on a charitable man show how acceptable the service is to God. "Blessed is he that considereth the poor: the LORD will deliver him in time of trouble" (Ps. 41:1). "Blessed are the merciful: for they shall obtain mercy" (Matt. 5:7). These and such like innumerable

---

[1] I call *mercy to the poor an act of worship* for the same reason that I have treated of this duty in a performance, dedicated to the consideration of *religious worship*, its *general nature*, and *particular institutions*. The apostle's description of Christian beneficence, I apprehend, is a sufficient warrant for both, "Pure *religion* (θρησκεια), and undefiled before God and the Father, is this, to visit the fatherless and widows in their affliction" (James 1:27). The word rendered *religion* properly signifies *worship*; and there is no reason to depart from its natural meaning here; for as Manton on the place has observed, "Charity to the poor must be performed as worship, out of respect to God."

declarations of his mind, are incontestable evidences that God is greatly delighted in acts of charity; and consequently, that the saints should abound in them, as they have ability and opportunity, and thus walk worthy of the Lord unto all pleasing.

2. The *command of God* has made it the duty of saints to communicate to the necessities of the poor. And there are two very material circumstances in the representation of this command, in the writings of inspiration, that greatly strengthen this obligation. (1.) The precept concerning charity is *frequently* repeated. Everywhere throughout the Bible, God is calling us to cast our bread upon the waters (Eccl. 11:1); to do good, and to communicate (Heb. 13:16); to deal our bread to the hungry, and not to hide ourselves from our own flesh, nor stop our ears from hearing the cries of the poor (Isa. 58:7); he will have mercy rather than sacrifice (Hos. 6:6); and we are charged to be rich in good works, ready to distribute, and willing to communicate (1 Tim. 6:18). Numberless are the Scriptures where it is enjoined as a duty. (2.) The peculiar *fervor* and *forcible manner* in which this precept is delivered and urged discover the vast importance of the duty. What a variety of cogent motives and arguments does a merciful God make use of to induce and persuade us to show mercy! His terrible threatenings demonstrate with what high displeasure and angry resentments he regards the sordid miser, and ungiving churl. He that hides his eyes, shall have many a curse (Prov. 28:27); he shall have judgment without mercy, who has shown no mercy (James 2:13); whoso stoppeth his ears at the cry of the poor, shall cry himself, but shall not be heard (Prov. 21:13). The principal charge brought by our Lord against the herd of ungodly men is deficiency in this great duty; that they fed him not, when he was hungry; did not clothe him, when he was naked; did not minister to him, when he was sick and in prison; in a word, that they did nothing for him in his poor members (Matt. 25). Righteousness, joining hands with grace, enters into and adorns the character of the blessed God; and he has knit them together in the most lovely descriptions of his rational creatures. Mercy is made an inseparable companion or consequent of truth and righteousness. "By mercy and truth iniquity is purged" (Prov. 16:6). "Let not mercy and truth forsake thee" (Prov. 3:3). He is not a *righteous* man who is not *beneficent. God* having *showed unto men what is good*, requireth of them to *show mercy* (Mic. 6:8). Charity is a principal part of practical religion, "Pure religion and undefiled before God and the Father is this, To visit

the fatherless and widows in their affliction" (James 1:27). All pretenses to religion are vain without this; for if a man say, I love God, and loveth not his brother, he is a liar (1 John 4:20). "Whoso hath this world's good, and seeth his brother have need, and shutteth up his bowels of compassion from him, how dwelleth the love of God in him?" (1 John 3:17).

3. The *promises made to the bountiful hand* display the acceptableness of it to God. It is a branch of true godliness, which hath the "promise of the life that now is, and of that which is to come" (1 Tim. 4:8). The following passages may serve as examples of this.

> If there be among you a poor man of one of thy brethren within any of thy gates in thy land which the Lord thy God giveth thee, thou shalt not harden thine heart, nor shut thine hand from thy poor brother: but thou shalt open thine hand wide unto him, and shalt surely lend him sufficient for his need, in that which he wanteth. Beware that there be not a thought in thy wicked heart, saying, The seventh year, the year of release, is at hand; and thine eye be evil against thy poor brother, and thou givest him nought; and he cry unto the Lord against thee, and it be sin unto thee. Thou shalt surely give him, and thine heart shall not be grieved when thou givest unto him: because that for this thing the Lord thy God shall bless thee in all thy works, and in all that thou puttest thine hand unto. For the poor shall never cease out of the land: therefore I command thee, saying, Thou shalt open thine hand wide unto thy brother, to thy poor, and to thy needy, in thy land (Deut. 15:7–11).

> Honour the Lord with thy substance, and with the firstfruits of all thine increase: so shall thy barns be filled with plenty, and thy presses shall burst out with new wine (Prov. 3:9–10).

> There is that scattereth, and yet increaseth; and there is that withholdeth more than is meet, but it tendeth to poverty. The liberal soul shall be made fat: and he that watereth shall be watered also himself (Prov. 11:24–25).

> He that despiseth his neighbour sinneth: but he that hath mercy on the poor, happy is he (Prov. 14:21).

He that hath pity upon the poor lendeth unto the LORD; and that which he hath given will he pay him again (Prov. 19:17).

He that hath a bountiful eye shall be blessed; for he giveth of his bread to the poor (Prov. 22:9).

Cast thy bread upon the waters: for thou shalt find it after many days. Give a portion to seven, and also to eight; for thou knowest not what evil shall be upon the earth (Eccl. 11:1–2).

But when thou doest alms, let not thy left hand know what thy right hand doeth: that thine alms may be in secret: and thy Father which seeth in secret himself shall reward thee openly (Matt. 6:3–4).

Now when Jesus heard these things, he said unto him, Yet lackest thou one thing: sell all that thou hast, and distribute unto the poor, and thou shalt have treasure in heaven: and come, follow me (Luke 18:22).

But this I say, He which soweth sparingly shall reap also sparingly; and he which soweth bountifully shall reap also bountifully. Every man according as he purposeth in his heart, so let him give; not grudgingly, or of necessity: for God loveth a cheerful giver. And God is able to make all grace abound toward you; that ye, always having all sufficiency in all things, may abound to every good work: (as it is written, He hath dispersed abroad; he hath given to the poor: his righteousness remaineth for ever. Now he that ministereth seed to the sower both minister bread for your food, and multiply your seed sown, and increase the fruits of your righteousness;) being enriched in every thing to all bountifulness, which causeth through us thanksgiving to God. For the administration of this service not only supplieth the want of the saints, but is abundant also by many thanksgivings unto God (2 Cor. 9:6–12).

For God is not unrighteous, to forget your work and labor of love, which ye have showed toward his name, in that ye have ministered to the saints, and do minister (Heb. 6:10).

4. This duty has been *practiced* by an innumerable company of confessors for the truth, who have made it their business to open both their heart and hand, to assist the needy, and to supply the destitute. You that read the Bible must have observed that the anecdotes concerning their charity compose generally some part of the precious memoirs of the saints, contained in these sacred records. Time would fail me to reckon up the many, many examples of this kind you will find in the word of God. *Christ went about doing good;* and his people learn of him to love, and do good, upon the most useful and extensive scheme of unfeigned benevolence. The apostolic writings, both their *Acts* and *Epistles*, are the clearest proofs of this. Being compassed about with so great a cloud of witnesses, we should lay aside every weight, and the sin that doth so easily beset us, and contribute of our worldly substance for the relief of the poor, and especially of poor Christians, with a cheerful readiness.

Upon the whole, since God is *well-pleased* with this service, has *commanded* his saints to abound in it, and has *devised such great and precious promises* to the liberal man; and since the saints have so *generally practiced* it, both before and since Christ was manifested in the flesh, it follows that *this duty is of continuing obligation.* These arguments are the more convincing if we remember that the *providence* of God has always ordered human affairs upon such a plan, that *the rich and the poor meet together* in every age, and in every place; and as the Jews were told, that *the poor should never cease out of the land*; so Christ has told his disciples, that *the poor they would have always with them* (Prov. 22:2; Deut. 15:11; Matt. 26:11).

3. The Causes Why They Neglect It

The third point to be considered on this subject is to inquire whence this important duty comes to be so much neglected, by assigning some of *the causes why men shut up their bowels of compassion from the poor.*

1. Some are culpable herein, *by substituting a regard for other branches of religion in the room of this.* As there are some who seem not at all conscious of sin, even while they shamefully neglect the private and public worship of God; because they support a fair character among men, for their *justice* and *humanity*; so there are others, who enjoy peace in their minds, even while they do not conscientiously perform the duties of *justice, mercy,* and *charity*; because they are zealous for what they conceive to be truth, and

are regular in the services of divine worship. Thus were the Jews of old exceeding zealous for the rituals of religion, and grew, at length, to be very superstitious therein; insomuch that *they made void the commands of God, by the tradition of men* (Matt. 15:6), living in the notorious violation of the moral precepts of the eternal law of righteousness. This conduct of theirs gave occasion to the following, and many other severe reproofs, which we meet with in Scripture,

> Is it such a fast that I have chosen? a day for a man to afflict his soul? is it to bow down his head as a bulrush, and to spread sackcloth and ashes under him? wilt thou call this a fast, and an acceptable day to the LORD? Is not this the fast that I have chosen? to loose the bands of wickedness, to undo the heavy burdens, and to let the oppressed go free, and that ye break every yoke? Is it not to deal thy bread to the hungry, and that thou bring the poor that are cast out to thy house? when thou seest the naked, that thou cover him; and that thou hide not thyself from thine own flesh? (Isa. 58:5–7).

The real Christian feels the influence of the divine authority, in one, as well as in another of the commands of God, and labors to "stand perfect and complete in all the will of God" (Col. 4:12).

2. *Self-love*, which is condemned in Scripture (2 Tim. 3:2), amongst the most flagrant vices, is the very root of uncharitableness. It extinguishes tenderness and goodwill towards others. By it a man is so bound up in *himself* that, if he can but pursue his own inclinations, and gratify his desires, he is easy and content. In this manner he centers in himself, and makes himself his end, as if he bore no relation at all to his fellow-creatures, and was no way obliged to care for them, or to do them a good office. Thus many persons, under the powerful influence of a mistaken *self-interest*, as if born for themselves, shut up all bowels of compassion toward the miserable, who crave their assistance. And is there not a little room to suspect that some of the *gaudy ornaments of life* are the fruits of this bitter root of *self-love*, which operates to the prejudice of Christian liberality? A faithful conscience will tell us so, if the reason why we have little or nothing to spare for the hungry and the naked, is because we cannot retrench our superfluities, in the least, to assist them; but will gratify our vanity to the

utmost of our ability. A mind devoted to the love of the vain show of life will render us blind to all moving objects of charity, deaf to the cries of the poor, and hard-hearted towards the most miserable.

3. Another cause of the neglect of this duty may be *an overvaluing of earthly things;* for hereby a man is restrained from generous actions, for fear he should lessen that which he rates at much above its real worth. A man who will be ashamed to confess that he believes riches can make him happy can yet allow himself to set his heart on them, as if they could. He expects more satisfaction in them than in reason he ought, and takes a sordid pleasure in running his vast sums over in his own mind. He blesses his soul while he liveth, in thinking that hereafter it will be said of him, he died immensely rich, and that men of his own temper will praise him for having done well to himself (Ps. 49:18). So mean is the fare on which worldly minds can feed! They consider not wherein the true value of such things lies, *viz.*, in the ability they afford a man; of being useful in this world; and of laying up a good foundation against the time to come. And for want of that consideration it is, that many neglect so to employ them.

4. Too much *anxious thought* about futurity, and a *distrust* of the care of Providence, may be another reason why some men are backward to do good, and to communicate.

They have their *own families* to provide for, and therefore reckon they may very reasonably be excused; nor do their consciences much reproach them, for the cruel neglect of the poor, because they have persuaded themselves to think they have it not to spare this way. Without all question, every man ought to make proper provision for those of his own house; for he who does not this, "hath denied the faith, and is worse than an infidel" (1 Tim. 5:8). But here is the danger, lest men deceive themselves, while, under pretense of doing that which is lawful and necessary, they live in the neglect of some other branch of necessary and indispensable duty. What is *this making provision* for such as we may leave behind us? Is it nothing *less* than heaping together a prodigious portion of wealth for them? Must it be nothing *short* of advancing them to some eminent situation above their fellow-mortals? When once the minds of men come to be anxious about such things as these, and they govern not themselves by sober reason and Scripture, they naturally grow strait-handed in their charity, and are ready to grudge every sum they part with, to relieve their poor brethren.

Some having *little faith* in God and his providence, are really afraid *they shall want themselves* what they are solicited to bestow upon others; and for this reason, among others, they do not care to do much while they live; and are unwilling to part with what they have, till they can hold it no longer. Such persons may be said to *give as a matter of covetousness, not of bounty*, or goodwill (2 Cor. 9:5).

5. Many neglect this duty from a *want of that compassion*, and *tenderness of soul*, which the Scripture so much inculcates, and requires us to maintain. To cultivate this excellent temper, it is necessary for us often to consider the reasons and motives of that love we owe our fellow-Christians; such as, the wonderful love and pity of God to us sinners; and the grace of our Lord Jesus Christ, who, though he was rich, yet for our sakes became poor, that we, through his poverty, might be made rich; together with the multiplied exhortations of the gospel, to the practice of this duty. This would serve to excite our commiseration towards the necessitous and afflicted; it would be a means, under the influence of the Holy Spirit, to preserve this divine affection alive in our breasts; and it would dispose us to sympathize with, to pity and pray for, those we cannot help, and make us free-hearted and willing to assist those we can. But if we lay aside the Holy Scriptures, and their precious contents; if we suffer the views and motives of this world to possess our hearts; if we are overwhelmed in the busy affairs of life, or dissolved in luxury, ease, and pleasures—we shall hereby quench every spark of humanity, harden our hearts against the cries of the needy, and withhold our hands from this good work. And to add no more,

6. Persons' neglecting this duty is very much to be ascribed to their *forgetting that day*, in which they must *give an account of their stewardship, and be no longer stewards* (Luke 16:2). The estates that men now enjoy are God's property, and he has lent them the use of them a while. But the highest character they bear, who possess the things of this world, is that of *stewards of the manifold favors of God*. They are entrusted with these talents, and must be accountable to *the Lord of all* for the use they put them to. We are very apt to think these things to be more our own than they really are; and to dispose of them accordingly. We forget that as they are God's property, so he requires us to acknowledge this; and to do him homage for them, by allotting to his poor a due proportion out of them. The Scripture, therefore, when this duty is recommended, often directs men to look

forward to the great day of account, because particular inquiry will then be made concerning *works of beneficence* and *charity*, as our blessed Savior has assured us (Matt. 25), and every man will then reap according as he has sown (2 Cor. 9). A serious remembrance of this tremendous day, and of the account we are then to give of our stewardship, would excite in us a holy fear, lest we should be found to have abused the talents which God has entrusted us with, to other purposes than those for which he gave them us. But if we are so unwise as to live unmindful of it, no wonder, if, other motives prevailing on us to *forget to do good*, with the blessings God has given us, we lay a foundation for the unwelcome painful remembrance of our having been *unjust stewards* in a dying hour, and in the future world.

These are some of the most powerful and dangerous causes of people neglecting to embrace the opportunities which the providence of God is daily giving them, and which the authority of God obliges them to improve, for doing good to the indigent. They are all faulty, and some of them generally reckoned odious; and yet how extensive is their operation! I have endeavored to set them forth in their own light, that, when they are discerned to be what they really are, everyone that reads this account of them, may either carefully avoid them, or else be without excuse, if he persevere in this sinful course. I shall conclude the section with that beautiful passage,

> If I have withheld the poor from their desire, or have caused the eyes of the widow to fail; or have eaten my morsel myself alone, and the fatherless hath not eaten thereof; (for from my youth he was brought up with me, as with a father, and I have guided her from my mother's womb;) if I have seen any perish for want of clothing, or any poor without covering; if his loins have not blessed me, and if he were not warmed with the fleece of my sheep; if I have lifted up my hand against the fatherless, when I saw my help in the gate: then let mine arm fall from my shoulder blade, and mine arm be broken from the bone. For destruction from God was a terror to me, and by reason of his highness I could not endure. If I have made gold my hope, or have said to the fine gold, Thou art my confidence; if I rejoiced because my wealth was great, and because mine hand had gotten much; if I beheld the sun when it shined, or the moon walking in brightness; and my heart hath been secretly enticed, or my

mouth hath kissed my hand: this also were an iniquity to be punished by the judge: for I should have denied the God that is above (Job 31:16–28).

4. The Objects, Measure, Manner, and Season of It

I shall now attempt to give same proper *directions* concerning the *objects, measure, manner*, and *season* of Christian liberality to the needy, in their distressed situations.

1. The *objects* of Christian charity are described by the apostle, when he says, "As we have therefore opportunity, let us do good unto all men, especially unto them who are of the household of faith" (Gal. 6:10). The general object, about which this duty is conversant, is very large, and takes in *all mankind*. The *Jews*, who were in many respects *a typical people*, were prohibited familiarity with idolatrous nations, though they were expressly enjoined by their law to be kind to strangers, because they themselves had been strangers in the land of Egypt; and from this prohibition they took occasion to look upon themselves as perfectly discharged from all obligation of kindness to the rest of mankind. But our Savior hath rescued this law of charity from such corrupt glosses, and explained its natural and original extent, both in his sermon on the mount, and in the parable of the compassionate Samaritan, and in the whole scope of his ministry.

Love to mankind implies not only *wishing them well*, and *speaking well of them*, but *doing them all the good offices we can*, by friendly counsel, and by communicating to their necessities upon proper occasions. And here it may be profitable to observe the following rules. (1.) Cases of *extremity* ought to take the first place; and do for that time challenge precedence of all other considerations. If a person be in great and present distress, and his necessity so urgent that, if he be not immediately relieved, he must perish, this is so violent a case, and calls so loud for present help, that there is no resisting of it, whatever the person be. If our enemy be in extremity, then that divine precept takes place, "if thine enemy hunger, feed him; if he thirst, give him drink" (Rom. 12:20). (2.) The obligations of *nature*, and the *nearness of relation*, challenge a considerable preference; for there is all the reason in the world, if other things be equal, that we should supply the necessity of those who are of our blood and kindred, before the necessities of strangers that have no relation to us. Not only Christianity, but nature ties this duty upon us, "if any provide not for his own, and specially for those of his own house, he hath denied the faith, and is worse than an infidel" (1 Tim. 5:8), that is, he doth not only violate the law of Christianity, but he sins against the very dictates of nature, which prevail even amongst infidels. (3.) Obligations of *kindness and benefits* lay the next claim to our charity. If they fall into want, who have obliged us by their former benevolence, both justice and charity do challenge from us a very particular consideration of their case; and proportionably, if we have been obliged to their family, or to any that are nearly related unto them,

> And David said, Is there yet any that is left of the house of Saul, that I may shew him kindness for Jonathan's sake?... And David said unto him, Fear not: for I will surely shew thee kindness for Jonathan thy father's sake, and will restore thee all the land of Saul thy father; and thou shalt eat bread at my table continually (2 Sam. 9:1, 7).

(4.) The *character* of persons, and all the *circumstances* of their condition, are to be considered in the objects of our charity; and, upon a fair comparison, the industrious poor man is to be preferred to the sluggard in his rags; the man who had been liberal, to the churl; the wise man, to the fool; the aged, to the youthful; and the infirm, to the stout and healthful. (5.) Those whose distressed situation is *really known* to us are to be considered as the objects of charity sooner, at least in a larger measure, than those we do not certainly know.

But our charitable benefactions are *especially due to the household of faith*; that is, to the saints of the Most High, who have embraced, and make profession of, the faith of the gospel. God has mercifully provided a goodly heritage for his people, for all things are theirs, whether Paul, or Apollos, or Cephas, or the world, or life, or death, or things present, or things to come; all are theirs, for they are Christ's (1 Cor. 3:21–23). But notwithstanding this provision for their complete and everlasting welfare, an infinitely wise and gracious God, who hath not called many noble persons, but hath chosen the poor of this world to be the heirs of that kingdom, which was prepared before the foundation of the world—has, in many instances, especially under the New Testament dispensation, appointed them to an indigent depending lot; partly, to try their own faith and patience; and partly, to give an occasion to their brethren in the faith of the gospel, to show their liberality in doing them good, purely in obedience to the command of God, without looking for any worldly recompense. The poor saints have a very particular claim to the charity of the people of God: for (1.) They are heirs of the same everlasting, great, and precious promises with their richer brethren. (2.) They have no other dependence under God, being hated of the world for the sake of Christ. (3.) They are pensioned, so to speak, upon their fellow-citizens of the household of God, who hath commanded his people, with a peculiar view to such a case, to "not love in word, neither in tongue; but in deed and in truth," by substantial proofs of unfeigned affection (1 John 3:18). And (4.) They represent Christ himself unto his people; and therefore what is done to them, he reckons to be done to him; and what is not done to them, he reckons to be not done to him. On all these accounts, the apostle might justly place an emphasis on the charity of believers, requiring them to "do good...*especially* unto them who are of the household of faith" (Gal. 6:10).

2. The *measure* or *degree* of Christian beneficence comes next under consideration. It would be an easy thing with God to level men's estates, and to give everyone a competency; but he does on purpose suffer things to be distributed so unequally, to try and exercise the virtues of men in several ways; for instance, the faith and patience of the poor, the contentedness of those in a middle condition, and the charity and bounty of the rich. And indeed *wealth and riches*, that is, an estate above what sufficeth a person's real occasions and necessities, is in no other sense a blessing than as it is an opportunity and ability put into his hands by the providence of God, of doing more good; and if he does not faithfully employ it to this end, it is but a temptation and a snare; and the rust of his silver and his gold will be a witness against him, and he doth but heap up treasures against the day of wrath.

But what proportion our charity ought to bear to our estates is difficult precisely to determine. The circumstances of mankind have too much variety in them to admit of any certain rule. In general, it may be safely affirmed that, if there be first a free and willing mind, a man will be generous and bountiful to his power, for the liberal man will devise liberal things (Isa. 32:8). He will not only *look* with compassion on the distresses of mankind, but will *open his hand* to give his bread to the poor; nor will he think it enough to wish well to others, unless he be also ready to do them good. When he says, *Be thou warmed*, and, *Be thou filled*, he speaks the language of his heart; but he considers too that unless this temper of mind operates with strength enough to influence his practice, in a regular conformity to his expressions, his *charity* will be like that *faith*, which is *dead being alone* (James 2:16–17). The *liberal man* (and this should be the character of every man) has a bountiful soul, and his whole conduct is under the direction of *the law of kindness*. He doth not only spare to the poor what he is incapable of enjoying himself, nor only leave the execution of his charitable designs to others, when he is dead and gone; but he readily denies himself many gratifications in life, that he may be the better able to do his duty in this respect, and that he may indulge his heart in the noblest pleasure of doing good. Nor doth he only do a generous action *now and then*; but a series of goodness and charity runs through the *whole tenor of his life*.[2] (Gal. 6:10).

In order to enable us to "abound in this grace," as the apostle speaks (2 Cor. 8:7), it may be very useful to observe the following directions. (1.) Christians should contrive how to manage what they have acquired, by the blessing of God upon their honest labors, with the *best economy*; and should wisely study how to regulate all expenses upon their own persons and families, with such a frugality as may enable them to be the more liberal to the poor. The psalmist describes and commends this conduct, when he says, "A good man sheweth favour, and lendeth," and that he may be capable of doing so, "he will guide his affairs *with discretion*" (Ps. 112:5). (2.) They should *wisely consider* the case of the poor (Ps. 41:1), and order their distributions according to their several conditions and necessities. When, by the favor of an indulgent providence, their hands are at liberty, their hearts should be so likewise, that they may give something out of their superfluities to *others' conveniences*; out of their conveniences, to *others' necessities*; and out of what may be called their necessaries, to *others' extremities*. (3.) They ought to employ all their wisdom and prudence, in order

---

[2] Some have labored to prove that a *tenth part of our income* is the precise proportion of Christian liberality; because this was the measure of the charity to be contributed for the purposes of the Levites, and of the poor in Israel; but for aught I see, it will be as easy to prove that Christians should still have *all things common*, as they were for a time at Jerusalem in the apostolic age. Both the case of Israel, and the case of these primitive Christians, were *singular*, in some respects; and arguments from them are not absolutely conclusive. Sometimes Christians may not have a call to give one *twentieth part* of their increase in a year to the poor; and it is easy to conceive many cases wherein they are called to such extraordinary liberality that it would become their sin to reserve *any of their gains* in the course of a year, because the Lord hath need of them. The best rule is *"as we have opportunity"* (χαιρον; or *a convenient season and occasion*), *let us do good"*

to dispose of their bounty in the *best manner*, and to the most advantageous purposes, for the help and comfort of the destitute. And (4.) They should daily consider that all they have in a present world is the Lord's; and he has given them the use of it; but with this express reservation, that they shall *honor him with their substance* (Prov. 3:9). The most generous and liberal soul has good reason to say, when he has showed mercy to the poor to the utmost extent of his ability, *I am but an unprofitable servant, and have only done that which was my duty to do.* He may say of his and others' contributions to the poor what David said of his and his people's contributions for the temple,

> Thine, O LORD, is the greatness, and the power, and the glory, and the victory, and the majesty: for all that is in the heaven and in the earth is thine; thine is the kingdom, O LORD, and thou art exalted as head above all. Both riches and honour come of thee, and thou reignest over all; and in thine hand is power and might; and in thine hand it is to make great, and to give strength unto all. Now therefore, our God, we thank thee, and praise thy glorious name. But who am I, and what is my people, that we should be able to offer so willingly after this sort? for all things come of thee, and of thine own have we given thee. For we are strangers before thee, and sojourners, as were all our fathers: our days on the earth are as a shadow, and there is none abiding…I know also, my God, that thou triest the heart, and hast pleasure in uprightness. As for me, in the uprightness of mine heart I have willingly offered all these things: and now have I seen with joy thy people, which are present here, to offer willingly unto thee. O LORD God of Abraham, Isaac, and of Israel, our fathers, keep this for ever in the imagination of the thoughts of the heart of thy people, and prepare their heart unto thee (1 Chron. 29:11–17).

3. The *manner* of supplying the wants of the poor is to be considered in the next place. Here a variety of directions may be offered from the word of God, which teaches us to perform this service of love (1.) *In the privatest manner*, without any ostentation,

> Take heed that ye do not your alms before men, to be seen of them: otherwise ye have no reward of your Father which is in heaven. Therefore when thou doest thine alms, do not sound a trumpet before thee, as the hypocrites do in the synagogues and in the streets, that they may have glory of men. Verily I say unto you, They have their reward. But when thou doest alms, let not thy left hand know what thy right hand doeth: that thine alms may be in secret: and thy Father which seeth in secret himself shall reward thee openly (Matt. 6:1–4).

To give our alms before men has too much the appearance of doing it for our own sakes, that we may have praise of men; and not for the sake of God, and the comfort of the needy. That expression, "when thou doest thine alms... let not thy left hand know what thy right hand doeth," has a singular beauty, and intimates, that we should hide our acts of charity, even from the applauses of our own mind, and much more from our most intimate acquaintances. People offend against this rule when they take a pleasure in reckoning up the favors they have conferred, in order to raise their reputation for being very generous; whereas it would better become them to record these undeserved bounties of a kind Providence that enabled them to do such generous offices. (2.) *With great cheerfulness*, "Every man according as he purposeth in his heart, so let him give; not grudgingly, or of necessity: for God loveth a cheerful giver" (2 Cor. 9:7). Love operates with delightful satisfaction towards its object; constraint, which implies any force upon the mind to cross its own inclination, in doing what is disagreeable to its governing principles, is quite a different thing. Beneficence should always be *an act of love*, and therefore performed with delight, in opposition to all grudging, or necessity, reluctance, or constraint; for God loveth a cheerful giver, and none else. (3.) *According to our ability*, "Upon the first day of the week let every one of you lay by him in store, as God hath prospered him" (1 Cor. 16:2). Distinguished blessings of Providence demand suitable acknowledgments to the poor, for whom nothing of that kind is provided; and God, who giveth power to get wealth, demands this tribute to his poor, from these whom he hath placed in a comfortable situation. Is it decent, or reasonable, or grateful, to give with a sparing hand to a poor brother, when God has made our cup to overflow? And I may add, is it consistent with this rule, for people to make no advances in their charitable distributions, when Providence has kindly increased their substance? Shall men trade more largely for this world, and yet neglect to honor the Lord with more of that substance he hath given them? (4.) When we give alms, we should guard against every apprehension of *meriting* anything by what we have done. Our pride naturally inclines us to deal with God upon terms; and none appear to be more agreeable to a carnal mind than to secure the favor of God by giving a little of the superfluities of life we cannot enjoy ourselves; and then we fancy we have done something meritorious, because we suppose there was no previous obligation upon us to dispose of our worldly substance in that manner. Such *glorying is not good*; for we are not the original proprietors, either of what we have, or of what we give; and therefore the apostle's reasoning is pertinent and conclusive, when applied to this case, "For who maketh thee to differ from another? and what hast thou that thou didst not receive? now if thou didst receive it, why dost thou glory, as if thou hadst not received it?" (1 Cor. 4:7). "And if some of the branches be broken off, and thou, being a wild olive tree, wert graffed in among them, and with them partakest of the root and fatness of the olive tree; boast not against the branches. But if thou boast, thou bearest not the root, but the root thee" (Rom. 11:17–18). I proceed now to consider,

4. The *seasons* of showing mercy to the poor and indigent. The general rule on that head is laid down, "Withhold not good from them to whom it is due, when it is in the power of thine hand to do it. Say not unto thy neighbour, Go, and come again, and to morrow I will give; when thou hast it by thee" (Prov. 3:27–28). This is the general rule; and to render it useful and practicable in daily life, I shall suggest the following directions concerning it. (1.) Seasonably relieve such as are *falling into decay* in the world, as ye have opportunity. As the keeping of a man that is stumbling, from quite falling down, is much alike with helping him up when he is fallen; so the relieving of a man when he is at the brink of poverty is much alike with helping him in it. This duty I take to be aimed at, " love ye your enemies, and do good, and lend, hoping for nothing again" (Luke 6:35). And if we were more exercised this way, there would be fewer poor than there are. (2.) Do not fail to abound in *private distributions* to the poor, at your houses, or otherwise, as you have occasion, "to do good and to communicate forget not: for with such sacrifices God is well pleased" (Heb. 13:16). Occasions of this nature are common in daily life, which try what sort of stewards

you are of the good things which Providence has put into your hand. It was Job's comfort in his poverty, that, when he was wealthy, he had communicated of what he had to the poor (Job 31). (3.) Conscientiously give in to *the Sabbath's collections*, to be distributed by the church. God has enjoined these gatherings to be made every first day of the week, "Upon the first day of the week let every one of you lay by him in store, as God hath prospered him" (1 Cor. 16:2). And the Lord Jesus hath appointed church officers, particularly, to take the oversight of the poor (Acts 6:1–3). So that this matter of the *Sabbath-day's collections* is not to be looked upon as a business of mere fashion, or an indifferent affair; but as a divine ordinance in the church of Christ; a consideration which should make people, out of conscience towards God, to give into it, in a suitable proportion to the substance God has put in their hands. (4.) Grudge not *extraordinary distributions*, not only for the relief of those of *other congregations* you are connected with; but even of *other churches*, whom you never saw, and perhaps never will see, in the flesh; "it hath pleased them of Macedonia and Achaia to make a certain contribution for the poor saints which are at Jerusalem" (Rom. 15:26). This is a duty of the communion of saints; for all the churches and congregations of saints in the whole world make but the *one body of Christ*; and they who are at the greatest distance from one another, being the members of Christ, are brethren one to another. Therefore, do not reckon yourselves unconcerned in their distresses; and do not withhold that assistance their case requires. And (5.) Be ready to give of your substance for *pious uses*, towards the promoting of the good of mankind; and especially towards the advancing of the good of the body of Christ. There are several occasions people have of laying out their worldly substance for pious uses, which want of due consideration makes them either to neglect altogether, or to do grudgingly and sparingly. But if you have an occasion put into your hand, by *the mammon of unrighteousness*, to honor God, to bring about good to mankind, or to contribute to the good of the church, you are to look on it as an opportunity you ought to embrace, for bestowing it to a noble purpose. "Honour the LORD with thy substance" (Prov. 3:9). Compare Ecclesiastes 9:10, "Whatsoever thy hand findeth to do, do it with thy might; for there is no work, nor device, nor knowledge, nor wisdom, in the grave, whither thou goest."

This much shall suffice on the head of directions, concerning the objects, measure, manner, and season of Christian liberality to the poor. I shall now shut up the subject, by attempting, in the last place,

5. A Regard to the Duty Pressed

To press upon the conscience *a serious and practical regard* to this duty, by some arguments. This is a very large field for employing all the topics of persuasive eloquence that are calculated to strike the inmost principles of action in the soul with a commanding energy. I shall only suggest the following considerations to such as fear God; and may the Holy Ghost give them their due effect!

1. To be charitable to the poor is *conformable to right reason*, and *dictated by the natural conscience*. Reason teaches mankind not only to wish well to their fellow-creatures but to do them good, and to exert themselves, as there may be occasion, in acts of beneficence. Surely it does not become men, whom their Creator has endued with bowels of kindness, to point all their labors and endeavors at their *single-selves*, exclusive of those about them, who need their assistance. Nature teaches you, O Christians! that you were not born for yourselves alone. You are debtors, *as men*, to the community of beings to which you belong; and obliged, by the ties of natural relation and natural reason, to subserve the common interest of all, so far as it is in the power of your hands to do it, and to interest yourselves in the distresses of others, so far as to relieve, or even, if possible, to remove them. Do not render yourselves monsters, inhuman, and unnatural, by withholding more than is meet.

2. This duty *becomes your character*, as the people of God: I beseech you therefore, brethren, holy and beloved, as the elect of God, put on bowels of mercy and compassion, towards Christ in his distressed members (Col. 3:12). Your character, as *the elect of God*, whom he hath chosen to partake of one Spirit, to be justified in one righteousness, to be heirs of the common salvation, to have a suffering lot with his saints in a present evil world, and to be ever with the Lord in heaven, employed in concert with the church of the firstborn—this your character obliges you to put on *bowels of mercy and compassion*. And if you have no zeal in this service of love to the saints for Christ's sake, you would be more consistent with yourselves, to throw off all professed relation to him, rather than to shelter yourselves under a name, that will be a standing monument of your

shame, and will continually reproach your neglect of this leading duty of pure and undefiled religion.

3. "Remember the words of the Lord Jesus, how he said, *It is more blessed to give than to receive*" (Acts 20:35). Glorious and persuasive words! O that they were truly believed! then we would honor them in our daily practice. How powerfully do they impel the mind that is impressed with them unto a cheerful compliance with the duty! They are *the words of the Lord Jesus*, whose lips are like lilies, dropping sweet-smelling myrrh, and whose mouth is most sweet. *He said, It is more blessed to give than to receive*; which evidently implies that it is a greater happiness, comfort, and honor; more God-like, and acceptable to him; and derives a more signal blessing from him—to do good in acts of charity to the poor, than to receive benefactions from others, or even than to increase in worldly stores.

Has the great mercy of God put you in so comfortable a situation of life, as to have wherewithal to give unto him that needs? This is more blessed, and matter of more thankfulness to God, than if you were under a necessity of receiving. A poor man is reckoned a mournful character; his poverty calls for compassion. Remember, ye rich and affluent! that, having received more from the hand of God than others, you are under stronger obligations to scatter abroad, and to honor God by relieving his poor.

Are your circumstances more narrow? Observe that command, "Let him that stole steal no more: but rather let him labour, working with his hands the thing which is good, that he may have to give to him that needeth" (Eph. 4:28). And propose the apostle for your pattern,

> Yea, ye yourselves know, that these hands have ministered unto my necessities, and to them that were with me. I have shewed you all things, how that so labouring ye ought to support the weak, and to remember the words of the Lord Jesus, how he said, It is more blessed to give than to receive (Acts 20:34–35).

Does not the very act of *giving* afford pleasure to a generous mind? A bountiful man shall be satisfied from himself. He enjoys an inward delight and satisfaction in relieving the indigent, arising from an apprehension of usefulness to his fellow-creature, and from a conscious sense of having done a duty, which he knows to be a sacrifice well-pleasing to God. And,

Generous sentiments inhabiting a believer's bosom, and prompting his hands upon Christian principles to useful benefactions, will render the reflection agreeable, and will administer future pleasure; nor can he recollect his bounties without singular comfort and joy; for his charity will turn to him for a testimony in life, at death, and at the day of judgment. How widely different from this are all sensual pleasures, which soon die and vanish! But that is not the worst of them, they leave a sting behind them; and when the pleasure is gone, nothing remains but guilt, and trouble, and repentance.

Upon the whole, I beseech you who profess to believe in Christ, and to be followers of him, to remember the words of the Lord Jesus, how he said, *It is more blessed to give than to receive.* This was not *a bare speculation*, a fine and elegant saying, like those of *the philosophers*, who said great and glorious things, but did them not; but this was his *constant practice*, and the great business of his life. He who pronounced it the most blessed thing *to give*, spent his whole life in *going about, doing good.* This was the life which God himself, when he was pleased to become man, thought fit to lead in the world, *giving us herein an example, that we should follow his steps.* He made full trial of the blessedness of this temper and spirit; for he was all on the giving hand. And shall not his *words*, which are rendered more weighty from his *example* in the work of giving, and from his *experience* of being blessed in this deed, recommend this practice to his people? If these things have no weight with others, yet they must, and certainly will, constrain all who follow the Lord Jesus Christ, as dear children, to esteem and pursue the superior blessedness arising from their doing good to all men in distress, as they have opportunity, and especially to the household of faith.

4. Consider *the tendency* of liberality and of covetousness, which affords an encouraging motive to induce all that have any regard to the honor of God, or to their own interest, to be bountiful, and to beware of covetousness,

> The desire of the righteous is only good: but the expectation of the wicked is wrath. There is that scattereth, and yet increaseth; and there is that withholdeth more than is meet, but it tendeth to poverty. The liberal soul shall be made fat: and he that watereth shall

be watered also himself. He that withholdeth corn, the people shall curse him: but blessing shall be upon the head of him that selleth it (Prov. 11:23–26).

If we take the 24th verse to be allusive to the management of a husbandman in sowing his seed, the sense will stand as easy as the thought will be beautiful and just; for everyone knows, that the more plentifully the husbandman scatters abroad his seed, in proper proportions, he is so far from losing his corn, which he has sown, that, by the ordinary blessing of Providence, he reaps the better crop in its season; and, on the other hand, that he, who through a niggardly temper, will not allow a sufficient quantity of seed for sowing his ground, will certainly have but a scanty harvest. As this is evidently true in the literal sense, relating to the natural world, so it holds equally good when applied to the moral world, and particularly to the liberality of contributing to the relief of the indigent,

> But this I say, He which soweth sparingly shall reap also sparingly; and he which soweth bountifully shall reap also bountifully. Every man according as he purposeth in his heart, so let him give; not grudgingly, or of necessity: for God loveth a cheerful giver. And God is able to make all grace abound toward you; that ye, always having all sufficiency in all things, may abound to every good work…being enriched in every thing to all bountifulness, which causeth through us thanksgiving to God (2 Cor. 9:6–11).

5. Call to mind the *express command*, and the *daily example* of God, your heavenly Father, who is bountifully adding to your store of blessings, every season, every day, and every moment; and be stirred up to do this good and acceptable will of God,

> Give to him that asketh thee, and from him that would borrow of thee turn not thou away. Ye have heard that it hath been said, Thou shalt love thy neighbour, and hate thine enemy. But I say unto you, Love your enemies, bless them that curse you, do good to them that hate you, and pray for them which despitefully use you, and persecute you; that ye may be the children of your Father which is in heaven: for he maketh his sun to rise on the evil and on the good,

and sendeth rain on the just and on the unjust. For if ye love them which love you, what reward have ye? do not even the publicans the same? And if ye salute your brethren only, what do ye more than others? do not even the publicans so? Be ye therefore perfect, even as your Father which is in heaven is perfect (Matt. 5:42–48).

Last of all,

6. Consider "the grace of our Lord Jesus Christ, that...for your sakes he became poor, that ye through his poverty might be rich" (2 Cor. 8:9). In the preceding discourse, the apostle had been exhorting the Corinthians to a liberal abounding charity towards poor Christians; and that not from constraint, but willingly. He proposes to them in the verse I have quoted, as a powerful motive to this duty, that the everlasting, free, and sovereign love of Jesus Christ engaged him to do and suffer infinitely more to make his people happy than was required of them in order to the assistance of poorer saints. And could he offer a more mighty argument to those who knew the invaluable benefits of Christ's purchase, and his incomprehensible grace and condescension in making it for us? This argument loses nothing of its force by any length of time. Allow me to set it before your view in the following light:

Seriously and often reflect upon the surprising greatness of the free favor, love, and bounty of our Lord Jesus Christ, who, though, as the eternal Son of God, he was originally possessed of all the perfection, blessedness, and glory of the Deity, yet, in marvelous compassion to sinful and ruined men, he humbled himself, and became of no reputation, he became a man of sorrows, and submitted, in the form of a servant, to *the deepest poverty*, amongst all his other sufferings unto death; consider also his most benevolent *design* in all these condescensions, which was, that we who are wretched, and miserable, and poor, and blind, and naked in ourselves, might, on account, and by means of his extreme poverty, be enriched with all the blessings of grace and glory, and with as many of the good things of this life, as he sees to be best for us. Carefully think on these things; and if, after you have considered them, you remain destitute of compassion towards the poor and afflicted members of Christ; or if your contributions for them be disproportionate and scanty, how will ye in any measure answer the munificent *grace of our Lord Jesus Christ?* How do you conform to his *example*, which carries in it the highest obligation and endearment?

Ah! how obdurate must that heart be, how ungrateful and unfeeling that breast, which rebels against the command, disregards the example, and despises the love of a condescending, dying Savior, "who, though he was rich, yet for our sakes became poor?" Had the kind Redeemer such a concern for them that are poor in this world? and should not you reckon it one of the most honorable, and most delightful services you can perform, to contribute to the comfort of these, who shall by and by come out of all their tribulations, and enter into the boundless everlasting joys of their Lord?

Chapter 20
Swearing by the Name of God

The importance of this subject is universally allowed among all sensible men, and in every civilized country, where an oath for confirmation is used as the happiest means of putting an end to all strife. In this light it is represented in the book of God (Heb. 6:16); and it has been always considered by the wisest heathens, as the best expedient human prudence could ever devise for this purpose. It is the most solemn and authentic security upon mankind for *integrity* and *veracity*; to induce them to give an honest declaration of their inmost sentiments, and to bind them to a behavior corresponding to a determined plan. Whatever is most worthy of consideration on this subject, will naturally fall into one or other of the following heads, which I shall propose, and explain as briefly as I can.

1. To give a short account of the nature of an oath.
2. To show that it is warrantable for Christians, upon just occasions, to swear by the name of God.
3. To inquire in what manner an oath should be taken.
4. To represent the important purposes, for which it may be safely and honorably used.
5. To answer a few questions relative to it. And,
6. To deduce some inferences from the subject.

1. The Nature of an Oath

I proposed, in the first place, to give a short account of *the nature of an oath*. It may be defined, *A solemn invocation of God, or an appeal to him, as the witness of the truth, and consequently the avenger of the falsehood, of what men assert, or promise to one another, in weighty and doubtful matters.* This description includes the *two kinds* of oaths, which are usually taken notice of by writers on this subject; *viz.*, *assertory* and *promissory* oaths. *An assertory oath* relates to the *time past* or *present*; as when a person affirms of anything, that it was, or is, such as he relates it to be. *A promissory oath* refers to the *time to come*; as when a person promises to do a thing, or not to do it, as the nature and different circumstances of the case may require. When such promises are made to men, by solemnly calling upon God to witness them, and to avenge the breach of them, they are a formal oath.

In order to represent this matter in the easiest light, I shall make the following observations.

1. God is *omniscient, almighty, righteous*, and *unchangeable*. He is *omniscient*, for "the eyes of the LORD are in every place, beholding the evil and the good" (Prov. 15:3), "Hell and destruction are before the LORD: how much more then the hearts of the children of men?" (Prov. 15:11). "Neither is there any creature that is not manifest in his sight: but all things are naked and opened unto the eyes of him with whom we have to do" (Heb. 4:13). He is *Almighty*, and his right hand is full of power; he is "a consuming fire" (Heb. 12:29), neither is there "any that [can] deliver out of his hand" (Dan. 8:4). He is *just and righteous*, "surely God will not do wickedly, neither will the Almighty pervert judgment" (Job 34:12), "the righteous LORD loveth righteousness" (Ps. 11:7), and will exercise it, in judging the world, "by that man whom he hath ordained" (Acts 17:31), and in revealing his wrath "from heaven against all ungodliness and unrighteousness of men" (Rom. 1:18). And he is *the Lord that changeth not*, being "the same yesterday, and to day, and for ever" (Heb. 13:8), whose eternal boundless perfection admits of no variableness, neither shadow of turning.

2. These perfections of God rise so naturally to the thoughts of mankind, when they consider him as the Creator, Preserver, and Governor of the universe; and when they reflect upon the suggestions, hopes, and fears of their consciences, aided by the instructions of others; that they are left without excuse, if they profanely attempt to suppress their conviction, by resisting the evidence, which is so clear, that *heathens* have confessed it, while the Scriptures abound in the most comfortable representations of the Deity, in reference to these perfections.

3. Mankind have many weighty concerns with one another, which depend entirely upon their *mutual confidence* in each others' *integrity* and *veracity*, as their best security; both for public good, and for private property, safety, and interest.

4. Mankind are become so ingenious in the arts of dissimulation and fraud that an *higher security* than their *bare word* is sometimes necessary for removing suspicions, and for establishing confidence. Hence all the useful devices of leading several witnesses concerning a fact that is past or present;

and of confirming and even combining obligations, respecting things to be performed at some future time.

5. There are some cases, so important in their nature, and yet so particular in their circumstances, that no adequate provision can be made to secure the confidence of mankind in one another, except by an appeal, in the most solemn manner, to the all-seeing, omnipotent, righteous, and unchangeable God, who made, upholds, and governs all his creatures; and who will judge the world at last, rendering to everyone according to his works (2 Cor. 5:10).

6. Such appeals to God, being the highest evidence that can be brought in favor of a person's veracity, and of his future conduct, are the *last resort* for putting an end to strife in important disputes about facts; and, where full evidence to the contrary cannot be had, should be acquiesced in, as finally decisive.

7. Oaths, or solemn appeals to God, are a part of the *religious worship* which is due to God only; "Thou shalt fear the LORD thy God…and shalt swear by his name" (Deut. 6:13). To *fear the Lord* is a general expression which comprehends every religious duty, and among others, that of *swearing by his name*, which is particularly mentioned as one instance. Hereby God is acknowledged as a sovereign Lord, as a present observer of our ways, as a righteous judge, and as the Most High, who is Lord of lords, and God of gods. A religious person is accordingly described to be one *that sweareth by the name of God* (Ps. 63:11).

8. The appeal which the swearer makes unto the Lord is either expressed in *words*, or manifested by *signs*, or it is showed by *both together*. Job's oath concerning his integrity (Job 16:19), the appeal of the *widow of Zarephath* (1 Kings 17:12), and of Ittai the Gittite (2 Sam. 15:21), are examples of expressing an oath in *words*, probably without any sign. It does not seem that all the priests and the Levites, the captains of hundreds, and the chief of the fathers of Israel, of whom Jehoiada took an oath (2 Kings 11:4), repeated the express words of the oath, but only manifested their acquiescing in a form of words used, by some confirming sign. But in many other cases the appeal was *both* expressed in words, and manifested by signs; as in the oaths of Abraham (Gen. 14:22–23); of Eliezer (Gen. 24:2–4); and of Joseph (Gen. 47:29–31).

9. Oaths are only to be used on *such occasions*, when the edification of our neighbors makes them expedient. To swear by the name of God with any other view would be to take his holy name in vain.

2. The Warrant for Swearing by the Name of God

I come now to show that it is *warrantable for Christians*, upon just occasions, to swear by the name of God. To swear by the blessed God is so far from being an evil and impious action that, on the contrary, when used on proper and necessary occasions, it is every way honorable and advantageous. For,

1. The *unavoidable condition of human affairs* hath made oaths necessary. The apostle takes it for granted that an oath is not only of great use in human affairs, but in many cases of great necessity, to confirm a doubtful thing, and to put an end to controversies, which cannot otherwise be decided to the satisfaction of the parties contending: "an oath for confirmation is to them an end of all strife" (Heb. 6:16). And indeed it is hardly imaginable that God should not have left that lawful which is so evidently necessary to the peace and security of mankind. Perhaps mankind are placed in such circumstances too, on purpose to oblige them sometimes to such an acknowledgment of the being and providence of God as is made in an oath. There is nothing that hath more universally obtained in all ages and nations of the world than to confirm things by an oath, in order to the ending of differences; which is the most certain indication that it is agreeable to the *law of nature*, and the *best reason of mankind.* And that this is no *degenerate practice* of mankind, like *idolatry*, is evident from this consideration, that when God separated a people to himself, it was practiced among them by divine authority.

2. This is an action highly *conducive to the honor of God*, whose glorious perfections are openly acknowledged in those solemn regular appeals men make to him, in such important cases, wherein there is no other way left to confirm the truth of what they speak. And, in such cases, the Jews were, by the law of Moses, not only *permitted*, but *commanded*, to swear by the name of God (Deut. 6:13), that being one branch of the religious worship due to him. It is for the honor of God that he is hereby openly acknowledged in all the considerable affairs of mankind; in which *never to interpose his name*, looks like a renunciation of his providence over the world, and tends to wear out of the minds of the generality, that natural sense of the Deity, which is very much kept up by the due and prudent use of oaths.

3. Swearing by the name of the Lord is *conducive to the public good.* In very many cases of the most important nature, we must wholly depend on human testimonies for finding out truth; and we can have no greater

20. SWEARING BY THE NAME OF GOD

assurance that men speak as they think, than their solemn appeal to God as the lover and witness of truth, and their dreadful avenger if they lie. It is reasonably supposed that if anything can oblige a man to a strict regard to truth, in what he deliberately affirms, this will. And charity prompts us to hope that men who have declared upon oath what they affirm, or deny, upon personal knowledge, would not abuse God's sacred name to support a known falsehood. An oath is naturally apt to make people more deliberately consider what they *depone [swear]* or *promise*, when otherwise they might be in danger of transgressing the law of truth, merely through inadvertency and heedlessness. And it is proper also to strike an awe into even those who have but little scruple of uttering a simple falsehood, while it is to be presumed, they would not willingly take divine vengeance on themselves.

4. If we consider the nature of an oath, and everything belonging to it, there is nothing that hath the least *appearance of evil* in it. There is surely no evil in it, as it is an act of religion; nor as it is an appeal to God, as a witness, and avenger in case we swear falsely; nor as it is a confirmation of a doubtful matter; nor as it puts an end to strife and controversy. But these are the chief ingredients of an oath, and the principal ends of it; and they are all so good that, instead of giving the least color of ground to condemn it, they rather commend it as a very useful and honorable action.

5. We have various instances in Scripture of God's condescending to confirm what he has spoken by an oath; wherein, because he can swear by none greater, he appeals to his own perfections, for the confirmation of our faith, that we may have the fullest assurance concerning his word. We have many examples of this in the Bible (as in Gen. 22:16–17; Ps. 89:35; 95:11 and 110:4; Heb. 6:17 and in many more passages). Now, admitting that these expressions are used in condescension to the *custom of men*, who confirm what they say in important cases by their oath, they strongly imply the lawfulness of swearing upon just occasions; because God would not have sworn, had an oath been unlawful in itself. That Being, who is glorious in holiness, cannot comply with men in an evil practice, and, by his own example, give countenance to it in the highest instance. For though he condescends to represent himself to us after the manner of men, he never does so in anything that is in its own nature evil and sinful. And,

6. The Holy Scriptures abound with *the examples* of godly men swearing on solemn occasions. The instances in the *Old Testament* are very nu-

merous, where we find it was practiced by the patriarchs, and the whole body of the Jews, with God's own allowance and command (Deut. 6:13). And, even in the *New Testament*, we have frequent examples of this kind. Our Savior himself did thus swear, when he was adjured by the high priest,

> And the high priest arose, and said unto him, Answerest thou nothing? what is it which these witness against thee? But Jesus held his peace. And the high priest answered and said unto him, I adjure thee by the living God, that thou tell us whether thou be the Christ, the Son of God. Jesus saith unto him, Thou hast said: nevertheless I say unto you, Hereafter shall ye see the Son of man sitting on the right hand of power, and coming in the clouds of heaven (Matt. 26:62–64).

Compared with Leviticus 5:1, "If a soul sin, and *hear the voice of swearing* and is a witness, whether he hath seen or known of it; if he do not utter it, then he shall bear his iniquity." *To hear the voice of swearing*, is to be solemnly *adjured*, as our Savior was, to declare the truth.[1] And there is no pretense to doubt of swearing being often practiced by the apostle Paul in his epistles, "For God is my witness, whom I serve with my spirit in the gospel of his Son, that without ceasing I make mention of you always in my prayers" (Rom. 1:9). "I say the truth in Christ, I lie not, my conscience also bearing me witness in the Holy Ghost, that I have great heaviness and continual sorrow in my heart" (Rom. 9:1–2). "Moreover I call God for a record upon my soul, that to spare you I came not as yet unto Corinth" (2 Cor. 1:23). "The God and Father of our Lord Jesus Christ, which is blessed for evermore, knoweth that I lie not" (2 Cor. 11:31). "Now the things which I write unto you, behold, before God, I lie not" (Gal. 1:20).

I might add that even the confession of adversaries is a considerable confirmation of my position. The Quakers are the only people in our land that pretend to deny the lawfulness of swearing; and yet Barclay, the best advocate for their cause, tells us that they are wont, on solemn occasions, to say, "We speak the truth in the fear of God, and before him, who is our witness, and the searcher of our hearts."[2] He indeed denies this to be an oath, as

---

[1] See Ainsworth, *Annotations*, on the place, and on Genesis 24:41.
[2] See Robert Barclay. *Works*, in fol. p. 553.

he also does the fore-mentioned expressions of the apostle Paul; but I take his denial to be contrary to the common sense of mankind, concerning the nature and import of an oath. So that it is rather *the name of an oath* they dislike than *the thing itself.*

Before I leave this head, I should consider the objection against the use of oaths, which is urged from our Lord's prohibition,

> Again, ye have heard that it hath been said by them of old time, Thou shalt not forswear thyself, but shalt perform unto the Lord thine oaths: but I say unto you, Swear not at all; neither by heaven; for it is God's throne…But let your communication be, Yea, yea; Nay, nay: for whatsoever is more than these cometh of evil (Matt. 5:33–37).

And this law the apostle James recites, as that which Christians should have a very particular and principal regard to, "above all things, my brethren, swear not, neither by heaven, neither by the earth, neither by any other oath: but let your yea be yea; and your nay, nay; lest ye fall into condemnation" (James 5:12).

But the very circumstances of these passages are sufficient to show *what kind of swearing* is forbidden in them, *viz.*, rash, unnecessary, and heedless swearing in common conversation; whereby men profanely swear by that which *by nature is no God*; as *by their head, by the heavens, by the earth*, or *by Jerusalem*, which were forms of swearing very usual among the Jews;[3] or *by their soul, by their life, by their troth, by their faith*, or the like, which are too too common among Christians. Nor should appeals to God be made at any rate, except in the *manner*, and for the *purposes*, to be explained in the two following sections. And therefore I proceed,

3. The Manner in Which an Oath Should Be Taken

To consider *the manner* in which an oath ought to be taken, that it may be used to the honor of that sacred name which is invoked by it.

Now, an oath being an appeal to God, made for the benefit of men, the *manner* of this appeal must be considered, both as it refers to *God, who is called upon*, and as it refers to *men, who are to be edified by the oath.*

---

[3] See Daniel Whitby. *A Paraphrase and Commentary on the New Testament*; and John Gill. *Exposition of the Bible*, on the place.

First, The *manner* of making an appeal to God, when we swear by his name, is to be considered *in reference to God*, who is solemnly invoked; and in this view it should be done,

1. With *profound reverence*; "For men verily swear by the greater" (Heb. 6:16). Far be it from men to indulge any levity, or to harden themselves in any pride of character and importance, when they are sisted [ordered to appear] in the immediate presence of the most high God, the possessor of heaven and earth. "Be not rash with thy mouth, and let not thine heart be hasty to utter any thing before God: for God is in heaven, and thou upon earth: therefore let thy words be few" (Eccl. 5:2). The name of the Lord is glorious and fearful; and therefore suffer not thy mouth to sin, by taking it in vain; wherefore should God be angry at thy voice (Eccl. 5:6)? The reverence due to God in swearing forbids men to use it about things of small importance; or about things that may be sufficiently confirmed without it; or with a light and unaffected temper of mind; for all these cases are instances of disrespect to the majesty of our Father in heaven.

2. Men should *swear in truth* (Jer. 4:2). There should certainly be a present conformity of the inward sentiments of their mind to the words of the oath in their common obvious sense, and as they are understood by those who require it, or for whose sake it is taken. The swearers should honestly speak what they think, with the strictest candor, and in the plainest words, without any equivocation, mental reserves, or secret meaning of their own.[4] *Perjury*, that horrid and shocking sin, which at once dissolves the strongest bands of humanity and religion, must be the consequence of persons declaring upon oath what they know to be false, or even of their declaring for truth, what they *do not know* to be so, although it may happen to be as they have declared; nor are they less guilty of this sin, who *never design* to perform what they solemnly swear to do. Can anything offer a viler affront, or be reckoned, in just construction, a higher contempt to infinite Majesty?

It is not enough that the thing sworn be a real fact; the deponent [oath-taker] must swear concerning it only from his *personal knowledge*. He is

---

[4] "To have an inward reserved meaning and sense of words in an oath, contrary to the common and ordinary acceptation of them, and that with a design to deceive, destroys the nature and end of an oath, which is to bring forth *nothing but the truth*; it opens a wide door to all falsehood and lying, contrary to Ephesians 4:25; and it unhinges the firmest bonds of society, that none can put confidence in another." *The Assembly's Shorter Catechism Explained by way of Question and Answer*, on quest. 53, 54.

perjured, if he go beyond the limits of his own knowledge, in either affirming, or denying. The reason is obvious: what he affirms may be false, and what he denies may be true, for anything that he knows. And, upon the same principle, it is evident that persons should cautiously forbear to give even *their sense* of men's words, or of facts, when they are called to give their evidence upon oath; since they may so easily mistake or misapprehend them, even where there is no design to injure truth, by a false representation of them.

Further, in all promissory oaths, our words must be followed and confirmed with *a punctual performance*. To fail in *the deed*, even though *the intention* was good, is *real perjury*, as well as to fail in *both*. And though the former being single is not so bad as the latter being double perjury, yet it is worse than perjury in the intention, which an after-repentance has prevented from becoming actual. Our very word itself, and much more the oath of God with it, lays so strong an obligation on our consciences that it is not in our power afterwards to reverse it ourselves. Others, to whom all the right has passed by our obligations, may cancel it; and, in case our power in the matter promised and sworn be subjected to superiors, they may disannul it (Num. 30). And if the condition expressed, or necessarily implied in the oath, shall fail, the obligation will cease of itself. But excepting these three cases, and that of the oath being in itself unlawful, every promissory oath is an indispensable tie upon us to do *simply and fully* what we have ratified by it, without any indirect evasions and forced interpretations, contrary to the genuine sense and design, even though they could *by some art* be reconciled to the literal words of it. To make use of such evasions would be to *swear deceitfully* (Ps. 24:4), and would destroy the confidence, and make void the security mankind intend to confirm by an oath. Not to enter on nice and intricate cases, this is certain in general, that *an oath is always binding against a man's own temporal interest*; so that, though great disadvantages should accrue from keeping the oath, they will not warrant his breaking it. If he happen to *swear to his own hurt*, he must *not change*; as it is the character of the godly man, that he does not, "LORD, who shall abide in thy tabernacle? who shall dwell in thy holy hill?... He that sweareth to his own hurt, and changeth not" (Ps. 15:1–4).

3. An oath should be taken *in judgment* (Jer. 4:2). The closest consideration, and the most deliberate attention to the nature, import, and obligation of an oath, are necessary, and every way reasonable, when per-

sons are called to swear it. The first point to be considered is *the thing to be sworn*, which should be carefully recollected, and digested by these who are called to declare what they know about it upon oath; and here it is a good rule never to exceed their own knowledge of any point, in the strength of *hearsay*, or *conjecture*, whenever they invoke God's name as the witness of truth, and the avenger of falsehood. They ought also to consider *the nature of an oath*, and with what godly fear they should serve the Lord, who is a consuming fire, and whose name is holy and reverend, when they take it. And finally, they must carefully ponder *the motives* that induce them, and *the ends* they propose, when they appeal to God; whether they have a holy, unfeigned desire to *glorify God*, by worthy acknowledgments of him as the fountain of all perfection; and to *promote the good of mankind*, by an impartial declaration of truth.

How contrary to this necessary caution and deliberation is the practice of many, who swallow down oaths with as little concern as they do their food; who have no thought or sense of God in what they are about; and who, instead of endeavoring to inform themselves as fully as they can, are willingly ignorant of what they swear about, or swear merely upon the credit they give to the testimony of men, or what they conjecture from circumstances? What is all this but trifling both with God and men, a present profanation of God's name, and a direct step to a further profanation of it in breaking such oaths? And,

4. An oath must be taken *in righteousness* (Jer. 4:2). When persons swear concerning *a fact*, they should conscientiously adhere to the truth, by giving a just representation of what they certainly know, in order that righteous judgment may be executed, in clearing the innocent, in punishing the guilty, and in putting an end to controversies. And when they bind themselves by *a promissory oath*, they should only swear to do things that are *lawful* in their nature, and that are *possible* to them.

Men should only promise upon oath to do things that are *lawful and honest*. It is the most aggravated impiety to convert the most sacred obligation into *a bond of iniquity*. The forty Jews who bound themselves with an oath to kill Paul (Acts 23:12–14), made the oath of God an instrument of unrighteousness unto sin. The case is not much better, where an oath is taken binding men to that which has a manifest tendency to an evil end, or which prevents their doing the good they ought; of which kind were those oaths which the *Jewish doctors* allowed, but our *Savior* condemned, for alienating even from parents what should be employed for their benefit (Matt. 15:5–6). Therefore should any be so unhappy as to be ensnared in oaths of this sort, which are in themselves null and void, and bind to nothing but to repent of them and renounce them, they must not add the guilt of *keeping* them to the sin of *making* them; but all thoughts and preparations towards the execution of them must be immediately laid aside. Herod did wickedly in beheading John the Baptist *for his oath's sake* (Mark 6:23–27). But David did worthily in forbearing to execute his rash oath, against Nabal's house (1 Sam. 25).

The matter of a promissory oath ought to be, humanly speaking, *in a man's power* to perform. Abraham's servant showed but a reasonable caution, when his master proposed to him to swear that he would go unto Abraham's country, and to his kindred, and take a wife unto Isaac. "Peradventure the woman will not be willing to follow me unto this land," said the servant. "Then thou shalt be clear from this my oath," replied his master (Gen. 24:5–8). This is an excellent pattern for all promissory oaths, which should be limited with every reasonable exception in the making of them; and being made, should be rigorously observed in the very letter of them.

Thus it appears that men should swear by the name of the Lord, *with reverence, in truth, in judgment*, and *in righteousness*. It is proper now to consider,

Secondly, The *manner*, or *form*, of making an appeal to God, *as it refers to men*, who are to be edified by the oath. What has been hitherto advanced on the manner of swearing has an immediate and principal respect to the inward temper of the mind, and the happy effect of just views of the divine character and perfections upon the soul; but what I am now to consider has an immediate and principal respect to the *outward evidences* of this temper, and *the tokens* whereby the judge, and all concerned, may be induced to believe, that the deponent swears with reverence of God, and in truth, judgment, and righteousness, and that he actually is impressed, as he should be, in taking an oath.

The *forms* of swearing, which imply these *tokens*, are very different in the several nations of the world. All have agreed in using, or referring to, such words as carry in them an appeal to a superior Being, who is supposed to know the heart, and to hate and punish dissimulation and falsehood; but in taking a formal oath before a judge, or to ratify a covenant, it would seem they used *some corporeal action*, besides the repetition of that form of words, or their acquiescence in the form that was read or repeated to them.

These corporeal actions were of *two kinds*: either (1.) Such as immediately accompanied the oath; or (2.) Such as were connected with it, though not considered as properly belonging to it.

The custom of *eating and drinking together* was generally reckoned a proper sequel, to seal a friendship confirmed by a solemn covenant and oath, as in the case of Jacob and Laban (Gen. 31:53–54), and of Isaac and Abimelech (Gen. 26:28–30). But this was not considered, I apprehend, as a circumstance belonging to the oath; but rather as an appendage to it, which testified the friendship of the parties, according to the tenor of the oath they had taken. My principal business is with *the corporeal actions that accompany the oath*, and are reckoned, *as tokens*, to pertain to it, for the purpose to be afterwards mentioned.

Among the Greeks, we find it was very common to swear, *laying their hands upon the altar*, which Aulus Gellius tells us, they reckoned the most sacred form of swearing. The Romans swore by Jupiter, *holding a flint-stone in their hand*, and afterwards flung it violently from them, with words to this effect: "If I knowingly falsify, God so throw me out of all my possessions, as I do this stone."

But as it concerns us most of all to consider what the Scripture has revealed on this point, I shall just touch a little at the *two tokens* of an appeal to God that are mentioned there.

1. There are two evident examples of persons swearing by *putting their hand under the thigh* of the person who required their oath: *viz.*, Eliezer of Damascus, who sware, *in this form*, to Abraham, that he would faithfully observe all that he had commanded him relative to the marriage of Isaac (Gen. 24:2–9); and Joseph, who put his hand under Jacob's thigh, when he sware to carry him out of Egypt, and to bury him in the burying-place of his fathers (Gen. 47:29–31). The oddness of this practice has induced some to suppose that there was something deeply *mysterious* and *extraordinary* in these two cases; and that it implied an appeal to God, either as having promised to multiply their seed; or, as having given them the sacrament of circumcision; or, as having promised the Messiah to come out of their loins.[5] But if people are inclined to amuse themselves with *the mar-*

---

[5] See Matthew Poole. *Synopsis Criticorum Aliorumque Sacræ Scripturæ Interpretum et Commentatorum*, Ainsworth, *Annotations*, Gill, *Commentary*, etc., on these verses.

velous, at great uncertainty, they may; and indeed all these opinions I have mentioned are advanced with a modest diffidence by every sensible writer that has adopted one or other of them. They have rather proposed them as *conjectures* than given them as their *own sentiments*.

But what is more certain is that Josephus affirms this gesture in taking an oath was an ancient custom that prevailed in these times; that many of the *best critics* derive the Greek word ορχος, which signifies *an oath*, from the Hebrew word (ירך), which signifies *the thigh*;[6] that this way of swearing is used still among the Indians, and some say among the Ethiopians too; and that it was not unusual in latter times; hence we are told, that "all the princes, and the mighty men, and all the sons likewise of king David, submitted themselves unto Solomon" (1 Chron. 29:24), or, as the margin has it literally from the Hebrew, *gave their hand under Solomon the king*. It is abundantly clear from the nature of the thing, and all expositors agree in it, that *an oath of allegiance* is included in this expression; and moreover, that it implies an allusion to some sign of appealing to God then in use.[7]

Upon the whole, I think it is *precarious and rash* to affirm, as some worthy men have done, that there was something *extraordinary* and *mysterious* in this form of swearing, which renders it unlawful to imitate it; and that it was rendered lawful, in the cases of Eliezer and Joseph, only in virtue of their singular situations, and the things their oaths referred to.

2. The other form of swearing, most frequently mentioned in Scripture, is by *lifting up the hand to heaven*, as a sign of the deponent appealing to God, whose throne is there. Thus Abraham expresseth the manner both of his prayer and oath, "I have *lift up my hand*...to the most high God" (Gen. 14:22). Thus *the Lord*, speaking after the manner of men, expresses himself, "For I lift up my hand to heaven" and swear (Deut. 32:40). In this manner also *the Angel*, which appeared to Daniel and John, sware (Dan. 12:7; Rev. 10:5–6). And to this sign of appealing unto God, there are many *allusions* in different places, as in Psalm 24:4 and 144:8, etc. As the oath, administered and taken with the hand under the thigh, implied *a*

---

[6] See Avenarium, Ainsworth, *Annotations*, Edward Leigh. *Annotations upon All the New Testament, Philological and Theological*, Stocklum, etc.

[7] "Positio manus sub femore juramentum exigentis, etc., *i.e.*, The putting of the hand under the thigh of him that required an oath (Gen. 24:2), was not for any mystical signification of Christ, but for a sign of subjection." Ames, *The Marrow of Theology*, book 2, chap. 10, sect. 38.

stooping posture; so this form of lifting up the hand, seems to have been connected with *an upright standing one*, "the Angel which I saw *stand* upon the sea and upon the earth *lifted up his hand to heaven, and sware*" (Rev. 10:5–6).

I shall not pretend to define *the meaning* of these circumstances, of *putting the hand under the thigh*, or of *lifting it up to heaven*; nor to inquire into any *particular reasons* for *this difference*; because I cannot find satisfactory lights from Scripture on these points. It is enough for my purpose to observe that *each of them*, as used by men, for the benefit of men, was *an outward sign of an appeal to God, as a witness, for the confirmation of what was asserted or promised*.

For setting the whole in the easiest light, I shall lay down these positions. (1.) The nature of an oath is no more, and no less, than *an appeal to God*, as the witness of truth, and the punisher of all falsehood. (2.) When an oath is taken before a competent judge, there must be *some external token*, or *some outward sign*, to assure the judge that the deponent has made such an appeal. (3.) These circumstances of *putting the hand under*, or *lifting it up*, were exacted as signs of this sort, and for this very purpose. And (4.) These outward signs, being principally intended for the satisfaction of men, did not enter into *the nature of the oath*; and therefore did not properly belong to *the act of worship*, performed in swearing by the name of God.

The *last* is the only proposition that any sensible person would hesitate about; and yet there is nothing more evident; for the *same act of divine worship* is required in *every oath*; but the *same outward signs* are not required in every appeal to heaven; yea, in many cases, *no outward signs* are either required, or used. We have many instances of this kind in the word of God, both in the Old and New Testament (as in 2 Sam. 15:21; 1 Kings 17:10; Rom. 9:1–2; and in many, many more examples, which the attentive reader will find in his Bible).

From the whole it appears that these outward signs are intended for the edification of men in swearing; but do not constitute any part of the worship performed to God in that service; or at most are *merely circumstantial*, and *not essential to an oath*, which is complete without them. This is still more evident if we consider that an oath is only to be used when the edification of mankind renders it necessary; and if this shall never point out a clear call to any particular person to swear by the Lord's name, it would be a sin to seek an occasion of doing it. And when an occasion offers, the oath is taken *to man*, as a party, *by God*, as the witness of the swearer's veracity and integrity.

To conclude this head, it shall suffice to add that there is no *outward sign* of a person swearing with reverence of God, and in truth, judgment, and righteousness, that carries so much simplicity and majesty, and that is so strongly recommended in Scripture, as that of *lifting up the hand*, which is invariably represented as the form of swearing used by JEHOVAH; unless we except that one instance, "the LORD hath sworn" (Ex. 17:16), or, as the marginal reading has it, *the hand upon the throne of the Lord*; that is, the Lord's hand is upon his throne, while he swears to have war with Amalek from generation to generation. But this is only a solemn declaration made by JEHOVAH, who in another place says, "The heaven is my throne" (Isa. 66:1), and evidently points our attention to things above; and the sign used in swearing among men best corresponds to this manner of swearing used by the Lord, when they lift up their hand towards the throne of God. But some give a very different sense of the words, to this effect: "Because the hand (of Amalek) is against the throne of the Lord, the Lord will have war with Amalek from generation to generation."[8]

4. The Ends for Which It Should Be Used

I shall now represent the important *purposes*, for which an oath may be safely and honorably used. This point may be discussed very briefly, because the case is abundantly plain.

1. An oath should only be used in matters that are of *great consequence*. Wherever we find any account in Scripture of God's swearing, it is always in some solemn and weighty business, where his own honor, or the happiness of man, are nearly concerned; as concerning the *eternal priesthood of Christ* (Ps. 110:4 compared with Heb. 7:20); concerning *every knee bowing to Christ, and every tongue confessing him* (Isa. 45:23); and concerning his *having no pleasure in the death of a sinner* (Ezek. 33:11). This authentic solemn ratification should never be prostituted by affixing it to a frivolous and trifling affair. The glory of God and the good of mankind being the ends of an oath, it should never be used, but in cases where they are interested in the thing men swear about.

---

[8] See Matthew Poole. *English Annotations on the Holy Bible*; Ainsworth, *Annotations*; Gill, *Commentary*, etc., on the place; John Weemes. *Works*, vol. 2, p. 174.

2. An oath should only be used where there is some reason to think the point to be confirmed thereby is *doubtful unto some*, whose interest is evidently concerned in being fully satisfied about it. It is a vile prostitution of an oath, to require or take it about things that are obvious and plain, or that are readily acknowledged, and cannot be denied. There is no need of an oath to prove that the whole is greater than a part; or, that the sun is risen at noonday. But the use of an oath is to clear up some obscurity, to resolve some doubt, to end some controversy, and to remove suspicions about what is so attested.

3. An oath for confirmation is *an end of all strife*, being the highest ground of faith and assurance that can be. It is the last security for truth and confidence among men; for if that will not oblige them to speak truth, we cannot suppose anything will. On this account, it is proper enough to demand an oath in such cases as the following, *viz.*,

To ratify covenants and treaties, that concern the good of many individuals (Gen. 26:28–31).

To confirm personal friendship, with a view to the benefit of posterity; or even with a view to personal safety in cases of extreme danger (1 Sam. 20).

To testify allegiance to a rightful sovereign (2 Chron. 23; Eccl. 8:2).

To give evidence in a court before a lawful magistrate, when duly called (1 Kings 8:31).

To purge one's own character from scandalous imputations, in some cases; though this should be used with great caution (Ex. 22:11).

To bind persons to fidelity in managing their trust, in important affairs (Gen. 24:2; 47:31).

There are several other such cases, when an oath may be properly required and taken; because it tends more to impress the conscience with an awful regard to truth and justice; and it gives the fullest reasonable satisfaction to all concerned, that the testimony may be depended on. Now, these are the great purposes of swearing at all, for "an oath for confirmation is to them an end of all strife" (Heb. 6:16).

5. Questions respecting It Answered

I shall now *propose and answer a few questions* concerning this duty of swearing, upon a regular call, and in obedience to lawful authority.

Question 1. Is it in any case lawful to *swear by creatures?*

Answer. By no means, for this is an honor due to God only, "Thou shalt fear the LORD thy God, and serve him, and shalt swear by his name" (Deut. 6:13). Even reason teaches us that creatures are not *omniscient*, and therefore it is absurd to apply to them for the deciding of matters that are known only to the Searcher of hearts and ourselves; and neither are they to be reckoned *avengers* of the cause of injured truth; for they have not a sovereignty over man, nor a right to punish perjury in such a way as God has. Therefore, to swear by creatures is to give them a branch of the glory due to the Creator, and is no less than *idolatry*.

We have in Scripture several examples of creatures being introduced into an oath. Thus we find Moses calling heaven and earth to record against the Israelites that he had set before them life and death, blessing and cursing (Deut. 30:19–20). And when David would represent the danger of his situation to Jonathan, with great earnestness, he uses this expression, "as the LORD liveth, and as thy soul liveth, there is but a step between me and death" (1 Sam. 20:3). And Abigail uses the very same words to David (1 Sam. 25:26). And there are several other examples much to the same purpose; and none of them are expressly blamed, as far as I have observed. But in none of these passages of Scripture, where creatures are introduced into an oath, have we the least appearance of an appeal being made to them. They are only referred to, as things that are undeniably evident and certain; and the person who swore by the name of the Lord, at the same time affirmed that the fact he attested was as real as the existence of such creatures as he named; and the creatures named in oaths were always such as the person, for whose benefit the oath was taken, had the fullest conviction of being really and truly what the deponent affirmed them to be.[9]

However, it is best not to draw this practice into *a precedent*; but, when we have a just occasion to confirm a thing further than by our simple declaration, to make use of God's name alone for this purpose; both because the promiscuous application of the same form of words to God and the creature carries the appearance of respect to the latter beyond what is due; and because it may be interpreted and used in this criminal sense by some,

---

[9] The *creatures* which are introduced in an oath, either *by actions*, as "putting the hand under the thigh," and "lifting it up to heaven;" or *by words*, as *taking heaven and earth to record, protesting by the rejoicing of the saints*, on whose account the oath is taken (1 Cor. 15:31), and using this form of speech, "As thy soul liveth"; I say, the creatures thus introduced are only *outward signs of the deponent's sincere appeal to God.*

without observing this intended difference; besides, that the name of creatures, liable, as all are, to sudden changes, is not proper to give a sanction to our words.

I know, some would reckon such forms of speech as that, "As thy soul liveth," or, "I protest by your rejoicing in Christ," only *strong asseverations*; but this is a weak expedient, and liable to be abused by such as may think too light of the occasions that would warrant the use of them.

Question 2. In what sense should the words of an oath be understood by the swearer?

Answer. He ought to understand them in that obvious, literal, and unforced sense which the words naturally bear; for not the *arts of criticism* but the *common sense of plain-hearted honest men* must direct the swearer. Indeed, if a man shall be told that, by swearing an oath, which is conceived in the plainest terms, and has the most innocent meaning, he will be construed by the court to swear in some particular sense, which is inconsistent with a good conscience in the swearer's opinion, he ought not to swear, till that information be satisfyingly explained; not so much for his own sake, as for the sake of the person who told him; that he may not give him occasion to think he approves of what he really detests. "An oath is to be taken in the plain and common sense of the words, without equivocation or mental reservation."[10]

Question 3. May a judge require an oath of a suspected person, concerning *his innocence* or *guilt*, in reference to the crime imputed to him?

Answer. It is against all reason to require a person to clear himself upon oath, of a crime which he is not charged with by some accuser; for secret things of this sort belong unto the Lord. And, if one is accused of a crime that cannot be proved against him by sufficient evidence, he ought not to be compelled to clear himself by oath; for it is against nature, for any person to take any step towards his own punishment; and it exposes a person to dangerous and violent temptations to perjure himself, when the issue is suspended upon his own oath. But, if a person, accused of some crime, is acquitted upon trial, because the charge against him is not supported by sufficient evidence, he may be allowed to purge his character from dishonorable suspicions upon oath, if he voluntarily demand the privilege of doing so; and if the court shall reckon the cause of suspicion so strong, as to warrant the use of an oath in the case (Ex. 22:11).

---

[10] *Westminster Confession of Faith*, chap. 22, sect. 4.

Question 4. Is there *any particular form of words* to be used in an oath, *preferable to another?*

Answer. Some *form of words* is highly proper to be used in swearing; though it would be rash to say that even this is *absolutely necessary* to constitute an oath. But the *particular form* of words to be used is not pretended by anybody to be prescribed in the word of God. We find a great variety on this head in the Scripture itself; where an appeal to God is expressed sometimes one way, and sometimes another; hence are these expressions, "I call God for a record upon my soul" (2 Cor. 1:23), "God is my witness" (Rom. 1:9), "God…knoweth" (2 Cor. 11:31), "I say the truth in Christ, I lie not" (Rom. 9:1), "as the truth of Christ is in me" (2 Cor. 11:10), etc.

But of the several forms, used in different countries, these are certainly to be preferred, which contain the *most direct and solemn appeal to God, as a witness and avenger*; and which are most likely to *affect the conscience* of the swearer, and to *give satisfaction* to the persons who have any concern in the issue of the oath. On this account, it must be considered as a piece of good policy to establish such a form of words as is both *awful* and *plain*, in every society where there may be occasion to administer justice by evidence upon oath.[11]

6. Inferences from the Subject

I shall finish this subject with *three inferences* that arise naturally out of it.

1. The view that has been given of an oath demonstrates *the deep and lasting obligation* it lays upon the conscience of the person who has taken it. "If a man…swear an oath to bind his soul with a bond; he shall not break [or profane] his word, he shall do according to all that proceedeth

---

[11] The form of the oath used generally in courts of justice in Scotland is to this effect: "I do swear by God, that I shall tell the truth, and nothing but the truth, as far as I know, in what shall be asked at me, without feud or favor, and that as I shall answer to God at the great day." Or, "As I shall answer to God, and by God himself, I declare that I will tell the truth, and nothing but the truth, in this matter."

The form of the oath used generally in courts of justice in England is to this purpose: "You shall declare the truth, the whole truth, and nothing but the truth: so help you God."

N. B., In Scotland the deponent repeats the oath, and therefore he speaks in the first person; but in England, the clerk of the court repeats it, and not the deponent, and therefore he speaks in the second person throughout.

Upon comparing these forms, it is very obvious the oath used in Scotland is much more solemn and expressive than that used in England.

out of his mouth" (Num. 30:2). Swearing is emphatically called, *the binding a man's soul with a bond*, which intimates that he who takes an oath *puts his soul in pawn*, so to speak, *for the truth of what he says*. Can any obligation be conceived of as weighty a nature as this, which brings the most awful and impressing views of the Deity immediately home to the conscience; which represents him as the God with whom the swearer has to do; and which strikes his hopes and fears by the most encouraging or most terrible prospects? The person who, in these circumstances, will take the liberty to utter falsehoods, or to conceal and disguise the truth, must be under the power of a reprobate mind, and his heart must be hardened through the deceitfulness of sin.

And in regard to *promissory oaths*, everyone that has taken them should steadfastly adhere to his engagement, in everything lawful and possible, unless the party to whom the oath was given shall dissolve the obligation. Length of time cannot make the obligation void. Human authority cannot set it aside. If the church of Rome has pretended to the right of loosing men from this sacred bond; it is only a proof that it is *the man of sin*, described by the Holy Ghost, "Who...exalteth himself above all that is called God, or that is worshipped" (2 Thess. 2:4). Though it should happen that the oath was made to *a wicked man* of *a different communion*, or possibly, to *an heretic*, or *infidel*, yet none of these or the like malignant circumstances can warrant any man to break his oath. In the sacred history we find that the several leagues and covenants, which the *patriarchs*, and other *holy men* of old, made with *heathens* and *infidels*, were solemnly ratified with mutual oaths, and were religiously observed, without any exception or abatement, on account of errors in religion, or transgressions in morality. There we see how sharply the *kings of Judah* were reproved by the prophets, and punished with heavy judgments, for their guilt in breaking their oaths of fidelity to the wicked and idolatrous *kings of Babylon*. And there we have an account of the fearful punishment of *Saul's sons*, on account of their father's sin, in stretching forth his hand against the Gibeonites, who had by lies and fraud obtained an oath of friendship from the *elders of Israel*, in the days of Joshua. Every one that has taken such an oath should be of the same mind with David, when he says, "I have sworn, and I will perform it" (Ps. 119:106).

2. Because an oath is so very solemn and binding, it must be a dreadful sin to take God's name in vain, by a common heedless use of it, upon trivial

and needless occasions, in ordinary conversation. How exceedingly wicked is this practice though, alas! it is become very general! Many sober heathens have detested it; and they will doubtless rise up in judgment against such profane swearers, as call themselves by the Christian name. Is there any name so glorious and fearful as that of *the Lord our God?* And shall these who live, and move, and have their being in him, blaspheme and curse, lie and deceive, by irreverent and profane abuses of it?

Tell me, *ye swearers,* whether your fearless use of an oath does not tend to make that tremendous ordinance a common and familiar thing to your minds? Does it not involve you in perjury daily; and does it not prepare your minds for perjury before a court? Does not your practice of confirming everything by an oath argue a perpetual distrust of your own reputation; and expose you to just suspicion among all sober men, who fear an oath? Is not your swearing an unmeaning expletive in your conversation, which affronts God, and offends sober men, who cannot be supposed to hear the great and glorious name of God so irreverently tossed upon every slight occasion, without grief and pain? Can you say that it is a real ornament to the discourse of your children, servants, and neighbors; and if you dislike it in them, how can you practice it yourselves? Can any reasonable charity find out a way to reconcile your practice with a serious belief of Christianity? Have you any excuse for your sin, except that it is common, and you mean no harm by it, or you do not know of it? Do you think the same excuses would justify a child in speaking as disrespectfully of his parents, or a servant of his master, or a subject of his prince, or even a man of his neighbor? Whether should you follow the fashions of that part of the world that lieth in wickedness, or obey the Holy Ghost, who gives that caution in reference to swearing, "Thou shalt not follow a multitude to do evil" (Ex. 23:2)? What profit[12] have you in practicing this sin? "Against whom do ye sport yourselves? against whom make ye a wide mouth, and

---

[12] "Take not his name, who made thy mouth, in vain:
   It gets thee nothing, and hath no excuse.
Lust and wine plead a pleasure, avarice gain:
   But the cheap swearer through the open sluice.
      Lets his soul run for nought, as little fearing:
      Were I an *epicure,* I could bate swearing.

"When thou dost tell another's jests, therein
Omit the oaths, which true wit cannot need:

draw out the tongue? are ye not children of transgression, a seed of falsehood" (Isa. 57:4). Are you in such haste to be with your everlasting companions, the *devils* and the *damned*, that you will needs hasten your judgment, and bring upon yourselves a swifter destruction? May God impress these alarming words upon your minds,

> As he loved cursing, so let it come unto him: as he delighted not in blessing, so let it be far from him. As he clothed himself with cursing like as with his garment, so let it come into his bowels like water, and like oil into his bones. Let it be unto him as the garment which covereth him, and for a girdle wherewith he is girded continually (Ps. 109:17–19).

Before I proceed to another point, I must observe that the unnecessary *repetition* of oaths, and particularly the exacting of a renewed swearing of the same oath, without any pretense to charge the person with any foregoing breach of it—are not much better than *taking the name of God in vain*; and ought to be industriously avoided by all who would maintain a tender conscience, void of offense towards God and towards men.

3. The due consideration of the nature, importance and design of an oath manifests the heinousness of the sin of *perjury*. Persons may be guilty of this sin several ways: as (1.) When they assert upon oath what they know to be otherwise; or promise what they do not intend to perform. (2.) When they are *uncertain*, whether what they swear be true or not. (3.) When they do not use the greatest plainness and simplicity in oaths, but answer doubtfully, and have secret reserves in their minds. And (4.) When they do not perform what they have promised upon oath, even though they intended to do so at the time when they took the oath. In all these

---

Pick out of tales the mirth, but not the sin.
  He pares his apple that will cleanly feed.
    Play not away the virtue of that name,
    Which is the best stake, when griefs make thee tame.

"The cheapest sins most dearly punish'd are;
Because to shun them also is so cheap:
For we have wit to mark them, and to spare."
    —George Herbert. *The Church-Porch: Perirrhanterium*

cases, persons become *really perjured*; and I need not use many words to aggravate this sin.

Deliberate perjury is directly against a man's knowledge, so that none can commit it without staring his conscience in the face, and sinning against light; which is one of the greatest aggravations of any crime.

It is equally a sin against both tables; being the highest affront to God, and of most injurious consequence to men. It is a horrible abuse of the name of God, an open contempt of his judgment, and an insolent defiance of his vengeance. And, in respect of men, it is not only a wrong to this or that particular person who suffers by it, but treason against human society itself; subverting at once the foundations of public peace and justice, and the private security of every man's life and fortune.

Perjury defeats the *best and last way* that can be taken for the decision of doubtful matters; and wherever it takes place, the foundations of confidence are destroyed among men, and all is thrown loose and uncertain.

Solomon very fully and elegantly expresseth the destructive nature of this sin, "false witness against his neighbor is a maul, and a sword, and a sharp arrow" (Prov. 25:18); intimating, that amongst all the instruments of ruin and mischief that have been devised by mankind, none is of more pernicious consequence to human society than perjury and breach of faith. This is as the pestilence that walketh in darkness; it spreads destruction by a secret stab and blow, against which, many times, there is no possibility of providing any defense. Those who fear not the oath of God will never regard the welfare of men; but these that honor God will love their neighbor also. And finally,

This is it that the Lord hath said, "Thou shalt not take the name of the LORD thy God in vain; for the LORD will not hold him guiltless that taketh his name in vain" (Ex. 20:7). Such guilty criminals may, and often do, escape punishment from men; but the Lord, to whom vengeance belongeth, will not suffer them to escape his righteous judgment; and it is a fearful thing to fall into the hands of the living God, who will not fail to assert the honor of his name at the dreadful expense of such impious wretches.

Chapter 21

Vowing to the Lord

Perhaps the difference between oaths and vows may not seem to be very material, in the opinion of many; and the rather it may be thought inconsiderable, because vowing is sometimes called swearing in Scripture, as in "I have sworn, and I will perform it, that I will keep thy righteous judgments" (Ps. 119:106), where swearing is only another word for vowing. But, as *an oath*, in the strictest sense, *is made to a creature, by God*, in which light I considered it in the last chapter; so *a vow is made to God himself*; and the same solemnity is required in both. For opening this subject, I shall endeavor to do these seven things.

1. To explain the nature of a vow.
2. To represent the warrant Christians have to vow unto the Lord.
3. To consider the matter these vows should refer to,
4. To inquire for what purposes religious vows should be made.
5. To speak of the obligation of them.
6. To show in what capacity Christians may vow to the Lord. And,
7. To add some directions relative to their vows.

1. The Nature of a Vow

For understanding *the nature of a vow*, it may be necessary to observe (1.) That it is only to be made *to God*. This is sufficiently intimated in all the places of Scripture where it is mentioned, as in "Vow, and pay unto the LORD your God" (Ps. 76:11). The whole tenor of the Scripture is to the same purpose, and gives no countenance to the impiety and sacrilege of *Popish vows* made to *saints* or *angels*. But these who pray to creatures are consistent enough with themselves when they also vow to them; for the object of prayer and of vows is the same. (2.) That which is *a promise* among men becomes *a vow* when it is used with reference to God; for as we bind ourselves to men by a promise, so a vow is a sacred promise to God, whereby we bind ourselves to him. (3.) A vow may be made several ways: as by *inward purpose and resolution of soul*; by *express formal words*; and by *significant actions*.

1. A person, or persons may vow to the Lord *by inward purpose and resolution of soul*. I know an inward purpose of mind cannot bind a man to his neighbor; there must be some declaration of it, or else he is as free as ever. But God sees and searches the heart, he knows the inward thoughts, and is a constant witness to all the thoughts, purposes, and desires of men; and therefore if there be an inward resolution, there is a bond upon the person before God. Hannah's vow did really bind her, though it was only an inward resolve of her heart, and she did not express a word (1 Sam. 1:10–13). We speak to God by the inward exercise of the soul, and converse with him by the language of the heart, as truly as we converse with men by words.

2. Persons may bind themselves to God *by express words*, as we have many examples of the saints actually doing. It is hardly possible, if the purpose of the heart is fixed, sincere, and strong, to forbear declaring it by words; for out of the abundance of the heart, the mouth will naturally speak. A mind deeply impressed with a sense of the importance and advantages of its inward resolutions, will readily incline to express them by opening the mouth unto the Lord.

3. Persons may vow to the Lord by some *significant actions*, though they say nothing with their lips. The *giving of the hand* did engage in suretiship, and testified consent, among the Jews, though the person said nothing (Prov. 6:1). And submission to the ordinance of *circumcision* made a man a debtor to do the whole ceremonial law, without speaking a word (Gal. 5:3). In like manner, *baptism* implies an obligation upon Christians to cleave unto the Lord with purpose of heart.

These who vow to the Lord should always be hearty, deliberate, and sincere in this solemn service, because they have to do with the most High God. And, if there is only a hearty determined purpose, this is, by reasonable construction, a real vow, to cleave unto the truths and service of God, according to what a man hath purposed in his heart, even though he never open his mouth. But if his mouth shall utter, and his lips express, the purposes of his mind, the vow is more formal, but not of deeper obligation in the sight of God. And if some significant action, simple and scriptural in its nature, is used to impress the mind more sensibly and effectually, with a strong conviction of the obligation of the vow, then the service is as solemn and formal as it can be.

Because a vow is made to *God only*, it cannot refer to anything but *matters of a sacred or religious concern*, either in their own nature, or in their tendency. And because a vow is of the nature of a promise, it must have a respect to some *future time*; and the things vowed are always supposed to be *lawful and possible*; for otherwise the vow would be a bond of iniquity, which ought not to be made, nor, if made, to be fulfilled.

2. The Warrant for It

I shall now represent *the warrant* Christians have to vow unto the Lord their God.

> The use of vows is to be found in most religions. They made a considerable part of the pagan worship; being made either in consequence of some deliverance, under some pressing necessity, or for the success of some enterprise.[1]

The heathen writers abound with examples of this kind. As soon as the sea ceased from her raging, Jonah being cast into it, we are told, that the mariners "feared the Lord exceedingly, and offered a sacrifice unto the Lord, and *made vows*" (Jonah 1:16).

Long before Israel received the law at mount Sinai, when the Lord had taken them by the hand, and had brought them out of the land of Egypt; I say, long before that period, we find that Jacob vowed a vow unto the Lord at Bethel (Gen. 28:20–22).

Among the rest of the statutes and judgments which were delivered unto Israel by the hand of Moses, we have a very particular account of vows, and of the laws concerning them in various supposed cases (Lev. 27; Num. 30; and other places). But these appointments have almost all of them a respect to the particular situations of that peculiar people, or else to such particular cases as it does not belong to my main purpose to enlarge upon.

Some have taken occasion to say that all religious vows are improper under the New Testament, because we have no mention of them, except in *two instances*, and both of them refer to ceremonial things, which are now totally abolished (Acts 18:18; 21:23). But we reckon the sense of the Scripture is to be the standard of our faith and practice, and not the bare sound

---

[1] Broughton, *Dictionary*, etc.

of words; and if there is a plain intimation of *the thing* meant by a vow, in the New Testament, all dispute about *the name* is idle and unreasonable.

Now, if *a vow is a voluntary and deliberate engagement to God, about matters of a sacred or religious concern*, it will be easy to show that it is both *lawful*, and *convenient*, and *profitable* for Christians to vow in this manner to the Lord.

1. It is *lawful* for Christians voluntarily and deliberately to engage themselves, and their connections, and enjoyments, to be sacred to the honor of God. The Lord hateth robbery for burnt-offering; and all that he requires of his people is consistent with that rule of the law and the prophets, *to do justly*. But if it be denied that the people of God, preserving a proper practical regard to this golden rule, may warrantably surrender up and devote their own selves, with all that they are and have, in a solemn manner, to the honor and service, influence, government, and disposal of the Lord Jesus, as their Head, Savior, and King, the whole system of the apostolic church's fellowship and practice will become disputable. The Lord having made a new covenant with them, and having put his laws into their mind, and written them in their hearts, he became their God, and *they became to him a people* (Heb. 8:10), that is,

> they were inclined and enabled, by his grace, to answer their obligations to him, in a way of faith and love, duty and obedience, and of owning him in a becoming profession of his name, as his peculiar covenant-people.[2]

Besides, they yielded themselves unto God, as those that were alive from the dead, and their members as instruments of righteousness unto God (Rom. 6:13). And they knew that they were not their own; for they were bought with a price: and therefore they glorified God in their body, and in their spirit, which were God's (1 Cor. 6:19–20). Moreover, they "gave their own selves to the Lord" (2 Cor. 8:5).

These were some of the principles of their religious fellowship, which account fully for everything in their system of holy communion; and these principles imply all that is essential in a religious vow. This is a much more decisive proof of the lawfulness of vowing under the New Testament, than

---

[2] Guyse, *Paraphrase*, on the place.

would arise from an induction of many examples of particular persons; as it shows that it was not only warrantable, but necessary, in the constitution and fellowship of the Christian church.

2. It is *convenient* for Christians to devote themselves unto the Lord. Two things render it very becoming for them to do so. (1.) God who cannot lie, hath condescended to swear unto us, that by two immutable things, wherein it is impossible for him to lie, we may have strong consolation; and shall not we, who are in the utmost danger of drawing back from God, reckon it expedient to bind ourselves in the strongest manner to his service? The firmest obligations best become us in so good a cause, where everything concurs to recommend the service. (2.) It become us to testify our concern about eternal things and our unfeigned affection to the ways of religion, by every possible demonstration of our regard and esteem. A cold approbation of these supremely excellent things, is not adequate to their nature. A truly gracious soul thinks it can never be bound fast enough to God, and therefore doth not only approve his ways, or desire to walk therein, but firmly purposes to cleave unto him. No solemnity can be too great in a matter of such infinite importance, where the strength of esteem, delight, and desire, should carry the soul to every possible expression of faith and love, of duty and obedience.

3. It is *profitable* for Christians to vow unto the Lord, and that in several respects. (1.) Hereby the heart is more engaged in approaching unto the Lord; when the person considers that he has vowed, this stirs him up to pay his vows unto the Lord; when he has sworn, he will be thereby excited to perform his duty in a proper regard to the Lord's righteous judgments. How beautifully does the apostle unite these things, in giving an account of his relation to God! "God, whose I am, and whom I serve" (Acts 27:23), which implies his being dedicated to the Lord, and in consequence thereof, his making it the great business of his life to serve him, not only in preaching his gospel, but in all manner of holy conversation and godliness. (2.) Hereby the soul is more established in its esteem of the ways of wisdom, and in its persevering progress in them. A double-minded man is unstable in all his ways; he is like a wave of the sea, that is driven of the winds and tossed; let not that man think that he shall receive anything of God. But when the vows of God are upon the soul, they tend to unite the heart to fear and obey the Lord, and to establish it in the love of its duty, and in the belief of divine truths; and thus they prevent persons from being

led away with the error of the wicked, and thereby falling from their own steadfastness. (3.) Hereby the soul is better fortified against temptations to depart from the truth, and to deny the power of godliness, according to the apostle's reasoning, on different occasions:

> What shall we say then? Shall we continue in sin, that grace may abound? God forbid. How shall we, that are dead to sin, live any longer therein? (Rom. 6:1–2).

> Likewise reckon ye also yourselves to be dead indeed unto sin, but alive unto God through Jesus Christ our Lord. Let not sin therefore reign in your mortal body, that ye should obey it in the lusts thereof (Rom. 6:11–12).

> Wherefore, my dearly beloved, flee from idolatry. I speak as to wise men; judge ye what I say. The cup of blessing which we bless, is it not the communion of the blood of Christ? The bread which we break, is it not the communion of the body of Christ?…Ye cannot drink the cup of the Lord, and the cup of devils: ye cannot be partakers of the Lord's table, and of the table of devils (1 Cor. 10:14–21).

> Be ye not unequally yoked together with unbelievers: for what fellowship hath righteousness with unrighteousness? and what communion hath light with darkness? and what concord hath Christ with Belial? or what part hath he that believeth with an infidel? and what agreement hath the temple of God with idols? for ye are the temple of the living God; as God hath said, I will dwell in them, and walk in them; and I will be their God, and they shall be my people (2 Cor. 6:14–16).

These considerations, that represent vowing to the Lord as a lawful, convenient, and profitable exercise, are sufficient to convince us of the warrantableness of the practice, in a general view of it; and have the same weight, when they are applied unto *personal* and *social vows*, in all the particular cases that concern Christians, upon the scheme of their fellowship delineated in the New Testament.

3. The Matters Which Vows Refer to

I come now to consider *the matters which vows refer to*; or what Christians may and should vow unto the Lord. On this head the following things are obvious and natural. (1.) Nothing should be vowed to the holy One of Israel, but what is lawful to be done; hence is that express prohibition, "Thou shalt not bring the hire of a whore, or the price of a dog, into the house of the LORD thy God for any vow: for even both these are abomination unto the LORD thy God" (Deut. 23:18). Upon this account, the vow of these forty men, who bound themselves with a curse, that they would neither eat nor drink till they had killed Paul (Acts 23:12), was impious and profane. This exposes the iniquity of these vows, much used among the Jews, in our Savior's time, and approved by the scribes and Pharisees, whereby, without regarding the necessities of parents, a man bound himself by a vow or oath, to devote to religious uses, what he might and ought to have spared for the relief of his poor father or mother (Matt. 15:5–6; Mark 7:11–12). (2.) Things that are *doubtful to a person*, are not fit matter for his vow. To make a vow in a dubious case is as much against all reason as for a man to run blindfold upon a precipice. Therefore we must never make a vow till *we are sure* the matter of it is lawful; and either a moral duty, or subservient to instituted worship. (3.) We should never vow anything which is *impossible*, for that would be both a mocking and a tempting of God.

A religious vow should *only* be taken about things that are either *morally good*, or else *immediately subservient to the worship of God*, though otherwise indifferent in their own nature.

1. These *duties that are required in the moral law* are fit matter for a religious vow. It is not improper, and it cannot be rash, for men to swear to keep God's righteous judgments (Ps. 119:106). The authority of God obliges us to do so; and our vows only recognize that obligation. Jacob's vow, for the substance of it, was of this nature,

> If [or seeing] God will be with me, and will keep me in this way that I go, and will give me bread to eat, and raiment to put on, so that I come again to my father's house in peace; then [or therefore] shall the LORD be my God: and this stone, which I have set for a pillar,

shall be God's house: and of all that thou shalt give me I will surely give the tenth unto thee (Gen. 28:20–22).[3]

That remarkable passage is of the same import, "One shall say, I am the LORD's; and another shall call himself by the name of Jacob; and another shall subscribe with his hand unto the LORD, and surname himself by the name of Israel" (Isa. 44:5). There are many inconsiderate persons, who forge chains to bring their souls into bondage, by needless vows, that set too narrow limits to their Christian liberty; but this ordinance is chiefly intended for the weightiest concerns of religion, and not for by-matters; for promoting real godliness, and not for spreading a spirit of superstition.

2. Such things as are conducive to holy living are proper enough to be the matter of a solemn vow. Whenever we open our mouths to God in such cases, we must take heed; that the matter be very grave and serious, and weighty; that it be something in our own power to dispose of; and that our vow about it do not contradict any part of our duty to God or man.

But if these essential limitations be duly observed, and if the just boundaries of holy Christian liberty be carefully maintained, it seems to be as safe, and, in some cases, as expedient to make solemn fixed purposes concerning the helps to powerful godliness now, as ever it was. Our Savior has

---

[3] Jacob made no conditions with JEHOVAH in this vow, as the words of it in our translation seem to imply; but, under the fullest conviction of the mercy, faithfulness, and power of God, who had spoken to him from heaven, he set his seal to what had been said, and constrained by the love of a promising God, he poured out his soul before him in these words, "*Seeing* God will be with me…*therefore* shall the LORD be my God," etc. (Gen. 28:20–22).

To support this translation, I might refer the reader to the passage itself, and leave him to judge, whether this manner of speech does not best become one, who was favored to see and hear so much of the Lord's goodness passing before him. Similar passages of Scripture might be compared (as Ex. 20:2–3; Titus 2:11–12). And, finally, the conjunctive Hebrew words in the vow, which are translated in our Bibles *if* and *then*, are frequently understood in the sense I have given of them, as in "*If* Mordecai be of the seed of the Jews," etc. (Est. 6:13), where the meaning certainly is, "*Seeing* Mordecai is of the seed of the Jews." "*Sith* thou hast not hated blood," etc. (Ezek. 35:6), the original word is, "*If* thou hast not," etc. And whoever has the least knowledge of the Hebrew language must be able to recollect many examples of the conjunctive particle, translated *then* (Gen. 28:21), being understood as implying that what follows is *the consequential effect* of what went before. I shall only add that the expression, "then shall the LORD be my God," has obviously this sense, "I will acknowledge him now and henceforth to be the Lord my God, and will, in his strength, worship and glorify him accordingly."

confirmed the covenant Job made with his eyes not to look upon a maid (Job 31:1), in his sermon on the mount (Matt. 5:28). And the apostle speaks of his firm resolution to preach the gospel without any expense, in these expressive terms, "As the truth of Christ is in me, no man shall stop me of this boasting in the regions of Achaia" (2 Cor. 11:10).

In everything that concerns *moral duties*, our resolutions should be positive and absolute, without pretending to add any limits or conditions; but whatever comes, whatever we want, or however we are dealt with in any respect, we must heartily give up ourselves, and our all, to obey and submit to the will of God, endeavoring, in a dependence upon his grace, to follow the Lord fully. In all that pertains to the *helping us in religious duty*, we should form our purposes and vows for binding our souls, with such reservations as are consistent with the moral obligations that lie upon us, in our several stations and relations; lest we make void the law of God, under a pretense of observing it more exactly. And we cannot be too careful, in the improvement of these helps to the ends we had originally in our eye, and in using them with cheerfulness and pleasure, without grudging or fretting at the restraints we are under, or making inquiry, after we have vowed, what pretenses we can find to justify our breaking them with the best color of reason. But this will fall to be considered, when I come to the *fifth section*. And therefore I shall proceed,

4. For What Purposes They Should Be Made

To inquire *for what purposes* religious vows should be made. And here I may observe the following things, that are sufficient to answer the end I propose by this inquiry.

1. Vows are to be used as *an acknowledgment of the sovereignty of God*, who has the first and most absolute right to our persons, services, and possessions. When we vow and pay to the Lord our God, we do not, we cannot, make God a debtor to us; for we only serve him with his own. His original right can never be alienated; and our vowing is only an acknowledgment of it. He has an undoubted right: to dispose of us at his pleasure; to demand our belief and confession of whatever he reveals; to be obeyed in all his commands; to be worshipped in spirit and in truth in every ordinance; and to prescribe the use to which we ought to put all the enjoyments of this world, which he confers on us. The vows we are called to make unto the Lord are only a recognition of this divine, uncontrollable

right; and to vow for this purpose is a most noble employment, every way worthy of intelligent creatures.

2. Religious vows are many ways *useful to men*; and should be used for enjoying the advantages arising from them, as an ordinance God hath appointed, and doth bless, for manifold good to mankind; *viz.*,

To engage the soul to an exact regard to the service of God, after signal deliverances from dangerous and alarming calamities; thus we find that, after the Lord had helped David, when the sorrows of death compassed him, and the pains of hell gat hold upon him, he expressed himself in these words, "O Lord, truly I am thy servant; I am thy servant, and the son of thy handmaid: thou hast loosed my bonds…I will pay my vows unto the Lord now in the presence of all his people" (Ps. 116:16–18).

To bind the soul unto God under severe and grievous distresses; thus Job expressed himself, when the hand of God lay heavy upon him in every shape; "Though he slay me, yet will I trust in him" (Job 13:15).

To promote an ardent love to the truth, when it is corrupted, or denied, or any way opposed; thus Joshua, fearing a revolt of Israel from the service of the living God, nobly declared his fixed purpose; "as for me and my house, we will serve the Lord" (Josh. 24:15).

To produce steadfastness in adhering to the truths and ways of Christ, when such cleaving to the Lord becomes perilous to Christians; thus the apostle gives a solemn charge to the church at Philippi;

> Only let your conversation be as it becometh the gospel of Christ: that whether I come and see you, or else be absent, I may hear of your affairs, that ye stand fast in one spirit, with one mind striving together for the faith of the gospel; and in nothing terrified by your adversaries (Phil. 1:27–28).

To fortify against temptations, which might lead into error, or vice, or indifference to the weighty concerns of real religion; thus the apostle exhorts Christians,

> that ye should earnestly contend for the faith which was once delivered unto the saints. but ye, beloved, building up yourselves on your most holy faith, praying in the Holy Ghost, keep yourselves in the love of God, looking for the mercy of our Lord Jesus Christ unto eternal life (Jude 3, 20–21).

These, and many other purposes, highly beneficial to the people of God, and through them of extensive advantage to the world, are set before the saints, as objects of great consequence, when they vow unto the Most High God; and a proper attention to these ends of vowing must determine persons and societies in fixing *the seasons*, and in making a prudent estimate of *their call*, to open their mouth with peculiar solemnity unto the Lord in this matter.

5. The Obligation of Them

I shall now attend to *the obligation of religious vows.* Here it will be necessary to explain the *nature*, the *grounds*, and the *extent* of their obligation.

1. The *nature of the obligation*, which religious vows lay upon the conscience, is to be considered. This is not a point of form, or conveniency; for if that were all, the obligation would be exceeding vague. But a vow, being made unto the Lord, is a bond wherewith a person doth bind himself; and shall not God require it? The obligation is of the most weighty nature; and cannot be dispensed with, except by God to whom we have opened our mouth,

> When thou vowest a vow unto God, defer not to pay it; for he hath no pleasure in fools: pay that which thou hast vowed. Better is it that thou shouldest not vow, than that thou shouldest vow and not pay. Suffer not thy mouth to cause thy flesh to sin; neither say thou before the angel, that it was an error: wherefore should God be angry at thy voice, and destroy the work of thine hands? (Eccl. 5:4–6).

> This is the thing which the Lord hath commanded. If a man vow a vow unto the Lord, or swear an oath to bind his soul with a bond; he shall not break his word, he shall do according to all that proceedeth out of his mouth (Num. 30:1–2).

It has been observed already that vows may be lawfully made, both concerning things that are moral in their nature, and concerning things that are conducive to a holy life. I shall consider the nature of their obligation in both cases.

When persons devote themselves, and their services, and substance, to the Lord, in obedience to the precepts of the moral law, the obligation that follows is neither greater nor stronger than they were under before they made this solemn dedication; for moral obligations can neither be increased nor multiplied, enlarged nor strengthened, by anything creatures can do. But, if the obligation of the moral law appears to the views of men so reasonable, so holy, so just, and so good, as to prevail on them to take its yoke upon them as easy, and to delight in its paths as pleasant; surely they will be much more criminal, if they burst these bands, and cast away these cords from them, after they have been so far enlightened, convinced, and affected, as to make these confessions. My meaning may be illustrated by the following example. Solomon sent and called for Shimei, and said unto him, Build thee a house in Jerusalem, and dwell there, and go not forth thence any whither; for it shall be, that on the day thou goest out, and passest over the brook Kidron, thou shalt surely die; thy blood shall be upon thine own head. And Shimei said unto the king, The saying is good. But at the end of three years, Shimei arose and saddled his ass, and went to Gath, to bring back two of his fugitive servants. Solomon, being informed of his going to Gath, and of his return again, sent for Shimei, and reminded him of his own command, and of Shimei's oath of obedience, and caused him to be slain for his contempt of the king's authority (1 Kings 2). In this history we see that the king's prohibition was the reason why Shimei must not go out of Jerusalem; and if Shimei had never promised any subjection to it, he would have been obnoxious to death, in case he went abroad; but having sworn by the Lord to obey, his offense was greatly aggravated; although his promise and oath neither gave Solomon a better right to prohibit his going out of Jerusalem, nor to put him to death for his disobedience. Solomon's right to do both was founded in his princely authority. Though the cases are not exactly parallel, this may serve to illustrate my position.

If vows are made concerning things which are not antecedently required in the moral law, but are *helps* to a sound faith and a holy life, the obligation to fulfill the vow is moral, and is founded upon the vow itself. Many of the Jewish vows were of this sort (Num. 30); and such was the dedication of Ananias and Sapphira (Acts 5); while their possession remained, it was their own; and after it was sold, it was still in their own power; but having professed to dedicate the whole of it to the Lord, and kept back part of it, they lied not unto men, but unto the Holy Ghost, and were remarkably punished for their sin, which was, by just construction, the deepest and grossest perjury.

2. The *grounds of the obligation of religious vows* must be represented, in the next place. These are various; but the influence of them arises from the whole combined together, and not from one, or two, or a few of them, taken singly. Particularly,

The matter of a vow is supposed to be something which is lawful, and in the power of the person that has vowed; and to be either required in the moral law, or to be a proper help towards religious worship.

It is supposed to be made in truth, judgment, and righteousness (Jer. 4:2). For this is no less necessary in a vow than in an oath.

It is made unto *God only*, as the party concerned in it. And the law is, "Thou shalt not forswear thyself, but thou shalt perform unto the Lord thine oaths" (Matt. 5:33).

The end of making a vow is to honor the sovereignty of God; and to promote the best interests of men, who are hereby many ways profited.

It is a just thing to perform our vows; for that God who hateth robbery for burnt-offering, will not be mocked by idle pretenses for neglecting to fulfill our engagements to him.

It is but grateful for men to do what they have vowed, "Praise waiteth for thee, O God, in Sion: and unto thee shall the vow be performed" (Ps. 65:1).

God hath no pleasure in these fools, who do not pay their vows (Eccl. 5:4). If any man shall put his hand to the plow, and look back, he is not fit for the kingdom of heaven (Luke 9:62).

The same motives that prevailed on us at first, to vow unto the Lord, should persuade us to keep our vow, whatever falls out; for God is the same, and his promises are all yea and amen in Christ.

Now, unite all these persuasive, powerful considerations, and you will immediately perceive the firm grounds of the obligation to perform, either personal or social vows.

3. The *extent of the obligation* which arises from religious vows is now to be explained. Here, I apprehend, it is a safe rule that, as nothing should be vowed, about the truth, lawfulness, and expediency whereof a person has any doubt, so, in performing his vow, he should leave nothing undone that he imagines he is thereby bound to do.

A private personal vow should be fulfilled, if it only respects such helps as are conducive to religious duties, in the sense he meant it (supposing that to be a good one), when he opened his mouth to the Lord. His words may imply more, or less, than he meant; but as a man "thinketh in his heart, so is he" (Prov. 23:7).

A social vow, relative to *such helps* as I have mentioned, binds in the full extent of what is engaged to, agreeable to the word of God; and moreover, the credit of religion, and the edification of his brethren, require that everyone concerned in such a vow should have a great regard to the very letter of it; in order that the ways of God may not be evil-spoken of through them, and that they may dwell in unity, as brethren.

But if a vow, whether personal or social, is made concerning things that are of a moral nature, the person or persons who have vowed should consider its obligation, as extending to the whole breadth and length of the divine law; for otherwise they would make void the law of God through their vows, which would in this case become a snare to the conscience. But, without enlarging further on the sacred obligation of religious vows, or entering on any nice and difficult questions, relative to their obligation in particular cases, I shall go on,

6. In What Capacity Christians May Vow

To show *in what capacity Christians may vow unto the Lord.* And, in general, they may engage themselves to him, either as *individual persons*, or as *united in holy societies.*

1. Christians may vow unto the Lord, as *individual persons*, devoting themselves, and all their concerns, unto the government and disposal of their Father who is in heaven. With Jacob, they may vow that *the Lord shall be their God* (Gen. 28:21). With David, each Christian may swear *to keep the righteous judgments of his God* (Ps. 119:106). With the apostle, every saint may say, "For me to live is Christ" (Phil. 1:21); and with all that believe on the name of Christ, may reason thus, "How shall we, that are dead to sin, live any longer therein?" (Rom. 6:2); and should not only *believe with the heart unto righteousness*, but *make confession with the mouth unto salvation* (Rom. 10:10). All this is the allowed privilege, and, on proper occasions, it becomes the bounden duty, of Christians, as individual persons.[4]

---

[4] Whoever want to be instructed in *the true nature* of this duty, and directed in *the right manner* of setting about it, may find an useful guide in Boston, *A Memorial concerning Personal and Family Fasting*, subjoined to Thomas Boston. *A View of the Covenant of Grace from the Sacred Records*, chap. 2, sect. 3, direct. 8.

2. Christians may make *social vows in a state of holy union and fellowship*. These social vows have a more extensive design than personal vows: the last being only intended to impress the person's own conscience with an awful and serious regard to the truths and ways of Christ; whereas social vows are likewise designed to beget and promote mutual confidence in the persons that make them, concerning each other's faith and practice, and to bind them to one another, in the same faith, love, and obedience of the truth. Social vows were very frequent among the Jews (Deut. 29; Josh. 24; 2 Chron. 15; 23; 34; Neh. 9; 10).[5] Their vows or covenants, first and last, were "an avouching of the Lord to be their God," engaging, through his all-sufficient grace, "to walk in his ways, and to keep his statutes, and his commandments, and his judgments, and to hearken unto his voice," according to the full extent of the revelation God had favored them with, above every other nation; all grounded upon, and referring to, that distinguishing covenant he made with Abraham (Gen. 17), whereby "he avouched them to be his peculiar people, as he had promised them" in that original covenant; the scope and intent whereof was, that they should keep all his commandments, and be made high above all nations which he had made, in praise, and in name, and in honor, and that they might be an holy people unto the Lord their God, as he had spoken (Deut. 26:17–19).

When God entered into covenant with Abraham, he said, "I will establish my covenant between me and thee and thy seed after thee in their generations for an everlasting covenant, to be a God unto thee, and to thy seed after thee… Thou shalt keep my covenant therefore, thou, and thy seed after thee in their generations" (Gen. 17:7–9). Thus he avouched them to be his peculiar people, and separated them *in their root*, that they might be holy above all people. And neither the law of ceremonial observances, nor of political ordinances, delivered unto Israel in the wilderness, four hundred and thirty years after, could disannul this covenant, confirmed before of God in the Messiah, with Abraham his friend, with a particular view to them, as his seed. All their institutions for worship and government were planned to manifest, and to improve, that covenant-relation between God and them, by carrying it forward to all its honorable and advantageous con-

---

[5] The engagements the Jews came under on these occasions were not only *oaths*, for the purpose of assuring each other of their united views concerning their faith and practice, but they were properly *vows*, wherein God was *the party* to whom they devoted themselves with the greatest solemnity; as well as *the witness* of the transaction.

sequences, in everything that pertained to Israel, as *a holy nation.* Hence *this covenant-relation*, which is strictly *religious* and *ecclesiastical*, is everywhere represented in the Scripture, as the source of all their privileges and obligations, and as the reason and design of every appointment, relative to their priesthood and jurisprudence. To collect the proofs of this observation, that appear almost in every page of our Bibles, would be a tedious, and a needless talk, while it is so manifestly implied in the passage lately quoted (Deut. 26:17–19).

This being the case, *the whole body of the Jews* became *a holy nation*, and accordingly they had a system of holy ordinances given them, to regulate their conversation, and to sanctify them to the purifying of their flesh; that they might be *holiness to the Lord*, as the phrase is (Jer. 2:3). The branches of that numerous people were all sanctified, in a political sense, in the root; and continued to be reputed holy, in virtue thereof, until they became degenerate plants of a strange vine unto God, by breaking through all the sacred bonds of that covenant of peculiarity, which God had made with them in Abraham; and then such branches were broken off, and the Lord regarded them not (Heb. 8:9).

All Israel were obliged to join *as one man* in these vows or covenants; and it was very proper for *their rulers* to use all their authority, *to cause them to acknowledge and stand to the words of God's covenant*, as Josiah did (2 Chron. 34:31–32). But it must be remembered that *Jewish princes* sustained a peculiar character, and were invested with powers of a singular kind: for they ruled over the people of God; they had the whole system of their laws and government from God; they were authorized to administer justice, as guardians of both tables of the law; they were not indeed allowed to execute any part of the office of the priesthood, that being assigned to the tribe of Levi, but it was their province, to take order, that unity and peace be preserved in the church, that the truth of God be kept pure and entire, that all blasphemies and heresies be suppressed, all corruptions and abuses in worship and discipline prevented or reformed, and *all ordinances of God duly settled, administered, and observed*; and they were to execute their office upon the plan of that covenant of peculiarity, which God had made with Israel as his own subjects; so that the exercise of their authority was to be entirely subservient to the honor of the God and King of Israel, and to the welfare of that holy nation, by either constraining their allegiance to their heavenly King, or else punishing their rebellion against him; and by doing both or either, precisely according to the tenor of the covenant of peculiarity he had made with them as his people. These were circumstances of a very singular nature, and yet they were necessary, by the appointment and command of God, in the person that should rule over that peculiar and holy nation; and until we have found *another such people*, it is to very little purpose to dispute whether there are, or should be, *other such rulers*.

This view of Israel and their rulers serves to illustrate both *the nature of their covenanting*, and *the warrant their rulers had to cause all the people stand to the words of the covenant*. Their covenant was an avouching of the Lord to be their God, by a profession of their faith, and by a promise of their obedience, according to the whole system of his revealed will concerning both. And their rulers, being authorized by God, obliged them, on proper occasions, to give that testimony, and to make that expression, of their allegiance to the holy One of Israel their King, which their circumstances had rendered necessary, both for the honor of their God, and for their own interest. In this situation, everyone that refused compliance with this command of the prince who ruled over them, was *justly reputed* a rebel against the law of his God, and an enemy to the welfare of his people, and was *deservedly obnoxious* to the punishments provided in such cases. But to pretend this as a warrant for *compulsory civil laws* concerning any established system of religion, besides the singular case of the Jews, must appear highly absurd and ridiculous, for two reasons: (1.) Because the form of the Jewish church and state is now entirely vanished away; and (2.) Because the Christian churches are modeled in the New Testament, in a form that has no connection with civil powers, no dependence on them, and no assistance from them, considered merely as churches; which, it is well known, was never the case with the Jewish church, from the day that the Lord took them by the hand, and led them out of the land of Egypt.

Israel, being under a dispensation of divine mercy, and of special service, engaged to believe and obey accordingly; but their being *a peculiar nation*, and their avouching the Lord their God, *to observe all the ordinances of the ceremonial and judicial laws*—were *only circumstances of their vowing and covenanting*. I grant, they were *essential circumstances under* (what the apostle calls) *the old covenant*; but so were the whole ordinances of divine service, and the worldly sanctuary, before the coming of the *Messiah*. But, as the shadows and examples of the good things that were to come are done away by the substance, which endures forever, so the *singular circumstances*, wherein the Jews covenanted, are now ceased forever, and yet *the substance of their vow* remains, as an *imitable pattern for Christians*.

The substance of their covenanting was a profession of their united, conscientious, and resolved attachment to their God, according to their then circumstances. I suppose, nobody will scruple to admit, that the moral law, and even the light of nature, confirm the obligation upon every Christian to depend upon his God, to keep his commandments, and to hearken unto his voice, according to the circumstances Providence has placed him in. And it is equally reasonable that a Christian should maintain his dependence and obedience, in solemn deliberate converse with God, avouching him to be his God, whose word he will believe, whose law he will observe, and to whose disposal he will be entirely resigned. This service is every way reasonable, and against it there is no law. Now, if we suppose that a number of individual Christians, who are agreed in one view of the faith and order of the gospel, are in such circumstances as clearly point out the necessity of their making some eminent profession of their faith and obedience, or of manifesting in the presence of one another, and perhaps of the world too, their joint and determined attachment to the truths, ordinances, and laws of Christ, according to the tenor of the New Testament system—then we put them and their covenanting on a foot with the Jews and their covenanting. Both of them vow, or covenant, upon *the same principle*; for they both profess their conscientious attachment to the will of God, only with this difference, that they are not in the same circumstances; but each of them is supposed to have their eye upon their own circumstances, and to engage themselves accordingly. Here the difference of circumstances has but an accidental connection with the substance of the duty, which is the same, be the circumstances what they will.

I shall not affront the reader by replying to the cavils of such as would represent this branch of the Jewish service, as peculiar only to their dispensation. I only beg leave to observe, as the sum of all that I have said on this point—that the circumstances of the Jewish covenanting were peculiar to that holy nation, even as the circumstances of Christian covenanting are peculiar to the New Testament dispensation; but the substance of both Jewish and Christian covenanting is the very same, and is originally founded in the law of eternal righteousness.

This being a point of some consequence, deserves the most careful attention. And for setting my thoughts about it in the clearest light, I shall consider the Jewish and Christian covenanting separately; and endeavor to state the singular circumstances of the covenanters, and the scriptural form of their covenanting, under each dispensation. The Jewish covenanting claims our first regard; and here we must observe what lights the Scripture gives us concerning the *singular circumstances of the covenanting Jews*, and *the form of their engagements* in these circumstances.

First, I shall mention some of the *singular circumstances* of the covenanting Jews, that were peculiar to themselves; and belonged to the nature of the dispensation they were under. And (1.) Their *covenant-holiness*, as a nation separated to dwell alone, and not to be reckoned among the rest of the nations, was entirely peculiar to them. Their systems of worship and jurisprudence had a peculiar connection and influence. Every individual was in the same degree entitled to civil and religious privileges. The persons, services, and possessions of that people were all sanctified. Their church and state had the very same subjects; and the laws of both viewed each of these subjects in the same light, whether favorable or unfavorable. Hence the same laws that prescribed what was available for the purifying of the flesh from ceremonial defilement, pointed out the way for taking off the temporal punishment that their sins exposed them to, as they were members of the civil community under God, as their political King. These circumstances too, of the priests executing civil offices, and of their kings giving appointments concerning the things of the Lord, were singular, and pertained only to that people. (2.) The ordinances of worship and policy, which they covenanted to observe, were peculiar to themselves, and are now ceased; for they were either connected with the land of Canaan, or a hedge of separation from the Gentile world, or else they referred to the Messiah then to come. (3.) The authority of their rulers to oblige people to enter into the covenant of God was most reasonable and warrantable, as has been already observed; but this circumstance is not a sufficient precedent for any other magistrates to attempt to compel their subjects to profess and practice religion, as they think fit to direct them. Upon these views of their circumstances, it appears that their covenanting was as much *a national affair* as anything could be, and was in fact an oath of allegiance to their God; and that it was strictly *a religious transaction* between them as the people of God, and JEHOVAH as their sovereign, whose revealed will was the rule and the reason of their obedience. But to urge the circumstances I have enumerated, as if they, or any of them, were common to any other people, is extravagant and foolish. I shall now explain,

Second, The *form of the vow*, or *covenant*, whereby the Jews bound themselves unto the Lord, and to his service. As far as we have any light on this head from Scripture, their form was very short and simple; a point that should be carefully attended to in all oaths and vows. It was also plain and familiar, scriptural and safe, for everyone concerned, to swear it in truth, in judgment, and in righteousness. There was no ambiguity in the words of their vow, and the thing they vowed was intelligible to the meanest capacity. The Holy Ghost has left us a variety of hints, sufficient to give us all reasonable satisfaction about the form of their vowing (see Josh. 24:14–28; 2 Chron. 15:12–15; 34:30–34; Ezra 10:1–5; Neh. 9:38; 10:28–39). The reader may examine these texts for himself, and he will find that their engagements on all these different occasions were founded on the same principle, and had the same meaning with that in "Thou hast avouched the LORD this day to be thy God, and to walk in his ways, and to keep his statutes, and his commandments, and his judgments, and to hearken unto his voice" (Deut. 26:17). This was the general form or purport of their covenant-engagements; although even then, their engagements sometimes bound them to services that were judged expedient only upon reasons of prudence, in their situation, when they entered into these covenants, though they were not required expressly in the law, "Also we made ordinances for us," etc. (Neh. 10:32), which is mentioned as something over and above their having "entered into a curse, and into an oath, to walk in God's law, which was given by Moses the servant of God, and to observe and do all the commandments of the LORD our Lord, and his judgments and his statutes" (v. 29). But these ordinances they made for themselves were evidently suggested by *a prudent regard to their circumstances*, and were highly expedient, if not necessary, for serving the Lord according to his own appointment, while they continued in that situation.

This shall suffice for some account of the *nature*, the *foundation*, the *manner*, the *peculiarities*, and the *form of Jewish covenanting* or *vowing to the Lord*. But that dispensation being now superseded, it is needless to enlarge on these points; nor should I have said so much on them, had it not been with a view to place, in the easiest light, *the substance*, and *the circumstances* of that *occasional service*, which the Jews performed with so great solemnity; and to make it evident that, when the circumstantial peculiarities of it are abolished, the substance of their service still remains, as *an imitable example to Christians*, who live under the best and last dispensation of the grace of God in this world. Some observations on the *particular circumstances of covenanting Christians*, and the *form of their vow or covenant*, shall shut up this section, as I have already proposed.

First, I shall enumerate some of the most remarkable and *distinguishing circumstances of covenanting Christians*, who vow unto the Lord in a state of holy union and fellowship. I may observe concerning these in general, that they are all to be planned on the scheme of *Christ's kingdom, which is not of this world* (John 18:36). If they exceed this model of Christian duty, they are not the ordinance of Christ; and he will reprove them, with good reason, as an addition to his words. According to the constitution of the gospel-church, it is obvious (1.) That the matter of their vows should be *the revealed will of God*, concerning their faith, worship, and practice, as Christians; for how can they, with any sense, or propriety, call their covenanting, or vowing, a religious Christian service, if it refers to anything else? If an engagement concerning anything else be sanctified by the name of a Christian vow, surely the name is profaned by such misapplication of it. (2.) The persons that engage in these vows are supposed to be *in a state of holy union and fellowship,* and to have one heart and one mind, in these matters they vow about; and consequently do not act in *a national*, but in *a church-capacity*, when they open their mouth unto the Lord. To pretend to graff the whole system of civil government and administration upon national schemes of religious engagements has many inconveniences, both: to *the magistrates*, who must either compel their subjects into uniformity, or else break their engagement by granting a toleration, in very many instances; and also to *the subjects*, who must either be supposed to be brutishly ignorant, or else they will naturally fall into different sentiments, from any religious scheme that *state-policy*[6] will choose

---

[6] *State-policy will choose to countenance.* It is well known that the law of God, delivered by the hand of Moses, was the complete system of the jurisprudence of the Jewish commonwealth; but nobody pretends that the same system, or any other scheme in the word of God, is to be adopted as a complete system of government in any other nation. Therefore in every country where the Christian religion has been legally established, we see it has been adopted into the body of their laws, and continued there, in subservience to political views. The history of *Christendom* (as it is called), will abundantly justify this remark.

to countenance; and then the unhappy Dissenters must either be exposed to the penalties of the law for nonconformity, as in many Popish countries; or, at best live as indulged offenders, as in England. (3.) The Christian system does not admit of *carnal weapons* to be employed, either for bringing men to vow unto the Lord, or for keeping them steadfast in his covenant,

> For though we walk in the flesh, we do not war after the flesh: (for the weapons of our warfare are not carnal, but mighty through God to the pulling down of strong holds;) casting down imaginations, and every high thing that exalteth itself against the knowledge of God, and bringing into captivity every thought to the obedience of Christ (2 Cor. 10:3–5).

And (4.) It is a glorious peculiarity of Christian social covenanting, when managed upon scriptural principles, that, under the influence of the Holy Spirit, it is a happy means of impressing the minds of them that vow with such affecting views of the majesty, authority, and mercy of God in Christ, as powerfully and practically teach them, to adorn in all things the doctrine of God their Savior; to love one another, and to love all the saints, for the sake of the truth; to live peaceably with all men, as much as in them is; and to be dutiful, loving, and conscientious in every relation and station of life.[7]

Secondly, I shall now consider *the form of Christian vows and covenants.* This should be as simple and short, as plain and precise, as possible; it should be divested of every ambiguity, and bind to nothing doubtful or uncertain. As vows have a reference only to present or future practice; so the form of these engagements, which are lawful for Christians, must express their resolved attachment to the Lord as their God, according to the

---

[7] Perhaps ours is not the only age that has produced *examples* of persons covenanting, not so much with a view to obtain these glorious ends, as to set a hedge about their own connections. I am sorry too to have occasion to observe that such weight is laid by many upon the disputable circumstances of their *manner* and *time* of covenanting, or vowing, as would naturally alarm a considerate person with some apprehension about their design in this service. Such as are equally sound, faithful, holy, and useful with themselves, must be reproached and defamed—neither for ignorance, error, nor vice; but because they are not satisfied about their manner of covenanting. I shall only make one remark upon this conduct: that these who carry such a spirit to this service have reason to consider, with a suspecting jealousy, whether they do not improve their engagements to a purpose very opposite to the essential design of Christian vows.

nature of the New Testament dispensation. The most complete form of words for this service should be preferred; and the general draft of it should be a solemn declaration of an unfeigned consent "to wholesome words, even the words of our Lord Jesus Christ, and to the doctrine which is according to godliness" (1 Tim. 6:3); or, a resolution, through divine grace, to observe all things whatsoever Christ hath commanded (Matt. 28:20); or, a declared purpose to have a conversation, "as it becometh the gospel of Christ, that ye stand fast in one spirit, with one mind striving together for the faith of the gospel; and in nothing terrified by your adversaries" (Phil. 1:27–28), so as to deny the truth, in order to avoid suffering.

This is the original scheme, and the general draft of Christian covenanting or vowing; and the particular truths or duties, which circumstances render expedient in certain cases, are to be graffed upon it. The *reason*, or the *occasion*, of such vows, is the best rule for determining the *truths* or *duties* that should be particularized in them. And in *forming* all such religious vows, it is expedient to observe the following rules: (1.) To be sure that there is a clear call to such a duty. (2.) To limit the particulars of the vow to the particular reasons or occasions that demonstrate the clearness of the call, because a multitude of things confuse and distress the mind. (3.) To condemn and renounce error or vice, and to express their faith and duty, in the point, or points, their vow refers to, as much in the Scripture-phrase as possible. (4.) Whenever a vow is repeated, let the ordinance of God be kept pure and entire. Let it not be imagined that men are to vow an adherence to a former vow; but if circumstances require it, and the call is clear, they may repeat their former vow, which expressed their consent to the words of our Lord Jesus Christ, and to the doctrine which is according to godliness; and this they should do, not because they had so vowed on any former occasion, but because the Lord calls them to do so at the time they vow. And (5.) A vow should run in such a form as leaves no room to suppose that it superadds any obligation to that of JEHOVAH's law.

Perhaps a more direct proof of the warrant Christian societies have to covenant together, and to vow unto the Most high, will be demanded. And, if it were not that I have partly endeavored to state that proof in another book,[8] I would willingly obey the call arising from my present subject to represent it here. All that I apprehend to be further necessary on this

---

[8] See Hall, *Scriptural View of the Gospel Church, of the gospel-church*, chap. 7.

head is briefly to mention the following observations. (1.) That the substance of social religious vowing is nothing else than a solemn profession of Christians in a state of holy union and fellowship, to cleave to the Lord, with purpose of heart, according to the tenor of revealed truth and duty in the Scriptures. (2.) That the first commandment of the moral law obliges Christians, both as single persons, and as united in sacred connections, to know and acknowledge the Lord to be their God, and to worship and glorify him accordingly. (3.) The covenant which God made with Abraham (Gen. 17:7, 9), was the foundation of Israel's avouching the Lord according to the whole tenor of the ordinances connected with that covenant under the Mosaic dispensation. These ordinances were to continue only till the times of reformation, and then they were to cease (Heb. 9:10). But the substance of the covenant remains unchanged,

> Repent, and be baptized every one of you in the name of Jesus Christ for the remission of sins, and ye shall receive the gift of the Holy Ghost. For the promise is unto you, and to your children, and to all that are afar off, even as many as the Lord our God shall call (Acts 2:38–39).

Now since the change of the dispensation has made no change in the original covenant, as to its best privileges and noblest obligations, which are for substance the same that ever they were, and hence *Christians* are said to be "Abraham's seed, and heirs according to the promise" made to him (Gal. 3:29), it is but reasonable to allow that believers may, under the gospel-dispensation, expressly engage to do and observe all that the Lord Jesus Christ hath appointed and commanded in his church, not only as individuals, but as brethren in holy society.[9] Such personal obligations are implied in *baptism*; and such social engagements are as strongly implied in *receiving the Lord's Supper* (1 Cor. 12:12–13; Gal. 3:27 compared with Rom. 13:14; Rom. 6 throughout, 1 Cor. 10:14–22). And if these engagements are implied in the most solemn ordinances of the gospel-church (even as similar engagements were contained in the Jewish circumcision and the passover), then there is nothing in religious covenanting inconsistent with the genius of the gospel-church, its constitution, or admin-

---

[9] See John Owen. *The True Nature of a Gospel Church and Its Government*, chap. 2, where this way of reasoning is largely and judiciously confirmed.

istration, when it is managed upon New Testament principles, and in a proper form.

The *peculiarities of the gospel-church*, and the *rules concerning the form of her covenanting*, which have been described, may be of some service to set the *nature* and *obligations* of the *public vows* of Scotland, and afterwards of Scotland, England, and Ireland, commonly called *The National Covenant of Scotland*, and *The Solemn League and Covenant*, in a safe and easy light.[10]

7. Some Directions Relative to Their Vows

A few *directions* concerning the *matter*, the *manner*, the *season*, the *end*, and the *performance of religious vows*, shall finish this subject. And,

1. Let *the matter* of them be both *lawful* and *possible*, *expedient* and *profitable*. *Lawful*: for it is the height of impiety to profane the name of the Lord, by vowing anything which his soul hateth; or even to bind the conscience with an engagement in any point that the person does not know to be lawful and warranted in the word of God. He that doubteth is self-condemned, if he eat. *Possible*: for God is not to be mocked, by men engaging to such services as they cannot perform. The end of vowing is the performance of their vow, which cannot be, if the vow is an obligation to anything out of their power, in the way of ordinary providence, and the usual supplies of the Spirit of Jesus Christ. *Expedient*: for the duty is only *occasional*, and the occurrences in providence must determine the propriety of doing it, at a particular time, or for particular purposes. The expediency of what we vow must be estimated by a prudent regard to the end we propose; and consists in the fitness and propriety of this measure to obtain that purpose. *Profitable*: for, though we cannot be profitable to the Lord by any of our services, yet every *good work is profitable unto men* (Titus 3:8). The matter of our vow should be prudently fixed, in order to impress our minds with a seasonable view of the sovereignty of God, and to confirm and establish our faith; to fortify us against strong temptations,

---

[10] For a full account of this matter the reader is desired to consult the preface to McEwen, *Select Set of Essays*, pp. 88–96. And John Brown (of Haddington). *An Historical Account of the Rise and Progress of the Secession*.

I refer to these writings, because I could not explain my views of the point, without setting the transactions of these periods before my readers, at greater length, than the limits and design of this discourse will permit.

to engage our hearts in present duty, when it is either important, difficult, or perilous, and to stir us up to a spirited active zeal in the ways of pure, undefiled religion.

2. Let *the manner* of religious vows be carefully pondered, as well as the matter of them. They ought to be made with *reverence, faith, consideration, sincerity*, and *pleasure*. *With reverence* and godly fear: for our God is a consuming fire (Heb. 12:28–29). Blessed is the man that feareth always; but in a particular manner, every tender conscience should and will *fear an oath*; especially an oath where the Lord is both *party* and *witness*. The person who can be irreverent in this work can never be rightly affected with a sense of the majesty of God in any other. *With faith*: "for whatsoever is not of faith is sin" (Rom. 14:23). In all matters of a religious nature, whatever we do not believe to be founded in, and authorized by the word of God, is very sinful for us to practice, or comply with. When we vow, we should be careful to have the fullest evidence, and the firmest assurance, that our vows are good in their matter, plain in their form, seasonable in their juncture, becoming our circumstances, and taken in truth, judgment, and righteousness. *With deliberate consideration*: for this service is only to be done by such as have knowledge and understanding (Neh. 10:28). A rash forward resolution is not a vow that becomes the divine Majesty. The whole Christian service is *reasonable* (Rom. 12:1). Hence is that striking passage,

> Keep thy foot when thou goest to the house of God, and be more ready to hear, than to give the sacrifice of fools: for they consider not that they do evil. Be not rash with thy mouth, and let not thine heart be hasty to utter any thing before God: for God is in heaven, and thou upon earth: therefore let thy words be few. For a dream cometh through the multitude of business; and a fool's voice is known by multitude of words. When thou vowest a vow unto God, defer not to pay it; for he hath no pleasure in fools: pay that which thou hast vowed (Eccl. 5:1–4).

With unfeigned sincerity: for the searcher of hearts doth not see as man seeth, nor judge as man judgeth (1 Sam. 16:7). He abhorreth goodly words, when they proceed from a deceitful heart (Ps. 78:37). Hypocrisy is both sinful and foolish, when we have to do with the Lord, whose eyes do see, and whose eyelids try the children of men; while he is delighted with truth in the inward parts. And *With pleasure*: for this, and every part of the ways of wisdom, is really pleasant (Prov. 3:17). Vows should be undertaken with cheerfulness; not as a piece of bondage we cannot avoid, but as a branch of liberty we voluntarily choose, and cordially delight in. There should be no hesitation, nor cold reserves in our affection, when we open our mouth unto the Lord; but we should lift up our whole heart with our hands unto God in the heavens (Lam. 3:41). What can be expected as to the performance, if there be hesitation in the undertaking?

3. Let *the seasons* of making religious vows be prudently weighed and chosen. Two things must be considered on this head of directions, *viz.*, That only such seasons are to be chosen for this duty as are proper for it; and that every such season is to be embraced and improved. (1.) Let such seasons be chosen for this duty as are most proper for it. Every thing is beautiful and useful in its season: "to everything there is a season, and a time to every purpose under the heaven" (Eccl. 3:1). Our world is full of changes, and the several events of time, and conditions of human life, are vastly different one from another; and we are continually passing from one of them to another. But every change concerning us is unalterably fixed and determined by the purpose and disposal of JEHOVAH, who hath appointed every event that befalls us, and hath pointed out our duty in every situation. This accounts for all the *occasional institutions* of the Scripture, which direct our practice, and command our obedience, *only* when we are in the condition which these institutions severally refer to. Whoso is truly wise will observe these things. Vowing to the Lord is an occasional duty; and therefore the circumstances that guide and oblige us to observe it should be carefully attended to, if we would honor the divine appointment. (2.) Let every proper season be embraced and improved: "Whatsoever thy hand findeth to do, do it with thy might; for there is no work, nor device, nor knowledge, nor wisdom, in the grave, whither thou goest" (Eccl. 9:10). "Wherefore is there a price in the hand of a fool to get wisdom, seeing he hath no heart to it?" (Prov. 17:16). The slothful servant, who knoweth his master's will, and doth not stir up himself to do it, is both wicked and unfaithful. We should endeavor to be always ready, and prepared unto every good work. No excuse is sufficient, no pretense can be sustained, to justify a disregard of the ordinance of heaven, when his word and providence concur in manifesting *present duty* to the conscience.

4. Let *the ends* of religious vows be strictly pursued, as well as judiciously directed. I have already mentioned several of them, on *the fourth section*; and shall only add, on this head, in the words of Mr. Marshall,

Think not to bring yourselves to good by vows and promises, as if the strength of your own law could do it, when the strength of God's law doth not. We bring children to promises of amendment; but we know how well they keep them. The devil will urge you to vow, and then to break, that he may perplex your conscience the more.[11]

5. Let every lawful religious vow be *exactly performed*; for this is the command of God, "Vow, and pay unto the LORD your God" (Ps. 76:11). He is a jealous God, and will by no means clear the guilty, who presumptuously vow unto him, and having vowed, neglect to fulfill their engagements. This direction may be branched into the following heads. (1.) Perform *what* you have vowed. Do according to all that hath proceeded out of your mouth. Every lawful vow is a bond to bind your soul. Thereby you acknowledge yourselves to be the Lord's devoted servants, and profess that you are not your own. You have owned your obligations, and therefore must conscientiously discharge your duty, unless you would run the fearful hazard of that servant who promised but never performed obedience to his master's will (Matt. 21:28–32). Your nonperformance will be a sin against God, and against the light and challenges of your own conscience; and may harden the profane, and grieve the hearts of the generation of the righteous, so far as they have access to observe and compare your vows with your practice. (2.) Perform them *in the manner* you have vowed; that is, with the same spirit of reverence, faith, consideration, sincerity, and cheerfulness, which prevailed when you made them. Maintain a sense of the honor, advantage, and obligation which conspire to enforce this glorious service. The same holy inducements that prevailed in vowing should operate with no less vigor in paying to the Lord. His people shall be willing in the day of his power. (3.) Perform your vows *in due season*. Consider the season for every duty, and the duty you are called to at every season. Such a well-judged scheme of practical religion glorifies God, adorns the gospel, and edifies the world. And, finally (4.) Perform your vows *with honorable intentions*. Do not so much as seem to affect any preeminence, on account of anything you vow or perform. Do not despise others who do not concur with you in social engagements. Do not go about to reproach, censure, and condemn your fellow-Christians, who maintain every material point

---

[11] Marshall, *The Gospel-Mystery of Sanctification*, direction 13.

of truth and duty you swear to observe, but cannot judge it their duty to join in your oath, either because they think *the season* or *the manner* of it wrong. Perform your vows in order to testify your gratitude, zeal, and humility; and to bind you more firmly to the service of your God. It is a most wretched *profanation of social vows*, when they are made subservient to the pride, interest, or humor of a party of professing Christians; and not rather used to impress the conscience, to affect the heart, and to engage all the active powers of the soul, to serve God with purpose of heart, in every branch of personal godliness and social religion.

Chapter 22

Casting of Lots

Whatever is necessary for instruction, caution, or direction, about the use of lots, will fall under the following heads, which shall be considered as briefly as possible.

1. The principles upon which this ordinance proceeds, must be represented;
2. The nature of lotting explained;
3. The purposes of it laid open;
4. The abuses of it held forth to public view in a just light; and,
5. Some directions concerning the lawful use of lotting must be suggested, for preventing these abuses; that it may be managed to the glory of God, when there is a just occasion.

1. The Principles on Which This Ordinance Proceeds

I proposed, in the first place, to represent *the principles* upon which the ordinance of casting of lots proceeds; and there are chiefly the five following.

1. That the providence of God extendeth to all his creatures, and to all their actions. There may be a great variety of second causes employed, in a most beautiful and harmonious concurrence, to bring about some ends; but the God of providence is the first cause, that guides and directs every secondary influence. In him we live, and move, and have our being. His kingdom ruleth over all. Two sparrows are sold for a farthing, and one of them shall not fall to the ground without his pleasure. The greatest things are not above, nor the least and most inconsiderable below, the care and influence of his holy providence.

2. That, in ordinary cases, men are furnished with sufficient means of discerning truth, and discovering their duty, for all the purposes of human life; but there are some things of very great importance to the welfare of mankind, that are not sufficiently provided for by all the exertions of

human prudence; and therefore must be referred to the decision of God, whose judgment is according to truth, and who, being the judge of all the earth, will certainly do right.

3. That many events fall out in such a manner, in the course of God's holy, wise, and righteous providence, that no creature can foresee, or any way influence them. These events are accidental, in respect of created intelligence, as no reason can be assigned, either before or after they happen, for their falling out one way rather than another, except that it seemed good unto the Lord, who "is wonderful in counsel, and excellent in working" (Isa. 28:29).

4. In some weighty cases, it is lawful for men to make an appeal unto the decisions of Providence, upon points that cannot be determined by human prudence to the satisfaction of contending parties, "The lot causeth contentions to cease, and parteth between the mighty" (Prov. 18:18). And,

5. The issue of the lot should be cheerfully acquiesced in, as manifesting the sovereign pleasure of JEHOVAH, who was appealed to, when the lot was cast, "The lot is cast into the lap; but the whole disposing thereof is of the LORD" (Prov. 16:33). I shall now attempt,

2. The Nature of Lotting

To explain *the nature of lotting*, as it refers to the principles I have mentioned. I understand it here in the sense which it constantly bears in those passages of Scripture, that speak of *casting lots*, where it plainly signifies the submitting a matter to be decided by way of *lottery*, which is some method purposely so contrived, as to put the decision quite out of the direction or influence of any mortal. For in appointing or fixing the particular form in which the lot shall be cast, the utmost care is professedly taken, that there may be no ground of probability upon which to form a judgment, nor the least room left for making any rational conjecture beforehand, which way the event of the lot shall fall.

Here then it should be carefully observed that it is not merely the *uncertainty*, or *contingency of any event*, that gives it the denomination of *a lot*. But in a lot strictly so called, some method must be taken *on purpose*, and *with a design*, to put it utterly out of the power of man to determine, or order, what the event shall be; or to bring to pass that event which he would desire, rather than another which he would not choose. And that which properly constitutes *a lot*, so as to distinguish it from other fortuitous or casual events, is *this careful design* of putting things into such an absolute state of contingency. This *purpose* is absolutely and essentially necessary to *the casting of a lot*. If this care be wanting, how casual, unexpected, or uncertain soever an event may be, yet there was no lot cast; nor can it properly be said that the event came to pass *by lot*. But when this care is agreed to, designed, and practiced, then, and then only, can it justly be said that recourse is had to a lot.

Further, since by *the use of a lot* it is intended that the decision of the case shall be put absolutely beyond the power of man, the necessary consequence of this is that hereby *the decision* is referred to *a superior agent*; even to *God* himself, whose name alone is excellent, and whose kingdom ruleth over all. And he has assumed and appropriated to himself solely, the high prerogative and glory of *the whole disposing of the lot* (Prov. 16:33). It argues therefore very gross stupidity, if not impiety itself, in any that are favored with the divine revelation contained in the Bible, to imagine that *the event of lots* comes either from the stars, from fortune, from the devil, from any of the saints or holy angels in heaven, or from blind chance; or to deny that it comes from God only.

The consideration of all this makes it evident that *a lot* is an ordinance of the like *sacred* and *religious nature* with *an oath*; and, as in *taking an oath* upon any just occasion, God is to be regarded as the heart-searching and omniscient, as the righteous and tremendous Judge of all; so in *the use of a lot*, God is to be regarded as the immense Governor of the world, who knows all things, and who is able and has a right to control, direct, and dispose of all as he sees fit. The very *nature of an oath*, likewise, implies *an appeal* to the great JEHOVAH, as the supreme Witness and Judge of all; so, also, *the nature of a lot* implies *the referring some matter to his decision*, as he is the infinitely wise Superintendent, and righteous Governor of the universe. The lot is a special, particular, and solemn appeal to God, and supposes that he is present to determine the event which is put upon the issue of it, as an oath supposes that he is a present Witness of what is sworn.

The amount of the whole is, that a lot is a direct appeal to God, that he would, by his immediate providence, give a present decision about some matter in question, without any use of means, or second causes, to influence that decision.

3. The Purposes for Which It Should Be Used

The *purposes for which a lot should be used* must now be laid open. From its sacred nature, as it carries in it a reference of some matter to the supreme Being, it is plain, a lot should not be used, any more than an oath, upon any frivolous or trifling occasion; but only when a matter is to be decided which is, either in itself, or in its consequences, of some importance: which may be the case when *strife* is to be prevented, or *contentions* made to cease; though the things themselves, about which the contention is raised, should not be of very great moment.

We may likewise conclude that a lot is not appointed for a man's *private direction in the management of his own affairs* for when it is said, "The lot…parteth between the mighty" (Prov. 18:18), there is a plain intimation that the cases in which it is to be used are such, in the decision whereof *more persons than one* are concerned. Nor is there an approved instance in Scripture of its being used in any particular case which related to a single person only, or to a man's private affairs, in which none but himself had any concern.

It may be further remarked that a lot is not to be used till *other proper means* of discovery or decision fail. As an oath in witness-bearing is a matter of such solemnity that it should not be required, or taken, till other satisfactory evidences of truth are wanting; so neither should a lot, which is of the like solemnity, be used, till we are at a loss how to come to a decision or determination of the matter in dispute by other means; that is, till we cannot find how to make a just and righteous determination of the case, by a faithful consulting the word of God, by a due attention to the rules of equity, or a careful exercise of human wisdom, judgment, and penetration.

Each of these remarks may be well supported by a due consideration of those instances of the *regular use of a lot*, which stand upon record in the Scriptures. From these we learn that the people of God had recourse to the lot only in *doubtful cases*, and such as were of *some importance*, where *several people* were concerned; and this only when *other methods* of discovery or determination failed; and then they used it as a solemn way of *referring the decision* to the Lord himself.

Thus it was used upon various occasions, relating to things respectively, both of a *religious* and *civil* nature. For instance, it was used: in the *dividing of lands*, as when Joshua required a description of the land to be brought to him, that he might cast lots for the people before the Lord

(Josh. 18:6); in *finding out secret offenders*, as in the case of Achan (Josh. 7), of Jonathan (1 Sam. 14:42), and of Jonah (Jonah 1:7); in *choosing officers*, as when Saul was chosen king of Israel (1 Sam. 10:20–21) and Matthias was made an apostle (Acts 1:26); in *ordering the courses of the priests* that were in office (1 Chron. 24:5; Luke 1:9); in *appointing the scapegoat* (Lev. 16:8); in *settling controversies* or disputes among men about their private property, to make contentions cease (Prov. 18:18); and it was used likewise in a case that related to a *public* or *state-affair* after the Jews returned from their captivity; for some peculiar difficulty then attending the inhabitants of Jerusalem, we read, that "the rest of the people also cast lots, to bring one of ten to dwell" there (Neh. 11:1).

And I cannot but observe that in all the cases I have mentioned, and in all others that are contained in the book of God, the matter to which the lot related was referred by the godly to the decision and determination of the great JEHOVAH; and so it always ought to be, when a lot is cast upon any occasion whatever. When those that have recourse to the lot do not intend to refer the matter to God, they profane his ordinance by using it in a way of mockery; since they make a show by their actions, of what is not so much as aimed at in their hearts. However, whether they intend it or not, the very use of the lot is an open manifest declaration that the affair to which the lot relates is avowedly submitted to the determination of God, who is infinitely superior to men in his influence, wisdom, and all other perfections. Since actions have a voice, this must be, by fair construction, the language of all men, both good and bad, in casting lots.

Upon the strictest review of the many cases in which the Scriptures tell us the people of God had recourse to the lot, there is not so much as one instance to be found of their ever using it in *a lusory [light]* manner, or upon occasion of any diversion, sport, or pastime; as is become too common among many professing Protestants in our day. There is no part of the word of God that can justly be thought to warrant the liberty they take in their vain practices of *playing at cards* or *dice*. These are ways in which the footsteps of God's ancient flock are not to be seen, nor traced.

From the whole, it is evident that a lot should be used only upon weighty and necessary occasions; and then it should be used (1.) As an acknowledgment of the wisdom, sovereignty, and influence of the holy providence of God, who is the Judge of all the earth; and (2.) As a final decision of some dispute, or contest, wherein the interest of many is concerned, that all contention may cease, in consequence of the verdict of heaven upon the litigated cause. These are the grand purposes that should be kept in the view of all who have a call to be any way concerned in casting lots before the Lord.

4. The Abuses of It

The *abuses of the ordinance of lotting*, which must now be considered, are almost endless. I shall only mention a few of them, leaving it to the judgment and observation of my readers to enlarge the catalog.

1. It is a fearful abuse of this ordinance when lots are cast in a way of *divination*, in order to discover things that are secret, or to learn beforehand things that are to come. "Secret things belong unto the LORD our God: but those things that are revealed belong unto us" (Deut. 29:29). Things to come are in the hand of God, and it is highly presumptuous for creatures to intrude into them, which is but an imitation of the ancient sorcerers and soothsayers. The ways and means of coming to the knowledge of futurities must not be devised by men; for this would be to set limits to the holy One of Israel.

2. Lots are much abused, when they are cast about *trivial things*, of no moment, either in their nature, or in their consequences. A lot is an ultimate judge and decider, even as an oath is, for ending all controversies. *It is*, as one saith, *like unto Moses, the greater matters should be referred to it.* Yea, a greater than Moses is here, even God himself, who passes a decision in every lot, by his providence. And therefore to call for a lot in frivolous and trifling cases is no better than sporting with that glorious and fearful name, *the Lord thy God.*

3. It is a gross profanation of this ordinance when people cast lots in *a careless unthinking manner*, without considering in whose presence they are, and to whom they make their appeal.

4. It is an abomination in the sight of God to use lots in *any game* or *pastime*, as in *playing at cards*, or *throwing the dice*, or any other diversion, where the event is designedly put out of the reach of human foresight, and referred to a casual decision, either in whole or in part.

Nobody can deny that *tossing up money* to determine who shall be partners in a game; or *drawing cuts*; or any kind of *throwing dice*, by whatever means, are *lottery*. And,

That there is *a lot* in the way of *dealing out the cards*, is undeniable; because in that method of proceeding there is a concurrence of those very circumstances, which make up the distinguishing property of a lot, and which constitute its peculiar form. For instance, let the case be closely viewed, and it must be acknowledged that *by the deal*, there is some matter to be decided and determined; and this is, who shall have *the best hand of cards* to play the game with. Again, this decision and determination is put absolutely beyond the influence of all human power, or the direction of human skill. This is evident from the care taken in *shuffling* and *cutting the cards*, before the deal. Yea, all this is done on purpose, and with a design that no man may know beforehand what the event of the deal shall be; and by this voluntary, designed, and chosen method of *dealing out the cards*, the *event of the deal* is left to be determined by some *superior agent*; that is, in plain terms, by *the holy One of Israel*, the sovereign Majesty of heaven and earth. For when the determination is *designedly* put above the power of man, it must of necessity be referred, and that immediately unto him; as he alone is the immense Being, whose influence and rule extend to the most minute contingencies, as well as the greatest events, upon earth, and reach to every single *hair of the head*; for these are all numbered by him (Matt. 10:30). And the *fall of a card*, let it be by what means or in what manner soever, can be no more beyond the extent, or below the notice of his government, than the fall of so inconsiderable and small a thing as *a single hair*. And here it becomes us to take notice that the universal extent and exactness of the divine providence cannot be illustrated in a more striking manner than it is by this instance; for it plainly shows that *the fall of a card*, as well as *of a hair of the head*, is as truly and absolutely under the sovereign direction of the Lord as any the most important event, whether relating to life or death. And to deny that the providence of God is concerned about any one contingency or circumstance in life, even *the most minute*, leads directly to a total denial of his government of the world. It is plain therefore that *the determination of the deal* must be of the Lord, who has the whole *disposing of the lot* (Prov. 16:33).

Though some have supposed *the dealing of the cards* to be a mere *casual action*; yet we may venture to say that it is impossible for men to contrive or frame *a lottery*, in which the event shall be *more a lot* than it is in the method of *shuffling, cutting*, and *dealing the cards*. It is an undoubted maxim that to whatever the just *definition* of a thing agrees, as bearing the distinguishing properties thereof, to that the *name* of the thing does justly belong. And if the observations we have taken from Scripture be duly weighed, and compared with the circumstances that attend *the dealing of the cards*, it must then appear to any considerate mind that the *definition of a lot* does so exactly agree to *the deal* as to show that it ought to bear *the name*. However it may be pleaded that there is an exercise of *memory, judgment*, or *skill*, in playing the game, yet this does by no means alter the nature of *the deal*, or make it cease to be a lot, any more than the skill of a gamester at *backgammon* can alter the nature of *throwing the dice*, or strip *the cast* of these circumstances which properly make it *a lot*. Thus I shall leave this point to rest upon the evidences now produced, and submit it to the well-informed judgment, and careful reasoning of every attentive reader, whether they do not incontestably prove that there is really *a lot* used in *dealing out the cards*.

I shall now endeavor to prove that *lots ought never to be used in gaming*. Nothing but the vices of the age could ever make it necessary to expose such a shameless corruption of God's holy ordinance. But since it is well known that bad things acquire importance by general practice and custom, it may appear to be no contemptible labor to divest them of their pretended significance, and to represent them in their own colors; that, being seen, they may be detested. To this purpose I would observe concerning lots, when they are used in gaming (1.) That there is no *matter of importance enough* to warrant an appeal to the Lord for a decision. It is most absurd and presumptuous to pretend that the lucre of the stakes makes the affair momentous; for, without any proper call from God or man, the parties refer it to the lot to decide whether that which is undoubtedly their own already shall be their own still; or shall pass to another. Who is so thoughtless, or ignorant, as not to see that this is a horrible profanation of a lot? (2.) There is *no necessity* for a lot in such cases; unless we shall say, it is necessary, that the manifestation of the divine counsels and providence be called in to subserve the covetousness, or recreation of mankind, which is too gross to be thought of without abhorrence. (3.) The *manner of using a lot in sport and pastime is too wanton* for that sacred ordinance. Would it not be grieving to any that truly fear God, to hear the solemn expressions Joshua used upon an important occasion (Josh. 18:6), uttered by persons, when in a vain sportive humor they are just going to enter on *an idle game?* It must greatly shock a pious ear, if one of the company should express himself, just before *throwing the dice*, or *dealing the cards*, to this purpose: "Come, let us cast lots for ourselves here before the Lord our God, and thus refer it to the holy One of Israel, the supreme Governor of all things, which of us shall win, or have the greatest advantage for winning the game, and triumphing over the rest." Yet if the action of casting a lot be duly weighed, what less than this can be the just construction of its language? The only excuse can be alleged for this profanation is that the parties have no thoughts of God in the affair. But why then do they refer away the decision from themselves to his disposal, without any consideration? If this excuse were allowed, it would only prove them guilty of a stupid ignorance, and of all the profligacy of a careless empty mind. (4.) The unhappy *consequences*, or *attending circumstances*, of sportive lots, demonstrate the sin and danger of using them. They are a great temptation to waste precious time unprofitably, to lying and cheating, to pride and passion, to peevishness and quarreling, to heathenish sentiments, heathenish language, heathenish affections, and heathenish practices.[1] So much for sportive lots.

5. The warmest advocates for *state-lotteries* must allow of several abuses in managing of them, such as (1.) That it is highly improbable, even in the judgment of the statesmen who plan the scheme of them, that a spirit of disinterested patriotism will induce the subjects to encourage them, with a view to the good of the public; and therefore they entice them with some very large prizes. Only a few indeed can be the better for these capital prizes; but everyone that puts in, considers one of them as his reward; so that public-spiritedness is out of the question on all hands. (2.) As covetousness is the great motive that induces people to engage in state-lotteries, so it is incredible that, under that spirit, they should be properly resigned in their hopes and wishes to the divine will, to whose disposal they have referred the matter. (3.) They are miserably abused by many, who ruin themselves and families, and injure their connections, by running imprudent ventures in them. And perhaps there are few arguments that can be urged against *private gaming*, but will retain much of their force when they are applied to *state-lotteries*.

---

[1] See Samuel Pike and Samuel Hayward. *Some Important Cases of Conscience Answered at the Casuistical Exercise, on Wednesday Evenings, in Little St. Helen's, Bishopgate-Street*, case third.

6. The last abuse of lots I shall mention is of a very dangerous and criminal nature, *viz., the using of God's holy word as a lot*. I must, however, observe that an infinitely wise and sovereign God, no doubt, has, and does many times overrule events in his holy providence, to a very happy issue, in behalf of his people, by guiding both their thoughts and eyes to such passages of Scripture as are particularly suitable to their case. But that which I censure, under the name of *Bible-lottery*, is a practice which has no connection with this; a practice too, which I know is too common; it is the professed purpose and design some people have in opening their Bible at random, in order to find direction or comfort, in the first passage that comes in their eye; looking upon that as an immediate intimation of the will of God, for their present duty or consolation; and this they will repeat as often as they want the counsel of the holy One of Israel, perhaps several times a-day. This practice is a just parallel to the use heathens made of the writings of Homer and Virgil; and it is a dangerous way of tempting the Lord; for (1.) The counsel of God is to be asked, and expected, in the way of prayer, and comparing Scripture with Scripture, that we may understand its doctrines and duties. (2.) Such persons as follow this practice, are in great danger of wresting the Scripture to God's dishonor, and to their own hurt. (3.) The Lord is righteous, if he give them over to strong delusions, and answer them according to their idol of jealousy, because they do not seek him after the due order of his own appointment; accordingly such unwarrantable abuses of the word of God generally keep pace with a spirit of *enthusiasm*, and produce effects which bring discredit upon the good ways of religion.

I might also have considered the regards many pay to *omens* and *appearances*, which they look upon either as *lucky* or *unlucky*. An example of this is recorded in Ezekiel 21:21, "the king of Babylon stood at the parting of the way, at the head of the two ways, to use divination: he made his arrows bright, he consulted with images, he looked in the liver." The fashion of divination may alter, as the fashions of other things do; but the sin is still the same, though it be practiced in other and new invented forms.[2]

---

[2] See Durham, *A Practical Exposition of the Ten Commandments*, on the third commandment—and, Anonymous. *Thoughts on the Nature and Use of a Lot*.

5. Directions concerning the Lawful Use of Lots

I shall now shut up this subject with a few *directions* concerning the lawful use of lots, in order to prevent these abuses that have been mentioned, or others of a like nature.

1. It should only be used in *a religious manner*; not in wantonness and diversion; not to kill time, or to furnish mirth. It is the ordinance of God, and therefore should be used with holy reverence, and a religious awe of the wisdom, sovereignty, and power of the divine Majesty and perfections.

2. A lot should be used with a special *exercise of faith*, both with regard to the divine Omniscience, and to the Lord's wise and righteous superintendency over all events, both great and small. In casting lots, men should look to their Maker, and their eyes should have respect to the holy One of Israel.

3. A lot should never be used by any *individual person*, in order to discover the mind of the Lord concerning anything that relates to *his own affairs*. The casting of lots is everywhere in Scripture represented as *a social deed*, and never as *a personal business*, except where that use of it is set forth in a criminal light (as Ezek. 21:21; Est. 3:7).

4. A lot should never be cast in any case, till we are satisfied that the matter in dispute is of such importance that we can, with a good conscience, make an appeal to God about it, and desire his immediate decision upon it; for it is a fearful thing to take that glorious name in vain.

5. It is unwarrantable to cast lots, where human prudence has not been first employed in doing all that can be done to decide in the dispute. A lot was only instituted to supply, where the prudence and wisdom of men should fall short of giving a satisfactory decision.

6. When the lot is to be cast, the parties should be determined to submit the affair in doubt to the decision of the Lord, with a humble and serious purpose, through his assistance, to acquiesce in his determination, when the event of the lot has manifested his pleasure, as to the matter about which the appeal or reference was made.

7. The use of a lot should be attended with *prayer* and *invocation*. Herein we have the example, not of king Saul only, who said unto the Lord God of Israel, "Give a perfect lot" (1 Sam. 14:41), but likewise of the apostles themselves, of whom we read that before they gave forth their lots, "they prayed" (Acts 1:24). And before we give forth ours upon any occasion, so should we.

8. As all fraud, or anything which might have influence, as a second cause, to mar or bring out the decision by the lot, should be carefully avoided, lest we mock God by pretending to put the decision to him, and yet endeavor to give the answer ourselves, so after the lot, there should be a reverend acknowledging of God's mind, without fretting or grumbling, and a cheerful submission to it, as an event appointed for us by the will of heaven.

These are the principal rules necessary to be observed in casting of lots, which I have not enlarged on, because they are either generally allowed, or such of them as are disputed have been explained and confirmed in the *preceding sections*. I shall only further observe that all the errors about the use of lots contradict some or other of the directions I have offered; and they are generally committed, not so much for want of *evidence* on the other side, as for want of *consideration*.

Appendix

There are certain practices, which have obtained in the Christian church that are supposed by some to be standing religious services, appointed by the Lord Jesus Christ, to continue till his second coming: *viz., Love-feasts, the holy kiss, washing the disciples' feet,* and *abstaining from the eating of blood and of things strangled.* Though it does not belong to the system of ordinances relating to gospel-worship to consider these points, yet as they are very plausibly urged by some, and generally omitted by many others, in their systems of religions institutions, I shall give my opinion of them severally.

Love-Feasts

That the primitive Christians were wont to *table together*, as opportunities and conveniences offered, sometimes at one house, and sometimes at another, is evident from Acts 2:46, "And they…breaking bread from house to house, did eat their meat with gladness and singleness of heart." This was the effect of their *having all things common*, and gives us a lively view of the spirit that ought to govern every true believer; though the *manner* and *degree of its exercise* were peculiar to the circumstances of those times, and were not designed for the imitation of all after-ages. But besides these occasional friendly entertainments, which were made at the common expense, and which were observed only for a season, and ceased probably in the apostles' time, when that equality of possessions had a period—there were feasts observed, in testimony of mutual love, and as a means of increasing their knowledge of and affection to one another, by these saints who loved as brethren. The entertainment was common; the rich furnishing the provisions, and the poor, who had nothing, being invited; and they partook of the entertainment together. They had certain fixed days for this service, when, it is said, they also received the Lord's Supper. It has been contested whether these feasts went *before*, or followed *after*, their receiving the Lord's Supper. Perhaps it will be most agreeable to truth to allow that they sometimes preceded, and sometimes followed, their eating the Lord's Supper.³

Tertullian gives this account of the *love-feasts* observed in his time:

> Our supper carries its reason in its very name; for it is called *agape*, which signifies *love*. We therewith relieve and refresh the poor. We do not sit down before we have first offered up prayers to God. We eat and drink only to satisfy hunger and thirst, remembering still that we are to worship God by night. We discourse as in the presence of God, knowing that he hears us: then, after water to wash our hands, and lights brought in, everyone is moved to sing some hymn to God, either out of Scripture, or as he is able, of his own composing. Prayer again concludes our feast, and we depart, not to fight and quarrel, or to abuse those we meet, but to pursue the same care of modesty and chastity, as men that have fed at a supper of philosophy and discipline, rather than a corporeal feast.⁴

This is one of the most favorable descriptions of them; for such excesses were committed at them in length of time, that the councils of Laodicea and Carthage totally prohibited the observation of them, some time between the years of our Lord 348 and 400. And supposing all the passages in the New Testament that are thought to refer to these feasts, to relate to them, as some have warmly contended, yet it cannot be refused that the irregularities attending these religious banquets, even in the apostolic age, were scandalous and shameful.

> When ye come together therefore into one place, this is not to eat the Lord's supper. For in eating every one taketh before other *his own supper*: and one is hungry, and another is drunken. What? have ye not houses to eat and to drink in? or despise ye the church of God, and shame them that have not? What shall I say to you? shall I praise you in this? I praise you not (1 Cor. 11:20–22).

> These, as natural brute beasts…count it pleasure to riot in the day time. Spots they are and blemishes, sporting themselves with

---

³ See Suiceri, *Thesaurus Ecclesiasticus*, on αγαπη.
⁴ See Tertullian. *Apologeticus*, chap. 39.

their own deceivings while *they feast with you*; having eyes full of adultery, and that cannot cease from sin; beguiling unstable souls (2 Peter 2:12–14).

These filthy dreamers defile the flesh, despise dominion, and speak evil of dignities... These are spots in *your feasts of charity, when they feast with you, feeding themselves without fear*: clouds they are without water, carried about of winds (Jude 8–12).

But if we examine carefully these texts, which are the only proofs alleged out of the word of God, perhaps it will appear, at least, doubtful, whether they contain any divine warrant for the practice, or not. They indeed intimate that it was not unusual among the primitive Christians to observe such feasts; but do not seem to contain any divine appointment, nor to carry the most distant intimation about their continued use in the Christian church.

That passage in 1 Corinthians 11:20–22 is supposed to be the most clear and decisive proof of the heavenly original of this practice. But

I see no just reason to suppose, that the apostle here refers at all to the *love-feasts*: for in verse 20, he mentions only the Lord's Supper; and all that he speaks of afterwards, admits of an easy application to their gross irregularities in partaking of that ordinance, while many of those things can admit of no other construction: and for the cure of their abuses of it, he brings them back to the original institution of the Lord's Supper (vv. 23–27); and then directs them how to celebrate it in such a manner, as might prevent their so unworthily receiving it (vv. 28–34).[5]

To show the force and evidence of this remark, I shall favor the reader with that excellent writer's paraphrase on the whole text of 1 Corinthians 11:20–22:

When ye professedly meet together, as New Testament churches use to do, in one place, for celebrating the Lord's Supper, which he instituted to be a memorial of his death, the way, in which many of you

---

[5] Guyse, *Paraphrase*, note on 1 Cor. 11:20.

manage on those occasions, is such as is not really partaking of that divine ordinance, according to the true nature and design of its institution, but is turning it into another sort of festival, than Christ intended. For in your disorderly manner of keeping that spiritual and sacred feast, ye eat and drink, as though it were appointed for the refreshment of the body, rather than of the soul: instead of the whole church's partaking of one bread, in testimony of their communing together with brotherly love, and of their having joint fellowship with Christ, each party bring their own provision, and eat their own supper, when it is ready for them, before another eats theirs: and instead of taking only a little of the bread and wine, which is enough to answer the end, some of you make a full meal, contrary to the plain design of the institution, which was at the close of the paschal-supper, after the hunger of the disciples had been satisfied, by their eating at that festival. And as there is a great difference in worldly circumstances, between some and others among you; so they, who, through their poverty, are incapable of providing for themselves, are neglected by the rest, and go away as hungry as they came, while the rich bring plentiful entertainments for their own and their friends' use, and eat and drink to the full, if not to a degree of excess, and *that* at a time when they ought to be most sober, self-mortified, and serious, and to exercise a compassionate love to Christ's poor, in distributing to their relief.

What an incongruous, absurd, and scandalous practice is this! If feasting to please and satisfy animal nature be your design, have ye not families to eat and drink in for this purpose, privately at home? Or, do ye think so lightly of the church of God's own institution, for the celebration of divine ordinances in their solemn assemblies, as if common and sacred things were to be blended together in its administration, and its poor members were to be thought beneath your notice, though they are as dear to Christ, and cost him as much to redeem, and have as much right to this holy ordinance, as the rich? And are ye minded to expose and discourage, and to pour contempt and scorn upon such members of the church, as have no provisions of their own, nor are admitted to partake of yours? What shall I say to such an extreme disorder and corruption among you, as this? Shall I commend you for it, as I did for your following my orders in other things? (v. 2). No, by no means; in this particular I cannot do it, but must faithfully reprove you: since herein you have, instead of keeping, notoriously departed from what I delivered to you about this very ordinance.

This view of that passage seems to be most consistent, plain, and natural. But if, after all, any should think the apostle meant *the love-feasts*, what he here says is no great commendation of them. In the beginning of the chapter he praises the Corinthians, because they remembered him in all things, and kept the ordinances, as he delivered them to that church (v. 2). Now, if we suppose that the irregularity he censures among the members of that church, in verses 21–22, refers to their love-feasts, he must be understood to correct it in the following verses, by reducing every part of that service to the original standard of divine institution. And when he explains what he had *received of the Lord*, and *delivered to them*, he makes no mention of a divine appointment of these feasts; he speaks nothing in defense of this custom, nor urgeth it upon them; but only presses the divine institution of *the Lord's Supper.* He entirely gives up the point as to these supposed love-feasts, and instead of proposing a remedy for the miscarriages at them, he only urges a proper respect to be paid to the standing ordinance of *the Lord's table.*

Upon the whole, I think it is really doubtful whether the apostle speaks of *love-feasts* at all in that place; but if he does, he seems rather *to condemn* than to give the smallest countenance to *the observation of them.*

The other two texts, 2 Peter 2:13 and Jude 12, are evidently of one import, and refer to the same thing. But all that can be gathered from them is not sufficient precisely to determine whether *the entertainments* mentioned were in token of *civil friendship*, or of *religious affection*; whether they were *stated*, or *occasional*; or, whether they were *public*, or *private*. To clear up these points with satisfactory evidence is highly necessary in deciding this question; but neither can that be done from anything in the texts themselves, nor from the analogy of faith, nor from compared passages of Scripture, in order to show *that love feasts were an ordinance of church-communion in the apostolic age.*

It is evident that *the infamous characters*, described by Peter and Jude, would be a scandal to *any social feast of entertainment*, whether it was held in the way of *civil* or *religious friendship*; and this consideration takes away all pretense to restrict it to *sacred connections*. And, if *the richer sort* in a congregation were to invite and entertain *the poor*, on proper occasions, agreeable to our Savior's advice about making a feast (Luke 14:12–14), the original nature and design of Christian love-feasts would be completely obtained; and this would be just such an instance of their unfeigned love now, as those feasts of charity were at that period.

The Holy Kiss
What considerate person would be so mad as to attempt the fruitless task of accounting for the characteristic manners of different nations, and different ages of the world? The sources of knowledge are so remote, the principles so uncertain, and the occasions of introducing their customs so accidental, that prudence forbids the useless waste of time and abilities, in a study that can never arrive, in the most of points, even at probable conjecture. It is generally best to take things as we find them, and accommodate ourselves to them the best way we can, as far as a good conscience will admit. In order to this, it is supposed that these manners are at least *innocent*, if not also *useful*, in civil life; because otherwise they ought to be abolished. Different places and periods have very different manners; while human nature may operate to the same end, and with the same ease, under very different appearances. This is an observation that must have occurred to the thoughts of all that know the world, either by reading, or experience.

The conversation of Christians should be universally holy, that they may adorn the doctrine of Christ in all things. Every creature of God, every condition of life, and every innocent custom of men they are connected with—all is good, being sanctified by the word and by prayer. And Christianity requires that the saints be holy in all manner of conversation, so far as it relates to their situation and social intercourses. Says Dr Owen,

> Mention is made in the Scriptures of sundry things practiced by the Lord Christ and his apostles, which, being then in *common use* amongst men, were occasionally made by them *symbolical* instructions in moral duties…but there being no more in them but a *sanctified use* directed unto the *present civil customs and usages*, the commands given concerning them, respect not the *outward action*, nor

appointed any continuance of them, being peculiarly suited unto the state of things and persons in those countries[6]

Such was *the salutation* Christ prescribed unto the seventy disciples, "into whatsoever house ye enter, first say, *Peace be to this house*" (Luke 10:5). And such was *the holy kiss*, or *the kiss of charity* or *love* wherewith the Spirit of God commanded Christians, in the apostolic age, *to greet* or *salute one another* (Rom. 16:16; 1 Cor. 16:20; 2 Cor. 13:12; 1 Thess. 5:26; and 1 Peter 5:14).

Saluting one another on the face, in token of respect and friendship, was an *ancient* and *common custom* among both Jews and Gentiles; and particularly among the Egyptians, Romans, and Grecians, it was continued for a considerable time among the primitive Christians, in their religious assemblies. They used it frequently *before*, and sometimes *after* the celebration of the holy supper.[7] The *apostolic constitutions* inform us, that this religious kiss was given by the clergy to their bishops, and by the people one to another, by the men apart, and, by the women apart.[8]

It is well known that the best things have been abused, and, through the depravity of human nature, perverted to purposes totally foreign, yea, altogether opposite to their original meaning. This observation is so generally true that nothing but a little experience of life is necessary to carry the most determined skeptic beyond all hesitation about it. *Salutation by a kiss* is a clear example of the position. It was undoubtedly meant, at first, as a token of the most hearty friendship and respect; but, among the many delusive arts of refinement in the mystery of iniquity, which is never practiced so successfully as under the fair appearances of virtue; *this* too has undergone very material alterations. By a violence and deceit, directly contrary to its most obvious intention, it has been employed: to conceal the

---

[6] John Owen. *A Brief Instruction in the Worship of God*, pp. 43, 44.
[7] Suiceri, *Thesaurus Ecclesiasticus*, on φιλημα ασπαζομαι, and ασπασμος.
[8] *N. B.*, These *apostolic constitutions*, or *canons*, were not composed by the apostles themselves; nor do they savor, in many points, of that simplicity which is in Christ. They are generally allowed, even by *the church of Rome*, to be a human work, that is not worthy of an inspired pen. We cannot certainly say when, or by whom they were compiled. The judicious Mr. Daille is of opinion, they were not collected till about the latter end of the fifth century. My design in referring to them is obviously no more, than barely to vouch for a matter of fact.

basest treason (Matt. 26:49); to flatter and deceive (2 Sam. 15:5); to plead the cause of lust and whoredom (Prov. 7:13); and to procure an undeserved fatal confidence (Prov. 27:6).

The Holy Ghost nowhere requires *simply* the use of this salutation by a kiss; which is everywhere in Scripture, supposed as *a common custom*, that was generally practiced. He only prescribes *the manner* and *purposes* of this salutation, that it might answer its original design, under the influence of Christian principles; which are so far from destroying, that they admit, and even carry on to the highest improvements, whatever is either honorable or advantageous to human nature and society.

The kiss which the Scripture commands the saints to give to each other must be both *holy* and *loving*. (1.) It must be *holy*, "Salute one another *with an holy kiss*" (Rom. 16:16), as if the apostle had said,

> As saluting one another is customarily used in civil society, and in the churches of Christ, in token of their most hearty friendship and respect; see that ye give this testimony of your brotherly regards one to another, by such a kiss, as is attended with *the utmost chastity, sincerity*, and *spiritual affection*, as becometh saints that love one another with a pure heart fervently.[9]

And (2.) It must be *loving*, hence called *the kiss of charity* or *love* (1 Peter 5:14). It ought not to be the deceitful kiss of an enemy, but an expression of love without dissimulation; not an idle compliment, but a visible instance of cordial affection; not an unmeaning act of common civility, but a token of Christian friendship grounded upon the faith and hope of the gospel.

The word ασπαζειν which is promiscuously rendered sometimes *to greet*, and at others *to salute*, is the same; and signifies any courteous, engaging, and respectful way of expressing, by word or action, our good wishes for the happiness and prosperity of those whom we address. But as custom regulates everything relative to *the manner* of expressing these wishes, and the customs of *times* and *places* are very different; it is neither necessary nor proper to establish *one invariable mode* and *token* of manifesting friendship among Christians in every situation they might be brought

---

[9] Guyse, *Paraphrase*, on the place.

into. A sanctified use of the present civil customs of any country and age is unquestionably the most proper way of signifying the unfeigned love of the saints to one another, in order to make their light shine with influence and observation among men. Indeed, where divine authority is interposed to point out the will of God concerning any service, which is enjoined for standing use among the saints, and has a promise annexed to it, and some grace of the new covenant represented or exhibited in it; such a service ought to be observed without any regard to the *manners* and usages of mankind, because both *the substance* and *the manner* of it are *the institution of Christ.* But the primitive *holy kiss* was only a temporary occasional token of entire affection, which may be as well expressed by any sober usage of salutation among men, that has the same meaning, and is applied to the same purpose.

The amount of the whole may be collected in these three positions. (1.) That *kissing* is a manner of salutation, not commanded by Christ for itself, but comprehended in the exhortations relating to it, as a well known practice, whereby men use to testify their love and respect to each other. (2.) The Holy Ghost only enjoins Christians to rescue that token of friendship from the abuses of it, and to employ it to its original purpose, *in holiness* and *love.* And (3.) Other tokens of friendship which are established by custom, in different countries and periods, may as effectually answer the same purpose, if they be used with that *holiness* and *love*, which should adorn the Christian character in all things; such as, *shaking hands*, and *bowing respectfully*, or any other decent, sober, and friendly method of salutation.

Washing the Disciples' Feet

Now before the feast of the passover, when Jesus knew that his hour was come that he should depart out of this world unto the Father, having loved his own which were in the world, he loved them unto the end. And supper being ended, the devil having now put into the heart of Judas Iscariot, Simon's son, to betray him; Jesus knowing that the Father had given all things into his hands, and that he was come from God, and went to God; he riseth from supper, and laid aside his garments; and took a towel, and girded himself. After that he poureth water into a bason, and began to wash the disciples' feet, and to wipe them with the towel wherewith he was girded. Then cometh he to Simon Peter: and Peter saith unto him, Lord, dost thou wash my feet? Jesus answered and said unto him, What I do thou knowest not now; but thou shalt know hereafter. Peter saith unto him, Thou shalt never wash my feet. Jesus answered him, If I wash thee not, thou hast no part with me. Simon Peter saith unto him, Lord, not my feet only, but also my hands and my head. Jesus saith to him, He that is washed needeth not save to wash his feet, but is clean every whit: and ye are clean, but not all. For he knew who should betray him; therefore said he, Ye are not all clean. So after he had washed their feet, and had taken his garments, and was set down again, he said unto them, Know ye what I have done to you? Ye call me Master and Lord: and ye say well; for so I am. If I then, your Lord and Master, have washed your feet; ye also ought to wash one another's feet. For I have given you an example, that ye should do as I have done to you. Verily, verily I say unto you, The servant is not greater than his lord; neither he that is sent greater than he that sent him (John 13:1–16).

Here we see the marvelous grace of our Lord Jesus Christ, who, though he knew that the Father had given all things into his hand, and that he was come from God, and was a-going to a state of the highest glory and exaltation in his Father's house, humbled himself to perform the office of the meanest servant, in *washing the feet of his disciples.* He loved them to the end; and therefore had compassion on their infirmities, and provided suitable antidotes against every unworthy suspicion of his goodwill. He was about to leave the world, and go to God; and therefore he would not leave them comfortless, under an apprehension of his being too eminent to regard their miseries, or condescend to their meanness. He was separate from sinners, being holy, harmless, and undefiled; and therefore he would not suffer them to continue ignorant of that most important branch of his mediation, as he is the Author of sanctification by the efficacy of his blood, by the power of his Spirit, and by means of his word. Ambition and pride, self-love and envy, these works of the flesh, are enmity against God and his people, and are implacable rebels against the authority, honor, and interest of the Lord Jesus Christ; and therefore, before he left the world, he would give his followers a most convincing proof of his abhorrence of these ungodly tempers, by exhibiting a perfect contrast to the whole of them, while he set them an imitable example of humility, kindness, and love, to the refreshment and comfort, purity and welfare, of their fellow-Christians and fellow-servants, in doing the meanest offices of friendship unto them, as occasions might require.

With a view to all these important purposes, our blessed Lord rose "from supper, and laid aside his garments; and took a towel, and girded himself. After that he poureth water into a bason, and began to wash the disciples' feet, and to wipe them with the towel wherewith he was girded" (John 13:4–5).

Hereby he assured them of his continued abiding love; confirmed their faith of his invariable regards to them, when he should ascend to his Father; instructed them in the mystery of sanctification, through union to his person, and the supplies of his Spirit; and strongly enforced the obligation upon them, to stoop, on all occasions, to the meanest and most laborious services, for testifying their mutual love, and affording reciprocal assistance to one another, being all on a level, as fellow-servants and brethren, in the kingdom and family of Christ.

His argument to enforce this obligation is peculiarly striking: "Ye call me Master and Lord: and ye say well; for so I am. If I then, your Lord and Master, have washed your feet, ye also ought to wash one another's feet. For I have given you an example, that ye should do as I have done to you" (John 13:13–15).

The *customs of the ancients*, in these parts of the world, being referred to by our Lord, when he says, "He that is washed, needeth not save to wash his feet, but is clean every whit" (v. 10), must be attended to, in order to understand the meaning of those verses. It is well known, *they* were wont to travel frequently *barefooted*, or *with sandals* bound upon their feet with thongs; that many places in these countries are sandy, and all of them hot at certain seasons of the year, and dirty at others; and that all these circumstances put together, rendered *bathing*, and *frequent washing of the feet*, both useful and necessary. They practiced both of them accordingly. One part of the entertainment, expected from every hospitable friend by every guest, was *water to wash his feet* (Gen. 18:4; 19:2; 24:31; Luke 7:44). This was expedient after a journey, both for the refreshment of the traveler, and for the decency of his appearance. And it was proper also, when a person was returned from the bath, where he was clean washed every whit, and only needed to wash his feet, that had been defiled in returning from it; and when one was to sit down, in the manner of these times, on a couch, to partake of an entertainment. Servants were usually employed in performing these mean, but friendly offices, to their guests; for it was thought to be rather beneath the dignity of the householder, to condescend to such a servile, laborious work himself, in ordinary cases (1 Sam. 25:41).

Our blessed Lord, who saw many instances of ambition and pride among his disciples, while he was with them, and who knew what would afterwards fall out among these who named his name, recommends unto all his people, by the washing his disciples' feet, these three things. (1.) To be very *humble*, and to learn of him who is meek and lowly in heart (Matt. 11:29). Humility is the noblest ornament of a true Christian. (2.) To be very *serviceable*, as well as humble. Washing of feet was a real service in these times; and we should embrace every opportunity to do good unto all, but especially to them that are of the household of faith. And (3.) To contribute all that we can to *the sanctification* of our fellow-Christians, by watching over one another, and provoking each other to love, and to good works. The saints should be fellow-laborers under Christ, in promoting their mutual interests, in point of universal holiness;[10] for this may be inferred from their washing one another's feet, by the same reasoning, as Christ's washing their feet signified his cleansing them from their sins by his blood and Spirit; in like manner, they should contribute all they can, by instructions, admonitions, encouragements, cautions, reproofs, and examples, to discourage sin, and promote the interests of true religion, among themselves. All this no way interferes with the glorious office of Jesus, who saves his people from their sins; because *every means* derives its efficacy from him, and not from any virtue either in itself, or in any creature concerned in the use of it.

Some have understood the command of Christ, concerning *the disciples washing one another's feet* (John 13:14–15), in a literal sense, supposing that this was intended for a standing ordinance in the church. Ambrose of Milan, and some others, practiced this service literally, because they believed it to be Christ's appointment. Ammonius, Theophylact, Oecumenius, and the generality of the ancient writers, thought it was not to be limited to that practice alone, but included every office of love, whereby one Christian might refresh, comfort, and help another, on any occasion whatever. These who insist for the literal observation of this practice in later times are

---

[10] See Matthew Henry. *Exposition of the Old and New Testaments*, on the place.

not of one mind about it. I shall not spend time on the *apish imitation* of our Lord's washing his disciples' feet, which the *Roman pontiff* pretends to, by annually washing the feet of so many poor people on the *Thursday of passion-week*: an instance of feigned humility, which is also practiced by many *Christian kings*, who wash the feet of a certain number of poor people on that day, though not with their own royal hands, but by the hands of their lord-almoner, or some other deputy.

There is a society which makes the highest pretensions to an exact regard to all divine institutions, that has given their opinion on this head, in the following terms: "Since our Lord tells his disciples that *they ought to wash one another's feet*, according to the example he gave them (John 13:14–15), we think this also incumbent upon us, *whenever it can be an act of kindness to a brother so to do*."[11] But this is no more, I suppose, than many would do in such circumstances as they mention, who cannot, however, agree with them in supposing that our Lord intended to institute *the washing of feet*, as an abiding ordinance of religious fellowship. Who will pretend to affirm, that our Lord's washing his disciples' feet was at *that time* necessary, either for refreshing or cleansing them? And it is plain, there is no such kindness in washing the feet, in our age and place of the world, when the legs and feet are properly covered and shod, both for comfort and defense; and where the situation of the climate is more equal and moderate every way than in Palestine and Canaan, and consequently, that service is generally forborne.

Moreover, we nowhere read that the apostles ever washed one another's feet. The only passage that seems to intimate that Christians did or should do so, is 1 Timothy 5:10, where the apostle, among other characters of a widow who should be honored by the church as a widow indeed, says, "if she have washed the saints' feet." But we have a key to that expression in the foregoing clause, "if she have lodged strangers." The *saints*, whose feet were to be washed, were *strangers*, who were either scattered by persecution, or traveling to spread the gospel; and as they were wont either to walk barefooted, or only to wear sandals, washing their feet was a part of their entertainment, and a great kindness to a traveler, though in itself purely *a civil act of friendship*. And if it shall so happen, which may sometimes be the case, that one Christian, who is on a journey, lodges with another, and

---

[11] See Samuel Pike. *A Plain and Full Account of the Christian Practices Observed by the Church in Saint Martin's-le-Grand*, p. 14.

has occasion for this very service to be performed to him, I believe it will be cheerfully allowed by everybody that his hospitable landlord should cheerfully contribute in *that* and *every other point*, to the comfort of his guest. The deed itself would be an act of civility, and a means of refreshment, to his weary brother; and the principle of his generous hospitality should be of a more noble kind than merely *civility*, or even *compassion*, to a man in distress; for he should do all to him *in the name of a disciple*. But it is ridiculous from all this to infer an *express divine appointment* of the disciples washing one another's feet, in ordinary cases, and without an evident call to promote the comfort of a brother by that service.

Abstaining from Blood, etc.

Sacrifices were a part of the solemn services of the church, probably from the first intimation of the mercy of an offended God to our guilty first parents, until the sacrifice of Christ, which was thereby prefigured, set them aside, and abolished them forever. And immediately after the flood, God having blessed Noah and his sons, and given them every moving thing that liveth for meat, was pleased to add the following restriction, "But flesh with the life thereof, which is the blood thereof, shall you not eat" (Gen. 9:4).

After Israel came out of Egypt, God gave them a system of laws for their worship and order; a system every way adapted to their circumstances, and profitable for their instruction about the good things that were to come by the Messiah. One of the points wherein the will of God was made known thereby related to their abstinence from blood, and from things strangled,

> Only be sure that thou eat not the blood: for the blood is the life; and thou mayest not eat the life with the flesh. Thou shalt not eat it; thou shalt pour it upon the earth as water. Thou shalt not eat it; that it may go well with thee, and with thy children after thee, when thou shalt do that which is right in the sight of the LORD (Deut. 12:23–25).

This law, with *the reason of it*, is recorded at large,

> And whatsoever man there be of the house of Israel, or of the strangers that sojourn among you, that eateth any manner of blood; I will even set my face against that soul that eateth blood, and will

cut him off from among his people. For the life of the flesh is in the blood: and I have given it to you upon the altar, to make an atonement for your souls: for it is the blood that maketh an atonement for the soul. Therefore I said unto the children of Israel, No soul of you shall eat blood, neither shall any stranger that sojourneth among you, eat blood. And whatsoever man there be of the children of Israel, or of the strangers that sojourn among you, which hunteth and catcheth any beast or fowl that may be eaten; he shall even pour out the blood thereof, and cover it with dust. For it is the life of all flesh; the blood of it is for the life thereof: therefore I said unto the children of Israel, Ye shall eat the blood of no manner of flesh: for the life of all flesh is the blood thereof: whosoever eateth it, shall be cut off. And every soul that eateth that which died of itself, or that which was torn with beasts, whether it be one of your own country, or a stranger, he shall both wash his clothes, and bathe himself in water, and be unclean until the even: then shall he be clean. But if he wash them not, nor bathe his flesh; then he shall bear his iniquity (Lev. 17:10–16).

The reason why the eating of blood was forbidden to the children of Israel was that the life of the flesh is in the blood, and the Lord had given it them upon the altar, to make an atonement for their souls: for it is the blood that maketh an atonement for the soul (Lev. 17:11). And from this passage it seems evident that the prohibition was ceremonial, because the original reason of it was to cease in the sacrifice of Christ who was prefigured in all these typical atonements (Heb. 10:1–10).

Here the dispute would cease, if we had not the prohibition repeated in the New Testament, and with the solemnity of *a synodical decision*, "it seemed good to the Holy Ghost, and to us, to lay upon you no greater burden than *these necessary things*; that ye abstain from meats offered to idols, and *from blood, and from things strangled*, and from fornication: from which if ye keep yourselves, ye shall do well" (Acts 15:28–29). And this decision which was originally intended for *Gentile Christians* is referred to and repeated as obligatory (Acts 21:25), and some think also in Revelation 2:24–25, "I will put upon you none other burden. But that which you have already hold fast till I come." In these texts, *the eating of blood, and of things strangled*, is condemned along with *fornication*, which is confessedly *a moral evil*; abstinence from eating them is represented as *a necessary thing; it seemed good to the Holy Ghost* to forbid the use of them, even to the Christians that had been heathens before their conversion; and consequently were never under any obligations to observe the law of Moses, in any point of Jewish services; and the Lord Jesus Christ is supposed to command the church at Thyatira to hold fast everything enjoined in that synodical decree, till his second coming. This I apprehend is the strength of the reasoning from the New Testament, against *Christians eating blood, or things strangled*.

A careful attention to these arguments is both reasonable and necessary, that we may understand the extent of that liberty wherewith Christ hath made us free. For this purpose, I shall state the case to the reader with all the exactness I am able; and then submit the whole to his own judgment.

A famous church having been gathered at Antioch, where the disciples were first called *Christians*, it continued some time in a flourishing condition, sound in the faith, and walking in the fear of the Lord, and in the comforts of the Holy Ghost. But their comfort and harmony were soon interrupted by "certain men which came down from Judea, and taught the brethren," who had been called from heathenism, "that except they were circumcised after the manner of Moses, they could not be saved" (Acts 15:1). Paul and Barnabas, who then ministered at Antioch, had no small dissension and disputation with *these men*, because they were to be blamed for attempting to bring this church into bondage, under a yoke which the Jews were not able to bear. But their resistance to such an imposition not being so successful as to defeat the intentions of these teachers that came from Judea, a resolution was formed, and universally acquiesced in, to refer the whole affair in dispute to the apostles and elders at Jerusalem; and to depute commissioners on each side, to lay the cause before that venerable court. The apostles and elders came together, and reasoned upon the cause referred to them; and after *much disputing* (vv. 6–7), they at last agreed in delivering the sentence upon that question, which has been already quoted (Acts 15:28–29).

From the short, but useful memoirs of that dispute and decision, recorded in Acts 15, I would beg leave to make the following remarks. (1.) That the Christians at Antioch were originally free from all obligation to observe the law of Moses; being called immediately to the faith, obedience, and liberty of Jesus Christ, according to the New Testament. (2.) Both

Jews and Gentiles were called to one faith, and one hope of their calling, in consequence of the gospel being preached to every creature. (3.) God, who had permitted several things to Israel, on account of the hardness of their heart, permitted also several things to the believing Jews for a time, on account of their fond attachment to the law of Moses. This is implied in Acts 15; but it is clearly asserted in Acts 21:20–27. (4.) Whatever had a tendency to interrupt the fellowship between the believers, called from among the Jews, and from among the Gentiles; or to offend one another; or to set one against another, must be both *sinful* and *hurtful*: *sinful*, because it made a schism in the body of Christ; and *hurtful*, because it hindered their prayers, destroyed their mutual love, and gave place to the devil. (5.) A dispute having arisen at Antioch, wherein Gentile and Jewish converts were like to state themselves parties against each other, the cause became, for that very reason, important, and demanded all the attention the apostles and elders gave it. (6.) The question was occasioned by *the Jews*; for "there rose up [at Antioch] certain of the sect of the Pharisees which believed, saying, That it was needful to circumcise [the converted Gentiles there], and to command them to keep the law of Moses" (Acts 15:5). This occasioned the disputation at Antioch, and the reference to Jerusalem. (7.) The synodical sentence was intended to preserve the liberty of the Gentile church from which the reference came, without giving any offense to the believing Jews that were zealous of the law. The scope of the reasoning both of Peter and James (Acts 15:7–19), is evidently in favor of the Gentile converts, as well as that part of the synodical epistle, in verses 23–24. And that they intended to guard against any occasion of stumbling or offense to the Jews is manifest from the reason James gave for the motion he made in the court, "to write unto [the Gentiles], that they abstain from pollutions of idols, and from fornication, and from things strangled, and from blood. *For Moses of old time hath in every city them that preach him*" (Acts 15:20–21). This is the ground of his opinion, and obviously carries the following sense:

> As the civil polity of the commonwealth of Israel still, in measure, subsists; and as the utmost care should be taken to keep the converted Gentiles at the greatest distance from everything that looks like favoring the idolatrous worship which they have renounced, and to prevent their giving offense to the believing Jews; it may be

very necessary, for uniting both parties into one civil society, and one Christian church, in the present circumstances of things, that we write a letter to our Gentile brethren, to recommend their abstaining from such things, as the proselytes of the gate have hitherto been obliged to, by the law of Moses, in order to their enjoying civil and religious privileges among the Jews; as particularly, that they abstain from eating or drinking anything that is offered or devoted to idols; and from all impure embraces, that are condemned by Moses' law, and have been used in the heathen temples before their gods; as also from eating the flesh of such beasts, or fowls, as were strangled to prevent the separation of the blood from their flesh; and from eating or drinking the blood itself, that has been taken from any animal; for as fornication is in itself sinful, so abstaining from the other things, as well as that, is needful to prevent offense to the Christian Jews, and secure a quiet enjoyment of privileges to the converted Gentiles; and so to promote mutual love and communion between both. For the law of Moses, which forbids these things even to the proselytes of the gate, is still, according to ancient custom, explained in every city, where there are religious assemblies of Jews; his writings being constantly read in their synagogues, at their times of public worship, every Sabbath-day: and therefore as they have been brought up, all their lives long, in a reverence of this law, and will still frequently hear it read, they will be exceedingly offended to find, that the things there expressly prohibited, should nevertheless be practiced by the uncircumcised Gentile converts, who, by the gospel, are brought into the same church and communion with themselves, and who, upon abstaining from these things, will have as good a claim to civil privileges, that are allowed by the law to strangers of the gate, as if they had been all devout Gentiles before.[12]

Agreeable to the opinion of James was the determination of *the synod*, which was expressed in these words, "it seemed good to the Holy Ghost, and to us, to lay upon you no greater burden than these necessary things; that ye abstain from meats offered to idols, and from blood, and from things strangled, and from fornication: from which if ye keep yourselves, ye shall do well. Fare ye well." These words may be thus paraphrased:

---

[12] See Guyse, *Paraphrase*, paraphrase on Acts 15:20–21.

It has pleased the Holy Ghost, as appears by the intimations he has given in ancient prophecies of the calling of the Gentiles, and by his extraordinary descent on Cornelius and his friends at Caesarea (Acts 10:44, etc.), and afterwards on the idolatrous Gentiles (Acts 13:46, etc.), though neither of them were circumcised; and it has accordingly been judged fit and proper by us, under his direction and influence, to enjoin your observation of nothing further, that might be looked upon as of a burdensome nature, than the few following things, which, considering all circumstances in the present state of the Jewish constitution, and of the gospel-church, are necessary to set you upon good terms with your believing brethren of the circumcision; and they are, that ye refrain from meats and drinks offered to idols, as partaking of them would be construed a countenancing of the idol itself, in opposition to the only true God; that ye forbear eating or drinking of blood, that has been taken from any animal; and from eating the flesh of any fowl or beast, that has been strangled to prevent the taking away its blood, as feeding upon either of these would be deemed symbolizing with idolatry, and would give such offense, as to prevent all free correspondence and brotherly communion with Christian Jews; and that ye never defile yourselves with any kind of unlawful use of women, as that is not only abominable on account of the impurities of that kind, which have been practiced before the heathen-idols in their temples, but is likewise destructive of God's ordinance of marriage, and of the peace, harmony, and welfare of families, and is directly contrary to the express command of our Savior (Matt. 19:3–9). If ye carefully avoid these four things, ye will do all that is needful, on your part, to take off exceptions against you, merely because ye are not circumcised, and do not think yourselves bound by the Mosaic law; and ye will commendably pursue the things, that make for the glory of God, the tranquility and comfort of the church, and the furtherance of the gospel. We add no more, than our hearty prayers, that your souls may abundantly prosper in light and grace, holiness, love, and peace, and may be saved forever.[13]

The *same author* very justly observes,

---

[13] Guyse, *Paraphrase*, on the place.

Though all these particulars were at that time necessary for avoiding offense, and promoting civil and sacred harmony, love, and peace, as things were then circumstanced between the believing Jews and Gentiles, who were to be incorporated into one church; they were not said to be *absolutely* or *alike* necessary in themselves: and therefore, it cannot be concluded from thence, that eating of blood, as well as fornication, is in its own nature sinful; or that abstaining from the first of these is at all necessary, now the reasons of the prohibition are ceased; though avoiding fornication will always be so, as long as God's ordinance for marriage, the laws of society, and the New Testament dispensation last. For if these things were necessary at all, on any account whatsoever, and particularly with relation to the case, which occasioned the writing of this letter; *that* is enough to answer the force of the expression, which calls them, in this view, *necessary things*. See Leland's *Div. Author of the Old and New Test.*, vol. 1, pp. 415–419. And as it is certain that many other things, besides these, were necessary to the Christian character, it appears that, when these only were spoken of as *necessary things*, it relates not to Christians as such, but merely to the then present state of the church.[14]

Upon the whole, it may be fairly concluded, from the circumstances of the judgment which the synod of Jerusalem passed concerning *the eating of blood, and of things strangled*, that it was not *a standing ordinance to the New Testament churches*; and that it does not make *our* abstinence from them any act of religious obedience, because it was only *a temporary institution*, and *the period of it is long since determined*. This will be still more evident, if we consider (1.) That the original ground of forbidding men to eat blood is *ceremonial* (Lev. 17:10–11). (2.) That the Jews were allowed to give or sell a creature that died of itself, and consequently in its blood, to a stranger, that he might eat it; which would not have been permitted, if eating of blood had been *a moral evil* (Deut. 14:21). And (3.) That all difference of meats is entirely abolished under the New Testament (Rom. 14:14, 17; 1 Cor. 8:8; Col. 2:16, 20–22; 1 Tim. 4:3–5; etc.). So that we are at *perfect liberty* in this matter.

---

[14] Guyse, *Paraphrase*, note on Act 15:28.

The objections against this liberty, which I formerly mentioned, have been partly answered already. What is further needful to be suggested, shall be now proposed on each of them.

1. "The eating of blood, and of things strangled, is condemned along with fornication, which is certainly a moral evil; and therefore so is the former." But it is well known, there are many sentences in the word of God, as well as in every other writing, that cannot bear this test of argument, if it may be so called. Examples of this kind are so frequent that particular instances are almost needless. What proves too much cannot infer any conclusion. Upon this principle it would be easy to demonstrate that the system of ceremonial and judicial laws was of moral obligation; because they are conjoined in the appointment of them, and are expressed in the same connection (Deut. 26:17–18; Luke 1:6).

2. "Abstinence from eating of blood, and of things strangled, is represented as a necessary thing (Acts 15:28–29)." But that abstinence was only necessary to serve *a particular temporary purpose.* The necessity of it arose from this consideration, that "Moses of old time had in every city them that preached him, being read in their synagogues every Sabbath-day" (v. 21). *That reason* of necessity is now ceased, and of course *the necessity itself* is now at a perpetual end; unless some new considerations should revive it.

3. "It seemed good to the Holy Ghost, to forbid the eating of blood, and of things strangled" (Acts 15:28–29). And from his character, as *the Spirit of truth and love,* we may be assured, that whatever tends to promote the union and fellowship of the saints seems good to him; and that prohibition, so far as it referred to the eating of blood, and things strangled, seemed good to the Holy Ghost *on that account.*

4. "This prohibition was enjoined upon the Gentiles." But it was enjoined on them for the sake of the Jews.

5. "It is referred to, several years after" (Acts 21:25). But, besides that a reference is only made to the fact in that passage, it must be observed, that the reasons of expediency and necessity still remained, and operated on that occasion very strong (see vv. 20–25).

6. "It is supposed, the faithful and true Witness refers to the decision of the apostles and elders at Jerusalem, when he says to the church of Thyatira, 'I will put upon you none other burden, but that which ye have

already; hold fast till I come' (Rev. 2:24–25)."[15] But the grounds of this supposition are so *weak* and *precarious* that it is needless to spend time in confuting them. The only reason that can be assigned for the conjecture arises from the similarity of the expressions: "I will put upon you none other burden," and, "it seemed good…to lay upon you no greater burden than these necessary things." It would be unpardonable credulity to admit conviction upon such evidence; unless some *concurring circumstances* strongly favored the supposition. But the obvious meaning of what our Lord commanded John to write unto the angel, and to the rest of the church in Thyatira, is to the following purpose:

> I will put no further injunctions or restraints upon you, than still to keep clear of these abominations before mentioned; nor the burden of any more mysteries, laws, or ceremonies, than are already established in my word. I only insist upon it, that ye still persevere in, and steadfastly maintain, your faith, love, and obedience, together with the purity of the doctrines and precepts, which ye have already received from me, and not count them grievous till I shall come the second time to your salvation.[16]

To conclude, "Meat commendeth us not to God: for neither if we eat, are we the better; neither if we eat not, are we the worse" (1 Cor. 8:8). But let every man that eateth blood be fully persuaded in his own mind; and let all eat, or forbear eating it, without either giving or taking offense.

---

[15] Poole, *Synopsis*, account of the religious practices, etc., p. 13.
[16] Guyse, *Paraphrase*, on the place.

Archaic Words

ampliation: enlarging, 232

compend: summary, 422

depone: swear, 573
deponent: oath-taker, 576, 579, 581, 582, 585, 587

frontless: shameless, 104

incontrollable: unquestionable, 136

lenity: gentleness, 412
letted: hindered, 330
lusory: light, 627

merchandise: commerce, 337

nervous: vigorous, 207

sisted: ordered to appear, 576

timeously: in good time, 334

Bibliography

A Defense of Some Important Doctrines of the Gospel in Twenty Six Sermons. Most of Which were Preached in Lime-Street. London, 1732.
Acts of the Council of Trent.
Ainsworth, Henry. *Annotations upon the Five Books of Moses, the Book of the Psalms, and the Song of Songs*. London, 1627.
Alsop, Vincent. *The Mischief of Impositions*. London, 1680.
Ames, William. *Conscience with the Power and Cases Thereof*. London, 1639.
———. *The Marrow of Theology*. London, 1642.
An Inquiry into the Nature, Obligation, and Advantages of Religious Fellowship: Together with an Attempt to Direct in the Proper Exercise of It. Glasgow, 1744.
Anno Primo Reginæ Elizabethæ. London, 1559.
Anonymous. *Thoughts on the Nature and Use of a Lot*. London, 1750.
Barclay, Robert. *Works*. London, 1692.
Bedford, Arthur. *The Scripture Chronology*. London, 1730.
Bennet, Benjamin. *The Christian Oratory*. Glasgow, 1776.
Boston, Thomas. *A Memorial concerning Personal and Family Fasting*. 1742.
———. *A View of the Covenant of Grace from the Sacred Records*. 1742.
———. *The Crook in the Lot*. Edinburgh, 1737.
———. "The Distinguishing Character of Real Christians". In *Works, Volume 4*.
———. *Works*. Edinburgh, 1767.
Bostwick, David. *A Fair and Rational Vindication of the Right of Infants to the Ordinance of Baptism*. New Brunswick, 1790.
Boyse, Joseph. *Remarks on a Late Discourse*. London, 1694.
Bradbury, Thomas. *The Duty and Doctrine of Baptism: In Thirteen Sermons*. London, 1749.
Bradbury, Thomas et al. *Practical Discourses concerning the Duty of Prayer: Preach'd at the Friday Evening-Lecture in Eastcheap by Several Ministers*. London, 1711.
Broughton, Thomas. *An Historical Dictionary of All Religions*. London, 1745.
Brown (of Haddington), John. *An Historical Account of the Rise and Progress of the Secession*. Glasgow, 1788.
Brown (of Wamphray), John. *De Causa Dei Contra Antisabbatarios*. Rotterdam, 1674.
Burnet, Gilbert. *An Exposition of the Thirty-Nine Articles of the Church of England*. London, 1705.
Calamy, Edmund. *An Abridgement of Mr. Baxter's History of His Life and Times*. London, 1713.

Calamy, Edmund. *An Account of the Ministers, Lecturers, Masters, and Fellows of Colleges and Schoolmasters: Who Were Ejected or Silenced after the Restoration in 1660, by or before, the Act of Uniformity; Design'd for the Preserving to Posterity the Memory of their Names, Characters, Writings, and Sufferings.* London, 1713.

Charnock, Stephen. *Works.* Edinburgh, 1840.

Chillingworth, William. *The Religion of Protestants a Safe Way to Salvation.* Oxford, 1638.

Clarkson, David. *A Discourse concerning Liturgies.* London, 1689.

Crofton, Zachary. *Catechizing, God's Ordinance.* London, 1656.

Cumming, John. *Dissertation concerning the Authority of Scripture-Consequences.* London, 1720.

Dickinson, Jonathan. *Familiar Letters to a Gentleman upon a Variety of Seasonable and Important Subjects in Religion.* Dundee, 1772.

Doddridge, Philip. *A Plain and Serious Address to the Master of a Family: On the Important Subject of Family Religion.* London, 1761.

Dunlop, William. *A Preface to an Edition of the Westminster Confession.* London, 1724.

Durham, James. *A Commentary upon the Book of the Revelation.* Glasgow, 1739.

———. *A Practical Exposition of the Ten Commandments.* Edinburgh, 1735.

Edwards, John. *A Complete History or Survey of all the Dispensations and Methods of Religion.* London, 1699.

———. *Theologia Reformata.* London, 1713.

Edwards, Jonathan. *A Careful and Strict Enquiry into the Modern Prevailing Notions of That Freedom of Will.* Boston, 1754.

Erskine, John. *Theological Dissertations.* London, 1765.

Erskine, Ralph. *A Short Paraphrase upon the Lamentations of Jeremiah, Adapted to the Common Tunes.* Glasgow, 1750.

Fleming, Robert. *The Fulfilling of the Scripture.* Boston, 1743.

Forbes, John. *Instructiones Historico-Theologicæ de Doctrina Christiana.* Geneva, 1680.

Gale, John. *Reflections on Mr. Wall's History of Infant Baptism.* London, 1711.

Gill, John. *Body of Doctrinal Divinity.* London, 1767.

———. *Exposition of the Bible.* London, 1763.

———. *The Ancient Mode of Baptizing by Immersion Maintained.* London, 1726.

———. *The Doctrine of Grace Cleared from the Charge of Licentiousness.* London, 1738.

Gurnall, William. *The Christian in Complete Armour.* London, 1662.

Guyse, John. *A Collection of Seventeen Practical Sermons.* London, 1756.

———. *The Practical Expositor: An Exposition of the New Testament, in the Form of a Paraphrase.* London, 1761.

Hall, Archibald. *An Humble Attempt to Exhibit a Scriptural View of the Constitution, Order, Discipline, and Fellowship of the Gospel Church.* Edinburgh, 1769.
Hammond, Henry. *A Paraphrase and Annotations upon the Books of the Psalms.* London, 1659.
Harris, William. *A Discourse concerning Transubstantiation.* London, 1735.
———. *Some Memoirs of the Life and Character of the Reverend and Learned Thomas Manton, D.D.* London, 1725.
Haweis, Thomas. *The Communicant's Spiritual Companion.* London, 1763.
Henry, Matthew. *Exposition of the Old and New Testaments.* London, 1710.
———. *Method for Prayer.* London, 1710.
———. *The Communicant's Companion.* Glasgow, 1761.
Herbert, George. *The Church-Porch: Perirrhanterium.* Cambridge, 1633.
Hervey, James. *Eleven Letters from the Late Rev. Mr. Hervey, to the Rev. Mr. John Wesley.* London, 1765.
———. *Rules and Orders of a Religious Society.* Edinburgh, 1779.
———. *The Cross of Christ the Christian's Glory.* London, 1753.
———. *Theron and Aspasio.* London, 1755.
Hoadly, Benjamin. *The Present Delusion of Many Protestants, Consider'd: Preach'd in the Parish-Church of St. Peter's Poor, in Broadstreet, November 5, 1715.* London, 1715.
Hopkins, Ezekiel. *Works.* London, 1701.
Horace. *Ars Poetica: The Art of Poetry.* London, 1735.
Hughes, Obadiah. *Sermons Against Popery, Preached at Salters-Hall.* London, 1735.
Jenks, Benjamin. *The Liberty of Prayer Asserted, and Guarded from Licentiousness.* London, 1695.
Jerome. *Dialogus Adversus Luciferianos.*
Kennedy, John. *A Complete System of Astronomical Chronology.* London, 1762.
King, Peter. *An Inquiry into the Constitution, Discipline, Unity and Worship of the Primitive Church.* London, 1691.
King, William. *A Discourse concerning the Inventions of Men in the Worship of God.* 5th. Edinburgh, 1713.
Leigh, Edward. *Annotations upon All the New Testament, Philological and Theological.* London, 1650.
———. *Critica Sacra: Philological and Theological Observations upon the Greek Words of the New Testament, in Order Alphabetical.* London, 1646.
Lightfoot, John. *The Harmony of the Four Evangelists.* London, 1644.
Mark, Johannes à. *Compendium Theologiæ Christianæ Didactico Elencticum.* Amsterdam, 1690.

Marshall, Walter. *The Gospel-Mystery of Sanctification Opened in Sundry Practical Directions: Suited Especially to the Case of Those Who Labour under the Guilt and Power of In-Dwelling Sin. To Which Is Added, a Sermon on Justification*. London, 1761.

McEwen, William. *A Select Set of Essays, Doctrinal and Practical*. Edinburgh, 1767.

"Of Prayer after Sermon". In *Westminster Directory for the Publick Worship of God*. London, 1644.

"Of Singing of Psalms". In *Westminster Directory for the Publick Worship of God*. London, 1644.

"Of the Place and Time of Prayer". In *Homilies of the Church of England*. London, 1757.

"Of Visitation of the Sick". In *Westminster Directory for the Publick Worship of God*. London, 1644.

Owen, John. *A Brief Instruction in the Worship of God*. London, 1676.

———. *A Treatise on the Sabbath*. London, 1829.

———. *An Exposition of the Epistle to the Hebrews*. London, 1684.

———. *The Complete Collection of the Sermons of John Owen*. London, 1721.

———. *The True Nature of a Gospel Church and Its Government*. London, 1689.

Pierce, James. *A Vindication of the Dissenters*. London, 1717.

Pike, Samuel. *A Form of Sound Words*. London, 1756.

———. *A Plain and Full Account of the Christian Practices Observed by the Church in Saint Martin's-le-Grand*. London, 1767.

Pike, Samuel and Samuel Hayward. *Some Important Cases of Conscience Answered at the Casuistical Exercise, on Wednesday Evenings, in Little St. Helen's, Bishopgate-Street*. Glasgow, 1762.

Poole, Matthew. *English Annotations on the Holy Bible*. London, 1683.

———. *Synopsis Criticorum Aliorumque Sacræ Scripturæ Interpretum et Commentatorum*. London, 1669.

Prideaux, Humphrey. *The Old and New Testament Connected in the History of the Jews and Neighbouring Nations*. London, 1749.

Rees, David. *Reasons for and against Singing of Psalms, in Private or Publick Worship, Considered with Candor*. London, 1737.

———. *The State of True Religion in All Ages, and the Charges Attending Divine Worship Consider'd*. London, 1726.

Ridgley, Thomas. *A Body of Divinity*. London, 1733.

Romanum Breviarium.

Scotland, Church of. *The Principal Acts of the General Assembly, 1708*. Edinburgh, 1708.

Shields, Alexander. *A Letter concerning the Due Boundaries of Christian Fellowship*. 1726.

Shower, John. *Sacramental Discourses*. London, 1726.

Smith, Walter and John Hepburn. *Directory; or Rules and Directions for Fellowship Meetings.* Glasgow, 1738.
Stillingfleet, Edward. *Irenicum: A Weapon-Salve for the Church's Wounds.* London, 1662.
Suiceri, Johann Kaspar. *Thesaurus Ecclesiasticus.* Amsterdam, 1728.
Taylor, Richard. *Discourses on Several Subjects.* London, 1719.
Tertullian. *Apologeticus.* Lutetia, 1613.
The Assembly's Shorter Catechism Explained by way of Question and Answer. Belfast, 1744.
Tillotson, John. *The Works of Dr. John Tillotson.* London, 1696.
Vindication of the Presbyterial Government and Ministry. London, 1650.
Wall, William. *A Defence of the History of Infant-Baptism against the Reflections of Mr. Gale and Others.* London, 1720.
Watts, Isaac. *Guide to Prayer.* London, 1715.
———. *The Holiness of Times, Places, and People.* London, 1738.
Weemes, John. *Works.* London, 1636.
Westminster Confession of Faith. London, 1646.
Westminster Larger Catechism. London, 1647.
Westminster Shorter Catechism. London, 1648.
Whitby, Daniel. *A Paraphrase and Commentary on the New Testament.* London, 1703.
Willison, John. *A Treatise concerning the Sanctification of the Lord's Day.* Edinburgh, 1745.
Witsius, Hermann. *De Œconomia Fœderum Dei cum Hominibus.* Leeuwarden, 1677.
———. *Exercitationes Sacræ in Symbolum quod Apostolorum Dicitur et in Orationem Dominicam.* Basil, 1697.

Scripture Index

Genesis

2 . . . . 314, 322
2:1–3 314
2:3 . . . . 312, 313
2:15 426
3:19 426
4:3 314
4:9 511
4:10–11 512
4:17 31
4:26 31
6:2 32
8:10–12 314
9:4 648
13:4 32
14:14 458
14:22 581
14:22–23 571
17 607
17:7 230, 235, 237, 243
17:7, 9 616
17:7, 19 233
17:7–9 607
17:7–14 243
17:9–13 231
17:9–14 238
17:9–27 243
17:10 232
17:12 244
17:17 251
18:2 4
18:4 645
18:17–19 501
18:19 51, 243, 331, 410, 458, 462, 498, 505
19:2 645
20:7 438
21:8 252
22 510
22:16–17 573
24:2 . . . . . . 581, 584
24:2–4 571
24:2–9 580
24:5–8 579
24:31 645
24:41 574
24:48 12
24:52 12
26:25 502
26:28–30 580
26:28–31 584
28:20–22 . . 595, 600
28:21 . . . . . . 600, 606
29:18–28 314
31 501
31:53–54 580
32:10 342
32:26 162
32:28 142
33:3 4
33:20 502
35:1, 3 502
35:2–3 498
37:31 212
39:9 510
47:29–31 . . . 571, 580
47:31 584
48:1 439

Exodus

3:14 166
4:25 199
12:11 296
12:14 280
12:22 212
12:48–49 . . . 243, 246
13:14–16 190
15 . . . . 32, 116
15:1 115
15:20–21 129
16:23, 26 315
17:16 583
20 452
20:2–3 600
20:4–5 24
20:5 . . . . 7, 14, 22
20:7 . . . . 396, 591
20:8 . . . . 319, 334
20:8–11 316
20:9 337
20:9–10 337
20:10 . . . 327, 331, 337
20:11 . . . . 314, 323, 338
20:12 410
20:14 395
20:24 . . 100, 175, 179, 187
20:24–25 24
22:11 . . . . . . 584, 586
22:28 405
23:2 589
29:4 . . . . 201, 206
31:17 320
32:5–6 296
32:10 162
33:4 358
33:19 32
34 362
34:5–6 32

Leviticus

4:6, 17 212

5:1 574	6:13 . . 5, 571, 572, 574, 585	24:27 252
9:22 173	6:20–25 189	**Judges**
9:22–23 173	7:3 506	1:15 209
10:3 . . . . 110, 303	7:6 236	5 32
10:11 71	12:23–25 648	5:12 353
16:8 627	14:2, 21 233	17–18 501
16:14–15 206	14:21 654	17:13 376
17:10–11 654	15:7–11 548	20 362
17:10–16 649	15:11 550	**1 Samuel**
17:11 649	17:8–9 71	1:10–13 594
19:3 411	17:19 52	1:12–13 138
19:30 318	23:18 599	2:7–8 544
23:2 350	26 32	2:30 530
23:10–17 233	26:17 612	7:5–6 369
23:24 130	26:17–18 . . . 370, 655	7:6 365
23:27 360	26:17–19 . . . 607, 608	9:12–13, 22 296
23:29 358	26:18–19 233	10:20–21 627
27 595	27:3 411	14:41 633
Numbers	28:47 5	14:42 627
6:22–27 . 32, 165, 166	28:58–68 20	15:9, 33 128
6:24 166	29 607	16:5 296
6:25 167	29:10–11 238	16:7 618
6:26 167	29:10–13, 29 239	16:12 296
6:27 168	29:29 . . . . . . 146, 628	20 584
10 130	30:6 . . . . 239, 240	20:3 585
15:19–21 233	30:19–20 585	25 579
19:18–20 206	32:39 136	25:26 585
28:24, 31 527	32:40 581	25:41 646
30 . . . . . 577, 595, 604	32:46–47 112	**2 Samuel**
30:1–2 603	**Joshua**	6:20 502
30:2 588	1:7–8 54	7 . . . . 342, 344
32:42 31	1:8 520	9:1, 7 556
Deuteronomy	5:7–8 246	12:16 . . . 358, 359, 362, 366
3:26 162	7 627	12:21–23 152
5:12 318	10:12–13 142	15:5 642
6:6–7 458	18:6 . . . . 627, 630	15:21 . . . . . . 571, 582
6:6–9 51	24 607	**1 Kings**
6:7 465	24:14–28 612	2 604
6:8 326	24:15 . . . 139, 505, 516, 602	

8 159	9 .... 362, 370	22:2–3 20
8:14 173	9:2 236	22:21 532
8:31 584	10:1–5 612	23:3 303
8:54–55 173		23:13 145
17:10 582	**Nehemiah**	25:4 236
17:12 571	1:3–4 365	29:13 115
18:12 419	2:1, 4 139	31 562
20:42 128	8:1–8 80	31:1 601
21 .... 362, 375	8:8 70	31:16–28 555
21:27 366	8:12 70	33:24 443
	8:13 70	34:12 570
2 Kings	9 .... 370, 607	34:32 365
3:11 205	9:1, 3 359	35:5–8 20
11:4 571	9:2–3 372	38:6–7 118
20:1 .... 439, 441	9:3 370	38:33 74
	9:38 .... 370, 612	42:8 438
1 Chronicles	10 607	
16:4–6 130	10:28 618	**Psalm**
23:13 173	10:28–39 612	1:1–2 .... 67, 520
23:30 32	10:29 612	1:2 .... 52, 114
24:5 627	10:32 612	2:11 353
29:10–18 354	11:1 627	3–5 125
29:11–17 559	12:43 349	5:3 .... 164, 377
29:14–16 25	13:15–17 328	10:5 147
29:24 581	13:19 334	10:17 161
		11:7 570
2 Chronicles	**Esther**	14:1–4 534
7:6 130	1:22 497	15:1, 3 398
15 607	3:7 633	15:1–4 577
15:12–15 612	4–7 362	18:23 394
17:8–9 71	4:16 .... 359, 479	19:2 527
20 362	6:13 600	19:10 67
20:3 369	9:26–32 350	22 344
23 584		24:4 .... 577, 581
29.25 130	**Job**	24:6 .... 142, 524
34:30–34 612	1:5 502	25:7 424
34:31–32 608	1:6 314	25:9 377
	2:11 439	25:12–13 511
Ezra	6:14 439	27:14 163
3:10–11 32	13:15 602	29:2 19
8 370	14:1–4 236	30 502
8:21 369	16:19 571	32:6 .... 148, 160

33:1 353	89:35 573	120:5 518
34:11 419	92:1–2 . . . . . 503, 527	130:5–8 163
34:19 432	93:5 306	136 . . . . 128, 354
35 437	95 19	137:1–2 478
35:13 . . . . 362, 365	95:1 116	137:2 121
37:3–7, 37 532	95:6 12	138:2 28
39:1–3 308	95:11 573	141:2 503
41:1 . . . . 546, 558	99:6 142	141:2–3 160
42:1–2 303	101:1 121	144:8 581
42:5–6 347	101:2–7 498	145 125
44:18–22 161	101:6–7 . . . . . 412, 517	145:10 354
47:7 . . . . 133, 160	102:17 164	147:9 135
49:11 31	103 342	150:2 347
49:18 552	103:1 133	
50:14 345	103:1–2 352	**Proverbs**
50:16–17 149	104 521	1:20 55
50:16–23 397	104:27 135	1:24–31 536
50:23 . . . . . 346, 352	106:47 345	1:24–33 . . . . 100, 400
51:5 236	107 . . . . . 350, 354, 521	2:2–6 53
55:13–14 478	107:40–41 544	3:3 547
55:17 . . . . . . 525, 527	107:43 . . 198, 354, 392	3:5–6 393
57:7–8 119	109:17–19 . . 396, 590	3:6 377
57:8 133	110:4 . . . . 573, 583	3:9 . . . . 559, 562
63:1 209	111:2 481	3:9–10 548
63:11 571	112:5 558	3:17 . . . . 348, 619
65:1 605	112:9 415	3:27–28 561
65:2 141	116:1, 13 342	4:4 458
66:1–2 117	116:12–19 355	4:7–13 253
66:16 . . . . . 478, 490	116:16–18 602	4:23–27 401
66:18 161	116:16–19 370	6:1 594
67:4 117	118:15 122	6:6 289
68:18–19 100	118:24 339	6:16–19 395
69:30–31 117	119 100	7:13 642
72:9 5	119:15, 23, 48, 78, 97, 148 521	8:4 55
75:6–7 544	119:18 68	10:18 397
76:11 . . . . . . 593, 620	119:54 119	11:13 397
77:17 205	119:97 67	11:23–26 566
78:37 618	119:106 . . 588, 593, 599, 606	11:24–25 548
80:17–18 28	119:164 524	14:21 548
81:10 154	120–134 125	15:3 570
84:9 28		15:8 146
85:8 163		15:11 570

15:22–23 91
16:6 547
16:31 425
16:33 .. 624, 625, 629
17:16 619
18:8 398
18:18 .. 624, 626, 627
18:24 418
19:17 ...... 546, 549
21:4 147
21:5 428
21:13 547
21:25 85
21:27 27
22:2 550
22:6 331, 410, 458, 462
22:9 549
23:7 606
23:26 421
25:11–12 91
25:18 591
25:19 417
26:20 398
27:6 .... 418, 642
28:9 146
28:14 366
28:27 547
29:15 408
30:6 .... 151, 370
30:17 399
31:10–31 408

Ecclesiastes

3 326
3:1 .... 346, 619
4:9–12 477
5:1–4 618
5:2 .... 159, 576
5:4 605
5:4–6 603
5:6 576
7:2 .... 439, 447

8:2 584
8:5 346
9:10 ... 288, 562, 619
11:1 547
11:1–2 549
11:4–6 148
12:13 ... 388, 420, 518

Song of Solomon

1:8 .... 439, 478
4:12 182
4:16 133

Song

5:1 290

Isaiah

1:3–13 301
2:8–9 14
6:2 13
6:2–3 18
6:13 ...... 233, 236
19:23 5
26:19 119
27:5 446
28:9–10 462
28:10 496
28:22 399
28:29 624
32:8 557
35:1–10 123
35:14 119
38:8 142
38:15 356
40:18 3
40:27–31 380
42:8 17
43:18 81
44:3 237
44:5 .... 32, 305, 600
45:20 136
45:23 583

48:17 68
49:22 173
49:23 5
52:1 236
52:7–9 123
52:8 115
53:5 271
54:1 123
54:10 169
55:6–7 ..... 147, 148
56:1–7 340
56:6 370
56:7 .... 139, 141, 330
57:4 590
58:2 301
58:3 .... 374, 376
58:3–7 374
58:4 375
58:5 359, 360, 375, 379
58:5–7 551
58:6–7 375
58:7 547
58:8–12 379
58:13 ... 319, 329, 336
58:13–14 340
58:13: 319
59:2 155
59:21 237
62:12 236
63:2–3 207
65:20 426
65:25 5
66:1 583
66:2 162

Jeremiah

2:3 608
2:5–8 224
2:9–13 44
2:10–11 140
3:4 421
3:15 88

4:2 . . . . 576–578, 605	8:24 233	3 362
6:16 44	9 . . . . 362, 370	3:4–9 366
6:28 397	9:1–3 366	3:5–8 360
8:6 375	9:3 362	
10:6–7, 10 18	9:20–21 370	**Micah**
10:25 . . 139, 497, 502, 512	9:21 359	6:6 12
11:16 234	9:24 269	6:8 547
17:19–22 328	10:2–3 . . . . 358, 362	7:7 164
23:18 81	10:3 358	
27:18 438	12:4, 9 182	**Nahum**
29:11–13 146	12:7 . . . . . . 233, 581	1:2–3 161
31:3 . . . . 169, 170		1:2–6 22
31:12 119	**Hosea**	
31:33–34 81	2:8 497	**Habakkuk**
36:6 359	2:8–9 345	2:3 164
50:4–5 . . . . . 364, 370	2:14–15 348	3:17–19 122
	4:6 . . . . 59, 108	
Lamentations	6:6 . . . . 358, 547	**Haggai**
1:18 442	7:9 426	1:5 369
3:22 342	11:4 101	2:8 429
3:41 619	14:2 139	2:11 99
	14:6 234	2:11–14 71
Ezekiel		
2:5 517	**Joel**	**Zechariah**
3:17 79	1:13 372	7:5 363
3:17–18 511	1:18 135	7:5–6 363
20:12 326	2 237	12:10 . . . 138, 153, 303
21:21 . . . . . . 632, 633	2:12 . . . 360, 364, 370	12:10, 12 360
33 493	2:12–13 370	12:10–14 524
33:11 583	2:15–17 361	12:12–14 358
33:31 . . . . . . 109, 328	2:17 438	
35:6 600	2:28 80	**Malachi**
36:37 . . . 142, 366, 435	2:32 32	1 516
44:23–24 71		1:13 336
	Amos	2:6–7 69
Daniel	5:8 504	2:7 . . . . . 71, 99, 463
2 344	8:5 . . . . 328, 336	3 144
2:17–18 478		3:7 44
4:32, 35 544	**Jonah**	3:16 . . . . 139, 332
6:10 . . . . . . 524, 527	1:6 140	3:16–17 476
8:4 570	1:7 627	
	1:16 595	**Matthew**
		2:11 13

3:1 69	10:16 401	23:8 475
3:5–6 210	10:20 154	24:20 . . . . . . 323, 324
3:6 . . . . 208, 215	10:28 402	25 308, 437, 546, 547, 554
3:11 208, 214, 226, 227	10:30 629	
3:16 209	10:40–42 545	25:26 426
4:2 362	11:9 111	25:30 86
4:8 209	11:29 646	26:11 550
4:10 . . . . 4, 7, 136	12:11–12 333	26:20–29 296
4:17 69	12:31–32 152	26:26–27 . . . 123, 179
5–7 71	12:34 144	26:26–28 . . 268, 304
5:1 209	13:4, 19 108	26:26–29 267
5:7 546	13:18 96	26:27 . . . . . . 268, 297
5:16 479	13:19 101	26:28 . . . 211, 273, 286
5:17 323	13:20–21 109	26:30 . . . 118, 123, 124
5:18–19 323	13:22 109	26:39 13
5:27–28 395	13:23 112	26:49 642
5:28 601	14:23 . . . . . . 209, 524	26:62–64 574
5:33 605	15:5–6 . . . . . 579, 599	27:46 271
5:33–37 575	15:6 551	28:6 339
5:42–48 567	15:9 . . . . . . xxxiii, 15	28:9 13
5:44 150	15:9, 13 24	28:18 180
6 . . 34, 143, 442, 452, 522	15:10 100	28:18–19 100, 191, 248
	15:22–28 162	28:18–20 218
6:1–4 560	15:25 13	28:19 . . . 179, 199, 212, 215, 226, 247, 254
6:1–6 122	15:29 209	
6:3–4 549	17:20 195	28:19–20 74, 181, 200, 217, 225, 228, 247
6:6 139	17:21 361	
6:9 . . . . . 141, 158, 396	17:27 209	28:20 . . . 25, 187, 247, 351, 615
6:10 150	18:3 113	
6:11 526	18:19–20 . . . 139, 478, 484	**Mark**
6:16–18 . 358, 361, 374		
7:6 . . . . 59, 60	18:20 100	1:2–8 217
7:7–8 141	19:3–9 653	1:8 208
7:24–27 97	19:5 235	1:35 . . . . 524, 538
8:2 . . . . 7, 13	19:14 . . . . . . 231, 233	1:40 13
9:13 81	20:22–23 211	2:27 . . . . 314, 323
9:15 362	20:23 214	2:27–28 319
9:18 13	21:13 330	3:11 13
10 93	21:22 161	4:2–3 212
10:1 79	21:28–32 620	4:24 100
10:5 79	22:37–40 530	5:6 13
10:6–7 70	23:3 308	6:13 . . . . 194, 195, 439

6:23–27 579	8:18 . . . . . . 100, 107	22:17 274
7:2–3 205	8:28 13	22:20 264
7:2–4, 8 204	8:41 13	22:41 13
7:4 205	9:51–56 37	23:43 219
7:4, 8 201	9:62 605	23:54 334
7:11–12 599	10 93	24:27 100
7:25 13	10:5 641	24:32 . . . . . . 97, 114
8:36 537	10:27–37 414	
8:38 275	11 . . . . . 34, 143, 522	**John**
10:14 231	11:2 158	1:19–22, 25 202
10:47–48 162	11:3–4 526	1:25 244
11:25 13	11:31 209	1:33 . . . . 208, 217
14:18–25 296	11:37–38 204	2:9–10 276
14:22–24 270	11:38 . . . . . . 205, 212	3:1–10 203
16:15 . . . . 70, 71	12:42 90	3:3, 5 222
16:15–16 213	12:47 . . . . . 143, 423	3:3, 5–6 215
16:16 . . . 101, 219, 226	12:47–48 471	3:16 384
	14:10 3	3:19–21 63
Luke	14:12–14 640	3:22 218
1:4 459	15 344	3:23 209
1:6 . . . . 25, 655	16:1 89	3:33 182
1:9 627	16:2 553	4:1–2 218
1:23 29	16:13 6	4:2 218
1:46–47 353	16:16 74	4:14 214
1:74–75 538	16:25–26 152	4:22 . . . . 15, 160
2:13–14 118	16:29 55	4:23–24 11, 15, 16, 160
2:25 5	16:31 59	4:24 . . . . 17, 133
2:36–37 . . . 358, 359	17:13 346	5:39 . . . . 47, 55
2:51 411	17:15 346	6:9 192
3:2 217	18 . . . . 143, 308	6:27 182
3:16 . . . . 208, 209	18:1 526	6:51 265
4 71	18:1–8 162	7:17 . . . . 68, 471
4:16 50	18:9–14 162	7:48–49 60
5:12 7	18:11–12 362	9:35 386
6:1–4 319	18:11–13 376	9:39–41 60
6:12 524	18:16 231	10:22 350
6:12–13 528	18:17 231	11:19 439
6:35 561	18:22 549	12:48 101
6:42 375	19:9 243	13:1 267
7:44 645	19:48 112	13:1–16 644
8:14 401	21:34 396	13:4–5 645
8:15 . . . . . 66, 111, 306	22:14–20 296	13:5 212

SCRIPTURE INDEX

13:8 212
13:10 645
13:13–15 645
13:14–15 . . . 646, 647
13:17 . . . . 114, 468
13:26 212
14–16 172
14:6 155
14:13–14 155
15:5 187
15:7 161
15:10, 14 351
15:14 114
15:16 138
16:8 172
16:13 82
16:14, 24 154
16:24 155
17:6–8 510
17:11 510
18:36 . . . . 37, 613
19:36 271
20 318
20:19 317
20:19, 26 479
20:19–20, 26 325
20:21 79
20:22 79
21 463

Acts

1:5, 8 208
1:24 633
1:26 627
2 291
2:1, 4 317
2:1–2 325
2:3, 17–18, 33 208
2:16–18 237
2:17 80
2:38 213, 216, 221, 222, 251, 256
2:38–39 229, 244, 616
2:38–41 219, 222, 230
2:39 . . . 224, 237, 239
2:41 . . . . . 213, 219, 251
2:42 139, 188, 263, 306
2:46 635
3:1 . . . . 159, 526
4:12 384
4:29–33 142
4:32 306
5 604
5:41 531
6:1–3 562
6:4 93
6:6 366
7:38 187
7:59 137
7:60 13
8:1–4 82
8:6 112
8:12–13 219
8:13 214
8:15–18 193
8:21 146
8:21–23 148
8:22 146
8:23 . . . . 146, 214
8:26 80
8:29 82
8:35 80
8:36, 38 214
8:36–38 213
8:37–38 230
8:38 . . . . 200, 209
8:38–39 209
8:39 209
9 200
9:10 200
9:11 . . . . 142, 524
9:18 219
10 362
10:2 . . . . 502, 524
10:14 236
10:28 236
10:30 . . 358, 359, 362, 502
10:33 . . . . 95, 112, 502
10:34 171
10:35 219
10:44 653
10:44–48 213
10:45, 47 219
10:47 . . . . . . 214, 227
10:47–48 219
11:15–16 208
12:5 139
12:12 479
13 71
13:1–4 82
13:2 29
13:2–3 366
13:3 361
13:15 . . . . 49, 80
13:46 . . . . . . 245, 653
14:15–17 . . . . . . 2, 19
14:21–22 75
14:22 100
14:23 . . . . 361, 366
15 . . . . 650, 651
15:1 650
15:5 651
15:6–7 650
15:7–19 651
15:20–21 . . . . 651, 652
15:20–25 655
15:21 . . . . 80, 655
15:23–24 651
15:28–29 . . 649, 650, 655
16:13 . . 479, 480, 486
16:14 . . . . 96, 112
16:14–15 213
16:14–15, 31–33 . . 243
16:15 244

16:15, 33 219
16:25 . . . . 118, 119, 122
16:31–33 . . . . 230, 250
16:32 244
17 19
17:2–3 100
17:11 . . . . 47, 111
17:14–15, 31–33 . . . 181
17:22–29 1
17:22–31 350
17:31 570
18:8 219
18:18 595
18:25 . . . . 91, 459
19:6 227
20:7 . . 100, 263, 298, 299, 317, 325, 331
20:20 381
20:27 . . . . 71, 89
20:28 . . . . . . 79, 269
20:34–35 564
20:35 564
20:36 13
21:8 200
21:20–27 651
21:21 459
21:23 595
21:25 . . . . . . 649, 655
22:16 . . . . 219, 221
23:12 599
23:12–14 578
25:25 171
26:20 377
26:22 100
27 368
27:23 597

Romans

1:9 . . . . 574, 587
1:18 . . . . 109, 570
1:18–25 9
1:20–21, 32 20
1:30, 32 398
2:14–15 20
2:18 459
2:28–29 . . . . 236, 239
3:2 54
3:23 383
3:25–26 446
4 238
4:3, 11, 22–25 230
4:11 . . . . 182, 213, 220
4:11–12 256
4:25 254
6 616
6:1–2 598
6:2 606
6:2–3 256
6:3–5 . . . . . 210, 256
6:3–6 254
6:4 . . . . 211, 221
6:4–5 223
6:4–11, 21–23 373
6:11–12 598
6:13 596
6:17 97
6:22 256
8:9 226
8:11 242
8:13 . . . . 172, 364
8:16 172
8:17 475
8:26–27 . . 147, 154, 172
8:27 137
8:33–34 255
8:38–39 170
9:1 587
9:1–2 . . . . . . 574, 582
9:6 236
10:10 606
10:12 88
10:14 75
10:15 . . . . 75, 78
11 76

11:16 236
11:16–17 . . . . 233, 237
11:17–18 561
11:24 235
11:25–26 76
11:33 199
12 79
12:1 . . . . . . 6, 14, 618
12:1–2 539
12:5 475
12:6 . . . . 184, 207
12:8, 13 545
12:11 162
12:20 555
13:6 405
13:14 616
14:5–6 352
14:14, 17 654
14:17 172
14:23 618
15:1–2 481
15:4 380
15:14–15 99
15:26 562
15:27 29
16:5 . . . . 122, 502
16:16 . . . . 641, 642
16:26 113

1 Corinthians

1:2 139
1:11–13 256
1:12 455
1:13 255
1:14 228
1:15 228
1:16 228
1:17 . . . . 87, 227
1:21 74
1:26–31 162
1:27–29 . . . . . 105, 187
1:30 180

2 82
2:4 104
2:4–5 .... 87, 104
2:6–7 101
2:9–16 154
2:12 172
2:13 105
3:5 185
3:5–7 ...... 187, 435
3:21–23 556
4:1 .... 185, 199
4:1–2 88
4:7 561
5:2 .... 358, 365
5:7 127
5:8 264
5:11, 13 292
6:11 216
6:15–20 395
6:19–20 14, 160, 224, 307, 596
6:20 .... 11, 15, 25, 132
7:5 361
7:14 235
7:29–32 ... 400, 429
7:39 506
8:8 .... 654, 656
9:7 93
9:13–14 93
9:14 .... 92, 93
9:27 363
10:1–2 205
10:14–21 598
10:14–22 616
10:16 .. 183, 264, 265, 268, 269, 272, 286
10:17 ...... 265, 287
10:21 ...... 263, 297
10:31 27
11:2 639
11:3 408
11:4–15 14

11:20 .. 199, 265, 266, 298, 312, 637
11:20–22 ... 636, 637
11:21–22 639
11:22 108
11:23 199
11:23–24 275
11:23–25 ... 183, 266
11:23–26 191
11:23–27 637
11:24–25 179
11:25 ...... 272, 275
11:26 ... 181, 215, 276, 283, 288
11:28 ... 181, 292, 293, 297, 299, 522
11:28–34 637
11:29 ...... 289, 304
11:30 289
11:32 290
12 .... 79, 83, 207
12:12 475
12:12–13 616
12:12–14 225
12:13 ...... 188, 291
12:13, 25–27 257
12:27 287
12:28 225
12:29 83
13:5–6 xxxiv
13:8 118
13:11 422
14 123
14:1, 31 83
14:15 . 118, 133, 160, 352
14:19 459
14:25 13
14:26 ...... 123, 464
14:34 124
15 223
15:29 ...... 223, 229
15:31 585

16:1–2 .. 317, 325, 326, 331
16:2 .... 560, 562
16:19 ... 122, 479, 502
16:20 641

2 Corinthians

1:10 348
1:23 .... 574, 587
2:15–16 112
2:17 84
3:8 .... 303, 335
3:12 86
3:12–14 101
3:17 .... 154, 188
3:18 .... 55, 101
4:2 ..... 37, 84, 101
4:3–4 101
4:5 85
4:7 187
5:10 571
5:11–21 94
5:14 170
5:14–15 285
5:20 78
6:2 426
6:14–15 506
6:14–16 598
6:18 222
7:7 358
7:10 378
7:11 376
8–9 464
8:5 596
8:7 558
8:9 567
9 554
9:5 553
9:6–11 566
9:6–12 549
9:7 .... 545, 560
9:13 113

9:15 305
10:3–5 614
10:4 37
11:3 470
11:10 ...... 587, 601
11:13–15 101
11:27 362
11:31 ...... 574, 587
12:9 155
12:14 409
12:15 85
13:5 .... 292, 300, 521
13:12 641
13:14 ...... 165, 168

Galatians

1:7–8 85
1:20 574
2:21 345
3:1 290
3:2 82
3:7, 9, 16–17, 27–29 238
3:7, 9, 29 243
3:8–9 230
3:13–15 273
3:14 234
3:17 230
3:26 475
3:26–27 .... 222, 256
3:27 ... 221, 224, 616
3:27–28 229
3:28 237
3:29 ... 230, 234, 616
4:3, 9–10 317
4:6 .... 138, 172
4:10–11 326
4:11 317
4:28 238
5:3 .... 225, 239, 594
5:16–26 185
5:24 172

6:2 .... 439, 478, 481
6:6 459
6:10 .545, 555, 557, 558

Ephesians

1:4, 6 307
1:13 182
1:13–14 172
1:17 .... 154, 160
1:17–18 172
1:19–20 241
2:3 236
2:8 538
2:8–9 385
2:12 234
2:12–13 237
2:14–15 117
2:19 475
3:6 234
3:8–9 100
3:14 ..... 13, 137, 141
3:18 171
3:18–19 170
4 .... 77, 207
4:1–5 224
4:4–6 255
4:5 228
4:7 483
4:8, 11 100
4:11–16 75
4:12–13 483
4:15–16 482
4:25 576
4:28 564
5:18–20 350
5:19 . 118, 123–125, 134
5:20 353
5:22–23 408
5:25–26 216
5:32 197
5:33 ...... 407, 408
6 164

6:2 410
6:4 . 51, 331, 408, 462
6:5–8 413
6:6 414
6:9 412
6:17 56
6:18 140, 150, 163, 369, 501, 526
6:18–20 91

Philippians

1:9–11 461
1:19 171
1:21 606
1:27 .... 306, 352
1:27–28 .... 602, 615
2:10 .... 13, 156
2:17 29
2:25 475
3:3 ..... 16, 240, 290
3:7–10 399
3:12 171
3:18–19 198
3:19 535
3:20 .... 198, 307
4:4 445
4:6 .... 140, 341
4:8 .... 377, 416

Colossians

1:7 88
1:21–22, 28 269
1:28 90
2:2 160
2:7 466
2:8–13 240
2:9 240
2:10 240
2:11–13 240
2:12 211
2:12–13 ..... 211, 257
2:13 211

2:16, 20–22 654
2:16–17 . 117, 317, 326
2:20, 22 257
2:23 266
3:1–2 ..... 257, 378
3:3–4 257
3:12 563
3:15 345
3:16 .. 53, 115, 118, 119, 123–126, 133, 134, 477, 480, 497
3:17 .... 134, 353
3:20 411
3:22 414
3:23–24 413
4:1 412
4:2 .... 501, 516
4:3–4 150
4:12 551
4:15 .... 122, 479, 502
4:16 50

1 Thessalonians

1:9 6
2:4 88
2:7–8 92
2:10 77
2:11 92
2:13 112
2:18 101
4:3–5 396
5:14 484
5:17 .159, 163, 526, 527
5:19 156
5:22 389
5:26 641
5:27 49

2 Thessalonians

1:10, 12 102
2:4 .... 297, 588

1 Timothy

1:11 89
2:1–2 405
2:1–3 ..... 149, 150
2:5 155
2:8 159
2:11–12 ... 124, 408
3:1 83
3:2 .... 77, 99
3:10 79
3:14–15 61
3:16 .... 75, 452
4:3–5 654
4:4 342
4:6 410
4:8 ..... 20, 148, 548
4:15 .... 85, 89
4:15–16 93
4:16 84
5:4 411
5:8 . 409, 511, 552, 556
5:10 647
5:22 78
6:1 413
6:2 413
6:3 .... 306, 615
6:9–11 428
6:17–19 430
6:18 ...... 545, 547

2 Timothy

1:7 26
2:15 77
2:16 17 43
2:19 182
2:22 420
3:2 551
3:5 519
3:15 ...... 51, 419
3:16–17 .... 85, 382
4:2 85
4:17–18 348

Titus

1:7 78
1:9 .... 72, 77
1:15 ...... 125, 235
1:16 378
2:1 84
2:1–3 425
2:6 420
2:8 104
2:9 413
2:9–10 413
2:10 225, 307, 348, 414
2:11–12 .170, 307, 530, 538, 600
3:1 405
3:4–6 223
3:5 .... 172, 213
3:5–6 ..... 208, 215
3:8 .... 539, 617

Philemon

2 479

Hebrews

2:1 113
2:2 96
2:14–15 285
2:16 271
3:12 402
3:13 ...... 478, 484
4:2 .... 96, 112
4:7 426
4:9 .... 318, 320
4:9 10 318
4:13 570
4:14, 16 .... 28, 141
4:14–16 155
4:16 162
5:4 .... 75, 199
5:11 99
5:12–6:2 460
6:4–6 110

6:7–8 346	13:17 .... 78, 85	3:16 416
6:10 549	**James**	3:20–21 211
6:12 398	1:5 68	3:21 214, 241, 253, 256
6:16 569, 572, 576, 584	1:6–7 161	3:21–22 257
6:17 573	1:19 99	4:1–2 257
6:17–18 189	1:21 .... 61, 113	4:7 526
7:20 583	1:23–25 108	4:10 .... 479, 483
7:25 141	1:26 5	4:11 89
8:6 29	1:27 ... 545, 546, 548	4:17 289
8:9 608	2:3 387	5:14 .... 641, 642
8:10 ... 222, 230, 596	2:13 547	**2 Peter**
8:10, 12 222	2:16–17 558	1:2–11 433
8:11 81	3:13 378	1:12 90
9:10 ... 201, 206, 616	3:15–17 455	1:18–19 377
9:13 206	4:6 162	1:19 xxxiv
9:14 6	4:9 .... 360, 365	2:5 69
9:15–17 ..... 273, 285	5:4 412	2:10 405
9:19 206	5:12 575	2:12–14 637
9:21 206	5:13 . 116, 119, 122, 365	2:13 639
9:22 206	5:14 194, 195, 437, 438, 447	2:20–22 110
9:23 206	5:14–15 194	**1 John**
9:27 152	5:16 142, 145, 150, 437	1:7 215
10:1–10 649	5:17–18 142	2 81
10:10, 14 298	**1 Peter**	2:3–4 471
10:14 28	1:3 242	2:20, 27 193
10:19–22 . 28, 141, 155	1:5 305	2:20–28 81
10:20 269	1:5–9 101	2:27 81
10:22 160	1:10–11 237	3:17 548
10:24–25 .. 478, 482, 493	1:11–13 101	3:17–18 543
10:25 100	1:15 326	3:18 557
10:29 303	1:23 101	4:1 114
11:24–27 531	2:5 14	4:19 .... 170, 277
12:1 394	2:13–14 405	4:20 548
12:25 100	2:15 308	5:14–15 155
12:25–28 101	3:1 408	5:16 152
12:28–29 173, 353, 618	3:6 408	**2 John**
12:29 570	3:7 501	4 420
13:8 570	3:12 141	8 336
13:14–15 119	3:15 .... 465, 471	
13:15 .... 344, 345		
13:16 ... 545, 547, 561		

Jude

3 72
3, 20–21 602
8–12 637
10, 13 288
12 639
14 69
20 . . . . 140, 153

Revelation

1:4 137
1:5 215
1:8 166
1:10 . 312, 318, 325, 335
1:18 220
1:20 79
2:2 466
2:10 101
2:24–25 . . . 649, 656
3:3 113
3:20 426
4:2–3 8
4:8–11 27
4:11 19
5 182
5:9–10 123
5:12 281
6:11 475
6:15 106
7:9–13 129
7:11 13
8:3 . . . . 141, 145
10:5–6 . . . . . . 581, 582
14:1, 3 123
14:3 119
14:13 321
15:2–3 115
15:3 123
19:1–7 129
19:10 7
19:13 207
21:7 230

22:8–9 13
22:18 370
22:18–20 42